THE BELGIAN BEER BOOK

ERIK VERDONCK | LUC DE RAEDEMAEKER

THE BELGIAN BEER BOOK

LANNOO

1. BELGIAN IS BEER — 11
Welcome from Erik Verdonck — 12
Welcome from Luc De Raedemaeker — 16
What is beer? — 20
Belgians about their beer — 21
Belgian beer in the world — 30

2. BEER HISTORY — 43
A healthy popular drink — 44
(300 up to 1500 AC)
Gruit or hops? — 46
A pure beer made with water, malt — 48
and hops
City beers under pressure — 52
(17th–18th century)
Industry and science take over — 59
(19th century)
Pils revolution (1842) — 62
War and crisis in beer land — 66
(1914–1945)
Economies of scale down to regional beers — 71
(1945–2000)
Microbreweries in the new millennium — 74
(2000–)

3. BELGIAN BEER CULTURE — 89
Popping into your 'local' — 90
Beer seeks café — 94
Enamel signs — 96
Beer labels — 100
Exchange fairs — 100
The Belgian and his beer glass — 105
Beer is fun — 106
Specialty beer cafés in Belgium — 110
Specialty beer cafés abroad — 165

4. BREWING PROCESS AND INGREDIENTS — 174

- Brewing method — 174
- Water — 198
- Hop — 200
- Yeast — 210
- Grains and malt — 217
- The malting process — 218
- Sugars and fruits — 223
- Herbs and spices — 223
- Wooden barrels: barrel or ingredient? — 226

5. BELGIAN BEER STYLES AND BEER TYPES — 233

- Abbey beer — 236
- Trappist beer — 246
- Spéciale Belge — 254
- Amber beer — 258
- Brut beer — 262
- Light blonde beer — 266
- Strong blonde beer — 274
- Triple — 290
- Strong dark beer, double and quadruple — 298
- Lambic and Faro — 306
- Gueuze and Oude Geuze — 310
- Kriek and fruit beers — 318
- Pils — 328
- Saison — 334
- Flemish red-brown — 342
- White beer — 356
- Scotch — 362
- Stout — 366
- Barrel aged — 372
- Wood-matured beer — 378
- India Pale Ale (IPA) — 382
- Beers with added wild yeast — 390
- Mix of beer styles — 394
- Extreme beers — 400

6. TAPPING, POURING, TASTING AND STORING — 409

- Learn how to serve a beer from the tap — 412
- Learn how to pour — 414
- Learn how to taste — 416
- Storing beer — 432

7. BEER KITCHEN AND FOOD PAIRING — 439

- Alcohol habituation — 440
- Hop shoots from the Westhoek — 442
- Beer with your meal — 444
- Brewing is cooking — 450
- Beer tastings — 451
- Beer with fish, crustaceans and seafood — 458
- Beer and burgers — 461
- Beer and game — 462
- Beer and chocolate — 466
- Beer and cheese — 470
- Beer and pasta — 476
- Beer and bread — 476
- Beer and pizza — 476
- Beer and the Eastern cuisine — 480
- Beer restaurants — 482

8. BEER TOURISM — 505

- Brewery visits — 506
- Beer festivals in Belgium — 678
- Beer events — 684

ADDITIONS

- Beer dictionary — 688
- Beer index — 692
- Brewery index — 694
- Beer and brewery musea — 697
- Beer festivals — 697
- Events — 697
- Cafés — 697
- Beer restaurant — 698
- Useful links and bibliography — 698
- Magazines — 698
- Television — 698
- Books — 699
- Thanks — 702

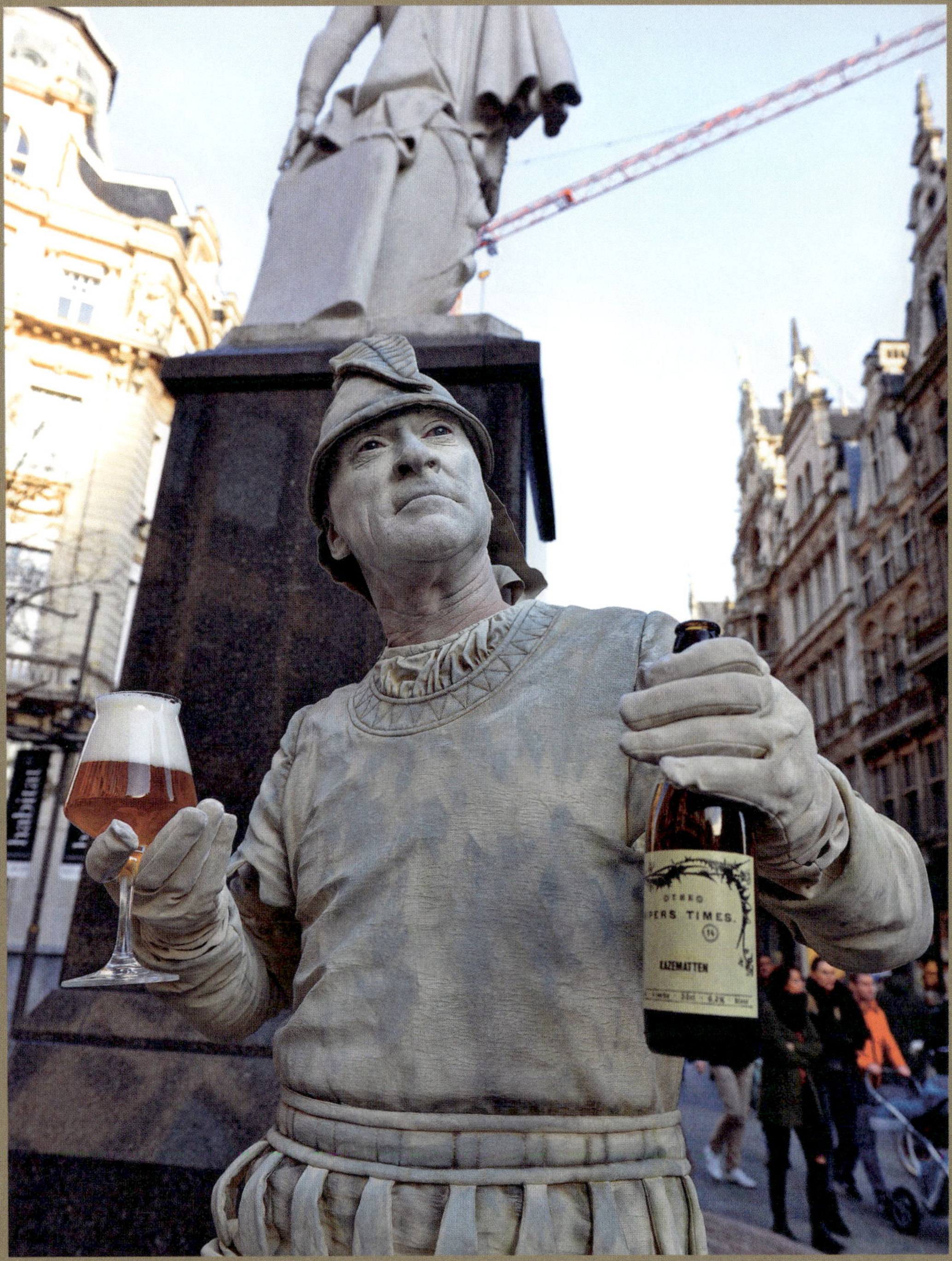
habitat
PERS TIMES.
KAZEMATTEN

BEER, IT'S THE BEST DAMN DRINK IN THE WORLD

Jack Nicholson

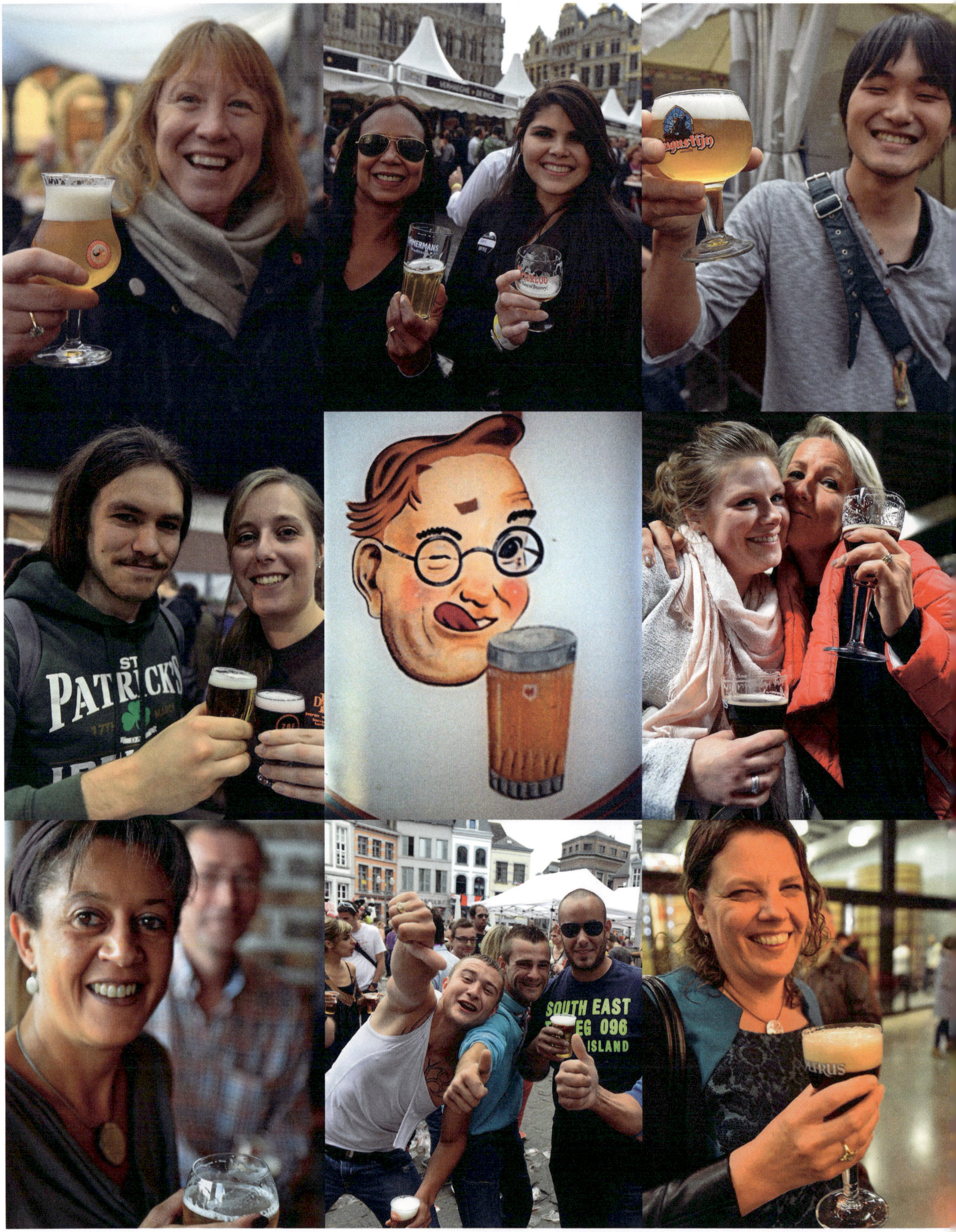
SOUTH EAST
ISLAND

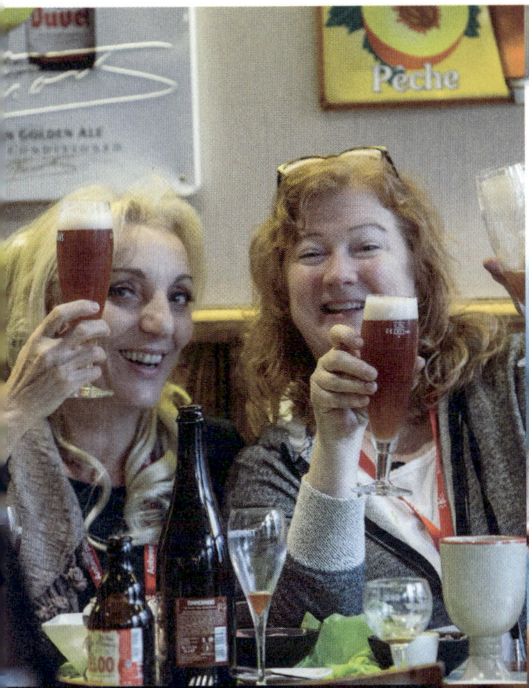
Pêche
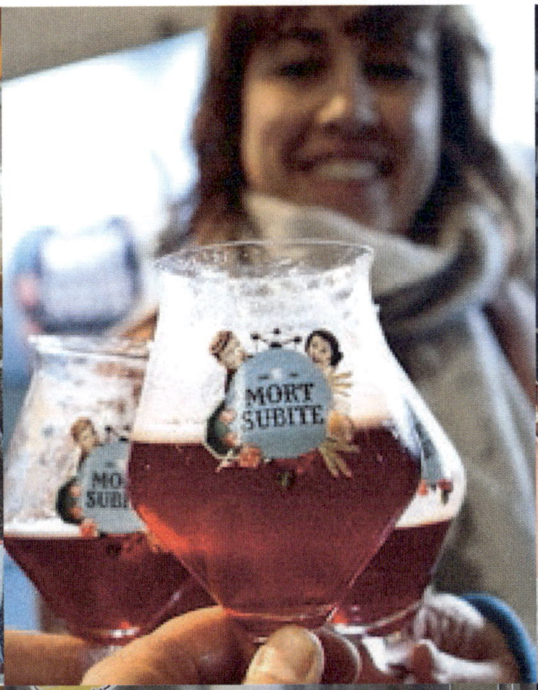
MORT SUBITE
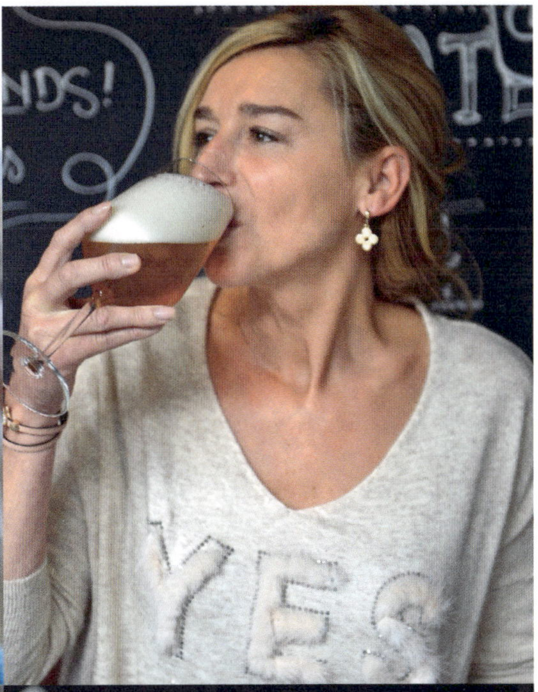
YES
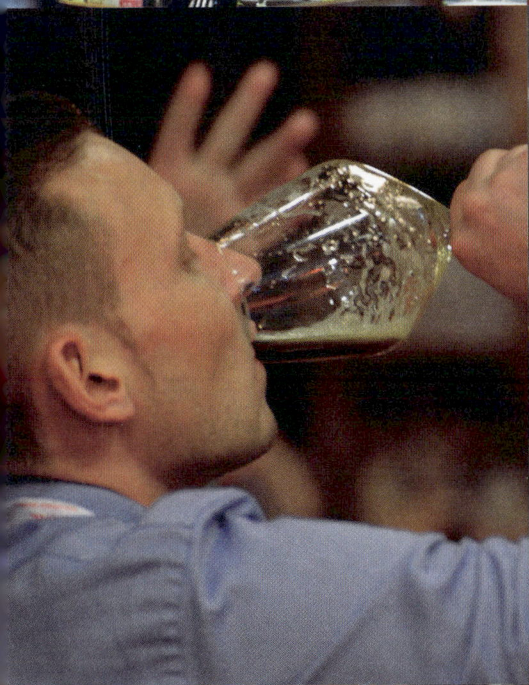
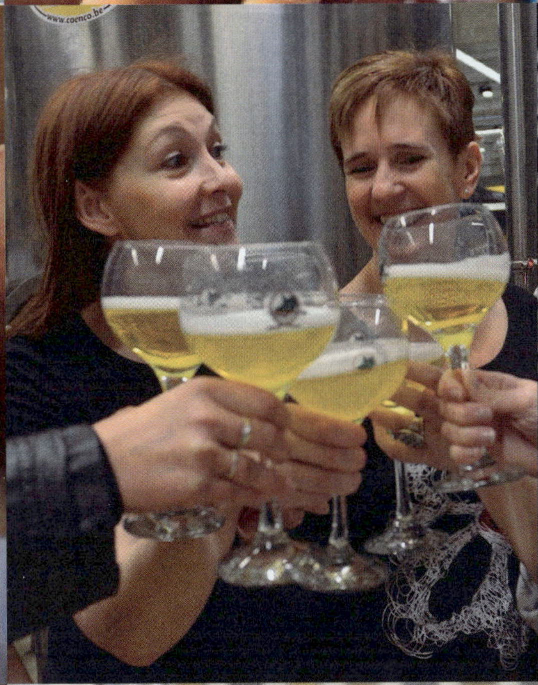
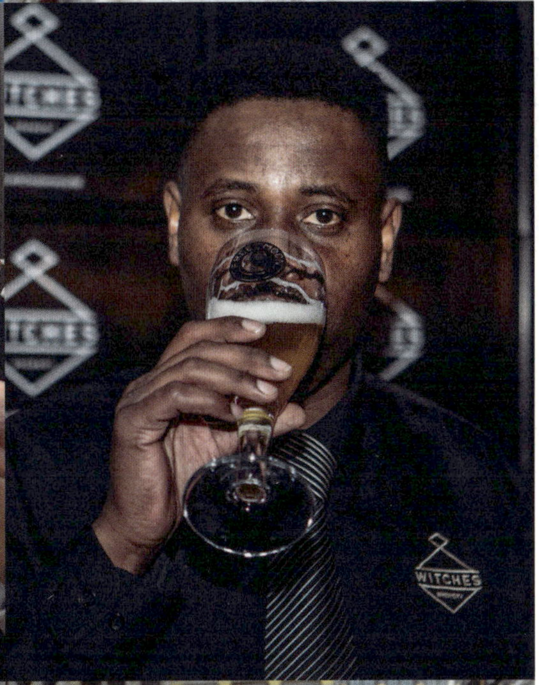
WITCHES
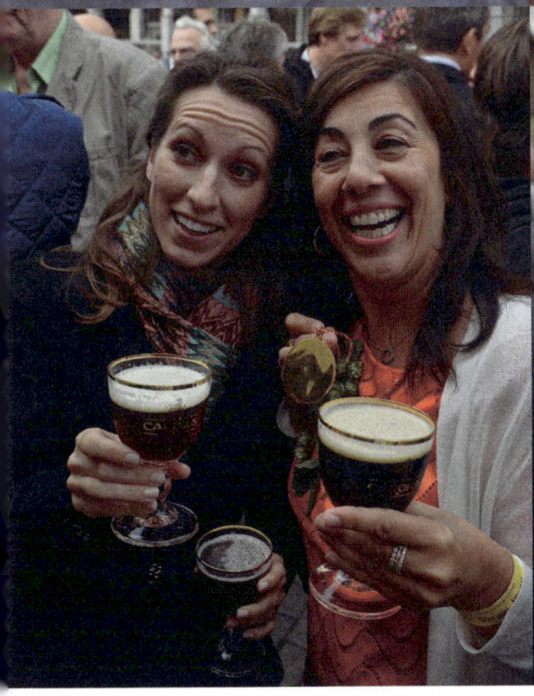
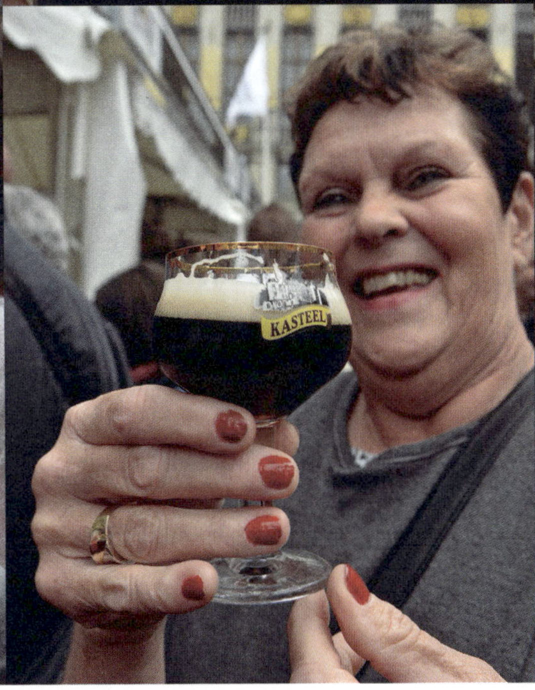
KASTEEL
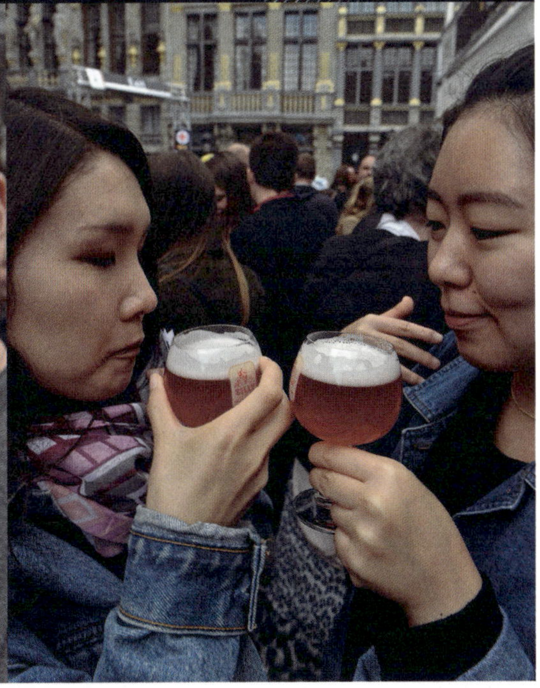

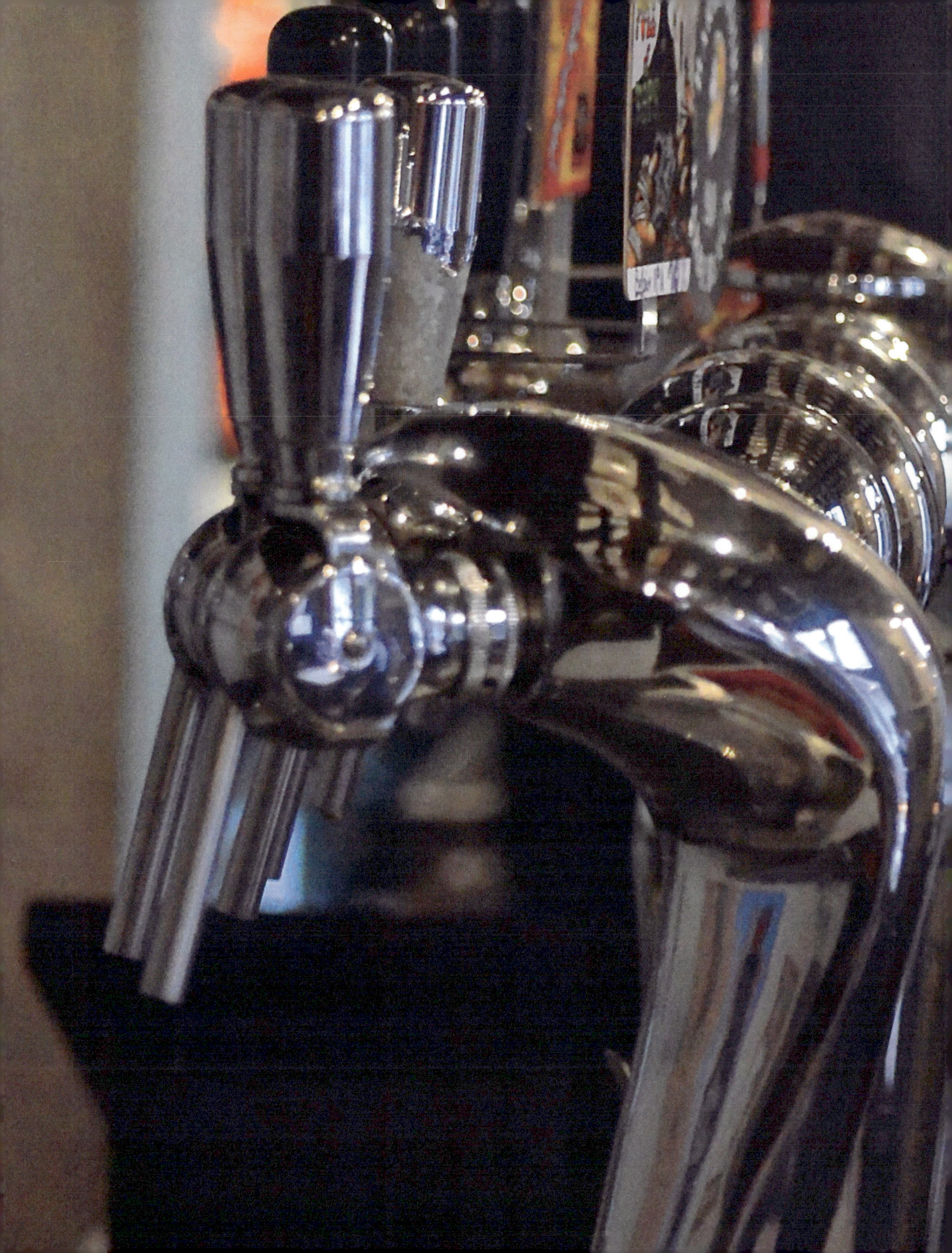

1
BELGIAN IS BEER AND BEER IS BELGIAN

INTRO

ALL THE WAY DOWN TO THE BOTTOM

Are you a beer lover? Then this situation will ring a bell with you. No doubt you remember that great bar chat the other day. No sooner had a round been poured before the next one appeared. You had to hurry up, empty your glass as quickly as possible to be ready for the next one and not fall behind in the beer race. With this book you can take a little more time. We're going down an entirely different road. No, we are not donning white gloves to uncork a bottle of beer. 'None of that nonsense', we can already hear our brewers say. 'source: Doe maar gewoon – just do as normal, However, we are really quite proud of our beers. We are doing them an injustice by just pouring them down our throats 'hijsen', we feel. Unless, of course, we are almost dying of thirst... To brew a tasty beer takes time, a lot of time. So why turn it into a drinking competition? A beer that is beautifully served from the tap or poured from the bottle is a work of art, pleasing to the eye and a caress for the senses. Find out for yourself. You may be working up a bit of a thirst when you are leafing through the pages of this book. You have been warned. Beer travellers do not set off unprepared. So what do you need? A beer of your choice, poured or served from the tap, at the correct temperature, in the correct glass/its own proprietary glass. All of this should go without saying. Above all, take time to enjoy your beer. Allow yourself to be seduced. Find out more about that single – secret – ingredient in your beer that prompts you to investigate further. Listen to the 'sssttt' sound when a bottle is uncorked, pour the beer slowly and carefully, source: schenk uit zonder te laten klokken, swirl it around in the glass, sniff the aromas, taste and allow the barley juice to unleash its devils. And now put a stop to your quest for the 'best beer'. With a little bit of luck, you have already found it. It is there in the glass right in front of you. The 'best beer' is the one that you fancy right now. In a little while, or tomorrow, you may reach for a different one or else, come back to your tried and trusted brew. You can be loyal or disloyal... the main thing is that you enjoy your beer. If you steer your course under the flag of Belgian beer you are certain to explore amazing horizons. Navigate your own course, at your own pace and rely on your own taste. This book aims to be your compass.

Why a book about Belgian beer? Look at art, at the great classical artists. Van Eyck, Memling and Rogier Van der Weyden are all painters who have earned their place in history with their timeless scenes, idyllic landscapes and lofty portraits. The Breughel era gives way to more down-to-earth scenes. Sweat is dripping on the fields, times are generally a bit rougher and thirsty throats are lubricated. Adriaen Brouwer gives you a sneak peek of the inn, amongst the players. Jordaens, Rubens and Van Dyck direct their gaze heavenwards once again. Permeke and Rik Wouters are staying closer to earth, to real life. And then there are the artists where nothing is what it seems, with Ensor holding up his masks in front of you, Magritte who delights in fooling you, Delvaux who lets you dream, Panamarenko who builds flying saucers that never take flight and vessels that are afraid of the water, Jan Fabre who tames the clouds, rides turtles and colours castles blue... Layered works of art where nothing is the way it is. Just like many Belgian beers that turn out to be far more complex than you would expect. You don't have to drain your glass all the way to the bottom. Take your time. Get lost in the beer world. Rely on your own taste. No-one knows it as well as you do. Have fun reading, tasting and drinking!

Erik Verdonck

PS This book is not an encyclopaedia. We are not listing all the beers and breweries but rather, we have made a personal choice. So, don't shoot the messenger! Achieving completeness can only be an illusion. Our lists, however carefully compiled, will already be dated at the time of going to press. We only aim to show the wide variety of Belgian beers and beer culture. Enjoy!

BRASSERIE DE L'AVENIR
A. DORIAUX-LEFEBVRE
ERQUELINES

BLONDE   BRUNE

Black, yellow and red. The Belgian tri-colour is often used in advertising, including that of the best-known Belgian pils brand, Stella Artois. Here, 'Triple' does not refer to the triple beer style but indicates that the beer has been 'filtered three times'.

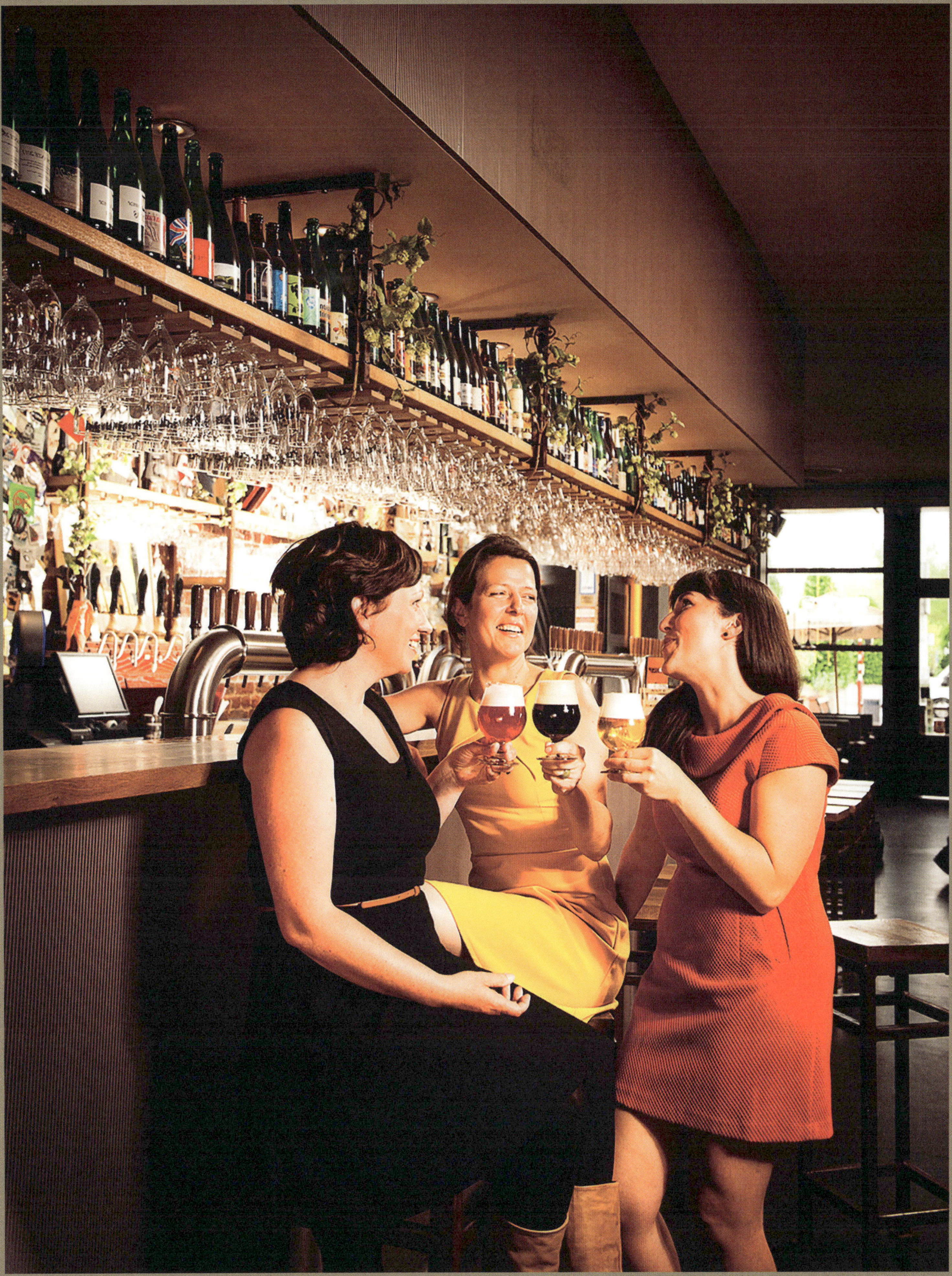

INTRO

BELGIAN = BEER

'For the Belgian, beer is a social lubricant. Snobbery doesn't come into it. At the bar, the plasterer is chatting with the lawyer and tongues are loosened.'

Where does Belgian beer stand on the global map? The main players have put our beers on the map. Abbey beers like Leffe, Grimbergen and Affligem have pointed the way towards specialty beers. In the 1990s gueuze beers enjoyed a revival in Belgium. This decade also saw the arrival of a new wave of microbreweries and classics. Het Anker brewery for example, rose from the ashes. Internet and social media gave the smaller players, such as the Cantillon lambic brewery or De Struise Brouwers, an entry into the wider world and some of them even grew into a hype. Marketing has left its imprint on the beer world. A genuine brewer will offer you a tasting first, more often than not without an explanation. He feels that his beer will sell itself. If marketing gains the upper hand, the beer tends to turn into a tool to sell brands. By the way, this is an international trend that can also be seen with the up-and-coming craft brewers. It is important that brewers, either large or small, manage the process and do not sell contaminated beer. If you are not a brewer yourself, team up with a professional who has earned his spurs. It takes time to perfect a beer. This is in contrast to the current rat race, where the aim is to produce new beers, tastes and styles all the time. Following the wave of IPAs (IPA = India Pale Ale) we are now being flooded by 'sour ale', said to be the 'new bitter'. We'll have to wait and see what this one brings as most people are not keen on the taste of sour. In the meantime, the results of the Brussels Beer Challenge, an international beer competition, are proof that the Belgians have mastered the craft of producing the Belgian beer styles – saison, Flemish red-brown, lambic, oude gueuze, kriek ... The Saison Dupont Biologique was recently crowned the best Belgian beer, but a classic such as the 'spéciale belge' amber beer from Palm also scooped an award. Genuine top-quality beers like the Westmalle tripel are perfectly balanced. Many Belgian breweries introduce innovations based on tradition and this is what makes us so special. Just take a look at the new, light and hoppy Ename Pater abbey beer from the Roman brewery or the light Tilquin gueuze from the tap. These beers are our response to the international trend for tasty and light 'session beers' and demonstrate how we manage to translate our rich past into the future time and time again. We are also rightly proud of our beer culture. Think of the expertise of our brewers that is rooted in tradition. They are top experts in specific beer styles. This idiosyncrasy can also be found in Belgian cafés. In Den Engel at Grote Markt in Antwerp or in Bahnhove, the railway station of the municipality of Hove on the edge of Antwerp, now converted into a café, you feel the typical atmosphere straight away. The beer card may be limited but you are guaranteed to find classic beers at prices that abroad, they can only dream of. This 'soul' is also alive in our breweries. Take a look at Het Anker, at Liefmans, De Brabandere, De Halve Maan or Brasserie de la Senne housed in a former industrial bakery ... All of these are brewing lovely beers. And even in the very modest canteen of a fourth-division football club, the Westmalle tripel will be served in the right glass. For the Belgian, beer is a social lubricant. Snobbery doesn't come into it. At the bar, the plasterer is chatting with the lawyer and tongues are loosened.

Luc De Raedemaeker

1 • BELGIAN IS BEER

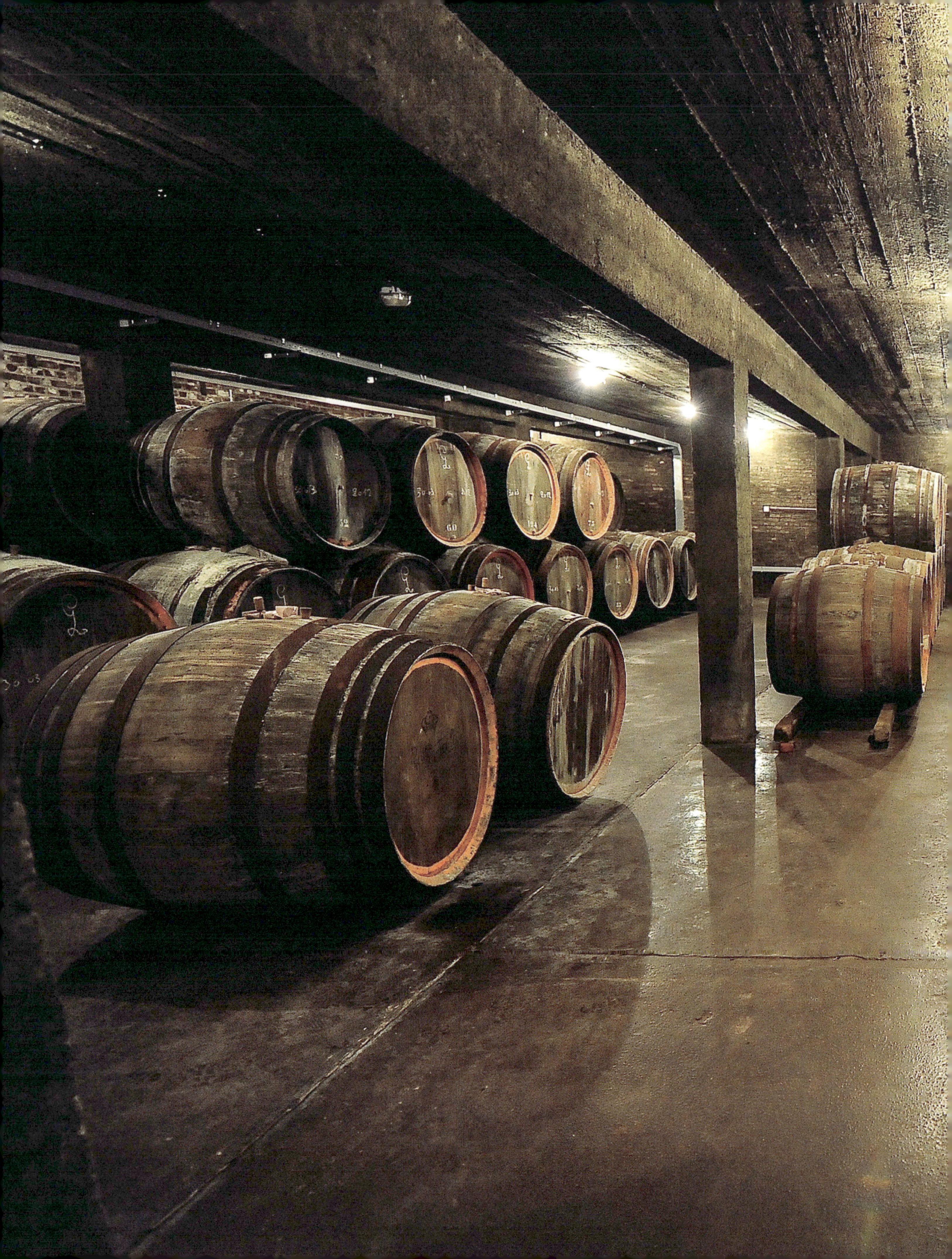

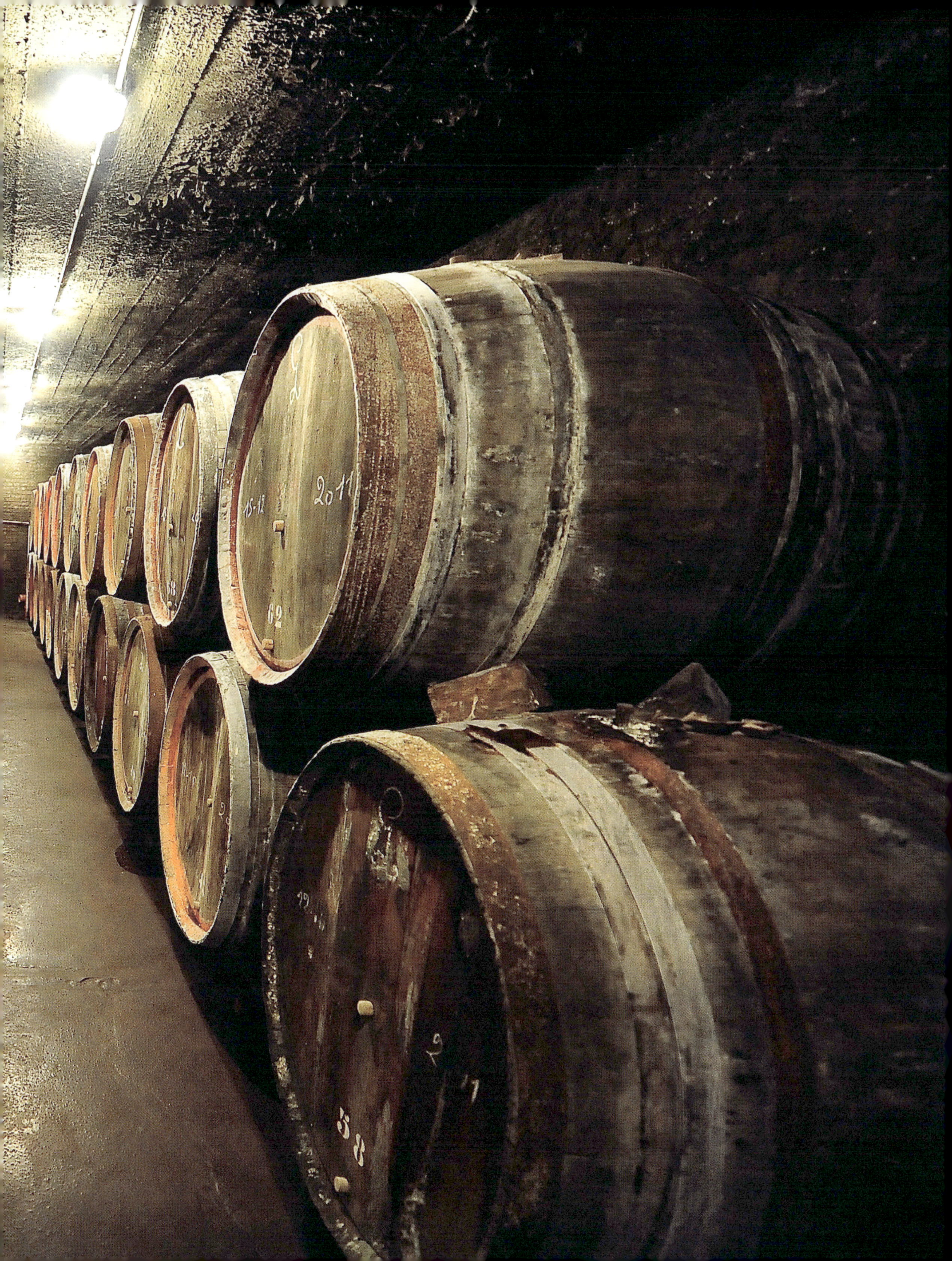
2011
62
58

What is beer?

A book about beer. But what exactly is beer? The dictionary tells us that beer is an alcoholic drink, yellow to dark brown in colour made from hop and malt and prepared through fermentation and boiling (Oxford Dictionary: an alcoholic drink made from yeast-fermented malt flavoured with hops). Belgian law defines it as follows: 'The drink obtained after alcoholic fermentation of a wort mainly obtained from starch and sugar-containing ingredients, of which at least 60% should be malt from barley or wheat, including hop, which can be in a processed state, and brewing water.' (Royal Decree 31/3/1993). According to Wikipedia, beer is an alcoholic beverage produced by fermentation.[1] Most beer is flavoured with hops, which add bitterness and act as a natural preservative. Fermentation produces a natural carbonation in beer.[2]

Admittedly, this is as succinct as it comes. We learn that beer is not wine and neither is it a distillate. It is a unique product with its own character. Beer is the magic combination of water, malt, hop and yeast. The brewer uses his talent to conjure up something beautiful in the glass. Besides the four basic ingredients water, malt, hop and yeast he has an entire arsenal at his disposal to give his beer the taste he is aiming for. In short, human genius in its purest and tastiest form. A thirstquencher and a drink to be enjoyed: that is what beer is. Unfortunately, this product of the noble barley plant often goes unappreciated at the table. This is completely unjustified. Beer has a huge amount of 'taste extremes' such as sour, sweet and bitter… and offers innumerable culinary possibilities. But there is more to it than romance. The brewer also has to pay his bills at the end of the month. Luckily, export growth and beer tourism are boosting the coffers.

Beer temple

A monument, on a par with a palace, is the opinion of the Belgian Brewers brewing federation, known in its own country as 'Belgische Brouwers'/'Brasseurs Belges'. They teamed up with the City of Brussels to make the **Belgian Beer Temple** a reality. This beer experience centre will be housed in the former Stock Exchange building and will open its doors in 2019. A stone's throw from the Grand-Place, the beer palace will be the best possible calling card for the Belgian brewers. The 'beer temple' is intended as a homage to the Belgian beer world. Don't expect a classic beer museum. This is going to be an interactive experience centre where you can discover, at your own pace, what is hidden underneath that robust head of froth. You wander the corridors and build up your own taste profile. Once you have worked your way out of this maze, you taste the beer that is the best fit with your taste profile. The bar, with its wide range of Belgian beers on offer, is beckoning.

Belgians about their beer

Sven Gatz, a former manager of the Belgian brewers, feels that Belgian beer culture is a piece of cultural heritage: 'What makes this country unique is the large diversity and the rich tradition. Granted, the world of beer is equally diverse in the USA, Germany and England. But there is no other country that unites diversity and tradition like we do. We have an eye for tradition and innovation. You could refresh your design and, at the same time, stay true to an original recipe. Or else you could go off the beaten track and launch an entirely new beer or a completely new beer style.' The Belgian beer world shows great diversity. You have the major players but there are plenty of medium-sized ones plus other participants varying from small to tiny. It is important to maintain this diversity. 'The Belgian beer culture is multi-layered and comes in all shapes and sizes', Sven Gatz concludes. 'There are many different stakeholders: brewers, café owners, chefs, zythologues, beer professors, collectors, owners of beer museums ...' A proposal was recently submitted to Unesco to include this rich Belgian beer culture in the **Unesco World Heritage** list. We are now awaiting approval. This book will give you an advance taster of what we feel our beer culture is about.

Jef Van den Steen

A silent taste revolution

Beer sommelier **Ben Vinken** has been advocating Belgian specialty beers for over thirty years. Ben Vinken: 'Balance and a centuries-old tradition - that is what we are about! That tradition does not stand in the way of creativity in any way. For example, many beers are now improved by re-fermentation or *dry hopping*.' And now, Ben is singing the praises of brewing education at Belgian universities and the phenomenal investments the brewers are making in new technology. Thanks to the impact of microbreweries, large breweries have updated their range more frequently and more quickly. They launch seasonal beers, limited editions or entirely new creations more often. We have to keep on surprising the beer lover with balanced quality beers. In the meantime, Belgian specialty beers have come a long way. Palm, Duvel, Hoegaarden, Leffe Blond ... all of these are milestones in Belgian beer history. There are even some beers that have managed to give rise to their own beer style. The most successful amongst them have built a bridge between thirstquencher and degustation beer. The 1990s saw a steep rise in the popularity of abbey beers which continues up to this day. You can now find an abbey beer with any possible aroma, colour or taste. In contrast, the success of the sweet krieken beers was only temporary and affected by increased consumption of soft drinks. Brewers started adding sugar to their products to seduce consumers who were no longer brought up with the taste of beer. The wave of white beers has also reached its crest. In recent years we have seen more genuine specialty beers with a noticeable touch of hops (IPA) or sour beers such as an 'oude gueuze' or a Flemish red-brown. Or else, the return of 'roots beers', the saison for example.

'The late beer guru **Michael Jackson** was right after all,' Ben Vinken concludes. 'As early as 1984 he predicted "*a quiet revolution of taste*", foresaw the advent of artisan brewers and made the case for "real ale". Michael taught us how to name and describe the different tastes of beer, how to pour them correctly and inaugurated us into the secrets of beer and food pairing. Really, there is nothing new under the sun.'

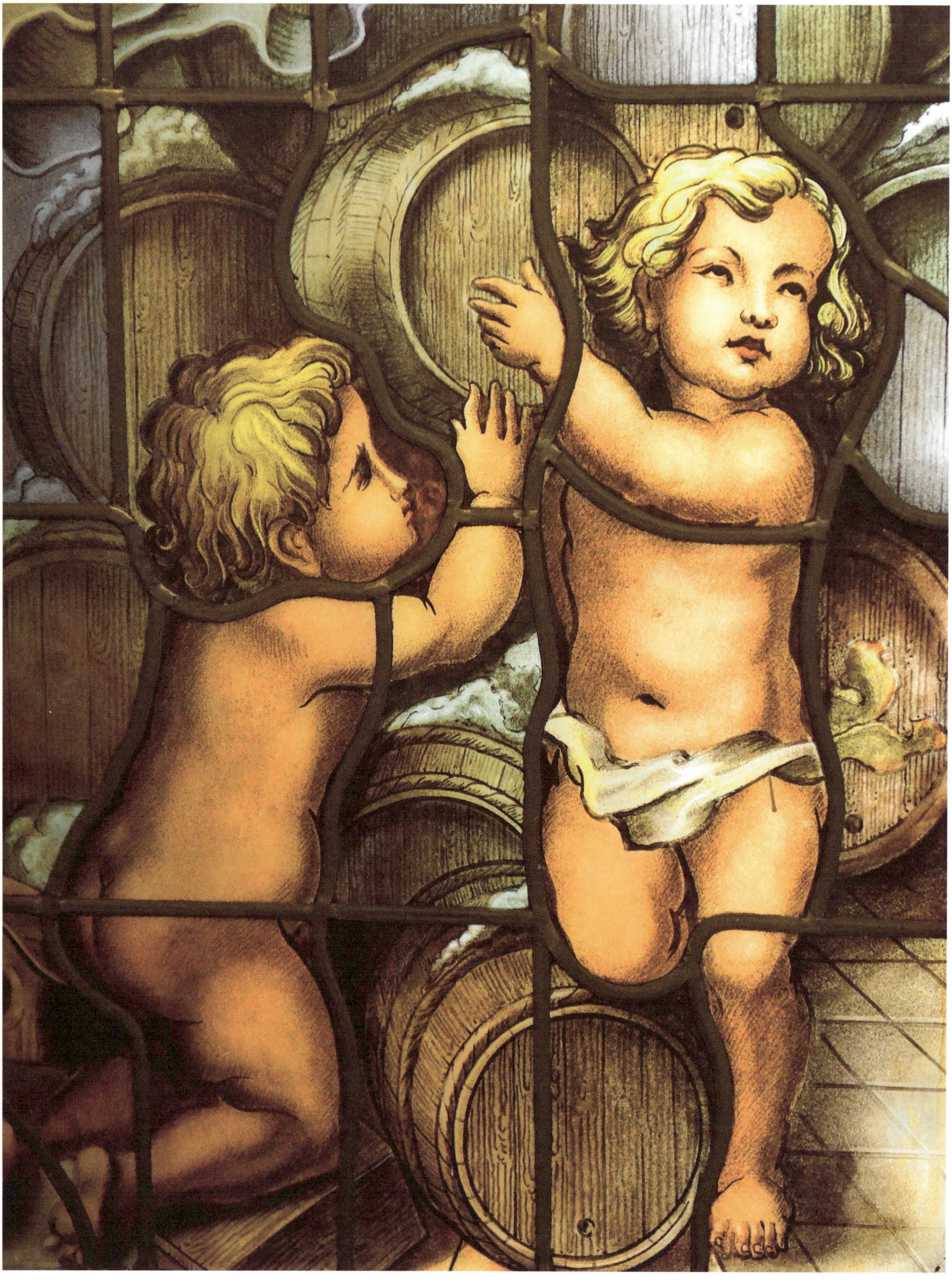

Thirst doesn't stand a chance

Belgian specialty beers are on the 'up', according to beer trader **Dominiek Geers**. The shelves at **Drankenhandel Geers**, not far from Ghent, are groaning under the weight of over eight hundred different Belgian beers. The beer trader is making a case for cooking with beer and beer pairing. Dominiek: 'More and more people are now cooking with beer and are serving beer with the meal. Also in restaurants, beer is starting to take up the place it deserves.' Dominiek has a soft spot for character beers with a distinctive, pure taste. 'I love dry and bitter beers of the saison or IPA type', he confesses. He mentions the slightly bitter, thirst-quenching beers made by Brasserie Dupont, Brasserie de la Senne, De Ranke and Brouwers Verzet. 'I'd like to be able to drink something else afterwards', Dominique explains. 'If a beer is too bitter or sour, it kills the taste buds straight away.'

Brewer, stick to what you're good at

Diversity, quality and balance, these are the trump cards played by Belgian beer, according to **Jef Van den Steen**, who is also brewing for **De Glazen Toren**. We are making a journey back in time to the early 1980s, when the tide started to turn in the Belgian beer world. In those days, Dolle Brouwers and Brasserie d'Achouffe were the pioneers amongst microbreweries. Specialty beers were enjoying a revival. A second wave brought ashore the beer firms, who sell beers that are brewed elsewhere. There are now over ninety of them. The internationally renowned Proefbrouwerij in Lochristi has served as the engine for this movement. The company is brewing on behalf of beer firms, from Belgium and further afield. It is not a guarantee of quality. At the end of the day, the content of the glass speaks for itself and the beer drinker seals the fate of the beer. Jef: 'Speaking as a brewer, I like to confine myself to beers that are truly perfect.' We are tasting a saison and an amber 'spéciale belge', both completely fermented, quite dry and perfectly balanced. 'I want you to fancy a second glass after the first one', Jef laughs. 'Many beers are said to be "exciting" or "interesting", but if you taste them, you will stick to just the one glass that is more likely than not to be your last. The brewer with the De Glazen Toren microbrewery focuses on his own interpretations of traditional beer styles such as a saison or white beer. Jef goes for simplicity. You can tell by his brewing equipment that has grown organically. He keeps both feet firmly planted on the ground and considers any improvements carefully.

Jef: 'We like to keep things on a small scale as we want to be one hundred percent certain of the quality.' He continues to learn every single day. Brewers are still looking to improve.

There is no such thing as the 'best beer'

A visit to Brussels beer shop **Délices & Caprices** is at the top of many a beer lover's wish list. **Ann** and **Pierre Zuber** are guiding you through the wondrous world of Belgian beer, with an open mind and without blinkers. Pierre: 'There are many shades of grey in the story of Belgian beer. Don't think that you really know a beer after only one tasting. If you carry on tasting it you will notice the difference between batches, just like with a higher quality wine. That stands to reason as the quality of the ingredients will be variable. You can taste that especially with the microbrewers. Their beers are subject to the caprices of nature.' Anne and Pierre feel that beautiful beers can be made by large as well as small brewers. Anne: 'We put a high value on consistency. Can the brewer produce the same brew the second time around? That is not always as obvious as it sounds. Is the beer pleasant to drink? Agreed, an extreme beer can be quite exciting. But will you order the same again?' Anne and Pierre are enthusiastically narrating the tales of their brewery visits. They tell the story behind the beer. Anne: 'We listen to our customers, we gauge their taste and only then will we recommend a beer. We will never force a product on a customer. If someone likes it sweet, we won't recommend an extremely bitter IPA. And why, if a customer has not tasted a gueuze in his or her life, would you sell them the sourest gueuze possible? Some beers, you just have to grow into. If you are tasting many different beers you will naturally expect more complexity. But what's wrong with a simple beer?' Belgians have grown up with beer. They don't often stop to think that it really is a complex product. Anne: 'Once again, the umpteenth hype is not what we are about. There is no such thing as the "best beer". The best beer for you is the beer that you want to drink right now. And that is different for everyone. At the end of the day, you decide what you are drinking.' Pierre comments in a jokey way: 'Ever tasted a Japanese lambic? Leo Imai is Japanese but lives in Belgium. Leo has had this Cuvée Chapeau lambic brewed by De Troch. There is one with Japanese plums and one using the blossoms of the Japanese cherry tree. Can you taste that saltiness? Such an explosion of aromas!' Both of us have fallen silent. The fruit of passion has suffocated the voice of passion.

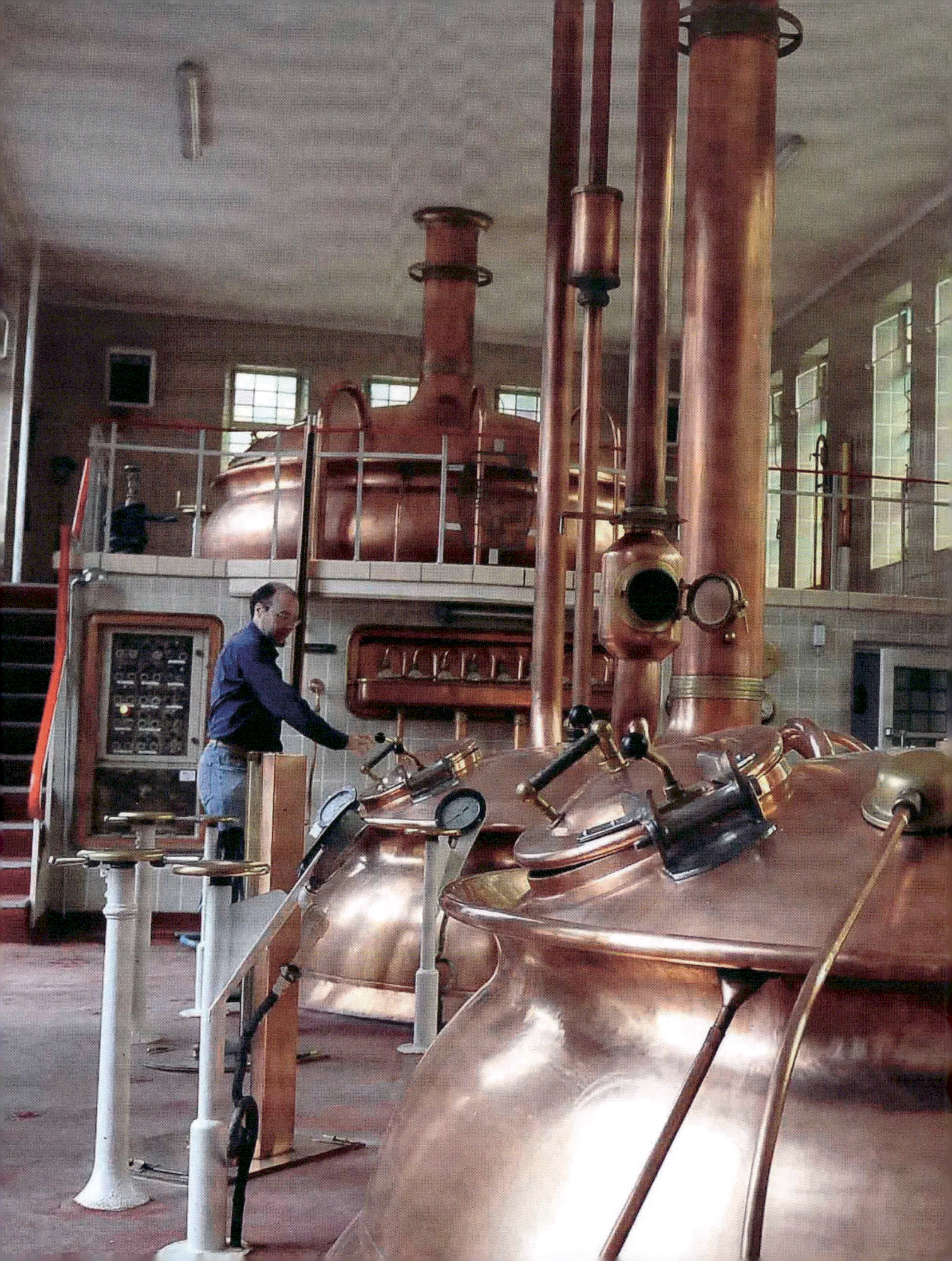

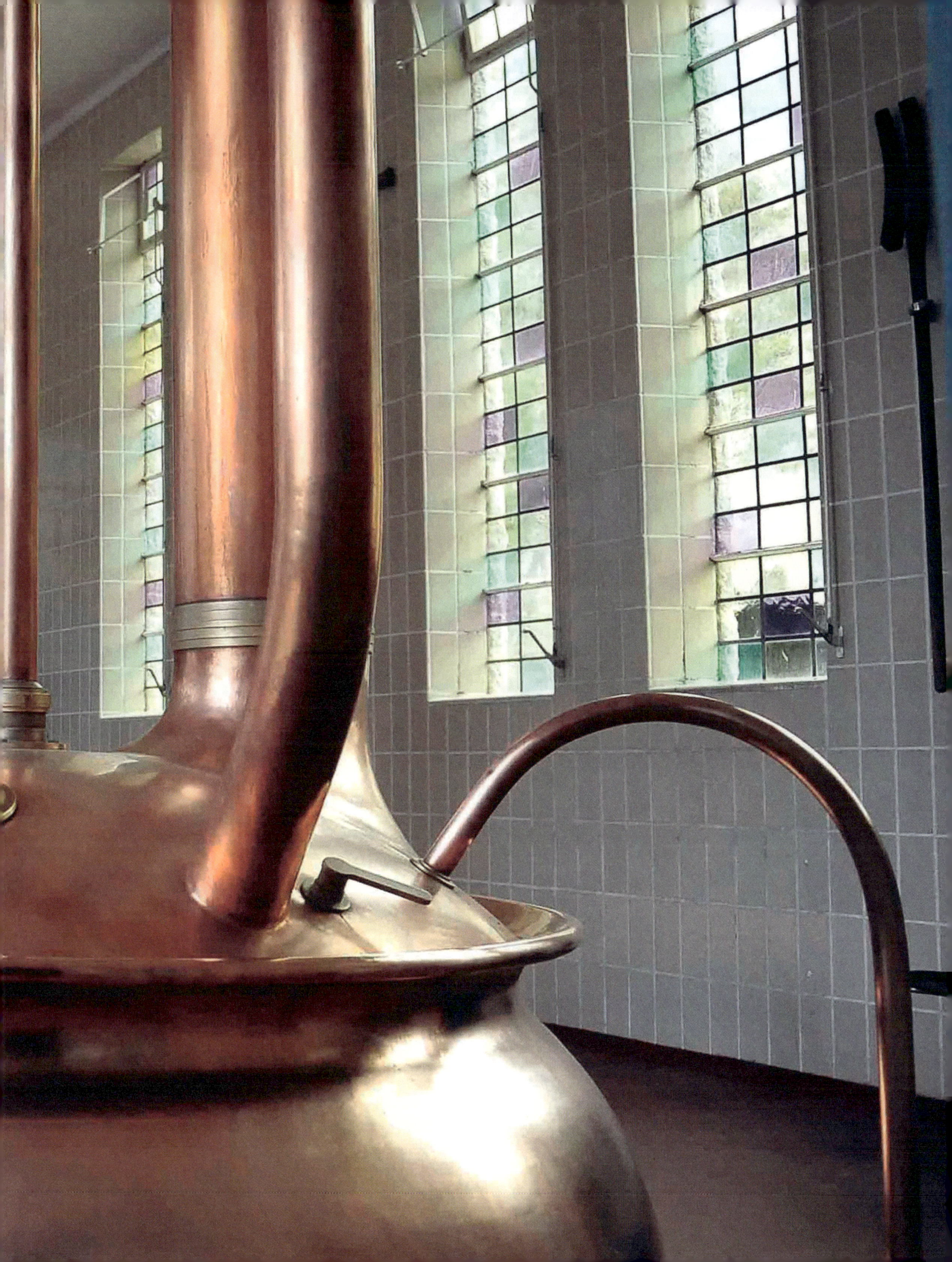

Today's beer landscape is in danger of fragmentation, Willem states. He holds both large and small breweries in much respect. However, he feels that brewers ought to limit themselves to brewing a small number of beers and concentrate on making these the best they can be. Otherwise, the risk of making unbalanced beers is never far away. And such a beer becomes boring very quickly. Willem: 'You are not brewing beer to make the *Guinness Book of Records*. Just admit it, it's not too hard to make the bitterest or sourest beer!'

Willem, in a former life, was a gueuzesteker with De Cam. He is singing the praises of lambic. 'So unique, with such a pure taste! Did you know that some lambics are hard to tell apart from white wine?' This beer expert is convinced that the unique Belgian beer culture deserves protection. 'Where else are they maturing their beers in wooden barrels or manage the art of re-fermentation that produces better beers that can be stored for longer? Belgium is also a country of "blenders" (gueuzestekers) and "cutters" of young and old beer. Adding young beer to old beer 'softens' it. On the other hand, the young beer improves in taste thanks to the old beer.' We cannot dispute that the result is very refreshing. Willem comments that many Belgian brewers pass on their know-how from father to son or share it with colleagues to safeguard the expertise of many years. 'That is the driving force of many family breweries. They always had a reasonably sound knowledge of the brewing process. Much of it is written down in ancient tomes. Up to 1850, people knew how to brew but when the beer tasted bad, they were unable to find out why. The tide turned in 1850. Pasteur conducted an in-depth investigation of beer yeast, another half-century later the secret of single yeast strains had been divulged and much insight had been gained into complex chemical processes.' Science slowly seeped into the beer glass…

Not aiming for a Guinness record

Willem Van Herreweghen had a thirty-year career with Palm Belgian Craft Brewers as their Production manager. He is now a brewery consultant with clients including Timmermans. They hired him to fine-tune their oude gueuze and lambic and Willem is also in charge of co-ordinating the opening of new microbreweries for the Anthony Martin Group, the owner of Timmermans. Let's have a round of beer history. Willem: 'Over here, traditions were usually passed from father to son. In Belgium, the trend towards globalisation occurred relatively late with Stella Artois (AB Inbev). Many small and medium-sized breweries managed to hang on to their traditional methods of brewing.'

Beers with a soul

'I only sell beers that I can support wholeheartedly.' Beer seller and sommelier **Christophe Gillard** of **Mi-Orge Mi-Houblon** in Aarlen (Arlon) does not beat around the bush. 'Many people want something other than a supermarket beer', Christophe finds. 'They are looking for authenticity and they want to know who is brewing their beer. I feel this personal relationship with the brewer is very important. Most of the brewers I work with are also my friends. I sell beers with a soul from brewers I respect.' With 350 beers, 70 percent of which are Belgian, Christophe's range shows the great diversity of Belgian brewing talent. Christophe makes a plea for respect of the Belgian brewing tradition. Our brewers must treasure the traditional beer styles and refine them. 'Why should a Belgian brewer copy IPAs from America?' Christophe wonders. 'Our true strength lies in brewing balanced beers. Real saisons, triples, red-brown beers... Let's focus on that to distinguish ourselves even more from "Belgian style" beers. I am calling on the brewers to always use the most appropriate yeast for their saison or triple.

> 'GOOD BELGIAN BEERS ARE COMPLEX.
> THE RE-FERMENTATION
> IN THE BOTTLE DEEPENS THE TASTE.'

If you are brewing a stout you should work with English yeast.' Christophe knows what he is tasting and, on an annual basis, we are talking about between 2500 and 3000 beers. His inner Belgian expects balance in the glass. He finds that many new microbrewers have too generous a hand when it comes to dosing hops or other ingredients, making their beer 'unbalanced'. If that happens, one single glass is sufficient. 'There is not too much of an art to scoring with a single batch', Christophe feels. 'But the best brewers manage to build up a consistent range. Take Brasserie de la Senne, De Ranke, Rulles or Cantillon. They have a basic offering with consistent quality. Besides, they give themselves room to experiment.' Christophe Gillard is helping to pave the road towards beer gastronomy. Within his own region he is responsible for the food pairings at Hostellerie Du Peiffeschof, La Grappe d'Or and L'Espelette. In Brussels he collaborates with La Buvette, Le Café des Spores and Hopla Geiss. A few years ago the sommelier entered into a partnership with Jean Le Chocolatier in Habay-la-Neuve. They work together to develop pairings for different pralines with beers made by Brasserie de Rulles, Sainte-Hélène and Cantillon, amongst others. 'Belgian beer offers a wealth of possibilities at the table', is Christophe's opinion. 'This is because good Belgian beers are complex. The re-fermentation in the bottle deepens the taste. Our beautiful beer styles have developed throughout the years. They are a piece of heritage that we need to treat carefully. I am all for creativity. But if I come across a "Double Blond" I start asking myself some questions. A Belgian "Dubbel" is dark by definition. It is a contradiction in terms, just like a "Black IPA".'

Balance required

'Balance in the glass, that really is the trade mark of Belgian beer', is the opinion of brewing teacher **Luc Pauwels**. 'It is in the DNA of our brewers. Don't come here if you are after an extremely sour, bitter or strong beer. Some may feel that our beers are too "well-behaved". But what we do offer are beers that are genuine classics. You cannot establish a tradition such as this from one day to the next. It translates into quality in the glass. I recently tasted a number of sour beers. Straight away I was able to tell the barrel-soured beers apart from the artificially soured beers. To achieve balance in the glass takes discipline, time, experience, know-how and continuity. You don't learn to brew in one day. Investing in technology also comes into it. Microbreweries often suffer from lack of resources.' Luc is taking a pragmatic view. He is teaching his students how to brew and taste in a way that is technically correct. He will not regale you with strange and unusual stories. But he will definitely teach you how to spot undesirable *off flavours*, diacetyl or DMS (Dimethyl sulfide) for example, in the beer and explains how to avoid them.

Pils land

Granted, our specialty beers enjoy an excellent reputation world-wide. We are in danger of forgetting that Belgium is a pils country at heart. Three in four beer glasses contain pils. Yannick Boes, who used to be the General Manager of Alken-Maes, and his colleague Robert Putman, a former Director of Production, set out to provide a detailed explanation. 'Pils revolutionised the beer world', Robert Putman tells us. 'This bottom-fermented beer provided a stable quality in the days when the beer was likely to turn sour quite quickly. Various factors contributed to the success of pils. First and foremost, there was Louis Pasteur, who identified beer yeasts and bacteria. Pasteurisation — a heating process — now renders the bacteria harmless and ensures a stable quality. At Carlsberg, Emil Hansen introduced the single, pure cell culture to propagate fresh yeast. The advent of refrigeration equipment was another key element.'

Pils was born in the Czech city of Plzen, or Pilsen (see Chapter 2). Over there, the brewers used naturally soft water, Saaz hops, large-grained brewing yeast from Moravia and natural cooling facilities. They were the first to use thermometers and densimeters. 'Pils took its time to reach Belgium,' Yannick Boes tells us. 'Stella Artois (1926) was a

Robert Putman, Yannick Boes

bottom-fermented beer but you could not yet call it a true pils. Cristal (1928) was the first genuine Belgian pils, brewed following the Czech tradition. In those days, the beer had a higher hop content (> 32 EBU) compared to modern times. The launch of the quarter-litre bottle turned Cristal into an icon. A great feat of marketing.' At the start of the 20th century Belgium counted 3,200 breweries. Only half remained after the First World War and after the Second World War, this number was halved again. In the meantime the Belgians had discovered English beers. The end of the Second World War heralded a time of rationalisation, consolidation and concentration in the beer world.

'Don't forget that pils is expensive to produce', Robert Putman continues. 'You have to invest in refrigeration equipment, in bottling plants and in marketing. This meant that gradually, the brewery evolved from a labour-intensive company into a capital-intensive one. An increasingly lower number of breweries but the remaining ones were a lot bigger in size.' The tide started to turn at the beginning of the 1960s. Belgians made a stand against 'uniform pils' and re-discovered their specialty beers. "Het Jaar van het Bier (1986 – the Year of the Beer) was initiated by the Federation of Brewers and played a significant role in promoting these beers," Yannick Boes assures us.

'That year saw us travelling around the entire country, mashing stick in hand, to promote our beers. At Alken-Maes we were giving beer gastronomy a step-up in the early 1990s with our book Beer and Gastronomy with its associated hotel, café and restaurant training."

The renaissance of specialty beers led to an increased appreciation of the existing breweries. New microbreweries found inspiration in beers and beer styles that had all but vanished, white beer and saison for example. Demand from abroad for Belgian beer also offered the smaller players a chance to survive. 'We are now living the 'moment de gloire' of Belgian beer', Yannick Boes comments. 'There is an explosion of creativity, particularly amongst craft brewers. Belgian brewers make their mark by innovating based on a rich tradition.' It turns out that this revival also provides great opportunities for bottom-fermented beers. 'Yes, a great challenge indeed', Robert Putman agrees. 'Take the new wave of 'session beers'. These are light beers with plenty of taste. It takes a great deal of expertise to make them as alcohol unites and re-enforces the taste. So how do you make a light beer with character? A challenge that pils brewers are more than happy to take up!'

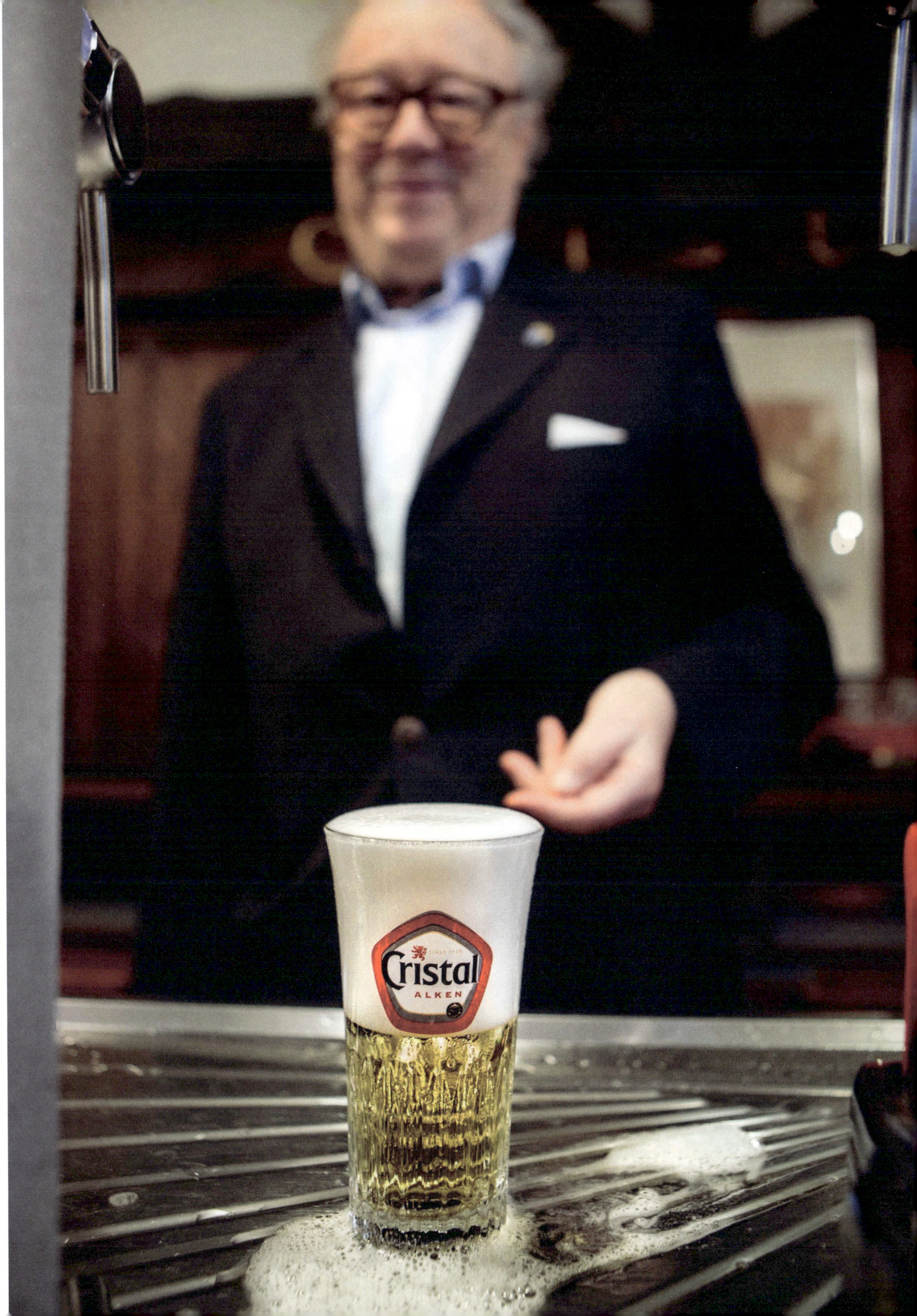
Cristal
ALKEN

Belgian beer around the world

Elisabeth Pierre

(beer author, France)

'Whenever I am blind tasting or am visiting a brewery, it gives me great pleasure to discover Belgian beers. You want to find out all there is to know about Belgian beers but, in fact, you will never really know them ... When I was taking part in the Rue de la Flandre event in Paris, I noticed that everybody, young and old alike, attended the tastings but for many of them this was the first time they were tasting a Belgian beer. At this event, people discovered our bruin, Flemish red-brown and white beers. They came to the conclusion that iconic brands often constituted a beer style in themselves. If you want to introduce the French to Belgian beer, you have your work cut out. You could explain to them how the saison came into existence and get them to taste a number of different saisons. Try the same with a lambic, oude gueuze, Flemish red-brown, Oudenaards bruin ... Whenever I organise tastings and food pairing sessions, a blind tasting of several Belgian beer styles invariably forms part of the programme. In this way, you "dive" into the glass straight away, put your blinkers to one side and discover the huge diversity. Also, I would advise everyone to discover the Belgian beer culture in the country where it was born, although I have to admit that I still have to meet quite a few brewers in their own breweries.'

Melissa Cole

(beer author, United Kingdom)

'Beer is in the Belgian DNA. This applies equally to global brands as to historic beer styles kept alive by stubborn brewers. The story of Belgian beer culture is unique. You travel from faro to white beer, stopping at triple or gueuze and traverse a world of tastes. And I am not even talking about the *single hopped*, strong blond beers, a Duvel for example, or the light but tasty session beers made by Brasserie de la Senne. It is like the Belgian sense of humour. You can't really put your finger on it (define it), it is just as personal as your fingerprint and is a source of inspiration for beer lovers across the world.'

A brewer's emblem with a mashing basin, malt blades, mashing stick and ladle and bucket displayed at the Beer Advertising Museum (Bierreclamemuseum) in Breda in the Netherlands.

John M. Brauer

(*Executive officer* European Brewery Convention (EBC), South Africa)

'Belgium is at the crossroads of the Roman and Germanic cultures in the heart of Europe. Having said that, international beer styles have never gained the upper hand on traditional local beer styles. A whole range of niche beers has survived throughout the centuries. Every single one has its unique roots and unique taste profile. No two beer styles are exactly the same, but there are quite a few similarities: some beers are lighter, some are stronger, they can be more or less hoppy... The list really is endless, the result of varying combinations of basic ingredients and brewing methods. Belgian beer has it all. It is a micro-cosmos of beers and beer styles. Rock musician Frank Zappa once stated that each real country has its own beer and its own airline. I wonder if he was aware of the rich Belgian beer culture and its incredibly diverse beer landscape.'

Stephen Beaumont

(beer author, Canada)

'Belgian beer was a revelation for people like me, who had grown up with British, German, Czech and North American beers in the 1980s. Our eyes were opened by Duvel, Chimay and white beers like Hoegaarden – when it still tasted right. We discovered a world of tastes and possibilities that prompted us to carry on searching. Besides bitter, pilsner, Hefeweizen and porter we explored a different, beautifully diverse world of unique beers. The North American beer tradition derived its inspiration from England and Germany to start off with. Then, the imported Belgian beers prompted the artisan microbrewers to innovate. I was born in the province of Québec, where Brasserie d'Achouffe used to sell one third of what it produced. Belgian beers were very influential here, owing to imports as well as the "Belgian style" beers made by Unibroue. Once Belgian beers became successful, creativity followed naturally. I think it is a shame that many young beer drinkers and brewers seem to go for an IPA straight away without first exploring the manifold world of tastes offered by Belgian beers, like we did in those days. I love hops and I understand that the North American microbrewers are inspiring the Belgians. But I remain convinced that we can learn a huge amount from Belgian beers.'

Brewers removing the bostel from the brewing kettle using a 'stuikmand', or filtering basket. Brewing day at the 17th century Paenhuys brewery at Bokrijk open air museum close to Genk.

Carsten Berthelsen

(beer author, Denmark)

'There is no doubt at all: Belgium has the best beers. Where else do you find such diversity? A golden-blond beer, with or without yeast residues, a full-mouthed dark beer, a sour beer, a white beer, a saison or an amber-coloured top-fermented beer... The world of Belgian beer continues to spin, however. In 1996 De Ranke introduced its revolutionary XX Bitter (6.2% alc. vol., 65 EBU). Quite an innovation at the time. Nino Bacelle and Guido Devos were challenging the taste buds of Belgian beer drinkers and their pale ale, made in the American mould, became a success. The Belgian breweries are now launching hoppy beers, the Duvel Tripel Hop made by Duvel Moortgat or the Saison Cuvée Dry Hopping from Dupont, for example. You will also come across porter and stout and beautiful wood-matured quadruples in Belgium. The key is to innovate and to experiment. We are living through the best beer years ever, the fruit of a successful marriage between tradition and innovation. My very best wishes to beer drinkers worldwide and, above all, in Belgium!'

Lisa Morrison

(beer author, owner of Belmont Station, USA)

''The USA has always been considered a melting pot of different countries and the same goes for the artisan microbreweries. The first wave of American microbreweries drew its inspiration from English, German and Belgian beer styles. The English and German styles lay at the basis of the first brews. The Belgian beers contributed an intriguing touch and sharpened creativity. The Belgians taught our brewers to let their beers mature in chambers, in wooden barrels, and how to "cut" (blend) them. They inaugurated them into all the secrets of spontaneous, wild fermentation. Thirty years on — at least in some parts of the USA — the American microbrewers have found their own direction. However, the unique and diverse beer styles of Belgium remain a source of inspiration for brewers from the USA and all corners of the world.'

John Holl

(editor *All About Beer Magazine*, USA)

'Gimmicks, hypes and experiments with fermentation that continue to push the boundaries are all features of the current beer landscape. The source of these trends lies in the past. Belgian beer is just like the perfect tailor-made black suit, classic and timeless. Blond, gueuze, lambic, double, triple, quadruple... The traditional beer styles and beer types have served to inspire poets and artists and prompted agnostics to embrace spirituality. They make café owners happy and instil pride in craftsmen. They provide a blank canvas for beer. Beer pilgrims travel to Brussels, to Flanders, to smaller towns and cities and abbeys, to Antwerp and further afield to drink from the original well and to experience living history. There is no other country that breathes beer culture quite like Belgium. You won't gain a full appreciation of Belgian beer culture if you don't come to Belgium and discover its beers in the place they are brewed.'

Tim Hampson

(beer author, president of The British Guild of Beer Writers (BGWB), United Kingdom)

'Belgium, boring? It is the birthplace of Stella Artois, the global Number One when it comes to beer. Nowadays this country brews more historic beer styles than any other place in the world. There are dark beers, red-brown beers, fruit beers, brut beers and spontaneously fermented sour beers. But you also find zesty white beers, saisons and brews that don't fit any particular beer style. Not forgetting the divine Trappists and abbey beers. Belgian brewing culture has had an impact on craft brewers around the world. There was a short time where Belgian brewers seemed a bit lost. No-one can claim to make the best beer in the world, as good beers are now produced all around the globe. Brewers in Belgium, Britain and Germany had been resting on their laurels. They were wary of experimenting, shied away from innovation and did not even draw on the past to gain inspiration for their new beers. Fortunately, times have changed. We now see a generation of brewers - in established breweries and also amongst the newcomers — who have an eye for the quality of the ingredients coupled with a passion for beer. Innovation and respect for tradition go hand in hand.'

Masayoshi Kaji

(beer connoisseur, Japan)

'Belgian beer is synonymous with great diversity. You could even state that every country in the world is aiming for the local, personal and original character of Belgian beer. Japan is no exception. We have excellent brewing technology as well as very enthusiastic and capable brewers at our disposal. But there is something missing: the ancient tradition of Belgian beer. In that sense, your story will always be different from ours. We discovered Belgium by drinking Belgian beer.'

Henri Reuchlin

(President European Beer Consumers Union (EBC), beer author, Netherlands)

'Ach, when I think that, for half my beer life, I gazed longingly at our Southern neigbours... They knew how to live well and produced such delicious beers! Back in those days, when the Dutch beer landscape looked like what you can see from your window (flat but refreshing), a friend used to bring me Belgian beers from time to time. Very appropriately, his name was Gruythuysen. Beers full of taste and aroma. Beers with plenty of colour. I even found out that a Rodenbach eventually leaves the body with a colour that would make our Royal Family proud. However, there is a paradox. In Dutch 'the dialectics of progress' mean that sometimes, when you are first you can also be left behind. Translating this to beer, these comfortable riches of taste do not provide a fertile ground for innovation. Other beer countries are experimenting to their heart's content albeit with varying outcomes. Compare that to the Belgian taste masters, who have been left behind in this respect. And that is a shame. Fortunately, in recent years Belgian beer has been going through some sort of renaissance, based on the ancient adage: change what you must but keep that what is good. And so far, this approach appears to be succeeding.'

Charles Leclef, proprietor of Het Anker brewery in Mechelen, is also a Knight of the Mashing Stick. These 'Knights' represent the honour of the brewing trade. The Knighthood has carried on the traditions of the 14th century Brewers' Guild that grew into the current Federation of Brewers.

Fedor Vogel

(publisher and editor-in-chief of *Bier! Magazine*, Netherlands)

'Belgian beer is the calibration point for every brewer and every beer lover. The beginning and the end. Alpha and omega. Anything in between was once derived from Belgian beer. At virtually all Belgian breweries tradition and craftsmanship go hand in hand. Innovation just for the sake of innovation is not something Belgian brewers like to do. Their motto is to retain what is good. Joining in with hypes or trends is unfamiliar to a Belgian. In contrast, what does the Belgian brewer credit, time and time again, is that he delivers stable quality and brews a consistent product. Is Belgian beer too sweet or too smooth or not distinctive enough? This may be the case now and again but this is also why the most quaffable specialty beers come from Belgium too. Belgian beer is popular with a global audience. Its success abroad proves it. And don't forget the marketing power and the high esteem in which the Belgian Trappists and abbey beers are held internationally. This has a great impact. It may sound a bit old-fashioned, but Belgian beer is the one and only reference for me in terms of high-quality specialty beer. The beer I go back to time and time again.'

Lorenzo Dabove

(beer expert, Italy)

'I discovered Belgian beer in the 1970s thanks to Michael Jackson's bestseller *World Guide to Beer*. Straight away I fell in love with the beautiful photographs, especially those of the "wild" lambic beers, oud bruin and Flemish red-browns. Ever since my first visit to Belgium I have established an intense relationship with the Belgians and their culture. It has grown out of the different Belgian beer styles. Lambic, gueuze and kriek now form an integral part of my life. I am not boasting when I say that I was, and still am, one of the major advocates of the revival of this traditional drink. Just like when I first came to Belgium, I like to hang around in busy cafés for a chat with the regulars, enjoying a saison in Hainaut, a Flemish red-brown beer in West Flanders, a double or a triple in a Trappist abbey tavern, and so on in the country that has now become my "second home". My passion has spread to thousands of Italian beer lovers. Each year, they are coming to Belgium in droves, not as tourists but as well-informed beer lovers. Belgium now forms part of my life. I am showing people what a traditional lambic is like, as if I were on a mission from God. Don't forget that I am the Prince of the Pajottenland!'

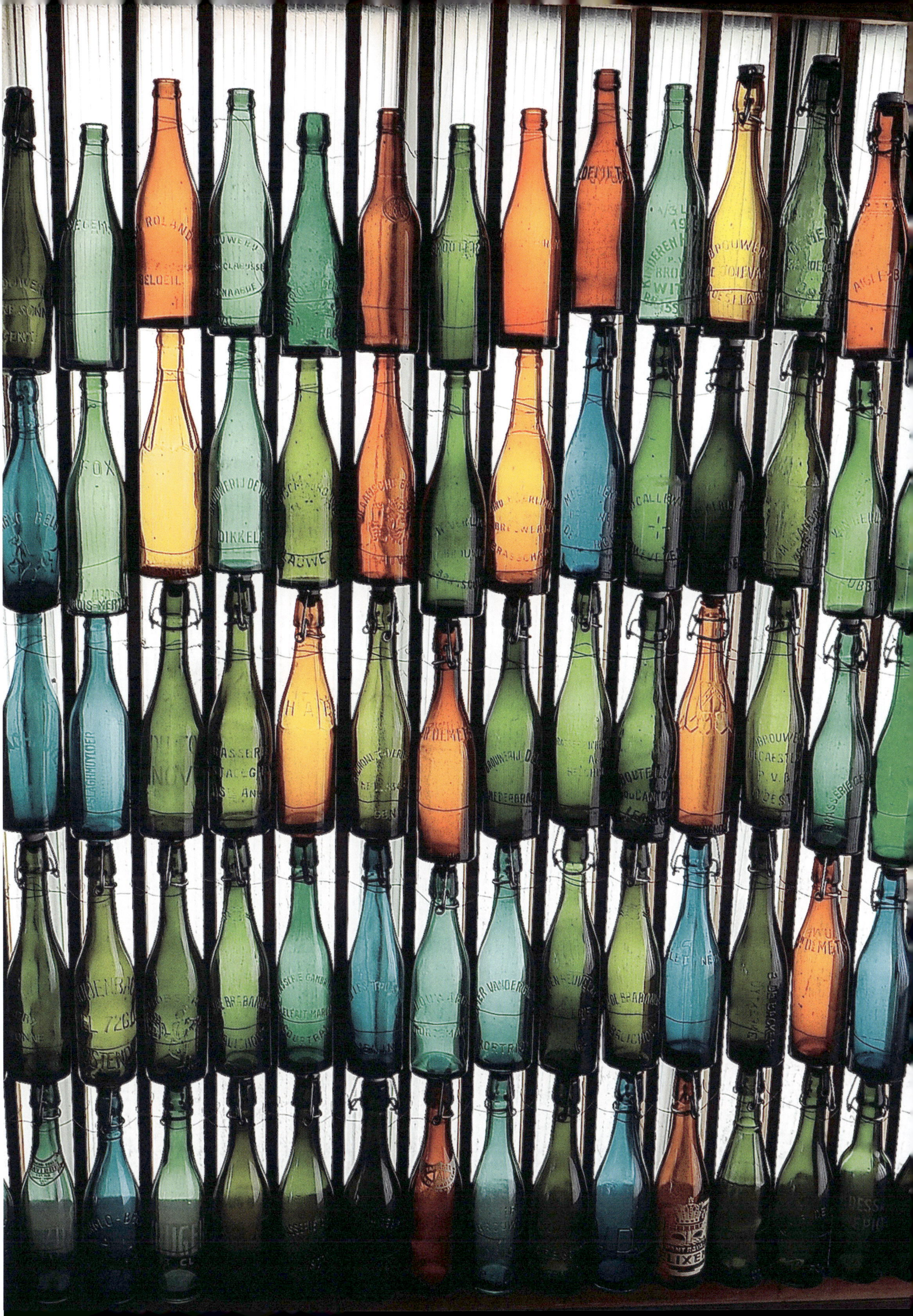
ROLAND
BELOEIL
FOX

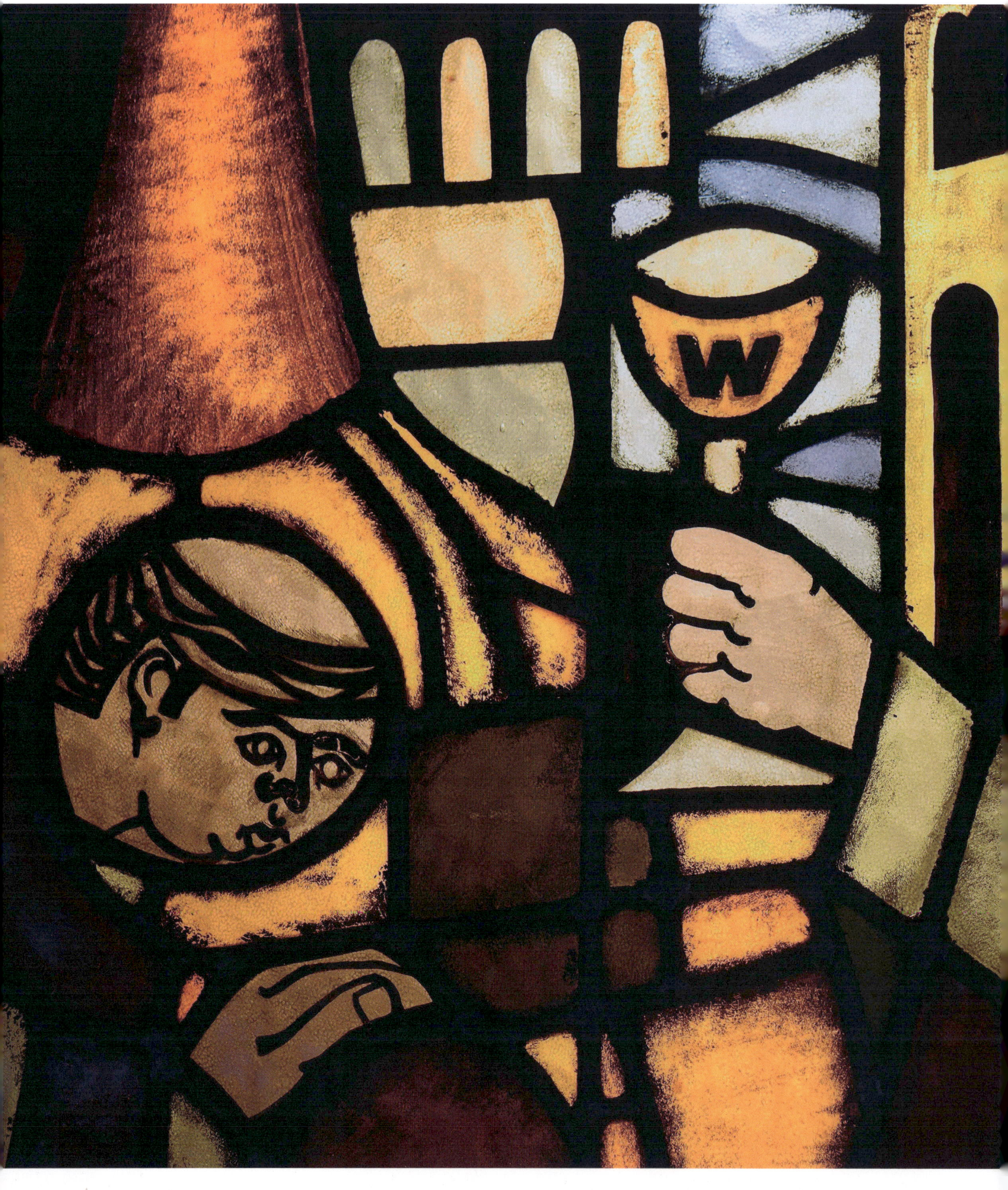
W

1 · BELGIAN IS BEER

Facts and figures

. . . .

Excise levied on beer: 196,464,000 euros
Exports: 11,222,701 hl (61.64%)
Investments: 180,300,000 euros
Production: 18,206,545 hl
Consumption per capita: 72 l
Employment (direct): 4516 persons
Employment (indirect): 45,000 persons

Source: Belgian Brewers — 2014 Annual Report

The greatest consumers of Belgian beer

. . . .

France: 3,248,799 hl
Netherlands: 2,035,877 hl
Germany: 1,325,241 hl
USA: 1,791,207 hl
Italy: 447,512 hl
Canada: 382,983 hl
United Kingdom: 280,606 hl
Japan: 122,156 hl

Source: Belgian Brewers — 2014 Annual Report

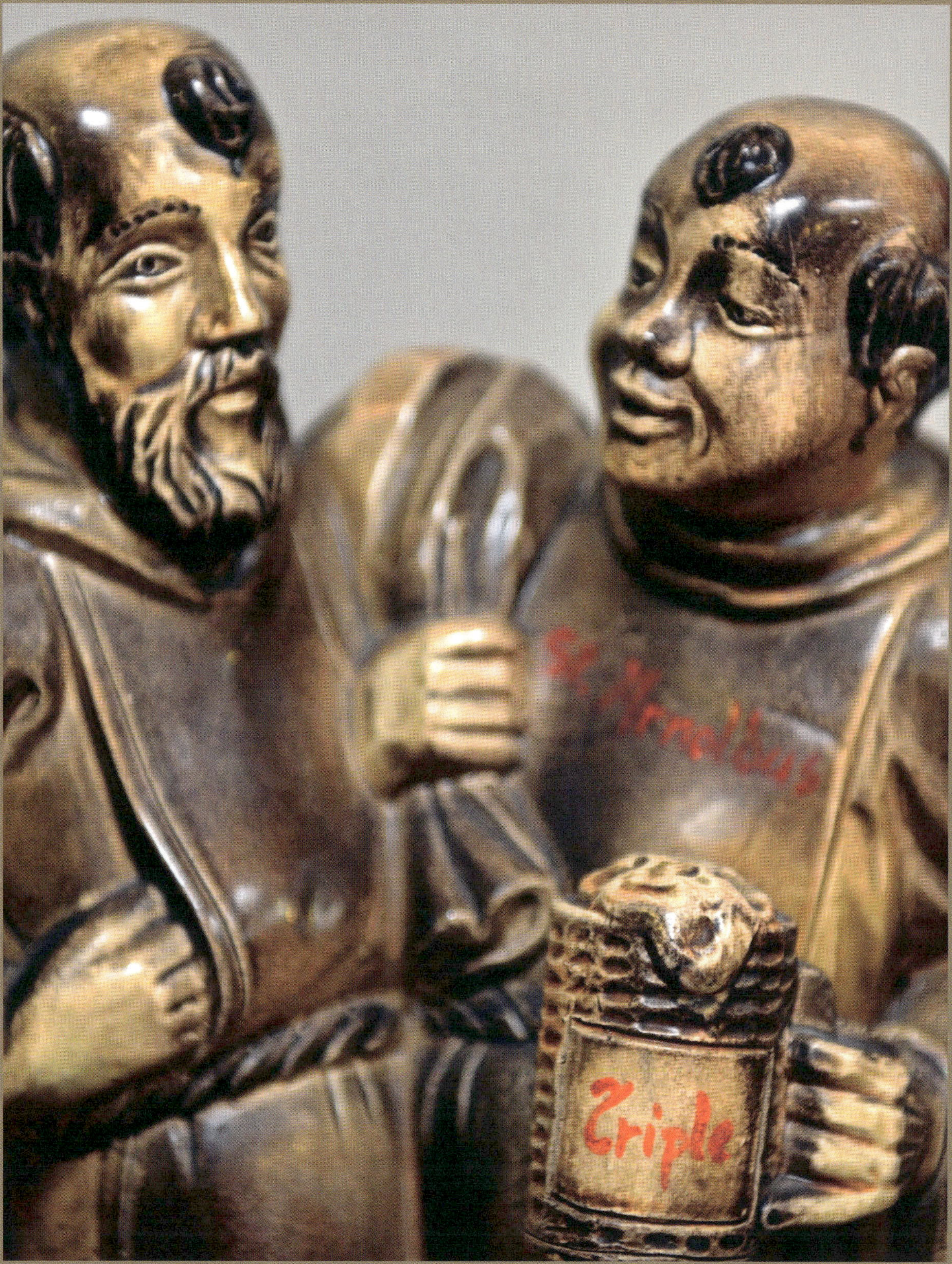
Triple

BEER IS PROOF THAT GOD LOVES US AND WANTS US TO BE HAPPY

Benjamin Franklin

SAISON
DUPONT
Biologique

DE HOORN

Battle of
Passchendaele
FLANDERS OFFENSIVE
31 juli 1917
To remember
FIRST
WORLD WAR
1914 / 1918

Tonneke
oud
BruinBier
BROUWERY - GOETHALS - MEULEBEKE

Brasserie d'Achouffe

Beer is the answer...
but I can't remember the question.
'T WAAGSTUK

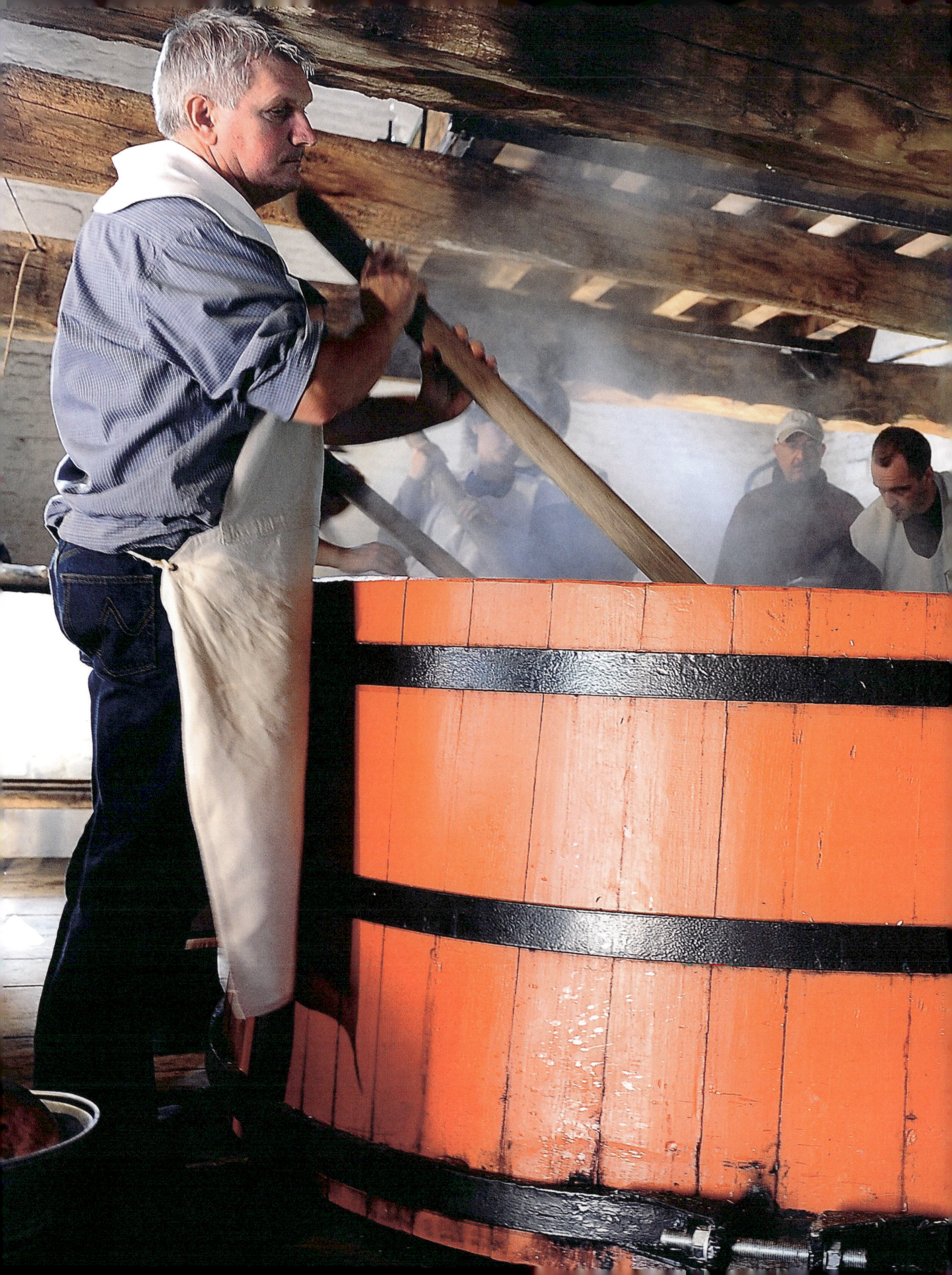

2

THE HISTORY OF BELGIAN BEER

THE HISTORY OF BELGIAN BEER

Beer is as old as... The earliest evidence of brewing activity can be traced back to ancient Babylon and Egypt. Also in China, brewing was done thousands of years ago. We are not going back in time quite that far. The history of Belgian beer starts in the early Middle Ages. Will you join us on our journey?

A healthy drink for everyone in the Middle Ages

(300-1500 NC)

Beer does not make you ill but water does. Beer is safe. This explains the success of beer in the Middle Ages when beer was essential to life as drinking water was heavily polluted. In what is now Belgium people consumed an estimated 300 litres of beer per annum. Rivers, ditches and canals were open sewers. Water was a source of germs and this is why everyone, young and old alike, was drinking beer. However, medieval beer is vastly different from the beer we consume today. It contained hardly any alcohol and had a sour and smoky taste. The populace was drinking 'thin' or small beer, boiled water in other words. During the third or first rinse the water was poured over the already exhausted remains of the grain used to produce beer for the well-to-do. The rich were able to afford 'thick beer', made with the first rinse. In those days beer was mainly based on oats and barley. Rye and wheat were used to a far lesser extent. The first professional breweries and abbey breweries also saw the light during this era. The abbeys with their literate monks developed into the knowledge centres of the beer world. Abbeys owned extensive lands that provided the ingredients for brewing. The monks acquired a vast knowledge of brewing techniques. They were predominantly brewing for their own use but also to sustain the many pilgrims. For example, the plans for the model abbey (820) of **Sankt Gallen** in Switzerland included no fewer than three breweries: one to brew the beer for the dignitaries, one for the beer for the simple pilgrims and one to produce the beer for the monks. Around 800, during the reign of Charlemagne, large professional breweries were created, where brewing was done for noblemen and their courts. This instantly put a stop to the role of women in the brewing world. Until then, brewing had mainly been carried out by women. But the gentlemen could not fail to notice that brewing was a (very) lucrative activity… In a number of regions, female brewers or women who dared to brew, ended up on the pyre. They were called 'beer witches'. The legend of beer king Cambrinus harks back to the Middle Ages. He may have been the Duke of Brabant, Jan Primus (1252-1294). He loved his drink and he loved to fight. After his victory in the Battle of Woeringen (1288) he staged a drinking feast. First of all, he drank the nobility under the table and then mixed with his soldiers, sitting on a beer barrel, holding a large beer jug. This is how he is usually depicted. Jan Primus liked women. Disguised as a troubadour he travelled through Flanders and Northern France and courted many women. When he entered into a liaison with the wife of Valseneuve, a knight, he was caught in the deed. Whereupon Valseneuve challenged him to a duel. In full gallop Jan Primus sped towards his rival to joust him from the saddle. His adversary exclaimed angrily: "Is it not a shame that a true knight is assisted by a helper?" Jan looked behind him for a split second. At that very moment his adversary pierced his heart. Valseneuve's retort: "Your helper was the jug of beer you downed before the fight. By calling him I was able to beat you." Jan Primus's body was boiled and his flesh was buried in Bar-Le-Duc in Northern France. His bones found their final resting place in Brussels and are buried in the former Franciscan abbey not far from the Grand Place. Here you can visit the catacombs and the grave of Jan Primus. Throughout the years the name of Jan Primus was corrupted and turned into Cambrinus or Gambrinus. Throughout Europe you will find beers and pubs that pay light-hearted homage to this historic figure. Just think of Primus pils brewed by Haacht, the Czech Gambrinus pils and the Dutch Hertog Jan. And, at Leuven's Grote Markt you will find the Gambrinus tavern. Saint Arnold was a knight from Tiegem (1040-1087). He embraced monkhood and in 1084 founded the Abbey of Saint Peter in Oudenburg. He wanted to prevent people from falling ill and advised them to drink beer. By doing so he saved many lives. Arnold was declared holy and, in later days, was promoted to Patron Saint of brewers. His statue, mashing staff in hand, guards many a brewhall.

Bruges – the city of beer

Bruges was home to many home brewers in the Middle Ages. Brewing activity was on a small scale, comparable with bread baking. In the middle of the 15th century the city numbered approx. fifty breweries. It was decided in 1622 that each citizen would be allowed to brew at home for his own usage. The new law resulted in 425 home breweries by 1680.

1. Miniature of Manfredus de Monte Imperiali, de herbis from Pisa, Italy (1320-1340), Bibliothèque nationale de France, Paris.
2. Cambrinus (1252-1294).

---

¹Reuchlin, Van brood tot Brood, p. 32 en 33.

In a clear voice

What did monks drink in the Middle Ages? Wine, mead, beer and water. Wine was a festive drink intended for religious ceremonies. Beer was an alternative to drinking water of suspect quality and provided a source of vitamins, especially when strict fasting was observed. On the floorplan of several abbeys you will find the brewery next to the bakery and the mill. Unsurprisingly, as the baker and the brewer used the same ingredients. Under the Rule of Benedict the monks were allowed to drink a limited amount of beer with their meal. Quite sparingly, as the monks had to be able to sing 'in a clear voice' during Holy Mass. Ancient written documents show that different qualities of beer were served in the abbeys. The best quality beer was made from barley and was served to guests. Oat beer was for the monks… who generally drank the lighter beer. This tradition has survived until today in the lighter monks' beers such as the 'green' Orval and Westmalle Extra.

Gruit of hops?

In the Middle Ages, brewers used the herbal mixture called 'gruit' that contained, amongst others things, yarrow, sage, Myrica gale, ginger and cumin. You would buy your gruit at your local 'gruithuis'. In this way the local authorities made some money out of it too. At the 'Gruuthuus' in Bruges the Lords of Gruuthuus would collect excise duties on behalf of the Count of Flanders. Abbeys were not obliged to purchase gruut and so they were the first to make the switch to hops. The hop plant officially reached our shores in 768. At Weihenstephan Abbey (Bavaria) the beer was flavoured with hops, with the added benefit of extending its 'shelf life'. In a charter dating back to 822 Adelard, Father Superior at Corvey Abbey, gave permission to his miller to work in the hop garden. In her writings on medicine, entitled *Physica* and *Causae et Curae*, German abbess Hildegard von Bingen (13th century) described a beverage made with 'hoppho' or 'hop'. This herb has a calming influence and tones down the male libido, the abbess wrote.

Emperor Charles IV (1316-1378) issued an edict under the name of 'Novus Modus Fermentandi Cerevisiam' in 1364. This new brewing method required the use of hops. This obligation applied to the Holy Roman Empire (the German Empire at the time), which also included the region of Imperial Flanders (the part of Flanders situated East of the River Scheldt). From then on, the beers from Imperial Flanders and Brabant would be different from those produced by the County of Flanders. The 'gruitrecht' remained in force for beers brewed to the West of the River Scheldt, as did fermentation by souring. For many years the use of hops was the subject of a hot debate. Both the nobility and judiciary, entitled to levy taxes on the use of gruit, tried to forbid its use. In the end, the beer drinker had the last word. There are now many countries where, conversely, you are not allowed to brew *without* the use of hops. Towards the end of the Middle Ages, males took over the brewing role from females who had traditionally been in charge of producing beer.

Breweries grew in size and there was (a lot of) money to be made from brewing. This prompted many men to take up the mashing staff for themselves.

1. *European Beer Museum at Stenay, France.*
2. *Miniature, Bruges (1525-1530), Pierpont Morgan Library.*

2 • THE HISTORY OF BELGIAN BEER

The brewing guild

Belgian Brewers: this is what the Belgian Brewing Federation calls itself today. Not to be confused with Belgian brewers in general. Not every brewery is a member. Belgian Brewers is one of the oldest professional associations in the country and even in the world, with roots that go all the way back to the powerful medieval Guild of Brewers that was founded in the 14th century. It is therefore no coincidence that the Belgian Brewers now occupy the historic location of the Brewers' House (1698) at Brussels' Grand Place. The Federation represents 100 large and medium-sized breweries. Together they account for over 90% of beer production in Belgium.

Ridders van de Roerstok

The Belgian Brewers inherited the traditions of the 14th century brewers' guild. The Knighthood of the Brewer's Mash Staff reminds us of these centuries-old traditions. The 'knights' represent the worthiness of the brewer's craft. Each year in February, the Belgian brewers celebrate the Festival of King Gambrinus. The summer months culminate in the annual Brussels Beer Weekend held at the Grand Place where Saint Arnold, the patron Saint of brewers, is paid due reverence. New Knights are appointed every year. An 'enthronement' such as this requires an elaborate ceremony held in Brussels Town Hall. Many brewers attend bearing their full historic regalia. This spectacle seems to make time stand still for a little while. So who is eligible for a knighthood? Honoraries include those who have made extraordinary efforts to promote the craft of brewing and those who can fulfil the role of ambassador on behalf of the Belgian Brewers. Think of importers and distributors from a range of countries as well as hospitality professionals including zythologues, cooks, beer sommeliers, academicians, media personalities or beer authors.

A pure beer made with water, malt and hops

In 1516 Duke Wilhelm IV of Bavaria issued a beer law also known as the *Reinheitsgebot*. From then on, brewing could only be done using water, malt and hops (yeast had not yet been heard of). This local law was to affect the beer market in a major way. The law on foodstuffs was intended to safeguard the beer drinker, impose limits on beer prices (that would depend on the season), protect the brewers' guild and consequently, it had an impact on the grain market. Originating in Bavaria, the law spread across the other German states. In 1871 (the Second German Empire) the law applied to the majority of German states. It became official throughout Germany in 1906 (with yeast as a fourth ingredient). The Reinheitsgebot was also enforced in Greece. Otto I, the first King of Greece (a German prince who became King of Greece after the Convention of London) implemented the law in 1832. In 1985, two years before the law was revoked, German professor Dr. Helmut Kieninger was condemned to a jail sentence. The reason: he had made a plea for the use of chemicals in beer. He committed suicide in his cell. After the fall of the Berlin Wall the ancient Klosterbrauerie Neuzelle fell foul of the law as they had been adding syrup to only one of their bottom-fermented beers. They were

1. A horse-powered mill at the Brewer's House in Antwerp.
2. Brueghel, The Peasant Wedding (1567-1568), Kunsthistorisches Museum, Vienna.

not allowed to market their 'Schwarze' for a while. The legal authorities granted an exemption in 2005 as the sugar had been added after brewing and filtration and therefore, it was not considered a component of the malt. To this days, most German breweries produce their beers in accordance with the rules of the Reinheitsgebot. Two German brewers, Sebastien Sauer and Peter Essel of Freigeist Bierkultur, are fighting the 'dictatorship' imposed by this ancient food law. Their beers are inspired by the period of history before the introduction of the Reinheitsgebot. Such a law reeks of protectionism, in the opinion of Sauer and Essel. Only those who follow the guidelines to the letter are allowed to sell their beer. On the other hand, the aim of the Reinheitsgebot is to guarantee a level of quality. Striving for quality is far from new in the brewing world. This takes us to the Brouwershuis (the Brewer's House) at the Brouwersvliet (Brewers' Kreek) in Antwerp. In the 16th century pure untainted water was a rare commodity in this city. Water drawn from the River Scheldt or the Antwerp canals could not be trusted. Clear pure water was transported into the city from Wommelgem by way of the Herentalse Vaart canal. Gilbert Van Schoonbeke, a building tycoon, developed an enterprise zone dedicated to breweries. The year 1556 saw the introduction of a pipe system that diverted the pure water towards the new Brouwershuis. It was pumped up by means of an ingenious system before being distributed to several breweries. The building had its own horse-drawn mill. Its function was to transport scoops (water basins) all the way from the basement reservoir to the top floor. The water would then be transferred to a smaller reservoir before being streamed towards the various breweries, using an intricate pipe system. The Brouwershuis initially supplied twenty breweries. The number then went down to sixteen. None of these breweries are still in existence. The unique equipment of the Antwerp Brewers' House was on display until 1993, the year the museum closed its doors for good. However, the building is still standing firm and the equipment is intact. In the 16th century Antwerp boasted around fifty breweries. They are no longer around owing to the increased popularity of pils beer after the Second World War. The Antwerp Beer Guild survived until 1962. Its members held regular meetings in the splendid meeting hall of the Brouwershuis. Its walls are clad in gilded leather.

JOUR ET NUIT
JOUR ET NUIT
VERBODEN TE PARKEREN 24u./24u. UITGANG GARAGE

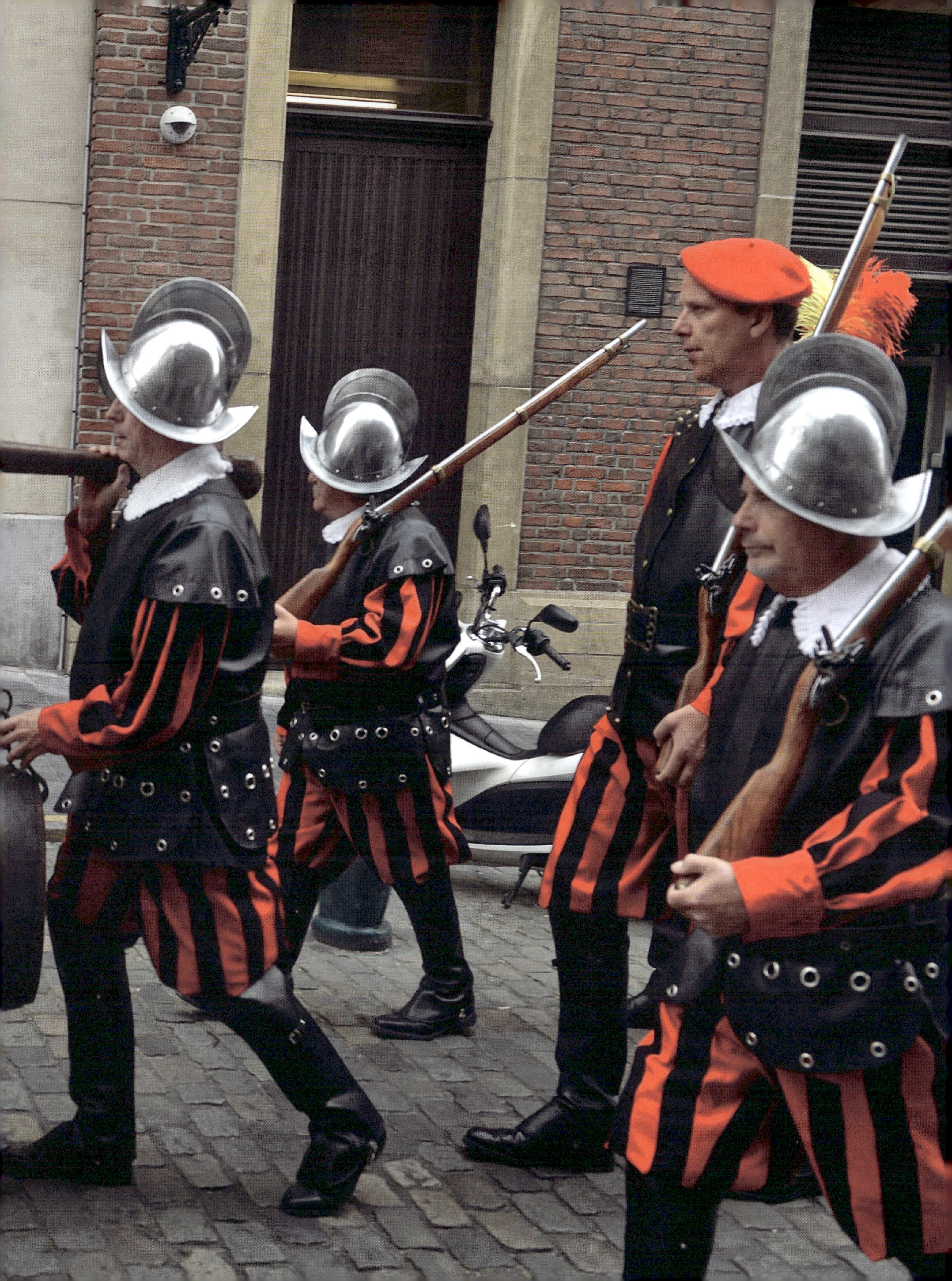

Brewing scenes from the now defunct Wieze brewery, displayed at the Huyghe Brewery Museum. >
Brewing Day at the Paenhuys brewery at Bokrijk Open Air Museum. >

City beers under pressure

(17ᵗʰ-18ᵗʰ century)

After the Middle Ages the city breweries came into their own. Towns and cities had their own special beers. There was a great variety in city beers as well as regional beers that can be explained by the quality of the water, drawn from a spring or a well, the ingredients used and differences in local brewing techniques. Just to mention a few examples: 'Brussels half en half', 'Antwerps gerstenbier' (*Antwerp barley beer*), 'Leuvense witte' (*a white beer from Louvain*), Henegouwse 'grisette' (*a 'grisette' from Hainault*), a 'saison' from Liège, a 'Caves' from Lier, an 'uitzet' from Mechelen or Herzeel, a 'kwak' from Dendermonde or a wheat beer from Hoegaarden. Not forgetting the brown beers of Oudenaarde, Zottegem and Diester. Caves, the city beer of Lier, is still brewed by the Verhaeghe-Vichte brewery, commissioned as ever by the venerable guild of 'Heren van Lier'. Caves goes all the way back to the 16th century. This brewery ceased to exist even before the First World War. However, in 1976, the local guild that went under the name of 'Heren van Lier' decided to breathe new life into this ancient city beer. Caves (5.8% alcohol volume) is a top-fermented, amber-coloured beer brewed with barley, wheat and hops, without any colouring preservatives or additional sugar. Alphonse Swartelee, brewmaster and beer historian, feels that, out of all of the beers on the market today, the sweetly sour Caves is the one that comes closest to medieval beer.

City breweries and regional breweries had a hard time of it in the 17th and 18th century. The 'new' world had been discovered and new beverages came onto the market: tea, coffee and chocolate. All of a sudden, beer drinkers were offered plenty of choice. At the same time, Dukes and Counts exempted the abbeys from paying tax as they made a real and tangible contribution to the general well-being. Towards the end of the eighteenth century, these privileges caused much unrest amongst burghers, craftsmen and traders, who felt that the abbeys were engaging in unfair competition. One of the Holy Roman Emperors, Joseph II, issued a decree that effectively dissolved the abbeys on the grounds that they were enjoying unfair advantages compared with other bakeries and breweries. From then on the abbeys were no longer allowed to practise brewing or baking. The French Revolution (1789-1794) heralded the – temporary or definitive - end for the abbeys and their associated breweries.

Brewing in the olden days
....

The open air museum of Bokrijk in Genk takes you back throughout the ages. It comprises an authentic 17th village brewery from Diepenbeek: 't Paenhuys. Come along in the third weekend in September to see the Demerdal beer lovers' guild practise brewing like in the olden days. A spectacle not to be missed. The stoker is firing up the wood to heat the water. The brewers are pouring bucketfuls of hot water into the open mashing basin. They are using mashing forks to

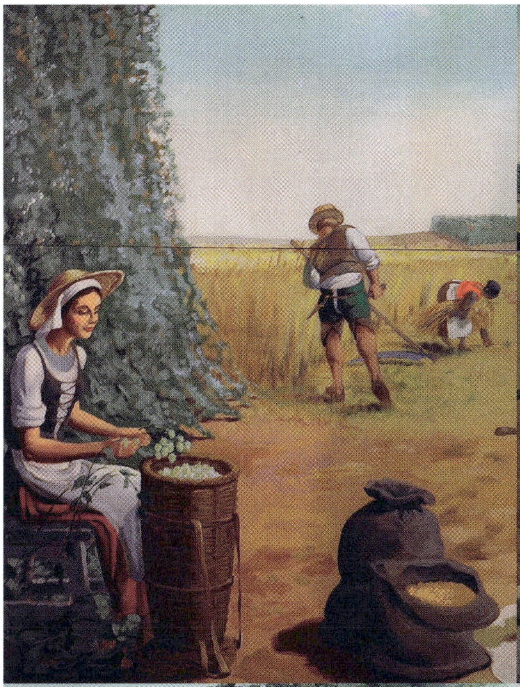
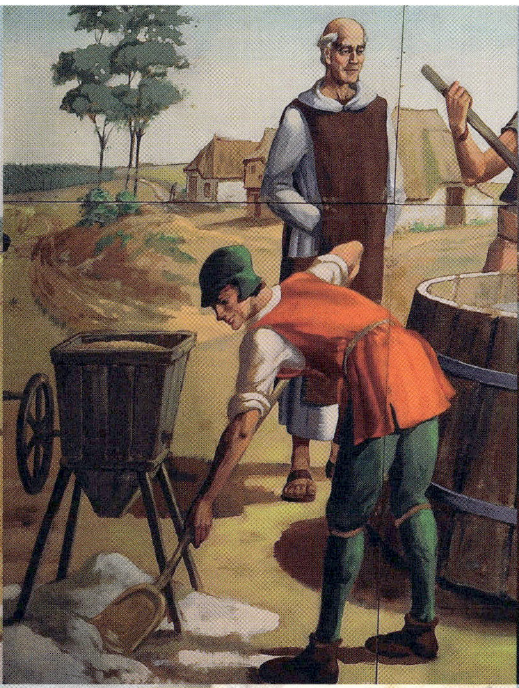
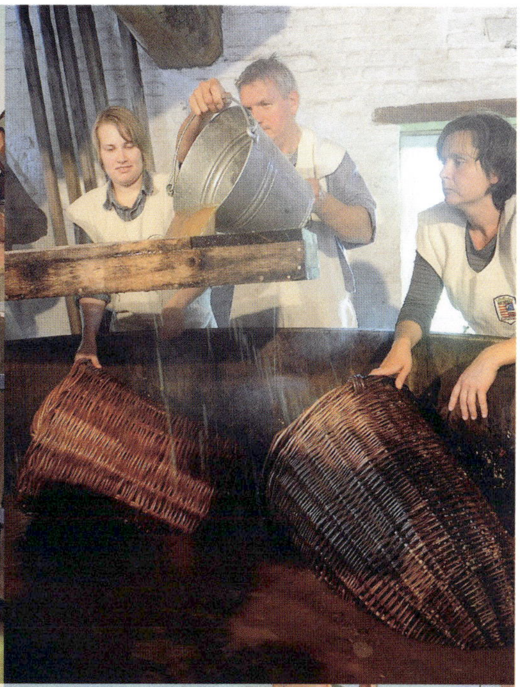
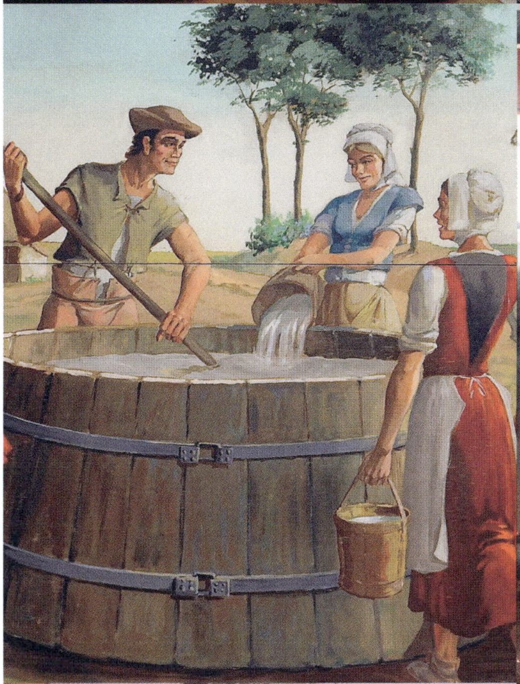
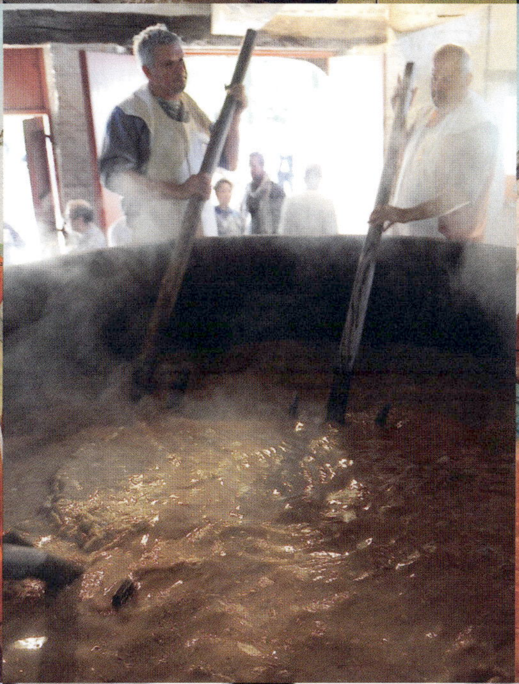
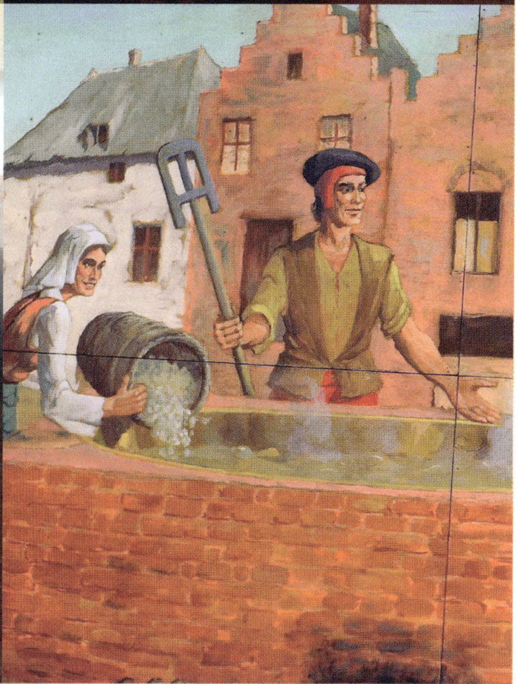
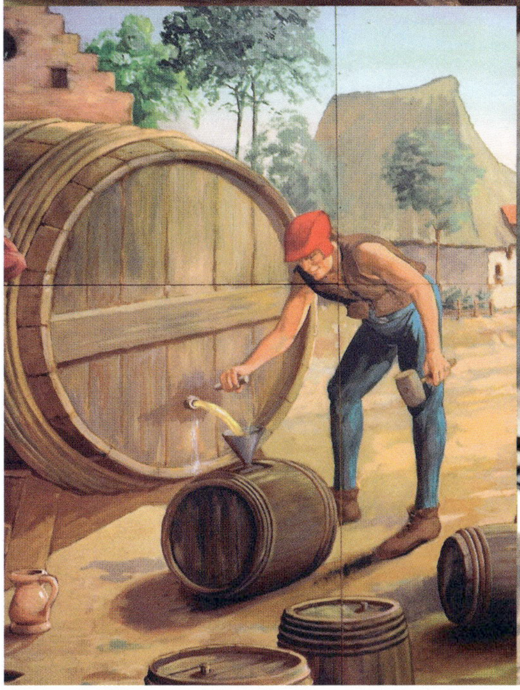
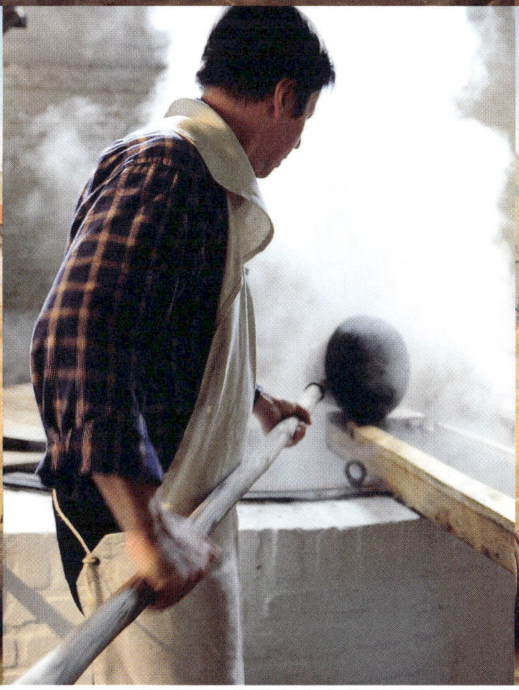
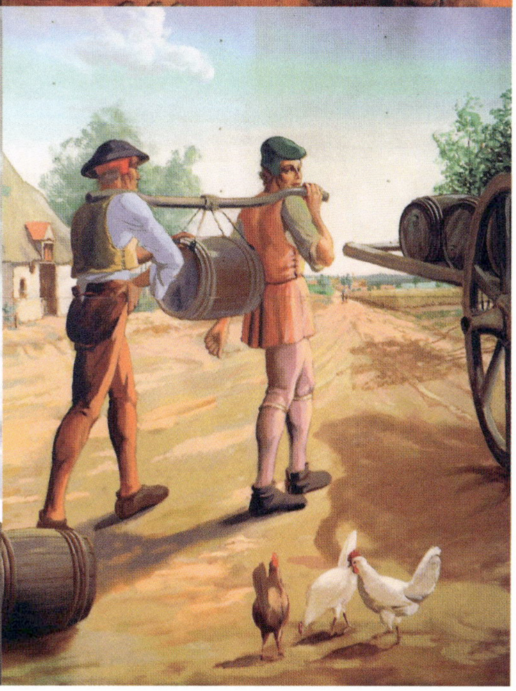

stir the crushed malt and add hot water from time to time to make sure the wort remains at the right temperature. Filtration is done in tall wicker baskets that sieve out the bostel (the remains of the grain). A local farmer comes along to collect it for his cattle – bostel makes an excellent cattle feed. In the next stage the wort is boiled and hops are added. After boiling, the wort is transferred to the open cooling basin where it will start to ferment. Yeast cells and other transient elements are caught by a lined mesh bag and disposed of. The beer will now be poured into wooden barrels where it will continue its fermentation. Sediment will sink to the bottom. The equipment on display in 't Paenhuys was retrieved from the former Tomsin brewery in Hoegaarden. Hoegaarden brewer Pierre Celis learned to brew white beer at Tomsin's before setting up his own brewery, De Kluis, in 1966. Celis used to work as a milkman. Between milk and beer…

Brussels Brouwershuis
....

The 14th century saw the appearance of the first stone-built houses at the Grand Place in Brussels, close to the splendid Town Hall built in the Gothic style. House 'De Hille', renamed 'Den Gulden Boom' in later years, stood on the site of the current Brouwershuis. The brewers' guild purchased 'Den Gulden Boom' at the end of the 16th century. However, in 1695 troops of French King Louis XIV shot the Grand Place to pieces. Fortunately the Town Hall survived. The brewers did not sink into despair. Rather, they financed the rebuilding of their Brouwershuis. The commission was given to the architect Willem De Bruyn. This edifice's splendid façade contains Baroque elements. The statue of a horse rider on top of the building was added around 1900. This rider is Charles de Lorraine, who was a great beneficiary of the brewers' guild. The rich Belgian brewing tradition is evoked in the cellars of the Brouwershuis. The tools, brewing kettles and yeast basins on display show how the craft has developed through the ages. The Belgian beer culture is brought to life by ancient beer jugs, antique porcelain and typical objects retrieved from an inn. The museum also highlights the latest brewing technology. You gain an insight into the ingredients used to make beer, the workings of a modern brewing hall and processes such as filtration, fermentation, cold storage and bottling or barrel filling.

Payment in beer

So, how much beer was consumed by the monks? The answer to this question depends on the era and the abbey in question. If you look at the history of abbeys, periods where ascetics and strict implementation of the rules dominated were followed by an era where the reins were loosened to some degree. And vice versa. An official tax census was held amongst 48 monasteries and abbeys in the province of Brabant between the years of 1781 and 1785. It showed that it was only city-based monasteries that did not have their own brewery and had to purchase their beer from elsewhere. Over half of the abbeys that did have their own brewery consumed over 90 per cent of their own output. Beer styles varied by region. White beer was popular in the area surrounding Louvain and Hoegaarden whereas a dark 'guild' beer went down very well in Diest. It is estimated that annual beer consumption in abbeys and monasteries lay between 97.5 litres and 317 litres per head per year. These numbers do require some explanation and modification. We are dealing with 'small beer', with an alcohol volume of between 2 and 3%, used as an alternative for bad quality drinking water. Beer was also used to pay salaries 'in kind'. Contractors often received part of their remuneration in the form of beer. This tradition survived for a long time outside the abbey walls. Just after the Second World War, a building contractor received half of his salary in kind, i.e. in beer.

European Beer Museum at Stenay, France.

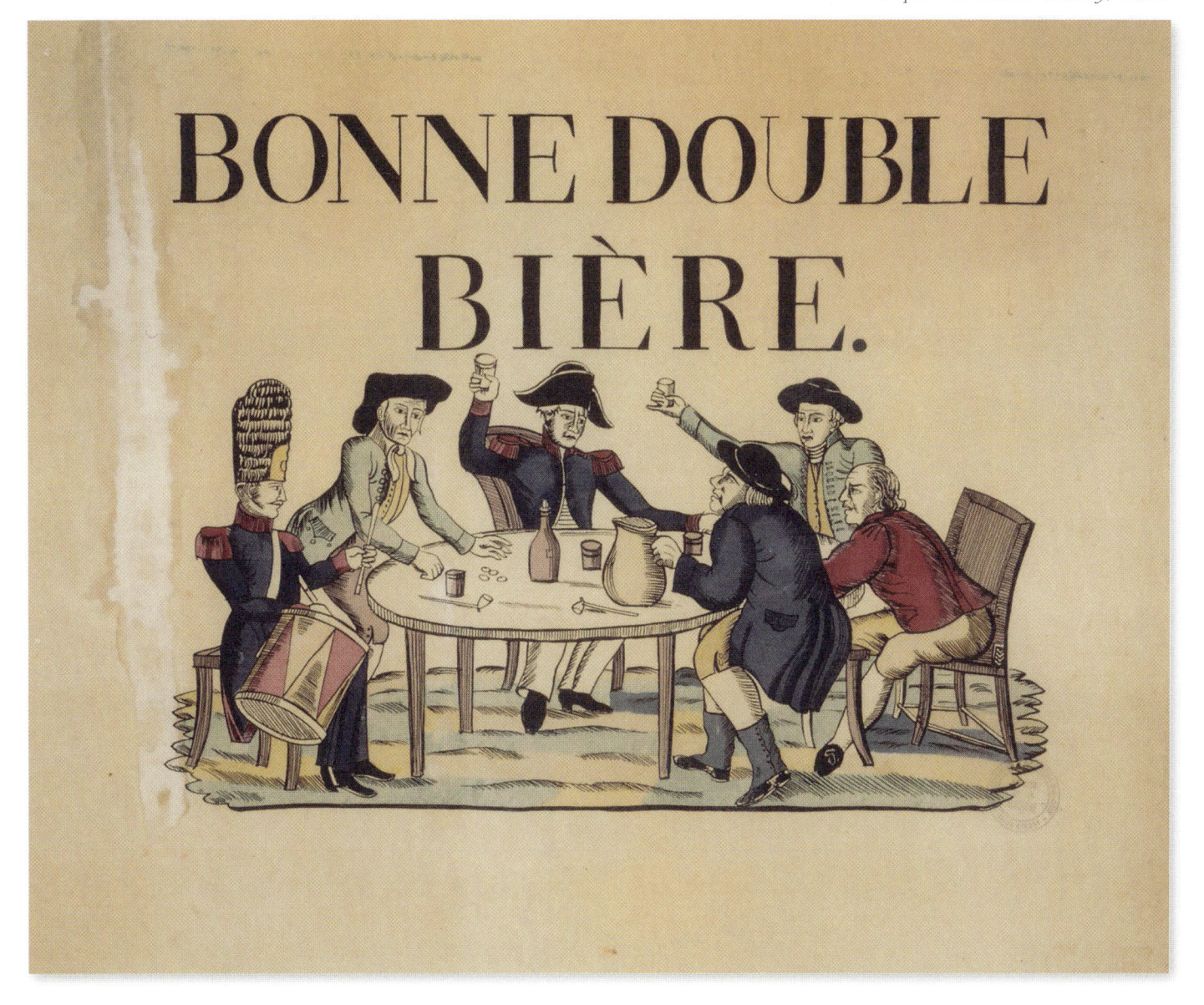

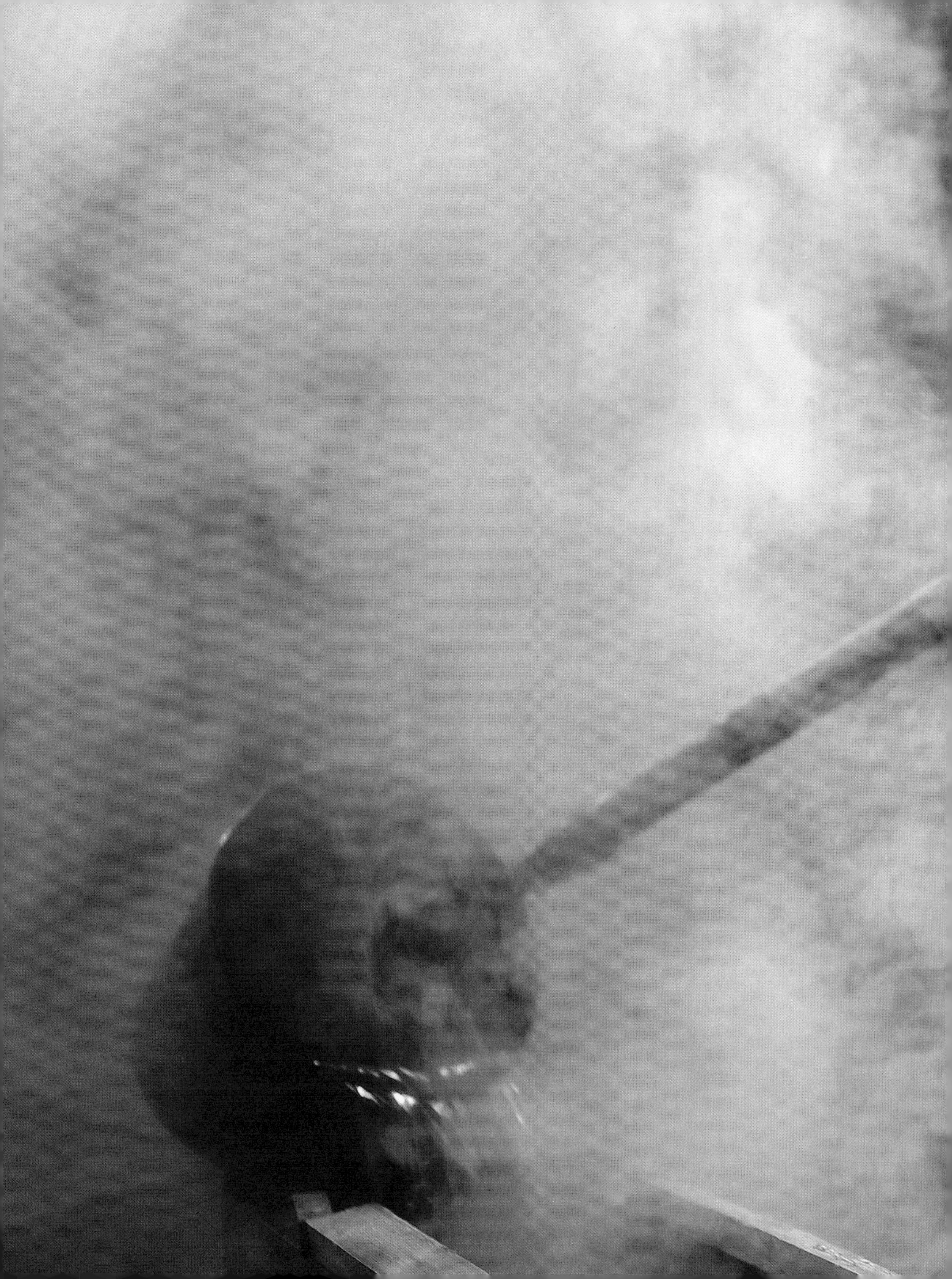

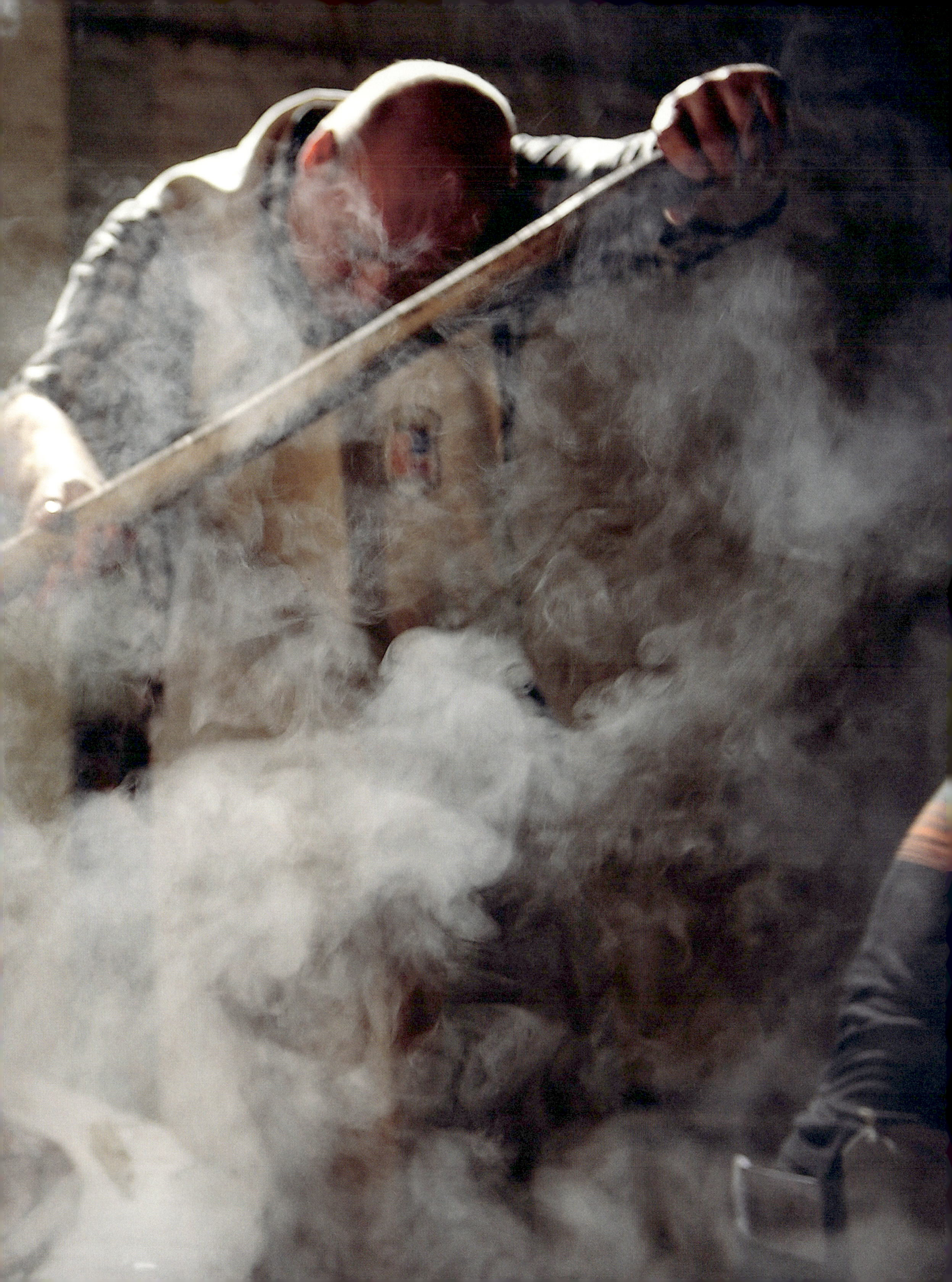

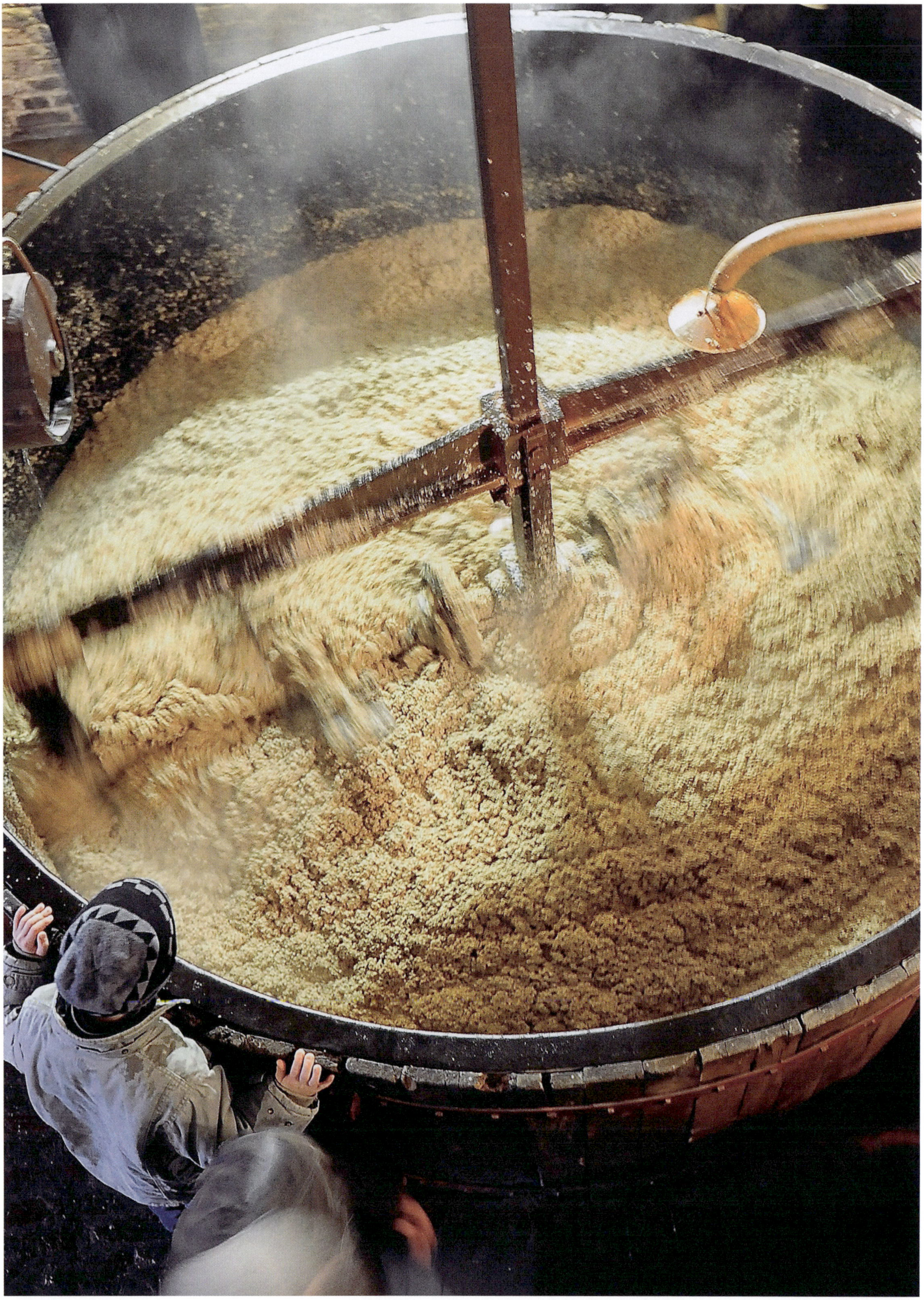

The fascination of industry and science

(19th century)

Brewing technology has advanced in leaps and bounds ever since 1760. Thermometers and saccharometers are now in standard use in the brewhall. Modern brewing techniques are rooted in knowledge of chemistry and biology. Frenchman Louis Pasteur discovered the workings of yeast. He published his pioneering work *Etudes sur la bière* in 1876. Pasteur demonstrated that all bacteria and yeasts will die and so cannot spoil the taste of the beer if you heat it to 70-80°C before bottling. Beer can be stored for a far longer period thanks to this 'pasteurisation'. Until the end of the 19th century beer rarely came in bottles. Glass was expensive. Moreover, these bottles could not be sealed properly. When Charles Goodyear invented rubber in 1842 bottles could be sealed hermetically and hygienically for the first time. The flip-top, invented by Carl Dietrich, followed in 1875. In the 1890s William Painter came up with the crown cork. You could now seal a bottle with a simple metal lid. The crown cork attaches itself to the bottle opening and it takes a fair amount of strength to remove it. The crown cork is eminently suitable for topping bottles of beer that contain carbon dioxide. The floodgates were truly opened when Painter launched the handy Capped-Bottle Opener in 1894. This little 'lever' conquered the world. The first metal can was developed by Englishman Peter Durand. He applied for a patent in 1810 but the drinks can only saw the light of day on 24 January 1935. American beer producer Kreuger's Beer was the first company to opt for this type of packaging. The beer can was five times heavier than it is today and had to be opened with the sharp awl that came with it. In 1963 Ermal Cleon Fraze thought up the current can opener: the ring pull. Production started in 1965. The brewing world was also fundamentally changed by the railways and refrigeration equipment (Carl von Linde). Brewers had increasingly large storage barrels built. On one, not so fine, day things went badly wrong at the Horse Shoe brewery in London's Tottenham Court Road. On 17 October 1814 George Crick came across an iron hoop that had fallen off a giant beer barrel. Apart from making a note for technical services he did not think anything of it. Suddenly an enormous bang reverberated all around the brewery. According to legend it could be heard seven kilometres away. A giant barrel had succumbed to the enormous pressure. A tsunami of beer poured from the barrel and the walls and roof of the brewery collapsed. Another barrel gave way and beer flowed down the street. Eight locals were killed in the explosion. The moral of the story? The wooden barrel has its natural limits.

Brewer-Mayor

In Belgium, brewing and politics were closely intertwined, a unique situation. The second half of the 19th century was characterised by a furious battle between Catholics and anti-Catholics. Both factions were after the mayorship in towns and villages. In many villages beer brewing was the main economic activity and the brewer was also the mayor. Most villages had two brewers: one Catholic, one anti-Catholic. For only a few hundred villagers there could be as many as ten beers. 'Export' to neighbouring villages was unheard of, as, after all, they had their own breweries. Such a combination of politics and brewing has never existed anywhere else. It goes some way to explain the flourishing of family breweries and the craftsmanship evidenced by the Belgian brewers.

---

[2] *Scoopers, A world full of beer, p. 126.*

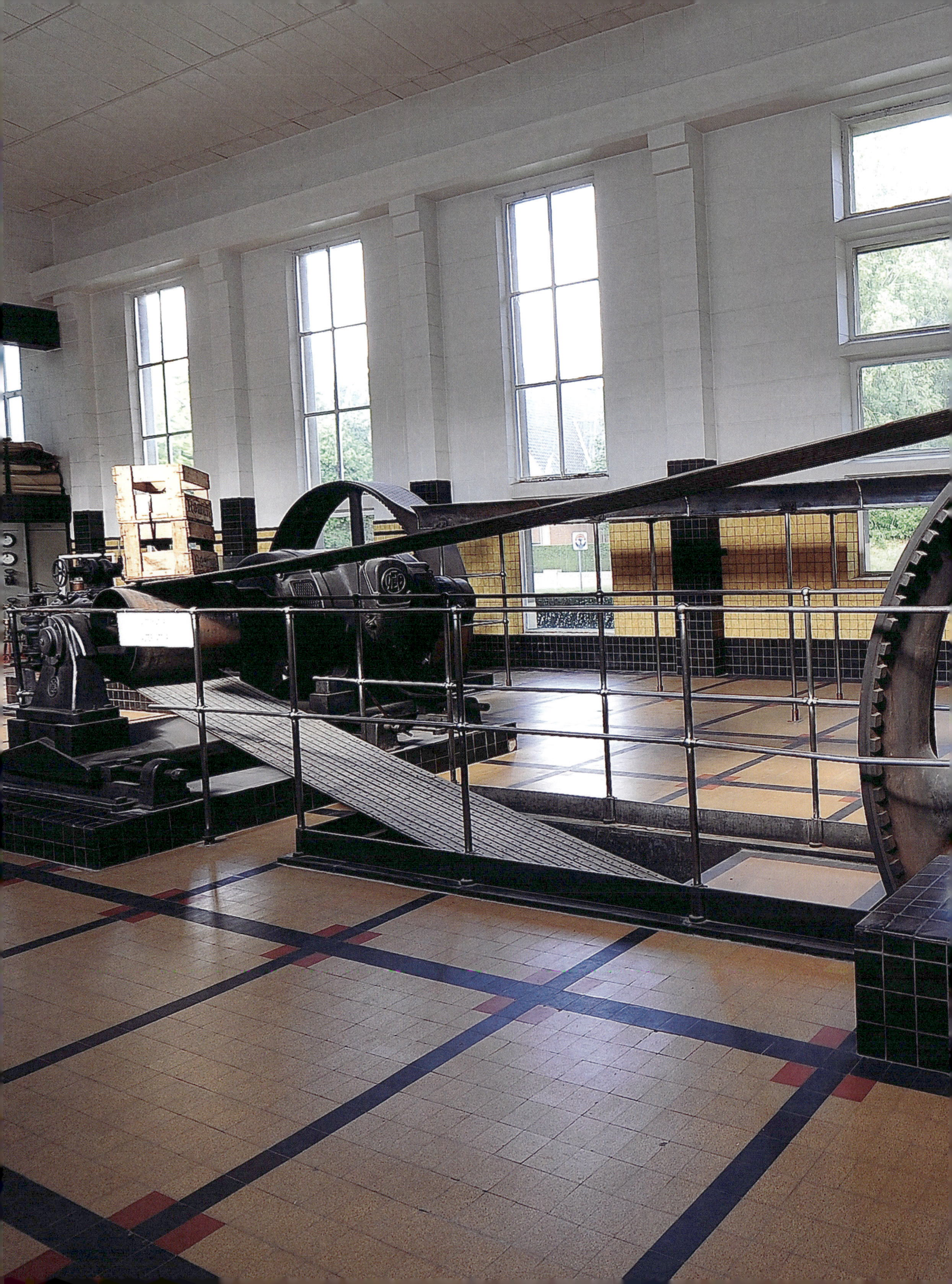

STOOMMACHINE
MACHINE à VAPEUR

The pils revolution

(1842)

1842 saw the start of the pils revolution that would shake the foundations of the entire beer world. The inhabitants of the Czech city of Pilsen were complaining about their cloudy and sour beer. In 1838 they poured 36 barrels of undrinkable beer into the city sewers whereupon the city council decided to have a new brewery built. Bavarian brewmaster Josef Groll achieved the impossible. He was the first to succeed in brewing a bottom-fermented beer. He made grateful use of the soft spring water and the sandstone subsoil of the area by having deep chambers dug out where the beer could be lagered (stored) at cool temperatures. The new 'pils beer' – clear, fresh, malty and hoppy with a golden colour – surprised his friends and enemies. Pils spread all across Europe. The Belgian brewers saw the way the wind was blowing and felt threatened by pils beers from abroad. In 1903 they launched the first national beer competition, the 'Concours pour l'Amélioration de la Bière Belge' – *the Competition for the Improvement of Belgian Beer*. The challenge was to brew a beer that was at least as strong as imported pils (with an alcohol volume of circa 5%) at a price that would be at least a third lower. Also, the new beer had to have beautiful pearlisation, a fine head of froth and contain more carbon dioxide than usual. Nobody took up the gauntlet... However, in 1905, 73 brewers took part in the third competition, called 'Concours National pour le Perfectionnement des Bières Belges' (*National Competition for the Perfection of Belgian Beers*). 57 of them entered a top-fermented beer, seven submitted a bottom-fermented beer whereas nine competed with a spontaneous fermentation beer. The Binard brewery from Châtelineau won the competition with its 'Belge de Faleau' bottled beer. This amber-coloured beer soon acquired a following. The 'Spéciale Belge' turned into the everyday beer for the working classes. It was an affordable luxury for those who worked on the land or in factories. The tradition of the 'Spéciale Belge' survives most notably in the beers made by Palm and De Koninck. Admittedly, the quality of Belgian beer left much to be desired in the 19th century. Many brewers put their trust in their own experience and intuition. Thermometers were not used and neither were densimeters. Beer quality was a worry for the authorities. Systermans, a people's representative from Brussels who was also the President of the Federation of Brewers, attended the 1880 brewers' congress where he advocated the foundation of brewing schools. His message bore fruit. In 1887 Ghent saw the opening of the École Professionnelle de Brasserie and at Louvain University, the Ecole Supérieure d'Agriculture was established. Five years on the École Technique de Brasserie, forming part of l'Institut Saint-Liévin opened its doors in Ghent. The brewing schools have educated brewing engineers, carried out scientific research and provided advice to breweries ever since.

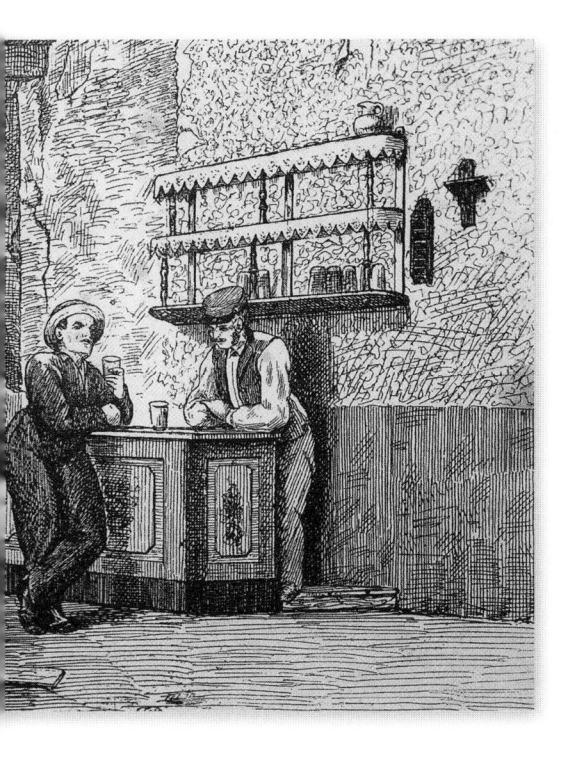

Brewers were cutters

"Just take a look at this!" Chris Vandewalle unearths an old leather suitcase containing an original, handwritten brewing handbook from 1856. "I can read it perfectly well, I know exactly what the brewer's intentions were, I compare it with my own study materials, couple my findings with my own experiences and finally, allow my gut feeling to come to the fore." Chris knows what he's talking about. Not only is he a historian, he also serves as the city archivist for Diksmuide and he is a home brewer to boot. Seizoensbrouwerij or 'seasonal brewery' Vandewalle, founded in 2011, fits in seamlessly with a family-based brewing tradition that goes all the way back to the second half of the 18th century. The family has ties to well-known local breweries that are still going strong, such as Van Eecke (Watou) and Leroy (Boezinge). The archivist is captivated by the history of the local brewers. His own brews go under the names of Reninge Bitter Blond and Reninge Oud Bruin. The well-hopped, blonde seasonal beer is brewed between September and May. The 'old brown' beer is produced in winter. "I am following the tradition of 'cut' beers (where a young beer is 'cut', or blended, with a beer that is one year old). Our 'old brown' will continue to mature in wooden foeders (casks)," Chris explains. "Brewers used to be 'cutters' first and foremost. They cut young beer with old beer to extend its longevity. Take, as an example, the gueuzestekers who, even now, blend several vintages of lambic. Up to the 1950s my family produced lambic in the Yser Valley and then cut it to produce a gueuze. This gave me the idea to start cutting lambic from Oud Beersel with Reninge Bitter Blond."

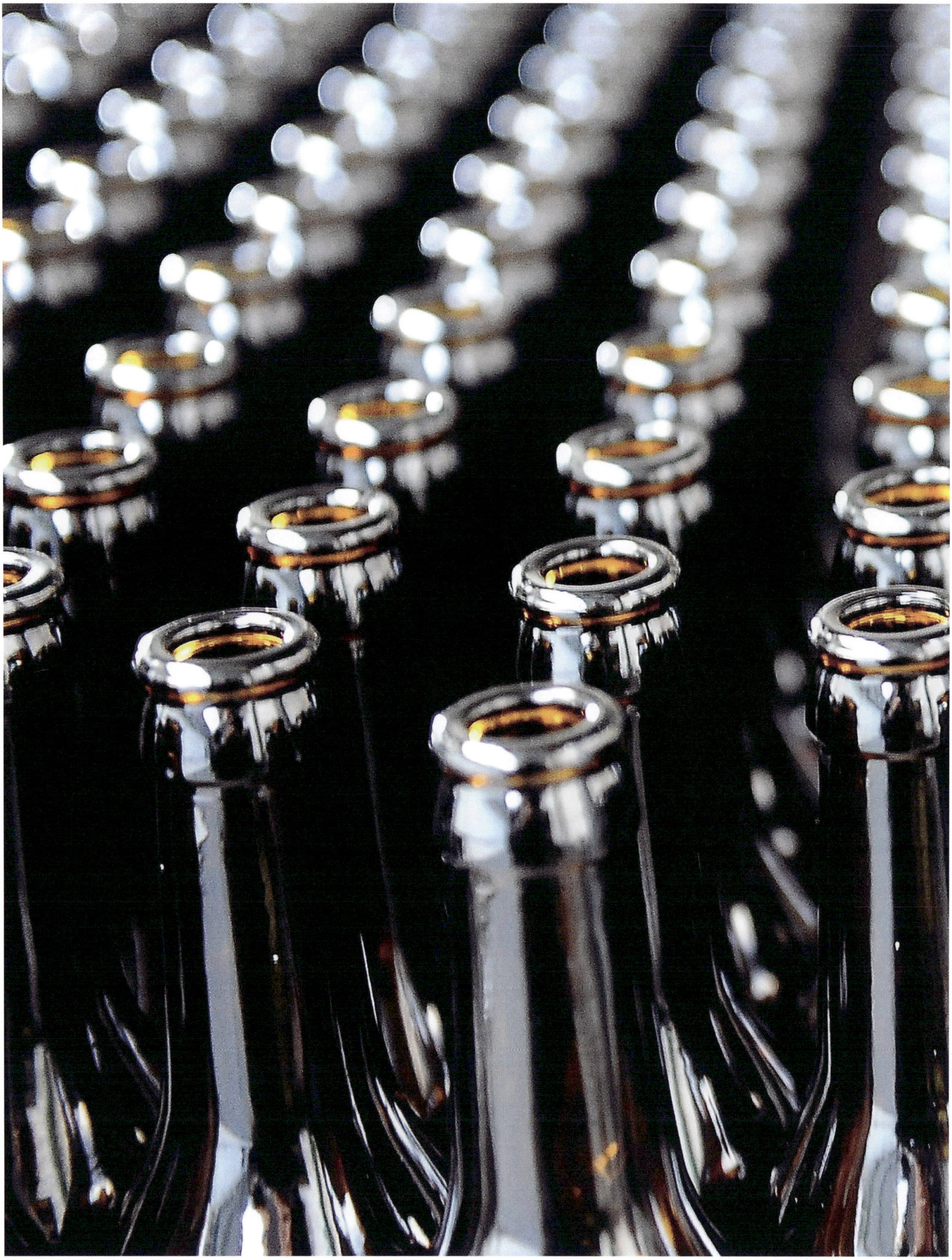

GUEUZE KRIEK

MORT SUBITE

GUEUZE

HANSSENS

DWORP

24-1/2 1978

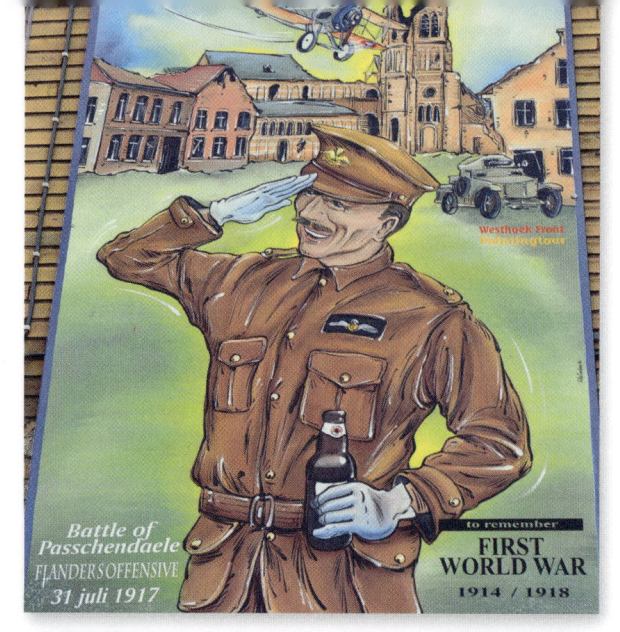

War and crisis in beer land

(1914–1945)

Around 1900 Belgium had counted around 3,200 breweries. The First World War sounded the death knell for many breweries. The German occupier requisitioned the copper kettles, the brewing equipment and the vehicle fleet. Ingredients were also in very short supply. Many breweries did not re-open after the war; half of them threw in the towel. However, in 1919, help arrived from an unexpected corner. The Belgian Vandervelde law prohibited the serving of spirits in cafés and strived to combat alcohol abuse amongst the pauperised population. The brewers jumped at this new opportunity and started marketing stronger beers. Another blow was only just around the corner though: the economic crisis of the 1930s followed by the Second World War. Once again, the copper disappeared into the hands of the occupier and raw materials were in short supply.

Having a glass of beer with your mates was not a whole barrel of fun during the war. You had to observe the curfew. The beer was also pale and tasteless, a miserly brew with an alcohol volume of only 0.8%. Not enough to make you drunk. In the end, 775 Belgian breweries managed to survive World War II. However, the British made a virtue out of necessity when they were engaged in the Battle of the Pacific. The British troops had a floating brewery installed on their HMS Menestheus mine-layer. The allies quenched their thirst with beer brewed at sea. Does this explain the final victory?

Razed to the ground

Chris Vandewalle is brewing beers inspired by the original beers from the area around Ypres and Poperinge. Chris: "Did you know that fruit beers like kriek were very common in the area? There were orchards covering up to four hectares. The area was known for its apples, pears, nuts and krieken cherries... up to the point when our 'Flanders Fields' were razed to the ground during the First World War. This put an immediate halt to local brewing activity. Many farmers diversified into brewing at the end of the 19th century. After the war some of them clubbed together and invested the wartime reparation money in the Brasserie Centrale Yproise in Ypres, where they started producing bottom-fermented beers, Ypra Pils for example. This brewery was shut down in the 1960s."

Belgium resists

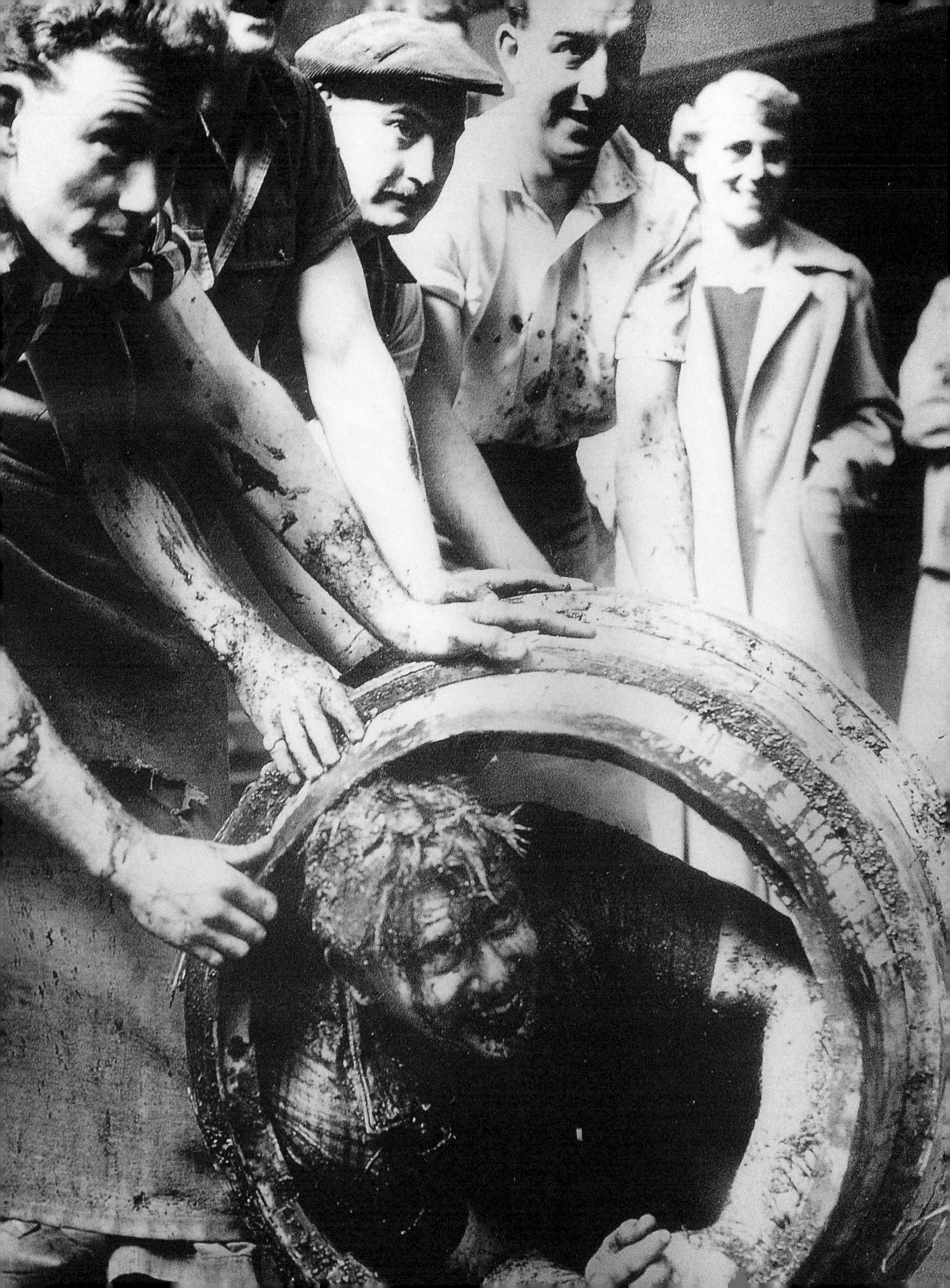

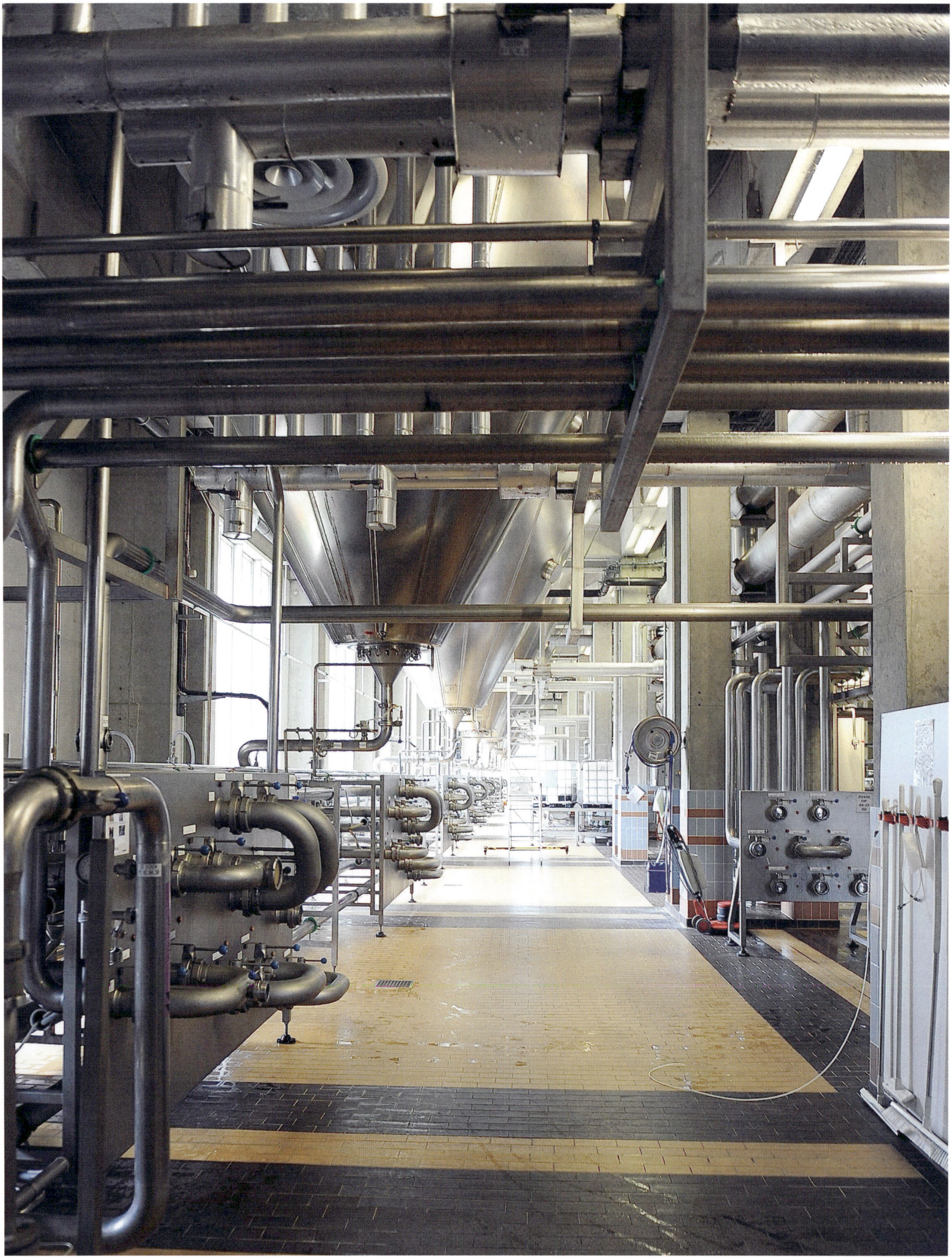

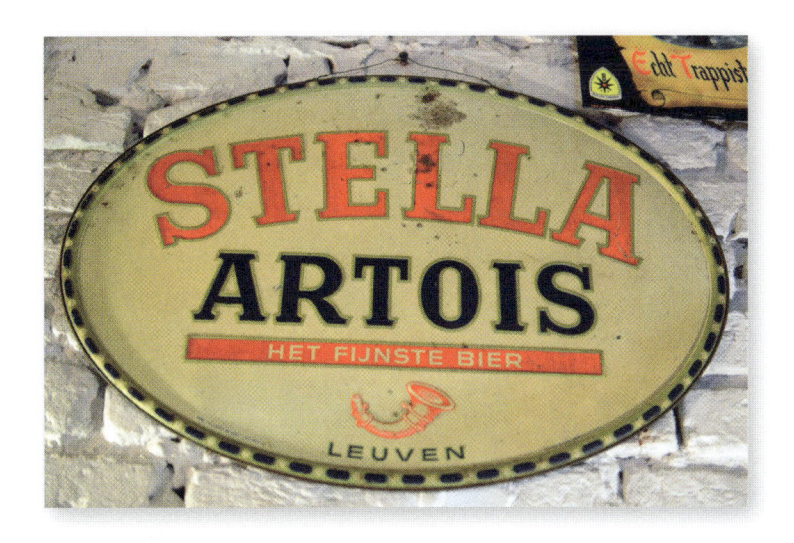

From economies of scale to regional beers

(1945-2000)

Consolidation in the brewing sector reached its height in the second half of the 20th century. Just bring to mind the explosive growth of the Artois brewery in Louvain, later called Interbrew, Inbev and now known as AB Inbev. Breweries took over their competitors leading to the closure of many brewing halls. King Pils reigned supreme. The diversity of the Belgian beer landscape came under threat. However, beer drinkers once again decided otherwise. At the height of the 'flower power' era, around May 1968, more and more people re-discovered their regional beers. They strongly opposed economies of scale and actively sought out beers made by small breweries. In defiance of beers 'that all tasted the same', they opted for beers with character. Kudos to them. Late British beer guru Michael Jackson (1942-2007) put Belgian beers on the global map in 1977. He achieved fame at the end of the 1980s with his television series, entitled *The Beer Hunter*, and penned various best-sellers on the topic of Belgian beer. The Federation of Belgian Brewers benefited from his success. 1986, the Year of the Beer (*Jaar van het Bier*) invigorated this campaign on a previously unknown scale. Once again, brewers started to believe in their products and sales increased. Having become familiar with German, Danish and English beers, Belgian beer lovers (re)discovered their own, home-grown beers. In the meantime, the major players enjoyed unprecedented growth. Louvain, the birthplace of the Artois brewery, is now home to the largest brewery in the world: AB Inbev.

The history of beer in Brussels is a good illustration of the trend towards economies of scale that saw many smaller players falling by the wayside. The Brussels Brewing Guild was founded in 1365. Beer was flourishing in the 15th century, particularly in the province of Brabant. Louvain, Brussels, Hoegaarden, Antwerp and Mechelen were all notable brewing centres. The province of Brabant was crossed by many rivers and there was plenty of good-quality wheat. It is no coincidence that both the white beer from Hoegaarden-Louvain and the lambic beers from the Brussels area are wheat-based. Brussels breweries enjoyed a large home market for their beers. The French Revolution put a spanner in the works, however. This era (1792-1794) not only saw the abolition of the guilds, replaced by private initiatives, abbeys also closed their doors and people started drinking more wine and champagne. In her *Bier en Brouwerijen te Brussel* (Beer and Breweries in Brussels), Patricia Quintens writes that there were 120 artisan breweries at the beginning of the 18th century. One hundred years on, only 29 remained. Another 14 disappeared after the covering of the river Zenne and the construction of central boulevards around the year 1866. Industrial breweries were set up predominantly in the outlying communities of Molenbeek, Anderlecht, Koekelberg and Vorst. Faro and lambic from Brussels were well-known in 1903. However, the pils beers from Germany (Bavaria) and Bohemia caused a revolution. The new pils quickly grew in popularity. Demand remained high thanks to the growth of the population and its increased purchasing power after 1860. Breweries such as De Koninck and Wielemans (1868) saw the light in this era. The Wiel's pils produced by Wielemans-Ceuppens dates from 1940, when raw ingredients were scarce and expensive. It was originally a 'fluitjesbier', Flemish slang for a weak and tasteless beer, with an alcohol volume of only 0.8%. At the Brussels World Expo in 1958 Belgian brewers promoted their beers in a replica of a historic town that was called Vrolijk België or Belgique Joyeuse. The fame of regional beers spread around the country. The Ekla pils from Brussels brewery Vandenheuvel is a case in point. The major Brussels breweries that were around in the 19th and 20th centuries are now primarily remembered for the brand names of their pils beers. Examples include Wiels from Wielemans-Ceuppens, Elberg from the Grande Brasserie de Koekelberg, Primus brewed by the Royal Brasserie of Laeken, the Three Star produced by Leopold, the Vox made by Brasserie de la Chasse Royale, Perle 28 from Caulier and, as mentioned before, Ekla from Saint-Michel-Vandenheuvel.

The 1960s was characterised by mergers whereas in the 1970s many breweries closed their doors. We are now seeing a renewed focus on specialty beers and, in the Brussels area, it is mainly the lambic breweries and 'gueuzestekerijen' that are benefiting from the increasing interest into all that is artisan, natural and traditional. Brussels and the Pajottenland region are now primarily known for their lambic beers, including faro, gueuze and fruit beers such as kriek.

Source: Michaël Bellon – www.beercapital.be

Belgian beer

The Association of Belgian Family Brewers (BFB) has twenty-one members. They are all medium-sized Belgian breweries that focus on specialty beers. What do they have in common? They have been brewing for at least fifty years within the same Belgian family. The stylised black-yellow-red BFB logo printed on the label is a guarantee of a unique beer that is not marketed under another name or with a different label. It is the hallmark of authenticity. The Belgian Family Brewers (BFB) came together in 2007. Belgian Family Brewers aims to increase the international exposure of authentic Belgian beers. Just like French wine or Scotch whisky, 'Belgian beer' is a strong brand. Belgian brewers are keen to use this quality label. They lay claim to the origins of traditional Belgian beer styles such as spéciale belge ale, Oudenaards bruin bier (Oudenaarde brown beer), Vlaams roodbruin bier (Flemish red-brown beer), saison, oude gueuze, witbier (white beer) or oude kriek which sets them apart from the numerous 'Belgian style beers' produced abroad.

The "Brabander"

Visit a brewery and you will find a treasure trove of images from the archives. Take a look at what is hanging on the walls or displayed in a hidden corner. You will come across pictures of every possible design of beer cart, often pulled by a span of robust draft horses. The best known breed of draft horse is the Brabander. It originates from the Brussels area. In the 'age of the horse', these members of the equine race were a coveted export product. They were shipped to destinations all over the world from small cities such as Halle to the south of Brussels. Their existence came into peril after the advent of the railway and the motorcar. Nevertheless, the brewers have not forgotten their Brabant draft horses. Far from it. Palm Belgian Craft Brewers in Londerzeel even has its own stud farm at Diepensteyn Castle at a stone's throw from the brewery. Here you can see the sorrel, or chestnut, horses with their cream-coloured manes galloping through the meadows near the Castle, not far from the hop fields. These splendid animals often take part in a parade, pulling a 'praalwagen', or float. Now and again they are even entered into competitions. The colour of their coat and mane is suspiciously close to the colours of the Palm spéciale belge amber beer. Surely, this has to be more than a coincidence? This famous and elegant Belgian draft horse from Brabant adorns the label of the Palm beers. When the brewery refreshed its image recently, young people were asked which elements of the logo they felt were dated and which ones they wanted to preserve. The general opinion was that the horse should not be allowed to disappear, and thus the label once again features a Brabander horse, albeit in a stylised version.

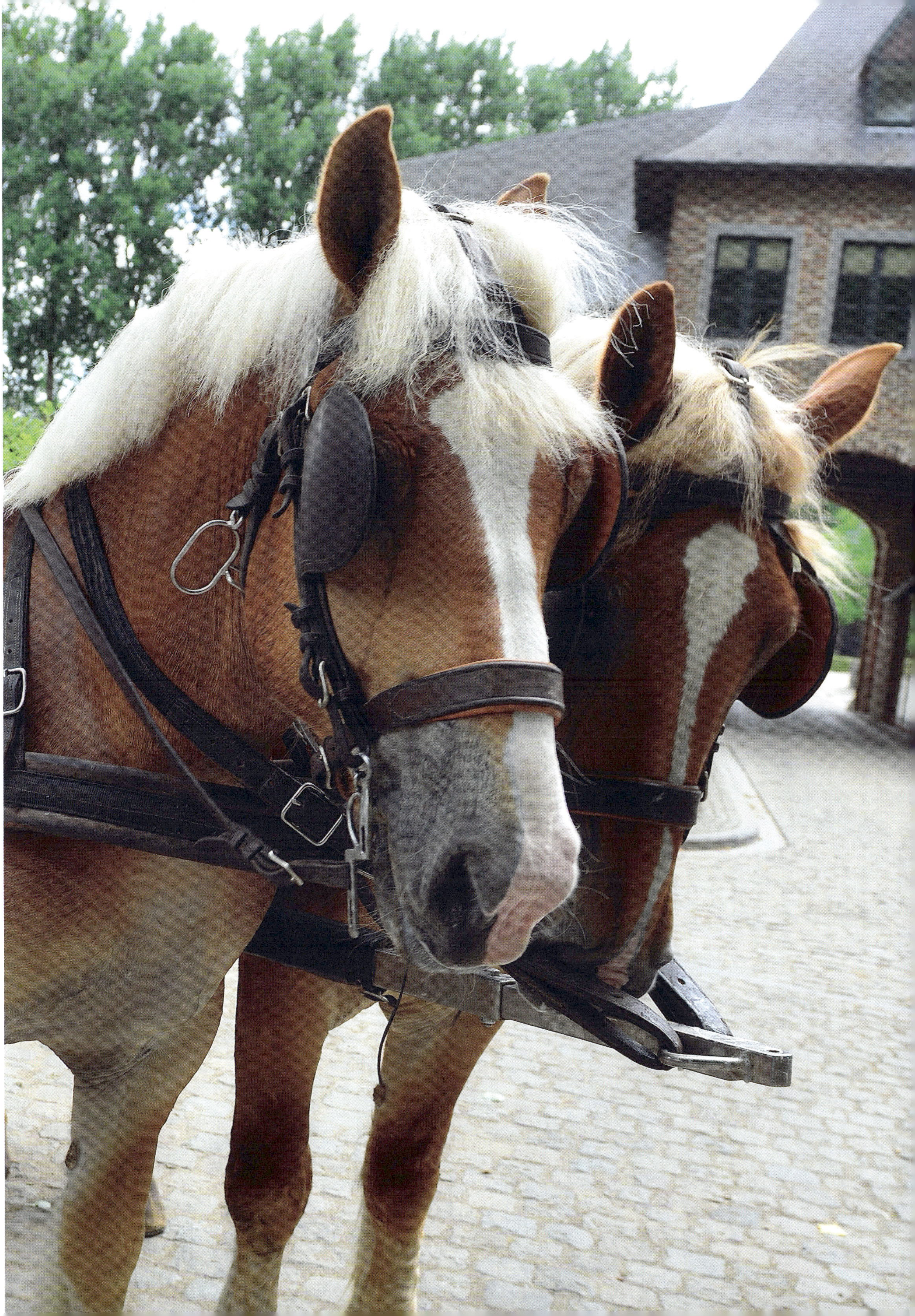

Microbreweries in the new Millennium

(2000-)

The new Millennium heralded the advent of a whole new range of microbreweries. These were often set up by microbrewers, some of whom have turned their passion into a profession. This trend has been going on in the USA for some time. The American brewers found their inspiration in imported Belgian beers. In turn, Belgian beers are now being influenced by new American beers made with powerful hop varieties that were previously unknown. Elsewhere in the world (Italy, Scandinavia, Japan) artisan, or craft, breweries are springing up. Women are starting to brew once again. Traditional beer styles are experiencing a revival. Lambic beers are taking off once more and demand for Flemish redbrown beers and saisons has increased significantly. Beer drinkers are in search of authenticity coming from local, artisan products. Microbreweries are taking advantage of this trend with organic beers and 'short-chain' beers brewed with barley and hops they have cultivated themselves. Three quarters of the beer drunk is pils and most beer consumption in Belgium takes place at home instead of in a café. The majority of Belgians opt for the familiar brands that are advertised widely. There is also an increasing group of, mainly young, beer lovers who swear by craft beers. Craft brewers are conquering the world. The USA now numbers over 4,000 microbreweries and the microbrewing trend is engulfing our fellow European countries: England, Germany, the Netherlands, France, Spain, Italy, Scandinavia... Belgian microbrewers are also involved but they put their own slant on the process. They are not mindlessly jumping on the bitter or sour bandwagon. They have far too much respect for our brewing tradition to make that leap. All well and good, but what exactly is a Belgian microbrewery? Brassigaume, a beer festival that takes place every year in

October in the village of Marbehan near Aarlen (Arlon) and is only open to microbreweries, imposes a production limit of 4,000 hectolitres per year. In some countries this would fall into the category of picobreweries or nanobreweries. Many Belgian microbrewers harbour ambitions that are really rather modest. Some consider brewing their main activity, albeit on a small scale. For others it is a side activity or simply a fun hobby. "I just brew the beer that I like best," is an often-heard statement. Or: "My favourite pastime is to make beer with my friends". In cases where substantial investments have been made, the conversation gains a serious undercurrent. If you are marketing a beer, you will not escape the strict food hygiene controls, excise duties and other obligations imposed by the authorities. This is why many microbrewers are happy to keep things small and simple. The world of microbreweries comes in all shapes and sizes. Small players may develop their beers at home and once they have fine-tuned the recipe, will outsource its production to larger breweries. The first microbreweries in Belgium took advantage of the revival of the specialty beers in the early 1980s after years of consolidation and industrialisation. Brasserie d'Achouffe (1982) outgrew its microbrewery status a long time ago. De Dolle Brouwers (1980), however, is still a microbrewery. This leading group is chased by a peloton made up of many different contestants with speeders and tailgaters amongst them. Compared to the 'Stone Age' of Belgian microbreweries, the current beer world has gained in professionalism. Food controls have become ever stricter and consumers have become ever more demanding to the extent that there is now no future for dabblers. Taste is always a subjective issue but today's beer drinker expects no less than a tasty beer that can be poured and served correctly, with a taste that fits in with the beer style advertised or else with a novel taste that is intriguing. Something he can talk about with his friends and acquaintances, a beer that prompts him to order seconds "if I can track it down". Every self-respecting brewer has to meet Olympic minimum standards. Large breweries possess all the facilities to guarantee consistent quality. This is why microbrewers often knock on the door of their big brothers to request lab analysis and technical support. Such a niche beer may be a one-off and fade from the market as soon as supplies are exhausted. The next brew, either similar or completely different, is marketed under a different name. Before long, the range reaches astronomic heights. An established brewer will then respond, with a smirk: "I told you, they are unable to brew the same beer twice!" Practised beer lovers don't mind this too much. They are after new discoveries all the time and are happy to put up with the high-fliers as well as

De Dolle Brouwers (above) and Brasserie d'Achouffe (below) started up in 1980 and 1982 respectively. At the time, they were brewing their 'gnome' beer called La Chouffe in a cowshed in the village of Achouffe. The brewery is now owned by Duvel Moortgat.

the duds. Don't forget that microbrewers are often drawn to extremes. They produce only small volumes and consequently they risk far less than the 'big boys'. Microbrewers can also respond to market trends far more quickly and the large breweries are well aware of this. Miraculously, Palm Belgian Craft Brewers recently opened its own De Hoorn microbrewery on its own site where they are busy developing beers in co-operation with sommeliers and chefs known to them. The Belgian microbreweries are now riding the wave of the success of Belgian beers abroad. Until recently they found it difficult to market their brews in their own country, as many cafés are owned by the large brewers. The same goes for supermarkets, who mainly stock the major brands. Therefore the microbreweries had been targeting independent specialty beer cafés and beer shops. Exports have now taken off substantially and several microbreweries and their beers have grown into a cult phenomenon.

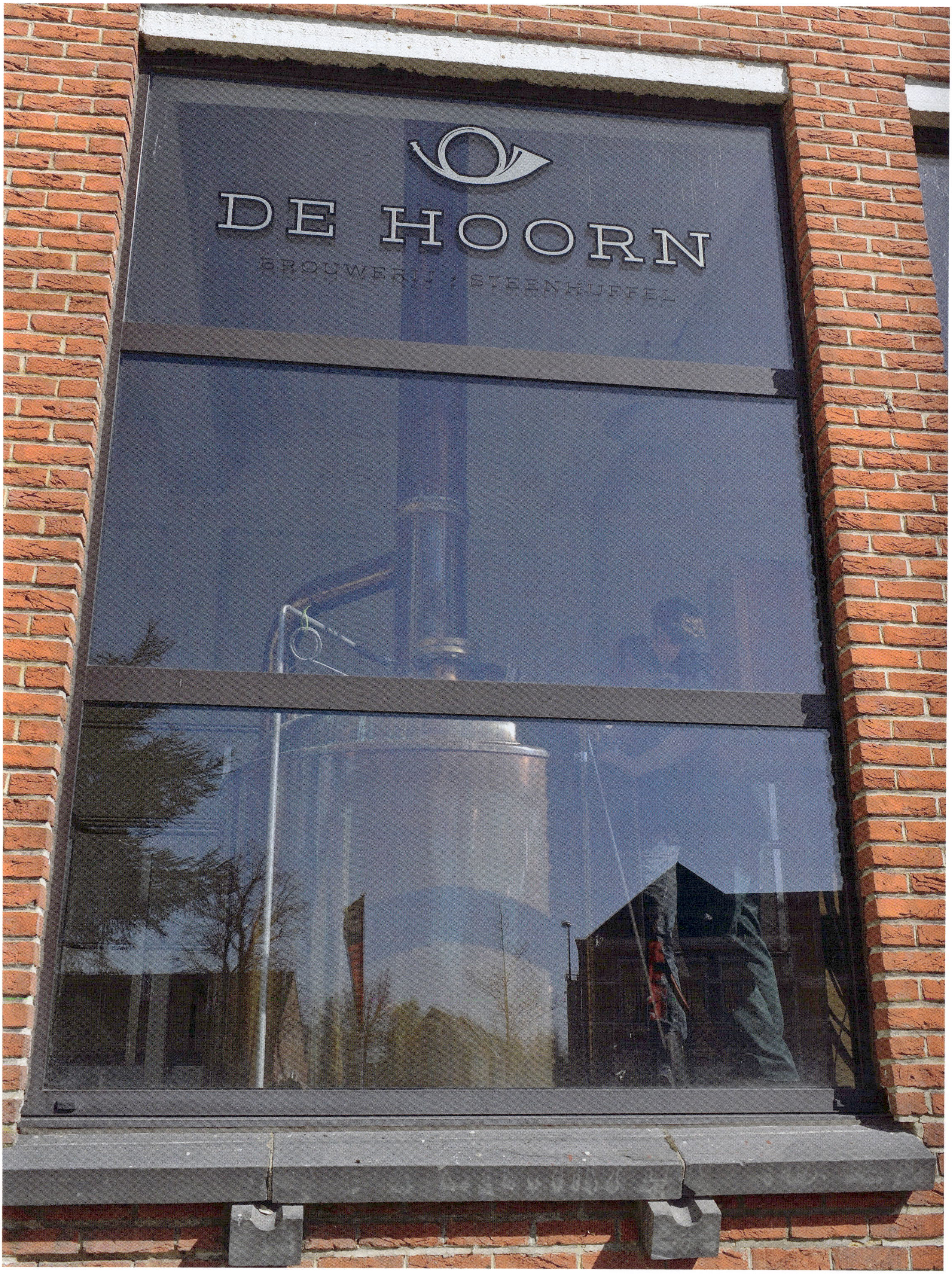
DE HOORN
BROUWERIJ : STEENHUFFEL

Quality label

Is 'Belgian beer' an indication of origin in the same way as the AOC for wine? You may be forgiven for thinking it, but no. Beer is an extract that uses ingredients from several countries. For example, Belgian brewers source large quantities of hops from Central Europe or the USA. And their barley or wheat often comes from abroad as well. The 'Belgian beer' label is more of an indication of the manner of brewing and fermenting and refers to local craftsmanship and tradition. Beer that has not been brewed and bottled in Belgium can only go through life as 'Belgian style beer'.

On the global map

The Brussels Beer Challenge international beer competition is on the up and up. The fourth edition was held in November 2015. Its beginnings were modest but in 2015, 1,100 beers from 30 countries were entered. Does this competition favour the main brewers or the microbrewers? "As far as the international jury is concerned, there is no difference," Thomas Costenoble, one of the organisers, assures us. "The tasting is conducted 'blind' so the beer experts — none of whom are brewers — have no way of knowing who is behind the beer that they are judging. They consider whether it is technically correct and how it fits in with the beer style in question. There are reference beers for each of the traditional Belgian beer styles. Think of Saison Dupont for a saison or Duvel for a strong blond beer. But there are many other lovely beers in the same style, made by other market players, both large and small." So how do you evaluate new and unknown beer styles, the Imperial Double White for example? Co-organiser Thomas Costenoble: "We keep an eye on the international beer competitions, compare the scores and decide whether we are dealing with a beer style or just a passing trend. If this beer style keeps popping up and it offers elements particular to this style that allow us to pass a verdict, it will be included in the list." Moreover, the quality of the beers has to be stable and consistent. This requirement remains a challenge, especially for microbrewers. We see plenty of 'one hit wonders' and quality sometimes takes a back seat at the expense of marketing.

Cult status

Lambic brewer and geuzesteker Armand De Belder of 3 Fonteinen enjoys star status amongst American beer geeks. He even receives requests to sign bottle labels. Whoever would have thought it? After all, in the early 1990s the craft of gueuzesteker was almost extinct. All microbreweries have great passion and creativity in common but between them, they can be vastly different. Millevertus specialises in herbal beers, Hof Ten Dormaal and Dochter van de Korenaar produce wood-matured beers, De Ranke and Brasserie de la Senne focus on hops, Brasserie de Bastogne and Kempisch Vuur opt for a stout, DijkWaert for a coffee beer, BOM Brouwerij uses home roasted malt. Den Toetëlèr, Den Tseut, Brasserie d'Erquelinnes and Grain d'Orge draw plenty of inspiration from local folklore, Seizoensbrouwerij Vandewalle and Brasserie de Cazeau are marketing traditional regional beers, De Glazen Toren brings a new interpretation of traditional beer styles, Dilewyns and Loterbol produce a triple gueuze that falls outside the existing beer styles. De Hoppeschuur is brewing for its brewery restaurant, Brasserie C and Brasserie des Légendes have brewery tourism in their sights, De Plukker and Jessenhofke choose to produce organic beers whereas both Alvinne and De Struise Brouwers like to experiment above all else. The advent of microbreweries is a blessing for beer lovers. There is no need to fear humdrum beers that are all the same. These days, if you really want to set yourself apart from the rest, you have to have a good story and, above all, a good glass of beer. Who will be next to take up the challenge?

Armand De Belder, 3 Fonteinen

BRASSERIE ST-JOZE

Jupiler

WILL TURA

Craft Beer Revolution

The USA may well be the most interesting beer country in the world at the moment. Increasingly uniform tastes will inevitably bring about a counter-movement, or so it would appear. The revolution in American beer culture is living proof of this. Let's take a moment to go back in time. The USA is built on the heritage of immigrants. The Europeans who tried their luck across the pond brought their brewing culture with them. And this is how all European beer styles ended up in the USA. During the prohibition era (1920-1930) this picture changed quite dramatically and most breweries were forced to close their doors. Only the large industrial breweries survived this 'dry' period. They started to specialise in the production of refreshing and thirst-quenching beer for the main public. American lagers such as these are closer to a 'vodka and soda'. In addition, the 'light beers' made their entrance in the mid-1970s. Bud Light is now the best-selling beer in the USA. Not until the 1960 was the artisan brewing tradition dusted off and given back the respect it was due. Fritz Maytag played a major role in all this. In 1985 he took over the ailing San Francisco-based Anchor Brewing Company and saved it from certain demise. He restored the brewery to its previous glory and became the main inspiration for all American Craft Brewers. This is why Fritz Maytag is considered their Godfather. In the 1970s Belgian beers started to trickle through into the US market. Many consumers discovered a wide range of tastes. American students travelling through Europe came across an entirely different beer culture and took their preference for specialty beers back home with them. Several inspired beer lovers started brewing at home. On 14 October 1978 the President, Jimmy Carter, approved the law that legalised home brewing (unless decided otherwise by the authorities). Many people took a step into the unknown and started up a professional brewery. The Craft Beer revolution had arrived.

---
[3] Kempen, *Beer's best kept secrets*, p.5.

What is a craft brewer?

An American craft brewer is *small*, *independent* and *traditional*.

'Small': maximum of 6 million barrels per year.

'Independent': 75% of the brewery must be in the hands of the owner(s). Only 25% of shares may be held by a different company.

'Traditional': 50% of the beers produced must be full-malted beers (without the addition of other flavours, or 'adjuncts').

Microbrewery: volume must be below 15,000 barrels per year and 75% of production is not sold on-site at the brewery.

Brewpub: volume must be below fifteen thousand barrels per year and 75% of production is sold in the brewpub/restaurant.

Regional Craft Brewery: situated between a Microbrewery and a Craft Brewery. Produces over 15,000 barrels per annum.

Macro Brewery: production exceeds 6 million barrels per year.

U.S. Brewery Count

	2012	2013	2014	2015	'14 to '15 % Chang
CRAFT	2,401	2,863	3,576	4225	+18.1
Regional Craft Breweries	97	119	135	178	+31.9
Microbreweries	1,149	1,464	1,971	2,397	+21.6
Brewpubs	1,155	1,280	1,470	1,650	+12.2
LARGE NON-CRAFT	23	23	26	30	
OTHER NON-CRAFT	32	31	20	14	
TOTAL U.S. BREWERIES	2,456	2,917	3,622	4,269	+17.9

An ode to experimentation

As a result of prohibition, the 'three tier system' is still in force in the USA. Breweries are not allowed to sell their products directly to consumers. Distribution is done through middlemen (wholesale and retail). This is not a problem in itself; however, the macrobrewers manage to control the middlemen using all sorts of legal constructions. For this reason, many Craft Brewers experience difficulty in distributing their products. At the end of the day, it is the consumer who loses out. In more and more places homebrewers decided to take their first steps into brewing, giving rise to small breweries. And, in the USA, they like their beers crazier and more extreme than anywhere else in the world. Take the Dogfish Brewery for example. Under the motto 'my hops are bigger than your hops' they created their IPA 12 that is so strongly hopped that you can smell it from one kilometre away.

Tradition does not mean too much in the New World. The brewers are not tied to a Reinheitsgebot as they are in Germany. They are mixing Belgian beer recipes with English or Japanese brewing methods to their heart's content. Beer made with lavender, chili, chocolate... imagine the craziest recipe you can think of and you can bet your bottom dollar that somewhere in the USA, it will be brewed. In the meantime, American brewers are serving as an inspiration to increasing numbers of European colleagues.

Extreme

Extreme beers are also rated highly in the USA. Sam Calagione, founder and owner of the Dogfish Head Brewery in Maryland as well as a well-known beer writer, describes extreme beers as follows: "Beers brewed with an extremely high dosage of traditional ingredients (Barleywine or Double IPA) or beers brewed with non-traditional, exotic ingredients." Greg Koch, owner of the Stone Brewery in San Diego, advertises his beers in this way: "This is an aggressive beer. You may not like it. It is highly unlikely that your taste buds are sufficiently developed to appreciate a beer of this quality and complexity. Therefore we recommend you stick to safer, more familiar territory that you may have heard of through a huge advertising campaign aimed at convincing you that this beer was brewed by a small brewery. Or else a campaign that tries to tell you that the tasteless, yellow beer will increase your sex appeal. Perhaps you think that mega campaigns make the beer taste better. You may already be drooling when you read this."

A sky full of stars

Beer has now made a breakthrough in gastronomic circles, too. A prime example is the Gramercy Tavern in New York, which has proudly held a Michelin star for many years. Not only does the Gramercy offer a comprehensive wine menu, it also offers a very appetising beer menu, culminating in an extensive collection of vintage and mature beers. Just like wine, beers can ripen and improve with age. Their taste will change and gain in complexity. The Gramercy's beer menu features a beer that was brewed as far back as 1998. Belgium's multi-starred chefs, be warned...

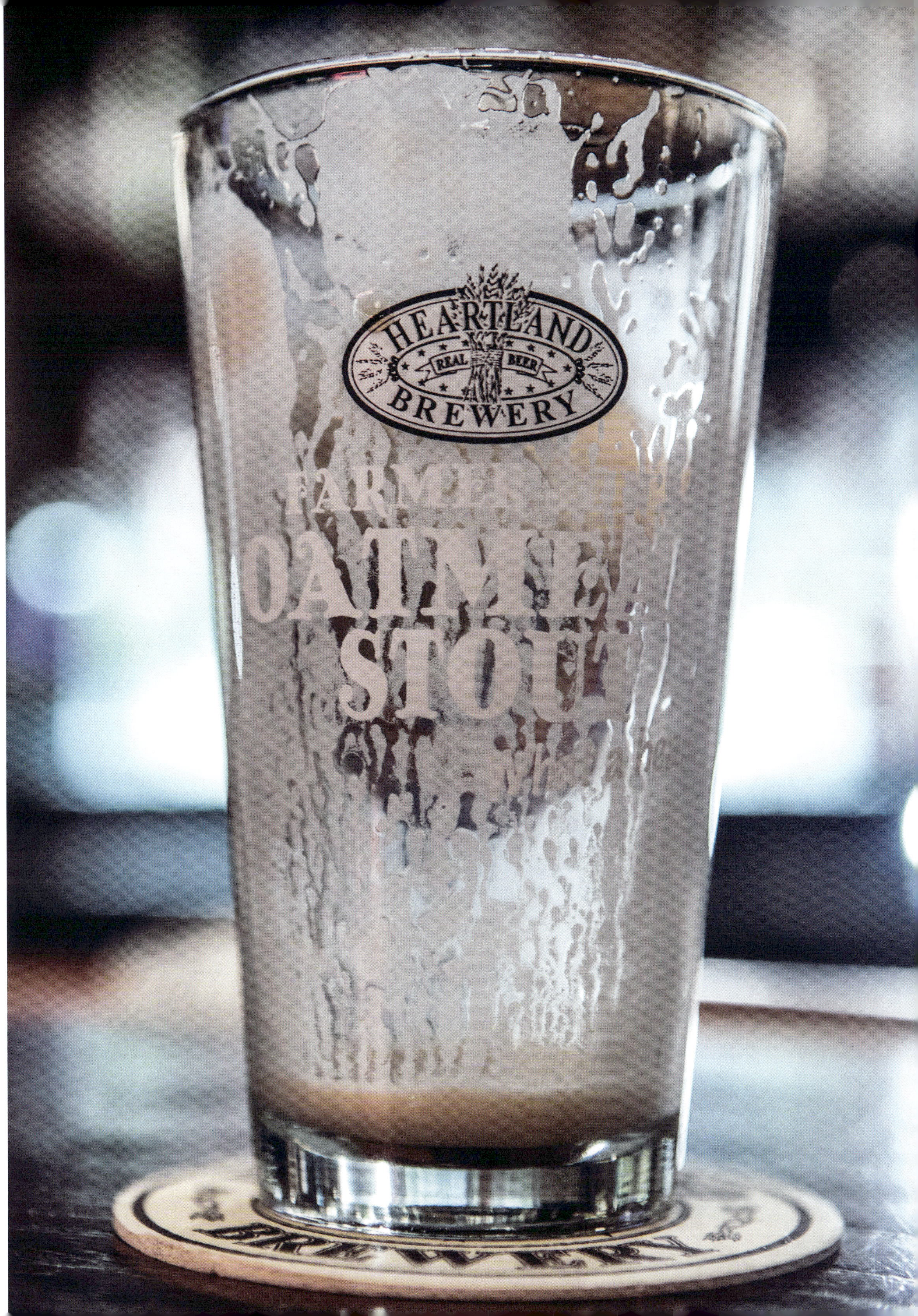
HEARTLAND
REAL BEER
BREWERY
BREWERY

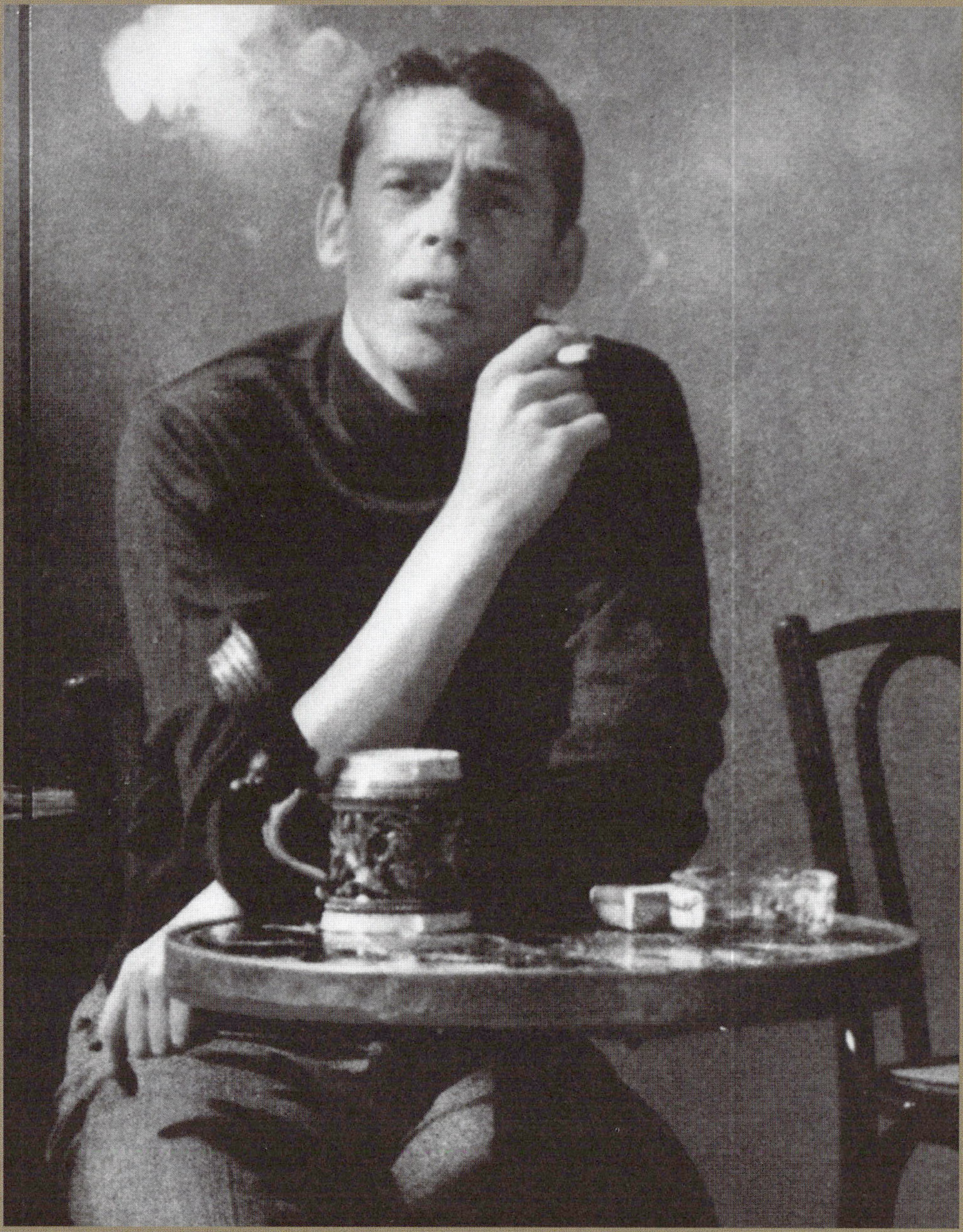

ÇA SENT
LA BIÈRE
DE LONDRES
À BERLIN,
ÇA SENT
LA BIÈRE
DIEU QU'ON
EST BIEN

Jacques Brel, Song: 'La Bière'.

BIEREN

BRUXELLENSIS
BRASSERIE DE LA SENNE

TIMMERMANS
MORT SUBITE
Oude Gueuze
FRAMBOISE BOON
KRIEK BOON
FARO
GEUZE BOON
CHAPEAU
GEUZE Mariage Parfait
FARO BOON
KRIEK BOON
LINDEMANS
GUEUZE
APPLE
FRAMBOISE
LINDEMANS

BELGIAN BEER

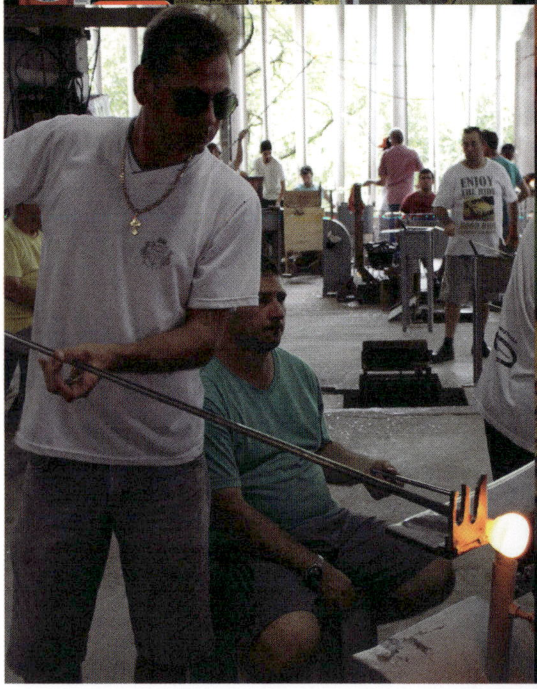

HELL'S PILS
HELL'S PILS

De Nieuwe Keizer
Hanny-D
ENAME

SINCE 1851

A
Atlas
RISMA PILS
ATLAS

FORCE
SANTÉ
STOUT LEOPOLD

ARE YOU
TOKKING
TO ME

VEDETT

BAVARIA
BIEREN
C.T.S
EXTRA SCOTCH

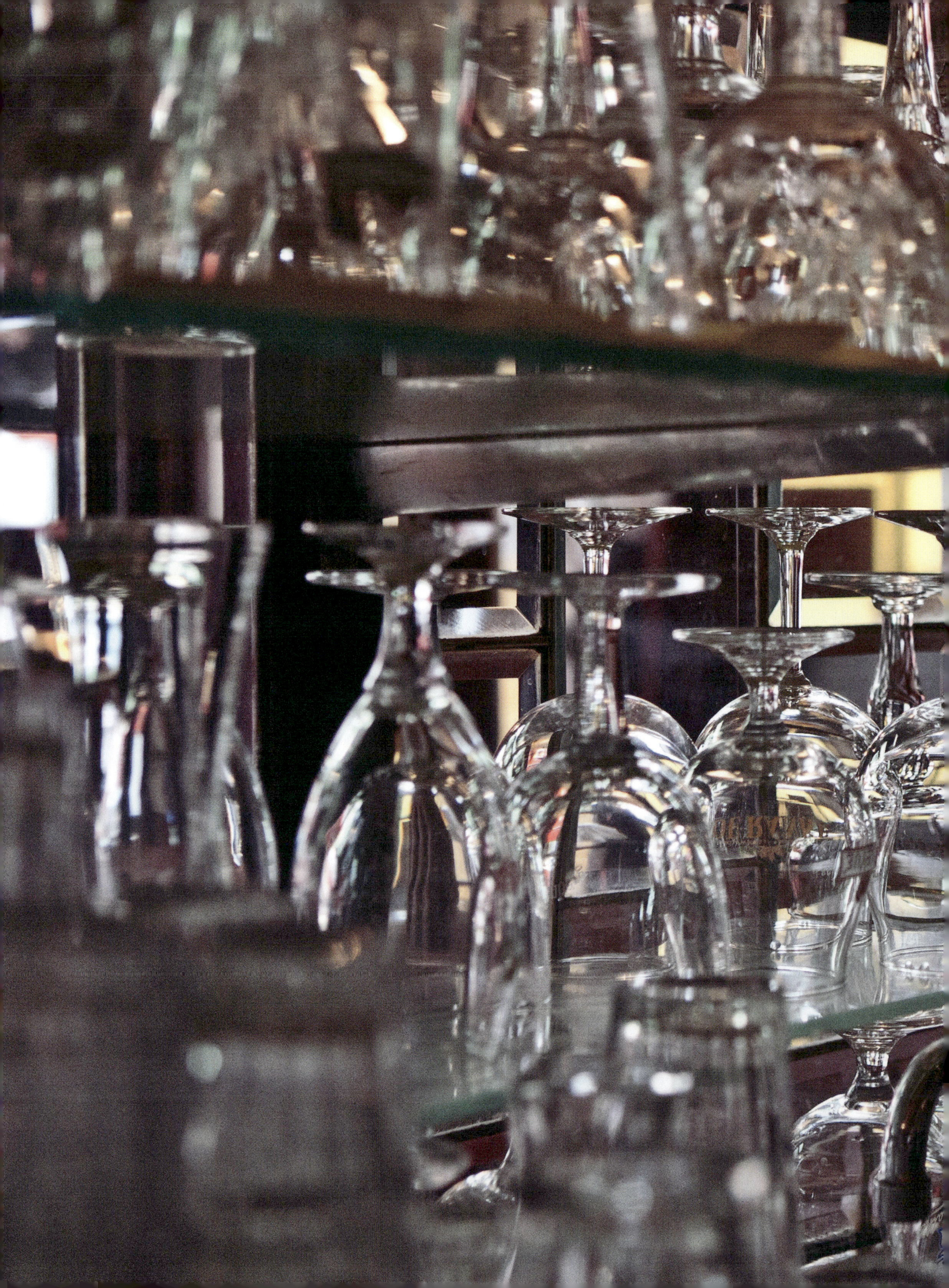

3

BELGIAN BEER CULTURE

BELGIAN BEER CULTURE

Belgium's beer culture is unique. Brewers, café owners, chefs, zythologues, beer professors, collectors, owners of beer museums and beer lovers; all of them contribute to this culture in their own way. In this section of the book we will delve deeper into the role played by the café. We will also take a look at beer advertising through the ages, bottle labels, enamel advertising signs, beer names and glasses. This chapter concludes with our own personal tips for the best cafés.

Popping into your 'local'

It should not come as a surprise that Belgian beer is so popular nowadays. Belgium is beer and beer is Belgium. It sounds like we are getting too big for our boots but really, we are speaking the truth. After all, beer is our national beverage. We have grown up with it. In Belgium, you can conjure up a can of beer from a vending machine and you can find beer on the shelves of your local supermarket or beer shop. Beer lovers are well served. And, of course, there is the café. It once started out as a 'home from home', or your 'local'. People used to live in cramped accommodation so they always had a good excuse to pop into their local café.

Clever café owners were running a shop as well as a bar. They were keeping an eye on their regulars' wallets as, after the umpteenth round, there should still be enough money left for 'the wife' to afford the groceries. Times have changed but your regular haunt, 'stamcafé' or 'local', remains the place where you arrange to meet your friends, where you put the world to rights at the bar, where you don't have to do anything but there is plenty to do if you want, where the 'patron' only locks up after the final customer has ordered his last pint. You will find cafés such as these in every town or village. Everyone is welcome and, fortified by a good glass, you will soon be involved in a round or two of bar talk.

Gueuze wars

Beer pops up everywhere, even where you least expect it. Sport and beer. It appears to be a rather strange combination at first sight. Not so in Belgium, where football and beer have gone hand in hand for many years. Jupiler, Belgium's largest pils brand, is the sponsor of the national squad, the Red Devils, and also backs the national Pro League. 'Men know why', the slogan has it. Posters of beer brands providing sponsorship are a firm fixture in the football stadium.

Before and after the match, emotions run high but are soon cooled down by a few mouthfuls of beer. In some stadiums they are unable to keep pace with the barrels and are tapping straight from the tank. The main focus is on pils and on… one round after another. In the 1970s the fierce competition between two brands of gueuze, Belle-Vue and Saint-Louis, blew over to the football stadium. The top match between Anderlecht and Club Brugge saw a 'gueuze war' between the sponsors of both first division clubs. The Van Honsebrouck brewery, based in West Flanders, had launched its Saint-Louis gueuze not long ago. They wanted to prove that you can produce a gueuze away from the Zenne Valley and also, that you can put up a good fight against a top team from Brussels, supported by Vandenstock, a brewer who even had a football stadium named after him. Tempers ran high but 'between pot and pint', the atmosphere reached more normal levels.

The beer sets the tune

Beer not only has its own culture, it has also had an impact on other forms of culture. A host of music festivals, both large and small, are sponsored by beer brands. Examples include Rock Werchter, Pukkelpop and Tomorrowland. At the mega-events you will primarily see pils brands. You can expect to see specialty beers sponsoring a jazz festival or castle concert or you may see them at a book fair or another, more modestly sized performance. As to books, the Grimbergen abbey beer is the subject of a whodunit, focusing on the search for the original recipe. In other words: a beer can write its own legend.

Drinking is ... saving

In origin, the Belgian café is a grocery store, a butcher's or even a barber's where the clients remained 'glued to the bar'. The grocer invited his customers to enjoy a pint. Free at the outset but they would have to pay later. This is how the café grew in size. The grocer received support from the local brewer. Each village had at least one brewery.

Five before midnight

The village policeman – the 'champetter' – used to check that cafés adhered to legal closing times. After all, the law dictated that each café had to shut its doors at midnight. But the love of beer is deeply ingrained in our little country on the North Sea. The Belgians were not defeated for long. Partying has no time limit. They introduced flexible closing hours so they could enjoy their beer for longer. The only solution the café owners could come up with was to fix the big hand of the clock at 'five to midnight'. Who's buying the last round?

EUROPEAN CUP SEMI FINAL
CHELSEA
25TH APRIL 2007
LIVERPOOL
1ST MAY 2007
BELGIUM
KONING BOUDEWIJNSTADION
WALES
16.11.2014
ANDERLECHT
MARSEILLE
LIVERPOOL
LIVERPOOL
SPURS
CAROLUS

NORWICH v LIVERPOOL
CARROW ROAD, SUNDAY 20th APRIL 2014
MANCHESTER CITY
FOOTBALL CLUB
WALK ALONE
CHAMPS LEAGUE 3rd
QUALIFYING ROUND
LIVERPOOL
STANDARD
LIEGE
ATLETICO MADRID
CLUB BRUGGE
Bier van het huis

Beer seeks café

There is no Belgian beer without a café. Ever since we can remember, the two have been inextricably linked. In all corners of Belgium you will find cafés in all flavours, sizes and colours, just like beer. There is always going to be a café where you feel at home and where you like to drink. Our regular café is our second home, where the bar is a great place to chat and the beer is flowing freely. Each self-respecting village will have a pub, café or 'staminee' in the shadow of the church tower. Trendy dance cafés attract a younger audience with their wave of decibels. If you look you will find little watering holes that time seems to have forgotten, dotted around small squares or on the corners of boring-looking roads. Loyalty is what brings a handful of elderly customers together. They have become part of the furniture, so to speak. The café owner knows them all by name, they play their game of cards or are crowded around the billiards table, pint never far away. In the brown café it doesn't matter who you are, what you think or what you wear. Pictures of rock and jazz icons are dotted around the walls. Now and again, the chairs and tables are pushed to the side and a small band begins to play. This is where the local brass band lubricates their throats, local clubs get together, politicians are sparring, personal anecdotes are exchanged and the world is put to rights over a glass of beer.

Premier league or fourth division

If you are walking around a city such as Brussels, sooner or later you will end up in an elegant brasserie or a similar 'drinking palace'. You will be served by a waiter dressed in an immaculate white shirt and typical waiter's waistcoat with gold buttons and black epaulettes. In a city café such as this, you are propelled back in time to the flowing curves of art nouveau. The floor is clad in splendid marble tiles and the interior just oozes class. The pumps are sparkling, the shelves behind the bar are displaying row after row of shiny beer glasses and large bottles are proudly on show. Outside the large cities, things are a bit more down-to-earth. Every village used to have its little café where the pigeon fanciers, cycling fans or fishermen got together. Where, on a Sunday, you used to play cards after attending Mass, got rid of the dust thrown up by a local bike race or cycling contest, or where tensions ran high when you were expecting the long-awaited return of the blue-scalloped racing pigeon. Before or after a movie, just on an ordinary weeknight, in-between, before or after a match… There is always a reason to pop into your local café. It is cosy and everyone receives a warm welcome. The interior testifies to tumultuous times. The walls are covered in dark wooden panels, you are seated on sturdy wooden chairs or on a wooden bench dented by many posteriors before yours. On the floor, wooden boards or beautifully decorated tiles. Often, the 'Leuvense stoof', a cast-iron wood or coal burner, was the centre piece of the café and served as a beacon of heat when the weather was chilly outside. The walls are covered in vintage photographs, beer advertising, maps, sports results and the obligatory poster stating the 'Law on Public Drunkenness' – which had to be displayed in every establishment where alcohol was sold.

Enamel signs

With a little bit of luck you may come across them at a brocante (flea market), a collectors' fair or an antiques shop. You'll need a well-stocked wallet to take one home, especially if you are coveting an original piece. We are, of course, talking about those handsome vintage enamel signs that used to adorn the walls of breweries and cafés to advertise their wares. Enamel is a durable material. The enamel layer, made of molten glass and applied to metal, served to protect the sign. Advertising such as this was meant to last. Over time the enamel board made way for more transient media like posters, newspaper and magazine advertising or, in the case of the larger breweries, advertising slots on radio and television. Nowadays the enamel sign feeds the hunger for nostalgia. Vintage enamel signs have turned into collectors' items. Belgium was once an important producer of enamel which the brewers were keen to use. However, they considered these signs from a practical point of view. If a sign was worn out or had become old-fashioned, it would be taken off the wall to end up in the attic, in the cellar or even just on the street. Early collectors used this to their advantage by going from brewery to brewery in search of handsome signs, which they could often purchase for a song. Jan De Plus, owner of the Bierreclamemuseum (Beer Advertising Museum) in the Dutch city of Breda is one of those. Over the years he managed to establish an impressive collection of enamelsigns. The museum is open every Sunday and on special occasions. Jan De Plus is an authority in the field of vintage beer advertising and regularly publishes articles and books on the topic of enamel signs.

A mosaic from Memory Lane

Undoubtedly, it looks splendid, such a wall covered in a mosaic of advertising signs from breweries that have since disappeared. Plenty of examples can be found. Take a trip to the Grange des Belges at jenever distillery Distillerie de Biercée near Charleroi; in the brewery cafés of La Binchoise, Den Triest and Duvel Moortgat; in the museums managed by lambic brewery Timmermans, by city brewery De Halve Maan and café brewery Brasserie des Fagnes; or pop into well-known specialty beer cafés like Delirium Café and Le Bier Circus in Brussels, 't Brugs Beertje in Bruges or 't Waagstuk in Antwerp. Around a hundred years ago the number of breweries in Belgium exceeded three thousand. All of them were competing for attention. If the brewery had a free-standing wall or chimney, a brand name would be painted on it before long. Alas, a few years later it would be anybody's guess as to what exactly was painted on the wall. Enamel signs removed all doubts. They lasted. However, these signs did far more than advertising the brand name and signposting the way to the brewery. Gaze at a wall covered in enamel signs and the work of an army of typographers, painters and designers is marching in front of your eyes. In the same way as fashion, you re-live the 'spirit of the times' with house styles characterised by the flowing shapes of the Art Nouveau or Jugendstil or the relics of modernism in the lettering or the Fifties Style design. Such a wide-ranging sample of Belgian beer culture on the wall is the ideal environment for relaxation with a good glass in hand. Don't forget to feast your eyes as well as your taste buds. Santé!

BRASSERIE
OUVRIERS REUNIS
CHARLEROI
Téléph: N° 16667
SPÉCIALE
OR
Stout
H
Stout
HAECHT
CAROLO
PILS
BRASSERIE
LES OUVRIERS REUNIS
SOCIÉTÉ COOPÉRATIVE - CHARLEROI
ABDIJ-BIER
POSTEL
1140
BAM
SUPER
PALE-ALE
BACCHUS
Bacchus
Pils
LION
EXPORT
BOCK
EXPORT
A. DEGREEF
RHODE-ST-GENÈSE (LEZ BRUXELLES)
ALLIED
STOUT

Bieren
ZÖLL
BRASSERIE OPSTAELE
BIEREN
BASS'
BASS
Primus
ROYALAEKEN

BIÈRE
HOUGAERDE
ANGLO BELGE
HOUGAERDE
ANGLO
BELGE
PECHEUR
Het beste bier
van
JOHN SMITH'S
BRUIN BIER
BIÈRES
& BLANCHE
d. Pré aux Moulins - BRUGES
Brune
FALSTAFF

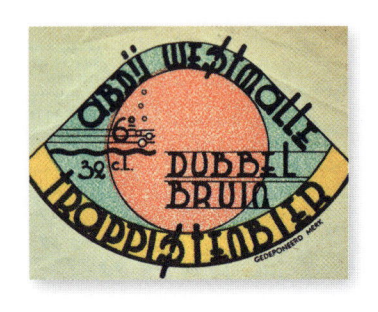

Beer labels

Almost every beer bottle is adorned by a label. This really is a brand's calling card, more so than the bottle or the glass as a label is more recognisable. Bottles and glasses come in various shapes and sizes that can be used by a number of brands. Browsing through a collection of labels, you traverse the history of a brewery and its brands. Belgian brewers used to look to the future rather than the past. They treated their archives in a sloppy way. And thus, an entire treasure trove of enamel boards, beer jugs and glasses, bottles with or without a label, crown corks and paperwork was consigned to the scrapheap, just like that. The tide has turned in recent years. What used to be put next to the bins can now be worth quite a bit of money. The beer label has graduated from an item offered at exchange fairs into a collectors' item in its own right. 'The internet has transformed the entire market', comments Marc Struyf, a collector. 'Traditional collectors' fairs have seen their business dwindle. You are now finding labels for sale on the internet'. And Marc should know. He is the proud owner of a collection comprising over 50,000 labels of Belgian breweries, including virtually every label that was introduced after the First World War. It turns out that a little bit of detective work helps to burst the bubble of certain well-established myths. 'The monks of the Abbey of St.-Sixtus in Westvleteren would swear blind that labels were never stuck on their bottles,' Marc laughs. 'I was able to show them these ancient labels.'

Exchange fair

The Hoegaarden Exchange Fair is one of the largest in Belgium. It is held every year during the first weekend of November. The fair was initiated by the Gambrinus collectors' club (www.gambrinusclub.be). The Gambrinus society was born in Louvain in 1978 where its first collectors' day was held. It turned into an official association in 1986. Gambrinus now organises four exchange fairs every year. The Gambrinus club magazines reports the latest news on labels, crown corks, beer glasses and beer mats and tips off the reader on new breweries. Belgium counts 500 Gambrinus members. The society is in regular contact with similar collectors' clubs abroad. The collecting bug knows no borders. The real work starts in the sports hall. Collectors launch themselves into a sea of beer mats, labels, bottles, posters, crown corks and promotional materials from times gone by. They are browsing the letterheads of breweries that ceased to exist many moons ago. Many collectors are interested in any possible item they can lay their hands on, others are looking specifically for beer glasses, mats, labels or crown corks, perhaps from a specific region or issued by one brewery in particular. This entire 'trade' is conducted without any involvement from the breweries. Even more, the brewers used to put their 'old rubbish' in the bin. These days antique brewery items are hard to find and worth a lot of money. Collectors from Belgium and abroad know each other and are well aware of who is in search of what. Ludwig Decaluwé has been around this collectors' world for a quarter of a century.

'My daughter started collecting beer mats,' he laughs. 'The beer collecting bug got hold of me very soon afterwards. Ever since then, my aim has been to obtain at least one object from every Belgian brewery: an invoice, letterhead, beer mat or a glass…' Everything is tidily sorted by brewery and the name of the town. Quite a bit of money goes around in the collectors' world. A pre-war beer glass from Moortgat brewery is quickly sold for 250 euro. Peanuts, really. Prices can go a lot higher. 'A brewer once told me that the original leaded windows from his brewery were offered for sale at a price of … 30.000 euro.'

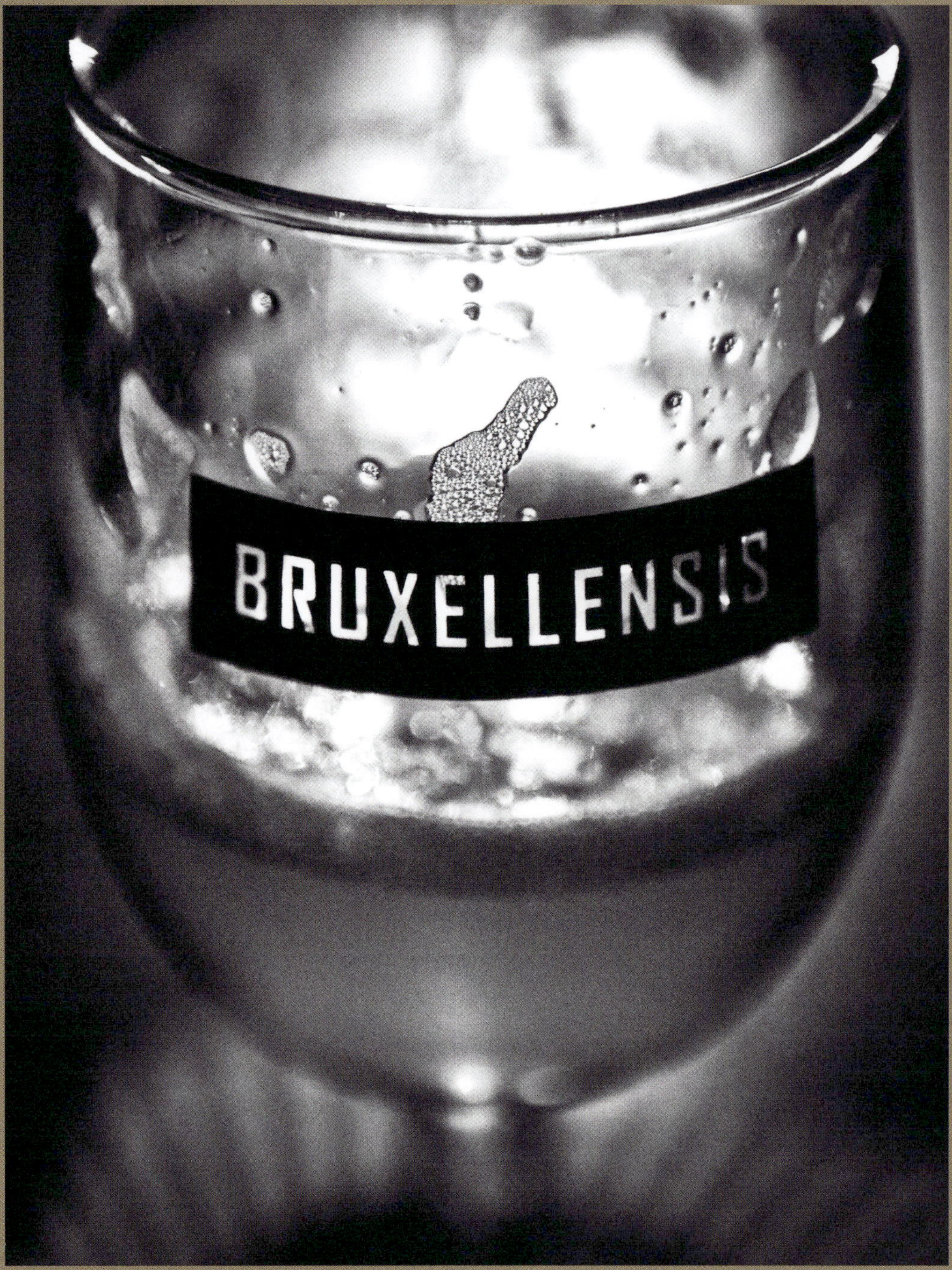
BRUXELLENSIS

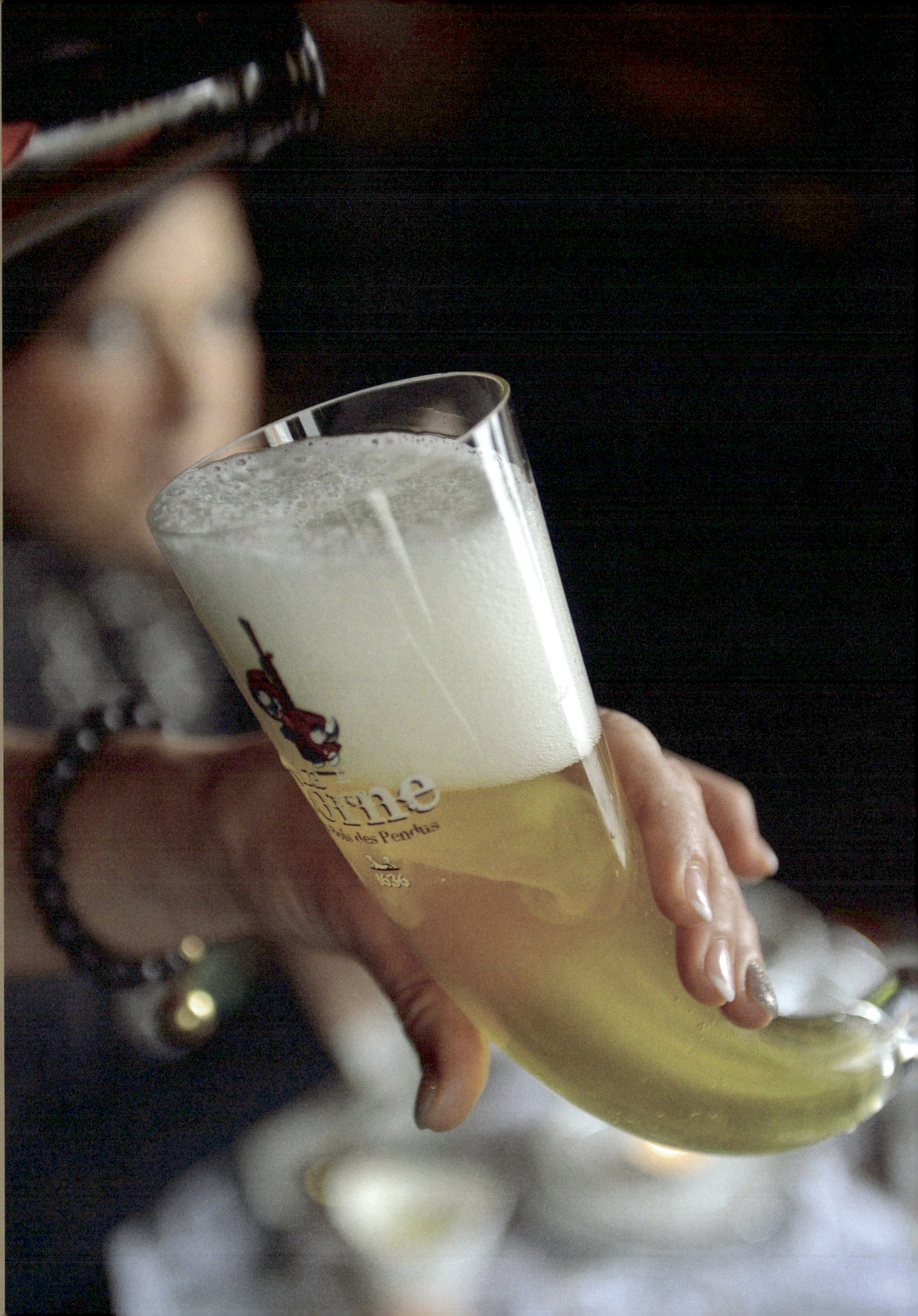

caves st pierre

Leffe
LA CHOUFFE
WORLD'S
SMALLEST TOAST

Moortgat
Blond

Imperial

"Bush-Beer

Gueuze
Caves Bruegel

Trappisten
Bier

Tripel
16 79
Karmeliet

Moortgat

The Belgian and his beer glass

Visitors from abroad are baffled when they look at our beer glasses. The Belgian beer glass really is in a world of its own. There is no other country with a greater variety of beer glasses. It is not only the shape that determines the identity of the brewery. Size and style also come into it. Our brewers are going one step further. They often feel that each beer deserves its own glass. Manna from heaven for collectors. They browse flea markets, collectors' websites and trade fairs. The hotel, café and restaurant trade does not always share this enthusiasm. After all, where do you put all those beer glasses? However, the Belgian beer lover has come to expect it. When he orders an Orval, Kwak or Chimay he wants to drink it from the correct glass.

Once upon a time

The tradition of the beer glass was born in the 19th century. Before then people drank their beer from receptacles made out of wood, ceramic, metal, porcelain, terracotta or enamel. In 14th century Germany introduced closed receptacles for foodstuffs to try and prevent the plague. Beer jugs were covered with a tin lid. This also protected the beer from insects crawling or flying in. The traditional wide, bulbous beer jug is reminiscent of Bavaria. The 'pint' is a reference to Great Britain and Ireland. This stable, robust and masculine glass turned into the trademark of Guinness. This glass fits well in the hand and thanks to its shape, slightly wider at the top, the aromas of the stout are done full justice. The jet black colour of this beer can be seen forming below the creamy head. In Belgium most beer glasses that were tied to a brand only made their appearance after the war. The current Orval glass dates back to 1947, just like the iconic 'Gaétan' pils glass with its ribbed bottom. That particular glass was blown using machinery but cut by hand.

The head

In recent years the market has been flooded with beer glasses. Marketing execs have been doing overtime and it is hard to find two glasses that are exactly the same. However, the main function of the glass shape is to do justice to the aromas and tastes of the beer. Furthermore, the glass helps to form a beautiful collar of froth that is different for each beer. The majority of beer glasses are a reflection of the beer style involved: the chalice for abbey beers and Trappist beers, the tulip-shaped glass for a strong blond beer or pale ale, the flat, wide, massive bock glass for white beer… The bulbous, balloon-shaped glass is suitable for dark beer and the ribbed glass is characteristic of pils. These iconic glasses belong to the beer, form part of its identity and are coveted collectors' items. Just think of Hoegaarden, Leffe, Orval or Chimay. Some breweries are breaking the tried and trusted codes: Dupont, Dubuisson and Van Steenberge to name but a few. They elevate the beer glass to a work of art. Others go for coherence by introducing one design across the board. Their beer glasses seamlessly fit the brewery in question, represent the 'soul' of the beer and give much tasting pleasure to the drinker. Examples include the Trappists, St-Feuillien, Bosteels (Tripel Karmeliet), De Brabandere (Petrus), Waterloo … The real classic drinking vessels remain the same throughout the decades. Even with closed eyes, you can recognise a Duvel glass. The same goes for the glasses of Val-Dieu, Brasserie du Bocq (Gauloise) and Grimbergen. And then you have the 'oddballs'. This is where originality gets the upper hand on functionality. These glasses 'tell a story'. There is no Kwak without a coach driver's glass. Equally, you cannot imagine a Corne du Bois des Pendus without a drinking horn or a Paix-Dieu Pleine Lune without its bulbous moon at an angle, resting on a tall stem.

The joy of tasting

Can the standard glass be consigned to the land of fairy tales? Granted, many attempts have been made to produce a universal, modern, balanced beer glass fit for many purposes, but these attempts have met with only varying degrees of success. Ritzenhof, Tradiglass and publishing company Becomev joined forces to develop a beer tasting glass for brewers, beer lovers and the horeca trade. This elegant degustation glass does justice to the aromas and tastes of the majority of Belgian beers. At home and in the café you would expect each beer to be accompanied by its proper glass, but in a restaurant you would expect the refined joy of tasting rather than brand recognition and image.

The joy of beer

With all the attention going towards to barrel aged beers, hop, hype, branding, marketing and science we are in danger of forgetting the simple truth that beer is fun. A good glass of beer is very tasty, loosens the tongue, cools down emotions or might just spark them off. You have a memorable conversation or a surprising encounter that sticks in the mind. In the best case, the aroma continues to excite the nose, the taste carries on caressing the tongue, and you re-live a moment of happiness. 'What exactly have I had to drink?' 'Hmmm, would a second glass bring back that feeling?' 'Brewers create fun', Pierre Celis stated many years ago. The man who put Belgian white beer – Hoegaarden, Celis White – on the map, was firmly grounded. All he did was to produce a good product with a good back story. He started off in the mid-1960s. Thomsin, a brewer, taught Pierre Celis, then a milkman, how to brew a white beer. Pierre showed plenty of courage and rowed against the tide of pils beers. The spirit of May '68 made itself felt. Creativity was the future. The non-conformity, simplicity and enthusiasm displayed by Pierre Celis fit the times perfectly. Who does not remember the iconic beer mat campaign from Hoegaarden, conducted in cafés? Email was still a long way off. You lost your heart, scribbled something on the reverse of a beer mat and put it up on the café wall in the hope that that the object of your affection would collect your message next time he or she popped in and perhaps leave you a message scribbled on a beer mat of their own.

Keep things simple

This small brewer from Hoegaarden quickly acquired a following. Chris Bauweraerts of Brasserie d'Achouffe was literally 'blown away' by the taste of this unfiltered, slightly sour white beer from Hoegaarden. In later years Pierre would remain an inspiration for this Ardennes brewery, known for its La Chouffe. Chris epitomises the slogan 'beer is fun' to a tee. You would be hard-pressed to think of a better representative. From nowhere, he conjured up an entire world of gnomes. Chris was a founder of the legendary Choufferie festivals and put the tiny village of Achouffe on the beer world map. Achouffe now hosts the world championship of 'beer crate climbing' where the gnome beer is streaming out of the tanks. Fun has been a marketing element that over the years, has been used cannily by breweries. Their enamel signs, labels and beer mats all depict fun and enjoyment.

However, genuine fun cannot be programmed. If, at the table, you are seated next to someone with whom you have very little in common, a stony silence will ensue. But when, on a Saturday, you knock on the door of the Erquelinnes village brewery, before long you will find yourself in front of a steaming plate of beef stew with a large bottle of Angélus on the side. Enjoyment is all that counts here. This is why the villagers get together to support their brewery. If the beer has run out, it's all hands on deck to produce the next batch.

But you have been warned: you never know if you will leave this brewery still vertical or crawling home.

DOPPIO MALTO - STRONG ALE

Ba

BIRRA BIONDA DOPPIO M

Vol - MAKASI BIERE FORTE BRUNE

bär

STRONG ALE MADE WITH HONEY

PONIKER & HONING BIER

BLONDE AU MIEL · SPECIAAL

SPECIALTY BEER CAFÉS IN BELGIUM

AALST

't Apostelken

Beer lovers make their way to this café-restaurant on the outskirts of the carnival city of Aalst. 250 beers are on offer, including a large number of regional beers and artisan oude gueuze and kriek. The café displays a unique collection of vintage and modern beer bottles, ordered by brewery. Plenty of bottles come from breweries that no longer exist. The collection also includes advertising signs, mirrors, vases and all sorts of other beer paraphernalia. It is normally kept behind lock and key. Ask Kevin, the café owner, if he is willing to open his Ali Baba's cave for you.

Apostelstraat 1 – +32(0)499/72 92 39
www.apostelken.be

ANTWERP

't Oud Arsenaal

Everyone feels at home in this people's café between the Vogeltjesmarkt, the theatre and the shopping Valhalla that is the Meir. Since it first opened its doors in 1924, this brown café has worn its age lightly. The interior is dominated by a leaded window and a range of beer objects. Antwerp citizens of a certain age, beer lovers and slightly lost tourists are exploring the beer menu and are pleasantly surprised by the reasonable prices. Traditional lambic beers such as oude gueuze and oude kriek are the showstoppers. Differences in class and wealth melt away at the bar. This is where the actor shares a glass with the postman, the teacher or manager. Unfortunately, the bar gets very crowded from time to time, especially when the market is held on Saturdays and Sundays. Nevertheless, don't miss out on this one.

Maria Pijpelincxstraat 4 – +32(0)3/232 97 54

SPA CITRON
Special
HEY-VA
STELLA ARTOIS
BIEREN HAMERKEN
Duvel
CHIMAY
Heyvaert
DE KONINCK
SPA MONOPOLE EAUX MINÉRALES
SCHMIDT
Arend dubbel
DELIRIUM
Antigoon

Kulminator

Beer geeks from abroad have no trouble finding their way to this café. The Kulminator is considered the best beer café in the world ever since the pub was awarded this honorary title in 2007 by www.ratebeer.com. Leen and Dirk, the owners, set up their café in 1974. They are now welcoming 'Antwerpenaars' as well as beer lovers from around the world. As far as the latter are concerned, the Kulminator is often the only reason to visit Antwerp. The beer menu includes over nine hundred beers, most of which are Belgian. However, De Kulminator mainly marked out its place on the map thanks to their stock of 'old beer'. With a little bit of luck, you can taste a Chimay Bleue from the 1980s or a Westvleteren that is even a decade older. Fancy tasting a beer brewed in your year of birth?

Vleminckveld 32 — +32 (0)3/232 45 38

Brasserie Bahnhove

Welcome to the renovated railway station of Hove on the outskirts of Antwerp. You can now order your gueuze, saison or Trappist from the former ticket office. Bernd Zwinnen, the owner, regularly surprises his customers with new beers. He also organises beer tastings. Each beer is served on its own beer mat. A great place to go during the summer months, when you can sprawl out on the lovely terrace and sample the beautiful beers on offer.

Kapelstraat 117, Hove — +32(0)3/294 96 13

't Been

A bland-looking building, located on the corner of two roads in a quiet and bourgeois area of the city, reveals a superb beer café at a stone's throw from Stadsbrouwerij De Koninck. An oasis of peace in a restless world where locals, the occasional passers-by, tourists as well as beer lovers are welcome to enjoy a delightful glass of beer. The beer menu offers a small number of beers on tap, one of which is always a guest beer. The range of bottled beers is quite idiosyncratic and changes regularly. The interior of this café, with its ancient tables, comfortable seats and old wallpaper is a great reminder of peaceful and nostalgic times.

Belpairestraat 28 — +32(0)472/85 50 56

Gollem

With 30 beers on tap and over 400 bottled beers this café, located near the Town Hall, should be highlighted on every beer lover's map. All of the well-known beer styles are on offer. The classics abound but you will also come across some hidden gems. The food menu includes burgers, world cuisine and snacks that taste even better with a beer on the side.

Suikerrui 28 — +32(0)3/689 49 89
www.gollem.be

't Antwaerps Bierhuyske

It would be easy to just walk past this unassuming café, one of umpteen in this busy, pedestrianised shopping street in the vicinity of Grote Markt. But its beer menu is worth a detour, comprising, as it does, quite a few beers from Belgian microbreweries. Moreover, this is one of only a few cafés in the world where you can order a beer from De Struise Brouwers, bottled or from the tap. Paul Meeusen, the owner, is a qualified zythologue and ensures that the service is impeccable. In this 'little beer house', you will find two hundred bottled beers as well as nine served from the tap.

Hoogstraat 14 — +32(0)475/89 49 64
www.antwaerpsbierhuyske.com

Bier Central

Bier Central, at a stone's throw of the most beautiful railway stations in the world, has an amazing range of 20 draught beers and 300 bottled beers. The beer menu reads like a thrilling novel. Missed your train? Are you waiting for the next one? Or did you end up on the wrong platform…? There are worse places to spend your time 'usefully'. Take a seat at a table converted from a yeast press or sit down in a foeder that has been cut in half. Busy city life disappears like magic at this old-style café. But, if you prefer the vibe of the city, make your way to the spacious terrace. Are you feeling peckish or ravenous even? Order a beer snack or a full meal. One thing there is plenty of, is beer.

De Keyserlei 25 — +32(0)3/201 59 80
info@biercentral.be — www.biercentral.eu

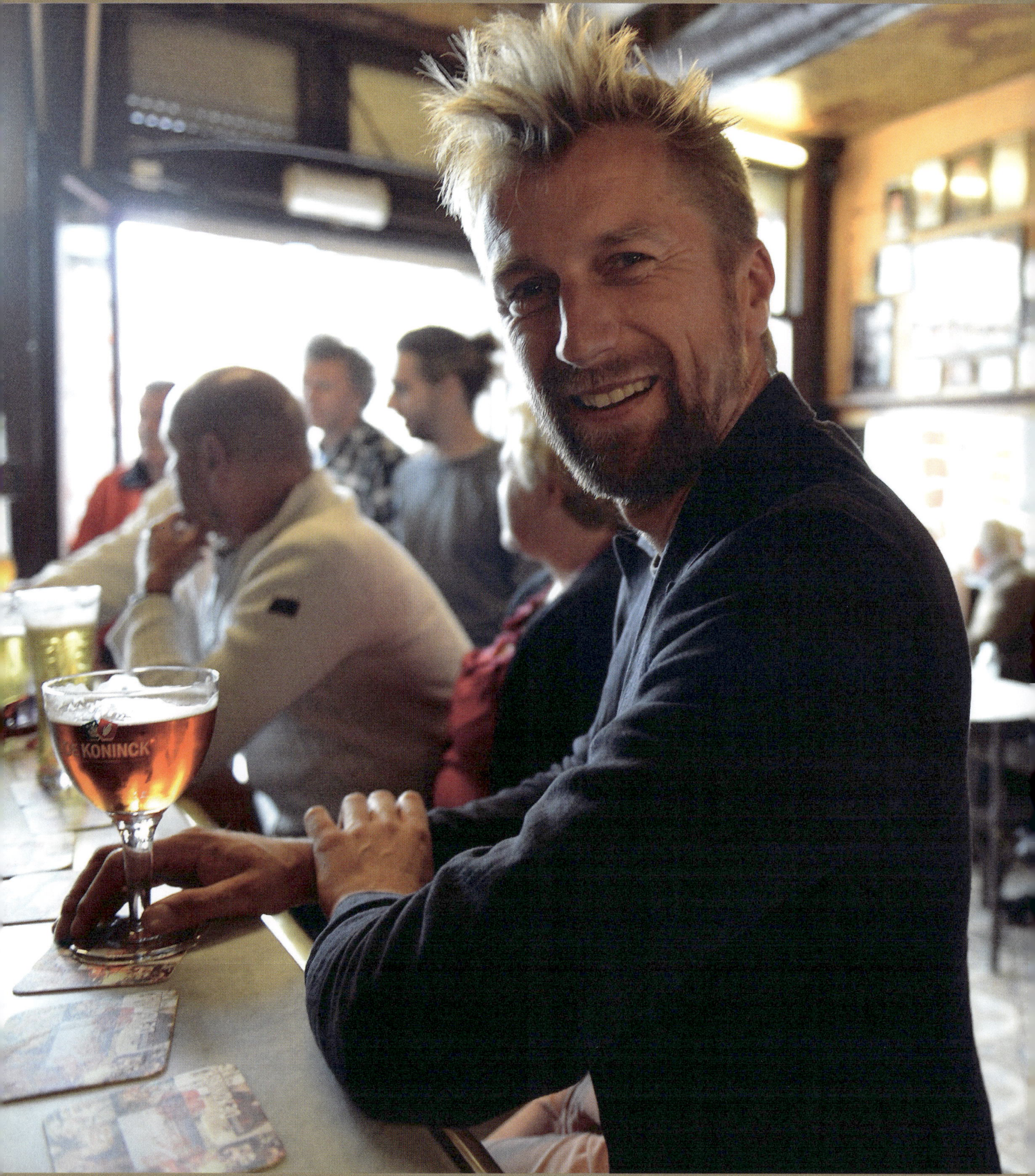
KONINCK

Café 't Oud Arsenaal at Antwerp's 'Vogelenmarkt' (Bird market) has escaped the ravages of time. Feast your eyes on the décor and your taste buds on its beers at the same time.

AUBECHIES

Taverne Le Saint-Géry

This is not by any means the centre of the world. However, pop into this village café and your visit will be well rewarded. This tavern is located in the shadow of a splendid Romanesque church, not far from the Gallo-Roman museum in Aubechies. The café itself could be called a living museum. The walls are clad in vintage enamel boards and you are almost at risk of tripping over the various beer items on display. The beer menu highlights local heroes, the saison made by Brasserie Dupont for example. Order a regional dish to go with it. There is a beer for every season and a dish for every saison.

Place d'Aubechies 2 — +32(0)69/67 12 74
www.taverne-saint-gery.be

BASTENAKEN/BASTOGNE

Brasserie Lamborelle

In the centre of Bastenaken, only 50 metres away from the Place McAuliffe where the famous Sherman tank takes pride of place, you will find the Brasserie Lamborelle. Almost like a beer hall, with heavy wooden tables and a wealth of beer paraphernalia, the Brasserie welcomes beer lovers with open arms. Its first floor is designed in a modern, quite minimalist way. Here, you can taste a beer in two different worlds. The 150 beers on offer include many local, lesser-known gems. Flambéed beers write their own chapter in the extensive beer menu.

Rue Lamborelle 19 — +32(0)61/21 80 55
www.brasserielamborelle.be

Bistro Léo

The Second World War still resonates deeply in the little town of Bastenaken (Bastogne), site of the horrific Ardennes Offensive also known as the Battle of the Bulge. Fortunately, in Bistro Léo the atmosphere is far more peaceful. This restaurant carriage has grown into an institution. Here, you can choose from over fifty beers, all served as they should be in a brasserie that would not be out of place in Paris. Order a regional dish with your beer and enjoy seasonal cuisine. Tip: whether you are looking for a 'young' or an 'old' Orval, this is a good place to go.

Rue du Sablon 6/8 — +32(0)61/21 14 41
www.wagon-leo.com

BERGEN/MONS

Le Sherlock Holmes

Step into this pub and board a train to Conan Doyle's London. Order a beer, a rum or a whisky to accompany one of the thirty meat burgers, veggie burgers, salads or *other pub food*. The prices will not put you off and the names of the dishes will bring you into the zone straight away. How about a Mary Jane Kelly veggie burger with courgette or a Miller's Court with aubergine? Can you withstand the challenge of the huge Jack the Ripper hamburger? Whatever you do, leave some space for the home-made tarte tatin. And don't forget to order a tasty beer on the side.

Rue du Miroir 3 — +32(0)65/31 49 09

La Lorgnette

To kick off a night on the town you meet up in this café close to the Grote Markt of Bergen (Mons). La Lorgnette is the place to be for beer lovers but fans of cocktails, including those made with beer, will also find what they are looking for. One of their classic offerings is the Pêche Mel Bush flambée. They set fire to it in front of your very eyes. You taste the result as a group, with your friends, when the large glass is put in front of you. Coming in from the cold, you are instantly warmed by the welcoming and convivial atmosphere of this watering hole, where everyone feels at home straight away.

Rue des Clercs 1 — +32(0)65/42 89 71

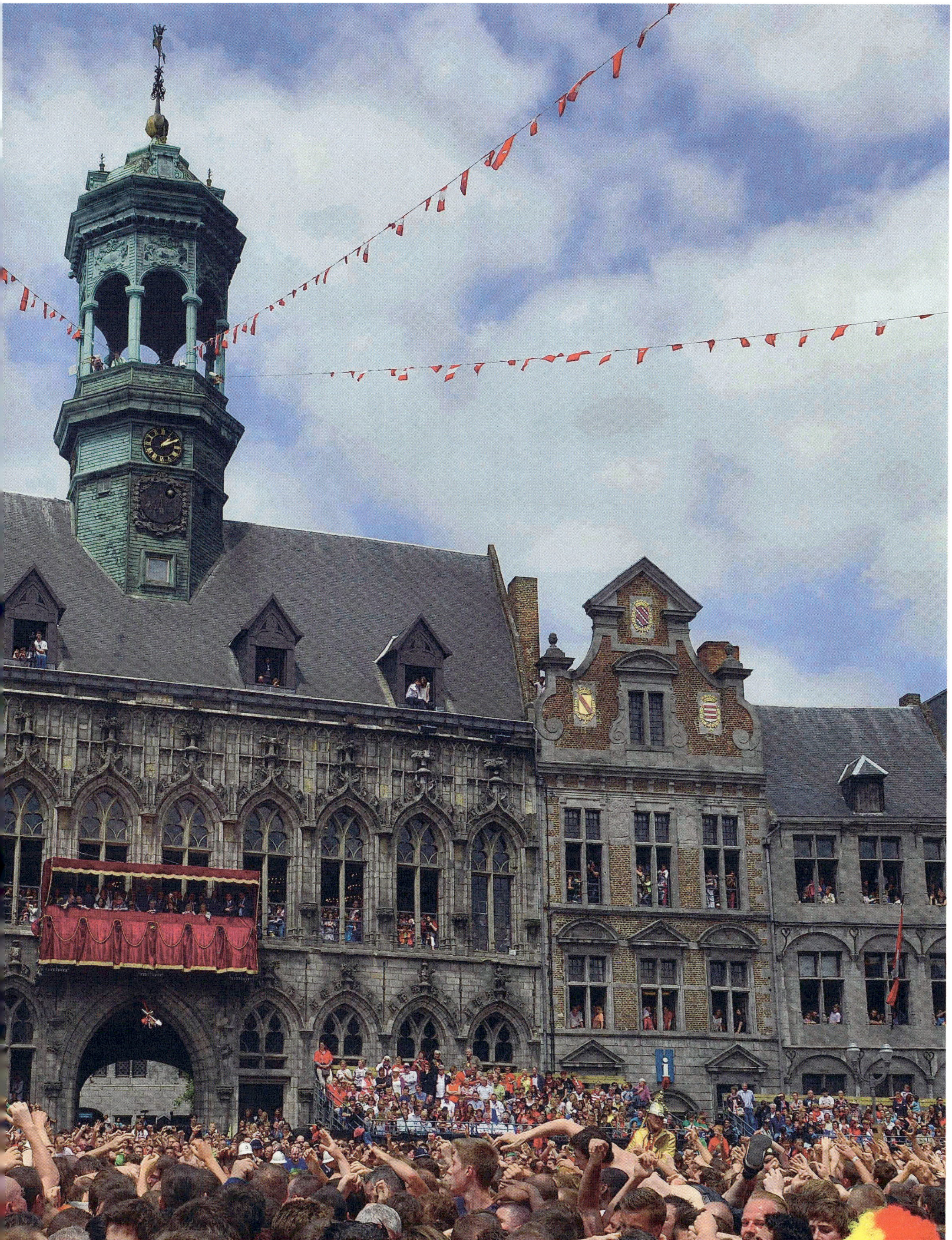

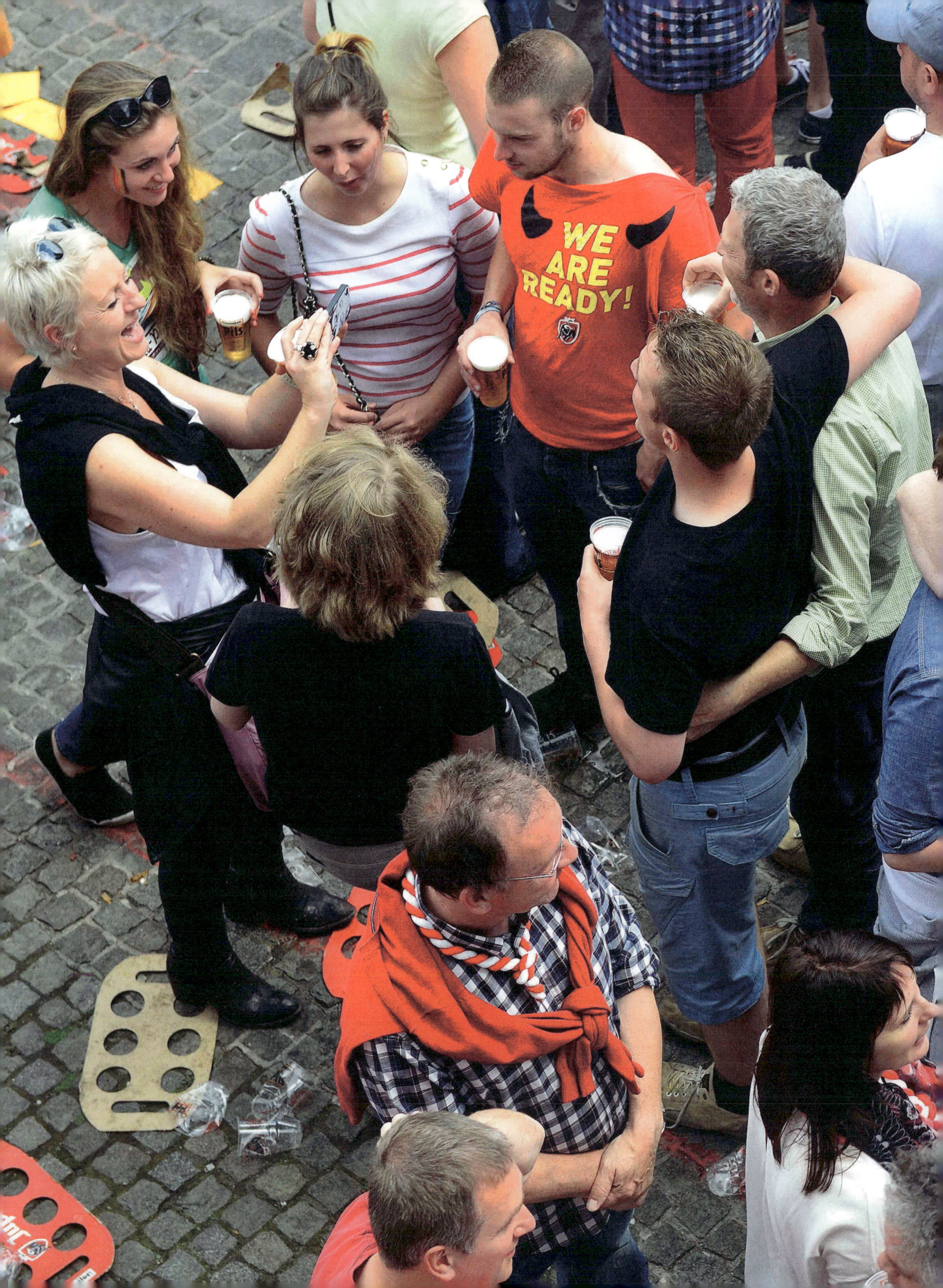
WE
ARE
READY!

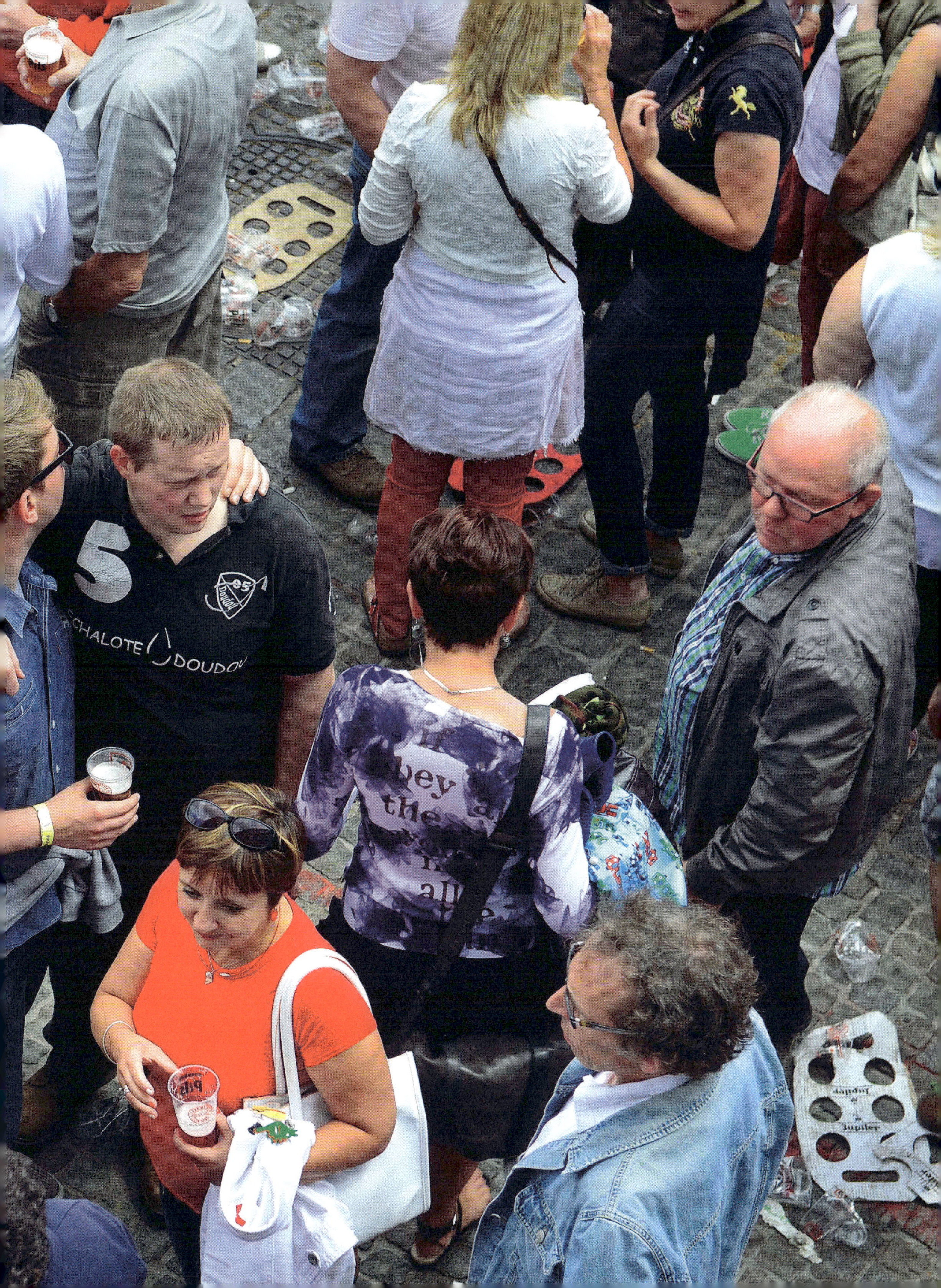
CHALOTE DOUDOU
Jupiler

BRUGES

't Brugs Beertje

Mecca in Bruges for the beer lover. This café has a beer menu comprising over three hundred Belgian beers. Daisy Claeys, who owns the café, is determined that pils will not be served in her establishment. The walls are covered in authentic, vintage enamel signs. Daisy is often credited with putting Bruges on the world beer map. We would not disagree in any way. Many beer lovers from across the world consider 't Brugs Beertje an unmissable stop on their travels. A wide range of Belgian beers is on offer here, with every single beer style and type represented.

Kemelstraat 5 — +32(0)50/33 96 16
www.brugsbeertje.be

Daisy Claeys of 't Brugs Beertje gives her verdict on the Straffe Hendrik Wild from De Halve Maan brewery.

Café Vlissinghe

Herberg Vlissinghe is the oldest café in Bruges. It is thought to date back to the 17th century. Its quirky interior contains many elements from that period. The main area was refurbished in 1869 in the so-called 'Flemish style' and acquired a marble fireplace and neo-Baroque furniture. The annexe in the garden was refurbished to resemble a Flemish parlour with a Gothic fireplace and wood panelling decorated with sayings meant to elevate your soul. This mini-museum was intended to be a meeting room. The ideal place to relax for a moment, away from the hustle and bustle of everyday life. We can also recommend the terrace in the beautiful garden.

Blekerstraat 2 — +32(0)50/34 37 37
www.cafevlissinghe.be

De Garre

The tiniest alley in Bruges takes you to a café where you discover a piece of Bruges beer history as well as 130 beers to a background of classical music. De Garre has a very central location close to the Grote Markt. Don't walk too fast — blink and you'll miss it. Before we forget to mention it: they have their own triple here. Hot and cold meals are also being served.

De Garre 1 — +32(0)50/34 10 29
www.degarre.be

Café Rose Red

Café Rose Red, a stone's throw from Bruges market, is full of character. Here you will find all of the Belgian Trappists. The beer menu also includes a 'beer of the month', often a hidden gem waiting to be unearthed. Highly recommended if you want to relax for a while with a good glass in front of you, either indoors or on the pleasant terrace. The café forms part of the Cordoeanier hotel.

Cordoeaniersstraat 16 — +32(0)50/33 90 51
www.cordoeanier.be

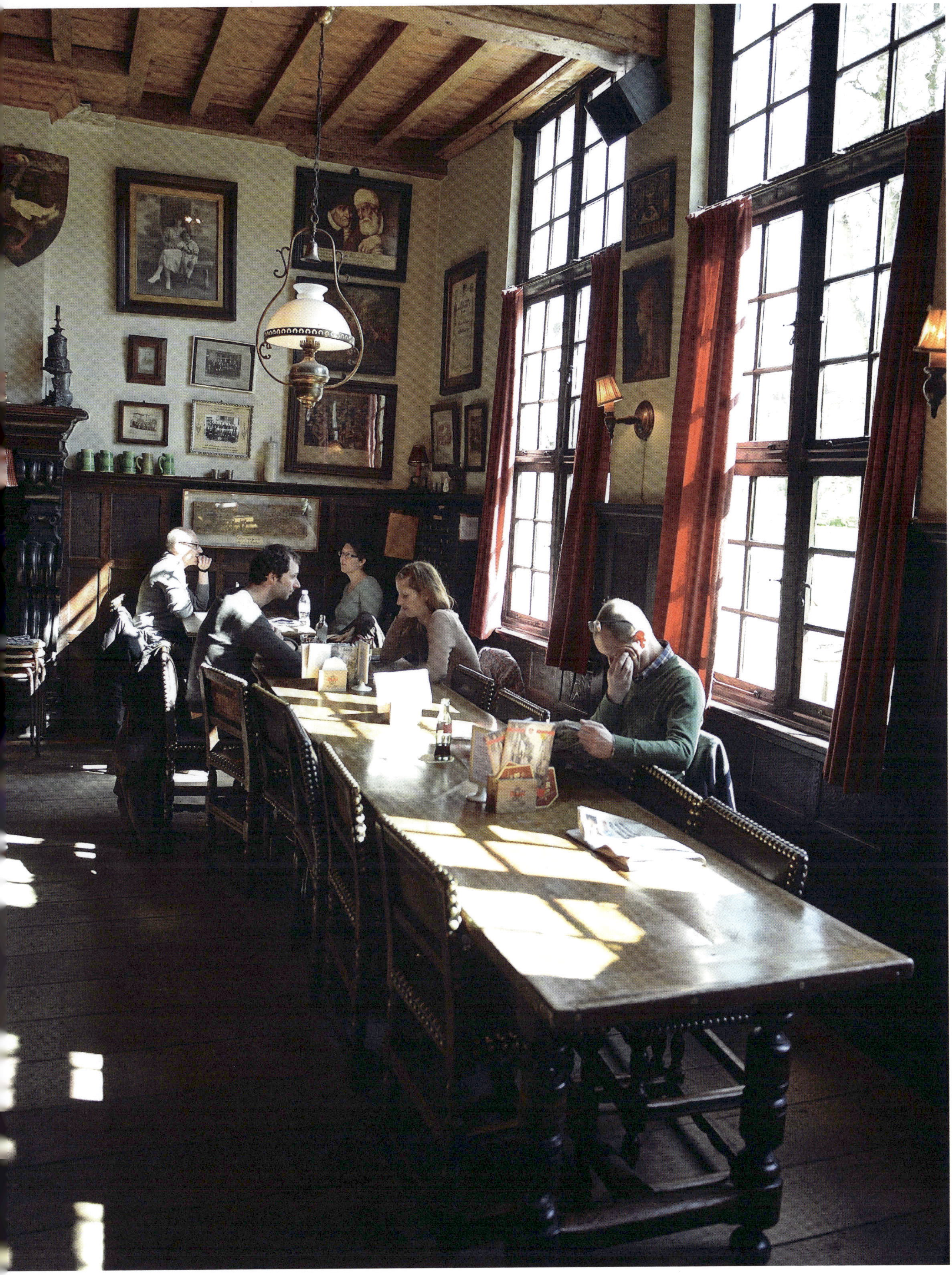

À la Mort Subite

NOS SPÉCIALITÉS BRUXELLOISES

TARTINE 1900
TARTINE FROM. BLANC

BRASSERIE VOSSEN
Mᵈ DE BIÈRES
7

NOS SPÉCIALITÉS BRUXELLOISES

GUEUZE et KRIEK
MORT - SUBITE

*A la Mort Subite is an iconic café in Brussels. It was named after a dice game.
If you lose the last round, you suffer sudden death, or a 'mort subite'. Game over.*

BRUSSELS

A la Mort Subite

This iconic café with its original interior dating back to the Belle Époque gave its name to the Mort Subite lambic brewery and its gueuze and kriek beers also. 'Mort Subite' is a reference to the dice game commonly called 'pitjesbak' that is played 'to kill time'. Round after round is played until one of the participants runs out of luck and is 'dead'. If you play the last round quickly, just to finish off or to attempt a swift win, this is called sudden death or 'mort subite'. Must be played with a glass of gueuze or kriek within easy reach.

Warmoesberg 7 – +32(0)2/513 13 18
www.alamortsubite.com

Au Dairingman 'Chez Martine'

This retro café, also known as Chez Haesendonck or Chez Martine, is situated between the Dansaertstraat fashion district and the canal. The guests here are of different plumage, from theatregoers and hipsters to 'ordinary' Bruxellois. On the walls, pictures of Elvis, Ella and other stars take pride of place as well as iconic Stella advertising from the 1950s. Leaflets and flyers are dotted around, showing everything there is to do in this city, from mainstream to alternative culture. A typical Brussels café with African music. Old, small, crowded and oozing with atmosphere.

Vlaanderenstraat 37 – +32(0)2/512 43 23

Bier Circus

Pop in here for the exceptionally rich beer menu with hundreds of beers. The barman hands you a beer menu seventeen pages long and advises you on your choice. Take a look at the blackboard that displays the seasonal beers and be on the lookout for hidden gems. In addition to the main area there are several separate chambers where the focus is on cartoons. A traditional Brussels beer pub that will not disappoint you.

Onderrichtstraat 57 – +32(0)2/218 00 34
www.bier-circus.be

Café le Coq

No-one knows why, but this is where you will find the greatest thinkers in the city. They come here for a fine glass of beer, a tasty snack and a sparkling conversation. What are they discussing? Society, politics and philosophy. Café le Coq is far from a tourist trap. In fact, few tourists find their way here. This typical Brussels café comes highly recommended for a good beer and a snack. Enjoy the convivial atmosphere amongst students, Brussels locals and beer lovers.

Auguste Ortsstraat 14 – +32(0)2/514 24 14

Hand-written beer list and menu at the Café le Coq in the heart of Brussels.

Moeder Lambic & Fontainas

The two entrepreneurs who breathed new life into Brussels 'institution' Moeder Lambic in the Savoiestraat (rue Savoie) took their know-how, enthusiasm and extensive beer menu to the city centre a few years ago. The focus here is on artisan microbreweries such as Dupont, De Ranke, 3 Fonteinen and Brussels breweries Cantillon and Brasserie de la Senne. A great place to taste something new or pure, bitter or sour, with or without cheese or charcuterie. Highly ranked on the map of Brussels beer cafés.

Savoiestraat 68 (Moeder Lambic)
+32(0)2/544 16 99 — www.moederlambic.com

Fontainasplein 8 (Moeder Lambic Fontainas)
+32(0)2/503 60 68 — www.moederlambic.com

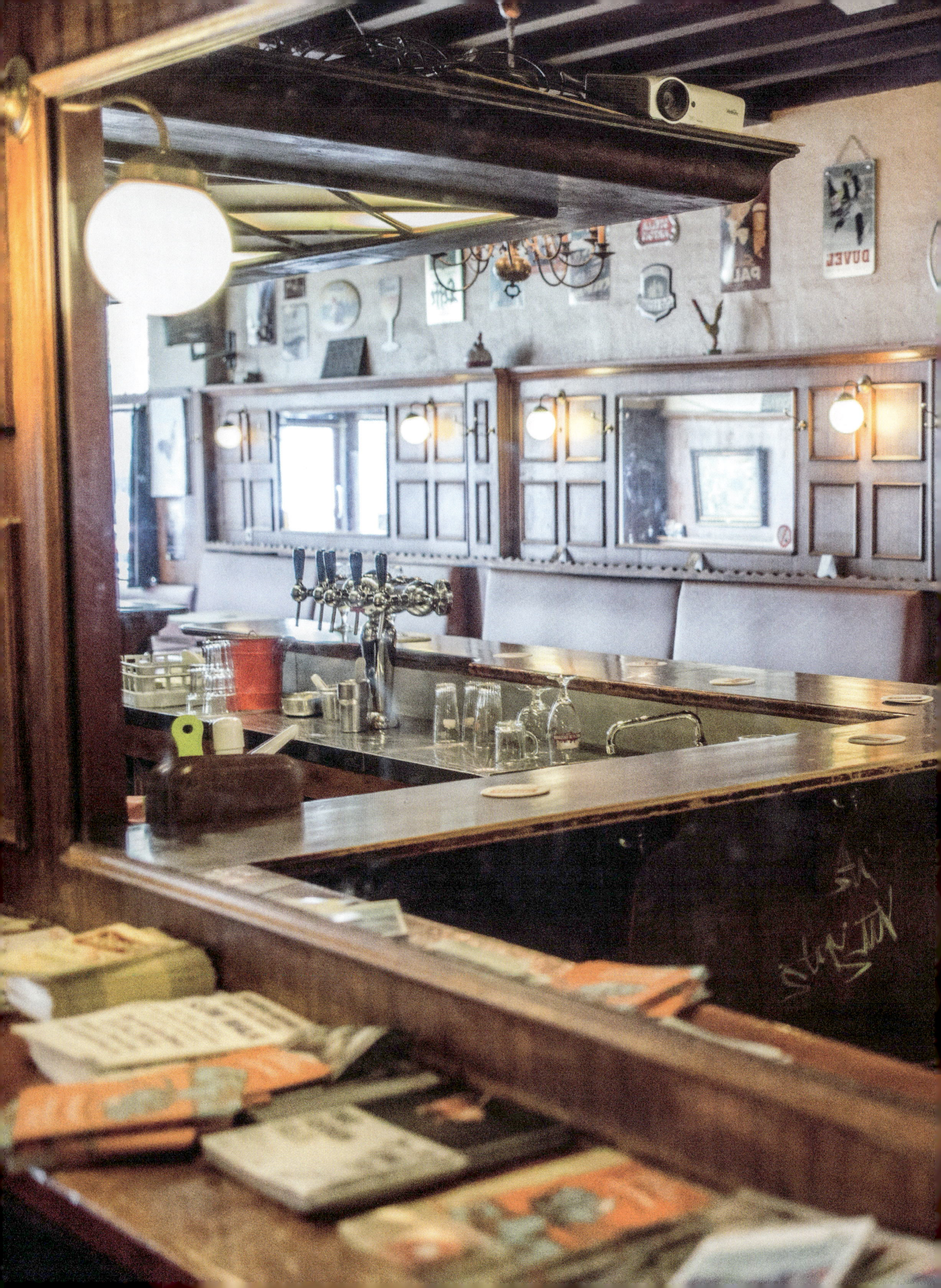
DUVEL

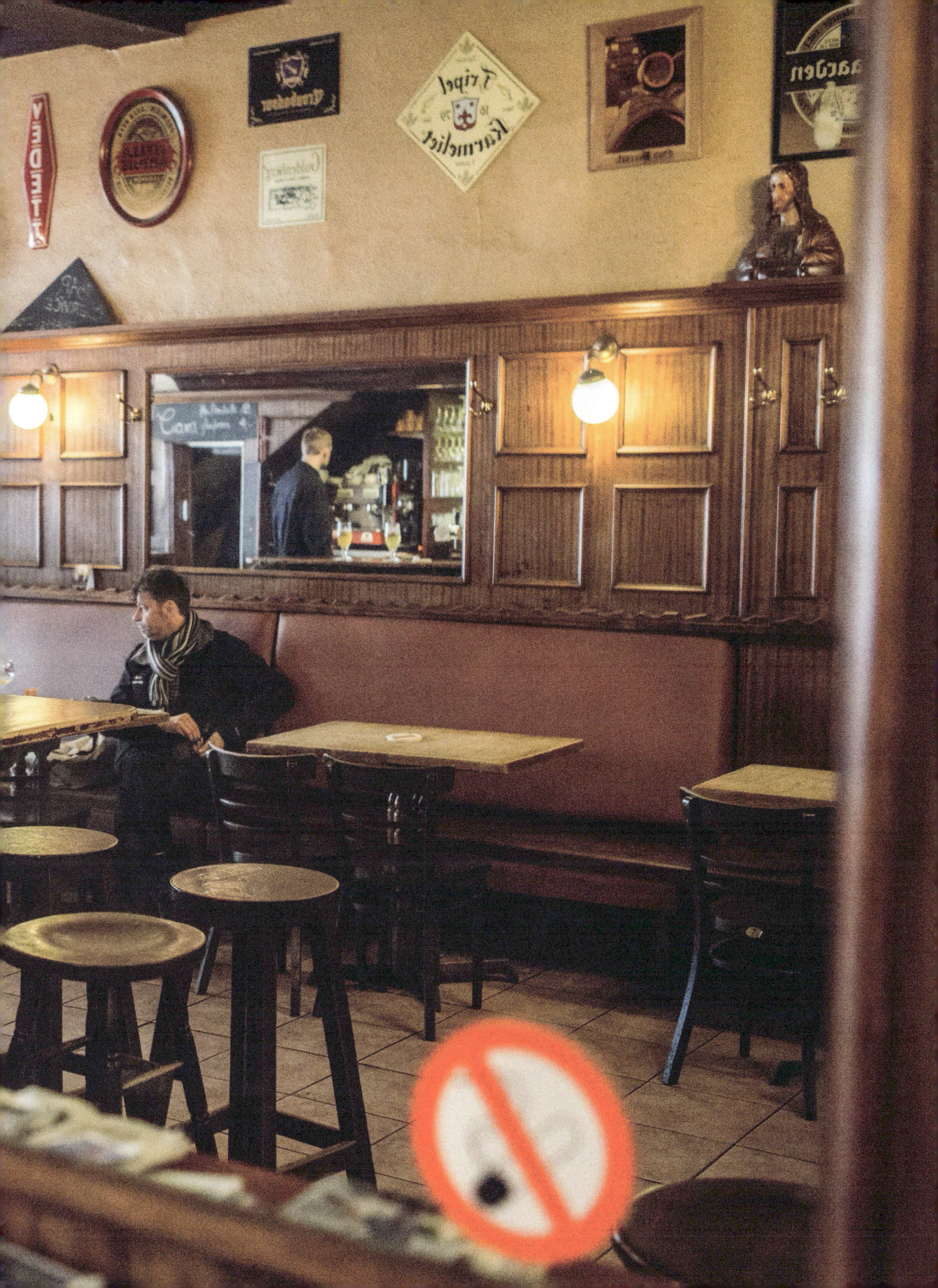

Poechenellenkelder
―

This café lies opposite Brussels' most eye-catching monument, the small Manneken Pis fountain, but it is a must-visit for other reasons. The convivial atmosphere hits you first of all. Poechenellenkelder is a café full of character. The walls are covered in puppets, vintage beer advertising, posters, depictions of Sherlock Holmes … You simply don't know where to look first. The well-stocked beer menu also requires some detective work. You enjoy a robust cuisine that includes steak tartare or a sandwich of brown bread, fresh cheese and radishes to accompany an oude gueuze. So who pops in here? Tourists on a quest to find Manneken Pis, 'Brusselaars' and really, just about everybody. Carry on past the bar and enjoy the view of the barrel chamber of a gueuzestekerij. You won't find anything more 'Brussels'.

Eikstraat 5 — +32(0)2/511 92 62
www.poechenellekelder.be

Het Goudblommeke in Papier
―

This café deserves to be called an 'institution'. Its retro interior is a treasure trove of photographs, manuscripts and items left here by famous visitors, including Hergé (Tintin), Jean Brusselmans and Magritte, as well as writings by local authors such as Guido Gezelle or the artist Jan Cox. Culture transforms into the glass as well. In an intimate setting you enjoy a splendid beer menu with a focus on the Brussels tradition of lambic, faro, kriek and oude gueuze. If everyone has the right to 24 hours of freedom each day, you could do worse than spending these hours in this characterful spot.

Cellebroersstraat 55 — +32(0)2/511 16 59
www.goudblommekeinpapier.be

Monk

The name of 'Monk' is a reference to jazz musician Thelonious Monk, but also points towards the Trappist monks. This hotspot is found in the trendy district around the Vismarkt and the Dansaertstraat, also home to the Brussels Beer Project further down the road. Here, tradition goes hand in hand with trendiness. The authentic interior of this café, with a back room in the art deco style that is included in the Monuments List, and its cosmopolitan atmosphere make for a scintillating cocktail. Feel the vibes that run through Brussels today. Enjoy the regional cheeses, the charcuterie and filled rolls (pistolets) to accompany one of the endless list of Belgian beers. Unmissable.

Sint-Katelijnestraat 42 — +32(0)2/511 75 11
info@monk.be — www.monk.be

Delirium Café

Delirium Café, in the heart of Brussels' 'Ilot Sacré', was initiated by Jean De Laet of the Huyghe brewery. This beer café deserves to be treated with respect. The menu includes over three thousand beers. There are even a number of tasting chambers decorated in separate themes. In brief, we guarantee that just having to choose will leave you stressed out. A few years ago this establishment acquired a little brother, the Little Delirium Café, at Kaasmarkt. The Delirium café concept is also popular across our borders. These ambassadors of Belgian beer culture are now found in all corners of the world.

Getrouwheidsgang 4A — +32(0)2/514 44 34
www.deliriumcafe.be
Kaasmarkt 7—9

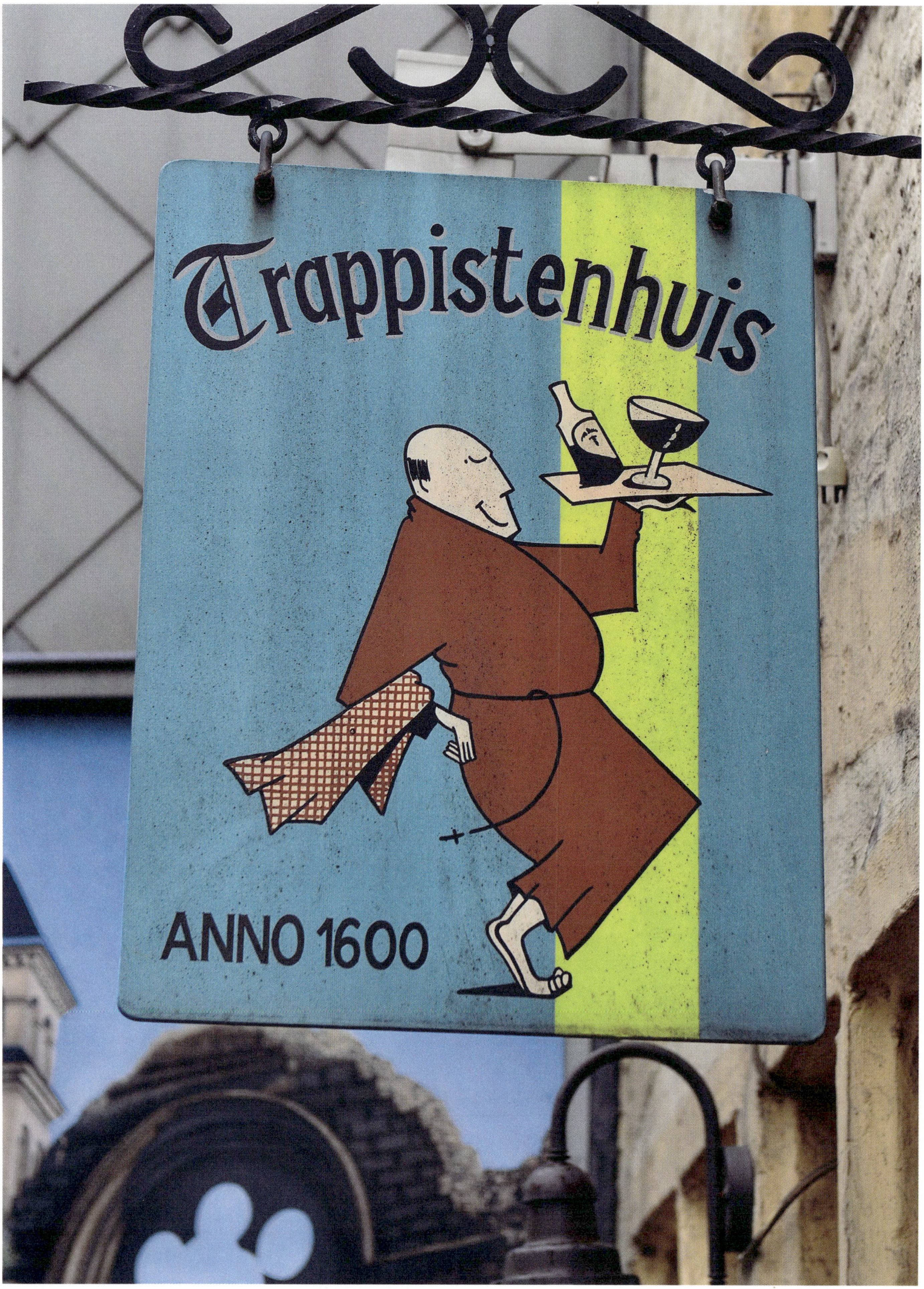
Trappistenhuis
ANNO 1600

DOORNIK/TOURNAI

La Vie Est Belge

The contemporary interior of La Vie Est Belge (LVEB) will surprise you with its many amusing references to the country that brought forth Tintin, Manneken Pis and Magritte. There are also LVEBs in Bergen (Mons) and Charleroi, where the local accent is ever-changing. Local artists are given a free hand. Great if you want to take a fresh look at our small country on the North Sea and the beers it has brought forth. Enjoy a good glass or cocktail with tapas made from regional produce.

Quai du Marché au Poisson 17, Doornik
+32(0)69/77 54 50 — www.lavieestbelge.be
Grand Place 40, Bergen
+32(0)65/87 20 25 — www.lavieestbelge.be
Rue de Marcinelle 12, Charleroi
+32(0)71/30 34 03 — www.lavieestbelge.be

GHENT

De Dulle Griet

Don't expect a shot from the cannon that bears the nickname of Dulle Griet. She has found her permanent home on the Vrijdagmarkt (Friday market). This is where you go if you want to choose from over 360 beers. Some of these may take an effort to obtain. If you are after a Max beer served in a coach driver's glass, you have to leave one of your shoes as security. This classic café has various rooms and you are certain the find the atmosphere you are looking for in one of them. The long bar accommodates a large number of guests so you need not worry about getting to the front of the queue. Tip: De Dulle Griet is known for its degustations of Trappist beers.

Vrijdagmarkt 50 — +32(0)9/224 24 55
www.dedullegriet.be

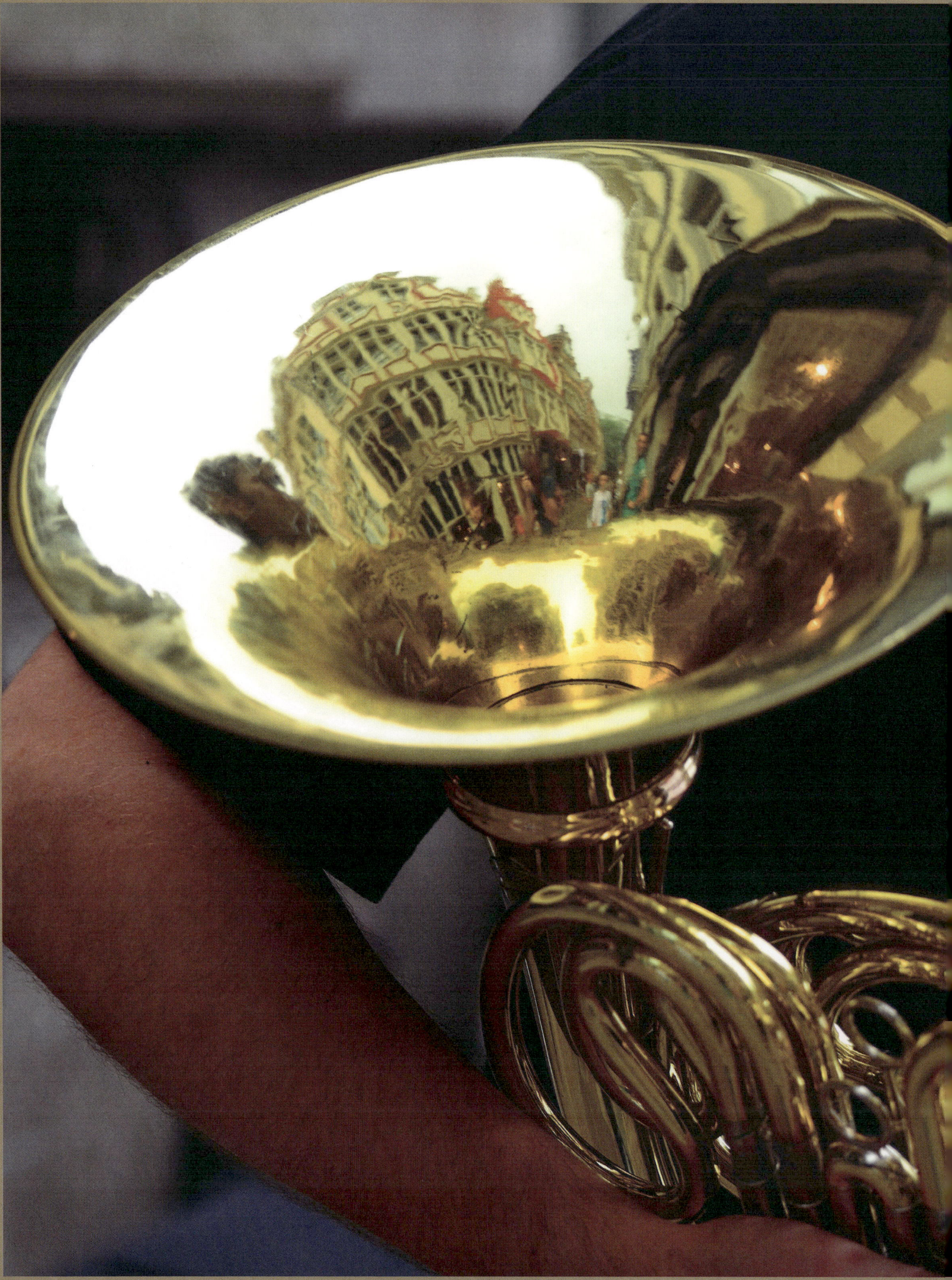

'Drinking by the meter' at specialty beer café De Dulle Griet in Ghent. The table top is resting on a wooden barrel previously used to mature lambic and krieken beers.

Den Trollekelder

Not far from Sint-Jacob's Tower you come across this convivial café where chat is by no means discouraged, quite the opposite. It is one of the places to be in Ghent, one of those brown cafés where you can spend hours at the bar, a regional beer or Trollenbier close to hand. The building was once home to a bookstore but now offers a fine glass of beer — or two. Just check out the almost endless beer menu. Seated below the vaulted ceiling of this café you can expect an intimate atmosphere. But what about these trolls…? The previous owner came from the Far North and trolls held no secrets for her.

Bij Sint Jacobs 17 — +32(0)9/223 76 96
www.trollekelder.be

Het Waterhuis aan de Bierkant

Perhaps they ought to have named this café 'Beer house on the Waterside' instead of 'The Waterhouse on the Beer Side'. At the bar, from underneath the hop cones, you select one of 165 beers that include the house beers Gandavum, Klokke Roeland and Mammelokker. Don't hesitate to ask your waiter for an explanation. He or she will be happy to provide it. And, as so often in Ghent, the medieval past is lurking just around the corner. This House is standing in the water and it used to take in wine and beer from the canal. In modern times you can still enjoy the view and the beer, either in its brown café or outside from the terrace.

Groentenmarkt 9 — +32(0)9/225 06 80
www.waterhuisaandebierkant.be

't Gouden Hoofd

The rough, unadorned industrial interior of this cosy bistro is a reminder of the meat wholesaler who once occupied this building close to the railway station of Gent-Dampoort. The focus here is on the eye-catching bar. You drink your beer in the industrial part and have your dinner at the front of the building, in the 'salon'. At least, that is what you would expect, but nothing stops you from doing it the other way around. We recommend this bistro for its international brasserie kitchen and the splendid beer menu.

Slachthuisstraat 96 — +32(0)487/20 65 01
www.hetgoudenhoofd.be

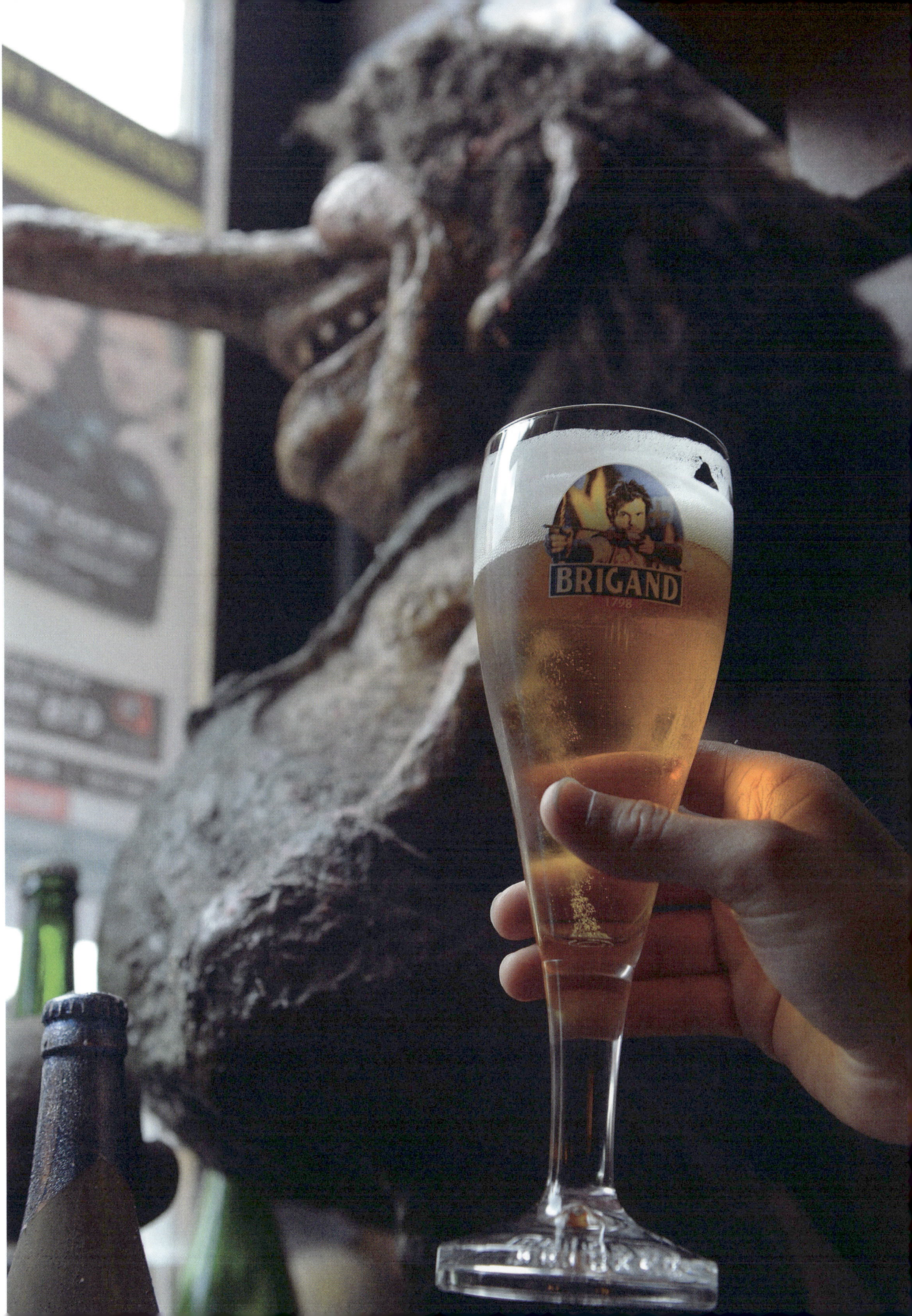
BRIGAND
1798

Pasta Fish Beef

Limburgse Witte
Corona
MARTINI
Pernod
RICARD
GANCIA
Bud KING OF BEERS
Hasseltse Jenever
CAMPARI
Jupiler
Coca-Cola
Rodenba(ch)
La Chouffe
Baileys
Hoegaarden
Speciale PALM
Bacardi
Brasserie DRUGST(ORE)

Caffè Coffee

ENPICK Corsendonk
Stibller
Leffe   JOHNNIE
OMER.
DE KONINCK

ELLA ARTOIS

Duvel   WALKER
SMIRNOFF

Carlsberg
J&B

Coffee House

THE K
MORT SUBI

HASSELT

In de Klein Hal

Each city has at least one classic watering hole. In Hasselt, this role is undoubtedly filled by In de Kleine Hal. Lots of wood panelling, decoratively plastered walls in the colour of egg white, a bar made out of stone and wood and a coat of arms crafted in wrought iron. Just add the buzz given off by the clientele and you have found the ideal atmosphere. For all those who like to enjoy a pint in the shadow of the Cathedral of St. Quintus. Enquire about the Beer of the Month.

Maastrichterstraat 30 — +32(0)11/22 96 17

Het Hemelrijk

The four hundred-and-something beers on the menu elevate you to heavenly realms in this quiet café close to the Grote Markt. You will find a wide range of oude gueuze and kriek and rare beers such as Pannepot and Stille Nacht. The beer card is listed alphabetically which helps you make a selection. Don't expect too much explanation here.

Hemelrijk 11 — +32(0)11/22 28 51

IEPER/YPRES

St-Arnoldus

No fewer than 25 regional beers are flowing out of the taps of this specialty beer café. You have come to the right place to enjoy a Sint-Bernardus or else a beer from De Struise Brouwers, De Ranke, Rodenbach, Omer Vander Ghinste or the city brewery of Ypres, De Kazematten. Trappists, oude gueuze and kriek are also making an entrance. All with the blessing of Saint Arnold, the patron saint of brewers.

Menenstaat 19 — +32(0)473/66 45 81

Kaffee Bazaar

Free live music, bring your own vinyl, hundreds of beers to choose from and a lively garden terrace. These are the trump cards played by this vintage watering hole. By all means, request little-known beers like the Hop Harvest on tap or the Cuvée Delphine made by De Struise Brouwers. This is the regular congregation place of beer tasting club Bierorde van Vauban ('the Beer Order of Vauban'). Keep an eye on the calendar to find out when tastings are held.

Boomgaardstraat 9 — +32(0)494/53 32 50
www.kaffeebazaar.be

KORTRIJK/COURTRAI

Gainsbar

This café is highlighted in the diary of every beer adventurer looking for a hidden pearl. The range comprises 120 Belgian and international craft beers. And they are proud to shout their love of hops from the rooftops. They frequently invite microbrewers to the café to present their latest creations. Have you ever had a beer tasting accompanied by a hand-picked musical scores in a DJ set? As to visitors from abroad, especially the Americans know how to find their way to the Vlasmarkt. The Gainsbar name pops up more and more online. The beer menu and the ten taps offering beers from Alvinne, De Ranke, Brouwers Verzet and Gulden Spoor ensure they keep coming.

Vlasmarkt 1 — stevie@gainsbar.org

Demandez les Bières de la Brasserie

Vraagt de Bieren der Brouwerij

H. VERMEULEN-MEYNNE
YPRES YPER

DEN BROSSER

STELLA ARTOIS

Jupiler

LEUVEN/LOUVAIN

The Capital

'My beer cellar is bigger than yours.' This café is quite open about its ambitions. Louvain, the home city of AB Inbev, the largest brewery in the world, claims to be the largest beer café in the country. However, so far, the Delirium Café in Brussels is still one size bigger. On the Capital's beer card, two thousand Belgian beers take pride of place. The entire stock parades before you in orderly ranks when you are looking through the glass floor tiles. Here, 'The floor is yours' can be taken quite literally. It is worth seeing when the beers that have been ordered travel to the bar on the elevator. Do you prefer your beer from the tap? In that case, you have to do an eenie-meenie-miney-mo between the twenty draught beers on offer.

Grote Markt 14 – +32(0)486/21 90 18
www.thecapital.be

M-Café

Art makes you thirsty. Are the pigments on the old paintings of Dirk Bouts part of the permanent collection…? This museum café has found its own solution. You can sample regional beers, with or without a snack, in a contemporary interior. Culture is flowing into the glass and a beer connoisseur will guide you through the beer menu. The home beer was baptised Rogier in homage to medieval artist and painter Rogier van der Weyden.

Savoyestraat 10 – +32(0)494/50 40 82
www.mleuven.be

Blauwe Kater

'Blue' is reminiscent of the Monday morning blues and a 'kater', Dutch for 'hangover', sounds like an evening spent hitting the bar or 'in de pinten vliegen'. It can all be done in this brown café where you will find over a hundred beers on the menu. Live blues or jazz is performed on Mondays. When the weather is fine, you move to the terrace to have a good chat with your friends. This is the first specialty beer café to open in this student city.

Hallengang 1 – +32(0)16/20 80 90
www.blauwekater.be

De Kastaar (Linde)

A former butcher's shop, now converted into a brown café and managed by 'den Erik', the quirky owner who knows exactly what he wants, is an accurate description of this establishment. A real village café where everyone is welcome: young or old, poor or rich. De Kastaar is located on a crossroads in the centre of Linden, the starting and finishing point of many walking routes and cycle trails. After exertion comes relaxation and it is lovely to spend some time lounging on the small terrace in the shadow of a linden tree.

Schoolbergenstraat 218, Kessel-Lo – +32(0)16/25 61 76

De Wiering

This ancient building on the River Dijle guarantees an excellent eating and drinking experience. The intimate atmosphere is heightened by hidden corners on different levels of the building. The apotheosis is the roof terrace with panoramic views of the city. There are over a hundred beers to choose from. Wooden floorboards, wood on the ceiling and wood panelling are the trade mark of this 'brown' brasserie. Here, nostalgia has the sound of an accordion on the wall or the look of photographs of royal families from times gone past or advertising for beers that time forgot. Add a candle and memories of Grandma's kitchen and the image is burnt onto your retina. Please spare a thought for the waiters, who are going up and down narrow and steep staircases to bring your beer to you.

Wieringstraat 2 – +32(0)16/29 54 83

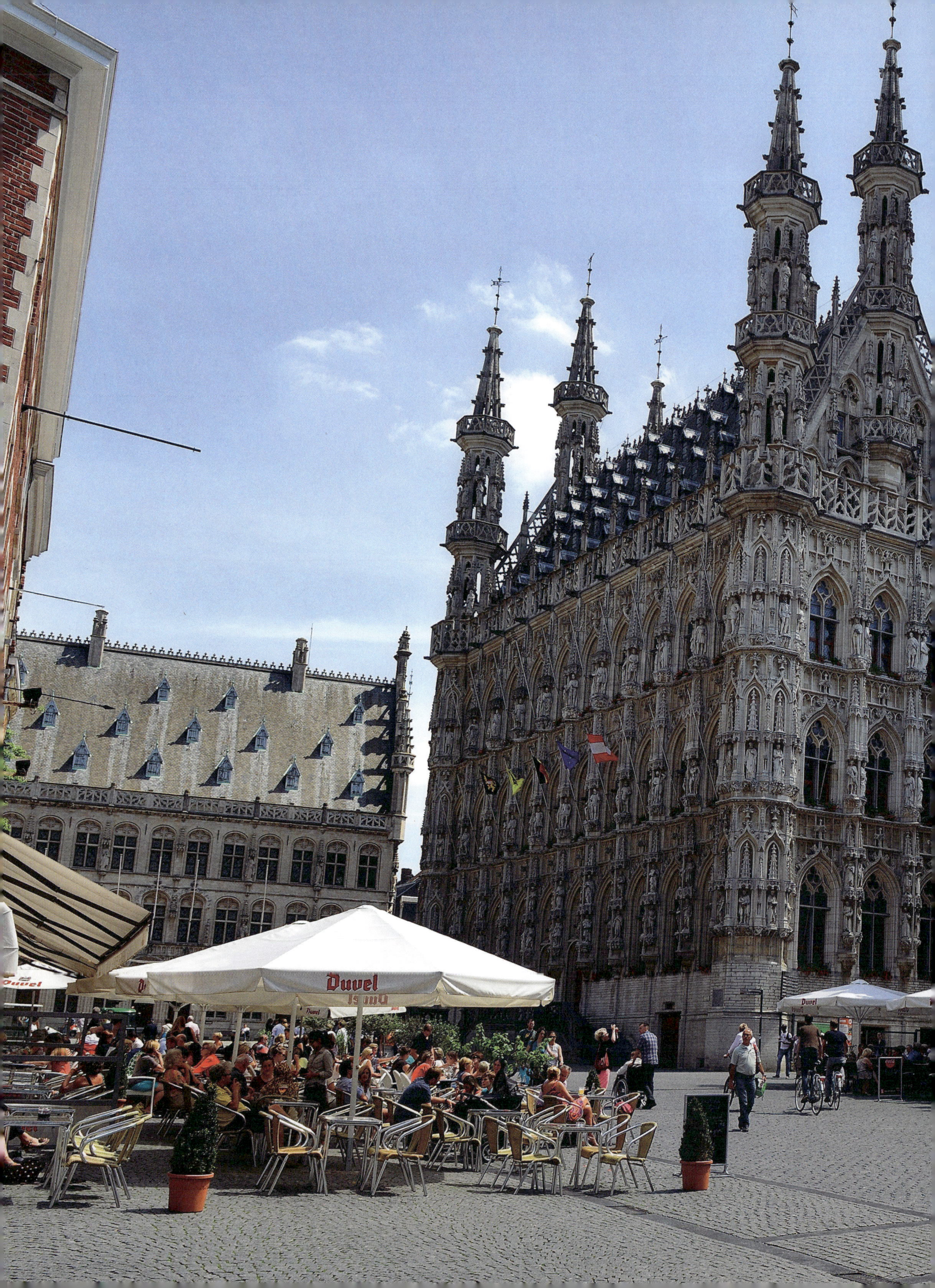
Duvel

IN 'T OUDE WOUD

SCRIPPENSHIS

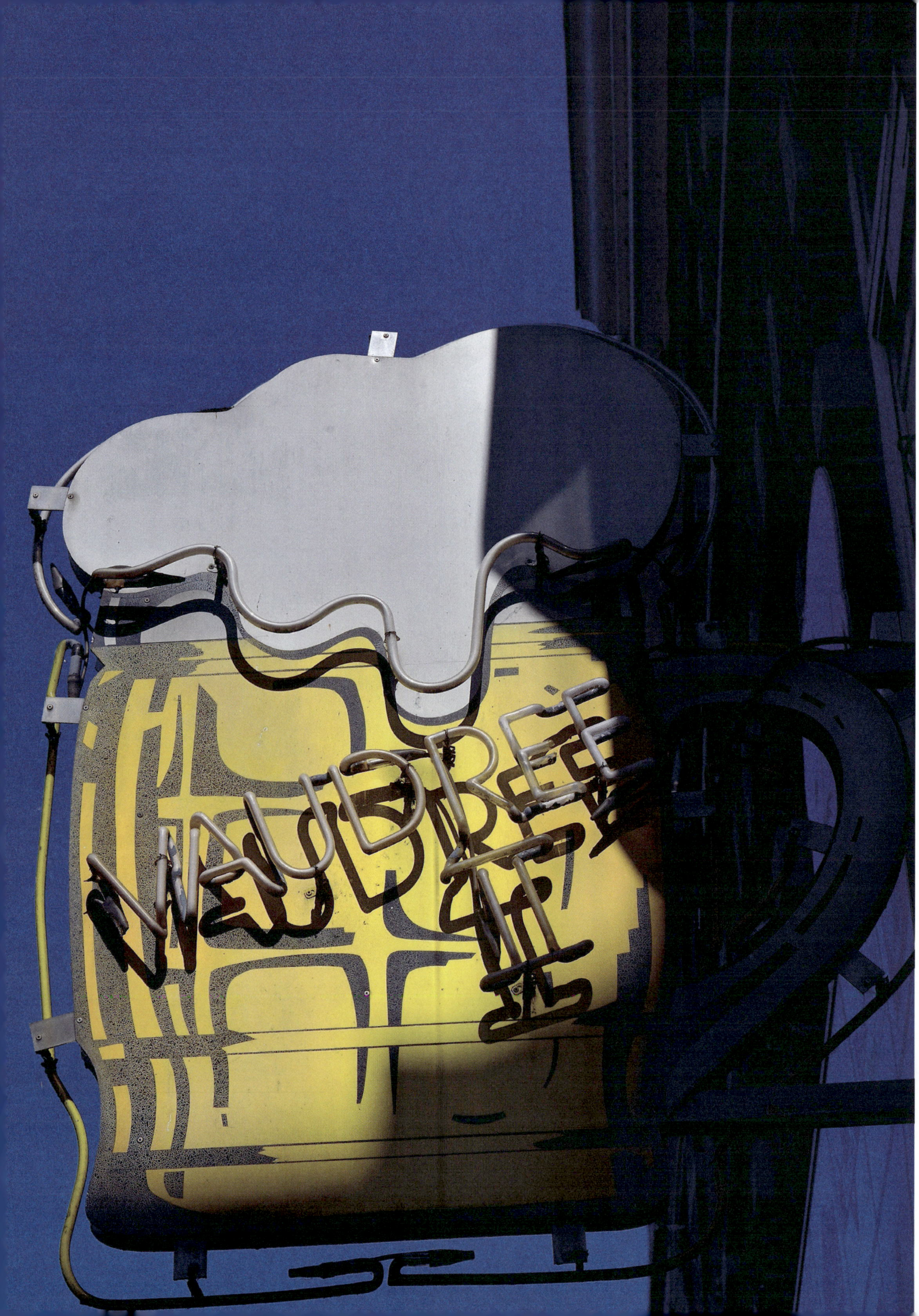

LUIK/LIÈGE

Le Vaudrée I, II & III

Much beer has flowed through the pipes ever since beer café Le Vaudrée opened its doors in Angleur in 1985. This rustic café with its 100 beers, 42 of which are on draught, has hit the mark. The same applies to its typical brasserie kitchen with beers to match. The Vaudrée family are now the proud owners of seven beer cafés in the Liège and Luxembourg regions. The formula is familiar but the execution is different every time. Both Le Vaudrée II in the heart of Liège and Le Vaudrée III in Juprelle extend a warm welcome to beer lovers in a setting of contemporary design that is popular with younger customers. This does not detract from the convivial atmosphere by any means. After all, you are finding yourself in the Fiery City, where they wear their hearts on their sleeve.

Rue de Val Benoît 109, Angleur
+32(0)4/367 10 61 — www.vaudree-concept.be
Rue St-Gilles 149
+32(0)4/223 18 80 — www.vaudree-concept.be
Chaussée de Tongres 13, Juprelle
+32(0)4/246 02 67 — www.vaudree-concept.be

L'Aigle d'Or

In this, the Golden Eagle tavern, the voice of the 'patron' is reverberating and salvos of laughter are echoing from the walls. After all, you are in the Fiery City of Liège, where beer takes pride of place. You can choose from a selection of a hundred beers or so, including ten draught beers. Trappists, microbreweries… they would not like to be left off the beer menu. Order a regional dish with your beer: Liège meat balls (*boulette*) with syrup, a vol-au-vent (*koninginnehapje*), steak or mussels with hand-cut fries, obviously fried twice as is the Belgian way…

Place Général Leman — +32(0)4/262 19 85
www.laigledor.beer

Beerlovers Café

Around 200 well-known and more obscure specialty beers are awaiting thirsty customers in this trendy café, located in the shadow of Liège Town Hall. Your beer is served in an elegant degustation glass on a tall stem. A 'bar to be' for beer lovers, terrace loungers and night owls alike. The café also has a shop where you can buy all these delicacies.

Rue de la Violette 9 — +32(0)4/221 39 77
info@beer-lovers.be — www.beer-lovers.be

Beer Lovers'

1 Saison Dupont	**4** Lupulus Brune	**7** Léopold 7
2 St Feuillien Triple	**5** Trouffette Blonde	**8** Bertinchamps Triple
3 Ducassis	**6** Chouffe	**9** Brussels Calling

13 Gueuze Tilquin − 3€   **14** Kwo

PARTAGE
convivialité
DEGUSTATION
& LOVE

BEERLOVERSCAFE
Rejoignez nous !
www.beer-lovers.be

asteel Rouge
urtius
obeline Fraise
- 2,20€

MECHELEN

De Gouden Vis

A listed 18th-century monumental building close to the Vismarkt with a handsome blue stone Louis XV entry gate and an art nouveau window is now home to a timeless beer café. The old café floor, the pillars that hold up the ceiling and the mirrors with bevelled edges bring back the atmosphere of the Belle Époque from the start of the 20th century. It is lovely to enjoy a glass amongst the vines in the old conservatory at the rear of the building or on the terrace that gives out onto the River Dijle and affords views of the former Lamot brewery. Only its name betrays that this establishment used to be a fishmonger's many moons ago.

Nauwstraat 7 — +32(0)15/20 72 06

D'Hanekeef

Welcome to the oldest café in Mechelen (1879). The 'savings banks' on the wall tell the story of regular customers who used to put money aside throughout the year to afford an annual knees-up. Good times are still to be had in this popular watering hole with a menu that includes over fifty beers. If you are brave enough to attempt one of the many pub games, you may be stung for one or more rounds. You may not be the ringleader amongst the parade of hens and cockerels depicted on the walls. Is the café owner obsessed with poultry? Far from it. This café owes its name to the chicken baskets, or 'hennenmanden', now empty, stacked up by the door. This is where the poultry farmers rinsed their thirsty throats after they had been to market. Mechelen is the birth place of the robust chicken variety known as the 'Mechelse koekoek', or Mechelen cuckoo. And where did the chicken eaters, or 'kiekenfretters' from Brussels go to buy their poultry? Exactly.

Keizerstraat 8 — +32(0)15/20 78 46

ARE YOU TOKKING TO ME

ATOMIC

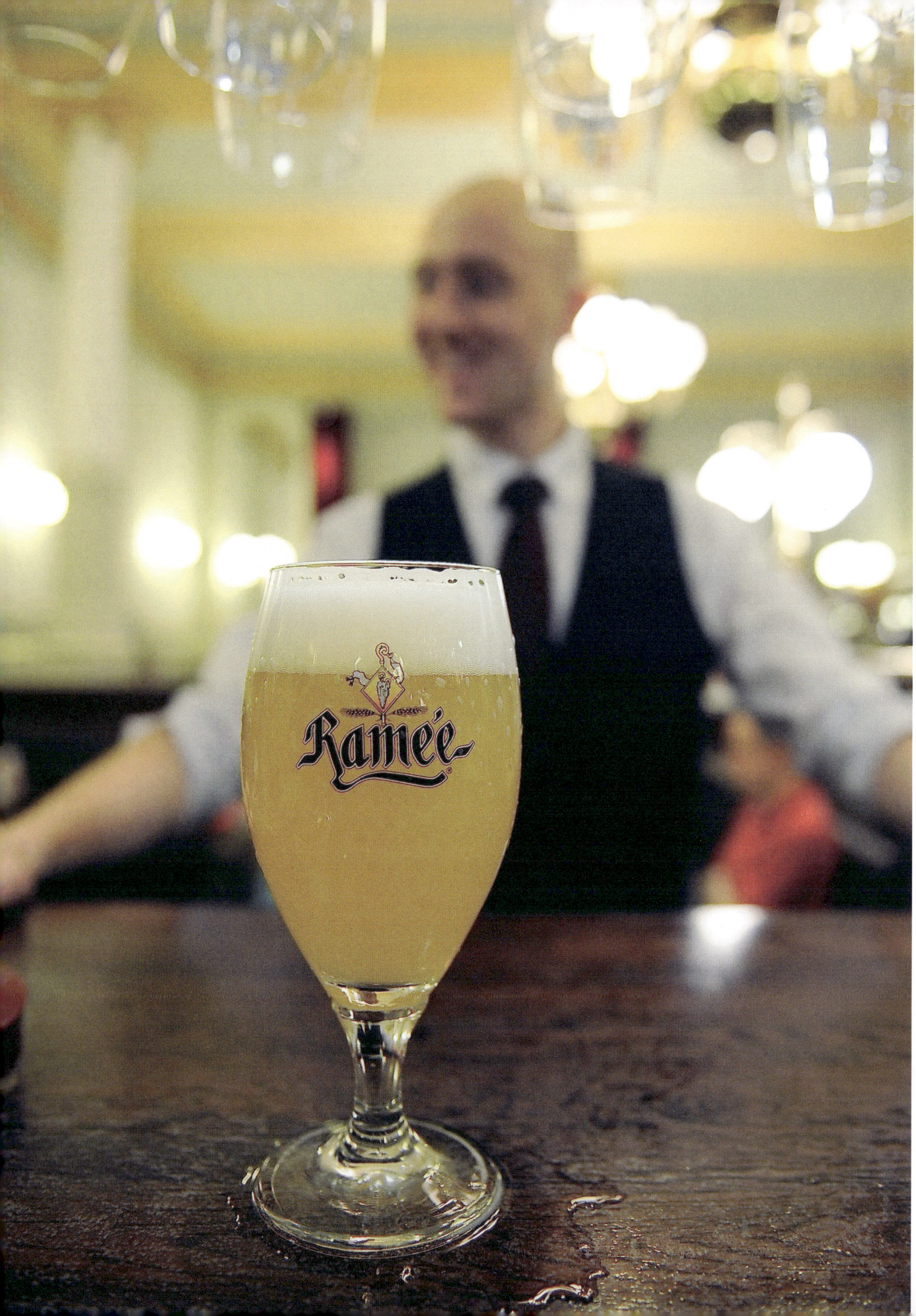
Ramée

NAMEN/NAMUR

Le Chapître

The focus of this café is on small and medium-sized breweries. Le Chapître is located next to the Cathedral of St. Aubain in the heart of Namur. A quiet spot to reflect on life whilst enjoying a Trappist. The regulars are full of praise for the beer menu that includes around sixty specialty beers. A vintage brown café. If the weather is fine, the terrace will be set up on the pavement across the road. This is how a bustling city embraces a village atmosphere.

Rue du Séminaire 4 — +32(0)81/22 69 60

OSTEND

Botteltje

We all know that the largest city on the Belgian coast has close ties with England. Pop into this pub and you may be mistaken for thinking that you are in Albion. There is a difference though: they are serving sixteen Belgian beers from the tap, all of the Trappists are available in the bottle and the splendid beer menu offers plenty of hidden gems as well as the 'evergreens'. At any rate, the name of this pub is promising. 'Bottel' means 'bottle' in the Ostend dialect. Does this sound familiar? Tip: if you have had one too many, you can spend the night at Hotel Marion, based at the same address, where you can also have a bit to eat.

Louisastraat 19 — +32(0)59/70 09 28
www.cafebotteltje.be

BELGIAN NORTH SEA BEER
PoppoLou
EXTRA HOPPY
BELGIAN NORTH SEA BEER
PoppoLou

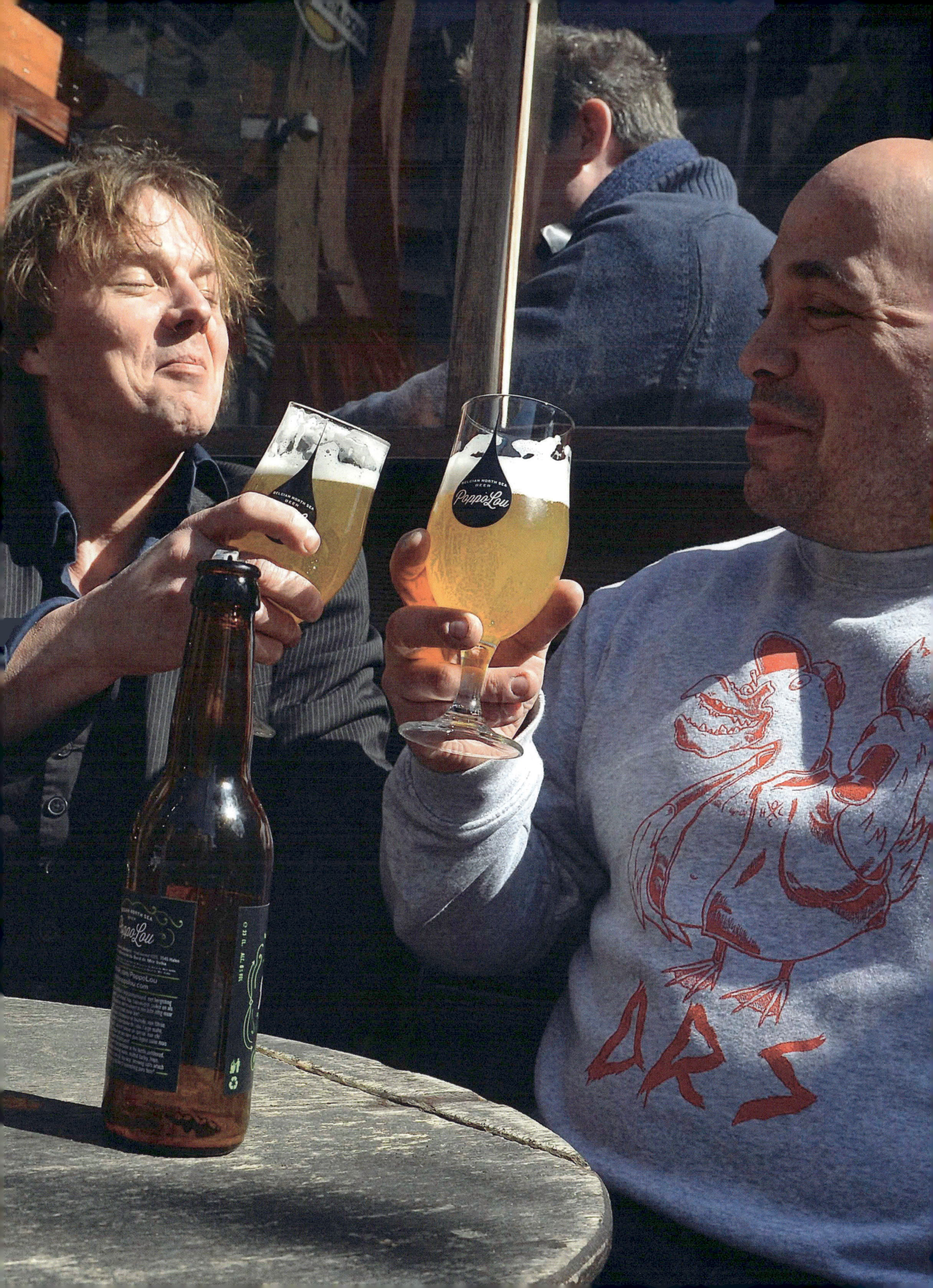
BELGIAN NORTH SEA
BEER

Manuscript

The story of 'dé Manu' reads like a thriller. Café owner Glenn Rotsaert spent some time touring with the American band Marky Ramone and The Speed Kings. And so he built up an extensive network, hence the legendary live concerts with big names as well as lesser-known acts on the bill. There is always a whiff of blues, soul, jazz or funk in the air. At the bar: a varied mix of tourists and locals from the seaside. At this brown café you feel at home straight away. The fresh sea air makes you work up a thirst. No idea what you would like to order? Take a look at the blackboard on the wall and choose from around one hundred Belgian specialty beers. Every beer style is represented. Never heard of Poppo-Lou? This is the name of the house beer, also known as the 'North Sea beer'. Besides the original blond version there is also a more strongly hopped beer (Hoppy). Café Manuscript owner Vanessa Demeij will tell you all about it.

Langestraat 32 — +32(0)59/51 11 88
www.manuscriptoostende.be

PAJOTTENLAND

Boelekewis

Meat from the grill, regional cooking and mussels are what attracts families to this restaurant near Halle. Whilst the little ones are having fun in the garden, the grown-ups are exploring the contents of the glass. Boelekewis is located in the heart of the Pajottenland, the birthplace of artisan lambic, oude gueuze and kriek. The BoelekeGueuze beer menu proudly presents the names of all the lambic brewers and gueuzestekers in the area. Fancy catching a few bottles? Then buy a 'Pajottenlandse Trots' containing a metre or half a metre of lambic beers.

Alsembergsesteenweg 856 — +32(0)2/380 44 14
www.boelekewis.be

De Cam

An ancient farm is now home to a gueuzestekerij, popular café and a museum of folk instruments. De Cam has revived the centuries-old farm tradition of brewing lambic during the winter for consumption in the following spring and summer. Gueuzesteker Karl Goddeau makes up his own 'blend' of young and old lambics which he will re-ferment to produce oude gueuze and kriek. Taste and compare several lambic beers in the café. If some members of your company are getting slightly bored, you can always give a pub game a go. Or you can ask Karl to play a tune on his bagpipes.

Dorpsstraat 67a — +32(0)2/532 21 32
www.lambicland.be

In de Verzekering tegen de Grote Dorst

This village café is a record beater. First off, there is the very long name. It translates as 'Insured against the great thirst'. No, this is not the work of an insurance company but rather the brainchild of the Panneels brothers. Besides, this café has the shortest opening hours you will come across anywhere... If you'd rather not end up in front of a closed door, we recommend you turn up on a Sunday morning, the only time that IDVTDGD is officially open. However, tastings are held from time to time to co-incide with events such as the Toer de Gueuze, Dag van de Kriek, Dag van de Lambiek or the Nacht van de Grote Dorst. And yes, we are talking about artisan lambic, oude gueuze and kriek in a café with a legendary cellar. Beer lovers, you have been warned.

Frans Baetenstraat 45, Elzeringen (Lennik)
+32(0)2/532 58 58 — www.dorst.be

't Klosken

A traditional farm inn in the heart of the Pajottenland serves regional dishes with their accompanying beers. Open the door, set foot inside and experience how any traces of stress just melt away. The main area, with its built-in man-height clock, hand-painted wainscoting and wooden benches, takes you back in time at least a hundred years. Just for a moment, it looks like someone is following your every movement. It is a life-size doll that has spent so much time next to the 'Leuvense stoof' heater that it has become part of the furniture. Who is he? No other than the original farmer and keeper of the inn. He must have enjoyed his lambic, oude gueuze or kriek in this very room. Does time really stand still?

Brusselsestraat 24, Lennik
+32(0)2/311 61 16 — www.klosken.com

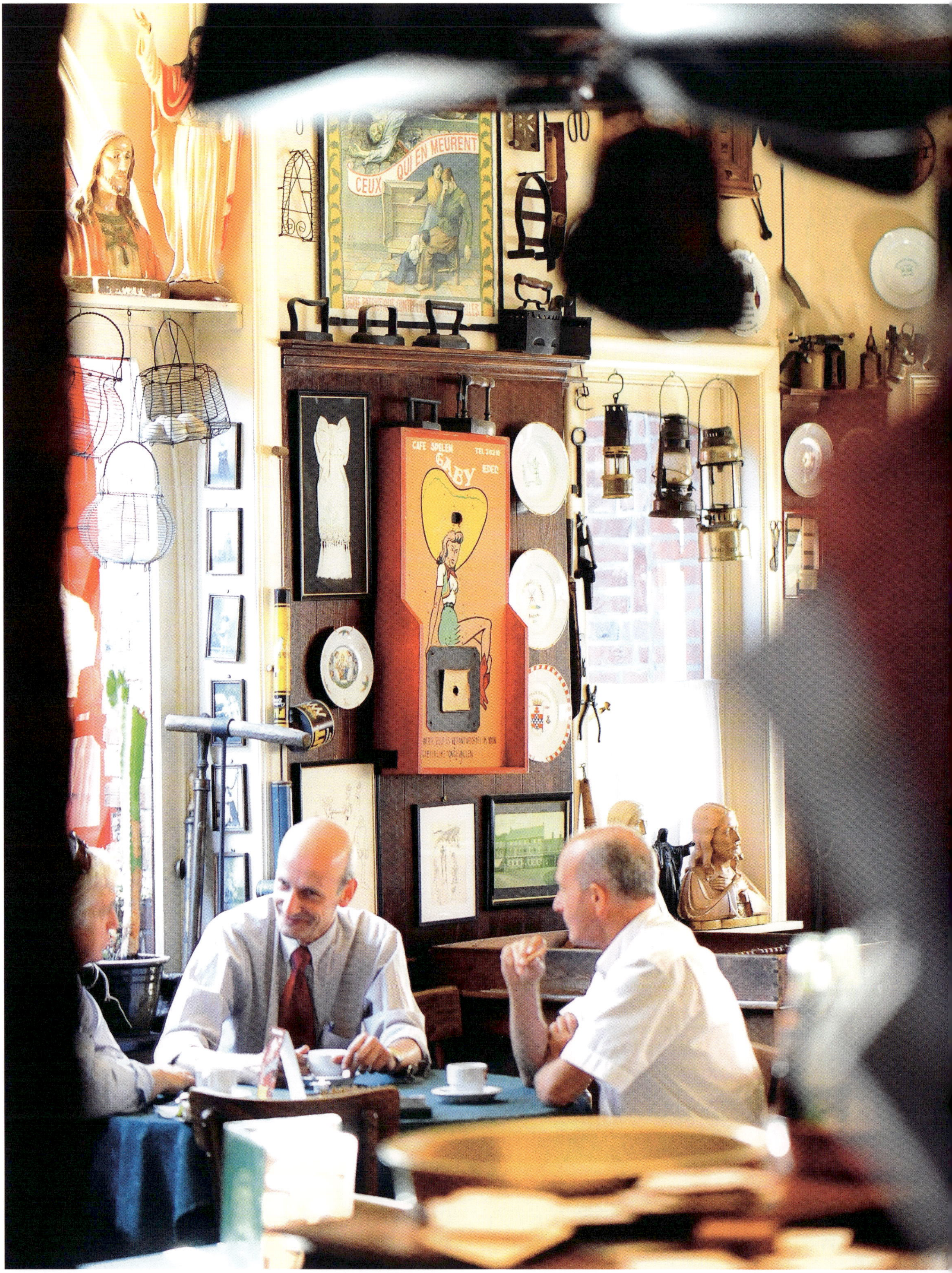

MEETJESLAND

Huyze Vacas

Stef Van Canneyt has worked his magic on the old town hall of Waterland-Oudeman and turned it into a specialty beer café. The bar, tables and chairs were sourced from other cafés. They bear the traces of their previous existence. Bar flies can choose from 350 regional beers. The café owner collects anything that is in any way related to beer. Only the 'tip of the iceberg' is displayed in the café. You can view old beer bottles and glasses as well as vintage enamel signs. 'I still have to sort out the rest', Stef sighs. Feast your eyes on all the items on show. Look for the giant bottle of Piraat, the pirate firing a cannon and the little boy who is carrying a Gulden Draak 9000 on his back. Schol!

Kerkstraat 30, Waterland-Oudeman
+32(0)9/344 55 72

WESTHOEK/HEUVELLAND

Het Labyrinth

A maze, a delightful garden and a cosy interior in retro style serve to attract bikers and hikers to Het Labyrinth. 'Sjoelbak' (a form of shove ha'penny) and 'trou madame' (bagatelle) are popular games that you play with others. The more, the merrier. The eye-catcher is, without doubt, the 'trabol' ball-throwing game that you play on the covered alley called a 'bolletra'. The well-stocked beer menu offers around forty regional beers and is well capable of quenching the thirst of the cyclist after the wobbly ride over the cobblestones of the Kemmelberg (11.6% incline). Take note: some specialty beers quickly go to your head and may affect balance! This café is a museum in itself. The walls are covered in beer paraphernalia, old smoking pipes, clocks and photographs from days gone by. The first floor is home to a genuine museum about the Celts who once lived in the area.

Dries 29, Kemmel – +32(0)476/60 76 86
www.hetlabyrinth.be

De Barbier

Open/Ouvert
vrij. ven. 18.
zat. sam. 18.
zon. dim. 12.
0032(0)57445924

At the barber's you used to enjoy a good glass of beer whilst having a shave.
Here, the digital era is still light years away.

This man, with his perfectly trimmed beard and moustache, entices his customers to order a beer. The barber alias café owner knows his customers' weak spots.

Le Temps des Cerises (Westouter)

Le Temps des Cerises has the fragrance of fruit orchards. But don't be mistaken. This is a conversational café where they sell vintage books, or is it the other way around? You lend or buy your books here accompanied by a foaming glass of beer.

Le Temps des Cerises, Sulferbergstraat 18
+32(0)57/42 12 04

De Barbier (Dranouter)

The barber used to have his own café within his shop. Nothing much has changed in De Barbier in Dranouter, although hair is no longer being cut and beards are no longer being trimmed. Whilst 'the Mrs.' was doing her grocery shopping, the men were boozing at the barber's, who made sure that his customers did not order too many rounds so the wives had some money left for shopping. This is how the till continued to ring. Peasants' wisdom.

De Barbier, Hillestraat 5, Dranouter
+32(0)57/44 59 24

Den Ekster (Dranouter)

A farm where world music, country & blues and bluegrass form the musical wallpaper. Unsurprisingly, Den Ekster just happens to be located in Dranouter which is known for its annual folk festival. On the menu are regional dishes and classics from the brasserie kitchen. How about a plate of 'rabbit with prunes in a dark Trappist sauce' with the same, dark beer on the side? Spoil your taste buds in tune with the seasons and meanwhile, enjoy the views of the undulating countryside.

Lettingstraat 42, Dranouter – +32(0)57/44 68 52
www.den-ekster.com

Blonde Idéale
ROELANTS
FORCE
SANTÉ
BLOND SPECIAAL
DENSITEIT VYF GRADEN
YPERSCHE
CENTRALE BROUWERIJ

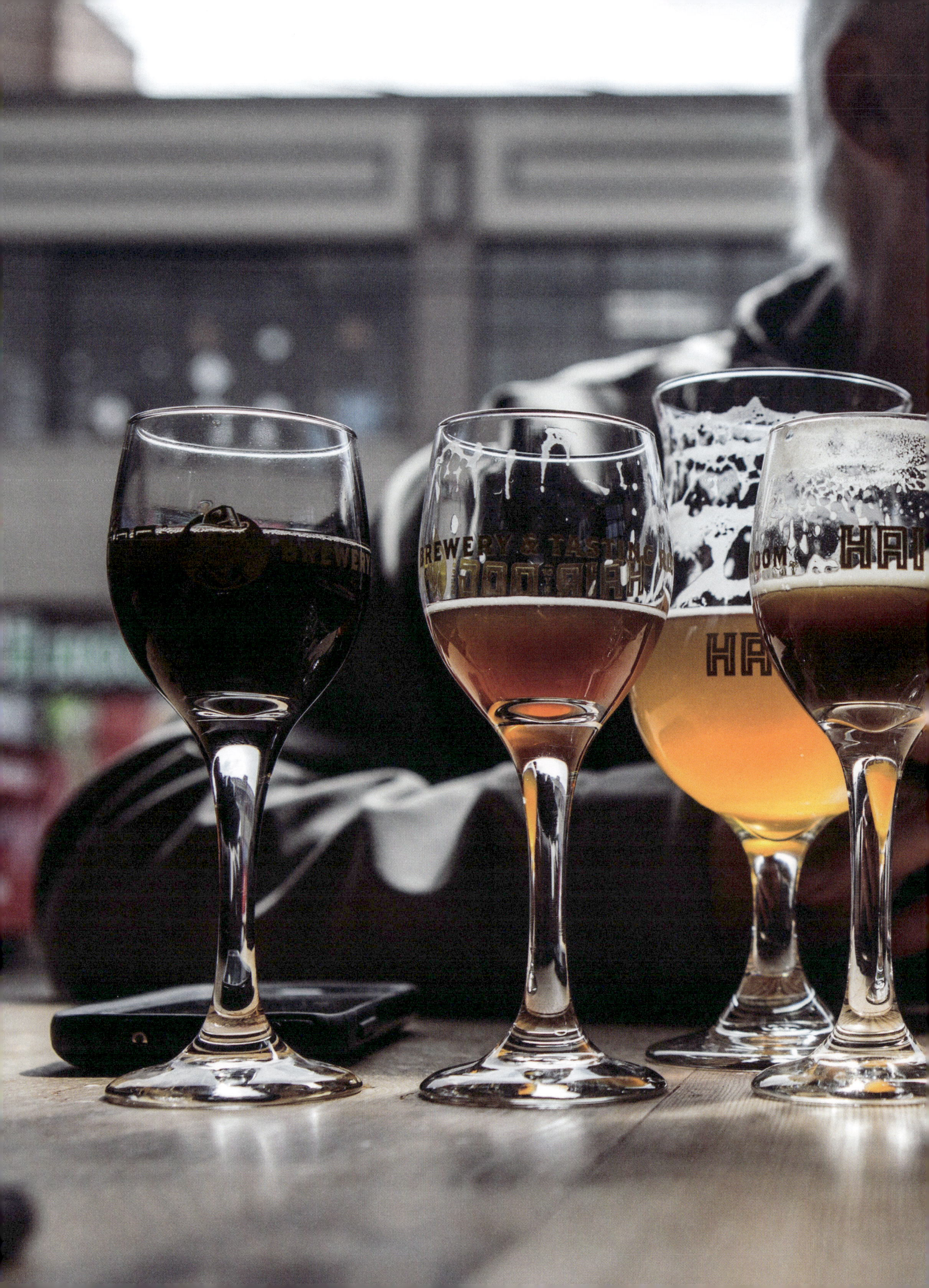
BREWERY

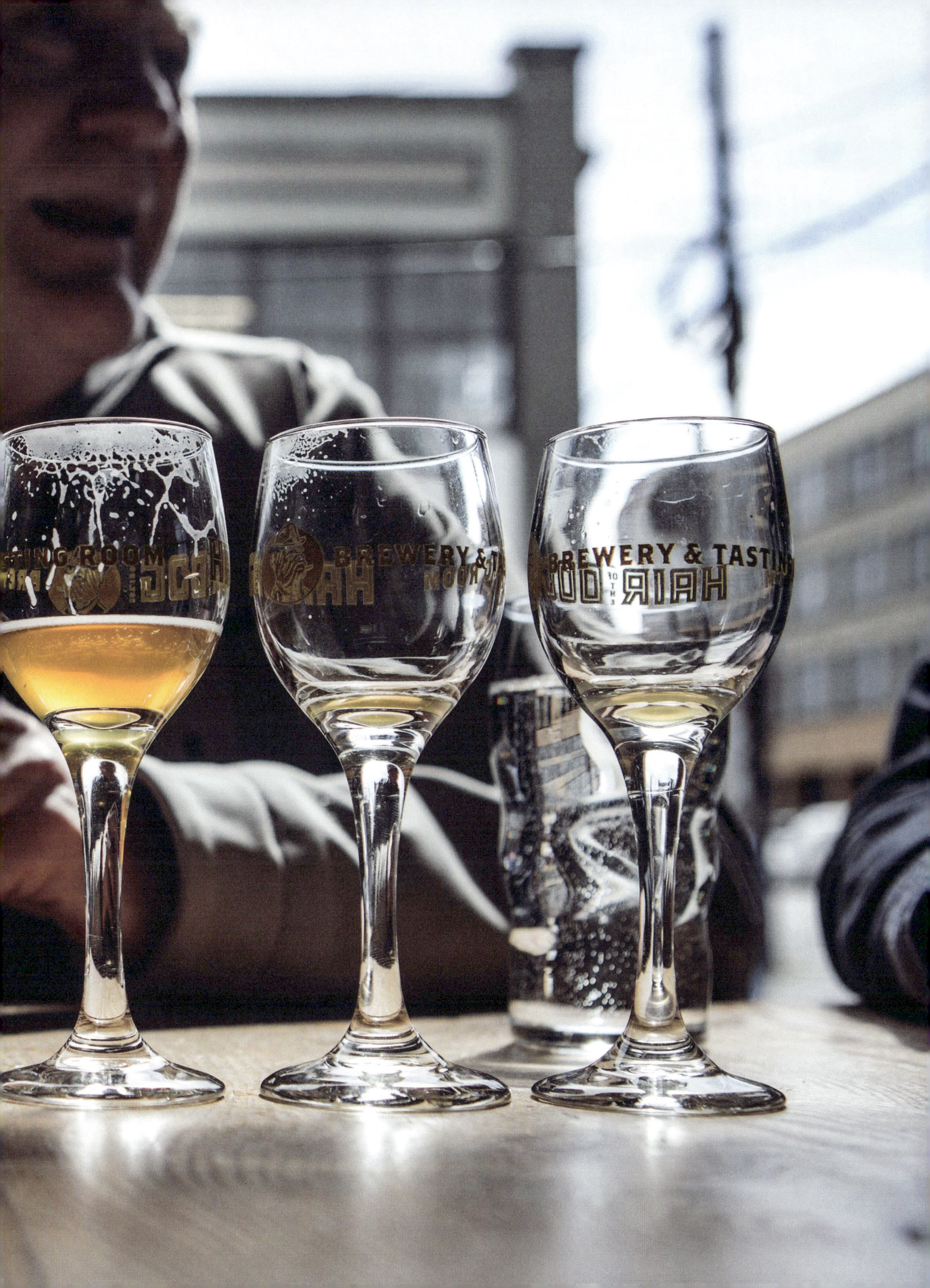
BREWERY & TASTIN

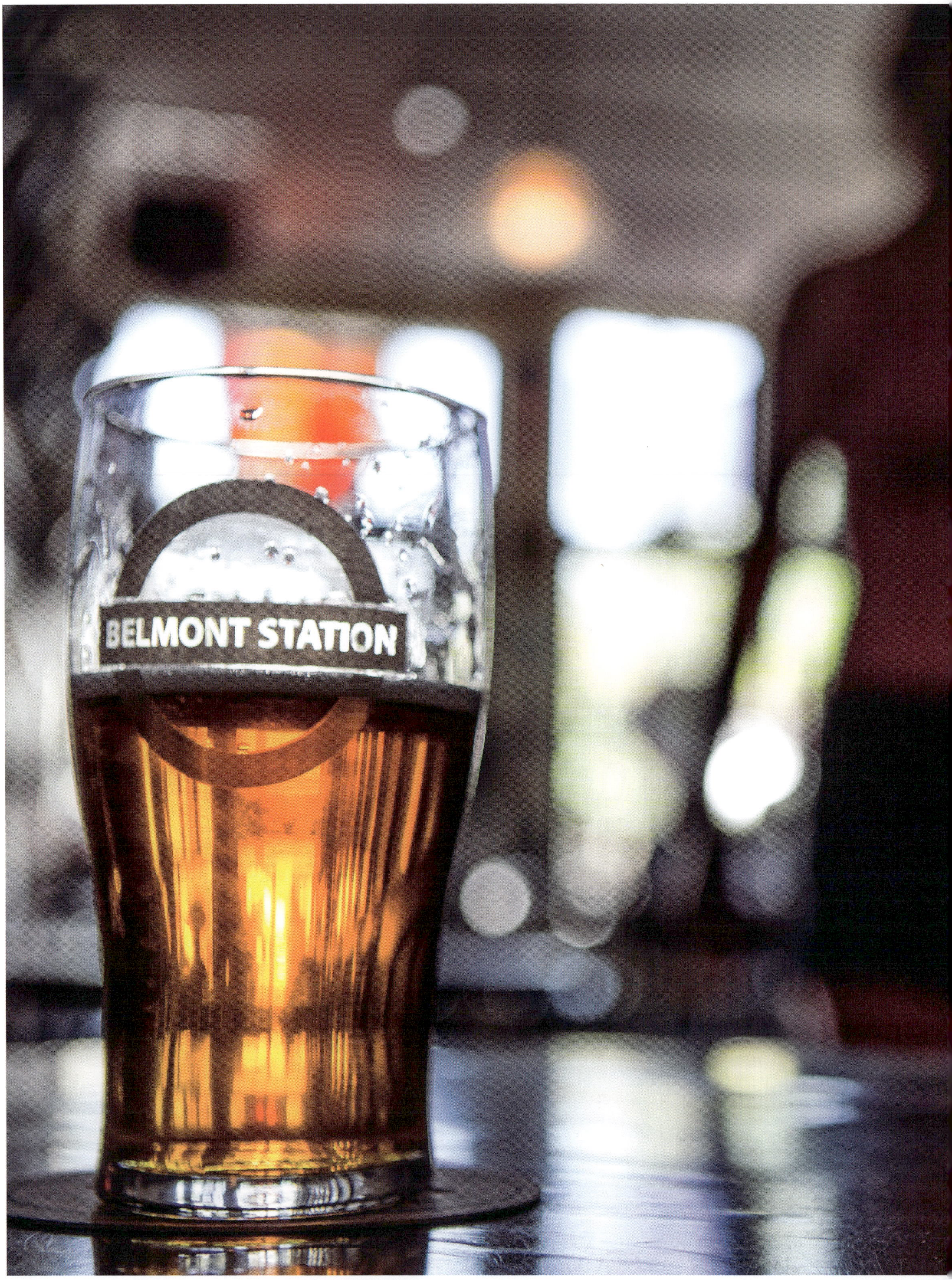
BELMONT STATION

SPECIALTY BEER CAFÉS ABROAD

London

The Rake
14a Winchester Walk, Borough Market SE1 9AG,
United Kingdom – +44(0)20/7407 0557
www.utobeer.co.uk

The White Horse
1–3 Parsons Green, London SW6 4UL,
United Kingdom – +44(0)20/7736 2115
www.whitehorsesw6.com

Paris

Bar Demory
62 rue Quincampoix, 4ème arrondissement
Métro Rambuteau/les Halles
+33(0)6/84 12 10 59
www.demoryparis.com

Le Supercoin
3 Rue Baudelique, 18ème arrondissement
Métro Marcadet Poissonniers – Jules Joffrin
+33(0)9/50 07 04 90
www.supercoin.net

Berlin

Das Meisterstück
Hausvogteiplatz 3–4, Mitte
+49(0)30/5587 2562
www.dasmeisterstueck.de

Tokyo

Ant n Bee
5 Chome-1-5 Roppongi, Minato
+81(0)3/3478 1250

World Beer Museum
1-1-2 Oshiage Sumida-Ku Tokyo, Tokyo Skytree Town,
Solamachi 7F – +81(0)3 5610 2648
www.world-liquor-importers.co.jp

Peking

Slow Boat Brewery Taproom
56-2 Dong Si Ba Tiao, Dongcheng District
+86(0)10/6538 5537
www.slowboatbrewery.com

Panda Brewpub
14 Dong Si Bei Da Jie, Dongcheng District

Portland

Belmont Station
4500 SE Stark Street – +1(0)503 232 8538
www.belmont-station.com

New York

The Pony Bar
637 10th Ave – +1(0)212 586 2707
www.theponybar.com

Philadelphia

Monk's Café
264 S 16th Street — +1(0)215 545 7005
www.monkscafe.com

Washington DC

Meridian Pint
3400 11th Street NW — +1(0)202 588 1075
www.meridianpint.com

Amsterdam

Proeflokaal Arendnest
Herengracht 90 — +31(0)20/421 2057
www.arendsnest.nl

In de Wildeman
Kolksteeg 3 — +31(0)20/638 2348
www.indewildeman.nl

Rome

Ma Che Siete Venuti A Fa
Via Benedetta, 25 — +39(0)6/6456 2046
www.football-pub.com

Open Baladin
Via Degli Specchi, 6 — +39(0)6/683 8989
www.openbaladinroma.it

Stockholm

Oliver Twist
Repslagargatan 6 — +46(0)8/640 05 66
www.olivertwist.se

Copenhagen

Mikkeller Bar
Viktoriagade 8 B-C — +45 33 31 04 15
www.mikkeller.dk

São Paulo

FrangÓ
Largo da Matriz Nossa Senhora do Ó,
168, Freguesia do Ó — +55.11.3931-2285
www.frangobar.com.br

Rio de Janeiro

Botto Bar
R. Barão de Iguatemi, 205, Praca da Bandeira
+55 21 3496 7407

Belgian cafés abroad

60 Belgian Beer Cafés world-wide
www.belgianbeercafe.com

14 Delirium Cafés world-wide
www.deliriumcafe.be/franchises

FOSTER'S
LAGER
TENNENT'S
CARLSBERG
SUGESTÃO
FRANGÓ
FONE:
*FRANGO GRELHADO
FRITA
E MUITA CERVEJA
Open
AQUI TEM

Remontez
le temps...
descendez une
Vieux-Temps.
Vieux-Temps
Vieux-Temps
AU FUT

THE PROBLEM WITH THE WORLD IS THAT EVERYONE IS A FEW DRINKS BEHIND

Humphrey Bogart

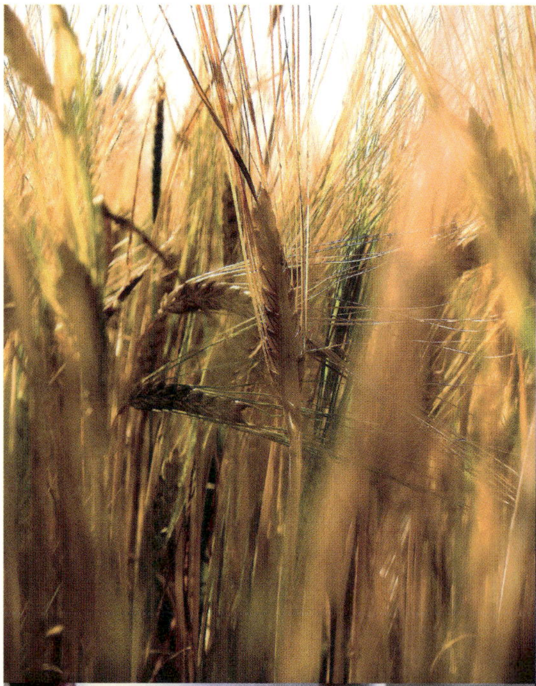

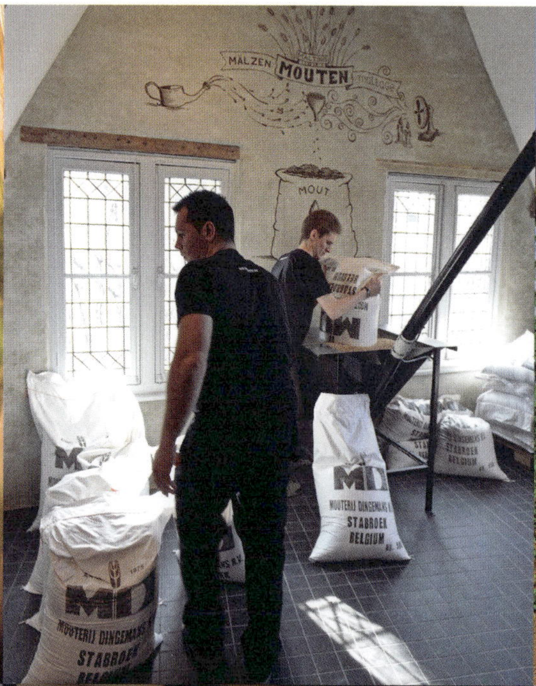

MALZEN
MOUTEN
MOUT
STABROEK
BELGIUM

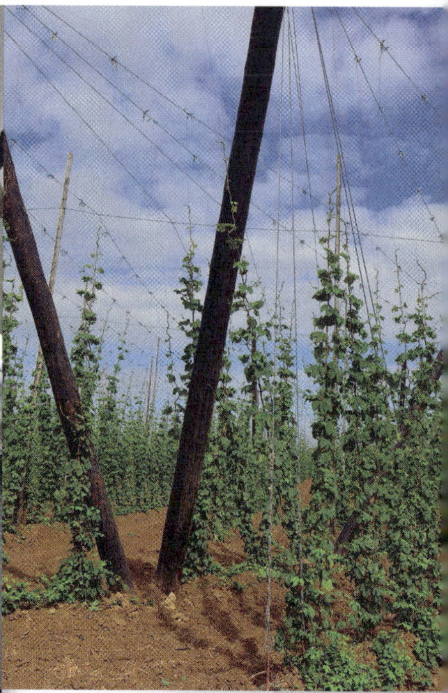

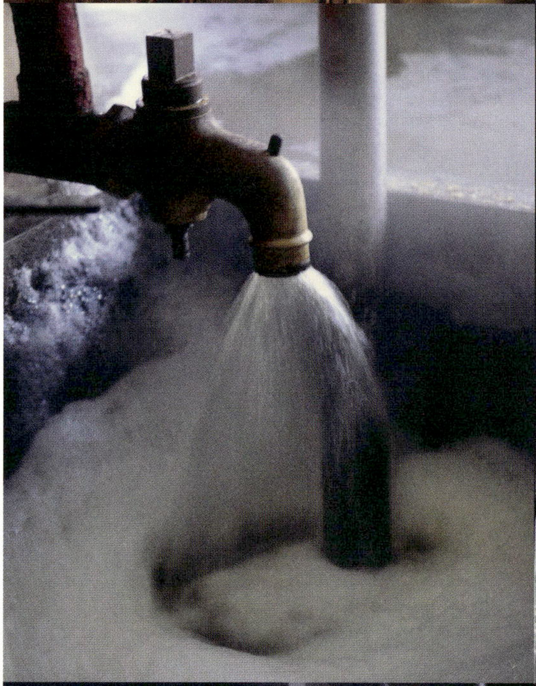

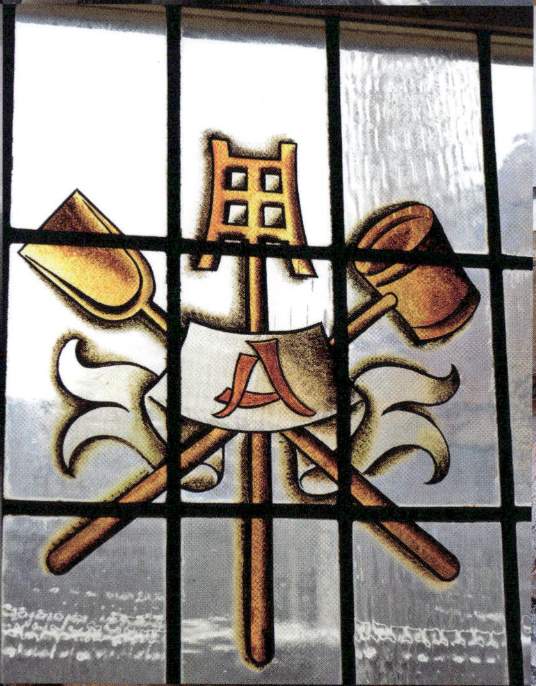

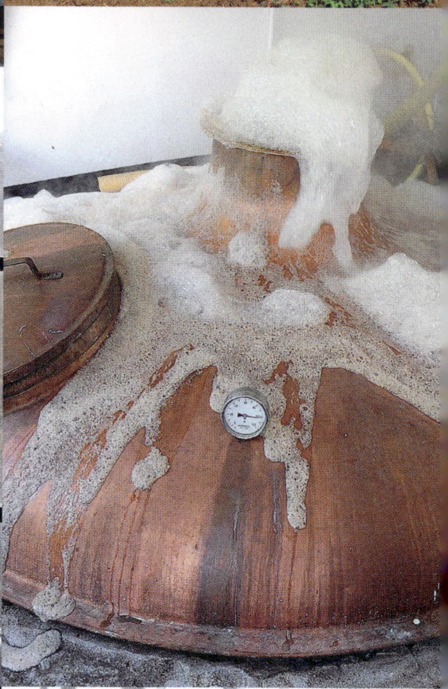

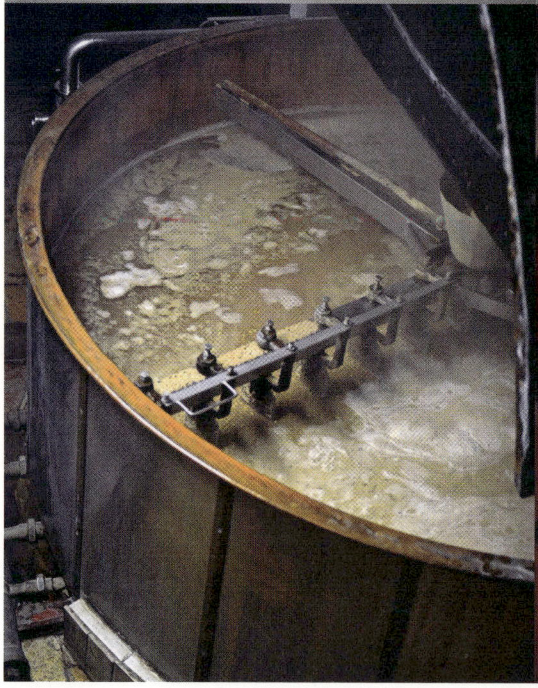

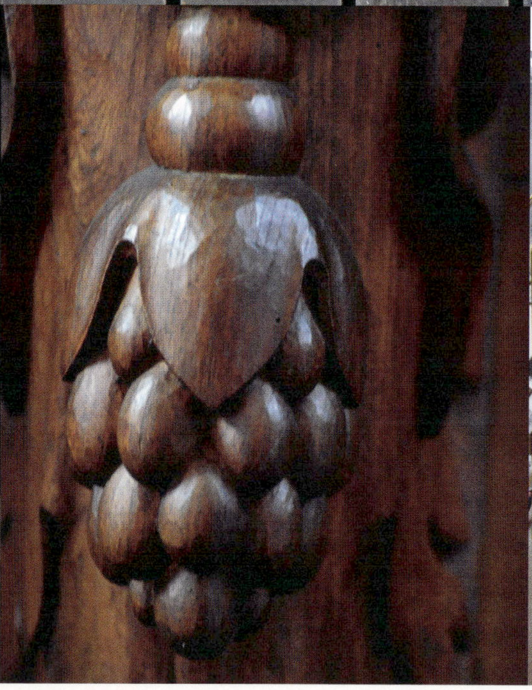

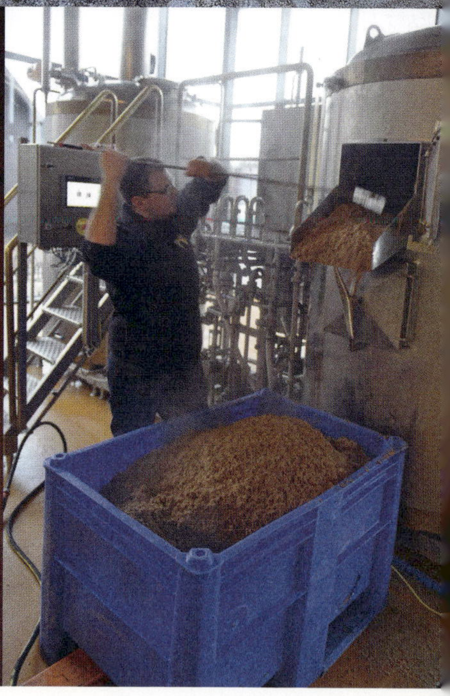

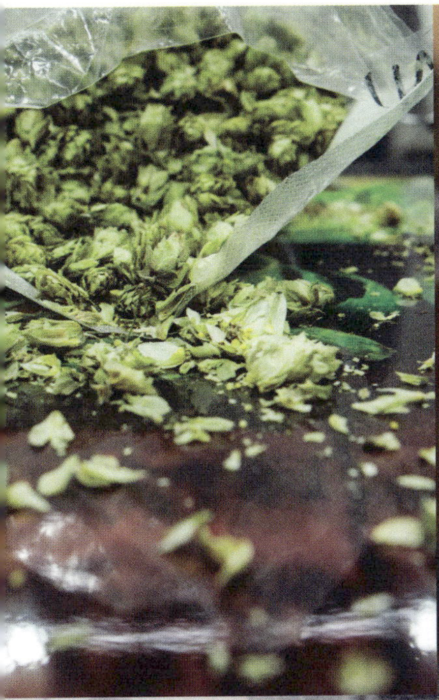
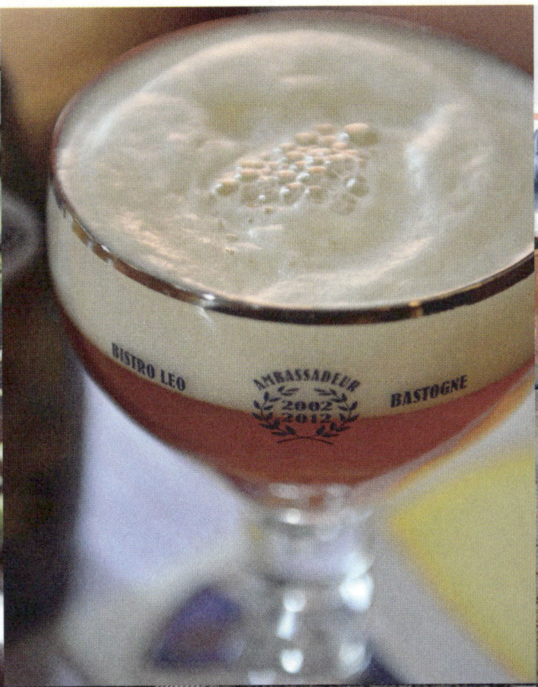
BISTRO LEO
AMBASSADEUR
2002
2012
BASTOGNE
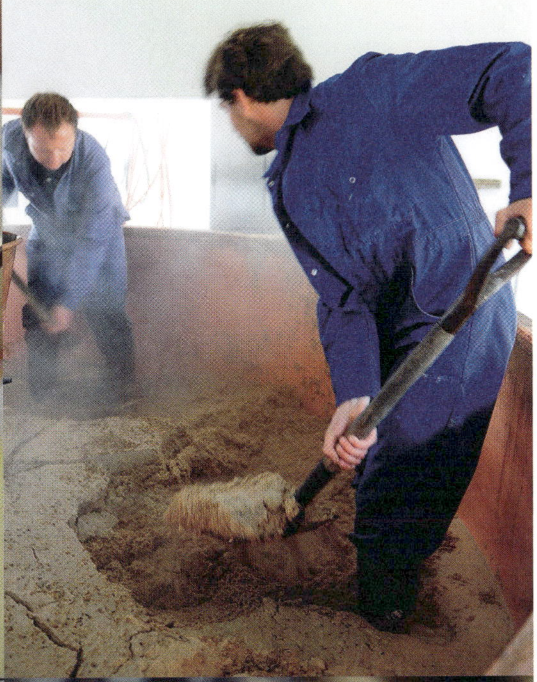
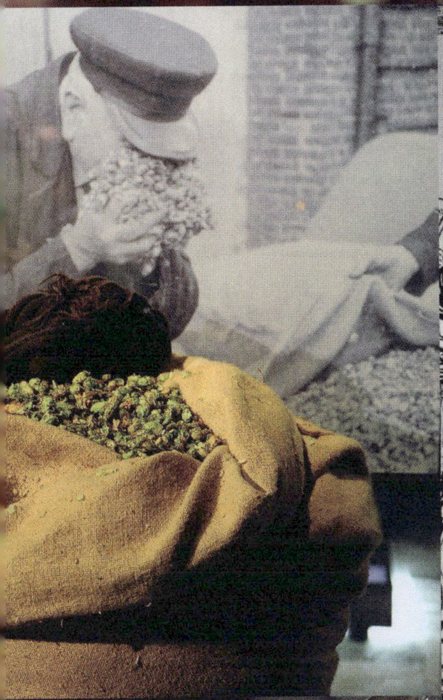
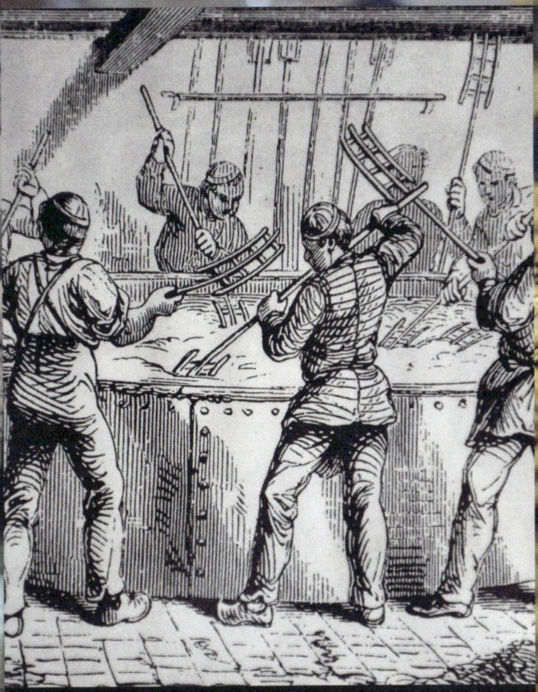
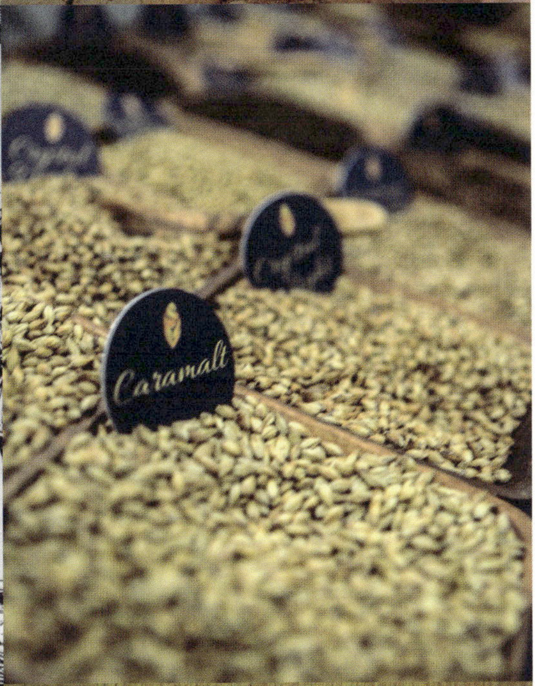
Caramalt
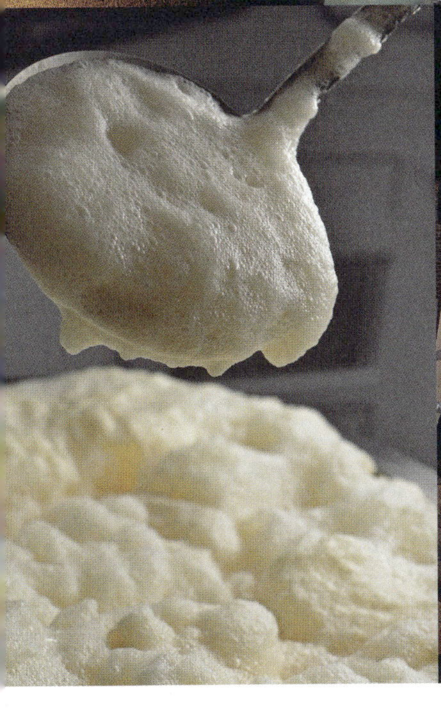
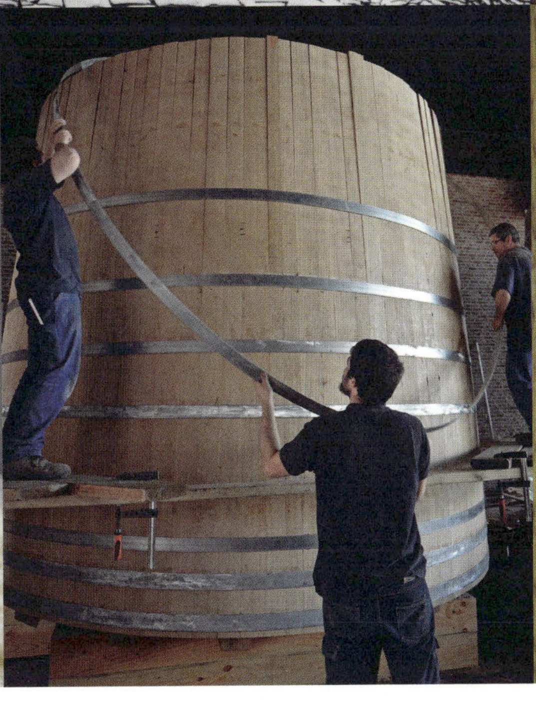
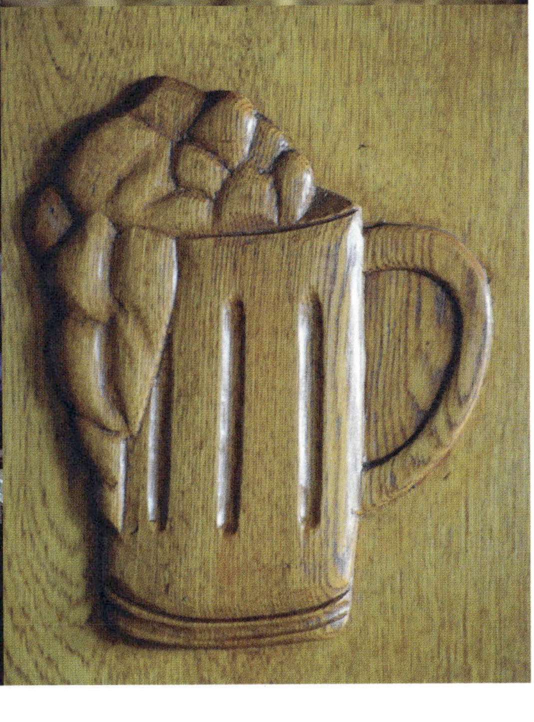

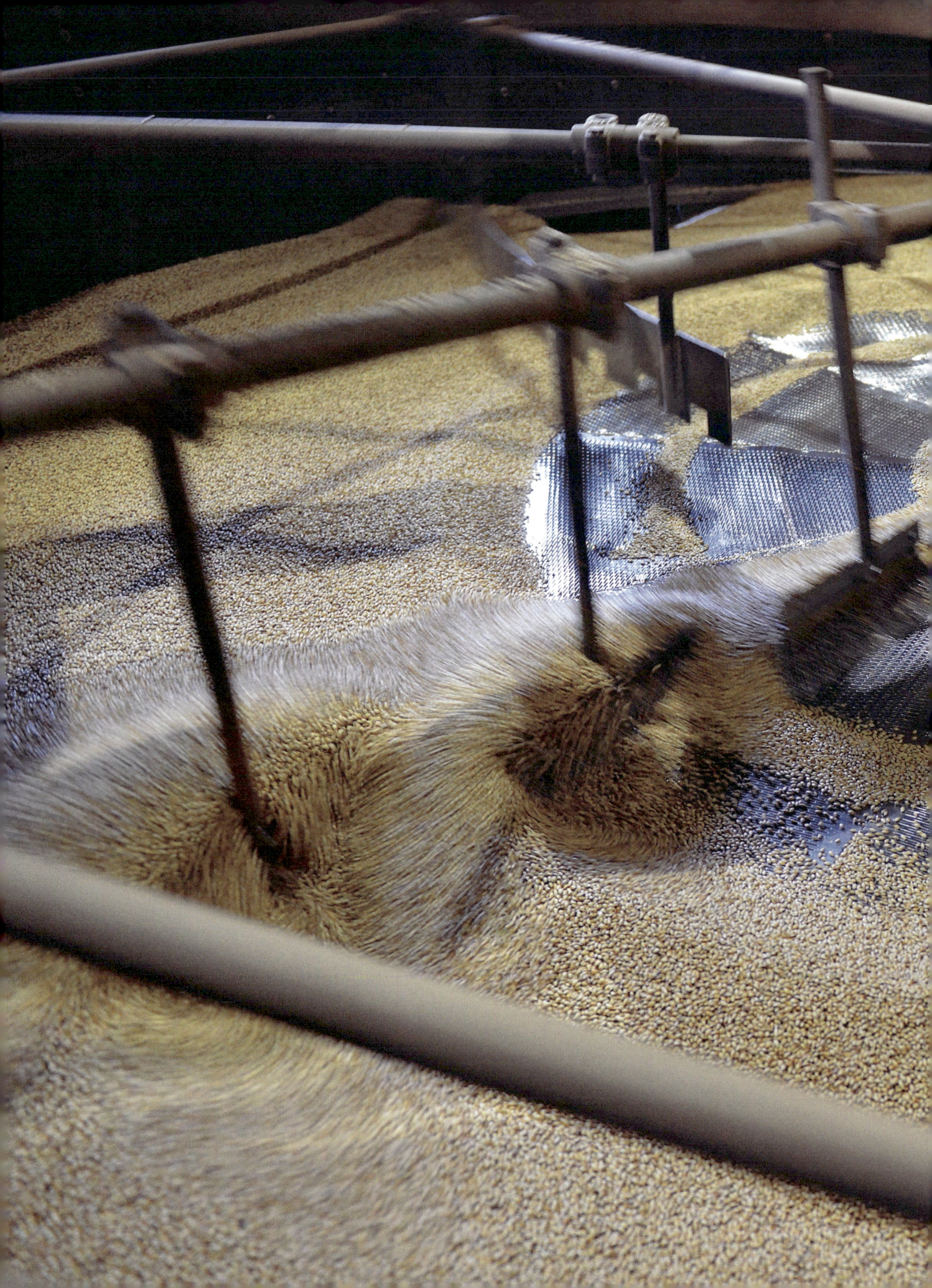

4

BREWING PROCESS AND INGREDIENTS

BREWING PROCESS AND INGREDIENTS

Making beer involves several major stages. Each of these stages comprises several procedures.

BREWING METHOD

Fritz Maytag of the Anchor Brewery in San Francisco feels that brewing is really quite simple: 'We brewers do not make the beer; rather, we mix the ingredients and the beer makes itself.' Modesty is a virtue but his statement contains a grain of truth. Bring the right ingredients together, use the correct equipment, follow the process step-by-step and you will end up with a drinkable brew. Below we will explain each stage of the brewing process in detail.

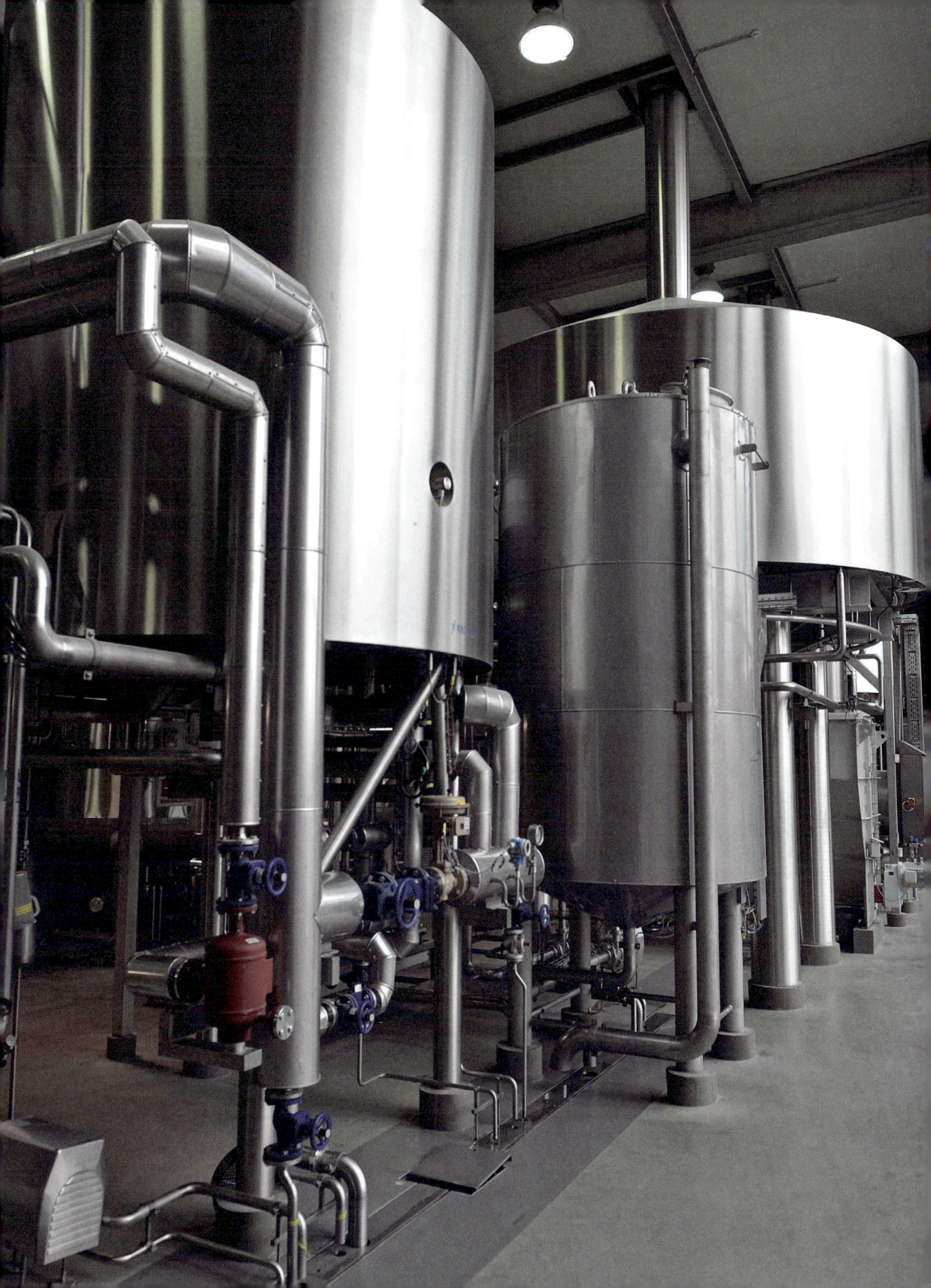

BREWING METHOD

1

'SCHROTEN'
or oarse grinding
a malt mill
is used to grind
the malt
coarsely.

malt

hop

2

MASHING
Starch is converted
into fermentable
sugars after
heating the
brewing mash
(water and malt).

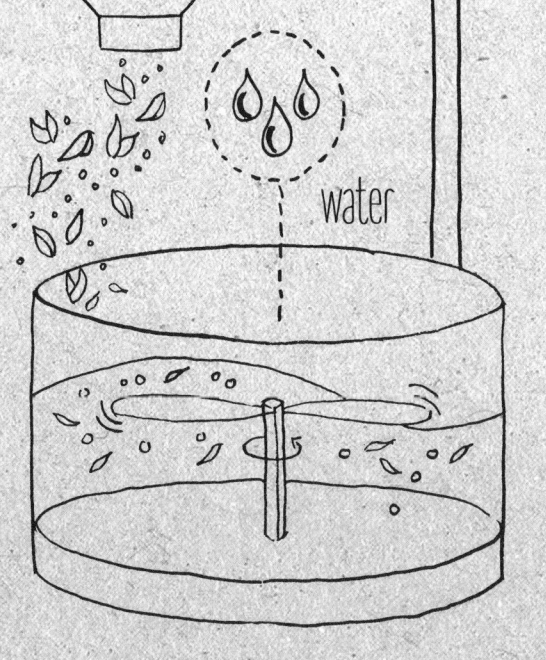

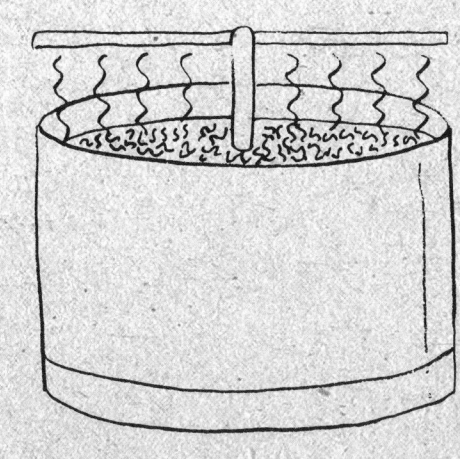

water

3

FILTERING
Separating the solid particles
or the 'bostel' from the liquid
particles called 'wort'.

4 • BREWING PROCESS AND INGREDIENTS

⬥ 6
COLD STORAGE

The beer is stored in a cool environment to enhance its taste. It will then be transferred to barrels or else used to fill bottles or cans.

⬥ 4
BOILING

The wort is boiled. Hop - and herbs (optional) - are added. Hop adds bitterness and/or aroma.

CO2

yeast

⬥ 5
FERMENTATION

The wort is cooled down and the yeast is added. The yeast converts the sugars into alcohol and carbon dioxide. We only use the term 'beer' after fermentation.

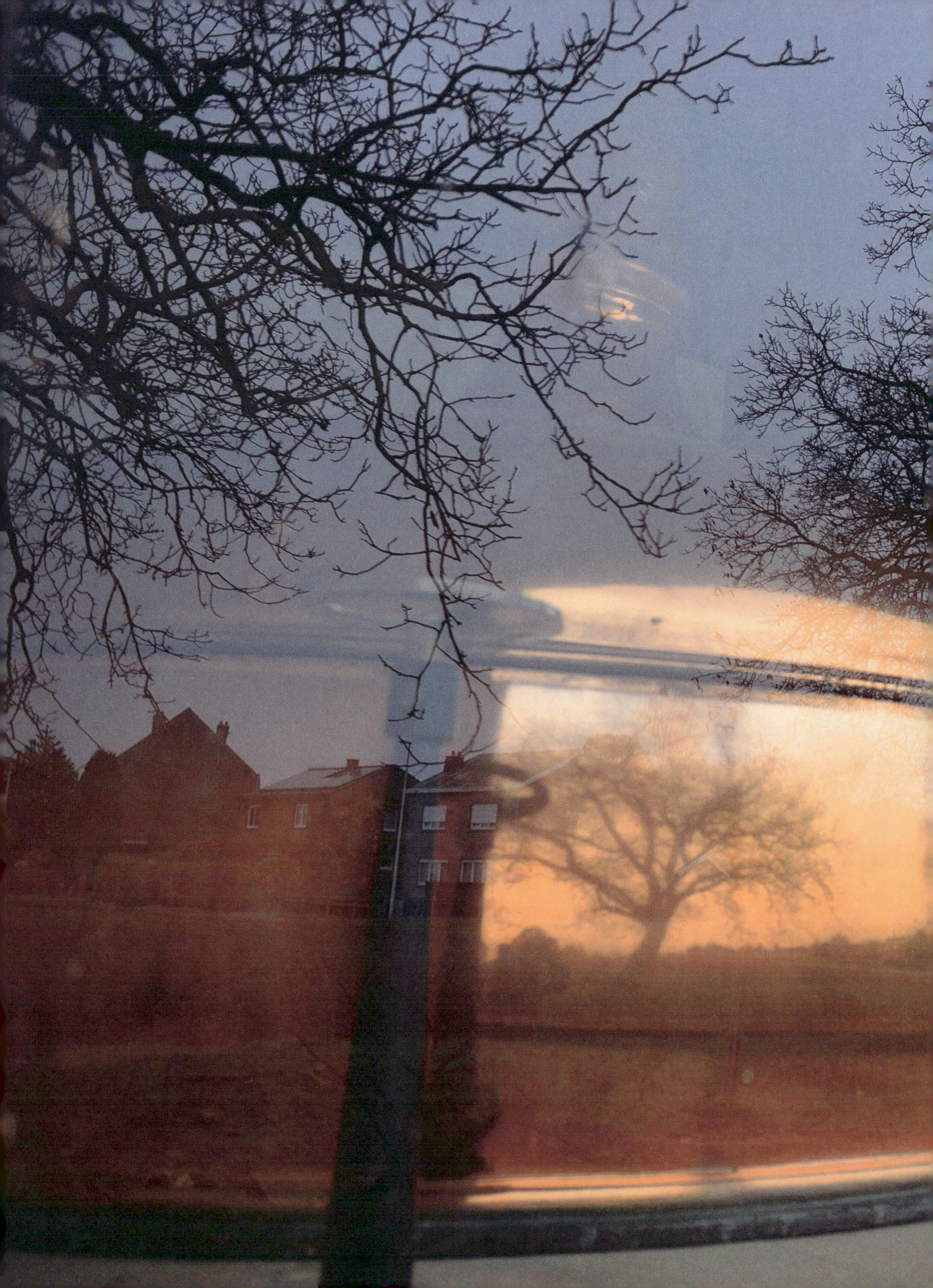

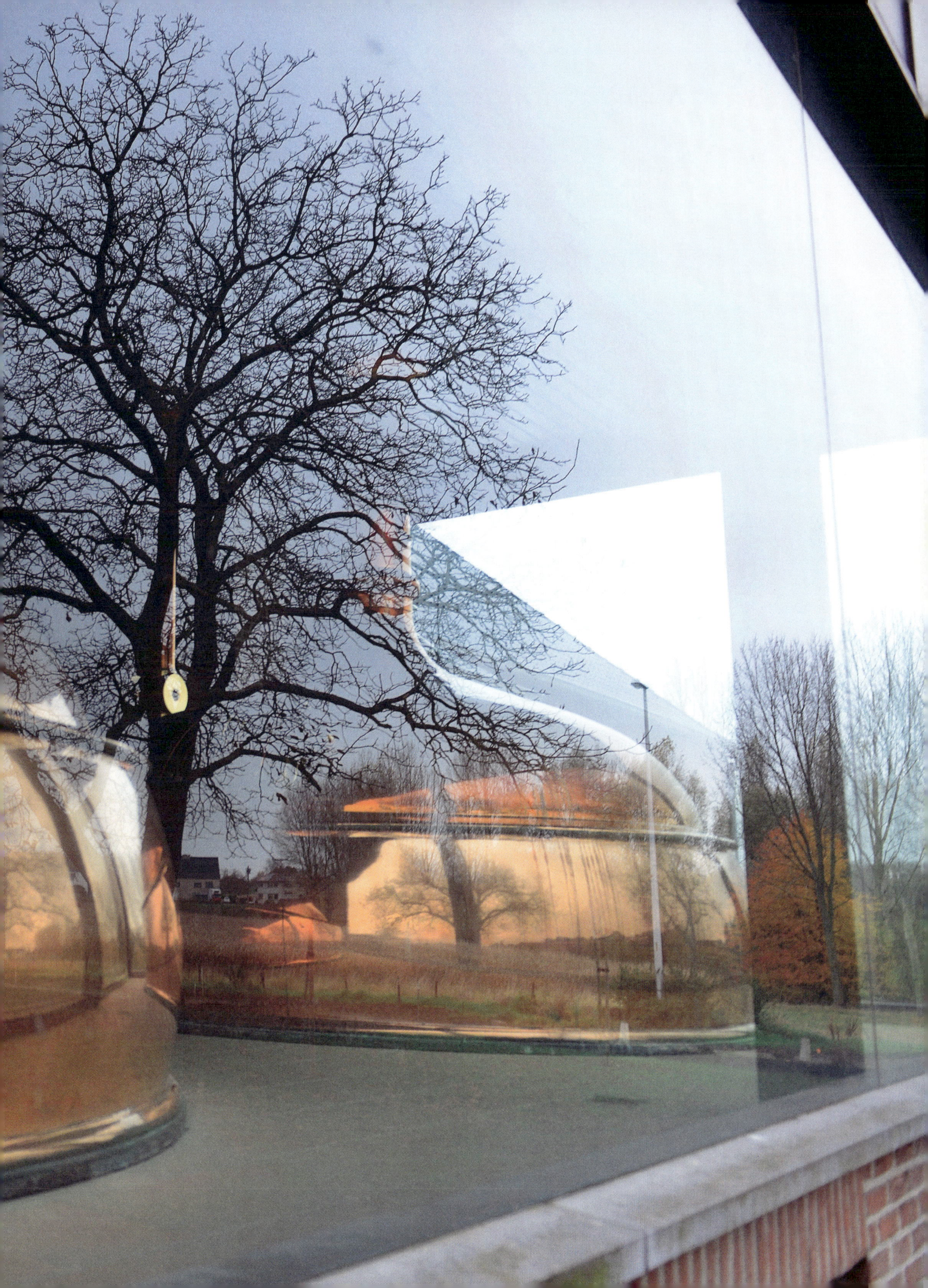

Coarse grinding or 'schroten'

The brewer grinds the malt to obtain a coarse mixture that can be dissolved in water. He takes care not to grind the chaff too finely as it will play a future role in the filtering process.

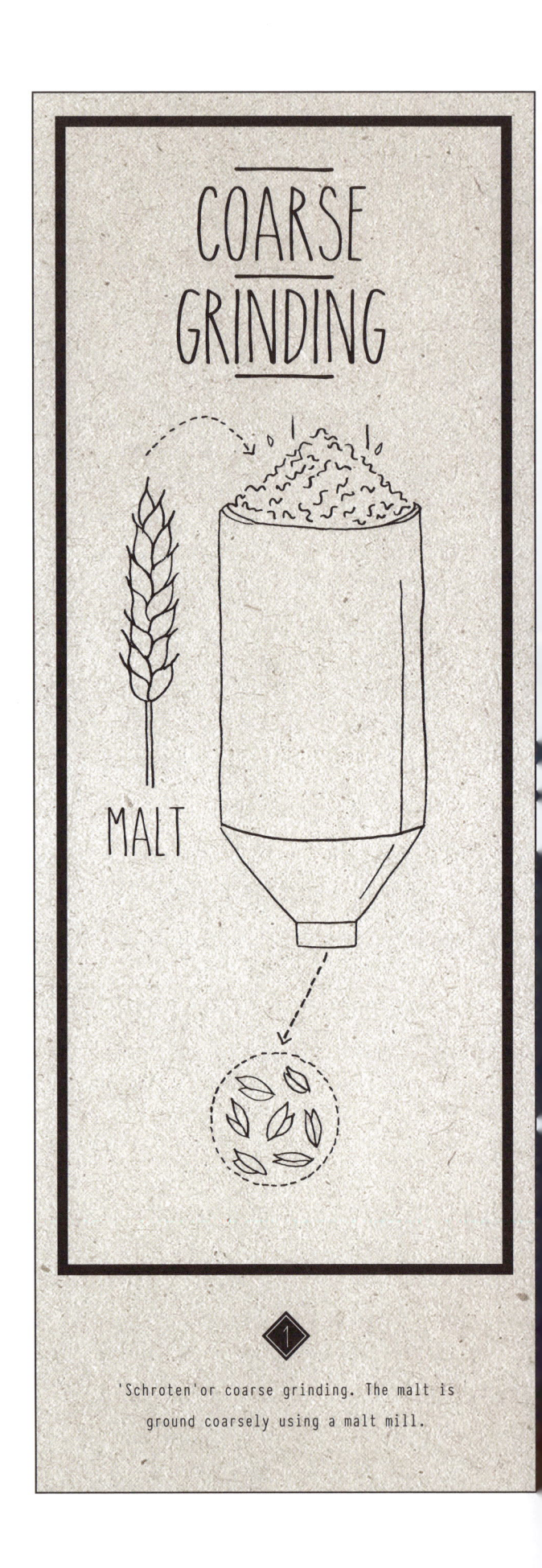

COARSE GRINDING

MALT

◆ 1 ◆

'Schroten' or coarse grinding. The malt is ground coarsely using a malt mill.

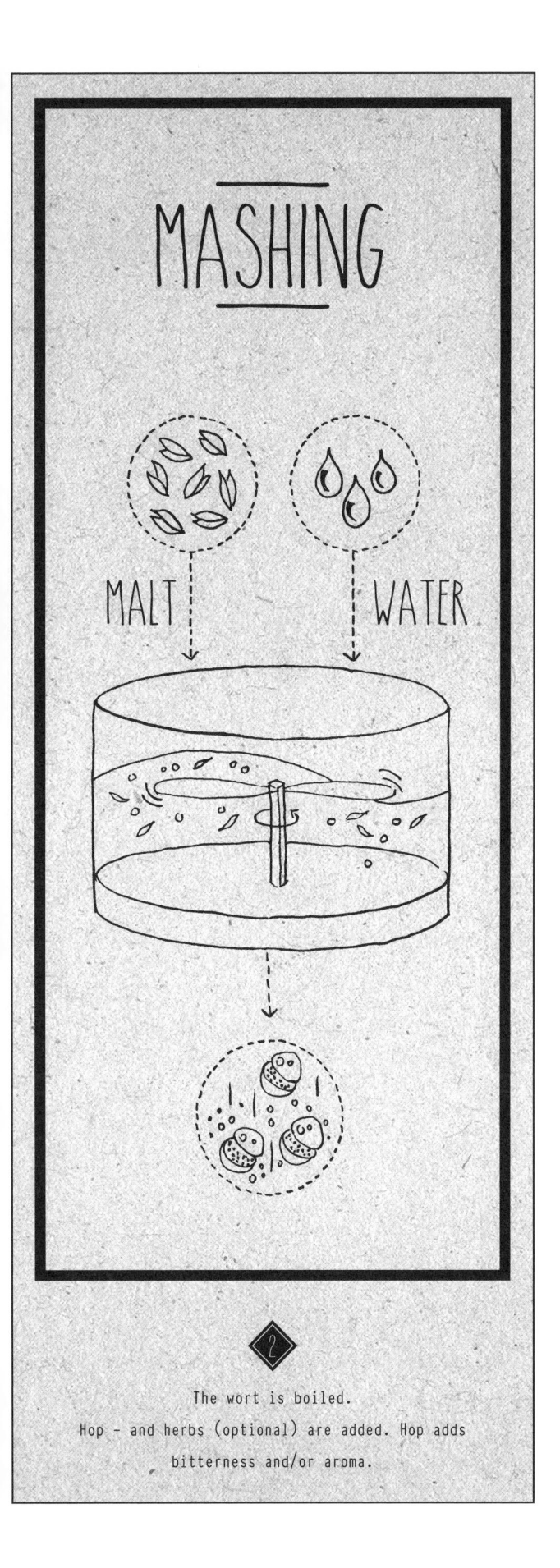

MASHING

MALT | WATER

The wort is boiled. Hop - and herbs (optional) are added. Hop adds bitterness and/or aroma.

Mashing

The brewer prepares a mash with the coarsely ground grain and brewing water. This mash is heated to the correct temperature in several stages. This process is also called maischen, using a German word. The mashing makes the grain dissolve and activates the enzymes contained in the malt. Each enzyme works in the optimum way at a specific temperature. The starch contained in the malt is composed of long chains of glucose molecules. The enzymes break down the long starch chains into smaller units: dextrines (cannot be fermented), maltose, glucose, ...

The yeast converts the maltose and glucose into alcohol and carbon dioxide (CO_2). The mashing process also helps to break down the proteins that make up the head of the beer. The brewer can adjust the proportion of fermentable and non-fermentable sugars in the wort by heating it for either a shorter or longer period at specific temperature stages. This is how he obtains a higher level of dextrin to give the beer more 'body'. Also, the acidity (pH) and the hardness of the water play a major role during the mashing process.

By means of the 'amylase' process, starch from malt and unmalted grains is converted into fermentable sugars:
- Between 45 and 55 °C proteins are broken down by the protease enzyme to create amino acids. These are the ones that feed the yeast and the medium-sized proteins that contribute to a firm collar of froth and the full mouthfeel.
- The beta-amylase process occurs between 61 and 63 °C and gives rise to fermentable sugars.
- At the alfa-amylase stage, between 73 and 75 °C, dextrines are formed.

Mashing is done using one of two methods: **decoction** or **infusion**. Using the decoction method, part of the maisch is removed and boiled separately before being added to the main blend. With infusion, the water is heated gradually.

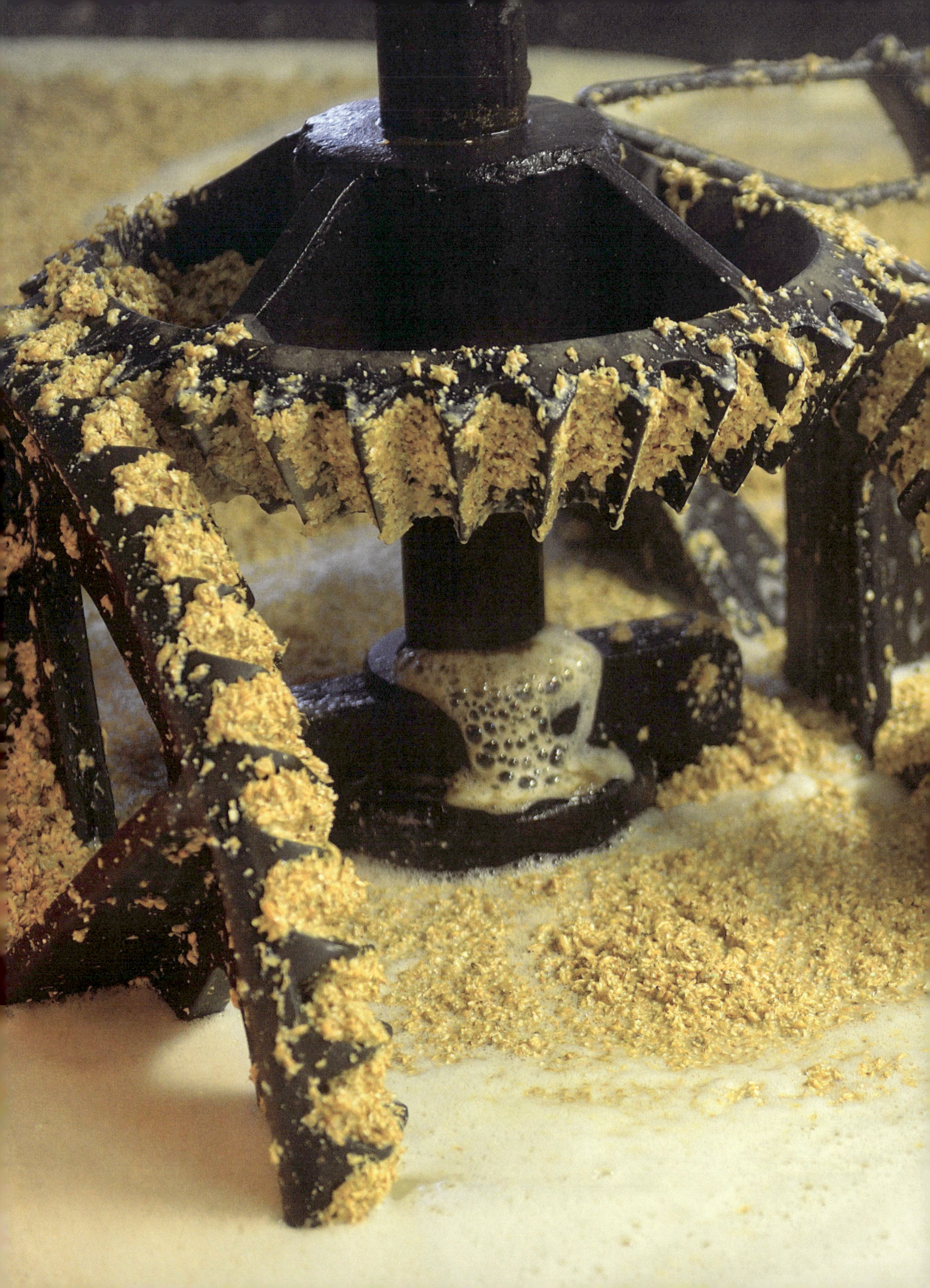

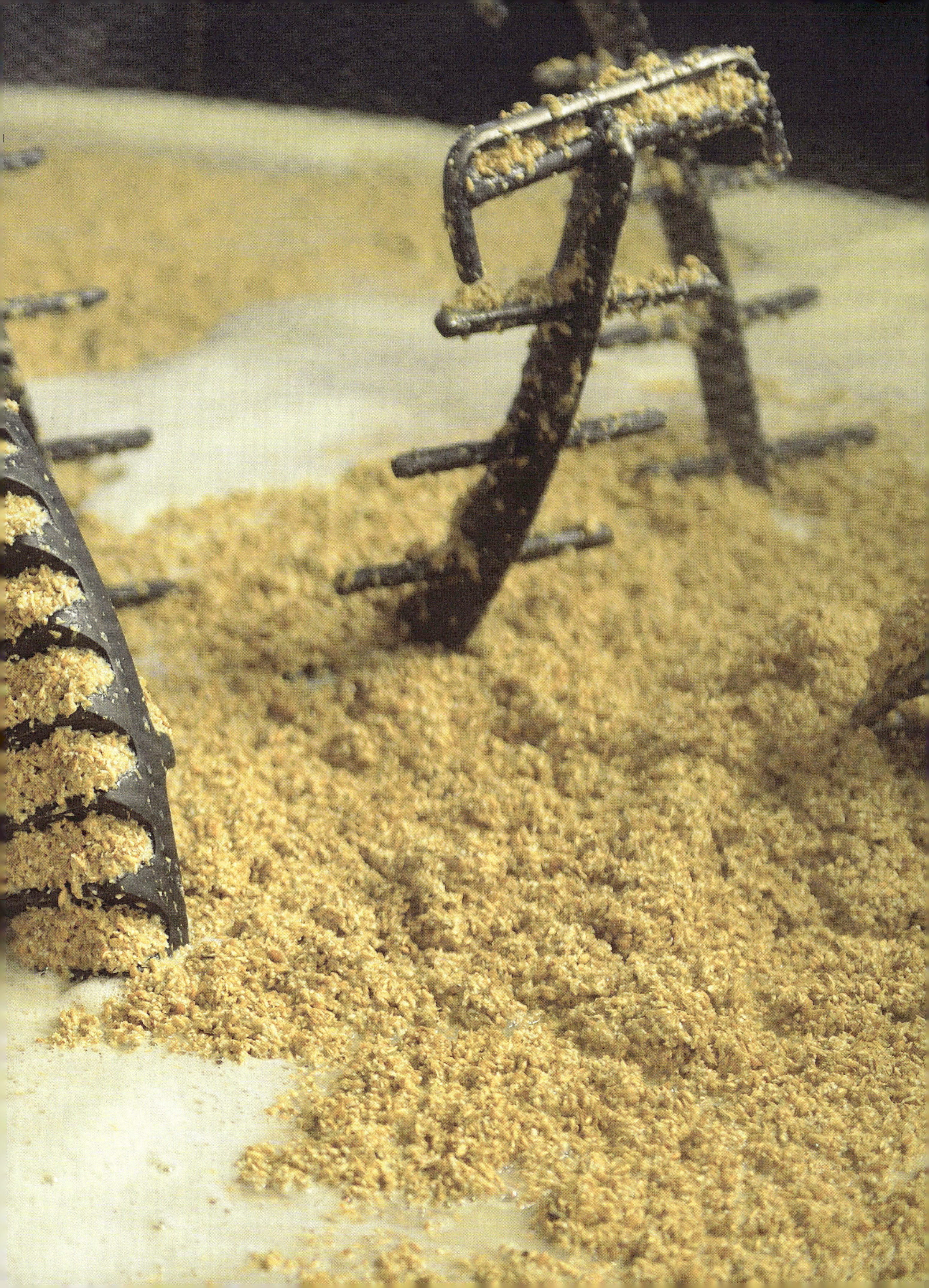

FILTERING

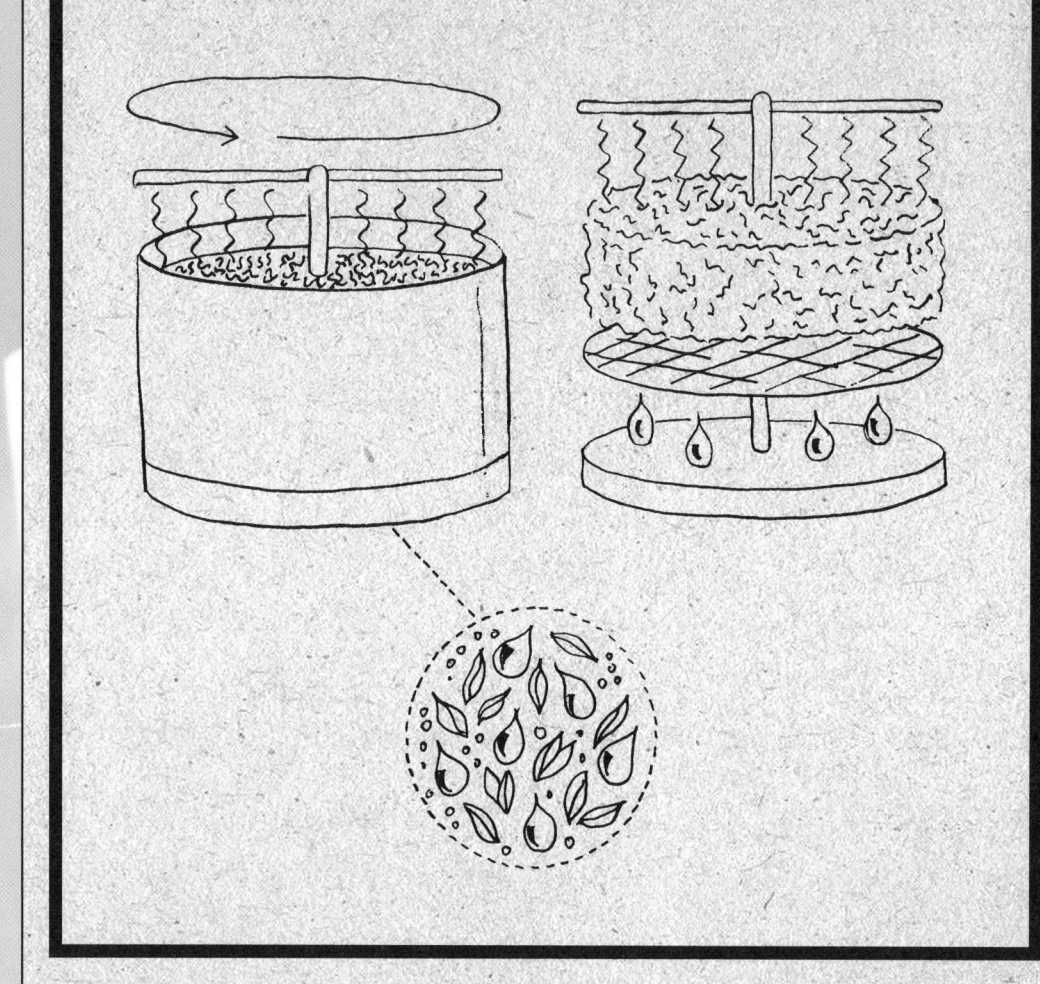

③

Separating the solid particles, or the 'bostel', from the 'wort', the liquid component.

BOILING

HOP

*The wort is boiled.
Hop - and herbs (optional) - are added.
Hop adds bitterness and/or aroma.*

Filtering

Once the mashing is done, the brewer separates the sugar-containing wort which is now liquid from the solid remainders of the grains (the bostel). The bostel will be used in cattle feed or as a basis for bread making. The chaff contained in the malt provides a natural filtering layer. This is why the malt is not ground too finely. The brewer will then rinse the bostel (the solid remains of the grain) to remove the sugars. Just before the layer of bostel is dried, the brewer will rinse or wash it with hot water at a temperature of around 80 °C. A thin layer of liquid remains on the bostel during the various rinses. This avoids air coming in contact with the bostel and prevents unwanted oxidation.

Boiling

The wort is now boiled together with the hops. The wort boiling process:
- Converts the bitter hop agents;
- Flocculates the large proteins;
- Evaporates unwanted volatile compounds;
- Sterilises the wort.

The wort will be kept on the boil for between sixty and ninety minutes. This high temperature converts the hop bitter agents and helps to create the typical bitter taste of beer. At the start of the boiling process many brewers will add bitter hops with a high content of alpha acids to ensure the beer is suitably bitter. Towards the end of the boiling process they will add aroma hops, each with their own specific aroma. The quantity and the type of hops added depend on the beer style.

During the boiling process large protein particles that have ended up in the wort during mashing will separate, or flocculate. After boiling the brewer will remove these protein flakes ('trub') as well as the hops by filtering the wort once again. This also allows undesirable organic compounds to evaporate. When all this is done the wort has to be sterilised to prevent contamination of the beer. Finally, the wort will cool down to 10–14 °C for bottom-fermented beers and to 15–25 °C in the case of top-fermented beers.

Dry hopping — adding hops during the fermentation process — increases the hop content of the beer, resulting in a more intense taste.

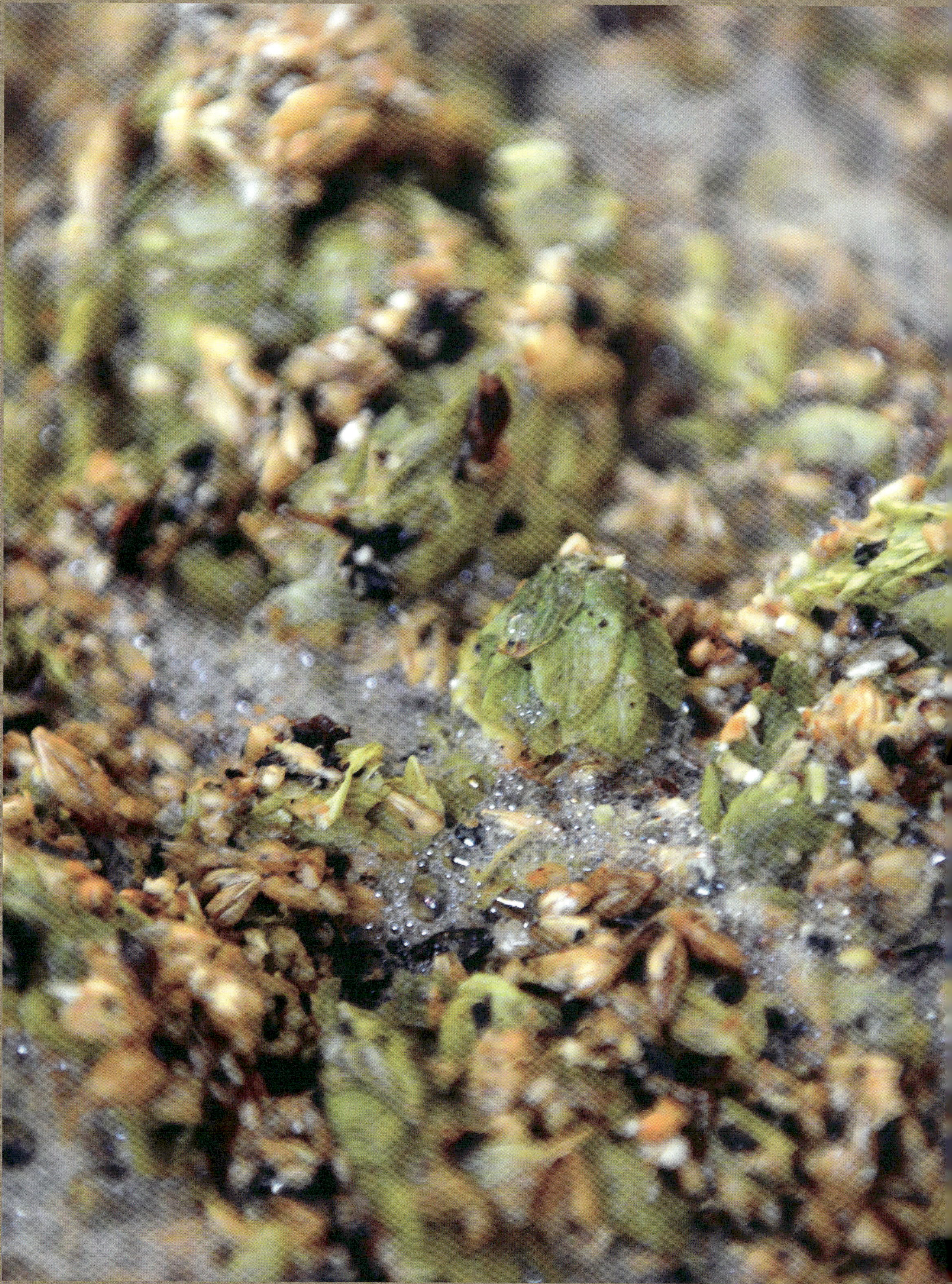

The hop is boiling under the approving gaze of Urbain Coutteau, brewer at De Struise Brouwers, who keeps a close eye on proceedings.

Fermentation

Yeast converts the sugars from the wort into alcohol and carbon dioxide (CO_2). We can only use the term 'beer' once fermentation has occurred. The strain of yeast used is largely responsible for the taste of the beer. Specific yeasts will create their own taste pattern (depending on temperature and composition of the wort) as they generate flavouring and aromatic agents as well as alcohol and carbon dioxide. During the fermentation stage and all subsequent treatments the young beer is highly susceptible to infections as the sugar-rich wort is a paradise for bacteria and yeasts. Consequently, hygiene is of the utmost importance.

Based on brewing technology beers are categorised by fermentation method. There are four separate categories: top-fermented, bottom-fermented, spontaneously fermented and mixed fermentation. Top as well as bottom fermentation mean that the brewer selects a yeast strain (originating from a single cell – 'reinculture) to add to the hopped wort.

Bottom fermentation

Bottom fermentation denotes the lower temperatures (maximum 14 °C) at which fermentation takes place and also points at the type of yeast (Saccharomyces carlsbergensis) that sinks towards the bottom at the end of fermentation. Bottom-fermented beers are a guarantee of a stable, consistent taste as at low temperatures there is only a small opportunity for wild yeasts to develop. Differences in taste used to occur more with top-fermented beers. However, thanks to improved hygiene procedures, it is now possible to produce pure beers at an ambient temperature. At low temperatures the yeast will produce fewer taste agents and aromatic agents. Example: pils beer.

Top fermentation

Top fermentation occurs at a higher temperature (15–25 °C) and denotes the type of yeast (Saccharomyces cerevisiae) that floats towards the top at the end of the fermentation process. Example: the majority of specialty beers.

Spontaneous fermentation

With spontaneous fermentation, wild yeasts attach themselves to the wort. After boiling the wort is poured into an open cooling basin, or 'koelschip', where it is exposed to wild yeasts (Brettanomyces lambicus and Brettanomyces bruxellensis, amongst others) and bacteria present in the surrounding air. These wild yeasts infect the wort and start off the 'spontaneous' fermentation. Post-fermentation the lambic goes into cold storage to continue its fermentation in wooden barrels. Examples: lambic beers, (old) gueuze, faro, kriek and fruit beers based on lambic.

Mixed fermentation

Finally, we have the mixed fermentation beers. These are fermented using a blended culture of top-fermented beers and lactic acid bacteria. After the main fermentation, part of the brew is pumped into vertical wooden barrels, or 'foeders' where it will continue to ferment on the basis of lactic acid. This process takes eighteen months or even longer and converts the organic acids into fruity esters. Afterwards the old mature 'foeder' beer is filtered and blended ('cut') with young, top-fermented beer, thus preserving the lifetime of the younger beer. Examples include: Flemish red-brown (Rodenbach) and Oudenaards bruin (a brown beer from Oudenaarde) (Liefmans).

FERMENTATION

YEAST

5

The wort is cooled down and the yeast is added. The yeast converts the sugars into alcohol and carbon dioxide. We only use the term 'beer' after fermentation.

Cold storage

At the end of the main fermentation stage the beer is pumped into the cold storage tanks where it spends some time maturing depending on requirements. At the cold storage or post-fermentation stage, the taste of the beer becomes more refined. It will continue to ferment and absorb CO_2.

Bottom-fermented beers require a longer storage period compared to their top-fermented cousins. During the cold storage period, the brewer will add hops to some brews, Orval for example, to obtain a hop aroma that turns into an intrinsic feature of the beer. This technique is known as dry hopping. After all, a large proportion of the original hop aromas will vanish during fermentation.

Filtration, bottling, packaging and pasteurisation

If the beer contains a yeasty residue, it will be cloudy. To obtain a clear beer, it must be filtered just before bottling or packaging. However, the filtration process removes some of the taste from the beer. It stands to reason that an un-filtered pils beer will be tastier than a filtered pils. The finished product is poured into barrels or used to fill bottles or cans. On micro-biological grounds, many brewers pasteurise their beers using a flash pasteuriser or tunnel-pasteuriser. The taste of pasteurised beers does not evolve.

Cold storage and filling: the beer is stored in a cool environment to enhance its taste. It will then be transferred to barrels or else used to fill bottles or cans.

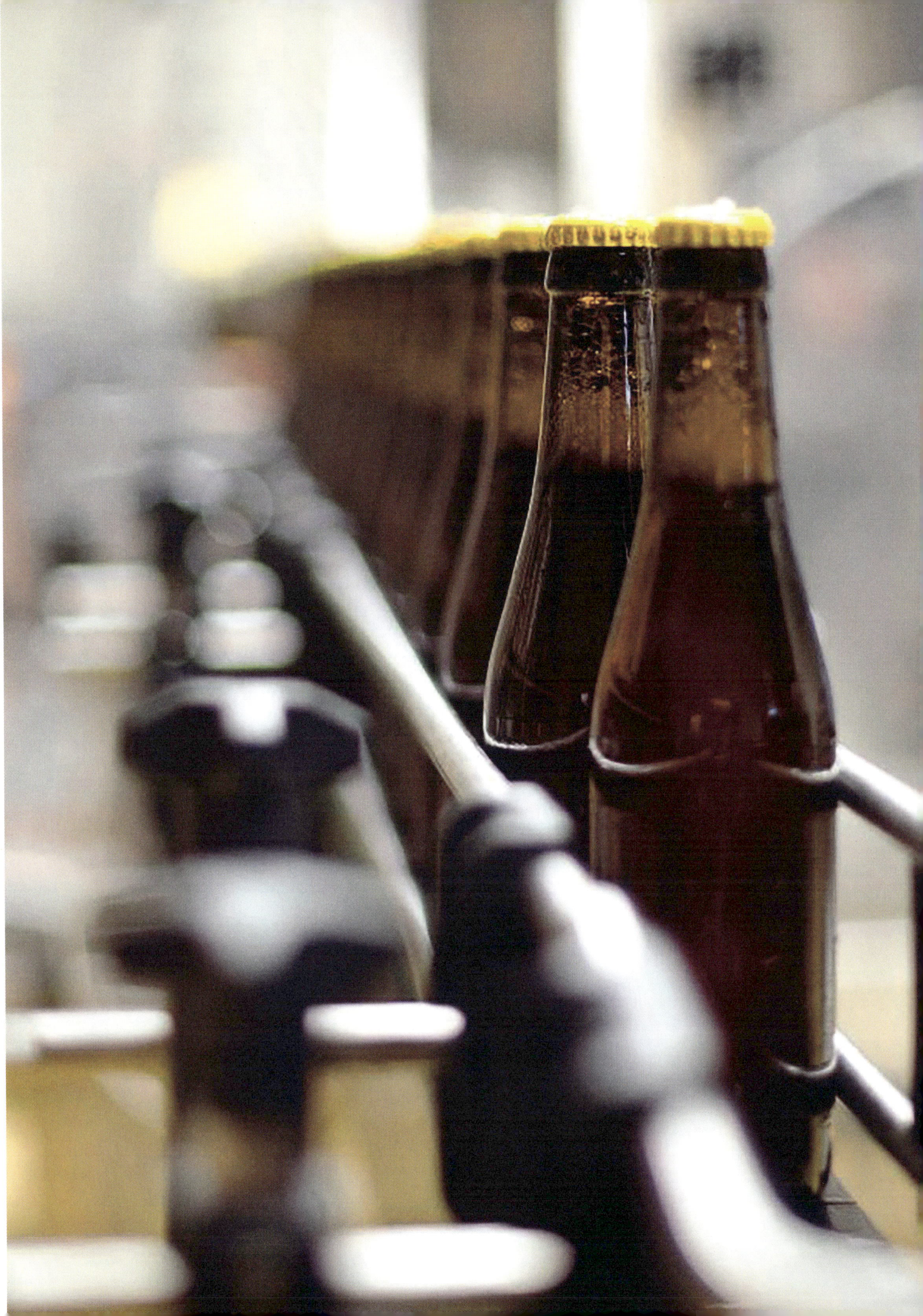

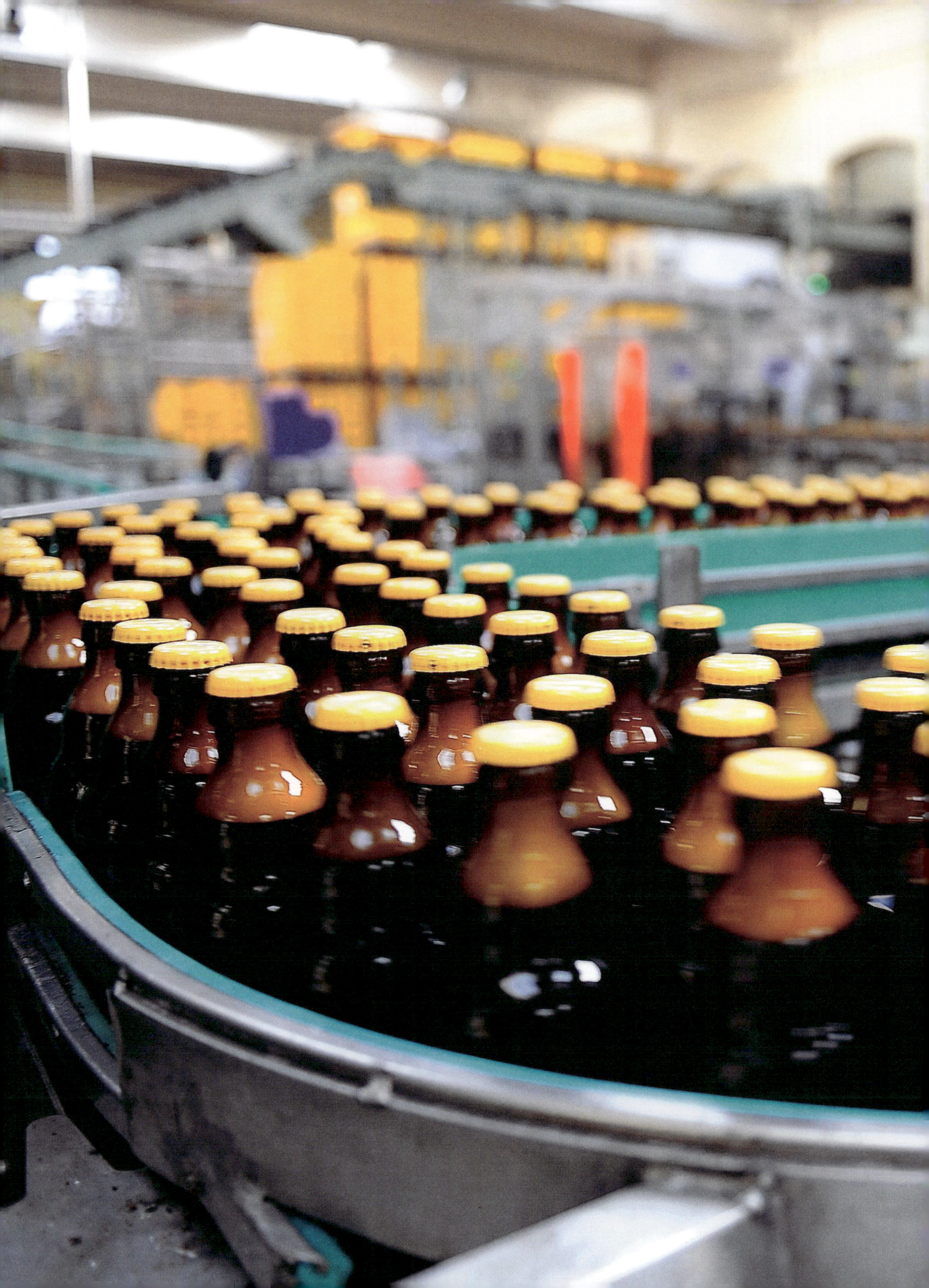

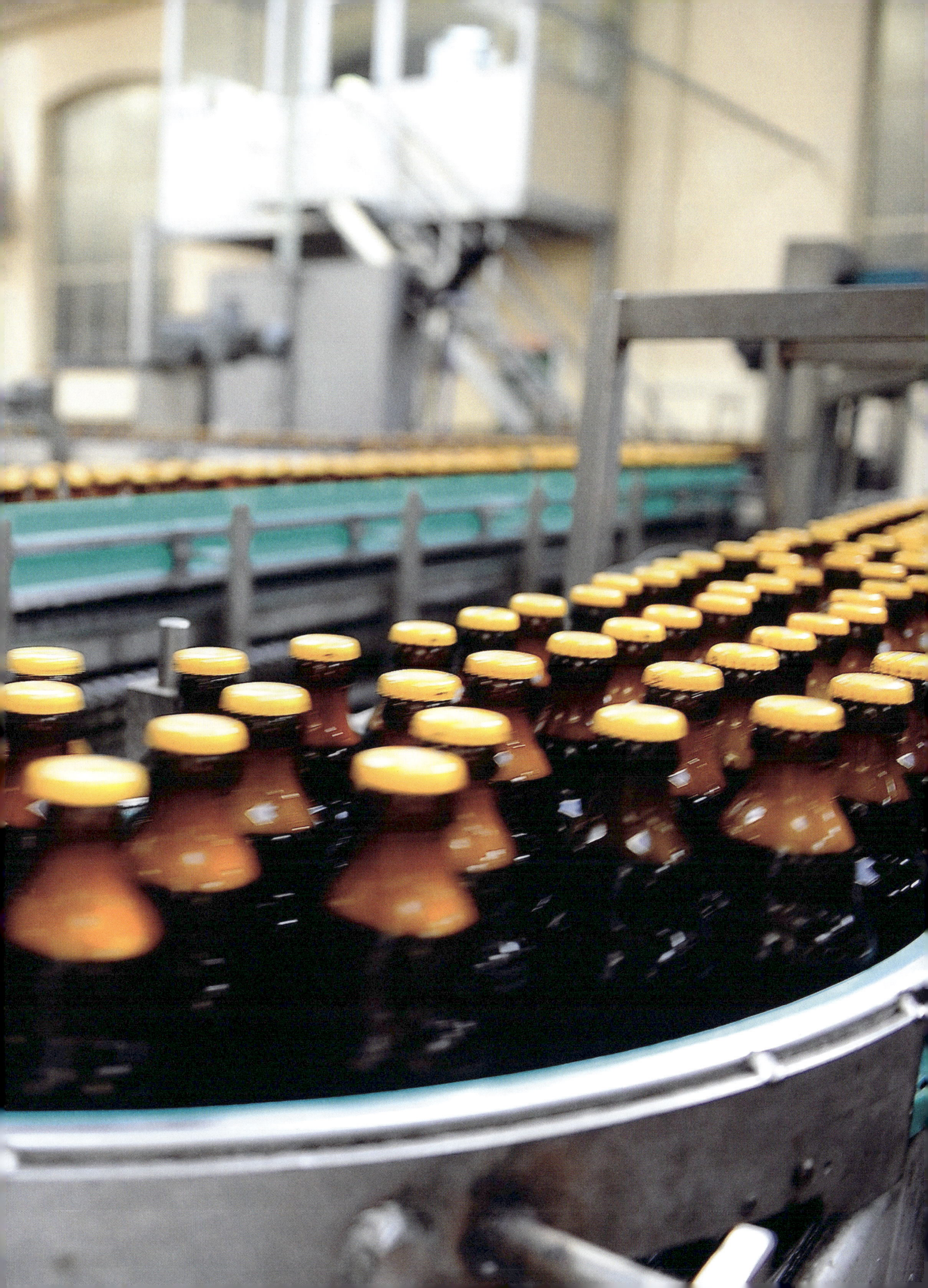

Second fermentation or re-fermentation

When the beer continues to ferment, or else re-ferments in the bottle, we talk about a second fermentation. The beer will produce a higher amount of carbon dioxide when sugars or yeast are added at the bottling stage, followed by a stay of between one and three weeks in a warm chamber (20–22 °C). The yeast present in the beer will protect it from less agreeable flavours that can be caused by maturation. Beers that re-ferment in the bottle are 'storage beers' that must be poured slowly and carefully. You are meant to leave the last centimetre of sediment in the bottle, to prevent the yeast from escaping and clouding the beer. The yeast sediment, however, is suitable for consumption and is, in fact, very rich in vitamin B. Various brewers serve the yeast along with your pint in a separate yeast glass, Hopus and Affligem for example. Breweries are now mainly using 'sticky' yeasts. These cling to the bottom of the glass and, when your beer is poured, there is only a minimal amount of 'rubbish' at the bottom. Also, different yeasts are now often used for main fermentation and second fermentation.

Brewing – art or science?
....

Brewing, is it an art or a science? A combination of both, is the opinion of the majority of brewers. As a brewer you must be in complete control of the fermentation process. Yeast is the most difficult ingredient by far. We are talking about living cells that only do their work correctly in an ideal environment. There is an art to developing a good recipe. That is far from all: you then need science to be able to reproduce it perfectly time and time again. Just like learning to cook, learning to brew means dealing with cooking temperatures, keeping an eye on the clock, giving it a stir from time to time... You have a goal in mind and can picture the end result, but how do you get there?

A treasure hunt
....

Brewing is in your genes or else you start off with a passion for food and cooking, as is the case with many chefs. If you don't like beer, there is no place for you here. You get to know the various beers and learn to tell them apart. Funnily enough, your birthplace affects your taste buds. If you are from Oudenaarde your taste will veer towards the sour. Westvleteren people have undoubtedly been influenced by the Trappists. Our tastes are shaped by our roots, by the way we were brought up on our home patch that was also home to our beer.

The process of making beer with only the basic ingredients of water, malt, hops and yeast, with a few simple actions, remains intriguing. The adjustments you make yourself, once you know what you are doing, determine the end product. Completely captivating. You can put your own slant on it, increase the bitterness, aim for a particular aroma or add fruit, honey or herbs. You experiment with varieties of malt, with the degree of sourness or with yeast – the brewer's secret. The brewer will cultivate his own yeast based on his own particular strain. All in all, to brew is to embark on a major treasure hunt. The most difficult aspect of brewing is to achieve a consistent taste. The problem faced by home brewers is that their brew has a different taste every single time. They do not have access to aroma panels that investigate the various components of the beer's aroma and neither can they make use of extensive laboratories, unlike the large breweries. Mass products have to taste the same anywhere and at any time. The large breweries make sure this is the case, even though the barley and hop harvest varies from year to year, in common with to grape vintages. More sunshine, a wet summer, all of this can affect the taste. With wine, it is accepted that vintages vary from year to year. But your average beer drinker will expect his tried and trusted taste in the glass.

Brewing the farmer's way

You could almost forget this when you walk through brand new brewhalls, admire towering tanks, watch armies of bottles flash by on a conveyor belt and manage a lucky escape from a fork lift truck racing to deliver pallets of beer to a large lorry. Breweries that have enjoyed continued growth have turned into factories, managed by highly technically skilled operators.

The brewing industry enjoys the fruit of automation. Efficiency is the name of the game. But take a good look around and traces of the past can still be seen. Brasserie d'Achouffe has preserved the look of an Ardennes farm. But who remembers, or can even imagine, that in 1982 they started brewing here in a cowshed? The architecture of a long-walled or square farmhouse indicates that many breweries started out as a farm. The farmers kept pace with the seasons. They would brew their beer in winter, when the fields lay bare, ready for the forthcoming spring. In those days the brewing process did not resemble a closed circuit, unlike today. Open mashing basins and cooling basins or 'coolships' were in regular use. If you were doing your brewing in winter, the risk of contamination was less and the beer could be stored for longer in its wooden barrels. The classic beers, the artisan lambic for example, have stuck to this tradition. Up to this day, they are only brewed during the winter months.

Brewer Bjorn Desmadryl of 't Gulden Spoor removes the bostel from the brewing kettle. It is used as cattle feed by farmers in the local area.

Joining hands at the kettle

It is an open secret that brewers collaborate behind the scenes. One brewer uses another's bottling line or knocks on the door of his big brother's lab to request an analysis. At first sight, brewing together seems rare. Nevertheless, this is happening more and more. The new wave of microbreweries in particular often brings new beers to the market that are the fruit of a collaboration with – usually – a colleague from abroad. Schieve Tabarnak, Black in Japan and Grey Jacket, all from Brasserie de la Senne in Brussels, are cast in the same mould. 'We will only brew with colleagues whom we rate highly. They have to share our vision on quality', brewer Yvan De Baets assures us. 'This is how we discover different methods of brewing and a variety of cultures, giving us room to experiment. We don't plan ahead for these *collaboration brews*. They have to come along spontaneously. First of all, we have to 'gel' – work well together. We will always try to work with our brewing colleagues on their own site. These *collaboration brews* are always a one-off. Brewing together keeps you on edge so you don't get stuck in your own familiar rut.' Examples abound. The Flemish red-brown Moaten is a joint creation from Two Brothers Brewing (USA) and Urthel. They added lactic acid bacteria and used champagne yeast. Garrett Oliver, the brew master at Brooklyn Brewery (USA), entered into a collaboration with Brasserie d'Achouffe, Gaverhopke produces the Bitter Sweet Symphony together with the Tired Hands Brewing Company (USA), for its Bronze Age, the Hof Ten Dormaal brewery worked with Still Water (USA) and Vicaris produced its Vicaris/Dock Street Philly Tripel together with Dock Street Brewing Company (USA). Larger breweries are also taking a peek over the wall. The various breweries sheltered by the Duvel Moortgat umbrella often work together. Gnomegang, a Belgian strong pale ale, is the fruit of a collaboration between Brasserie d'Achouffe and the Boulevard Brewing Company (USA). 'You could say that all the beers from our Ommegang Brewery (USA) resulted from a partnership, as all of their recipes originate in Belgium,' states Hedwig Neven, brewmaster at Duvel Moortgat. However, he is not referring to the physical process of brewing together

4 • BREWING PROCESS AND INGREDIENTS

to produce a batch. Brasserie St-Feuillien has been teaming up with Green Flash (USA) for years. The result of their collaboration includes the Black Saison in 2012 and the Belgian Coast IPA using a variety of hops (Simcoe, Columbus, Centennial, Citrus, Cascade), a special edition introduced to commemorate the 140th anniversary of this Belgian brewery. American brewer Chuck Silva was invited to work on this project.

Off the beaten track
....

The job of a geuzesteker is to blend lambic beers from a range of lambic breweries. In a way, you could call this a collaboration, although the various participants never get together in the brewhall. By the way, lambic can also be used to lend a surprisingly, freshly sour touch to other beers. This has given rise to the Vicaris Triple Gueuze, made by Brouwerij Dilewyns and the Duysters Tuverbol from the Loterbol brewery. The latter uses a lambic made by 3 Fonteinen. De Rulquin is a stout from the Ardennes. This re-fermented beer that spends several months maturing in oak barrels was created jointly by Brasserie Rulles and Gueuzerie Tilquin. The Japanese OWA Brewery has entered into a partnership with Brouwerij Van Den Bossche for its amber beer and stout. Its lambic beers are provided by the De Troch lambic brewery. At De Struise Brouwers and Alvinne, 'brewing together' is part of their creative DNA. A striking feature of *collaboration brews* such as these is that they are born in the spirit of 'camaraderie' amongst friends who have met before at beer festivals where both were present. A great example is Spanish exporter Zombier who has launched the Zombienation project in which several European breweries take part. Brewing is done in different locations and every brewer who joins brings along one more ingredients from his own country. Even though this project involves Belgian brewers, it does not necessarily follow that all the beers produced are strong. Alvinne launched a light ale in co-operation with Twickenham Fine Ales (UK). We hear that more beers in a similar vein are planned.

The blades cut through the mash whilst the wort is slowly being heated. Picture contributed by Brouwerij Cornelissen.

WATER

The main constituent of beer is water. Places where the local water has specific properties have given rise to typical beer styles. For example, the pale ale brewed in Burton on Trent (UK) owes its excellent quality to the local hard water. In contrast, the water in the Czech town of Pilzen is extremely soft, which makes it eminently suitable for pils brewing. These days, the components of water are adjusted by every large brewery, meaning that any style can be brewed anywhere in the world. Unfortunately, this has been detrimental to regional beers, causing them to lose some of their charm.

Brewing water

Water used for brewing is a reactive medium. In other words, the components that dissolve in the water may well interact with one another. Water is also a transport medium. For example, the water will permeate the kernel of the barley grain or the starch contained within and transport the enzymes to the place where they do their work. Last but not least, water plays an important role in causing chemical reactions, determines temperature and pH and is essential for the transport of energy and heat.

The main components are calcium, magnesium and bicarbonate. Together they determine the hardness of the water. The composition of the hardness has a major influence on the acidity or alkalinity (pH degree) during the brewing process. Depending on the presence and concentration of other elements, the brewer will adjust the brewing water to:

- Remove insoluble components
  - components that make the beer cloudy by filtering them out with the use of a sand filter,
  - bacteria by means of sterilisation.
- Remove soluble components by means of:
  - oxidation and filtration (iron),
  - deionization,
  - remove unwanted aromas and smells,
  - degasification,
  - decarbonisation (reduce the carbon dioxide content).

Water used for cleaning

Breweries require huge amounts of water to produce their beers and to clean their equipment. The ratio between beer and water is 1 to 7. In other words, the brewer requires 7 litres of water to brew 1 litre of beer. Many breweries optimise their water usage and aim for a ratio of 1 to 4. From a bacteriological point of view, the water used for cleaning has to meet the same standards as drinking water.

Stout de Gaume
Brune
Bière de Gaume
La Rulles
Triple
La Rulles
Saison
XIII

HOPS

The hop is the herb most widely used in brewing over the last four hundred years or so. Initially it was used as a conservation agent. However, beer drinkers became accustomed to the bitter taste of hops and so, bitterness became an essential component of the flavour of beer. The hop plant, alias *Humulus lupulus* (small wolf plant), is a fast-growing climber, related to hemp and cannabis, that grows naturally in Belgium. The hop vine has delicate, small tendrils it uses for climbing up trees, shrubs, poles and wires. Only the lupuline gained from the flowers of the female hop plant is used in the production of beer as male hop cones contain oleaginous components and oils that are detrimental to the head of the beer. In Belgium it is prohibited by law to grow male hop plants within a five-kilometre radius from a hop field.

Varieties of hops

Bitter hop
These hop varieties lend the beer its bitterness. Bitter hops are added at the start of the boiling process to get the most out of them. The main names when it comes to bitter hops are Magnum and Target.

Aroma hops
Aroma hops give off a zesty, flowery and occasionally citrusy fragrance. These aromas are extremely delicate. This is why the brewer adds these hops varieties towards the end of the boiling process to do full justice to the hop aromas. Well-known hop varieties include Saaz, Hallertau, Mittelfrüh and Cascade.

Dual purpose hops
Several hop varieties can be used as both aroma and bitter hops.

Humulus lupulus, originating from Eastern Europe, is now found in all areas that enjoy a moderate climate, including Poperinge in West Flanders. Large hop production areas elsewhere in Europe are Kent in England, Hallertau in Germany and Zatec (Saaz in German) in the Czech Republic. In the USA, hops grown in the Yakima Valley in the North-West of the country enjoy an excellent reputation. In the Southern hemisphere, hops are primarily grown in Australia and New Zealand.

ORIGIN OF HOPS

Originally from China

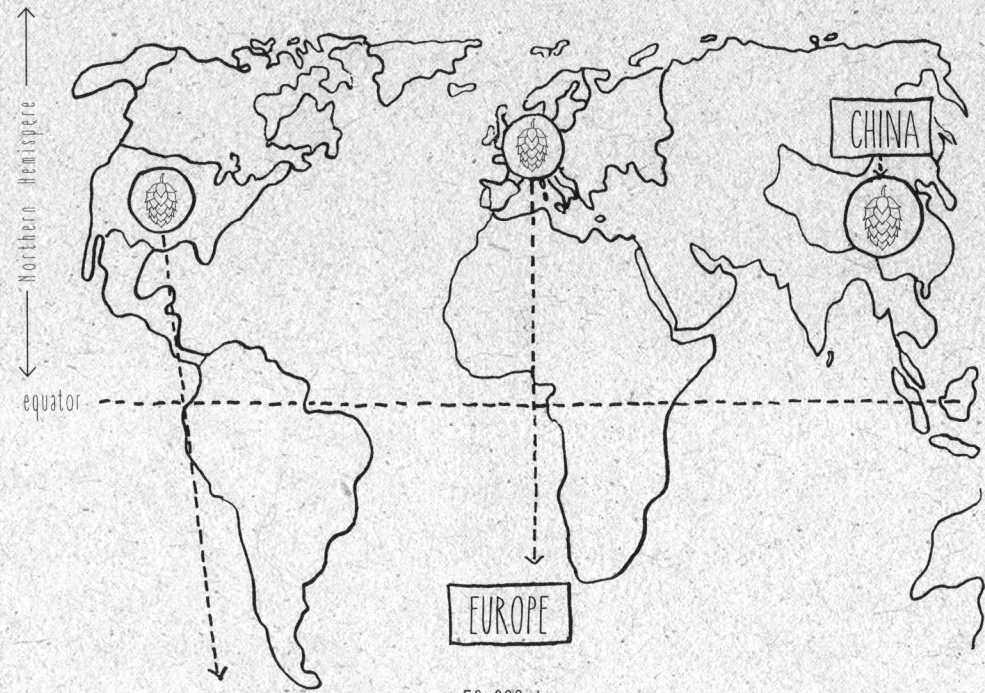

← Northern Hemisphere →

CHINA

equator

EUROPE

UNITED STATES

32,200 tons

50,000 tons
2,600 tons hop
Germany : 38,500 tons
Czech Republic: 6,200 tons
Slovenia: 2,300 tons
Poland: 2,000 tons
United Kingdom: 1,450 tons

PRODUCTION

All over the world:
80,000 – 100,000
tons per year
The largest beer
consuming area:
Russia, United States
and Japan

DID YOU KNOW THAT?

For 1 litre of beer you need 200g grain, 2g hops, a little yeast and 5 litres of water.
These proportions are used in the majority of beer types.

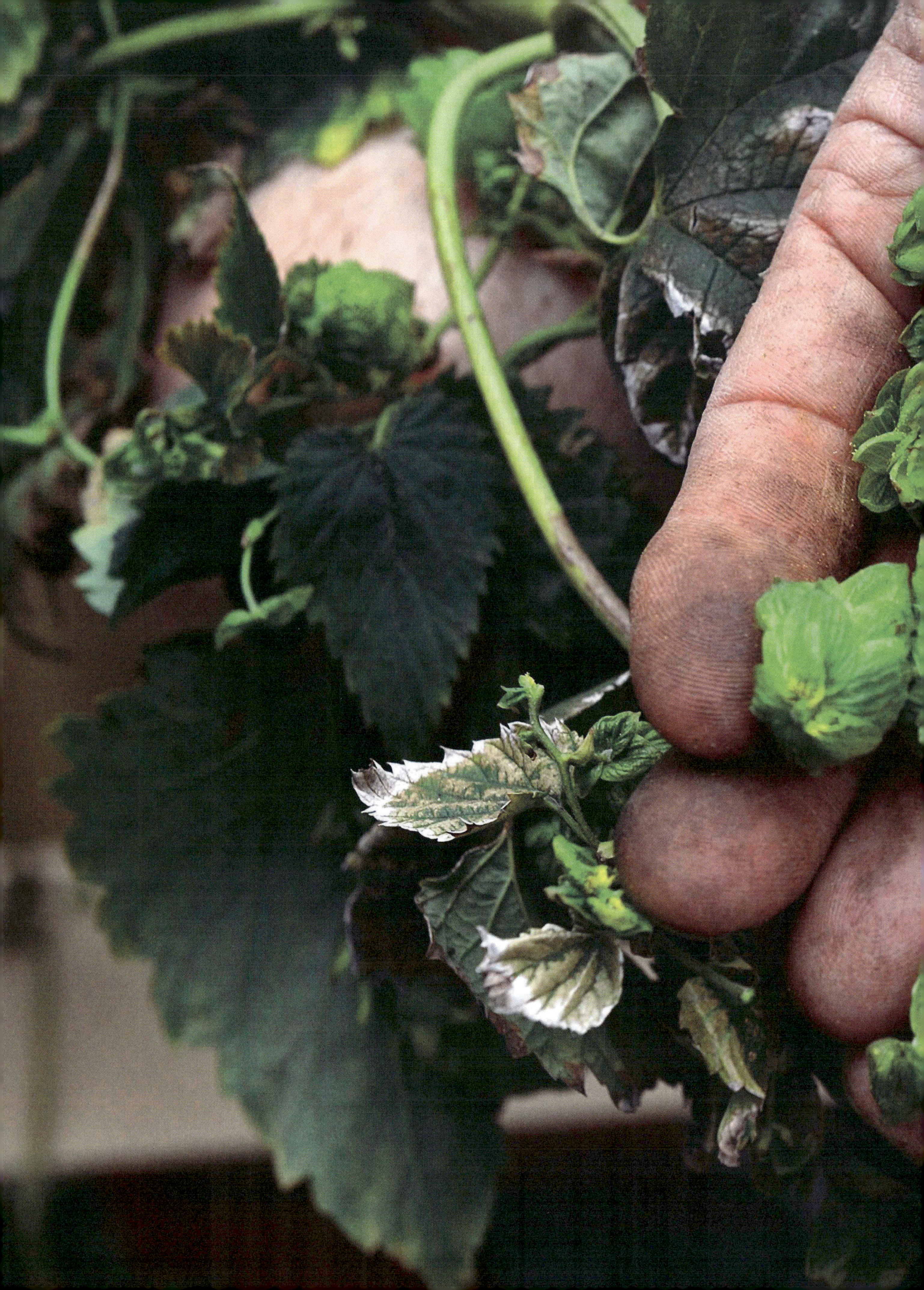

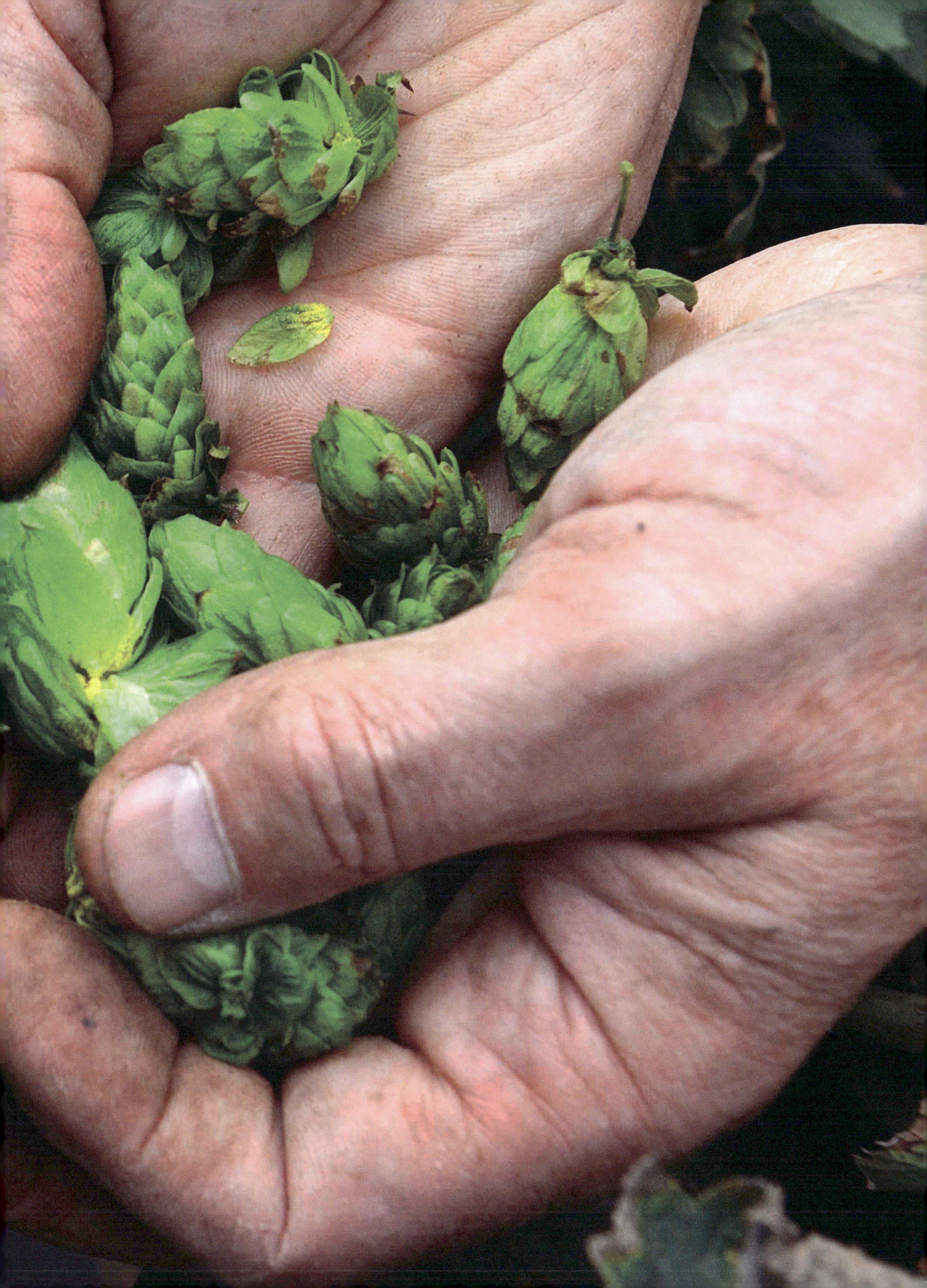

Hop cultivation

The hop vine, or rank, bounces up from the ground in April and usually reaches its final height in July. During that short season the plant will grow up to 7 or 8 metres tall. If conditions are right the hop plant can increase in height by up to 30 centimetres per day. The Latin name for hop, *Humulus lupulus*, is a reference to this high growth rate. The ancient Germanic term of '*Humulus*' means 'heaven' and '*Lupus*' is Latin for 'wolf'. Hop can only be grown at a latitude of between 35° and 55° as, the closer you get to the equator, there are fewer daylight hours. The Hop Devil symbolises the stormy wind that wreaks havoc and destroys hop fields.

Hop harvest

Harvesting is done between the end of August and the end of September, depending on weather conditions during the season. The hop is ready to harvest when the cone is completely closed but still has some elasticity. The hop cones are dried straight after picking. Speed is of the essence as the amount of natural liquids contained in the hop cone can encourage mould and cause the flowers to rot. Drying is done in a kiln.

Processing

The raw hop cones are used by the processing industry to prepare a variety of hop products:

Entire hop flowers
Its classic form is the dried hop cone, but only a few breweries are brave enough to go down this route. The reason: hop cones cannot be stored for long and may cause the loss of wort during the production process. A few breweries, De Ranke for example, use freshly harvested hop flowers.

Hop powder/hop pellets
Hop pellets, made with ground hop cones, are the most natural hop preparations. The hop powder is compressed and packaged using vacuum techniques or delivered in a metal canister filled with nitrogen or carbon dioxide. Preparing the hops in this way increases the bitter content by 10% to 15% compared to using pure hop cones thanks to the larger surface and greater ease of dissolving.

Hop oils
These are products made with essential hop oils. They are available as a water emulsion (oil droplets in water) and contain hop oils just like they occur in nature, with a highly aromatic character.

Source: Stibon, Nederlandse Bieropleiding, niveau 3, Les 7 (Stibon 2012) P.3-14.

An overview of hop varieties

The use of a specific hop variety determines the bitter quality and the hop aroma.

HOP TASTES

Hops are one of the ingredients that affect the bitterness of the beer as well as its aromas. The brewer has an almost endless arsenal of hop varieties at his disposal. This can be compared with cépage in grape cultivation. The use of specific hop varieties determines the degree of bitterness of the beer as well as the hop aromas.

→ **LUPULIN**
This substance is contained in the female hop flower and provides essential oils that prolong the storage period of the beer.

HOP VARIETIES	HOP TASTES
Germany and Czech Republic	
Hallertau Mittelfrüh (aroma hop)	zesty, wood, mint
Tettnanger (aroma hop)	zesty
Saaz (aroma hop)	zesty
United Kingdom	
East Kent Golding (aroma hop)	zesty, grassy, spicy
Challenger (double)	fruity, zesty
Fuggles (double)	wood, earthy
Target (double)	zesty, earthy, bitter
United States	
Cascade (double)	flowery, zesty, earthy
Citra (aroma)	fruity, zesty
Simcoe (double)	citrus, apricot
Amarillo (double)	flowery, tropical fruit, citrus
Centennial (double)	flowery, fruity
New Zealand	
Pacific Gem (bitter)	fruity, wood
Nelson Sauvin (double)	fruity, grassy, wine (Sauvignon blanc)

Hops in Belgium

In Poperinge and its surrounding areas the following types of hops are grown: aroma hops, bitter hops, dual purpose hops. 26 hop growers are still active in this region with fields covering a total of almost 60 hectares. Poperinge's mild maritime climate and its fertile soil, made up of sand and loam, provide the ideal basis to grow a rich palette of hop varieties. The Aalst area is one of the earliest hop growing regions. Nowadays six hop farmers are still based here. Together they cover an area of around eight hectares where aroma hops predominate (Hallertauer Mittelfrüh, Hallertauer Magnum, Saaz and Golding). Several breweries have also started to cultivate their own hops: Dubuisson, Palm Belgian Craft Brewers, Sint-Bernardus and others.

Source: www.belgischehop.be

Belgian Hop logo

The elevated level reached by Belgian beers is only possible due to the strong quality of the ingredients used, including Belgian hops. On 17 September 2011 a number of bodies (Vlaams Centrum voor Agro- en Visserijmarketing — Flemish centre for Agricultural and Fishery Marketing) (VLAM), the vzw (non-profit association) Vlaamse Hopregio, the vzw Hop and the City of Poperinge) jointly launched a campaign to encourage brewers to use Belgian hops.
Less and less of Belgium's arable land is used for growing hops. This has been going on for years to the point where the area covered is now less than 200 hectares. Really rather strange for a country that brews and exports huge quantities of beer. Both statements can only lead to one conclusion: not all of Belgian beer is brewed with Belgian hops.

The quality of Belgian hops has improved significantly in recent years. This is borne out by a new logo that serves as a hallmark of quality. Belgian brewers are not allowed to use this logo willy-nilly. When this quality logo adorns the label, it indicates that over half of the hops used in brewing the beer was grown in Belgium.

Hop is hip

'I am really surprised by the hype around hops these days. Hops used to be just an everyday ingredient,' finds Denis Dekeukeleire, a 'hops professor' at the University of Ghent. No-one is better placed to provide an analysis. After all, Denis Dekeukeleire is a globally renowned expert when it comes to the components contained in hops and their various applications. 'This plant is truly fascinating', this don commences his lecture. 'Did you know that lupuline, essential in brewing, contains around three hundred different components? It is an important bio-reactive agent, in other words, it becomes aware of its environment and reacts to it. In fewer than fourteen days, the flowers produce a powder, which is a concentrate of protective agents. This genetically determined survival mechanism allows the plant to survive viruses, bacteria, moulds, UV-rays... The more hostile the environment, the more effective the defence mechanism. The lupuline agent accounts for a third of the weight of the dry cone (flower) which must be a record in the flower world.' Lupuline contains bitter agents (alpha and beta acids) that are required for the taste, polyphenols to help the plant to survive and essential oils that determine the aroma and protect the plant from bacteria. Composition varies depending on the type of hop and its environment. We now have over two hundred varieties of hop. With bitter hops, the content of bitter agents will be between 10% and 25% whereas aroma hops contain a maximum of 5%. The 'dual purpose hops' are the best of two worlds, containing, as they do, over 10% of bitter agents with a highly desirable aroma. This professor is studying the unique structures of the iso-alpha acids and other components and their general effect on the conversion through boiling during the brewing process.

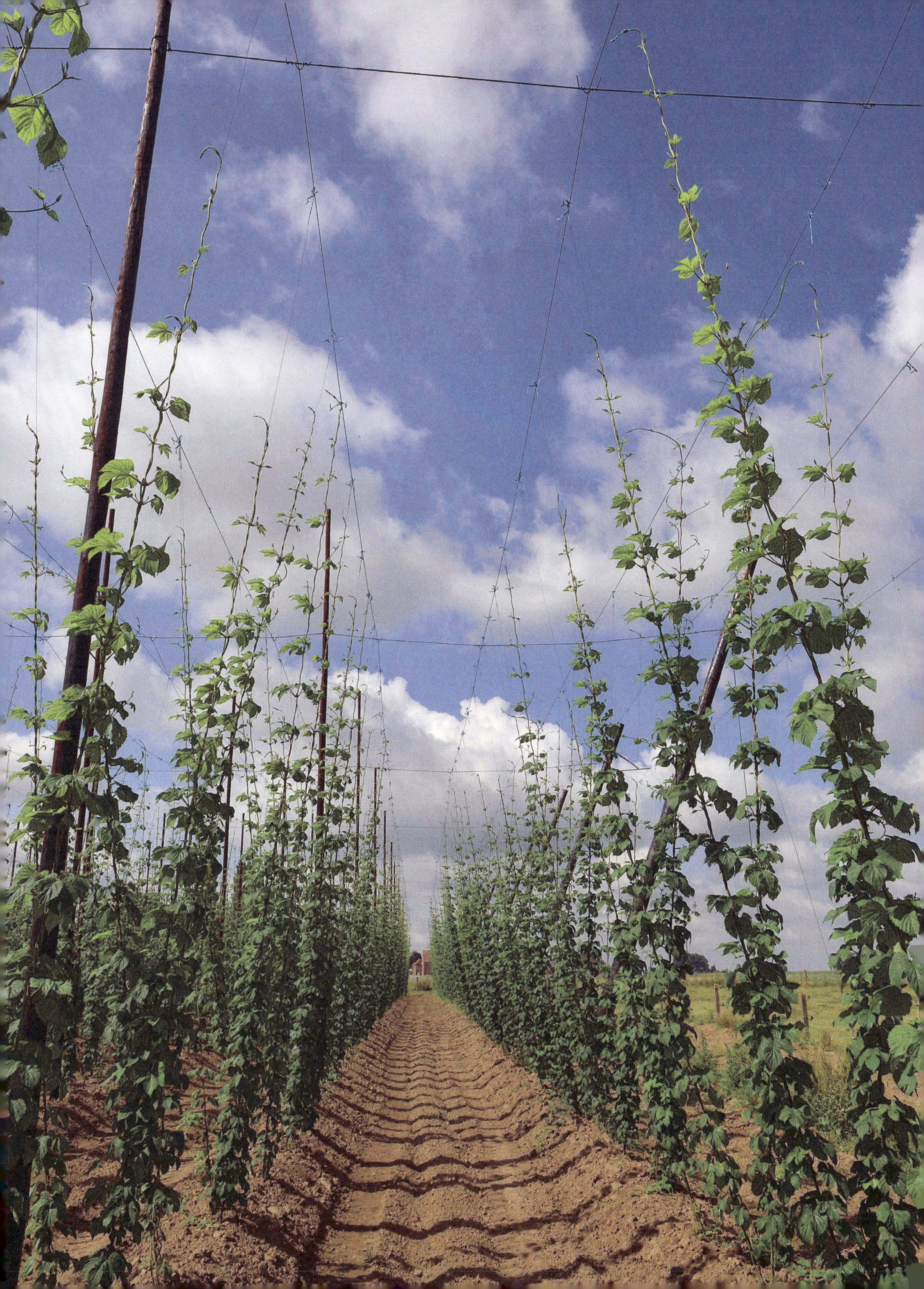

À la carte

....

Hops used to be an everyday ingredient. The brewer ordered his hops from his regular supplier and that was it. Much has changed since then. The heavily hopped IPAs (India Pale Ales) have conquered the world, we have witnessed the advent of dry hopping and the increasing popularity of exotic aroma hops. In the USA alone hop acreage has increased by 17%. Also, many brewers use four to ten times the quantity of hops than they used to, resulting in true 'hop bombs'. This has led to a hop shortage with prices going through the roof. In addition, the highly desirable aroma hops are more susceptible to diseases and so the yield per hectare is lower than for traditional bitter hops. This 'hop hype' brings its own dangers. If you are working with one variety of hop (*single hop*), you are more or less in charge of the process. If you use several varieties you end up with a more complex beer but often to the detriment of the taste. For example, the bitterness is toned down by the fruity aromas and the overall result is more uniform. Your beer is likely to come with an overriding aroma of lemon or grapefruit. Hops used to be a standard ingredient but now the composition is usually different for each beer. The hop-o-meter maps out every hop variety for you. Saaz, Amarillo and Cascade turn out to have a balanced composition but in Citra, the touches of citrus are dominant.

Beer 'cépage' – or the variety in ingredients

....

Hedwig Neven, chief brewer at Duvel Moortgat and University Professor at KU Leuven, feels it is fascinating how, using only pure basic materials, you can produce specialty beers with a broad and varied complexity. Every variety of hop has its own characteristics that, to a high degree, determine the taste and the aroma of the beer. The grape variety determines the unique character of a wine and, in the same way, the hop varieties used decide the taste and aroma of the beer. Hedwig Neven: 'Take a look at the Duvel Tripel Hop. When we want the character of the Citra hop to shine through, we will add this hop once more after the main fermentation in *dry hopping*. This ensures a continued strong presence of the fruity character in the beer.'

> *Hedwig Neven*

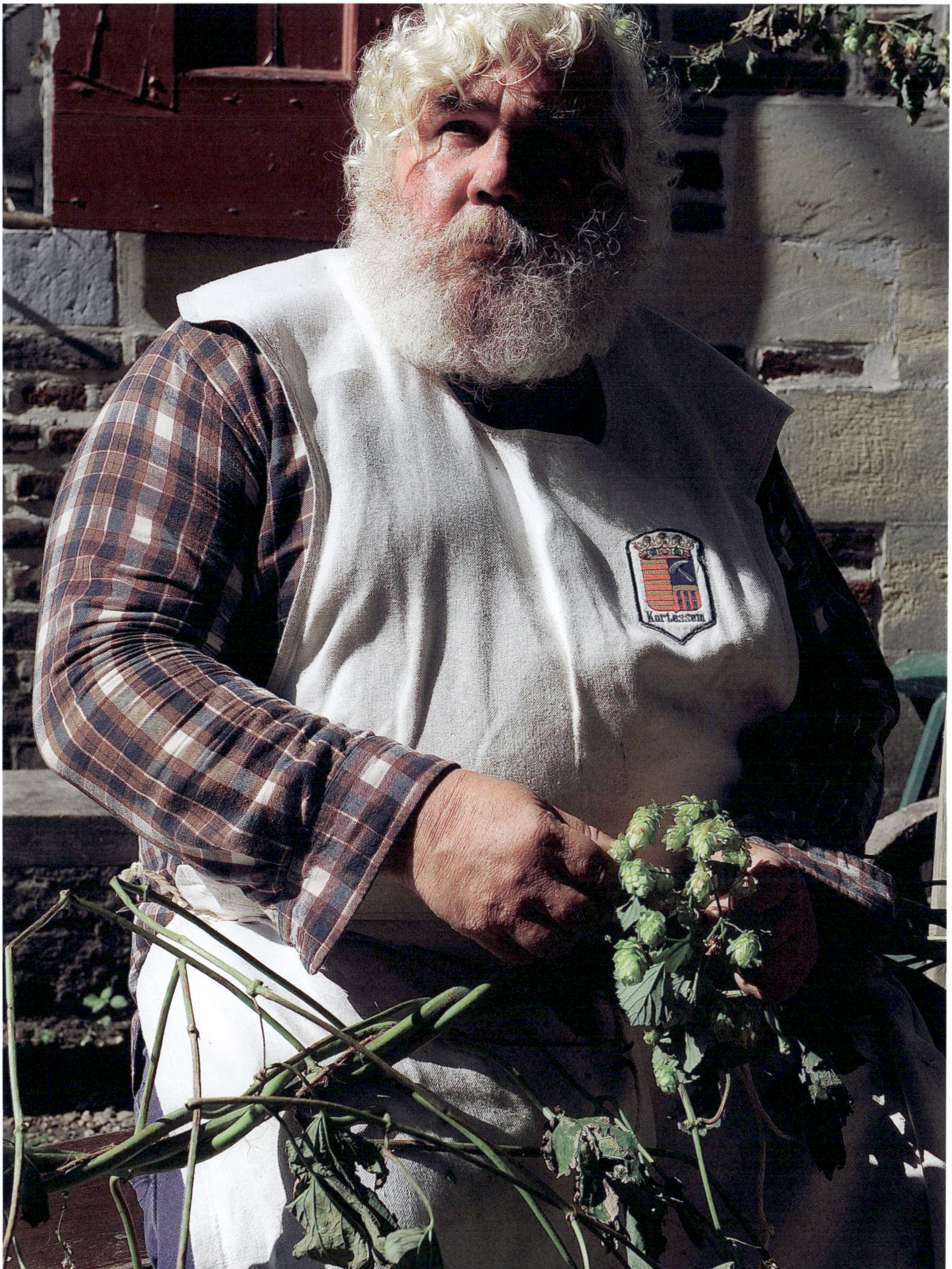
Kortessem

YEAST

The single-cell micro-organism called yeast is probably the main ingredient in beer. Microscopically small yeast cells convert the sugars present in the wort into alcohol and carbon dioxide. All breweries anxiously protect their yeast culture as this gives the beer its own identity, aroma and taste. With older Belgian beer styles (lambic and Flemish red-brown for example), that are also made with wild yeasts and bacterial flora, the fermentation process causes the beer to go sour (also see brewing process).

The 'soul' of the beer

'A brewer will sooner change his wife than his yeast.' A blunt statement but one that contains more than a grain of truth. To a large extent the yeast governs the soul of the beer. It is an important catalyst in the complex interaction between water, malt, hop and any other ingredients. Established breweries tend to keep a copy of their yeast strains in a yeast bank away from the premises. If a problem ever arises, they are able to start up a new yeast culture quickly so the beer is saved. There are hundreds of well-known beer yeasts. When a new yeast is discovered, the food technician investigates its suitability for brewing. Is it resistant to alcohol? Will it remain active up to the final fermentation? Does it convert the sugar from the wort into alcohol? Does the yeast sink to the bottom after fermentation so it can be removed properly? Test brewing allows experts to find the answers to questions such as these. They will, of course, also investigate the aromas given off by the yeast and whether unwanted aromas (*off flavours*) develop during fermentation. In the selection of brewer's yeast the parameters of 'fruitiness' and 'zestiness' are of the essence. Zestiness is a reference to the presence of phenolic aromas, also related to sulphuric components. Fruitiness means the presence of esters that generate aromas of banana, apple-anise, pineapple or apricot.

As a result of the boiling process, large protein particles float around the wort after mashing. The brewer will filter out these protein flakes after boiling.

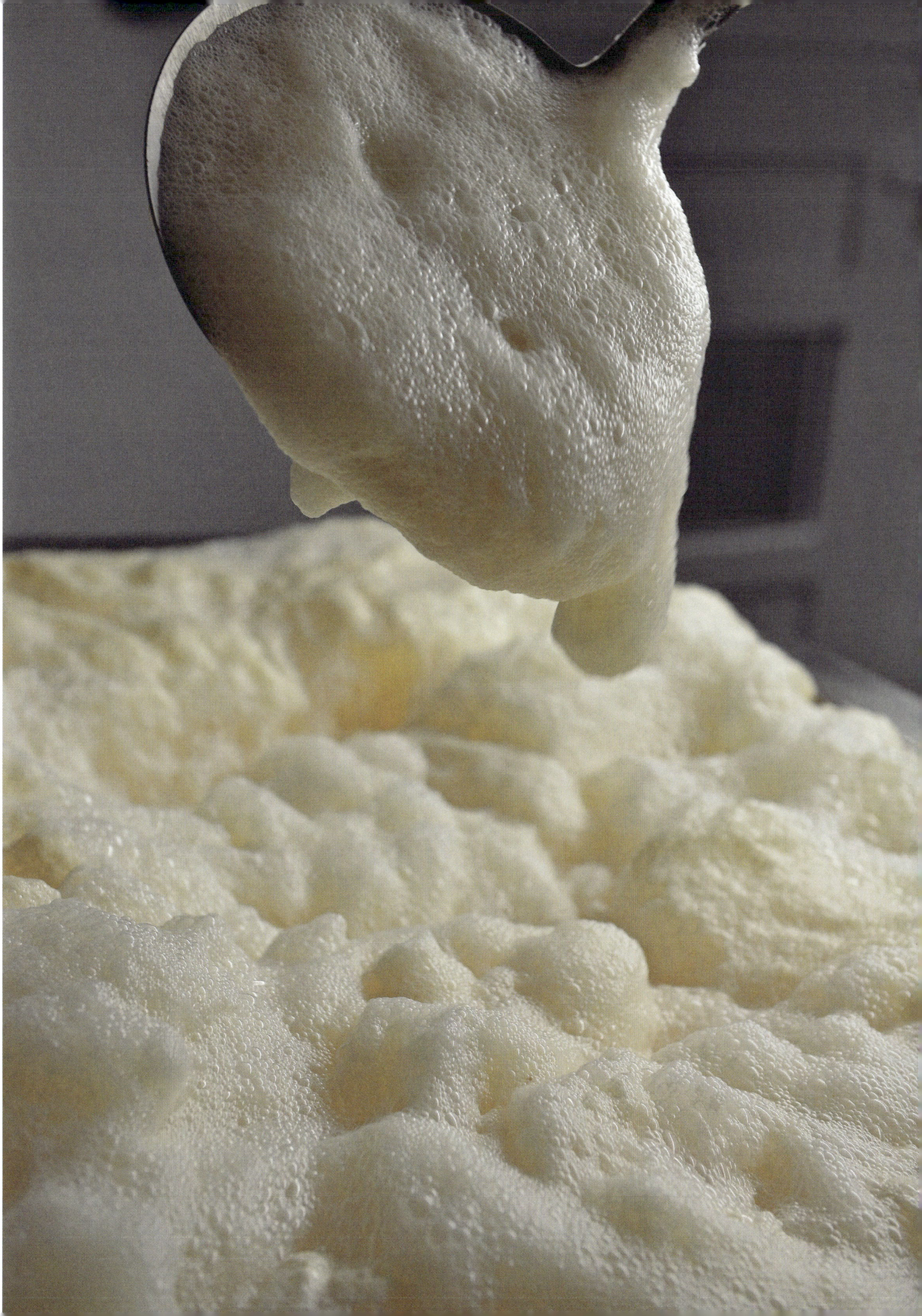

Belgian yeast?

Yeast is a living single-cell organism. Beer yeast is either *Saccharomyces cerevisiae* (top yeast) or *Saccharomyces carlsbergensis* (bottom yeast). A specific beer yeast produces alcohol easily and yields pleasant aromas. Traditionally, start-up brewers collect yeast from their colleagues. This yeast will gradually adjust to its new environment and start mutating, leading to the development of a specific beer yeast proprietary to the brewery. However, these yeast strains will still be related to each other. There is a Belgian yeast strain for example. Various factors affect the further development of the yeast: how it is fed and kept, the conditions in the brewery (hygiene), the raw ingredients, fermentation, brewing technology… It is perfectly possible to produce different beers using one and the same yeast strain. It is important that the yeast is in optimal physiological condition. Yeast experts investigate the DNA – the fingerprint – which allows them to draw up a family tree. During this process they will also look at how colonies are shaped. The yeast will then be used for brewing small volumes. Different yeast strains are added to wort contained in a number of fermentation tanks, enabling a comparison.

New beer

So, how do you go about developing a new beer? The brewer may base his new beer on an existing recipe. He or she may have a specific beer style and taste in mind but wants to build on it to create something new. Yeast plays a major role in this process. First of all, the brewer will see if he can achieve his objective with the use of existing brewery yeasts. Is this a high-quality yeast? Does it contain a sufficient number of young, active cells? Or do we have to go in search of a new yeast? Beginner-brewers often opt for a dry yeast available from trade stores. The disadvantage of this type of yeast is that its aromas and tastes differ from that of a fresh yeast. After all, it has been dried, which causes stress to the yeast. Established breweries prefer the propagation method, whereby they continuously grow fresh yeast in the propagator. You can also recuperate yeast from previous brews and store it for a limited time in yeast storage tanks. As stated before, brewing technology determines the success of the yeast and the resulting brew. How are you brewing and what do you use? And what is the beer the brewer is aiming for? If a new yeast is called for, the brewer has to invest a fair amount of time and money into research and development. Don't treat it as a race against time. Work on the basis that you won't get it right first time around. Yeast experts are best placed to conduct this type of research. They have plenty of time to select different yeasts and study how they develop during the brewing process. They will take into account the brewing method and the technology available. Each yeast is identified beforehand with a code and has its own log book describing its specific properties. It takes months, sometimes even years, to perfect a new beer. Such a beer needs room to 'grow'. After a while the brewer manages to deliver a beer with a consistent taste. He has to take different factors into account all the time, changes in the quality of the raw materials (vintages) for example. Market trends also come into play. Beer can be allowed to have a slightly hoppier taste if the beer drinker expects it. At the end of the day, the brewer makes a beer for himself, that he can support wholeheartedly, a beer with its own soul and the signature of the brewery. Belgian brewers are looking for balance in the glass. If the beer is perfectly balanced you are more likely to order another. Extreme beers are interesting but less suitable for daily consumption. After all, we prefer to drink what we really like.

Open fermentation

Up to a few years ago, breweries like Orval, De Koninck and Affligem used open fermentation. Cylindro conical fermentation tanks (CCT) have since been introduced and 'closed' fermentation is now the norm amongst brewers who would like to see their beer protected from oxygen and want to avoid any risk of contamination. However, we also see a handful of microbrewers making a deliberate choice for the traditional open fermentation method. This is different from the production of lambic through spontaneous fermentation as the brewer does add yeast. The beer ferments in open basins instead of closed tanks. These basins are usually long and shallow. Consequently there is little pressure coming from the height of the tank and the amount of liquid contained in it. The yeast is less susceptible to stress and forms more fruity esters. Open fermentation gives a broader taste spectrum provided that it is done correctly and that the process really suits the beer. The fermentation in open basins causes more carbon dioxide to escape from the beer. Carbon dioxide hampers the development of the yeast and delays its reactions. Fermentation is therefore different in open basins. The disadvantage of this production process is that you have to work in possibly an even more hygienic manner as the risk of contamination is greater compared to the use of a completely closed circuit.

Marc Coesens of the Liefmans brewery keeps a watchful eye on the fermentation process.

Cleaning

Most brewers shield their wort and beer from oxygen and contaminating substances. All tanks and pipes are airtight. The gas is able to escape without descending into the beer and it is impossible for air to enter. With open fermentation, the opposite occurs: the wort is in contact with the ambient air across a large surface. Some brewers prefer this traditional way of working. They skim the yeast from the top-fermented beer to re-use it in subsequent brews, giving a second life to their active yeast. Respect for hygiene is crucial to avoid contamination and oxidation, so the tanks and pipework have to be cleansed thoroughly. Advocates of open fermentation include microbreweries; Brasserie de Bastogne, Seizoensbrouwerij Chris Vandewalle and Brasserie de Rulles for example. Gregory Verhelst, who brews with Brasserie de Rulles, was instantly convinced of the benefits of open fermentation after serving an apprenticeship with the De Koninck brewery that had just switched to closed fermentation tanks. 'We compared the aromas achieved by open and closed fermentation and it was immediately obvious that you cannot achieve the same quality with closed fermentation,' is Gregory's opinion. 'In an open, shallow basin (maximum depth of 1.20 metres) the yeast is less susceptible to stress and produces far more fruity esters. The aromas are more delicate and appealing. Add to this the re-fermentation in the bottle and you get the type of beer that I want.'

Way of working rather than recipe

Every advantage has its disadvantage, however. Open fermentation requires more labour and is therefore costlier. You also need a well-insulated space that can be kept at a stable temperature. 'We sand down the fermentation basins by hand', Gregory laughs. 'You're not in this business for an easy life.' He emphasises that beer is a process rather than a recipe. 'Give me different equipment and the beer will be different.' The effect of the yeast on aroma and taste also varies quite considerably. In some beers you barely notice the yeast, in others it comes to the fore. Gregory finds that his beers are quicker to ferment compared to the closed fermentation method. They are also more homogenous. The Rulles beers are quite dry and mild. 'Over here we smell and see everything that goes on,' he explains. 'From experience and based on gut feeling, we know exactly when the beer is ready to go into cold storage. We pump the beer across to the lager tanks at exactly the right moment. The great aspect of brewing is that you enter into sensory contact with the yeast.' He uses a sieving spoon to skim off the yeast floating on the top. 'And now, witness the start of the next brew,' he laughs.

Something is brewing at De Kroon

Dad Freddy and son Filip Delvaux are members of the select club of beer experts that ensures Belgium's excellent reputation in the beer world. Freddy started his career as a brewmaster at AB Inbev before founding the beer laboratory at the University of Louvain which he headed for dozens of years. Filip was to follow in his footprints. Father and son act in an advisory capacity to the top Belgian breweries in the field of technology. Both are predominantly known for their expertise in the area of fermentation. If you want to test which yeast is best suited to your beer, if you are looking for a new yeast or if you just want to know how a particular yeast will develop based on the recipe that you have in mind, Delvaux is sure to have the answer to your question.

Beers from the olden days

Freddy and Filip have opened up their own Biercentrum (Beer Centre) in the heart of Neerijse in the vicinity of Leuven. De Kroon was a brewery that until 1983 predominantly produced table beers and regional beers, such as 'dubbel witbier'. A new microbrewery has now been set up on the site. This is where Freddy and Filip Delvaux are brewing their own beers on a limited scale and carry out testing on behalf of breweries. The Centre also includes a well-equipped laboratory. De Kroon has grown into a fully-fledged beer experience centre where you can join guided tours, discover the history of the brewery, learn how to taste beer and enjoy the Delvaux beers. Job (6%) is an unfiltered beer with fruity aromas of yeast. The Super Kroon (6.5%) is a dry, amber-yellow pale ale with a malty aroma of caramel, hop aromas, pronounced yeast aromas (pineapple, apple, truffle) followed by a delicate bitterness. Delvaux (8.5%) is a mild, slightly bitter special blonde, full in the mouth, with a vinous yeast, a complex fruity bouquet (Chardonnay) and touches of citrus and tropical fruits. De Kroon is also often engaged in 'translating' ancient recipes into modern beers: an ongoing investigation into the history of brewing. 'Great fun', Filip enthuses. 'We interpret vintage recipes, study how brewing was done in those days and then adjust the recipes based on modern-day technical requirements and consumer taste.' One of their achievements is the re-launch of the 'Seefbier', very popular in the Seef quarter of Antwerp before the Second World War. They researched far and wide and eventually found a yeast that originates in the bakers' world.

of useable yeasts. 'It has become a sport,' he smiles. We are now taking a one-hundred year leap back in time. One century ago, bottom-fermented beers (pils) pushed out the traditional top-fermented beers. Their advantage was that they remained stable for longer and turned sour less quickly. 'Before the introduction of pils the brewers mainly used mixed fermentation to extend the storage period', Filip explains. 'Bring to mind the cutting (blending) of young beer with soured old beer, as happens with the West-Flemish red-brown beers. The popular "tonnekensbier" (non-sparkling beer poured from wooden barrels, or 'tons') was consumed as quickly as possible, even before it had completed fermentation. Due to the lack of refrigeration facilities the beer did not store very well, especially in summer. A larger dosage of hops was added to the beer in an attempt to prevent the formation of lactic acid bacteria. Our Super Kroon harks back to this pre-war beer taste.' Each component affects the beer in its own way. This is why, when a new beer is being developed, regular comparisons are carried out between the same brews using different varieties of yeast, hop or malt. This can result in large differences. For example, replace the standard yeast used for a pils with a more aromatic variety and you get impressions of a specialty beer.

Mystery yeast

Filip is a bio engineer, just like his Dad. He gained his PhD on the topic of 'cloudiness in white beers' and was engaged for many years in carrying out audits on behalf of breweries. 'We take beer samples and analyse them,' he tells us. 'This is how we get involved in all aspects of the brewing process: the ingredients, production, technology and biochemistry... in summary, everything that may affect the quality of the beer. A brewer may want to invest in a new brewhall. In that case we will advise on the switch-over between the old and the new equipment. When you make a major change such as this, you always run the risk that the character of the beer might be different before and after.'

Yeast is by far the most mysterious component of beer. You can see the yeasts at work in an open cooling basin or through the window of a yeast tank, you can observe them under a microscope and smell the aromatic components they produce. Nevertheless, yeast is less 'tangible' than hops or malt. Beers can be recognised by the home yeast used by the brewery. This yeast is largely responsible for the DNA of the beer. Yeasts are found everywhere in nature. From time to time, Filip scrapes down the beams of the old brewery in search

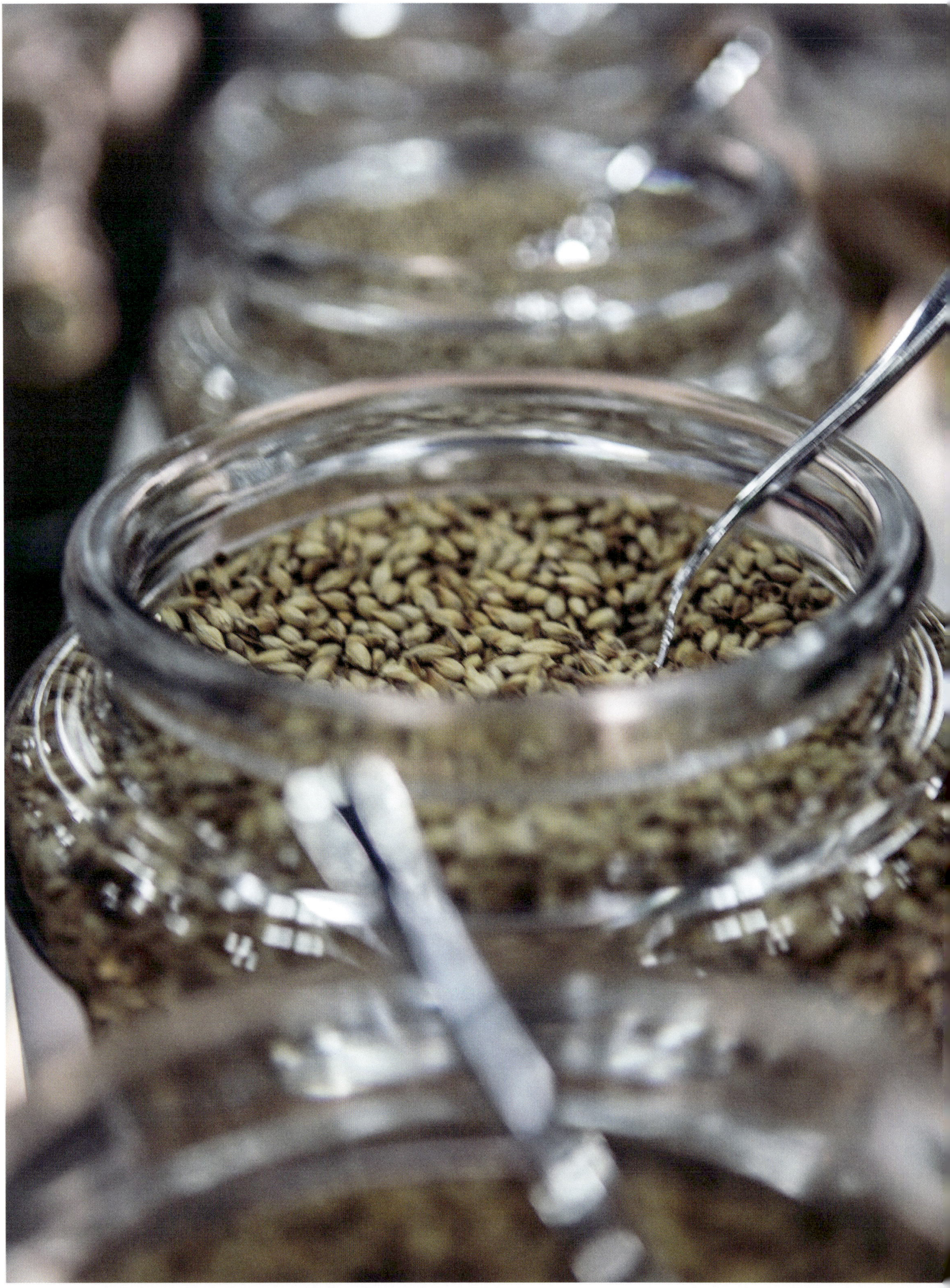

GRAINS AND MALT

Malted

Malt

In the main, brewers use barley especially cultivated for brewing, as barley has a layer of chaff, or husk, that sticks to the kernel (this means that barley stands up well to transportation and is easier to process in the malt works). The husk forms a natural filtration bed during the brewing process. Barley malt has a high return and provides an elevated level of enzymes, required for the conversion of starch into fermentable sugars. Barley (malt) provides all the nourishment required by the yeast during fermentation. Take note, not all barley is suitable for use in brewing. The brewers pose high demands as to protein content, grain size, capability to germinate and homogeneity.

Most of Europe's barley is grown in France. Talking in wine terms, the 'grand cru' of brewing barley comes from a region just to the South of Paris.

Wheat

Used in the brewing process either as wheat malt or unmalted wheat. Contains far less starch and more proteins compared to barley. Wheat gives the beer a characteristic taste that is both sharply sour and mildly sweet and yields a firm collar of froth. Both white beer and lambic are brewed with unmalted wheat, amongst other ingredients.

Spelt

Is a large-grained wheat variety and one of the oldest known grains cultivated by man. Spelt has recently grown in popularity (especially with those who like organic food). Spelt gives a pale colour and a robust but fresh mouthfeel.

Rye

Gives the beer a slightly fuller and zestier taste.

Oats

Lends a slightly greasy touch to the beer. Brewing with 100% oats is not particularly successful. Therefore, oats are always mixed in with barley. .

MALTING

Malting means preparing grain (usually barley) for brewing. The barley grains cannot be used in their natural form. The maltster will germinate the barley grains under the influence of water, heat and air. As soon as the enzymes have started to develop, the maltster will stop the germination process by drying the grain. After the malting process, the word to use is malt (barley malt, wheat malt, oats malt…).

Storage and sorting

When the barley arrives at the maltings, it is sorted, foreign elements are removed and the barley is stored in silos. Freshly harvested barley is not ready for malting as the kernels are not yet capable of germinating.

Steeping
The kernel of the barley grain will only germinate when the liquid content is 30%. This is why the barley is steeped in water for 24 to 48 hours.

Germination
After steeping, the barley will begin to sprout. This process takes five to six days and requires the grain to be aerated. The 'green malt' thus produced is turned over regularly. The maltster imitates nature by providing moist and warm weather conditions. The barley will begin to sprout as it would normally do in the spring. This germination process encourages the formation of proteases and amylases. Both are enzymes that, during the brewing process, will break down the protein and starch molecules.

Oastings
The maltster puts a stop to the germination before the barley kernels turn into a small plant. To this end he will add hot air during oasting. The higher the oasting temperature, the darker the malt. Pale malt varieties, pilsner malt and pale ale malt for example, are dried at low temperatures. If you increase the oasting temperature the malts will take on a darker colour. From light to dark: Vienna malt, Münchener, caramel malt… The maltster may caramelise part of the sugar freed in the process. At 110 °C all the enzymes are rendered inactive. To

achieve higher (read: darker) colours, the maltster will roast the malt. The choice of malt is largely responsible for the colour of the beer.

Polishing
The grain sprouts are removed after oasting. This is what we call polishing.

Storage
After malting, the malt is not yet ready to be used in brewing. It requires a rest period of approx. six weeks.

Malt, the silent helper
The furore around hops, thanks to the advent of exotic aroma hops, has reached such heights that you'd almost forget the importance of malt for the colour, the aroma and the taste of the beer. Visit a brewery and you are reminded straight away. The characteristic 'brewery smell' is mainly due to heated malt. Many breweries used to have their own maltings. The typical tall chimney you often see is a reminder of that era. Malting has now grown into a separate business. Over the years, industrial maltings have been created. They predominantly work for the major pils breweries. A handful of malt houses have developed specialty malts in accordance with the specific 'lastenboek', or list of requirements, of a particular brewery.

Malting
The least complicated process is the conversion of barley into pils malts. The barley is stored in silos and cleansed thoroughly. All extraneous grains and broken grains are removed. The brewing barley is then transferred to steeping basins with a humidity of 15% to 45% before moving to the germination chamber, where, thanks to the judicious addition of water and conditioned air, the ideal conditions for germination are created. The mass is stirred regularly to aerate it so the barley does not clump together. During germination, insoluble proteins and starch molecules are converted into soluble proteins and starch molecules. 'We must interrupt the natural germination process at exactly the right moment,' confirms Karl Dingemans of the eponymous maltings in Stabroek near Antwerp. The green malt is now transported to the oast house to be dried. 'Oasting is done by drying the malt in the oast. As a professional I know the exact amount of time the germinated barley has to spend on the oasting floor. This drying process determines the eventual colour and taste of the beer.

The sprouts are removed immediately after drying and used in cattle feed. The finished malt is stored in silos and transported to the breweries, generally in bulk.'

Roasting

Dark malts, caramel malt for example, are produced by roasting the green malt directly in the tin. This process can be compared with roasting coffee beans. The maltster sees, feels and tastes when the malt is ready. Stout is an example of a beer that derives its bitterness from the use of roast malt varieties. It is based on a very dark, almost charred malt with a taste reminiscent of coffee. Without a 'feel' for the malt, the finesse that is inherent to beer will never be achieved. The taste and colour of the roast malt result from a chemical reaction between proteins and sugars that occurs when the malt is heated. The maltster pairs his scientific knowledge with experience and intuition. He sees, feels, tastes and learns.

Quality time

Several breweries, both in Belgium and abroad, frequently carry out experiments with different types of malt. The brewers seek the advice of the maltster when they are developing new beers. As many as 20 parameters are used in the evaluation of malt. 'At the end of the day, the brewer will make his selection based on the criteria that he feels are most important to his beer', maltster Karl Dingemans tells us. 'The range of malts we offer is targeted as much as possible towards the requirements of the brewer. We also have to take into account the quality of the raw ingredients which is different every season. We may have to adjust our germination schedules, buy from growers in different regions or at other times of the year, etcetera. You are working with a natural product after all.' The maltster does not skimp on time to achieve a good result. It takes around 30 days to steep a batch. The barley will then sprout for five to five-and-a-half days and spend at least one day on the drying floor, sometimes one-and-a-half days. Then, dark malts will spend up to three hours in the roasting centrifuge at 125 °C. Just imagine the lovely smells.

Unmalted

Unmalted products are grains and other plants that have not undergone a malting process but do help to increase the extract content.

Maize

An inexpensive basic ingredient. It gives the beer a clear colour and a milder (and fuller) taste. Maize in its original state cannot be added to the brewing kettle: it is too high in fat and the outer layer of the grain is too hard. This is why brewers often use ground maize, maize flour or pre-stiffened maize flakes.

Rice

High in starch and low in protein. Rice ensures that the beer has less body (making it easier to drink) and gives it a rather dry taste, doing more justice to the hop. The beer will also develop a lighter taste.

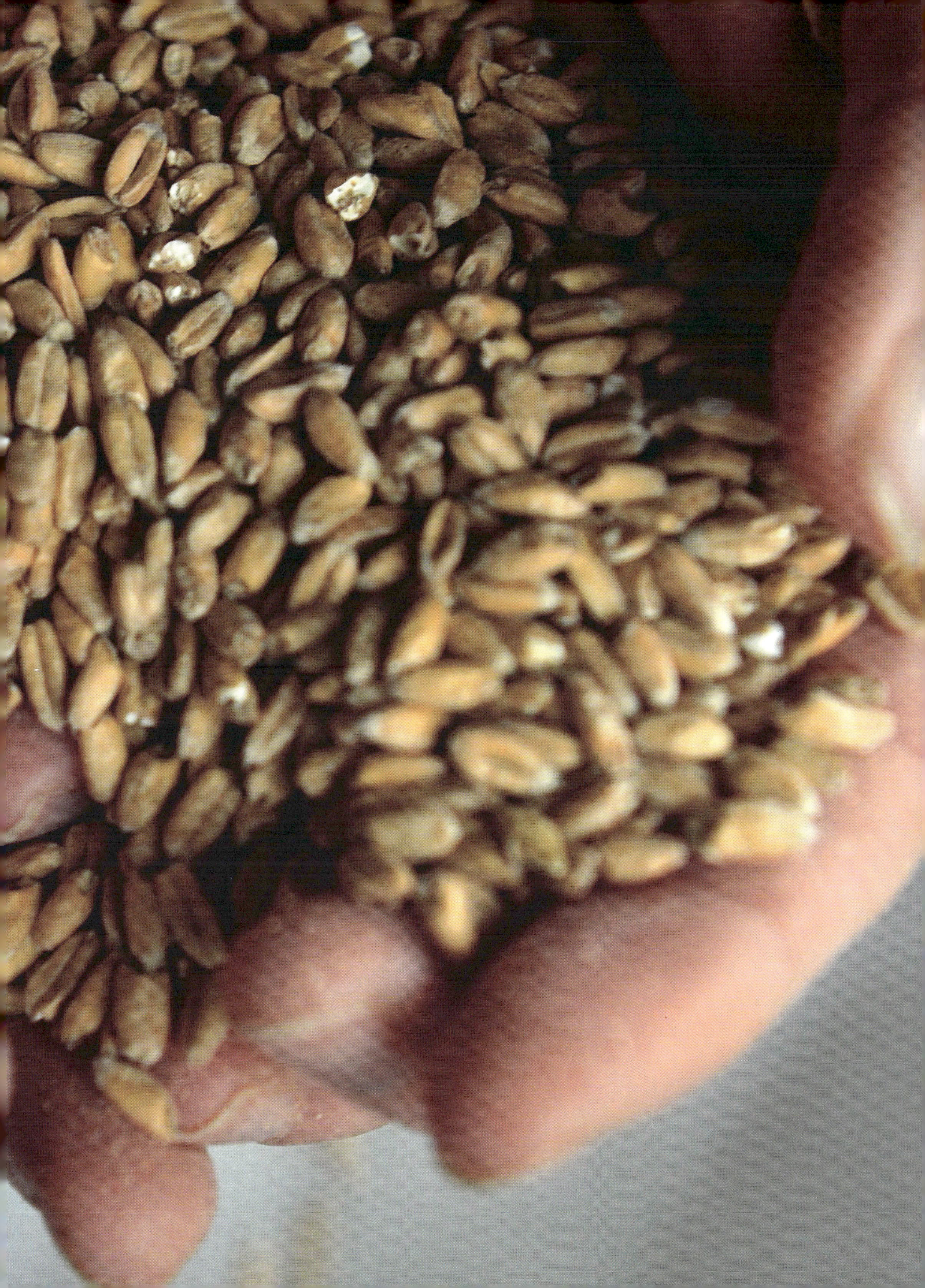

Caramalt

SUGARS AND FRUITS USED TO INCREASE THE TASTE

Sugars, sugar syrup and honey are all sugar extracts not included in the mashing process. Their purpose is to increase the level of sugar in the beer. They can be added at any time during the brewing process. The main points to consider when using sugar: At which stage are the sugars added? During the boiling process; before or after fermentation? What is the composition of the sugars? Are they simple sugars (monosaccharides) or compound sugars (disaccharides)? What are the aromatic components?

Just like honey, fruits provide sugars (extract) and aromatic components. In fruits, the presence of aromatic components is often far more noticeable than in honey. For the use of fruit in brewing, you can choose natural fruits, fruit extracts or aroma extracts. The effect of the fruit depends on the stage at which it is added. If the dosage takes place before fermentation, the character of the beer will be substantially different. These fruits are often used in brewing: apple, peach, raspberry, banana, cherry.

Adding sugar at Brasserie Caulier.

HERBS

In addition to hop, brewers use herbs or herbal mixtures, called gruit (or gruut) to lend a different taste to the beer. For example, many white beers are improved by adding a pinch of coriander. The brewer might also use curaçao liqueur or dried orange peel to provide a fresh, citrusy touch. Other herbs used in beer are Myrica, liquorice, rosemary, cinnamon, cloves, sage and bay.

Coffee can also be classified as a herb. It is often used in the production of stouts and porter beers. The taste profile of these beers is not dissimilar to that of coffee. This is due to the proportion of toasted/roast malt that gives a roasted flavour to the beer, as we also find in coffee.

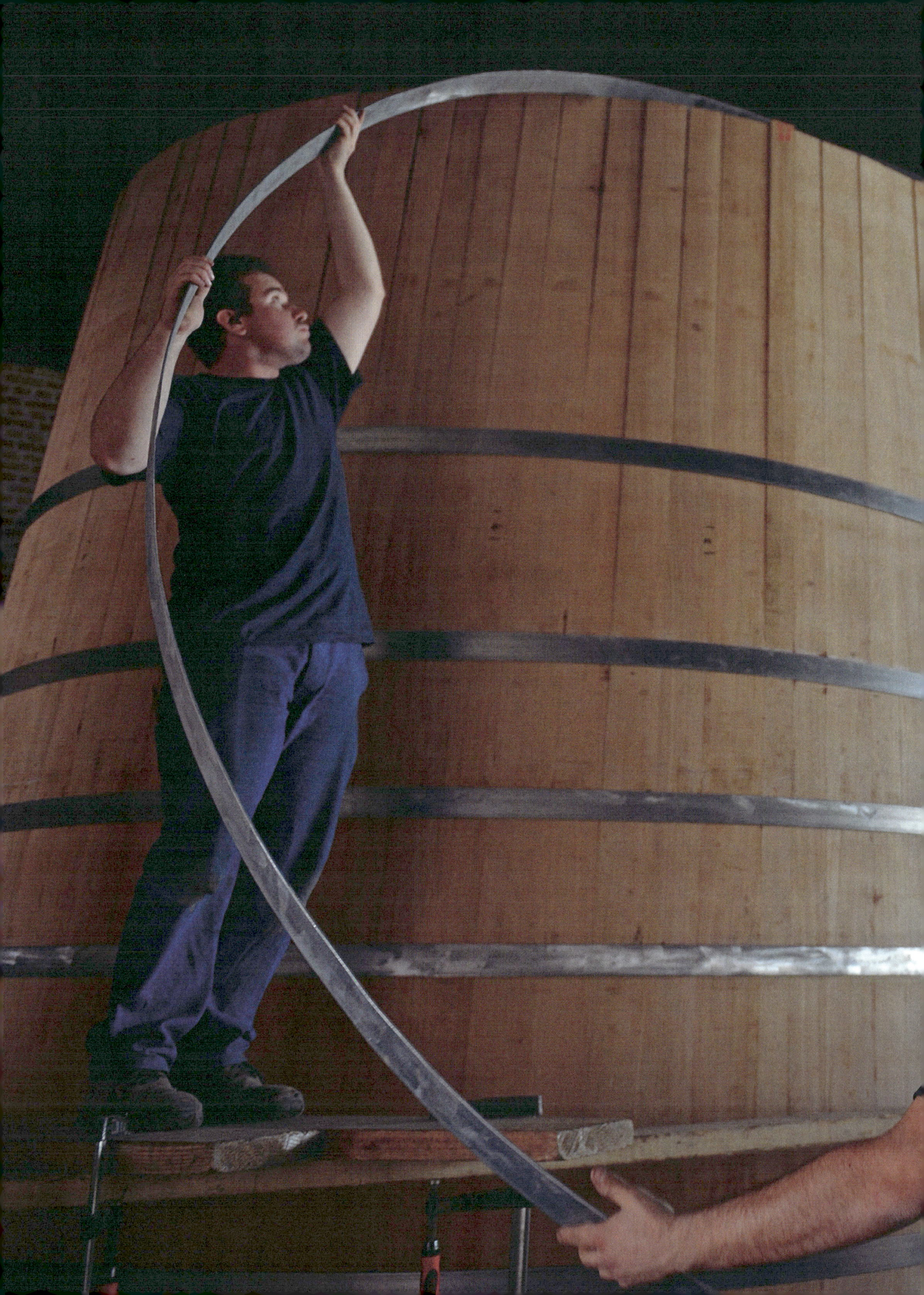

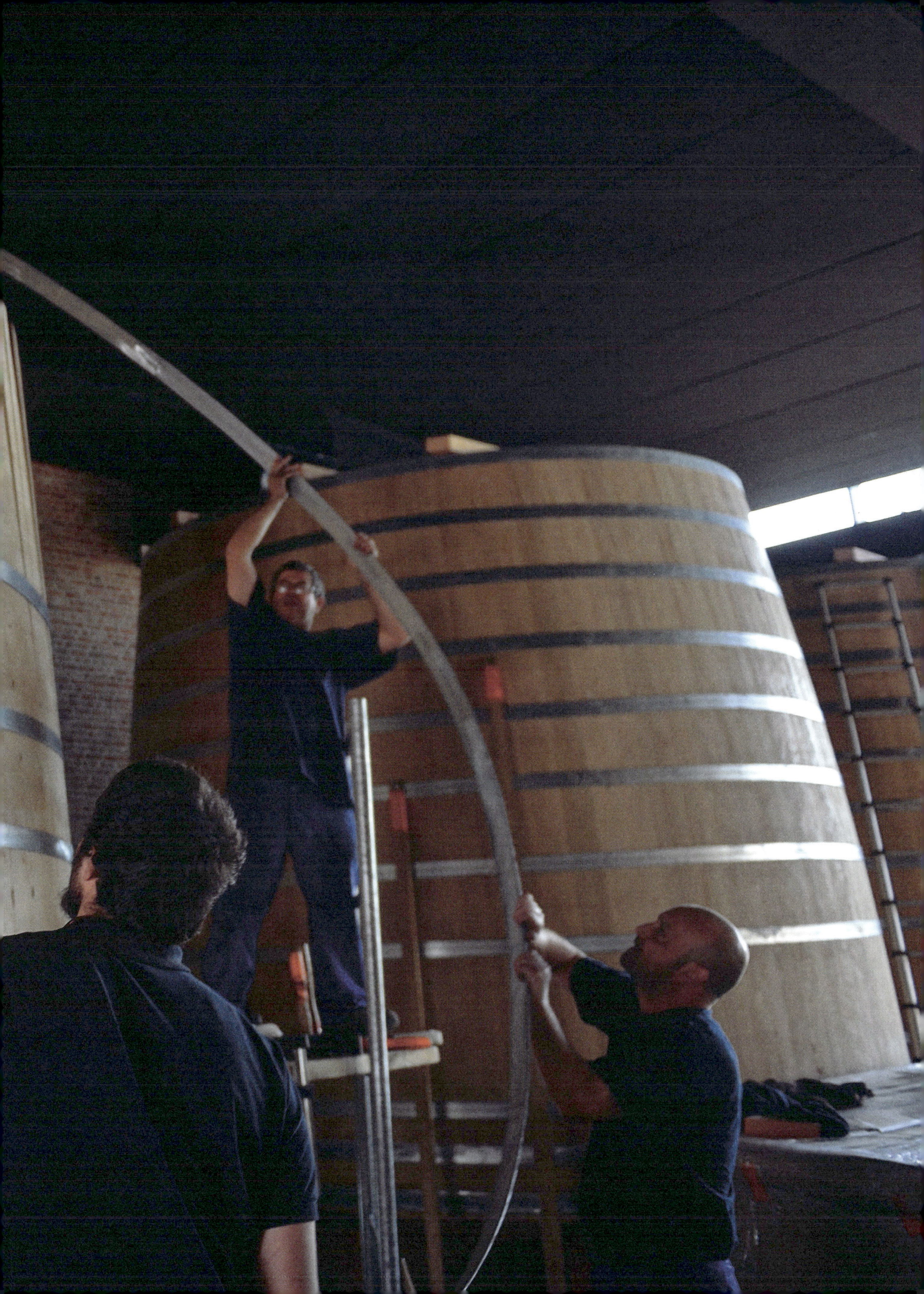

WOODEN BARRELS AND FOEDERS: JUST A BEER BARREL OR AN INGREDIENT?

Most wooden barrels are made from oak, sometimes from chestnut, which costs less. The oak comes from trees that are 120 to 150 years old. The wood is cleaved (no sawing involved) into planks that form the staves of the barrel. Only wood from the core of the tree will be used. Around four cubic metres of wood are needed to produce one cubic metre of stave wood. Wine and beer barrels are primarily made from summer and winter oaks. White American oak is traditionally used for bourbon and you will also come across it in the beer world.

Very large barrels are called **foeders** (also see Rodenbach). The staves of these huge barrels may be up to 10 centimetres thick. The largest barrels in the brewery contain a maximum of 200 hectolitres, with a few exceptions. Oak has different qualities depending on its provenance. The type of oak tree, its age and growing speed all determine its physical characteristics (permeability, size of the apertures in the wood …) and the chemical composition (tannins, aromatic substances).

Oak that is freshly cleaved comes with a humidity of 50% that has to be reduced to 15%. This is done by means of a drying and ripening process that can take from one-and-a-half up to three years. This enhances the taste of the stave wood and reduces the amount of bitter tannins emanating from it. Oven-dried oak is not suitable for use in beer barrels. Barrel making is a craft on its own. France produces around 800,000 new barrels every year. There are no longer barrel making firms in Belgium. However, Rodenbach and Boon still employ 'coopers' to maintain their foeders. The inside of an oak barrel contains both soluble and insoluble substances. Certain elements from the oak affect the taste of the beer. In this sense, wood could be included in the list of ingredients. The strong blond Cornet beer, made by Palm Belgian Craft Brewers, relies on wood to make an important contribution to the taste.

New barrels cannot be used in beer making. New oak contains too high a proportion of tannins that give an extremely sour bitterness to the beer. Unlike beer, wine is not made with the use of hops. Therefore, a wine can benefit from an extra dose of bitterness.

Wooden barrels can be coated or drained. These drained barrels will only produce a good beer once they have been filled two or three times. Every single brewer uses recycled barrels. A wide range of barrels can be used with the exception of those used for either wine or spirits made with herbs. It is up to the brewer to make a choice (also see *barrel aged* or wood-matured beers in Chapter 5).

Stibon, Nederlandse Bieropleiding, niveau 3, Les 7 (Stibon 2012) p. 15-18

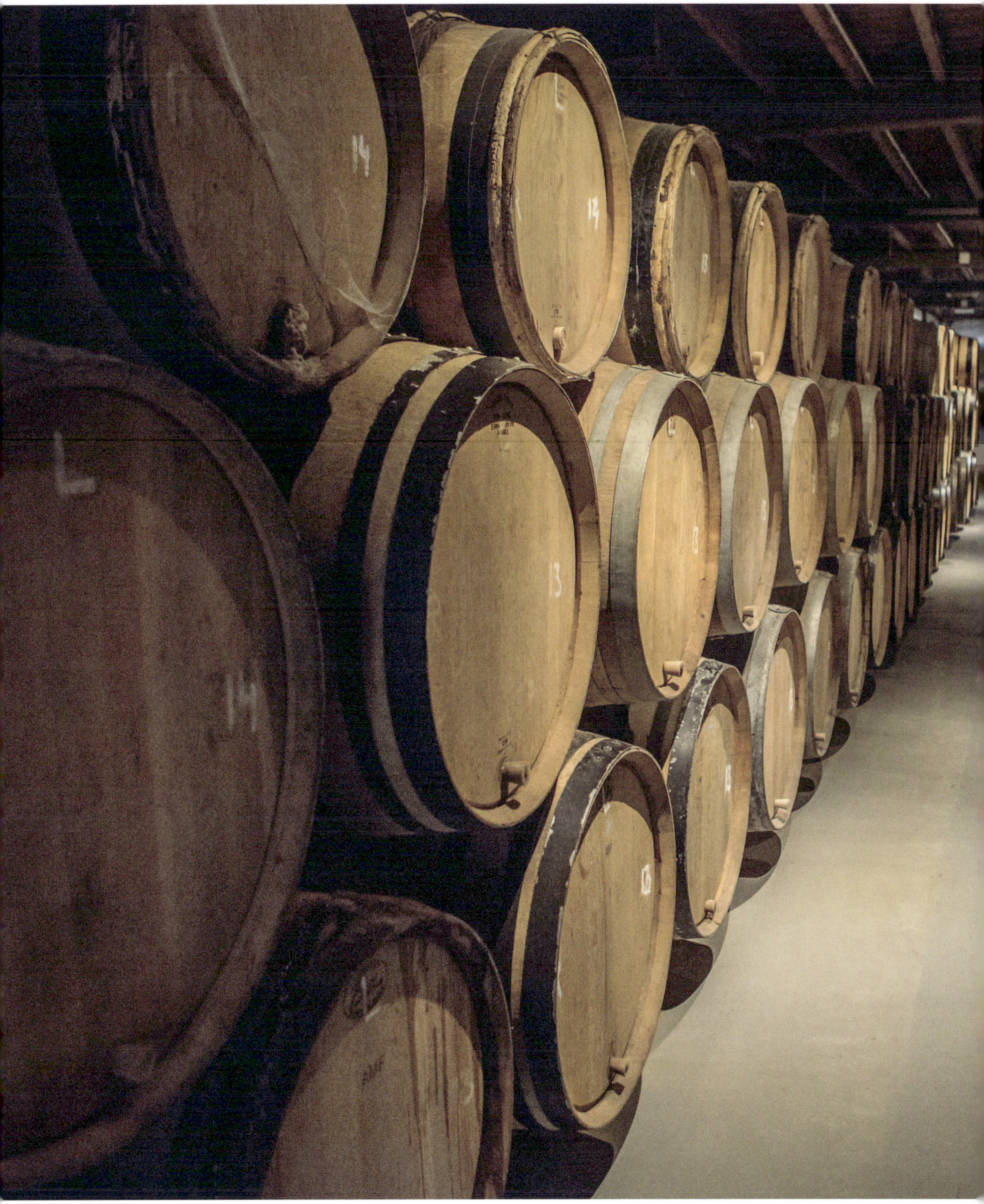

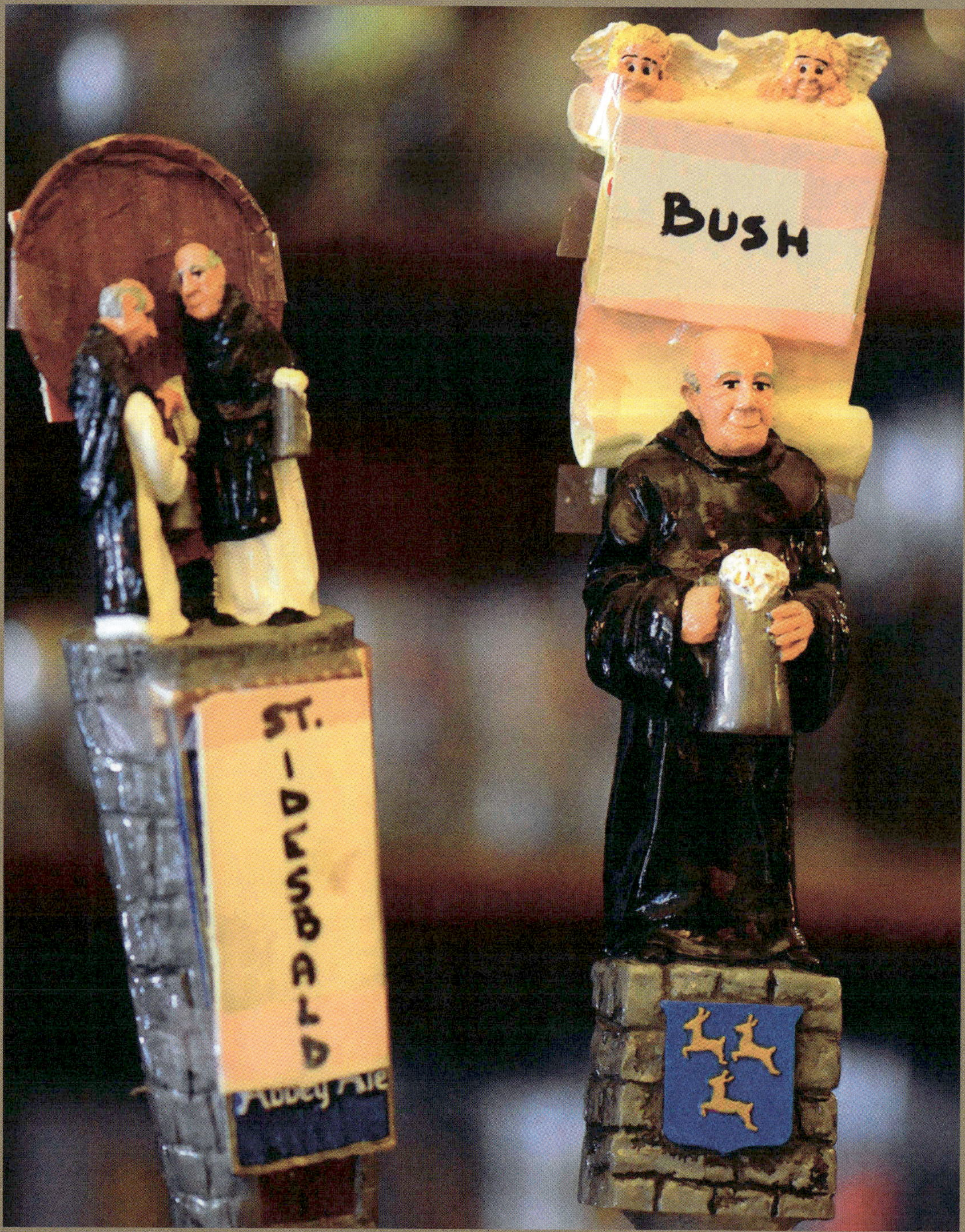
BUSH
ST. IDESBALD
Abbey Ale

THEY WHO DRINK BEER WILL THINK BEER

Washington Irving

GOUDENBAND
Liefmans
BROUWERIJ LIEFMANS N.V.
Oudenaarde
Tel.(055)31.13.91

Augustijn

TRIPEL • DUBBEL
Trappistenbier
Trappistenbier
WESTMALLE
TRAPPISTENBIER

Tripel
16 79
Karmeliet

Bornem
Double
Abbey Ale

Kriek
KLEIN 33 CL
GEFILTERD
GROOT 75 CL
GEFILTERD
GROOT 75 CL
ONGEFILTERD

classi

DE KONINCK
DE KONINCK
BIEREN
DE KONINCK
HOGE GISTING

TRAPPISTE
ROCHEFORT
une « bonne »
Trappiste
de l'Abbaye de
Rochefort

SEIZOENSBROUWERIJ
XII
LO-RENINGE
NINGE
BRUIN
RIJPT OP EIKEN VA

GRIMBERGEN

BELGIUM

Trappist
Westvleteren

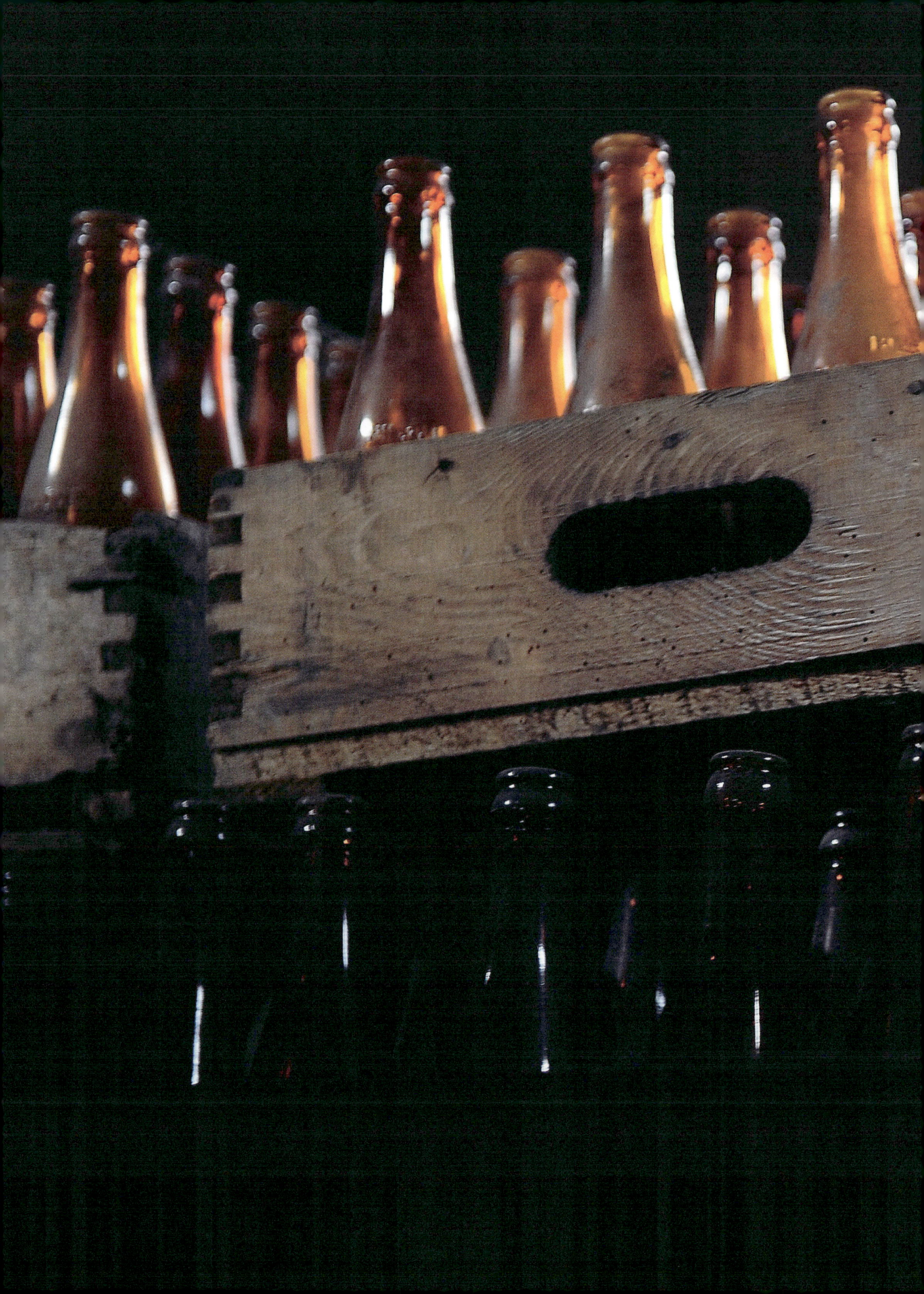

5

BELGIAN BEER STYLES AND OTHER BEER STYLES

BELGIAN BEER STYLES AND OTHER BEER STYLES

Many beers bear a strong resemblance to others. They share their colour, aroma and taste and as such, could be said to be interchangeable. Beers that have much in common with other beers in terms of their technical production as well as aroma and taste fall into the same category of beer style and type. Some of these are recognised beer styles and beer types whereas others exceed the boundaries.

This book introduces a selection of beers that is representative of what is on the market. We have made a personal selection, intended as a guidance only. Bear in mind that beers classed within one particular beer style or type can still be vastly different.

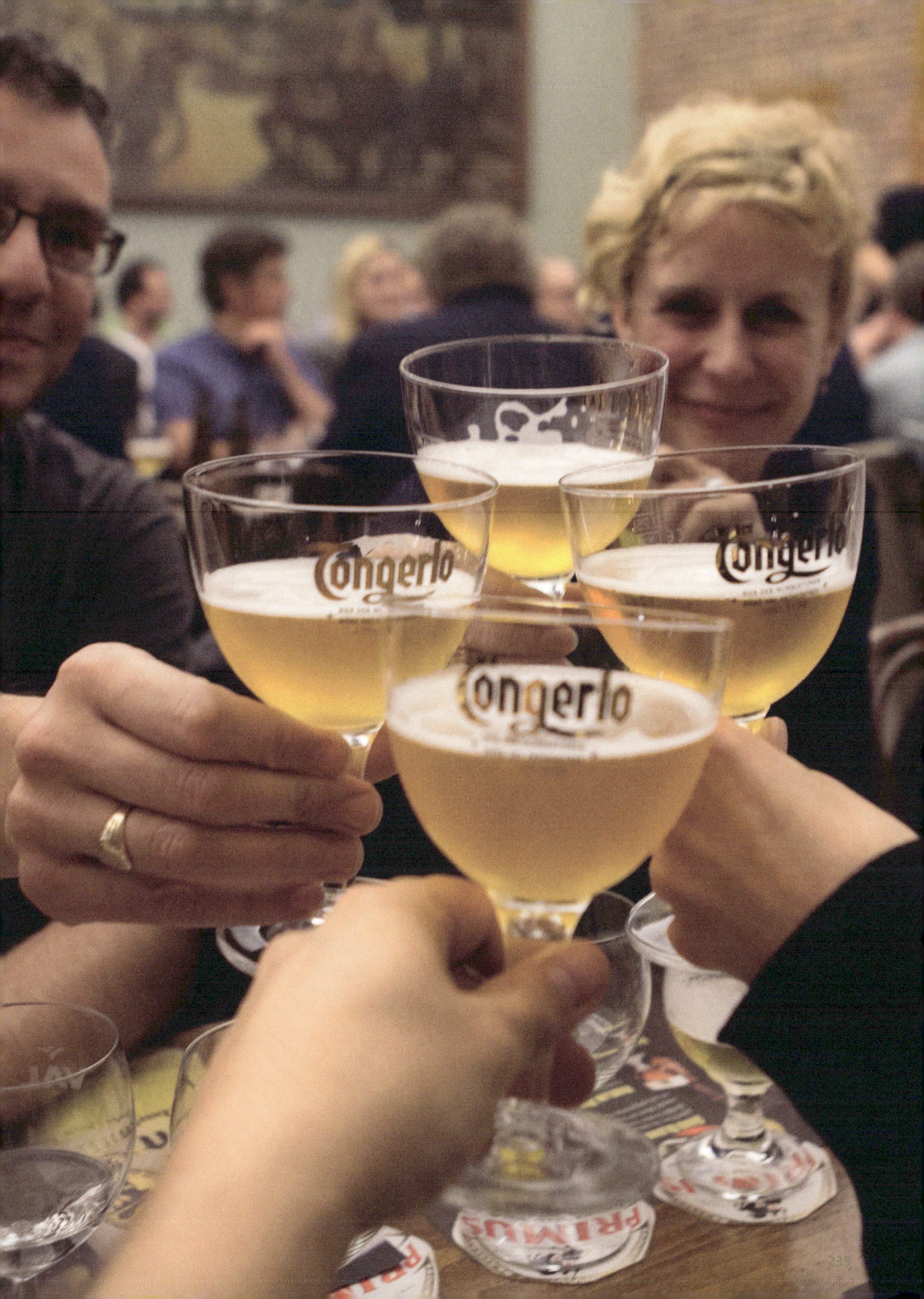
Congerlo
Congerlo
Congerlo
PRIMUS

ABBEY BEER

Abbey beers are typically Belgian. Our beer culture would not be the same without them. Some abbey beers refer to abbeys that still exist and where brewing has been done since time immemorial. Others remind us of abbeys that were wiped off the map many centuries ago. These days the majority of abbey beers is brewed under licence by breweries that have no relationship with the abbey. The brewery is allowed to use the name and, in return, pays royalties to the existing abbey. Abbeys that are still in operation will use these reimbursements for their own subsistence and to fund charitable activities. Abbey beer, or 'Abdijbier' is not a protected beer style. Rather, it can be compared to a denomination of origin (AOC). The Federation of Belgian Brewers brought clarity to this story in 1999 by introducing the 'Recognised Belgian Abbey Beer' label to combat commercial excesses. This label is a guarantee that there is a demonstrable historic link between the beer and an abbey, either still in operation or consigned to the history books. Proof could consist of ancient writings describing brewing activity, drawings or paintings depicting a brewery or even physical evidence of brewing found amongst the abbey ruins. Abbey beers are generally blond or dark beers with quite a high alcohol content but they can also include strong triples and quadruples. There is a great variety in aromas and tastes.

Abbaye de Brogne Brune (7,5%)

Organic dubbel

In earlier days, if you ordered a 'Trappist' – or any other robust specialty beer – you could count on a dark 'double' being placed in front of you. However, times have changed and the Belgians are now going mad for strong blond beers. Think of a dark double and a strong, full-mouthed beer with more than a hint of sweetness will spring to mind. Abbaye de Brogne Brune is the exception to the rule. This organic abbey beer proves to be relatively light and rather dry. The toasted caramel malts provide a slight coffee aroma. Abbaye de Brogne, launched in 1982 by Brasserie Desfosses, has been through quite a journey. It travelled to Affligem and Lefèbvre before ending up at La Binchoise. This beer has recently been flowing out of the tanks of a brand new brewery established at the site of the abbey, just like it does at Villers-la-Ville, another initiative by Bruno Deghorain, brewer at La Binchoise. Bruno strives to produce beers that give balance in the glass and with an easily recognisable signature. A good beer has to excite the nose and caress the taste buds. The beer drinker is intrigued, asks himself what he has just tasted and wants to order a second glass to get to the bottom of it.

———

This is quite a dry beer where the malt takes centre stage with its impressions of nuts and touches of coffee, chocolate and caramel. The roast malt does not affect the balance of this beer at any stage. A mild, tender, delicately bitter and fruity beer.

www.abbayedebrogne.be

Affligem Tripel (9,5%)

Complete with yeast glass

The abbey of Affligem can look back proudly upon a brewing tradtion that has been sustained for centuries. Monks started cultivating hops in this region. The recipe for the Affligem abbey beers goes all the way back to the original medieval Formula Antiqua Renovata, carefully stored at the abbey. The Affligem abbey beers are brewed with the very best summer barley malt and aroma hops. The yeast is considered the 'soul' of the beer. The fermentation method produces esters with impressions of tropical fruits. All Affligem abbey beers re-ferment in the bottle. After a fourteen-day stay in the warm chamber they emerge as complex and layered beers: strong blonde or amber-coloured top-fermented beers in which hops and malt are beautifully balanced.

———

A delicate aroma of malt with intense aromas of ripe fruits, bananas in particular. The onset is slightly sweet with nuances of stone fruits and citrus - emphasised by the re-fermentation in the bottle - that evolve into a pleasantly refreshing bitterness. This beer tastes full in the mouth and is richly layered. Exquisitely balanced despite the high alcohol percentage. With a long and enjoyably bitter finish.

www.affligembeer.com

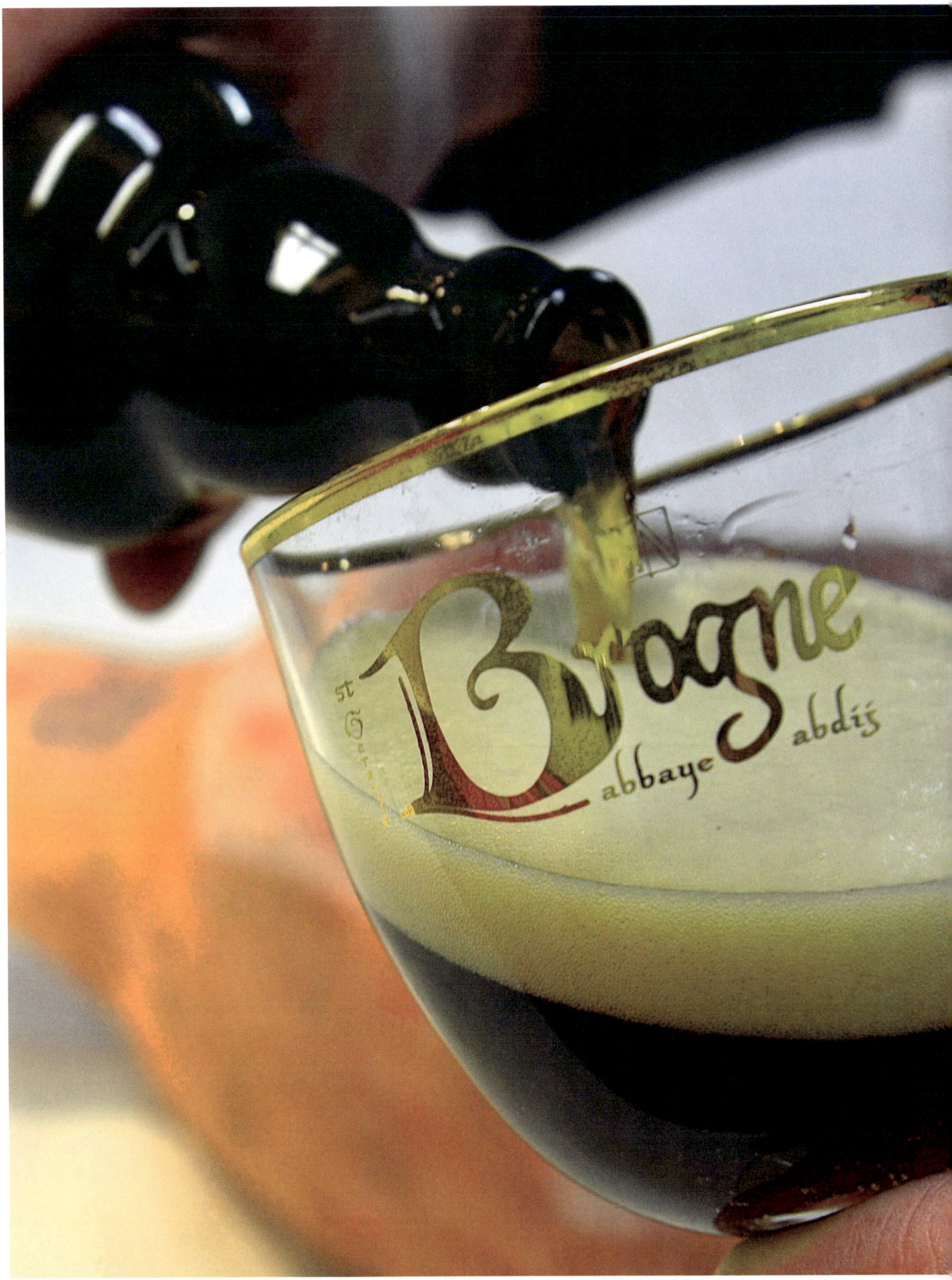
Brogne
abbaye
abdij

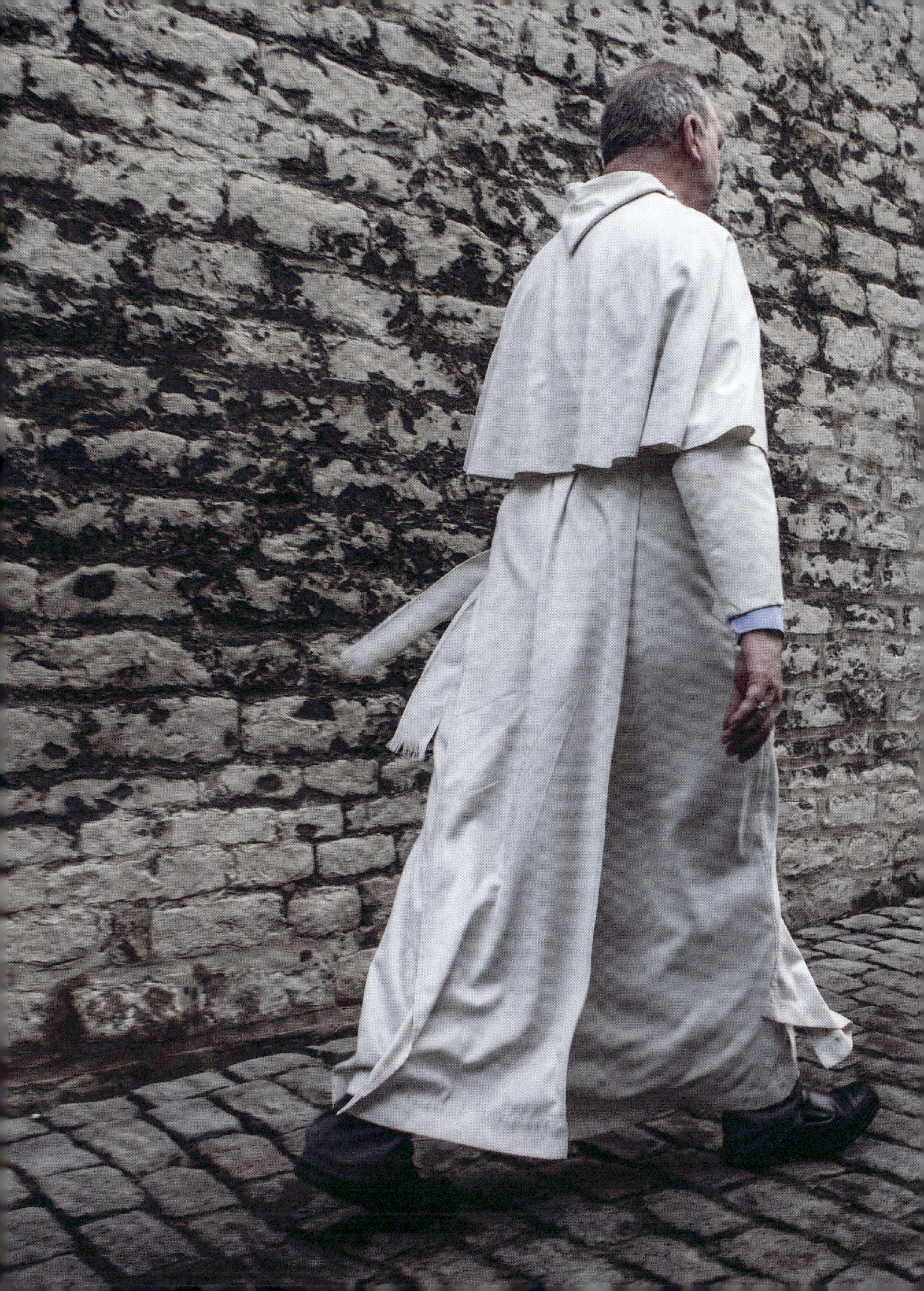

Augustijn Blond (8%)

From the abbot's barrel

1295. The year monks took up brewing in the Augustine abbey in Ghent. Brouwerij Van Steenberge has been responsible for production since 1978. The Augustijn abbey beers are top-fermented and re-ferment in the bottle. Yeast and sugar are added before bottling. The beer will then mature in a warm chamber at a temperature of around 20 °C to allow the yeast to do its work. Improvements to the traditional recipe have borne fruit. Enjoy this gold and amber-coloured beer with its luscious head of froth. In several countries Augustijn is better known as St. Stefanus.

———

Augustijn Blond possesses a hoppy taste on a malty background. Gourmands will also detect a slightly fruity vanilla taste.

www.vansteenberge.com

Averbode (7,5%)

Fragrant with hops

As well as producing its own cheese and bread, Averbode Abbey now also has its own beer, brewed under licence by Huyghe. At Averbode the monks themselves were engaged in brewing from the 14th to the 20th century. *Dry hopping* is used as part of the brewing process: one or more hop varieties are added either during fermentation or afterwards. This brings the hop aromas to the fore and lends a fruity, rather than a bitter, taste to the brew. This blond abbey beer that re-ferments in the bottle is brewed with special *dry hops*, pils and Munich malts. Since 2016 Averbode abbey beer is also brewed in a brand new microbrewery located within the abbey. This beer comes in barrels and is different from the bottled beer. It is only served at the abbey.

———

Averbode has a pleasantly hoppy character with a refreshing yet full finish. Its aroma is one of apples and flowers.

www.averbodia.be

Ename Pater (5,5%)

Light and hoppy

Ename Pater proves that an abbey beer can be light yet full of taste. Brouwerij Roman is responding to the growing demand for lighter beers with plenty of character. The cloudy veil is noticeable in this beer that has undergone less filtration than the other Ename abbey beers. The *dry hopping* gives impressions of hops in the nose and on the tongue. The Ename abbey beers derive their name from the former Benedictine abbey of Ename that was demolished during the French Revolution. Excavation of the ruins brought to light a small harbour town dating back to the early Middle Ages. Together, the foundations of the abbey and the harbour town now form an archaeological park.

———

A pleasant freshness in the nose with impressions of hop and malt. A slight zestiness is also makes itself felt. A refreshing taste with touches of malt and herbs, a beautifully integrated bitterness and a brief, dry finish.

www.roman.be

Grimbergen Blond (6,7%)

Risen from the ashes

The phoenix is the symbol of Grimbergen abbey. Both have risen from the ashes. Grimbergen is Belgium's oldest occupied Norbertine abbey, founded between 1126 and 1128. In 1816 the abbey was razed to the ground. All that remained were the church, the parsonage, the farm and the ancient entry gate. The interior of the 17th-century Basicila of Saint Servatius stands out through the remarkable way the light shines on its treasures. It is decorated with much splendour and is a venue for organ recitals. Even though no beer has been brewed in this abbey since the days of the French revolution, its abbey beer remains popular. Alken-Maes is now in charge of production and distribution. In addition to the Grimbergen Blond, the Grimbergen beer family includes the stronger, blond Grimbergen Triple, Grimbergen Goud and the dark degustation beer that goes under the name of Grimbergen Optimo Bruno.

———

A beer with a malty aroma and taste, mild, slightly fruity with a hint of bitter.

www.grimbergenbeer.com

5 • BELGIAN BEER STYLES

241

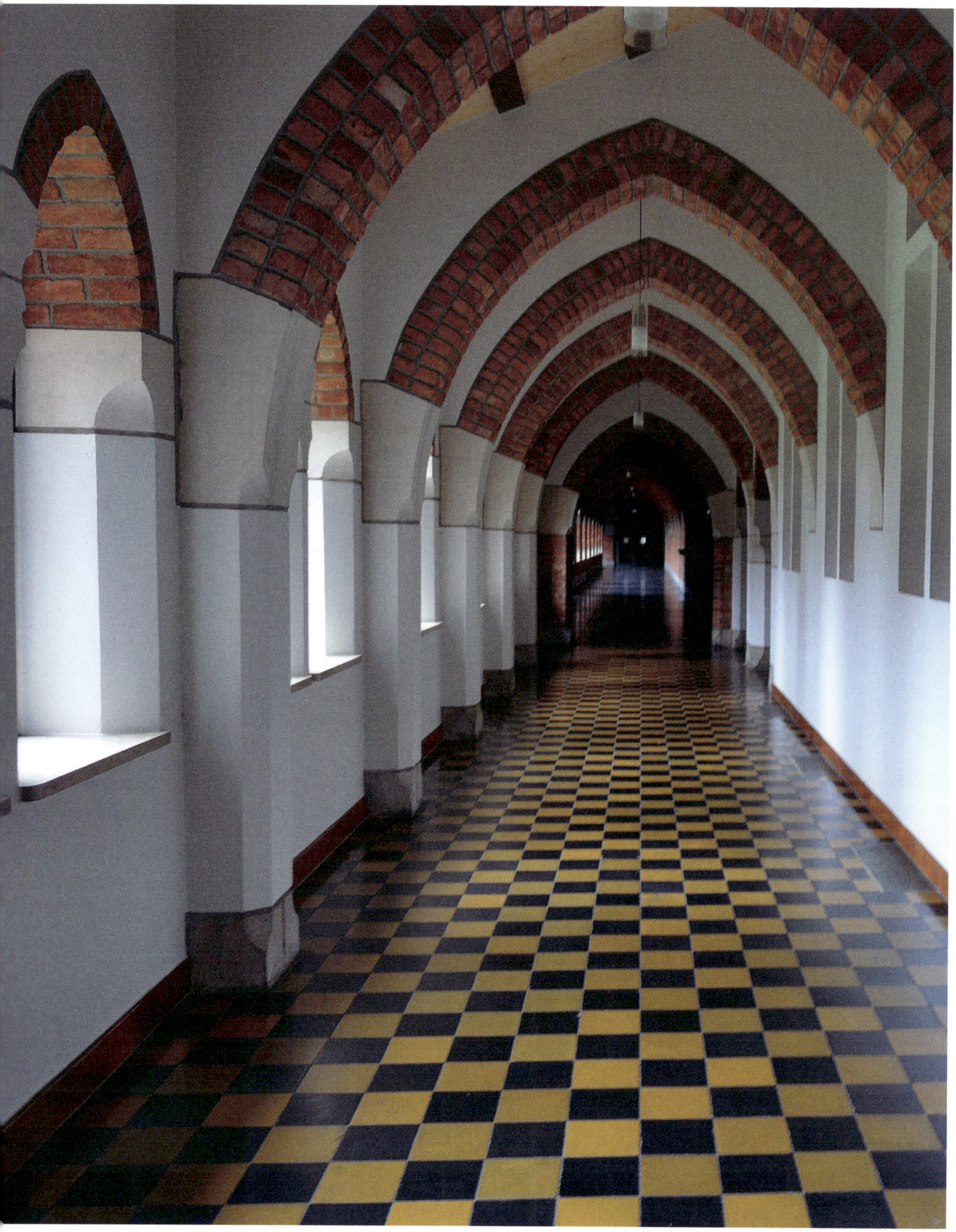

Herkenrode Bruin (7%)

Brave like a count with the elegance of an abbess

All that remains of the former abbey of Herkenrode, close to Hasselt, is the imposing and beautifully renovated abbey farm. Herkenrode has produced its own 'recognised' abbey beers ever since 2009: Herkenrode Bruin and Herkenrode Triple. Jef Cornelissen Sr. of the Cornelissen brewery (named Sint-Jozef Brewery in a former life) was asked to 'brew a beer with the bravery of the Counts of Loon, the elegances of the abbesses of Herkenrode and the aromas of the herb garden'. The resulting Herkenrode Bruin is an orange and amber coloured abbey beer brewed with Munich malts derived from summer barley with the addition of aroma hops. It spends a month maturing on wood, accounting for its stronger taste with smoky hints of vanilla. This beer goes down easily and is served in an elegant degustation glass. As this is an unpasteurised beer, its rounded taste is preserved to the full.

_____

The first tasting yields a noticeable bitterness thanks to the interaction between the roast malt and the aroma hops, followed by a zesty finish with a hint of sweetness.

www.abdijsiteherkenrode.be

Leffe Blond (6,3%)

Popular all around

This abbey beer is conquering the world. It has been a major, even a 'world' brand, for AB Inbev ever since 1987. The hop is prominent and emphasises the dry character of the Leffe Blond. Since its inception, the Leffe beer family has grown by, give or take, ten beers, including the Leffe Radieuse and the Leffe Royale. Leffe is now available in around sixty countries. Just a few hundred metres from Dinant city centre, Leffe Abbey was founded by Norbertine monks in the 12th century. Its brewing tradition harks back to medieval times. It is generally assumed that there was a brewery on this site from the 13th century up to the French Revolution, when most of the breweries closed down. In 1952, brewer Albert Lootvoet from Overijse gifted the beer from Leffe its second youth. The rest is history.

_____

Leffe Blond has a slight aroma of cloves. It has a mild and fruity taste with impressions of orange. However, it comes with a powerful finish.

www.leffe.com

Maredsous Bruin (8%)

Prescribed by the Father

Father Pierre Atout was keen to serve pilgrims with something other than water. This prompted him to create the recipes for the Maredsous abbey beers. The brown Maredsous Bruin is surprisingly subtle and balanced. First of all, you taste caramel, followed immediately by a very pronounced roast aroma, which makes the beer resemble coffee (mocha). Maredsous Bruin is easy to digest and not too heavy in any way. However, the robust alcohol content does come through in the taste. This beer's bitterness is derived from its nutty character and is supported by the roast aroma of dark malts. This is also noticeable in the lingering finish. The Maredsous abbey beers are brewed by Duvel Moortgat.

_____

Toasted and roast aromas with touches of coffee and dark chocolate. A delicate bouquet of caramel with subtle hints of dark fruits and chocolate.

www.maredsousbieres.be

St Feuillien Grand Cru (9,5%)

Perfectly balanced

Grand Cru tells us that here we have a top-of-the-range beer, usually the jewel in the crown of the brewery. The St Feuillien Grand Cru is a full-mouthed degustation beer with a pronounced character, re-fermented in the bottle. To explain the name of the beer and the brewery we have to go back to the distant past. In the 7th century Irish monk Folian travelled through the area that is now Belgium. In 655 he paid for his religious zeal with a martyr's death in the village of Le Roeulx, where the brewery is now based. In later years Folian was declared a Saint, much to the benefit of Le Roeulx. It turned into a pilgrimage site where, in 1125, a Premonstratensian abbey was founded. Up to this day and not surprisingly, the foundation date of the abbey is proudly printed on the label of the St Feuillien abbey beers. This Belgian abbey shared the fate of many others. In 1796 it fell at the hands of the French Revolution and was never resurrected.

A wide range of hop aromas with touches of fruit (orange, lemon, tangerine), wood, roast malt and impressions of wine. All in beautiful balance. From slightly bitter, the taste sensation flows into a more pronounced hop bitter, coming to the fore in the long and complex finish.

www.st-feuillien.com

Tongerlo Prior (9%)

A layered taste in your glass

A zesty, fruity and rather complex abbey beer from the Kempen region around Antwerp. Tongerlo Prior has replaced the sweeter Tongerlo Triple that was lower in alcohol. At Tongerlo Abbey the monks were engaged in brewing until the abbey closed its doors at the time of the French Revolution (1789–1794). The abbey was resurrected in 1840 to incorporate a small brewery. German soldiers confiscated the copper brewing kettles at the time of the First World War. Nowaways, the Tongerlo abbey beers are brewed under licence by Haacht.

Fruity aromas with pear in the foreground. This full-mouthed beer initially comes across as gentle but in the finish you will experience a brief but powerful burst of hop bitters. Quite dry but highly quaffable.

www.tongerlo.be

Val-Dieu Triple (9%)

A beer with body

The classics are beers that are well-balanced. This certainly applies to the Val-Dieu Triple, where you find sweet, sour and bitter without either of these being dominant. This characterful triple has plenty of body. In the finish, the alcohol makes its presence felt. All Val-Dieu beers re-ferment in the bottle. Monks have made an important contribution to the success of Belgian beers. They documented their brewing knowledge in recipes that are inspiring brewers up to this day. Val-Dieu Abbey has a tangible link with its monastic past as its beers are still brewed within the abbey walls.

Val-Dieu Triple yields surprisingly fruity aromas of citrus and spices with impressions of caramel and malt, always with a subtly bitter undercurrent. Its taste is beautifully balanced between sweet, sour and bitter.

www.val-dieu.com

5 • BELGIAN BEER STYLES

TRAPPIST BEER

◆

What is the difference between a Trappist beer and an abbey beer? There are only twelve beers in the world allowed to bear the Trappist name: those from Achel, Chimay, Koningshoeven (La Trappe), Mont des Cats, Orval, Rochefort, Westvleteren, Westmalle, Stift Engelszell (Gregorius and Benno), Zundert, Spencer and Tre Fontane. Belgium numbers six Trappist abbeys: Westmalle, Westvleteren, Chimay, Orval, Rochefort and Achel. Westvleteren was the first to start brewing a Trappist beer, in 1831, followed by Westmalle (1836), Achel (1846), Chimay (1862), Rochefort (1899) and Orval (1931). Trappist beer is not a protected beer style. The name is solely an indicator of origin, the Trappist abbey, and denotes the ethics followed. There are eleven Trappist beers that bear the 'Authentic Trappist Product' logo: Achel, Chimay, La Trappe (Netherlands), Orval, Rochefort, Westmalle, Westvleteren, the beers brewed by Stift Engelszell and by Zundert (Netherlands), Spencer (USA) and Tre Fontane (Italy.). The logo is only awarded if the following conditions are met: the beer is brewed within the walls of a Trappist abbey or in the vicinity; the brewery is of secondary importance to the abbey and its monastic life; brewing is done by the monks or supervised by them; the beer is not brewed to make a profit. Rather, the revenues from brewing fund the cost of living for the monks and the maintenance of the abbey and its surroundings. Any remaining money goes to charity.

The Trappist breweries strictly adhere to all of the standards in terms of health and safety and consumer information. As to marketing and advertising, they strive for honesty, modesty and understatement, in keeping with the religious environment in which the beers are brewed. As a rule, Trappist beers have a high alcohol content and a rich variety of aromas. Herbs are often used to lend the beer its characteristic taste. The majority of Trappist beers are generally categorised as blond, strong brown double and strong blond triple, but you will also come across amber-coloured Trappist beer.

Source: http://www.trappist.be/nl/pages/trappistenbieren

Achel Blond Extra (8%)

'Enjoy our light beers and get back on your bike!'

The sage advice from the Brother is not falling on deaf ears. After a bike ride we are now rewarding ourselves with a blond Trappist on the terrace that forms part of the interior court with a good view of the brewing hall. This triple from Achel is the bigger and stronger brother of the Achel Blond 5, a beer that can only be tasted in the abbey itself where it is freshly poured. The Achel Blond Extra was launched in 2001 but had a rocky start. It began as an unfiltered beer with yeast at the bottom of the bottle but then evolved into a bottle re-fermented beer. Third time lucky: topped by a silver crown cork, this triple was finally able to strengthen the 'silver fleet' of Trappist beers. Just like its brown 8% brother, the Achel Blond Extra makes for a good 'entry' Trappist. In other words, it appeals to a wide audience. The beer's image completely fits the understated chalice into which it is poured and the modest label that adorns the bottle. Brewery revenues help to support the Achelse Kluis abbey.

———

You can taste hops and malt. The robust head places the crown on this brewing effort. In this beer, an honest, sweet, malty palette comes to the fore, reminiscent of bread, complemented by the fruity touches of not overripe pear and banana. This beer is quite low in body. A tender thirst-quencher with, at the finish, a thin veil of bitter that fades quietly.

www.achelsekluis.org

Chimay Bleue (9%)

Beer and cheese

The Chimay Bleue was added to the standard range of this Trappist brewery as a 'Christmas beer' in 1954 and has taken pride of place ever since. This strong dark beer, also available in large bottles labelled 'Grande Réserve' with the vintage stamped on the label, has joined the selected ranks of beers that improve with age. Under the right circumstances, a Chimay Bleue will easily keep for five years or even longer. If you can muster the patience you will be rewarded with overpowering aromas of vintage port. Chimay Bleue is a powerful and complex Trappist beer that more than deserves it place on the table. Why not pair it with a semi-hard or mature, hard Chimay abbey cheese? You will even find a Chimay à la Bleue cheese. To produce this, beer was added to the curds and, moreover, the crust was rinsed in the beer. Still not convinced? Have a mouthful of Chimay Bleue paired with a toast with melted Roquefort...

———

The nose picks up surprising impressions of coffee, cocoa and dried fruits, followed by aromas of stony fruits or seeded fruits such as apricots and nectarines. The taste is dominated by mocha and coffee. The alcohol provides a warming finish to accompany the fresh and fruity aftertaste.

www.chimay.com

Orval (6,2%)

From the chalice

The odd one out amongst the Trappists. Orval provides the whole package: hops, yeast, barley malt, crystallised sugar with a hint of wild magic, all bathing in a warm glow. In its home region of the Ardennes, people tend to prefer the milder beer that has aged for at least six months. This is the 'vieil Orval', the result of the first bout of work from the wild yeasts. An Orval ages well. The wild yeasts take their leisurely time to convert all the residual sugars into alcohol and carbon dioxide. This is good news for diabetics: the old or 'vieil' Orval is free of residual sugars. Ever since its launch, this beer's recipe as well as the glass, the bottle and the label have remained unchanged. Pay a visit to the abbey tavern that goes under the name of L'Ange Gardien (the Guardian Angel) to sample the lighter, 'green' Orval, the monks' table beer that is only served in the refectory. The quality of the Orval beers is largely due to the pure spring water used for its brewing. By the way, the Orval spring features in an enchanting legend. In the 12th century the Countess Matilde, recently widowed after the death of her spouse Godfrey, nicknamed the Hunchback, sat down at the well to comtemplate her future. In an unguarded moment her wedding ring fell into the well. After fervent prayers to the Virgin Mary, hey presto, a trout jumped up out of the water and gave her back her wedding ring. The fish carrying the ring was to become the Orval emblem.

The slightly malty palette hides an abundance of fruitiness. An entire fruit basket is hidden under the veil of a prominently earthy, zesty and peppery bitterness that, with its mildly sour touches of citrus forms a perfect pairing with the pleasantly sour and wild character of this beer. Full in the mouth, creamy with a playful finish that fizzes on the tongue. The finish is dry.

www.orval.be

Rochefort 8 (9,2%)

Fresh caramel

This Trappist is a degustation beer that cannot be hurried. The Rochefort 8 saw the light of day in 1954 and is a neat fit between his little brother, number 6, and big brother number 10. All three beers have the same basic recipe with varying amounts of malt and candi sugar added. Throughout the ages the Rochefort Trappists have been brewing with the water of the calcium-rich Tridaine well. In the 'brewing hall cathedral', barley malt, wheat starch and hop pellets are added. Ever since the 1960s the house yeast has been responsible for the typical esters. The bottle indicates a 'best before' date five years into the future. However, it has been proven that much older beer is also perfectly drinkable. Up to three years into storage, the Rochefort acquires a rounder taste. Keep it for longer and its evolution slows down.

You taste the soft, milk-chocolatey caramel flowing into a malty bitter, more pronounced in the finish that yields impressions of cloves. Sweet but never boring. The same applies to the alcohol that will never overpower the subtlety in the glass. The complex house yeast is the first to come to the fore with a zesty dairyness and a sweetly spreading alcohol.

www.abbaye-rochefort.be

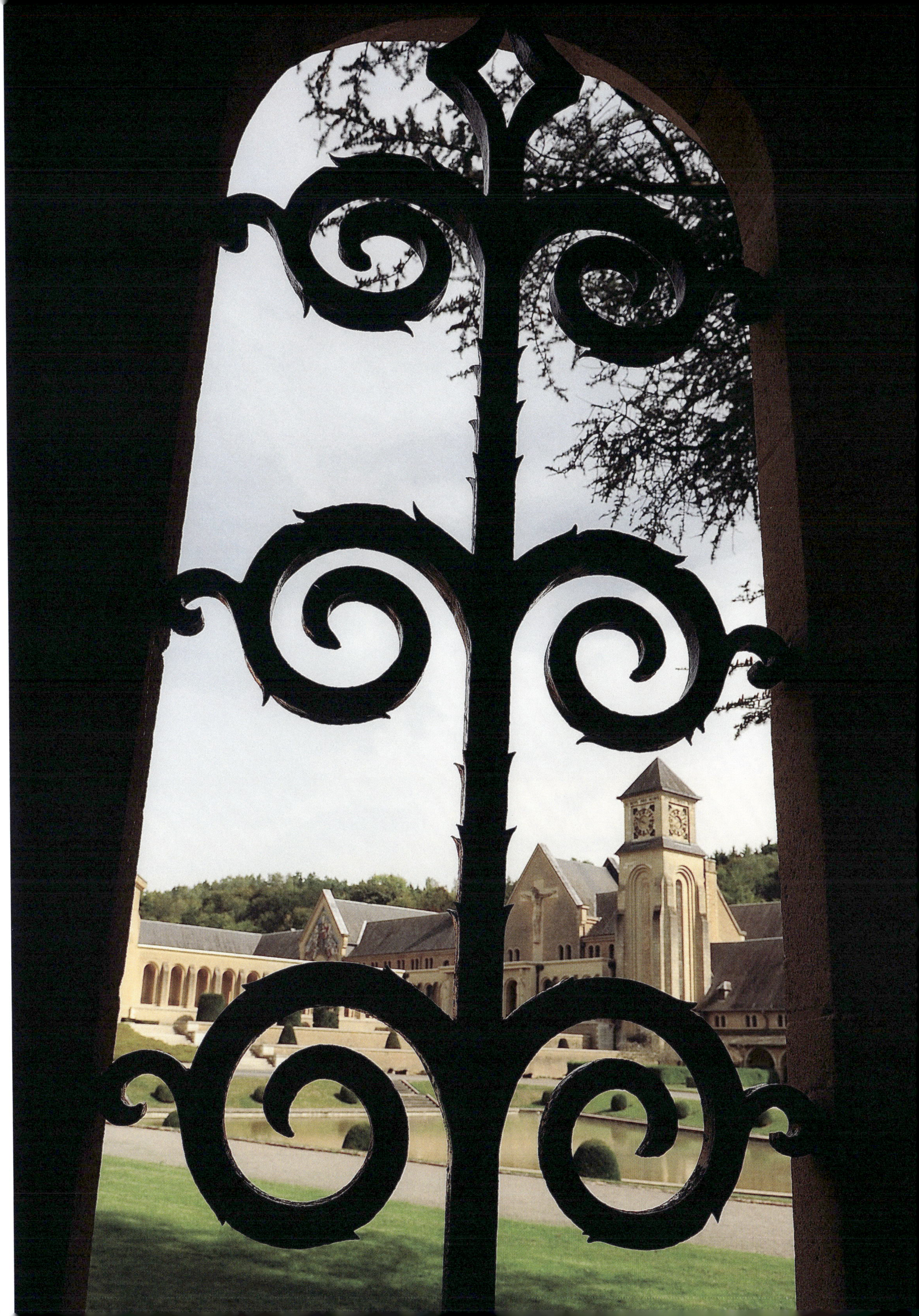

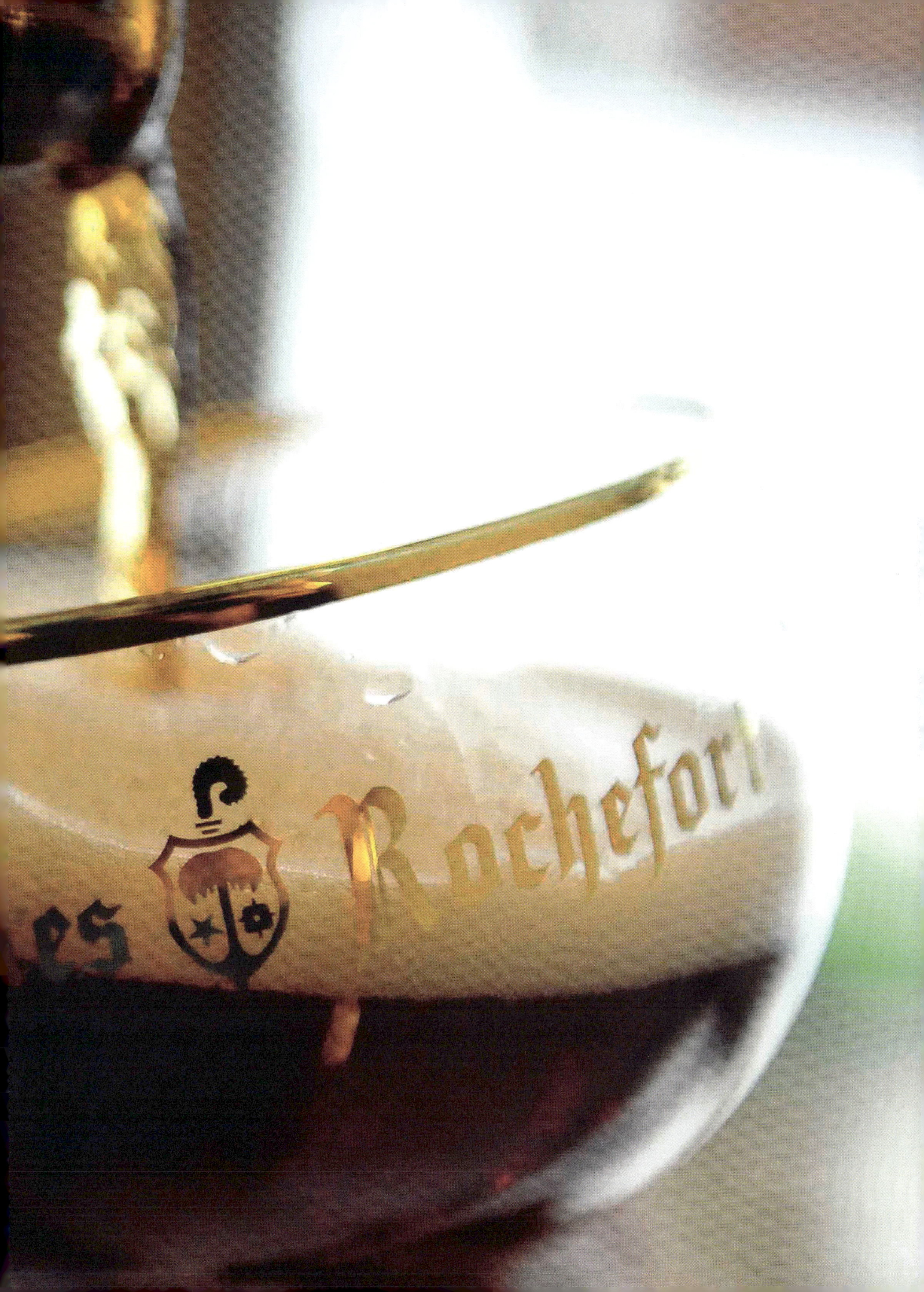
Rochefort

Westmalle Dubbel (7%)

Glazen boterham

Westmalle Dubbel is a full-mouthed, balanced abbey beer, zesty and fruity. A 'dubbel' is a heavy dark, sweet or bitter beer. The Westmalle Dubbel is offered fresh from the tap in around three hundred selected hotels, cafés and restaurants. The taste of the tap beer is slightly sweeter than that of the bottled variety. The first brewery was built at Westmalle Abbey in 1836 and in the same year, the first dark, sweet, top-fermented brew flowed out of the kettle. The brown table beer was joined in 1856 by a dark Trappist which became the predecessor of the current Westmalle Dubbel (1926). This beer, once the heaviest beer in Belgium, is still considered a reference for its particular beer style.

———

Aromas of banana and chocolate with gentle zesty touches of vanilla and aniseed. The taste yields impressions of milk chocolate joined by a mild espresso, followed by sweet alcohol and rounded off with hop. In the finish, slightly bitter chicory.

www.trappistwestmalle.be

Westmalle Triple (9,5%)

The mother of all triples

In 1934 the monks of Westmalle launched a new 'super beer' to celebrate the opening of their brewhall. The Westmalle Triple was 'super-heavy' for its time. Natural ingredients, including genuine hop cones and the finest barley malt provide its refined character. Hops are still measured by hand in Westmalle. Damaged hop cones are discarded. Westmalle Triple provides the utmost in balance, with a refined hop bitterness accompanied by a fruity sweetness. This mother of all triples now has multiple offspring. Triple is one of the most frequently brewed Belgian beer styles and the Belgians love their triples. The term 'triple' refers to a higher proportion of raw ingredients used. A triple is a heavy beer, usually blonde, with a strong taste of malt and/or hop bitters.

———

This triple seduces us with its sweet banana aromas. This aroma dance is performed to a background tune of hop bitterness. Its malty body is enriched by yeasty alcohol esters and hop cones. Its zesty and rather earthy character is enlivened by pearls of carbon dioxide, giving an airy feel to the whole.

www.trappistwestmalle.be

Westvleteren Abt (10,2%)

Liquid heritage

To even call the Westvleteren 12 an icon would be an understatement. This Trappist beer from the Abbey of Sint-Sixtus entered the world of legends when www.ratebeer.com pronounced it the best beer in the world. Many beer lovers put this beer on a par with liquid gold, as it is very hard to obtain anywhere other than at the abbey café, De Vrede. The monks embarked on brewing when the construction of the current abbey was finished in 1831. The Westvleteren 12 started off as a light refectory beer (2% alc.vol.), entirely different from the beer that is brewed nowadays. The Westvleteren 12 as we know it now was conceived at the start of the Second World War. Who would have thought that it would grow into the only monumental beer amongst the Trappists?

———

A full-mouthed beer with aromas of raisins, nuts, caramel, alcohol, tobacco and leather. It has a complex taste with impressions of malt and caramel with a long, dry and rather bitter finish.

www.sintsixtus.be

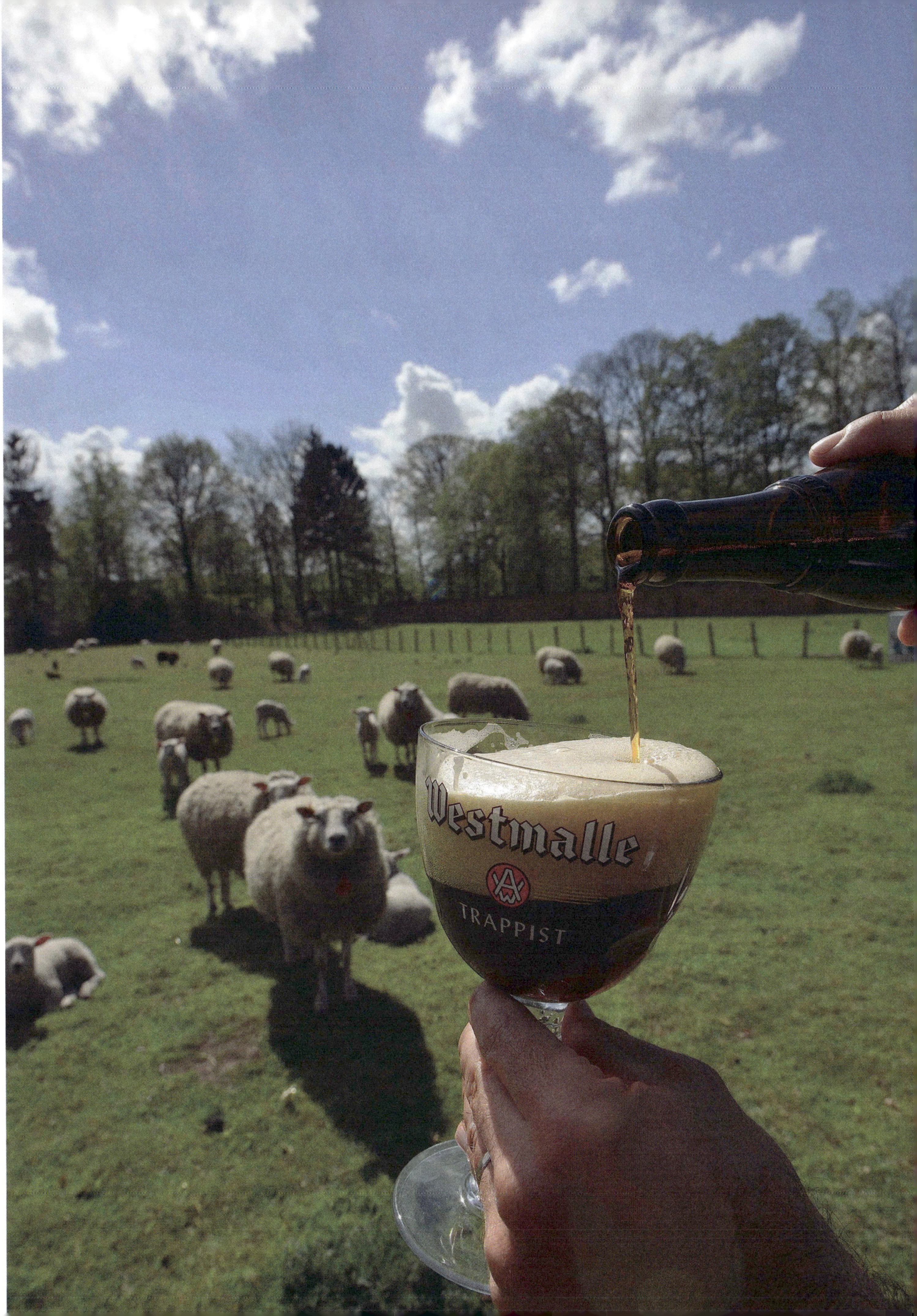
Westmalle
TRAPPIST

SPÉCIALE BELGE

When pils conquered Europe around the 1900s Belgian brewers felt threatened by its success. The brewery schools launched a competition challenging brewers to come up with a Belgian answer to pils from abroad. The goal was to produce beer of similar strength (circa 5%) that could be sold at a lower price, up to a third cheaper. The beer also had to come with a delicate pearlisation and a fine head of froth and it had to contain more carbon dioxide. No fewer than 73 brewers entered the 1905 contest, which was won by the Binard brewery from Châtelineau with its 'Belge de Faleau' bottled beer. The success of this beer was to inspire many other brewers to produce an amber-coloured Spéciale Belge. This Spéciale Belge turned into the quaffable beer for the middle classes and also represented affordable luxury for those who worked on the land and in factories.

De Koninck (5%)

Bolleke

In Antwerp they treasure their 'bolleke', named after its bulbous glass. This Antwerp classic was launched in 1913. With its intense mahogany colour and robust head of froth, its immediate appearance is striking. De Koninck is a complex beer with touches of coffee, chestnut and caramel and a slightly smoky aroma. There is an evident fruitiness, prodominantly banana, accompanied by a zestiness coming from the noble hops. All these elements come together in the pleasantly mild taste with a touch of nuts. This beer is quite bitter, as a real Spéciale Belge should be, but never aggressively so. The finish is full and creamy. A well-poured glass ensures a sufficiently creamy head. Down to the last mouthful, a layer of creamy froth remains in the glass. You lot behind the bar, please pay attention! To pour a De Koninck properly is no less than an art form. You pour the beer in two stages, first until the froth reaches up to one centimetre below the rim of the glass, then you let the beer rest for a few seconds before pouring more beer from the tap until the froth is bulbous/convex. Don't skim off the head! Schol!

———

De Koninck is a mild, very quaffable beer, almost treacherous in the way it goes down so easily. At first you can taste the malt, then herbs with a gingery fruitiness, followed by the delicate Saaz hops in the finish. This amber beer has a surprisingly zesty, dry and slightly bitter taste united by its malty aroma.

www.dekoninck.be

Palm Hop Select (6%)

From the hop field

This younger brother of the classic amber-coloured Spéciale Belge Palm is worthy of its name. The Palm Hop Select is hopped three times: once at the start of boiling, once again just before the end of the boiling process, followed by a *dry hopping*. This is done towards the end of the main fermentation with Hallertau Mittelfrüh-hops from Palm Belgian Craft Brewers' own fields. The composition of the malt and the choice of yeast indicate that this beer fits in with the Spéciale Belge beer style, of which the traditional Palm also forms part. The unique amber malts give slight tastes of caramel with a honey-like tenderness. The yeast provides the fruity character. The re-fermentation in the bottle lends the beer a stronger pearlisation and preserves the character of the hops. The nose picks up flowery and fruity hop aromas with hints of banana. A great combination of the full-mouthed taste of a Spéciale Belge amber beer and hop aromas.

———

The beautiful bitterness completes the picture. The taste is dominated by hop bitter. A fresh mouthfeel with some sweetness and a slightly bitter finish tempered by a sweet touch.

www.palm.be

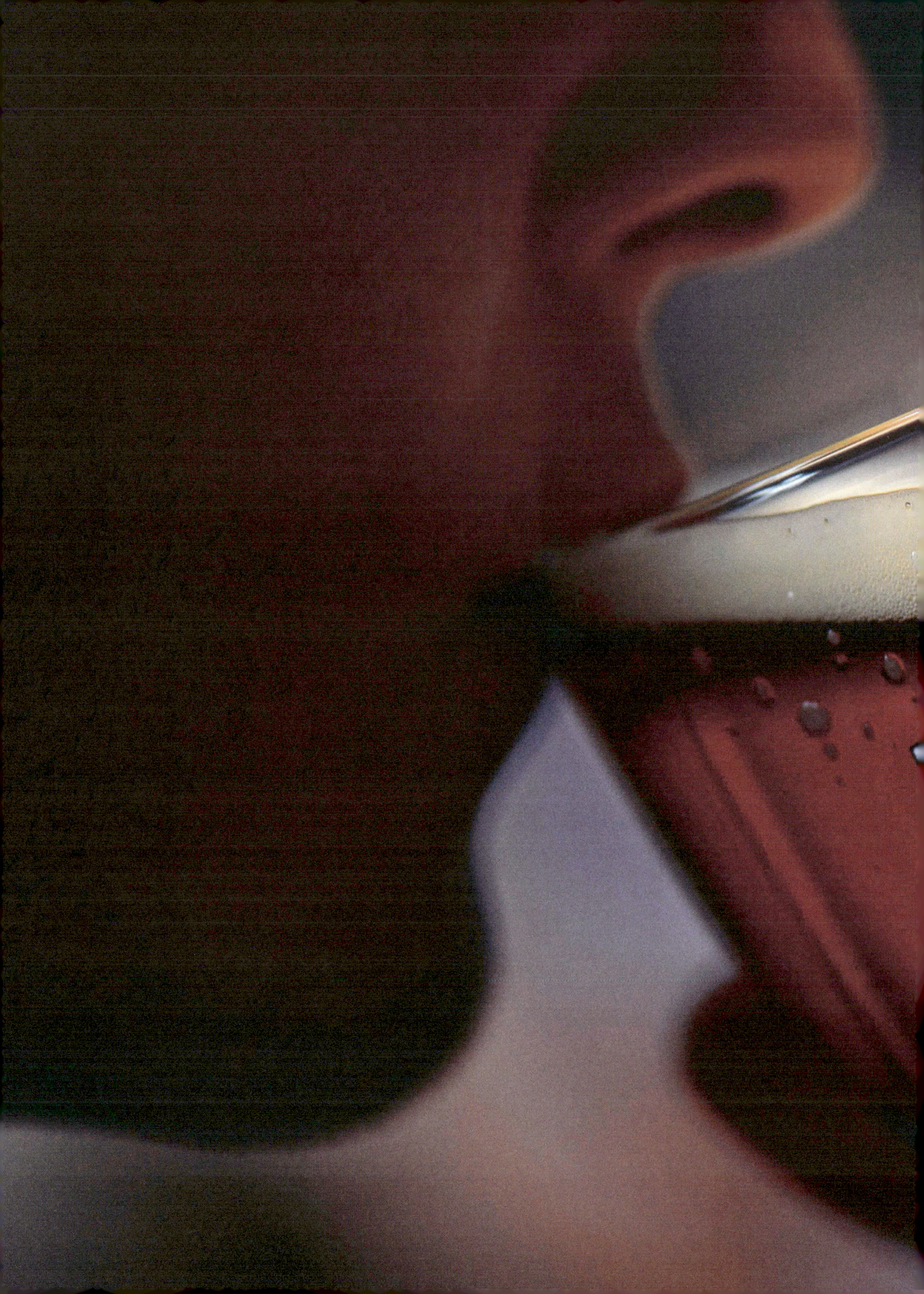

KONINCK
APA

AMBERBIER

Stronger amber beers do not fit into the Spéciale Belge beer style. This goes for, amongst others, the Bush Ambrée, one of the strongest Belgian beers and a classic from the 1930s, the Pauwel Kwak, also known as the 'coach driver's beer', and for the Zinnebir.

Bush Ambrée (12%)

Amber and alcohol

This, Brasserie Dubuisson's flagship beer, is one of the oldest specialty beers in Belgium. Bush Ambrée (Scaldis in the USA) was introduced in 1933 and contains only malt, hop, natural sugars, water drawn from the brewery's own well and the house yeast that has developed a high resistance to alcohol. The combination of a high quantity of malt and an active yeast produces one of the strongest Belgian beers. The beer is well saturated, easily digested and suitable for use as an aperitif as well as a digestive. Amber beer is a classic Belgian beer style. With its high alcohol content the Bush Ambrée could be called the odd one out.

The Bush Ambrée owes its bitter-sweet taste and consistency to the caramel malt used in brewing as well as the expertise and patience shown by the master-brewer. It has a striking aroma of roast nuts.

www.dubuisson.com

Caracole (7,5%)

At a snail's pace

At the Caracole brewery you are travelling back in time. This brewery is a living museum where a wood-fired burner is still used to heat the brewing kettles. Its brewer François Tonglet used to sell regional products from his store in Namen (Namur). After he discovered regional beers he set up his microbrewery. Where does the snail in the logo come from? 'I am from Namur', François Tonglet laughs. 'We do everything at a snail's pace and that includes brewing, tasting and drinking.' Dinant is just around the corner. Caracole's Saxo pays homage to Adolphe Sax, a local hero who invented the saxophone. The brewer emphasises the importance of using a particular yeast to achieve the taste, as well as specific varieties of malt and hop. But why is he still firing up his kettles with wood? 'The wood is our raw material, always available and affordable. Wood is a sustainable fuel and it gives off wonderful smells!'

An amber-coloured beer with a fruity nose. Its taste is rather surprising for a beer that is light in colour. Mildly bitter with a touch of roast malts.

www.brasserie-caracole.be

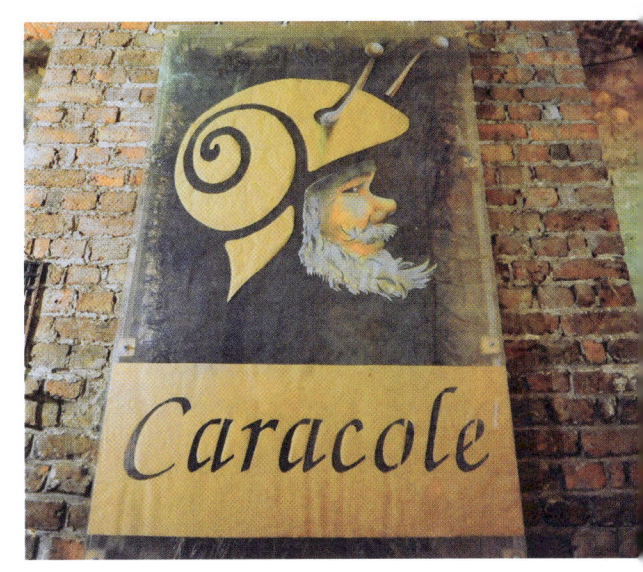

Pauwel Kwak (8,4%)

The coach driver's beer

Once upon a time… there was a brewer named Pauwel Kwak who lived in the Dendermonde area. He was brewing his own dark and heavy beer. He owned a coaching inn on the main road between Mechelen and Ghent where the mail coaches stopped. Under the Napoleonic regime, however, coach drivers were not allowed to share a beer with their passengers. They could not leave the coach to quench their thirst. Pauwel Kwak came up with a solution: he offered them his 'Kwakbier' in a special glass that could be fixed to the carriage.

Earthy aromas, a malty character with touches of liquorice, a robustness with hints of nougat and a warm finish reminiscent of caramelised banana. The first aroma is of yeast and red fruits, complemented by herbs. The caramel pops out from the beer in a lovely way, accompanied by herbs and orange peel. The finish is slightly bitter with more than a hint of zest.

www.bestbelgianspecialbeers.be

Zinnebir (6%)

A character beer

The two 'Zennebrouwers' have been reaping success with their Zinnebir and Taras Boulba. Both beers are easily recognised thanks to their maltiness, hop bitterness and fruity yeast. The duo is not following any particular plan. 'We make character beers that we like to drink ourselves. We are keen on sour beers, like Cantillon's lambic beers or bitter beers like those we produce ourselves. Just like the olden days when sweet beer simply didn't exist. We are only working with water, malt, hop and yeast. Above all, we are brewing lighter beers with a lot of taste.'

A light, complex, well-rounded beer with a noticeable presence of malt and hop bitters all the way to the slightly bitter finish.

www.brasseriedelasenne.be

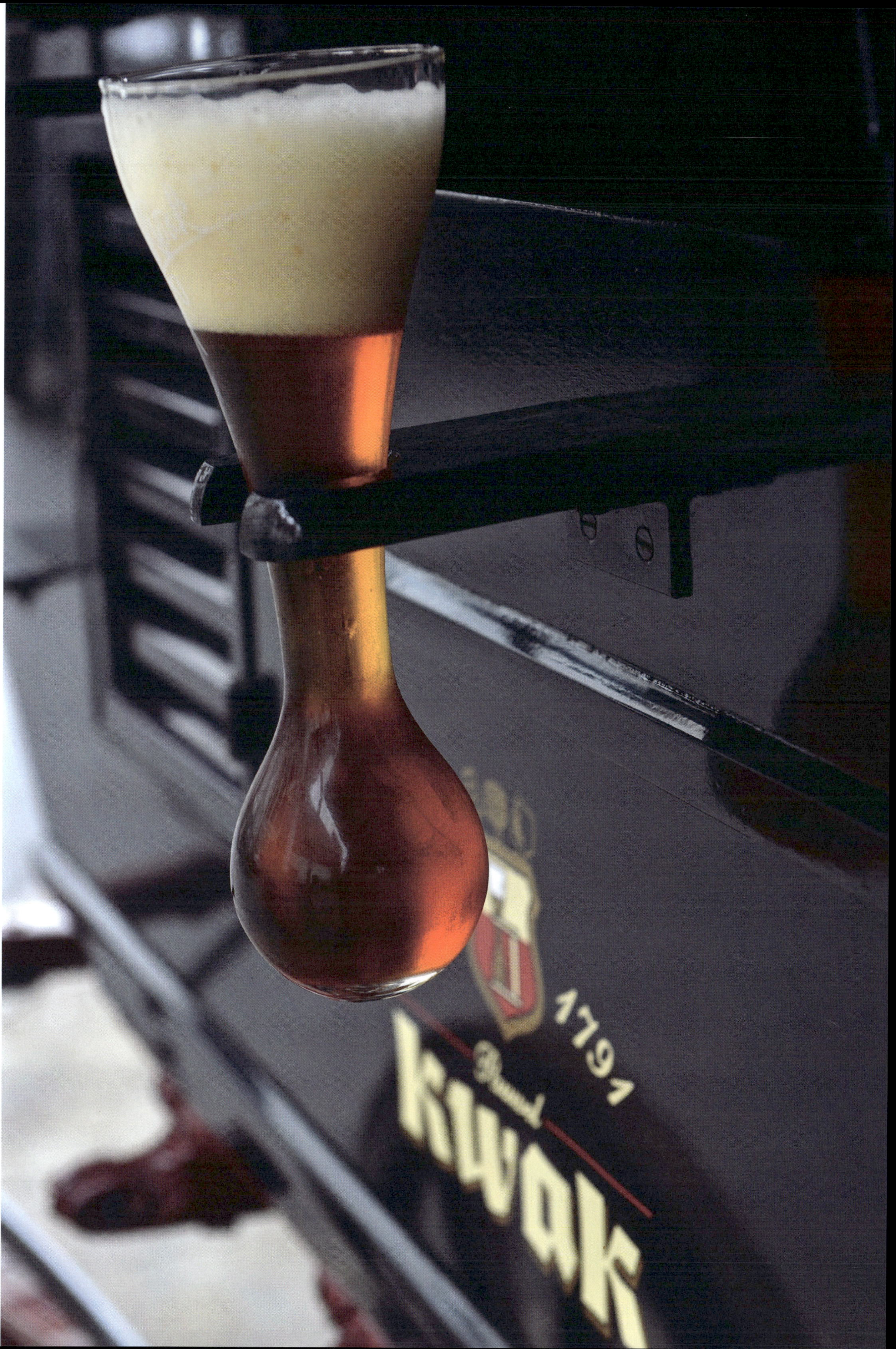
1791
kwak

BRUT BIER

It turns out that brewers can be inventive as well as creative. The two main producers of Bière Brut are De Landtsheer and Bosteels from Buggenhout near Dendermonde. Their Brut beers bridge the gap between beer and wine. Brut beer is made in the same way as champagne. The mother beer undergoes a first fermentation over ten days. The second fermentation takes about as long. After cold storage and filtration a dose of champagne yeast and white candi sugar is added. The in-bottle refermentation, once finished, is followed by the remuage (the bottles are turned until the yeast is in the neck of the bottle) and finally the dégorgement (freezing, removal of the yeast prop that has gathered in the neck of the bottle, followed by re-bottling). The result? Clear, sparkling beers. Strong but with a light taste.

DeuS Brut des Flandres (11,5%)

A party beer

The carefully chosen yeast strains contribute a mild taste of ginger. The finely balanced hop bitterness, selected ingredients and attention to each detail of the complex brewing process result in a beer that is halfway between beer and bubbles. DeuS is brewed using barley by the master-brewer. After a first fermentation and maturation the beer travels to the Champagne region, so to speak, where it spends a year re-fermenting and maturing. After this rest period a sediment has formed on the bottom of the bottles, laid out in a horizontal position. The *remuage* process – turning the bottles – ensures that the lees gather in the neck of the bottle. After three weeks or so the bottles are in a vertical position and all the sediment has gathered in the neck of the bottle. Now follows the *dégorgement*, or disgorging. The frozen yeast plug shoots out of the bottle and the cork is put in place.

———

Mild, sweet aroma, flowers, hint of citrus, ripe fruits. The flowery character is echoed beautifully in the taste where the ripe fruits make a come-back. Also a fine pearlisation. In the finish, a pleasant bitterness that concludes on a lovely dry note.

www.bestbelgianspecialbeers.be

Malheur Bière Brut (11%)

Beer or wine?

Beer and wine meet in the glass. The love of both pushed brewer Manu De Landtsheer towards the Brut beers. Malheur Bière Brut, launched in 2002, is based on the top-fermented Malheur 10 beer and is re-fermented in the bottle for up to three years. Just as with champagne the yeast is collected in the bottleneck. This yeast is frozen and, during the process called *dégorgement* or disgorging, the plug of ice containing the yeast is removed. The result is a delicate and sparkling beer with a tasty head of froth and an elegant aftertaste. It takes time to perfect a beer such as this. Manu De Landtsheer: 'An American brewer once proudly told me that he brews two hundred different beers. But brewing isn't a contest, is it? What we want is quality in the glass!'

———

Strong but extremely mild at the same time, with a zesty finish, very aromatic with impressions of peach and roses, apricot, vanilla, orange and lemon peel.

www.malheur.be

Bruut'n Triest (9%)

Effervescent

Brouwer Marc Struyf of Den Triest knows the world of microbrewing like the back of his hand. For his beers he often uses little-known European hops as well as aroma hops from New Zealand and America. His Bruut'n Triest lies at the heart of this 'champagnised' beer. His Bruut' Triest has spent four months maturing before the 'remuage', where the yeast gathered in the neck of the bottle is frozen and expelled, before the cork is replaced on the bottle. This beer is brewed with champagne yeast, hence the tiny pearls and delicate head of froth.

———

This is still a beer. If you swirl the glass around the fragrant hop aromas come to the fore. Afterwards you can taste apple, pear, grapefruit and a slight touch of lychees. The finish is bitter.

www.dentriest.be

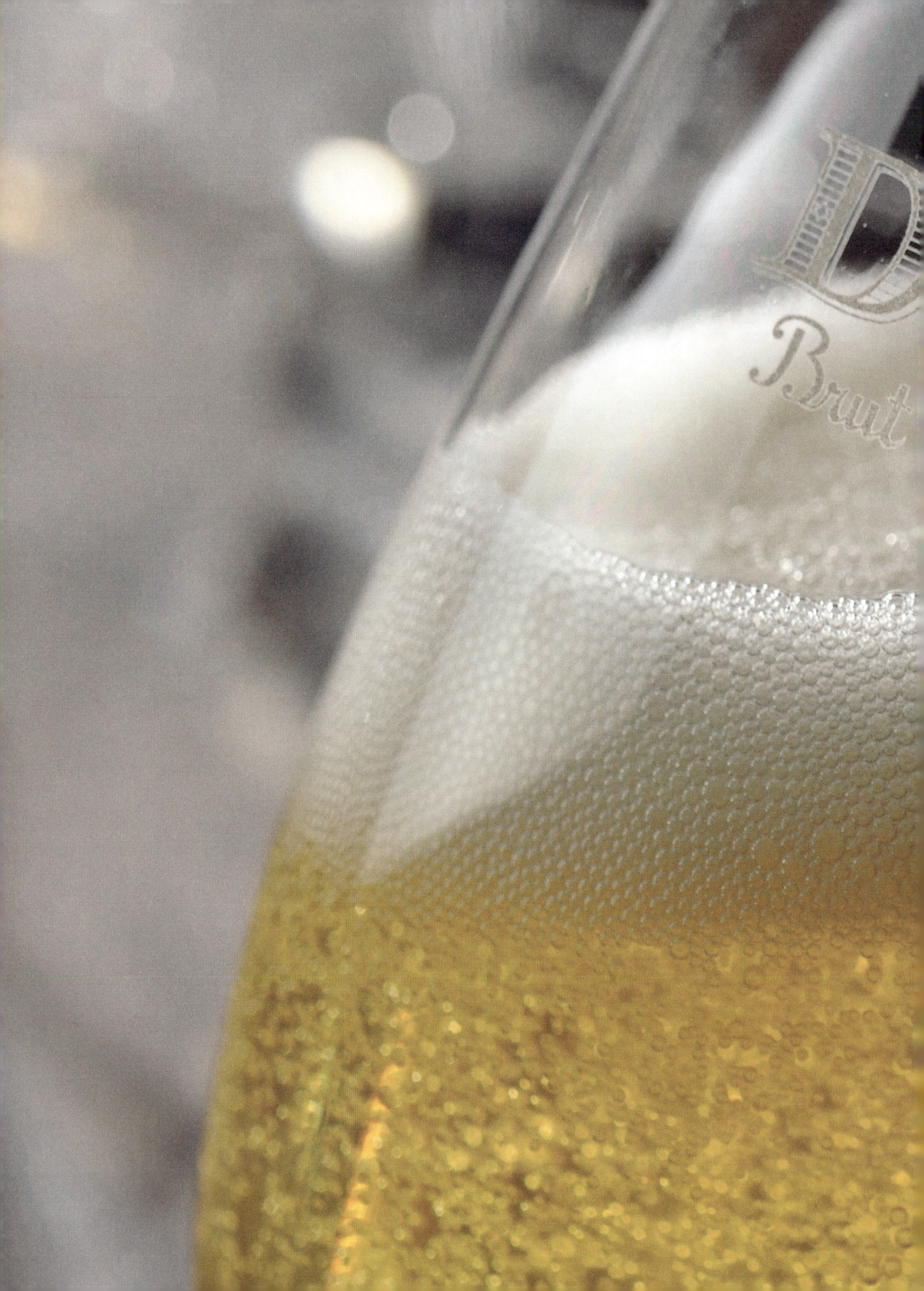
Brut

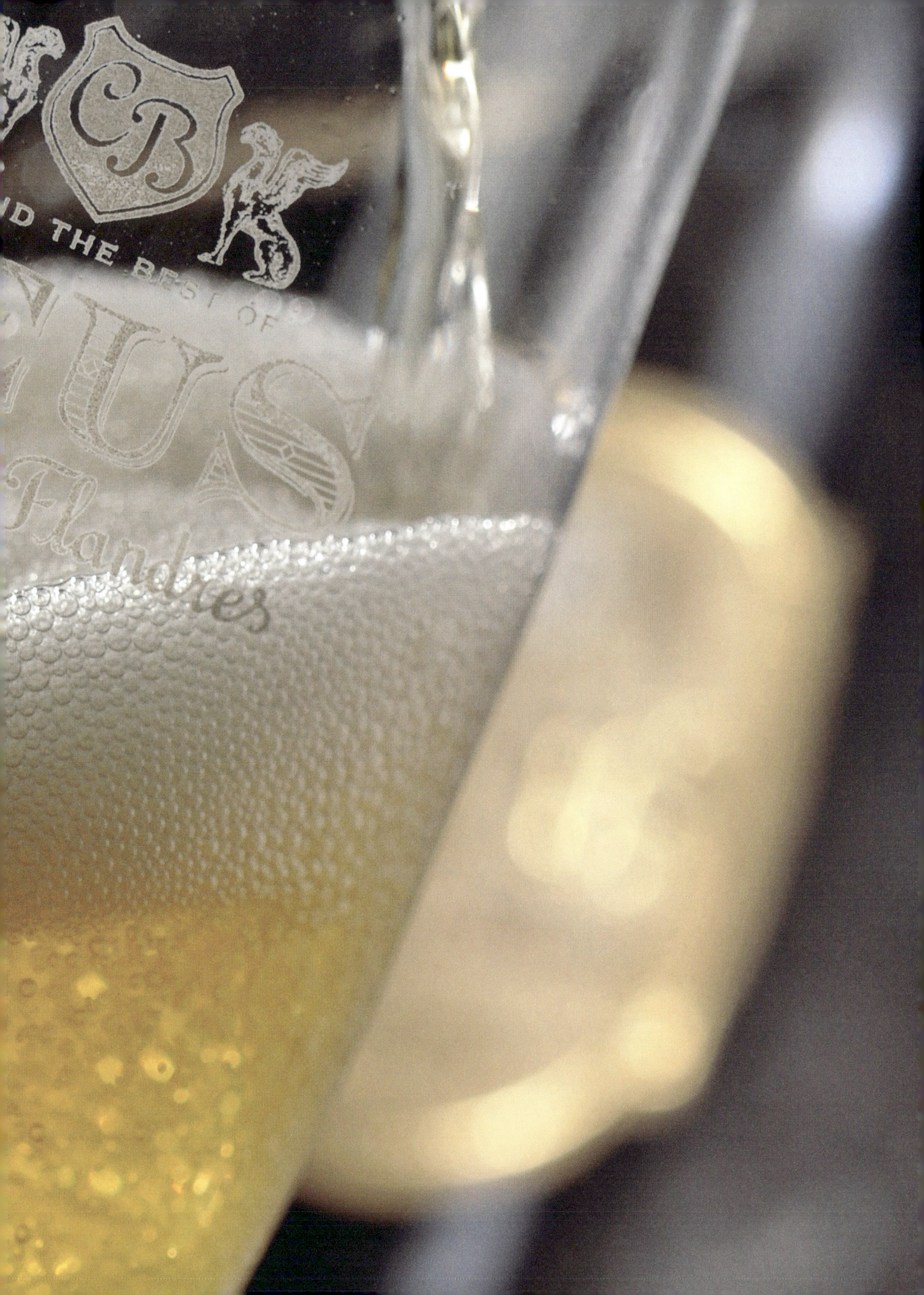
CB
ND THE BEST OF
EUS
Flandres

LIGHT BLOND BEER

◆───────◆

Light blond beers take on a golden-yellow colour in the glass and have a modest alcohol volume. The beer often sports a luxurious head of froth and has a mild, fruity and fresh taste. Very occasionally you will come across one that has a hoppy, bitter touch. This beer style is versatile and makes for a perfect thirstquencher or aperitif beer but is also a welcome guest at the gastronomic table. Tastes and aromas widely vary: from delicate and mild, the Quinto from the Dilewyns brewery for example, to well-hopped, like the Taras Boulba from Brasserie de la Senne.

La Binchoise is served in front of the statue of a Gille, a traditional carnival character from Binche.

Bière Darbyste (5,8%)

Refreshingly 'figgy'

Beer is liquid heritage. Before you know it, you have imbibed a piece of history. Take for example the Bière Darbyste from Brasserie De Blaugies, a light beer where the yeast is fed by fig juice rather than sugar. Its rather strange name is based on John Darby, the founder of the fundamentalist Plymouth Brethren who worked as a preacher in the Borinage region (around the city of Mons) in the 19th century. Marie-Noëlle Pourtois of Brasserie De Blaugies: 'In those days it was a very light drink for the workers. A mixture of water, wheat and figs was left behind the stove to ferment. It was poured into bottles that tended to explode the moment you touched them.' We sincerely hope that your bottle survives for a bit longer.

———

A refreshing, delicate bitterness, fruity, no added sugar.
www.brasseriedeblaugies.com

Binchoise Blonde (La) (6,2%)

Put on your masks

Talls hats made of ostrich feathers, colourful outfits stuffed with straw, wooden clogs dancing to the rhythm of the tambourine… Binche Carnival, now included in the Unesco World Heritage List, captivates the whole of this city and the Binchoise Blonde lubricates thirsty throats. This beer was introduced in 1995 and harks back to a light blond beer made by the local Meunier brewery in the 1960s. La Binchoise Blonde is now in the capable hands of brewer Bruno Deghorain, a 'Binchois' born and bred and one of the Gilles proudly on parade during the annual carnival. His fresh and fruity blonde thirstquencher has amazing aromas of citrus, orange peel and coriander that account for its zesty character. Thanks to the use of these last two ingredients, usually found in white beer, this blonde is halfway between blonde and white. The phenolic acids from the yeast re-enforce its zestiness. The yeast flocculates beautifully, clarifying this beer in the most natural way.

———

The nose picks up subtle aromas of hop, coriander and orange peel. A fresh, fruity, delicately bitter and very quaffable beer with a pleasant finish.
www.brasserielabinchoise.be

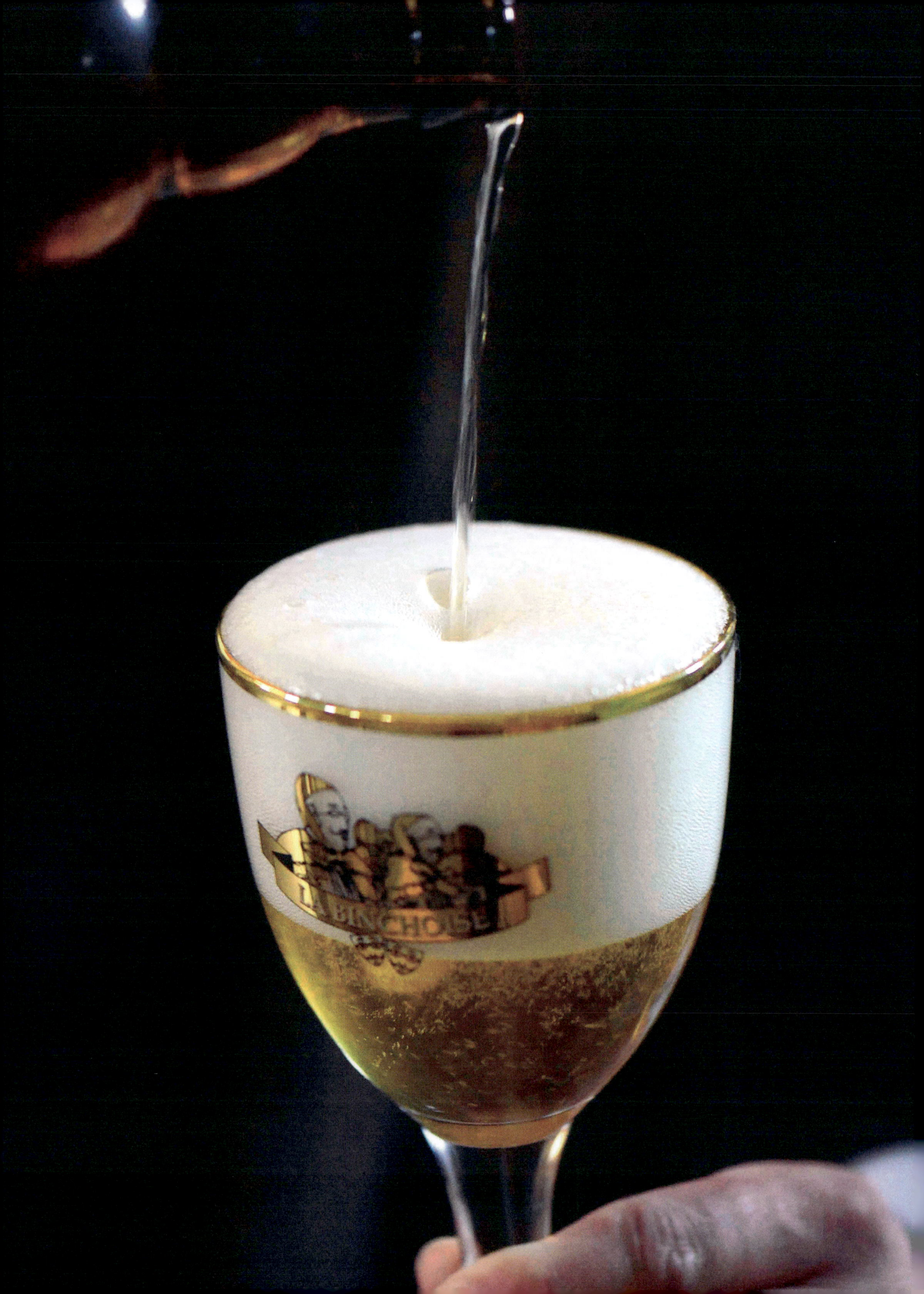
LA BINCHOISE

Bruno Deghorain, brewer at La Binchoise, in his Gille costume at the annual Binche carnival, pictured here in his brewhall. Only a few citizens are allowed to wear this outfit for the annual parade.

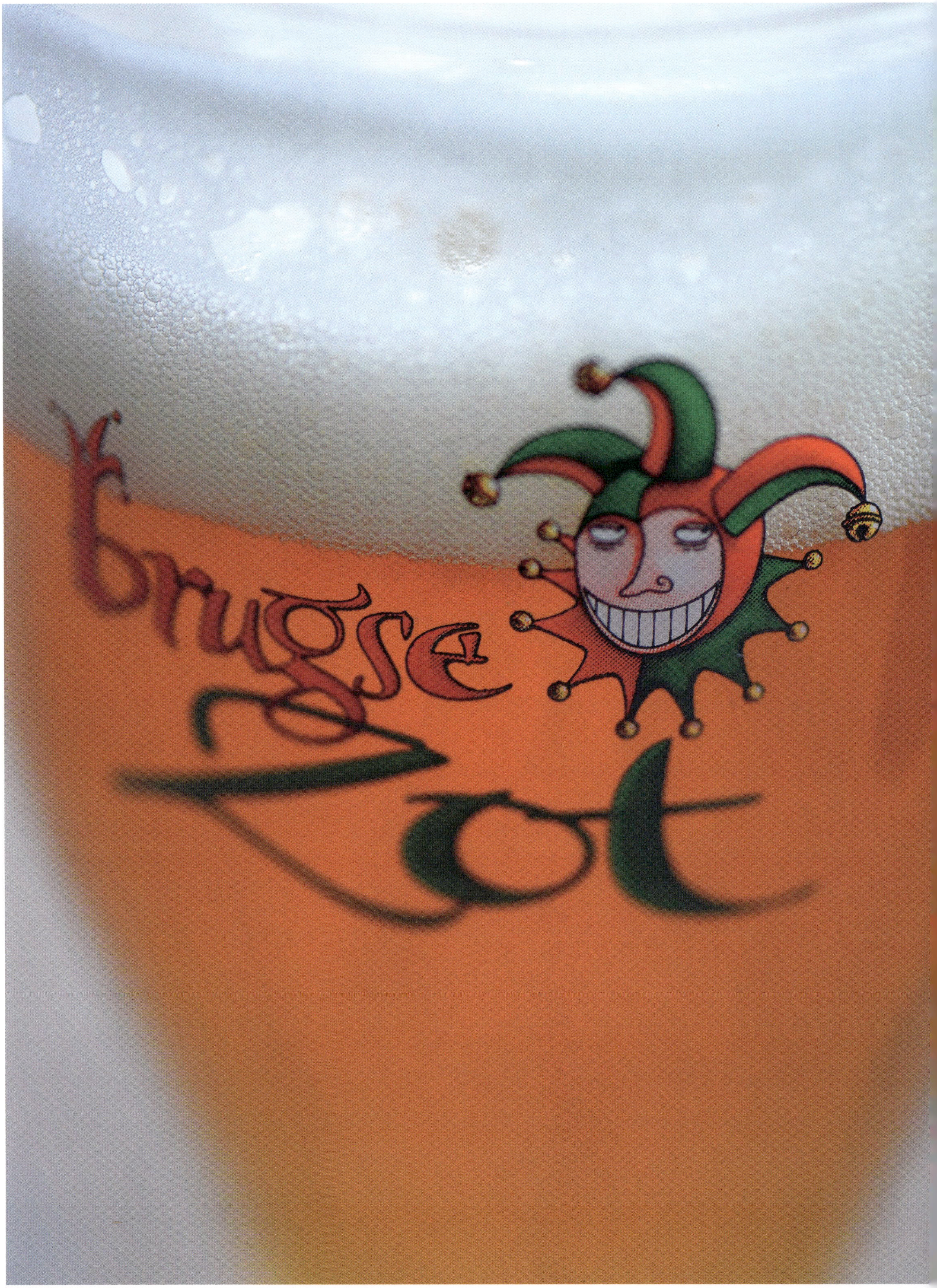
brugse
Zot

Brugse Zot Blond (6%)

A playful parade

From the label, a jester grins at you. City beer Brugse Zot was first brewed in 2005 but its name goes all the way back to the late Middle Ages, when Emperor Maximilian of Austria paid a visit to Bruges. A colourful parade of exuberant jesters and madmen (fools called 'zotten') was laid on to honour the Emperor. Afterwards, the citizens of Bruges asked the Emperor for a new 'zothuis', or madhouse. Whereupon the Emperor responded: "A madhouse is all I have seen today." Brugse Zot is a very quaffable beer with bags of character, brewed with four varieties of malt and two types of aroma hops. It re-ferments in the bottle, giving a more profound taste.

———

A very drinkable, sparkling and refreshing, fruity and zesty beer with aromas of citrus and hops coming to the fore. Taste impressions of malt and bread, lemon and herbs. The carbon dioxide causes an explosion in the mouth, as it were. A pleasant bitterness with a dry finish.

www.brugsezot.be

Curtius (6,5%)

The city beer of Liège

After a long wait Liège once again has its own city beer: Curtius, a light blond beer based on barley and wheat malt, subtly bitter, fruity and aromatic. This beer is neither filtered nor pasteurised, re-ferments in the bottle and comes in a stylish champagne bottle. Renaud Pirotte, its brewer: 'Our Curtius is made with three different hops: Styrian Golding, Magnum and Cascade. The latter is primarily responsible for its freshly sour aroma. The wheat malts make all the difference. We are using a higher dosage of wheat that results in a light beer with a more complex taste, somewhere between a white beer and a triple.' The name of the beer pays homage to a 17th-century entrepreneur from Liège who made his way up in the world and ended up a respected member of the nobility. His house, a Renaissance palace, is located on the banks of the river Meuse and is now a municipal museum.

———

A refreshing beer with touches of fruit, particularly citrus. Never overpowering.

www.lacurtius.com

Kwaremont (6,6%)

A calf-biter

De Oude Kwaremont is a steep hill, in other words a calf-biter, that forms part of the Tour of Flanders. This cyclist's beer has not stolen its name, far from it. Bike riders and cycling fanatics will testify to that. The race is often decided on the cobblestones of the Oude Kwaremont. In a tight pack, pushed on by the cheers of the roadside spectators, the riders are making their bumpy way up the hill. It feels like a mountain stage. Before you start the climb you have to make sure you are ahead of the peleton or else you can forget about winning the stage. And don't think that you have made it after the first steep climb as you will have to negotiate this hill twice more. These efforts call for a strong blond. You can bet your bottom dollar that the Kwaremont will be in full flow during and after the ride. This 'course beer' never misses out on a good party.

———

Full of character with a zesty spiciness. This beer, replete with malt, rewards your efforts with a hefty dose of liquid sugars.

www.brouwerijdebrabandere.be

Safranaise (La) (7%)

Colouring with herbs

Finding the right balance when using herbs and spices is quite a challenge. Brasserie de Millevertus, close to Orval, works its zesty magic. Daniel Lessire is a cook rather than a brewer. He is experimenting with saffron, pepper, ginger, aromas of smoky malt… 'Brewing is all about dosage,' he finds. 'A beer is only good if you are intrigued by it. What am I tasting here? You order seconds and you carry on your search. You have to learn the art of brewing with herbs and spices. It's a matter of judging the quality and trying all sorts of things.' All sorts of projects are going around in his head, making it buzz. The home-made bottle labels add a touch of humour. La Safranaise is brewed with four malt varieties, three American aroma hops and saffron from the city of Virton in Belgian Luxembourg.

———

Overpowering aromas of herbs, fruit, hop, malt and saffron. The taste is slightly sweet with a hint of bitter.

www.millevertus.be

Wilderen Goud (6,2%)

A thirstquencher

Wilderen Goud is drunk from a glass 'pot'. This golden-blond malt beer is quite fruity and dry. A powerful thirstquencher to enjoy after a walk or bike ride or when you hit the town. Unsurprisingly this beer sells well in student cafés. 'This is a beer for everyone,' is the opinion of Mike Janssen, its brewer. 'Neither complex nor extreme, but definitely oozing with taste.'

———

Fruity with impressions of peach and white grapes. Slightly bitter taste with touches of caramel and a mild finish.

www.brouwerijwilderen.be

Wipers Times 14 (The) (6,2%)

Drinking wartime papers

Ypres is steeped in First World War history. The city fortifications or 'Kazematten' precede the war as they form part of the 17th century city walls that were designed by Vauban, a military architect who served under French King Louis XIV. These subterranean areas were in use as barracks over the course of centuries and housed the printing press of the British soldiers' newspaper *The Wipers Times*. The 'kazematten' are now home to a city brewery of the same name. The Wipers Times 14 is a blond, multi-grain beer that is brewed with local hops and herbs, including the Saint Mary's Thistle that adorns the label.

———

Zesty aromas and impressions of cheese and vanilla. A very mild and creamy taste. Delicately bitter to start with, then zesty with touches of vanilla. Dry finish.

www.kazematten.be

Witkap Pater Stimulo (6%)

Beer with a soul

Witkap Stimulo has turned into a reference in the field of blond beers. A relatively light beer with a subtle bitterness, a sour freshness and flowery touches. The Witkap beers are the progeny of a former brewery: De Drie Linden from Brasschaat in the vicinity of Antwerp. The name refers to the white hoods worn by the Cistercian monks and does not denote any abbey in paraticular. This beer is now brewed by Slaghmuylder in Ninove, where the flag of tradition is always flown high. Brewery owner Bénédicte Slaghmuylder: 'We still brew with copper kettles. They are the soul of our brewery.' The Witkap beers are brewed with fresh hop cones.

———

The nose is replete with the floral and flowery scent of hops from Erembodegem near Aalst as well as the intensely fruity yeast aromas. The taste and finish are dominated by a refreshing hop bitterness.

www.witkap.be

5 · BELGIAN BEER STYLES

STRONG BLOND BEER

◆

Strong blond beers are extremely popular in Belgium. They use pale malt, which often makes them even lighter in colour than pils, but they are also far more complex. Strong blond beers go down very easily. This beer style has found its icon in Duvel. The secret resides in the choice of pale malts, fragrant Saaz and Syrian Golding aroma hops and an extremely pure production process aided by long periods of warm and cold fermentation.

Barbar Blond (8%)

Hop and honey

The number of honey beers in our country can be counted on one hand. Barbar, made by the Lefèbvre brewery, is made with Yucatan honey from Mexico. The taste of this honey, that is used throughout the brewing process, shines through. Water, barley malt, wheat, honey, sugar, hop, coriander, curaçao and yeast, the list of ingredients tells us. It takes an experienced hand to conjure a balanced full-mouthed and fresh specialty beer out of all this.

———

A slightly zesty perfume with touches of citrus, ginger and coriander. Quite rounded and powerful, subtle touches of honey, good level of bitterness right down to the finish, with vibrant liquorice coming to the fore. Sweet and dry all at once.

www.brasserielefebvre.be

Brigand (9%)

Rebels

In 1798, at the time of the Peasant's War, rebels called *brigands* were fighting the French occupying forces in the Kortrijk region. They suffered a defeat in Ingelmunster, the village that was home to the Van Honsebrouck brewery until its operations moved to the nearby village of Izegem. The rebellious Brigand is a dry and bitter blond beer that re-ferments in the bottle. It used to show up amber yellow in the glass but these days it pours a clear blond thanks to the use of pale malts, pils malts and unmalted wheat.

———

A beer with a full-mouthed taste with a strong presence of malt aromas. A slightly malty taste, zesty and hoppy. Hop bitters in the finish.

www.vanhonsebrouck.be

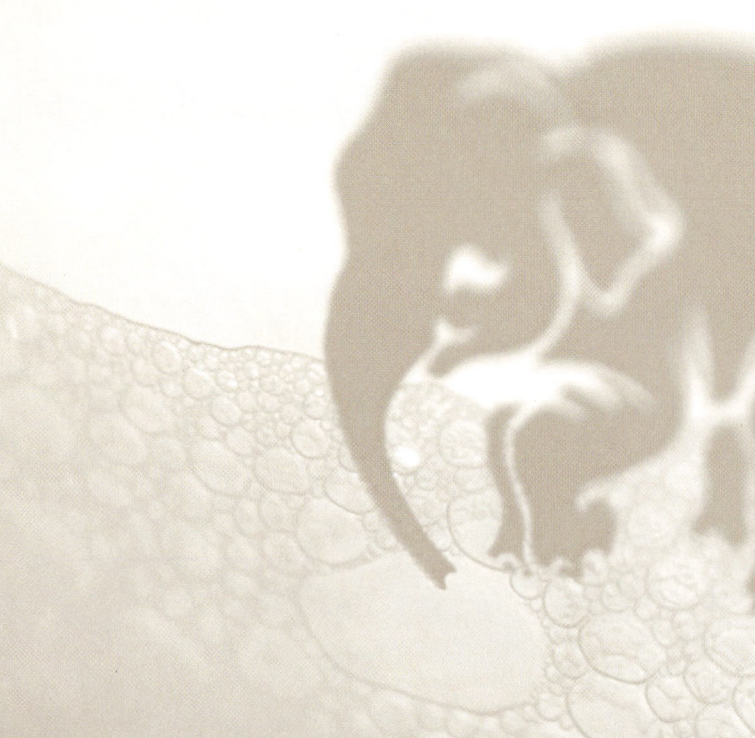

Delirium Tremens (8,5%)

Pink elephants...

...are not a figment of your imagination. The Huyghe brewery introduced Delirium Tremens in 1988. The bottle resembles a piece of stoneware from Cologne. The label features pink elephants, crocodiles and dragons depicting the various stages of inebriation you might go through after a glass or two, or three... The controversial name was thought up by a tax inspector as he grew aware of approaching intoxication. Delirium Tremens is a strong blond beer of the triple type. It re-ferments in the bottle and unusually, uses three different yeasts. The beer gained world-wide popularity, or should we say notoriety, thanks to the popular Delirium specialty beer cafés. Initially set up by the brewery in Brussels, they are now found in all corners of the world, from Japan to São Paolo. The pink elephant has turned into a cultural phenomenon. Pop into a beer festival and more often than not, you will see pink elephant hats staggering around.

———

Taste this triple and you will be surprised by its malty aromas and the fruity touches of orange peel and apricot. An alcoholic glow warms the tongue as well as the palate. Delirium Tremens tastes full in the mouth, with plenty of body and a long, dry and bitter finish.
www.delirium.be

Alain De Laet, owner of Brouwerij Huyghe, has the entire world on speed dial. Their 'pink elephant beer' Delirium Tremens is sold in 80 countries.

5 · BELGIAN BEER STYLES

Duvel (8,5%)

A strong blond

Does this beer need any further introduction? This strong blond became the symbol of an entire beer style. Its success story started in 1924 when a Duvel still took on a dark colour in the glass. Nowadays, the robust snowy-white head that forms when pouring is this beer's trademark. A Duvel is poured slowly into a dry glass and the residual yeast is left in the bottle. The bouquet is zesty and fizzes in the nose, with some citrus, even a hint of grapefruit, thanks to the use of aroma hops. These aromas return in the taste, well-balanced with a touch of zest and the well-known, typical beer character. The high saturation makes for a round mouth feel. Not only does a Duvel quench your thirst, it also stimulates the appetite. The dry finish is a bonus.

―――

Refreshing, subtle hop aromas. A light, moderately fruity beer with a gently bitter finish. High quality bitterness with a dry finish and intense pearlisation.

www.duvel.com

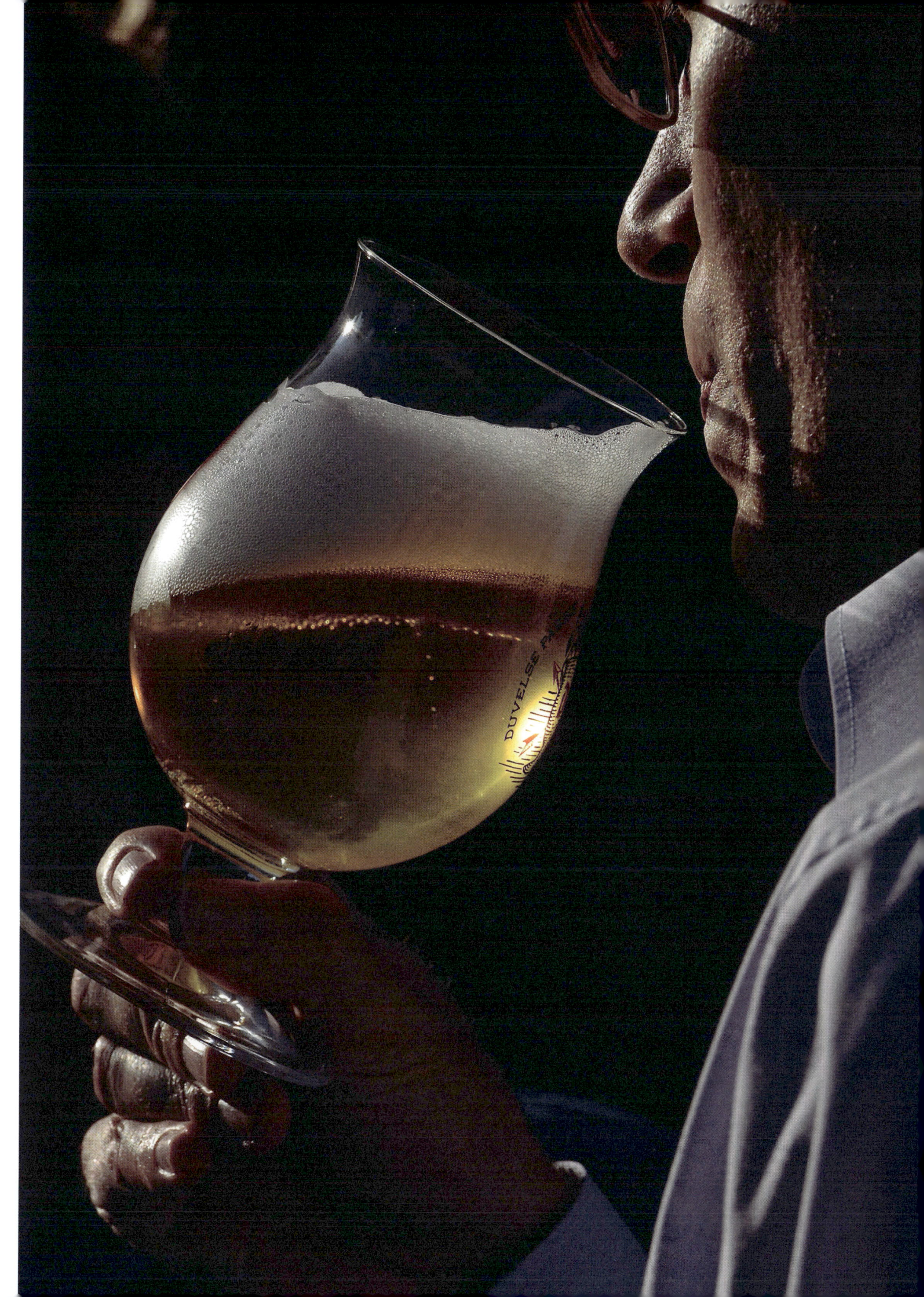
DUVELSE

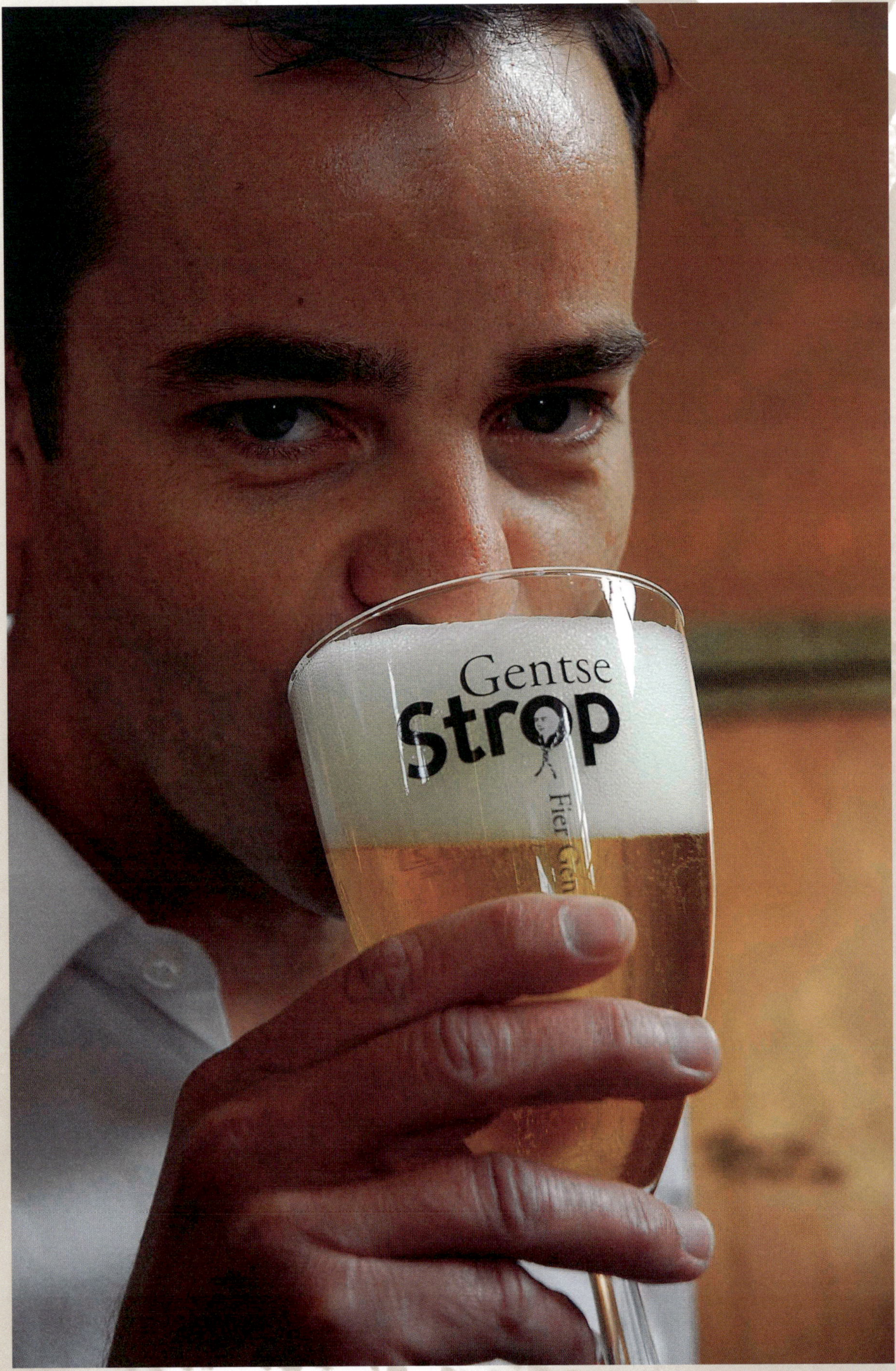
Gentse
Strop

Gageleer (7,5%)

As pure as can be

Gageleer is an organic, herbal beer brewed with Myrica gale, also known as bog myrtle or 'wilde gagel', one of the ingredients of the herbal mixture known as gruit or 'gruut'. It was used by medieval brewers before hop reached our shores. Buy a Gageleer and support nature conservation: revenues from this beer go towards the purchase of nature reserves. Bog myrtle still grows in abundance in one particular nature reserve: De Liereman between Oud-Turnhout and Arendonk. The extensive clumps of myrtle with their characteristic fragrance and colour palette contribute to the uniqueness of this area.

Aromas of resin, heather and herbs including bay, aniseed and mint. Slightly sweet to start off with, fruity and zesty, hints of pepper and liquorice with an undercurrent of bitter.

www.gageleer.be

Gentse Strop (6,9%)

Named by the Emperor

De Gentse Strop was introduced in 2011 and is a reminder of the historic ties between the cities of Oudenaarde and Ghent. Ghent was Emperor Charles V's home town, while his illegitimate daughter, Margaret of Parma, was born in Oudenaarde. And how about the 'strop' or noose referred to in the name of the beer? That was the punishment suffered by the rebellious citizens of Ghent.

In 1540 the Emperor Charles forced the dignitaries of Ghent to wear a noose around their necks to punish them for their opposition to his reign. The rebellious citizens of Ghent have borne the nickname of 'stroppendragers', or noose bearers, ever since.

This beer uses noble aroma hops that yield delicate, fruity aromas with a subtle hop bitter that continues to permeate the taste. Strikingly zesty touches of mild pepper and coriander.

www.roman.be

Gruut Inferno (9%)

Hop and herbs

In the early Middle Ages, before hops came across to Belgium, the brewers were using herbs to preserve the life of their beer. Annick De Splenter, brewer at the Gruut Ghent city brewery, draws her inspiration from that era, albeit with the use of modern brewing technology. Her Gruut Inferno, created in collaboration with De Brabandere, is the only beer in her range that contains hops. In medieval times the river Leie separated the city of Ghent into two administrative districts. The right bank fell under German rule and the brewers here were using hops (from the 13th century onwards). The brewers on the left bank were governed by France and they were using gruit. Landowners imposed a levy on beer that depended on the amount of herbs used. The gruit was blended differently in each area. The landowner was aware which herbal mixture was used and imposed his taxes accordingly. Hops gradually replaced herbs as they prolong the storage period of the beer.

Hop aromas are making their presence felt and are joining herbs, wood and hints of sugar bread. Full in the mouth and full of zest, sweet impressions with a mildly bitter finish.

www.gruut.be

Guillotine (La) (8,5%)

As sharp as a blade?

During the French Revolution, heads were rolling off the metaphorical conveyor belt. The guillotine was doing overtime. This sharp dropblade now adorns the label of this commemorative beer, launched by Huyghe two hunderd years after these grisly events. The blood-red label forms a great contrast with the creamy-coloured bottle that contains this golden-blonde triple. La Guillotine is brewed with barley, wheat and three varieties of hops. It also uses *dry hopping*. Fresh hops are added to the tank during cold storage.

The nose picks up aromas of herbs, fruits, citrus and hops. Quite neutral to start off with but then, the carbon dioxide fizzes on the tongue and the bitterness (apple, lemon) makes itself felt.

www.delirium.be

Beer lover Wanne Madelijns is looking chuffed, holding a personalised bottle of La Guillotine. Brouwerij Huyghe introduced this beer to commemorate the 200th anniversary of the French Revolution in 1989.

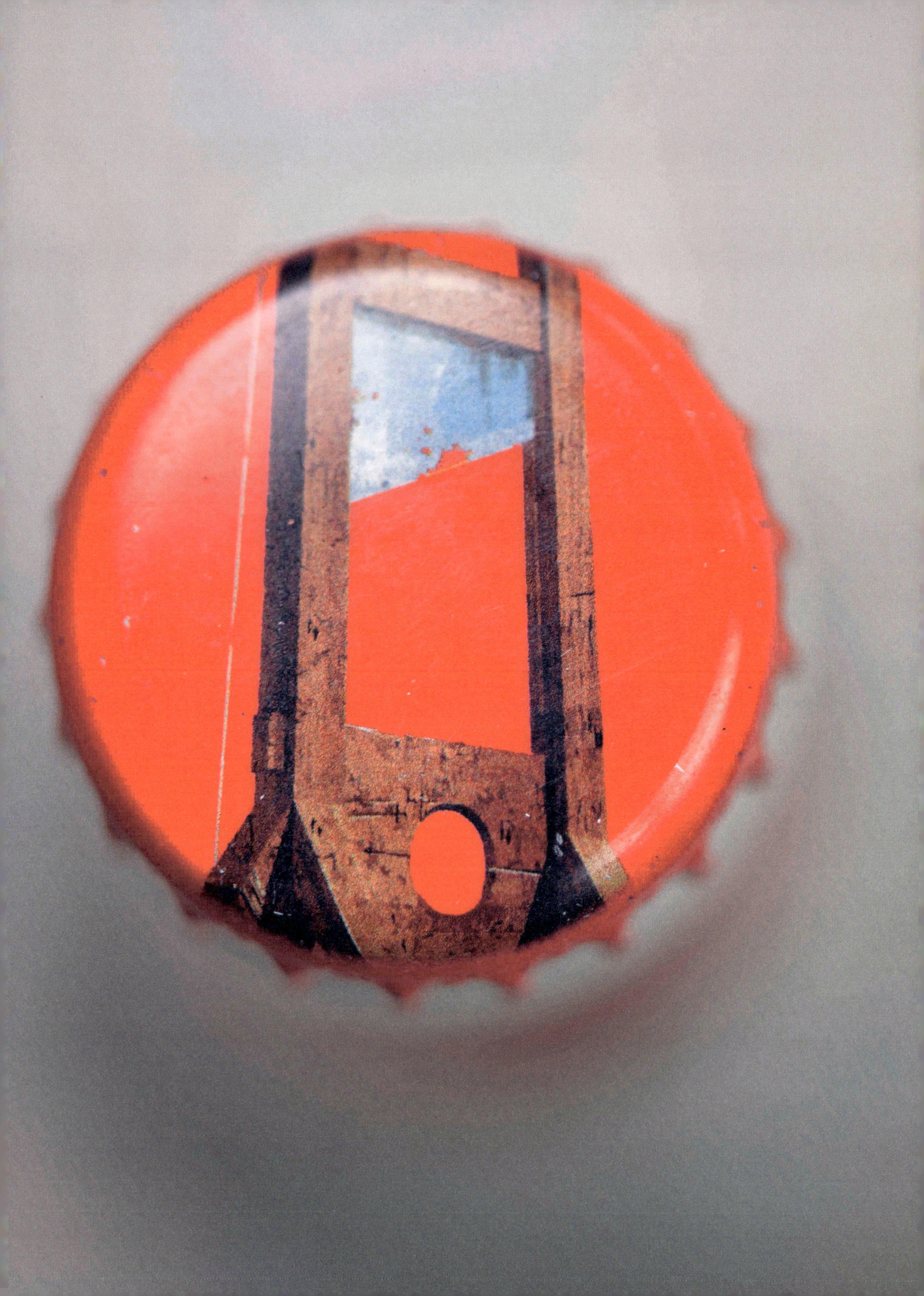

Hof ten Dormaal Wit Goud (8%)

Brewing endives

Endives brought prosperity to this region. All that remains now is memories of stoves giving off smoke and corrugated sheets. Hof ten Dormaal Wit Goud is brewed with chicory (the root of the endive plant) and pays homage to the cultivation of this crop. André Janssens, the brewer, drew his inspiration from his own childhood memories. 'I managed to translate the quite specific bitterness of endives into the taste of the beer', he tells us. 'It has turned out to be a perfect combination. Quite obvious really, as the bitterness in the beer normally gives it a deliciously fresh taste. We grow our own beer barley and hops. The energy comes from oilseed rape from our own fields. As we are also cattle farmers, we use the bostel to feed our cows. And this completes the circle.' The chicory is added 30 minutes before the end of the boiling stage.

———

Earthy, spicy and fruity aromas. Zesty taste with touches of pepper and a bitter undercurrent from the roast chicory.

www.hoftendormaal.com

La Chouffe (8%)

A gnome beer

Once upon a time, a gnome whispered the secret of his favourite beer into the ear of a brewer, deep in the Ardennes forest. The year was 1982. This Ardennes triple has now conquered the world. La Chouffe is an unfiltered blond beer, that re-ferments both in the bottle and in the barrel. It is pleasantly fruity, made with zesty coriander and gives off gentle hop aromas. Thanks to the golden-yellow colour and creamy head of froth, the sun seems to be shining in your glass. Zesty aromas make their playful entrance with citrus at the front, followed by the refreshing aroma of fresh coriander. This lends a flowery character to the whole, complemented by a banana-like fruitiness that flows over into the taste. The combination of these fresh and floral flavours ensures a light mouthfeel at any given time. The finish is pleasantly zesty and peppery.

———

A full-mouthed, very quaffable beer with the fruity aromas of peach and apricot, touches of citrus and coriander and a subtle touch of hops. A pleasantly surprising taste of spices, malts and fruits.

www.achouffe.be

Lupulus Blonde (8,5%)

The hop that keeps on giving

At Les 3 Fourquets they never stop tinkering with their beers. Their Lupulus is a hoppy, unfiltered Ardennes triple with a golden colour. It re-ferments both in the bottle and in the barrel. Refreshing and aromatic. Pierre Gobron, the brewer: 'Many microbrewers want to make far too many beers. I feel that it takes five years or so to perfect a particular beer.' We don't have a lot of time for chatting. The brewer is adding hops to the boiling barley liquid. He frequently checks his high-tech equipment. 'Brewing accounts for my long life', Pierre laughs. The brewery is housed in a splendid 18th-century farmhouse, next to a stream with clear water, surrounded by an oasis of green. Can you be any more 'Ardennes'? Pierre Gobron, co-founder of Brasserie d'Achouffe in a former life, drew his inspiration from the wolves that once roamed the Ardennes forests. It is said the wolves wandered across from Slovenia, just like the best hops. Coincidentally, these hops go by the Latin name of Humulus lupulus, that could be translated as 'modest wolf cub'.

―――――

Aromas of roast malt, hop, flowers, spices and citrus. In the taste you find hop bitter, seasoned with a hint of thyme and nut, rounded off by a slightly bitter finish.

www.lupulus.be

Hopus (8,3%)

Vijfmaal hop

There is a special art to pouring a Hopus. Open the flip-top bottle and hear the 'plop'. Then slowly pour the beer into its elegant glass. Leave a sufficient quantity of beer in the bottom of the bottle. Pour the yeast residues into the yeast glass. Drink them seperately or mix them in with the beer that remains in the bottle. As the name indicates, this is a hoppy and strong blond, brewed with five varieties of hop and bottle-fermented. During the 1960s the Lefèbvre brewery resolutely opted to produce specialty beers of higher strength, which have been flowing out of the tanks here ever since. The brewer swears by brewing the artisan way: 'We don't use filtration. Instead, we centrifuge the beer to preserve its natural taste.'

―――――

Hopus will astound you with its aromas of citrus, hop, malt, flowers and fruit that return in the taste, where the tone is set by bitter touches, followed by a long, slightly bitter finish.

www.brasserielefebvre.be

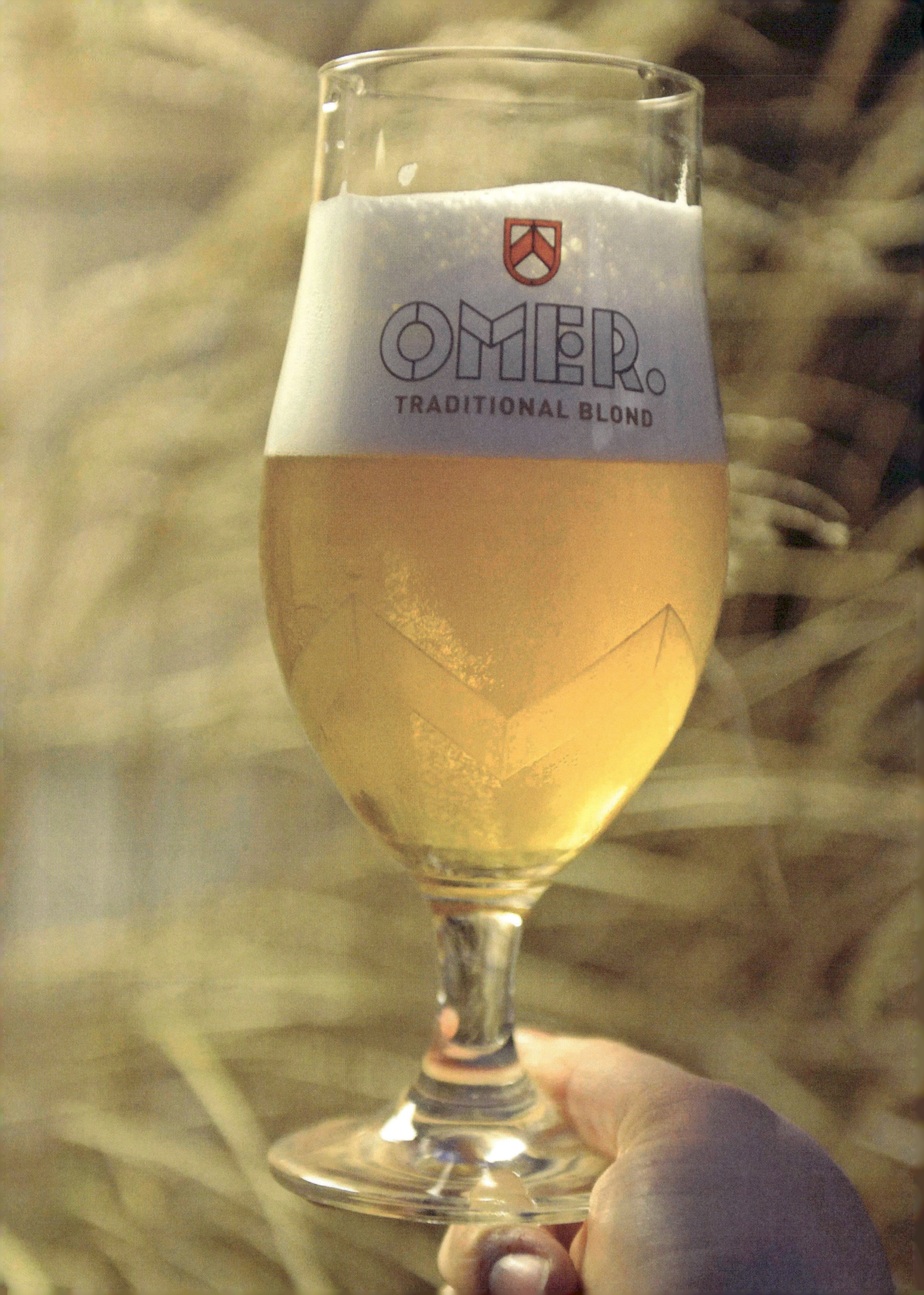
OMER.
TRADITIONAL BLOND

Omer (8%)

Dynasty

This strong, blond, top-fermented beer is the result of 120 years of craftsmanship. In the year 1892 Omer Vander Ghinste founded a brewery in Bellegem. To put his beers in the spotlight he had the name 'Bieren Omer Vander Ghinste' etched into the stained glass windows that adorned the façade of his café. The brewer's wife, Marguerite Vandamme, pointed out to her husband that changing those expensive leaded windows whenever the brewery was handed over to the next generation, would not really be feasible. And so, it came to pass that every first-born son would bear the name of Omer. The brewery was managed successively by Omer (1892–1929), Omer Remi (1929–1961) and Omer (1961–2007). Management as well as the well-kept brewing secrets are now in the hands of Omer-Jean Vander Ghinste. The hand-crafted, stained-glass windows still take pride of place in several cafés in the Kortrijk area.

―――

The nose encounters fruity aromas contributed by the yeast. The fruity character also shines through in the taste, when the hop makes its entrance with delicate touches of bitterness that culminate in a slightly bitter finish.

www.omer.be

Vapeur Cochonne (La) (9%)

Steaming ahead

At Brasserie à Vapeur in Pipaix you feel like you are on a movie set. Their brewing equipment is still steam-driven just like it was in the 19th century. The brewery was founded in 1785 and revived in 1984. Pulleys start to turn, belts move back and forth at high speed and the brewhall fills up with steam. The crushed malt is spewed out into the large, open mashing basin. Slowly, the brewing water comes up to the right temperature, starting off at 46 °C, followed by 55 °C, 62 °C, 68 °C, 74 °C… The mashing blades turn around and around until they produce a homogenous mash. The liquid wort is transferred to the boiling kettle and fills it up to the top.

Jean-Louis Dits, the brewer, is wearing his brewer's apron and fires off his instructions, not unlike an experienced conductor of an orchestra but with one difference: he is bathed in steam. Come and see this spectacle for yourself… and taste the Vapeur Cochonne.

―――

Hints of fruit, caramel and raisins steeped in rum. Aromas reminiscent of wine, hop, honey and orange with an undercurrent of alcohol.

www.vapeur.com

Paix Dieu Pleine Lune (10%)

Brewing by the light of a full moon

The Cistercian abbey of Paix-Dieu, close to Hoei, used to brew only when the moon was full. Today, this 'full moon beer' made by Caulier is a reminder of the lives of these monks, dictated by the calendar of prayers and work on the land, staying close to nature. It is said that the wort ferments better when the moon is full and that the beer will take on more body and have a fuller taste. Paix-Dieu Pleine Lune is a blond beer that re-ferments in the bottle. 'It is the first beer in the world that is brewed under a full moon', the brewer states. Look at the glass to find out what you are drinking. The tilted lunar globe on a tall stem, the top of the glass pointed towards the nose, all the better to sniff the aromas. Caulier beers are brewed in a natural way, using only spring water, pure malt, entire hop cones, yeast and natural aromas.

―――

Fruity and zesty aromas. A delicate bitterness supported by a touch of hops, leading towards a long finish.

www.paixdieubeer.be

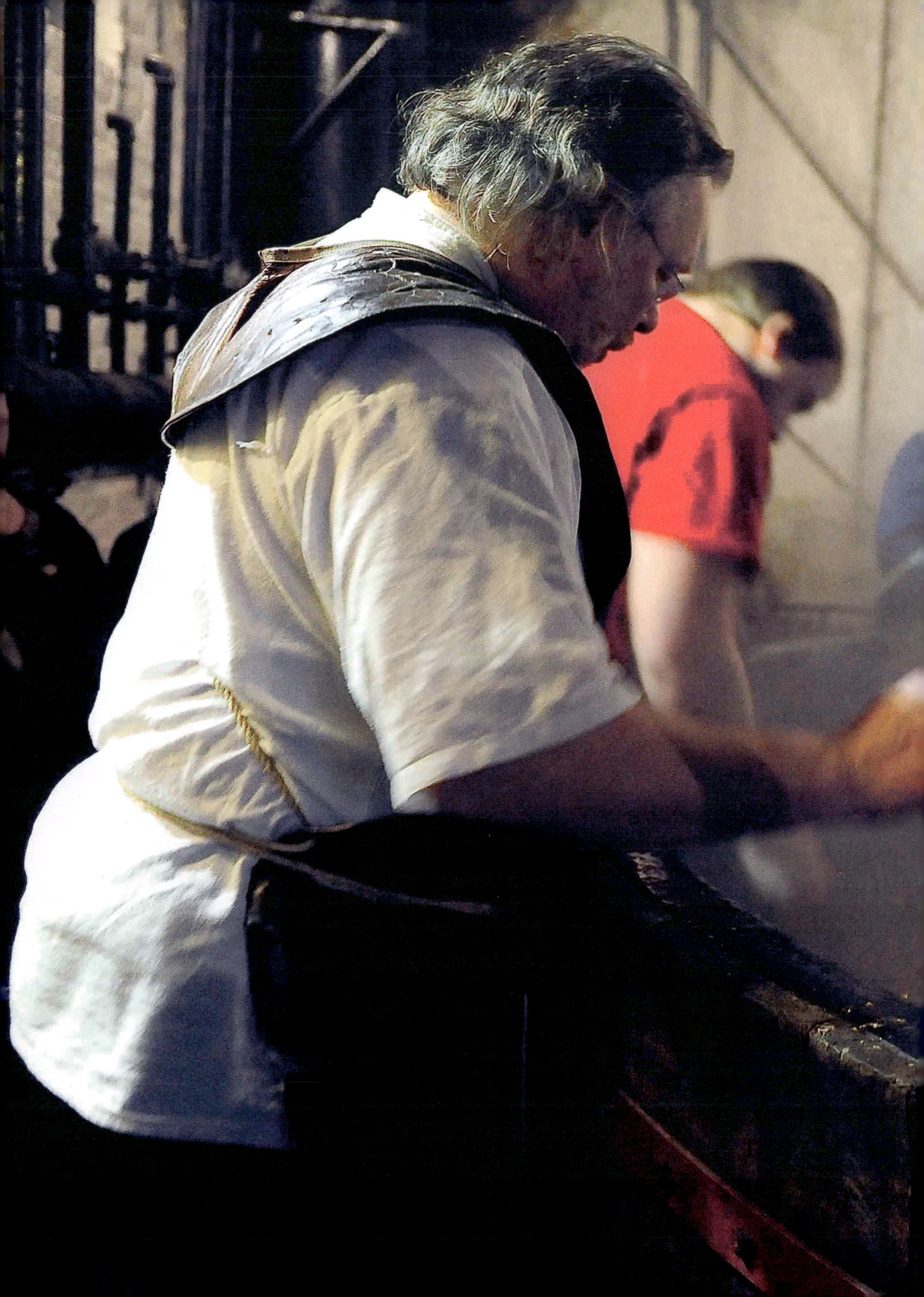

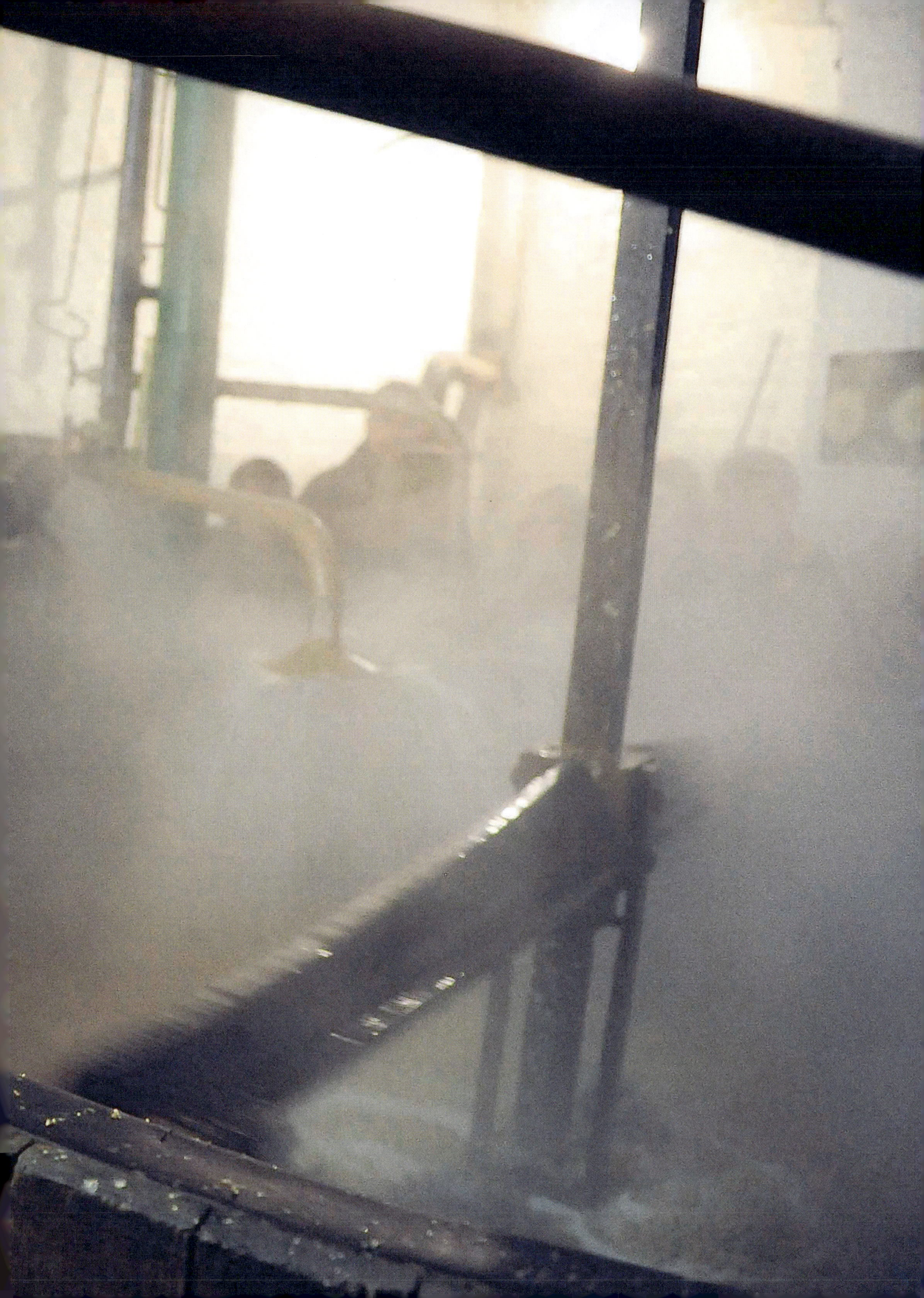

TRIPLE

◆

Triple is a term that refers to the quantity and density of the wort used in the beer. 'Triple' indicates a higher proportion of ingredients used in brewing. A triple is a heavy beer, usually blond, with a strong taste of malt and/or hop bitter. A modern triple is fruity and dry with just the right amount of carbon dioxide and a lovely bitterness. Triples tend to go down dangerously well. Triple is a generic term for a strong beer, blond to amber in colour, that re-ferments in the bottle. Westmalle Triple is considered the reference for this beer style. The triple was first brewed by Trappists but is now a generic term. Triples are a specialty of Belgian brewers. Belgian triples are beers with a predominantly golden-blond colour, slightly darker than strong blond beers and with a high volume of alcohol.

Mother An and daughter Miek De Ryck of the eponymous brewery. An brews, Miek sells.

Arend Triple (8%)

A high-flier

Arend Triple is a slightly cloudy, golden-blond, top-fermented beer that re-ferments in the bottle. An De Ryck brews nine artisan beers. This family brewery is rooted in the tradition of the Spéciale Belge amber beers. In 1920 the De Ryck brewery launched an amber beer of the Spéciale Belge type as an alternative to pils. This would be the only beer produced by the brewery for thirty years. In the 1950s a Christmas beer was added. Inspired by the British pale ale, it is the predecessor to the Arend Winter.

In 1886 Gustaaf De Ryck, a tanner, set up his own brewery in the heart of Herzele and named it Arend ('Eagle'). He had learnt his craft at Zum Golden Adler in Bremen, which inspired the name. After the First World War, the brewery carried on under the De Ryck name.

———

A hoppy aroma in combination with a mild taste of malt. A gently bitter and warming finish.

www.deryckbrewery.be

Brugge Triple (8,7%)

Powder keg

Many Belgian cities can boast their own city beer. Bruges brewery De Gouden Boom launched the 'Brugse triple' in 1987. The brewery was taken over by Palm Belgian Craft Brewers in 2004 when the beer was re-named Brugge Triple. Its roots go all the way back to the Middle Ages, even before the introduction of hops, when brewers used a herb mixture called 'gruut'. The Gruuthuus in Bruges is a reminder of those times, when the Lords of Gruuthuus, on behalf of the Count of Flanders, collected excise duties on the gruut used by the brewers. At any rate, the Brugge Triple is still full of zest

———

The Brugge Triple yields striking aromas of malt, banana, cuberdon sweets, caramel and chocolate accompanied by the smoky, toasted touches from the yeast. This triple has a powerful, bitter-sweet taste. A full-mouthed beer with a long, slightly bitter finish.

www.palm.be

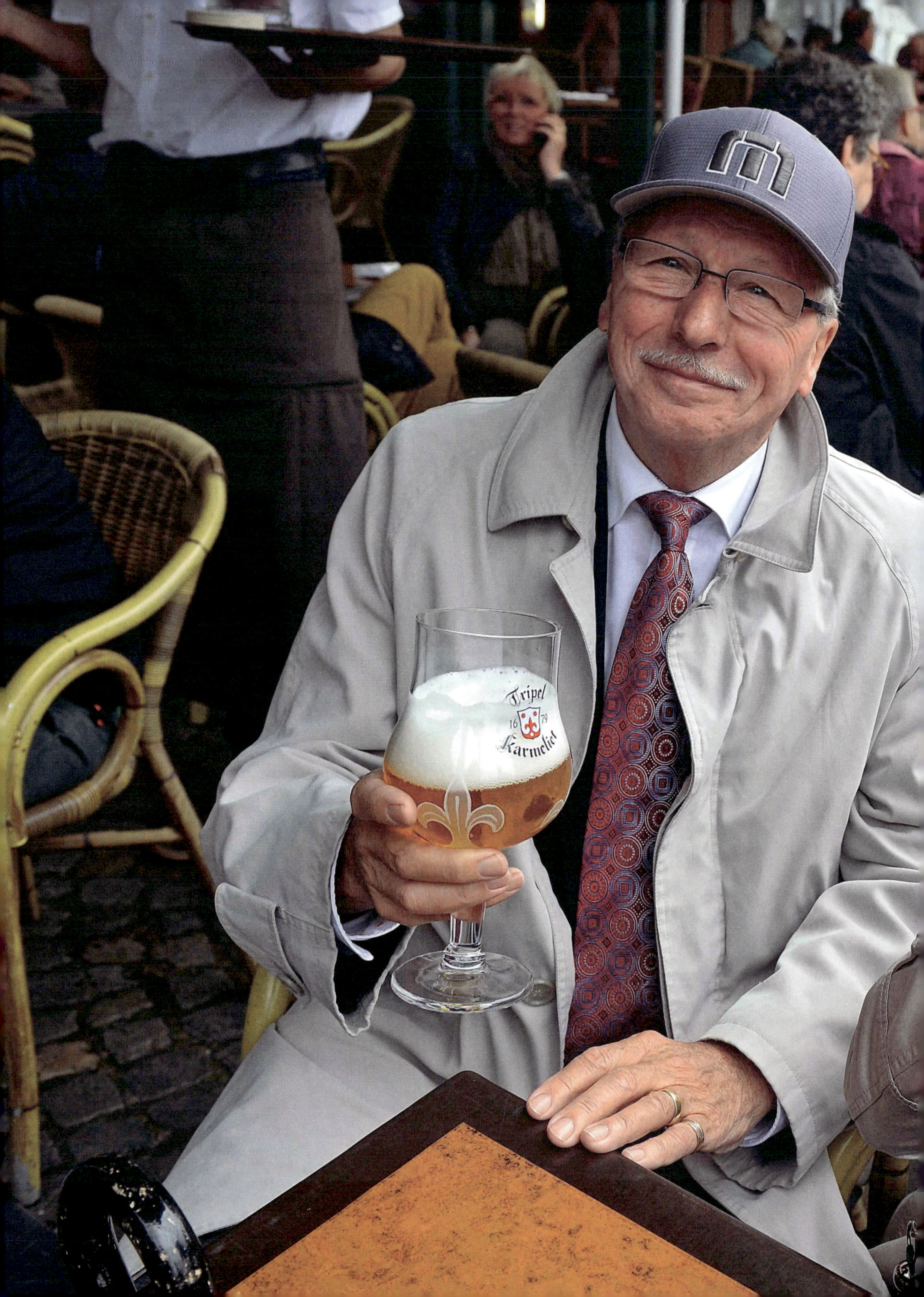
Tripel
16 79
Karmeliet

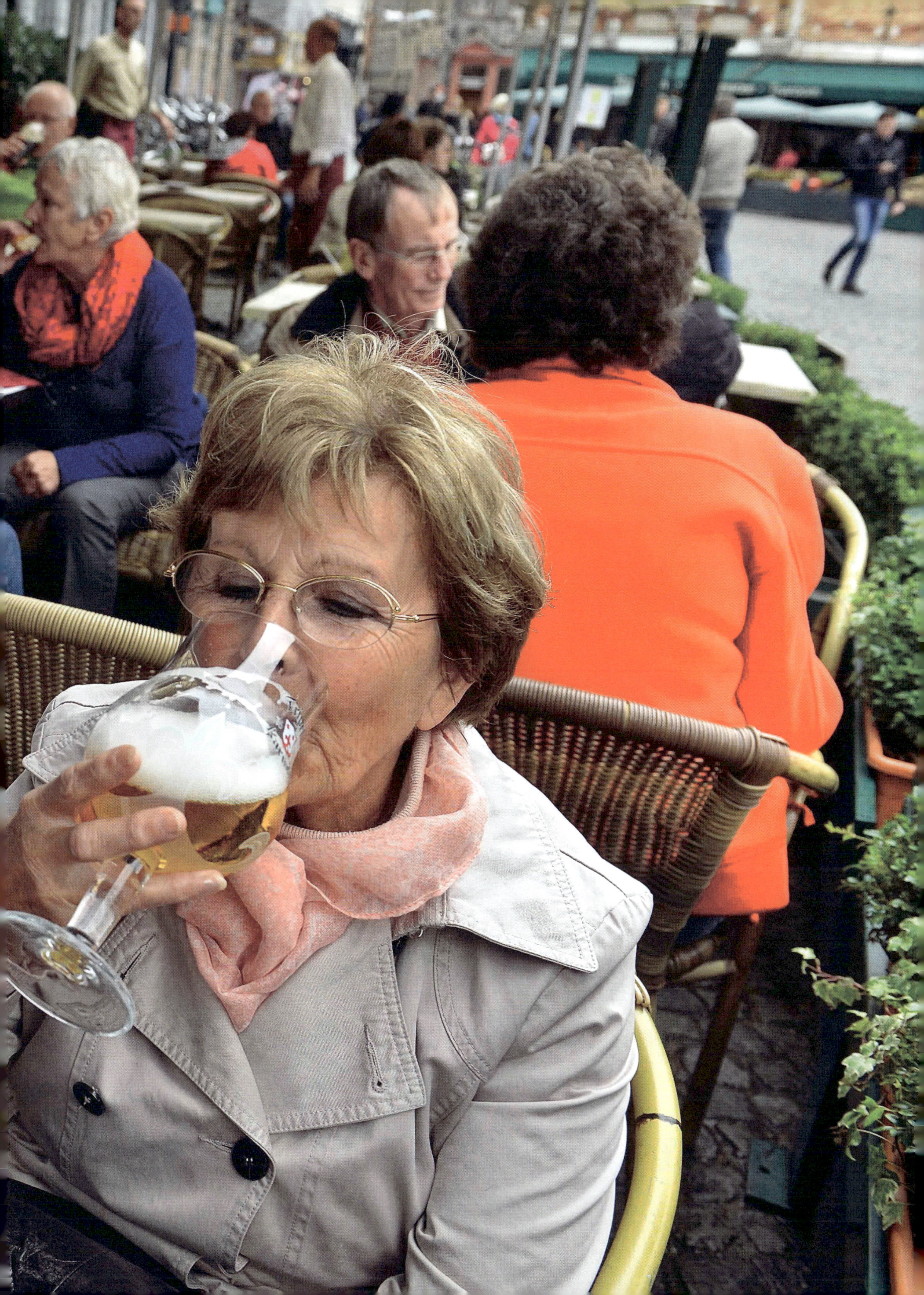

Jambe-de-Bois (8%)

Both legs firmly planted

The bitterest triple in Belgium? If you know Brasserie de la Senne, you are aware that they have a generous hand when it comes to adding hops. Their Jambe-de-Bois or 'peg-leg' is a reference to Jean-Joseph Charlier, a soldier in Napoleon's army. He lost his leg during battle and survived on a small pension. In 1830 he joined the Brussels revolutionaries in their fight against the Dutch occupier, making good use of a Dutch cannon that had been left behind. The entire story is brought to life on the label. Yvan De Baets, the brewer, makes no effort to hide his love of hops: 'Hops are our trademark. We make bitter beers. We brew with traditional European hop varieties cultivated in their country of origin.' Furthermore, Brasserie de la Senne are proof that light beers can pack a surprisingly characterful punch. The brewers allow themselves time to produce a quality product. 'The entire process takes us two months: main fermentation, cold storage, bottling, re-fermentation, resting in the warm chamber and in the depot…', Yvan explains. 'Our beers are fully fermented. You will not come across any residual sugars or sweetness. Or spices, for that matter.'

———

Hoppy, flowery and fruity aromas with hints of banana. The taste is dominated by malt, supported by a long and delicate bitterness that vibrates all the way through to the finish.

www.brasseriedelasenne.be

Triple Karmeliet (8,4%)

Won over by grains

A three-grain beer from Dendermonde. Karmeliet is a triple brewed with barley, wheat and oats. You could even talk about a six-grain beer as each variety is used raw as well as malted. In this beer, the lightness and freshness of wheat is coupled with the creaminess of oats and accompanied by the zesty, dry feel of lemon. The brewer was inspired by a traditional recipe for a three-grain beer found at Dendermonde Abbey.

———

A three-grain beer brewed with Styrian hops and judiciously used herbs. Owes its fruity character (banana and vanilla) to the house yeast. The vanilla merges with the orangey hop aromas. Plenty of citrus in the nose, also bitter lemon and sugar. On the tongue, a hint of malt accompanied by sweet ripe fruits. In the finish, citrus and sweet malts.

www.bestbelgianspecialbeers.be

Triple d'Anvers (8%)

For the 'sinjoor'

The citizens of Antwerp, commonly called 'sinjoren' (seigneurs), finally got their own triple. In 2010 Antwerp brewery De Koninck launched its first real triple, De Koninck Triple d'Anvers. It is a top-fermented beer that colours golden-blond to pale amber. De Koninck Triple d'Anvers is topped by an amazingly rich, white head. Its complexity clearly makes itself felt in the nose. The beer is mildly zesty and fruity thanks to the yeast, with aromas of pear and ripe banana. The pale malts are beautifully balanced with the caramel malts. At the outset, De Koninck Triple d'Anvers comes across as slightly sweet with a great balance between hop bitter and fruitiness. This triple owes its sparkling character to the re-fermentation in the bottle that lends the beer depth and complexity as well as a lingering finish.

———

Surprisingly fruity aromas with a subtle interaction of pale and caramel malts and a fine balance beween hop bitter, fruitiness and freshness. Full in the mouth and very quaffable.

www.dekoninck.be

Triple Kanunnik (8,2%)

Zesty and fruity

Mild, gently hopped and zesty. This is how you would describe the Triple Kanunnik. This pleasant, full-mouthed and fruity triple stands out through its malty aroma. This four-grain triple is brewed with barley, wheat, oats and rye as well as three different herbs and two hop varieties, one of which is an American aroma hop. Kanunnik Triple contains the same house yeast as Wilderen Goud, hence its fruity character. The Triple Kanunnik also forms the basis of the Eau-de-Bière house spirit.

———

A mild, zesty triple with a gentle finish. Impressions of citrus, vanilla, banana, peach, wood, malt and candi sugar. Coriander jumps to the front of the queue when it comes to spices.

www.brouwerijwilderen.be

Tripel Karmeliet
1679

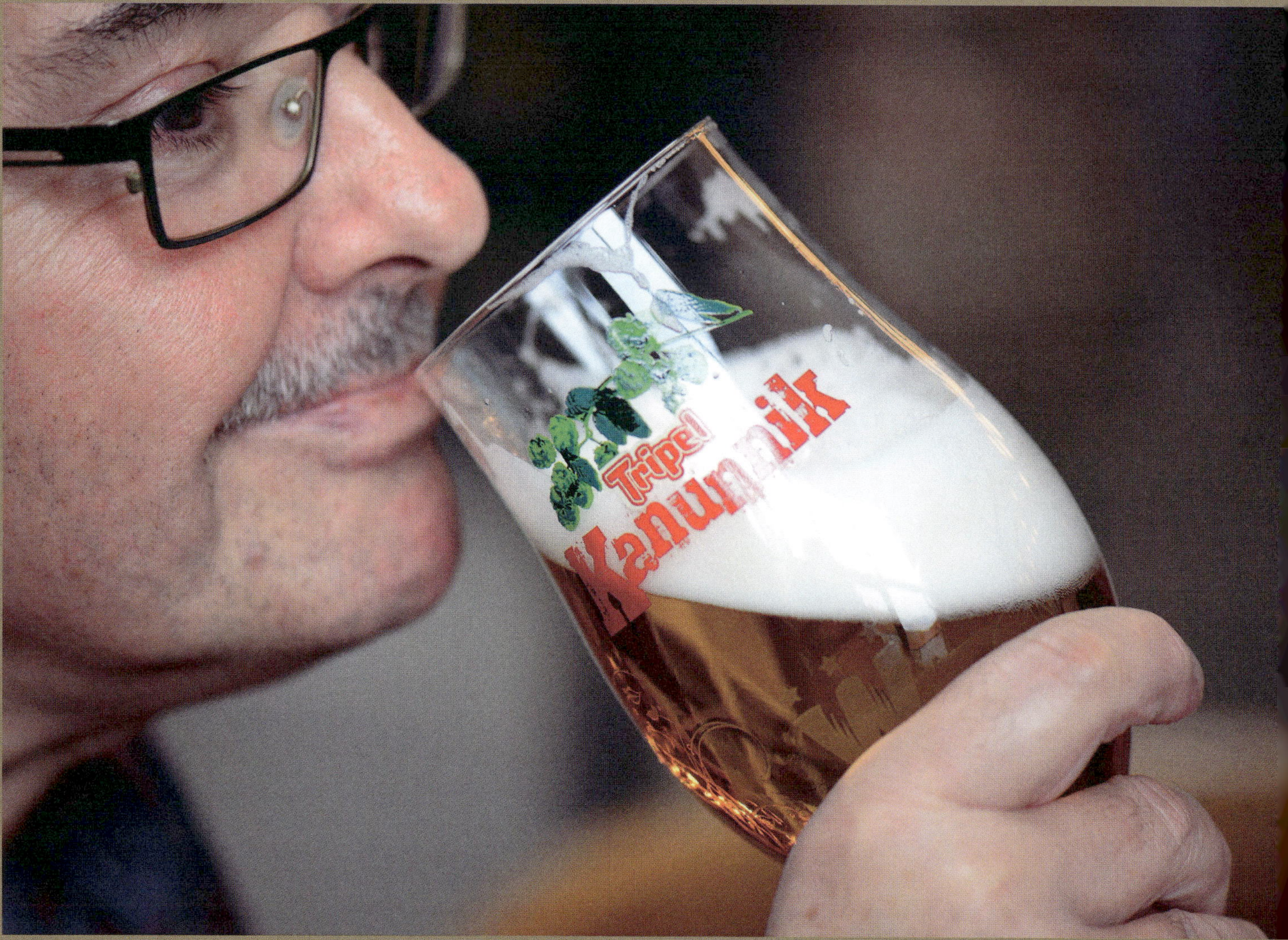
Tripel

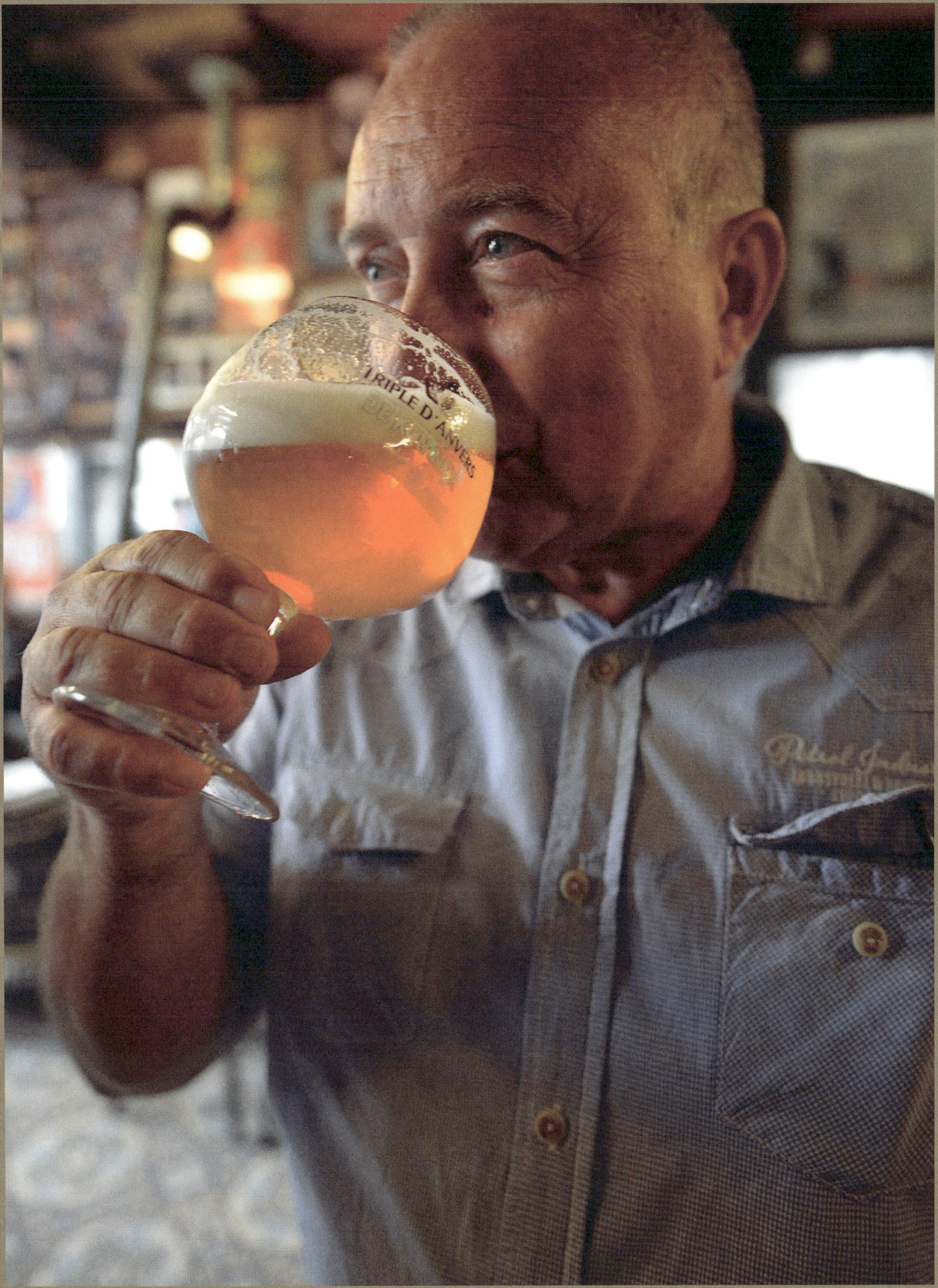
TRIPLE D'ANVERS

STRONG DARK BEER, DOUBLE AND QUADRUPLE

◆―――◆―――◆

Abbey beers and Trappist beers have many strong dark beers amongst the members of this beer style. These types of beer are also popular outside of these categories. In times gone by, if you ordered a 'Trappist', you would invariably find a strong dark beer in front of you. In the meantime, tastes have changed and at the bar you are equally likely to come face-to-face with a strong blond beer or triple. 'Dubbel' or double denotes the quantity of malt added and the density of the ingredients in the beer. Beers in this style category tend to have an initial sweet taste with touches of dried fruits and a dry, slightly bitter finish. A 'dubbel' used to come from abbey breweries but is now a generic term for a strong dark beer. The dark quadruple is stronger than the triple (+10% alc.vol). This beer type became popular in Belgium thanks to the quadruple brewed by La Trappe, a Dutch Trappist abbey.

Barista (11%)

From beer to coffee

Hot and cold. Two words and two worlds. Kasteel Barista bridged the gap between both. This descendant of the Kasteel Winter seasonal beer comes with a pronounced roast character thanks to the use of a variety of toasted malts. This degustation beer has been given a name that reminds us of the art of brewing a good cup of coffee and lives up to its name with its dark colour covered by a delicate, cream-coloured frothy collar. The warming glow of alcohol provides another reason, if needed, to award this beer the moniker of 'black gold'.

———

Kasteel Barista is fragrant with strikingly fruity aromas and touches of roast malt, caramel, coffee and chocolate. In the finish, bitter-sweet impressions of marzipan take centre stage, as does the warming alcohol.

www.vanhonsebrouck.be

Diôle Brune (8,5%)

Dark and pure

Many Belgian brewers limit themselves to producing a blond beer and a dark, or Christmas beer. The dark one has the colour and fragrance of roast malt and often comes with a hint of candi sugar. The brewer at Brasserie des Carrières also takes charge of the malting process. Julien Slabbinck oversees the quality of the malts produced at the Malterie du Château. He is a great supporter of 'terroir' and sources his ingredients as close as possible to the brewery. The barley is grown in the fields that are owned by the cousins of his mate, François Amorison, and is turned into malt according to his specific instructions. A characteristic element of the Diôle beers is the touch of caramel, that gains in intensity depending on the beer style, from blond across amber to brown.

The gentlemen brewers drew their inspiration from Brasserie Dupont, a global reference when it comes to saison. Here also, the mashing basin is heated on gas, which causes the malt at the bottom of the basin to caramelise slightly. Diôle Brune pours dark into the glass with a hint of red. The beer produces small bubbles below its head of 'café crème'.

———

This dark one is fruity and zesty with hints of biscuit. The alcohol has a warming effect and the finish is slightly bitter. This is an honest and pure beer, brewed only with the basic ingredients.

www.diole.be

Gouden Carolus Classic (8,5%)

History in the glass

Gouden Carolus Classic carries on the tradition of the Mechelsen Bruynen, the Mechelen city beer during the reign of Emperor Charles (16th century). In those days, Mechelen brewers referred to it as the 'Groot Keizersbier' (the beer of the Great Emperor). It was poured without restraint after the fox hunt and was bound to cheer you up, just like it does today. This beer's name refers to the gold coinage in use during the imperial reign. This classic beer is a strong, dark top-fermented beer that re-ferments in the bottle. It will only come onto the market after three months in cold storage. The Gouden Carolus Classic is made with caramel malts, aromatic malts, wheat starch, Belgian hops as well as curaçao orange peel and coriander, typical of a white beer. The Gouden Carolus Classic formed the basis for the development of the stronger specialty beer that goes under the name of 'Cuvée van de Keizer blauw'.

Raisins, prunes, toffee and caramel colour the aromas of this beer. The predominant taste is one of candi sugar and raisins, accompanied by touches of orange and passion fruit. This beer gains in complexity thanks to the roast malts, the yeasty esters with their fruity touches and the warm alcohol glow. The finish of this full-mouthed beer is zesty and dry.

www.hetanker.be

Gulden Draak (10,5%)

Tamed in the glass

The dragon that proudly dominates the top of the Belfry in Ghent has now been tamed in the glass. Gulden Draak is a dark triple. It was re-fermented with the use of wine yeast, which is why it should be properly referred to as barley wine. The Gulden Draak has also multiplied into a quadruple: the Gulden Draak 9000. Legend has it that Norse King Sigurd Magnusson displayed a Golden Dragon on the prow of his warship ('drakkar') when he set off to join the Crusades in 1111. This statue is said to have made a detour to Constantinople (Istanbul) before ending up in Bruges. When the citizens of Ghent conquered the Brughelians in 1382 the statue was looted... A great story but none of it is true. The dragon was crafted in 1377 at the request of Ghent city council. Towering over the belfy, it is keeping a watchful eye on the city. He is 3.55 metres long, 1.50 metres wide and 1.80 metres tall and weighs 398 kilograms. He is forever chained to the tower as he was made without legs.

Gulden Draak is a quaffable, full-mouthed and balanced degustation beer with aromas of fruit (apple, cherry) and spices, with a taste hinting at caramel, toffee, roast malt and coffee. The long and bitter-sweet finish is supported by a soft alcoholic glow.

www.vansteenberge.com

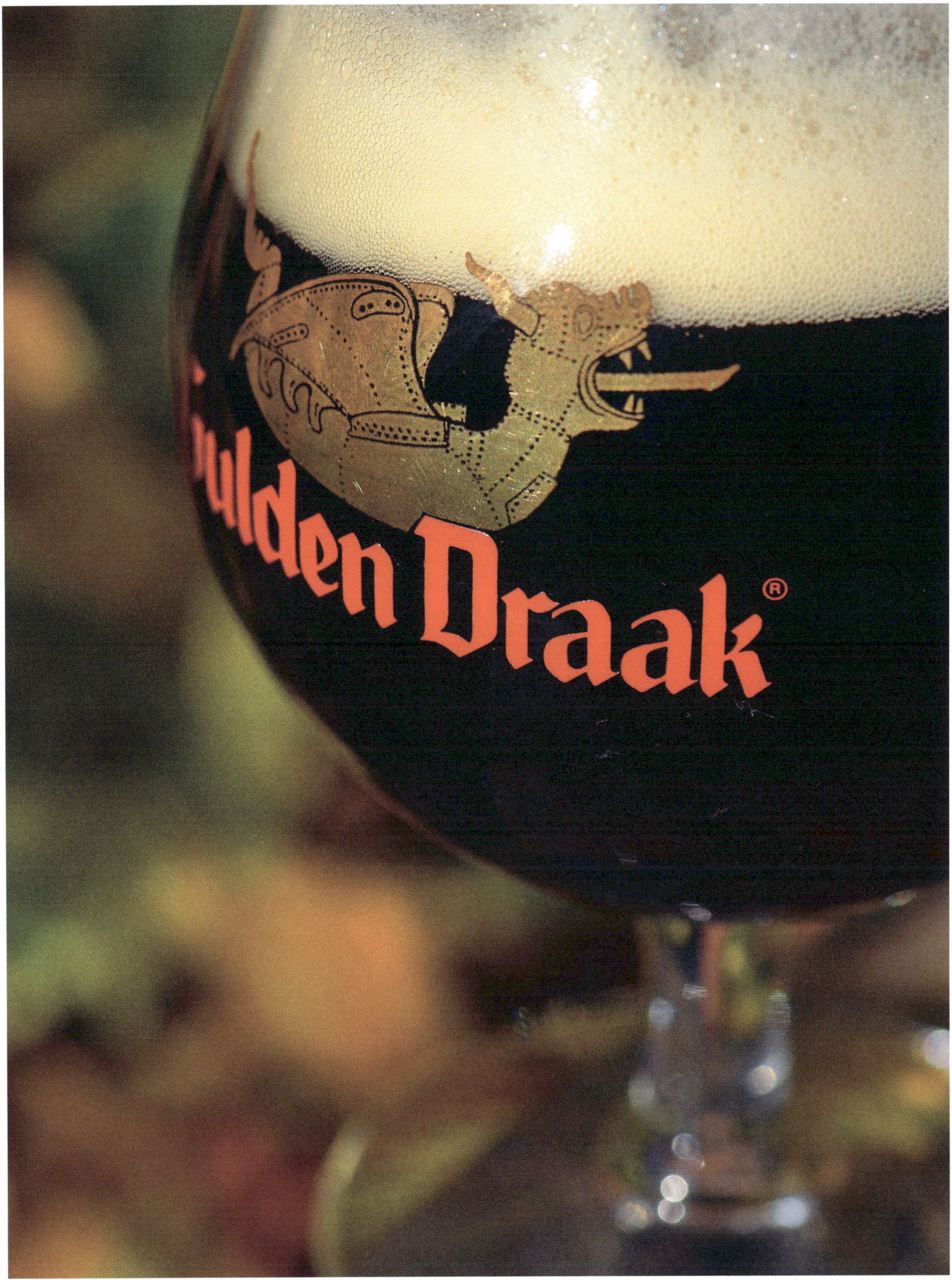
ulden Draak

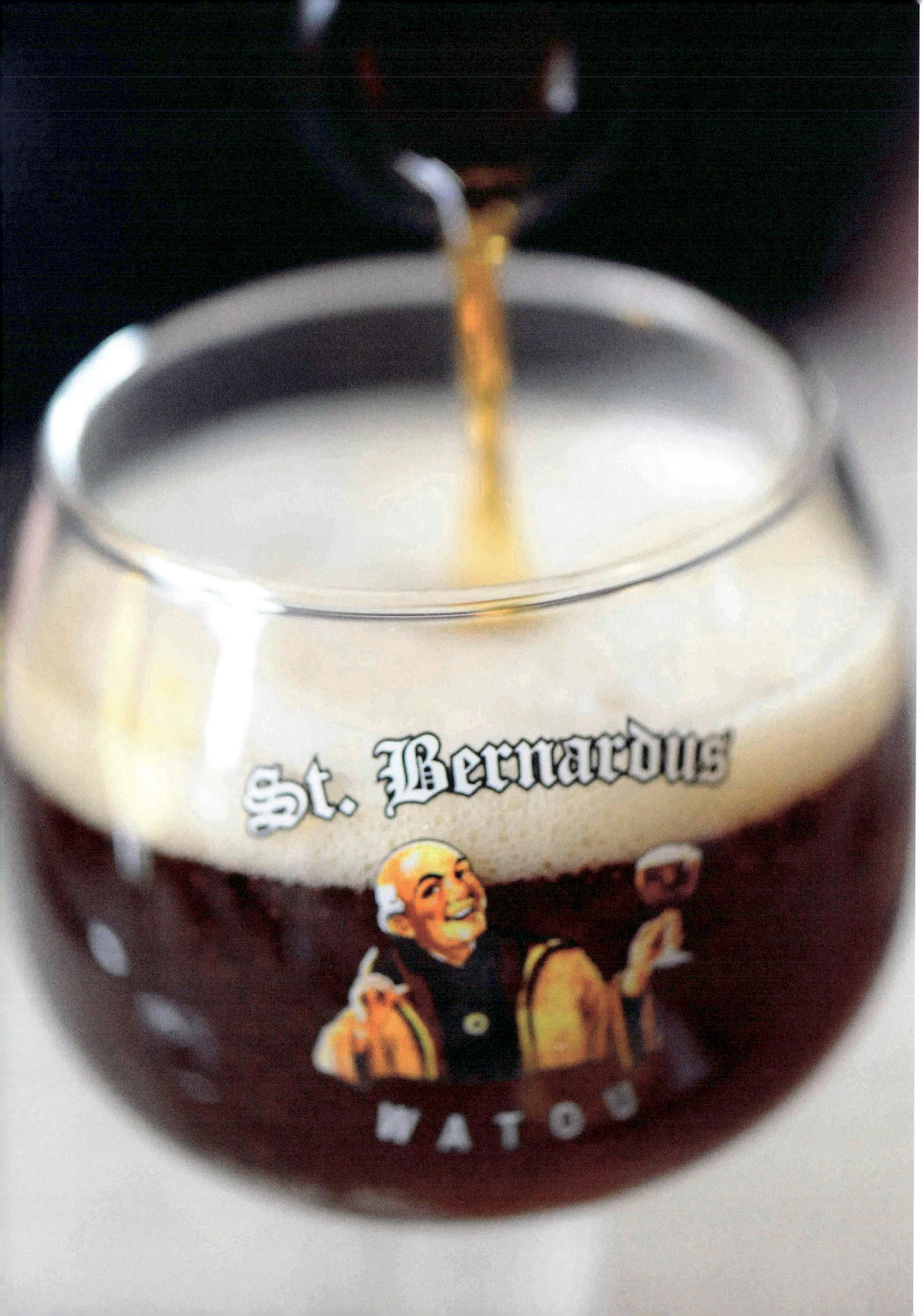
St. Bernardus
WATOU

Pannepot (10%)

Food as well as drink

In close proximity to Westvleteren, brewing heavy beers seems the obvious thing to do. 'Food and drink', as they say in the area. The Struise Brouwers made their name brewing beers of this type. On the basis of a good mother beer they are striving for a balance between different taste sensations. This beer veers between a strong dark quadruple and a stout. Each mouthful frees up complex tastes varying between roast coffee and sweet caramel. The brewers allowed their beer to mature in various types of barrel, giving rise to the Reserva and Vintage, amongst others. The Pannepot name is a reference to the sloops used by fishermen to trawl the North Sea. On the label, the ship can be seen sailing towards the far horizon.

———

A jet black degustation beer with a head resembling milky froth and understated aromas of grains, roast malts, candied fruits, sugarbread, chocolate, nuts, spices and mild hops.

www.struise.com

St. Bernardus Abt 12 (10%)

The other Twelve

The Abt 12 is a classic Belgian dark quadruple, brewed since 1946 on the basis of the recipe created by the monks of Westvleteren. In an abbey, the Abbot is the monk who holds the highest rank. The same goes for this Abt, in other words, he is held in high regard. This Abt is often compared with the Westvleteren Abt and that is far from a coincidence, as the Sint-Sixtus Trappist beers were brewed under licence at the St. Bernardus abbey until 1992. Up to the present day, the St. Bernardus abbey beers are made with the Sint-Sixtus house yeast. The brewer uses slightly salty, soft well water whilst the Westvleteren brewers use tap water these days. And brewing is now done in Westvleteren with Westmalle house yeast. A lesser-known fact is that the laughing monk on the St. Bernardus Abt label gives you a saucy wink from time to time. When exactly does he wink at you? When every thousandth bottle rolls off the conveyor belt.

———

Aromas of honey and frangipane (an almond filling). The roast malt frees up aromas of caramel and chocolate. A balanced beer with plenty of body with a noticeable but never dominant presence of hops. Characteristically salty impressions from the water used in brewing.

www.sintbernardus.be

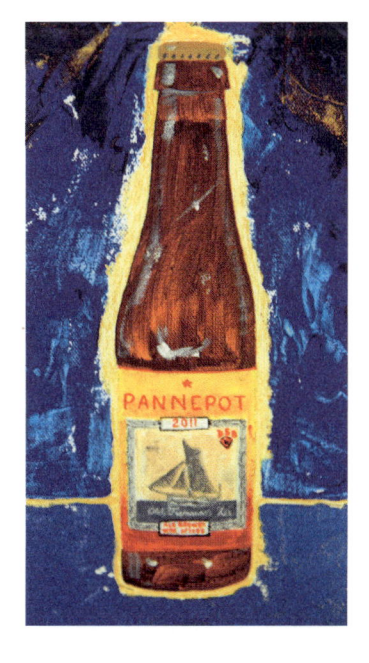

The monk gives you a wink whenever each thousandth bottle of St Bernardus Abt rolls off the conveyor.

> Pannepot being made.

Straffe Hendrik Quadrupel (11%)

A strong one from Bruges

At the Halve Maan brewery in Bruges, the era of degustation beers commenced with the Straffe Hendrik. They produce 'living' beers with a taste that continues to evolve thanks to the in-bottle re-fermentation. Straffe Hendrik is the star beer offered by the oldest brewery still in operation in the centre of Bruges. De Halve Maan has been brewing for nigh on 500 years.

A rich beer, intensely dark in colour, with a full-mouthed taste. It has a zesty and elegant aroma with touches of slightly roasted malt. Replete with the taste of coriander, dark fruits, aniseed and roast chestnut. Slightly syrupy finish.

www.straffehendrik.be

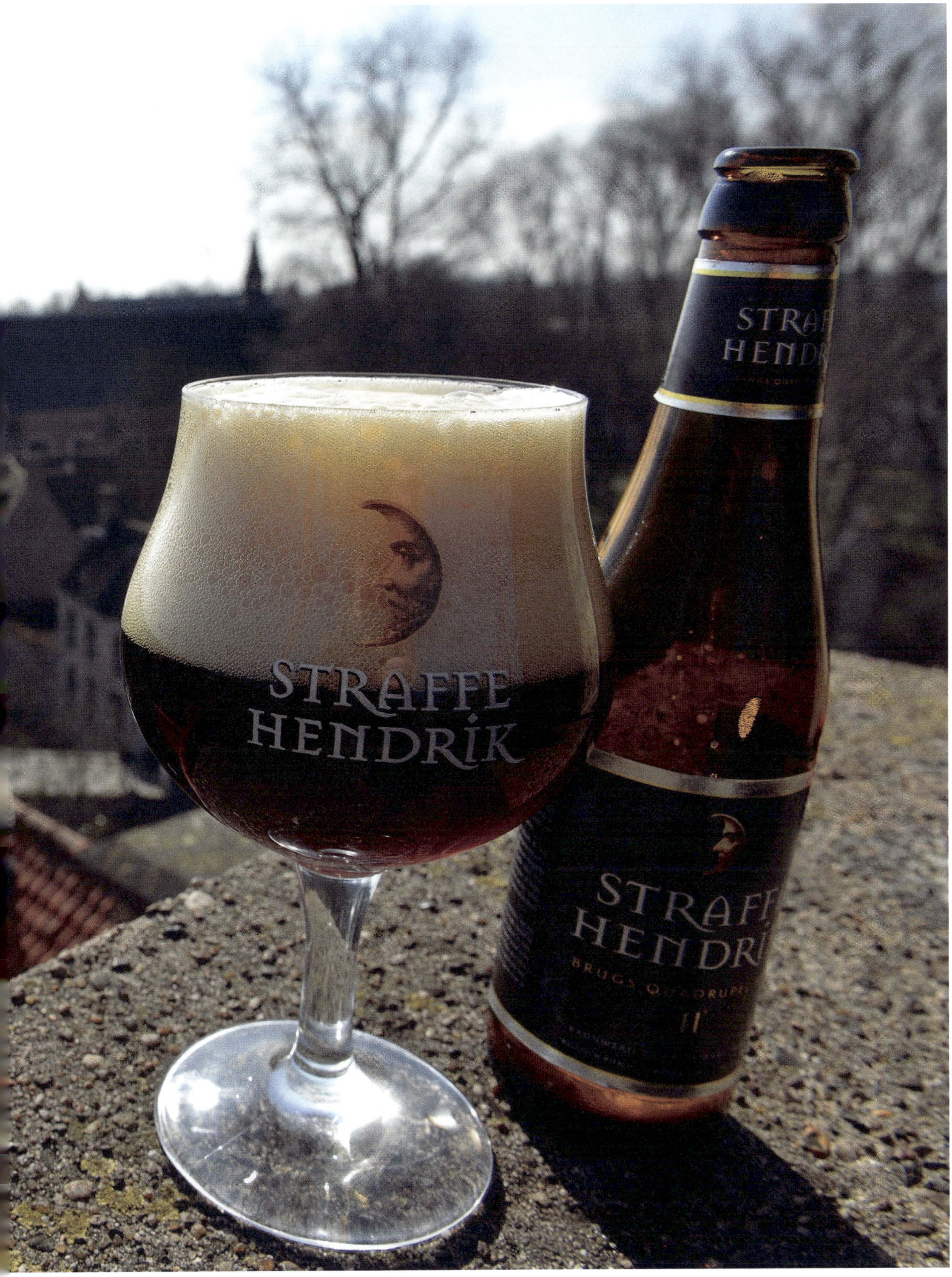
STRAFFE
HENDRIK

LAMBIC AND FARO

Lambic is one of Belgium's oldest beer styles. The colour of this beer veers between coppery blonde and amber-coloured. It is a spontaneously fermented flat beer (low in carbon dioxide, in other words), brewed with barley, wheat and hop. In the year 1420 Jan IV, the Duke of Brabant, decided that more wheat should be added to the beer to improve its quality. Nowadays, this beer must be made with at least 30% unmalted wheat. The hops have to satisfy three different conditions: two to three years old, only female hop cones can be used so the beer does not take on a bitter taste, and five grammes of hops per litre must be added to improve storage. The wort will boil for between two and five hours before cooling down overnight in an open 'koelschip'. When the wort cools down, the wild yeasts floating in the air around the brewery permeate the wort. The main yeasts used in this process are the Brettanomyces bruxellensis and the Brettanomyces lambicus. They determine the specific taste of the beer and are resistant to alcohol. Once the beer has cooled down, it is transferred to horizontal (oak) wood 'pijpen', 'pipes', barrels in other words, or else into large foeders where it will continue to ferment for months or even years. Lambic is traditionally brewed from the end of September to the end of April at a temperature below twenty degrees Celsius. Under these conditions, the wild yeasts are present in the correct proportions. Lambic is a flat beer with a sour taste. It makes for a good thirstquencher, especially during the summer months. Lambic is often used as the mother beer for faro, sweetened with candi sugar, or else it is used as the basis for a krieken lambic, a kriek or other fruit beers or gueuze, in particular an Oude Gueuze.

Chapeau Faro (4,7%)

A sweet lambic

The vagaries of time do not appear to have affected the De Troch lambic brewery. Crushed wheat is mixed with malted barley in the open mashing basin before being heated. The wort will then be transferred to the boiling kettle where it will boil for approx. 3.5 hours together with the aged hops. The boiled wort will then be left in a 'koelschip' – open fermentation basin – to cool down. It will be exposed to the open air, allowing the wild yeasts to 'infect' the wort. The following morning, the liquid is pumped into oak barrels where the young lambic will continue to mature. The sugars contained in the wort are converted into alcohol. The wild yeasts are doing their work and produce the complex tastes and aromas. Faro, typical of Brussels and its surroundings, is a sweetened lambic.

Aromas of marzipan, candi sugar, caramel and figs. You can taste apple, pear and currant bread.

www.detroch.be

De Cam Oude Lambic (5%)

The secret of the gueuzesteker

Taste a blend of unpasteurised three-year-old lambics matured in oak barrels that are a century old. At De Cam in Gooik, the lambic will ferment and mature in wooden barrels until Karl Goddeau, the geuzesteker, feels that it has reached its optimal taste. Here, the lambic comes from wooden barrels and is the result of spontaneous fermentation, cooled down in the open koelschip, unsweetened and unpasteurised. Karl is proud of the range on offer. 'I work with different lambics. Each barrel tells its own story. That is my secret.'

A velvety soft old lambic not dissimilar to wine, with impressions of apple extending to calvados and sherry.

www.decam.be

At a handful of cafés, including A la Bécasse in Brussel, freshly tapped lambic is poured from a stone jar. In Belgium, lambic is the odd one out as this beer is not sparkling and does not form a head of froth. This only occurs after fermentation, when lambic turns into gueuze.

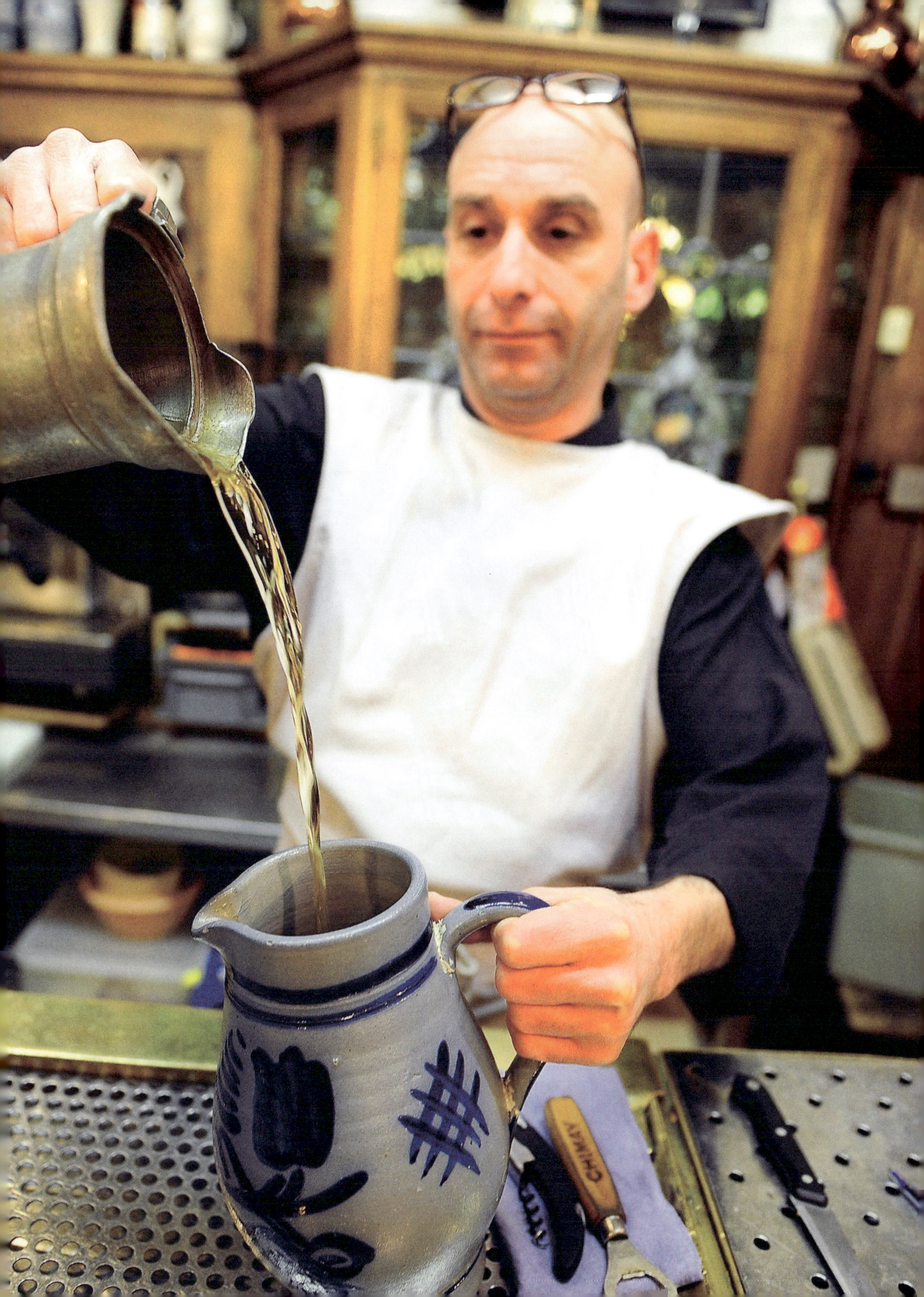
CHIMAY

GUEUZE AND OUDE GUEUZE

◆

Gueuze is a lambic that has re-fermented in the bottle. Other beers can be added but not necessarily. Geuze or gueuze is not brewed but it is 'cut', or blended. It is a cloudy but sparkling beer, matt gold to amber in colour, with a slightly sour taste. The lambic re-ferments in the bottle and consequently, the beer contains only minor traces of sugar, making it suitable for diabetics. In common with lambic, gueuze is an extremely delicate product. It takes years of experience to manage the spontaneous fermentation process. The end result is governed by numerous factors: the temperature, the maturation on wood, the workings of the wild yeasts… The proportion of old and young lambic – and possibly other beers added to the brew – is different for every gueuze. There is a preference for a 'tender' lambic (not too sour). The higher the proportion of old lambic added, the more aroma, depth and breadth in the beer. Gueuze is dry, tart and fruity but you will also find some with a roasted aroma.

St-Louis Gueuze Fond Tradition (5%)

Lambic on the river Leie

'It is perfectly possible to make a gueuze in the Leie valley'. Brewer Luc Van Honsebrouck was true to his word. In 1958, on the occasion of the World Exhibition in Brussels, he introduced a gueuze that was born in Ingelmunster, far away from gueuze's traditional heartlands. St-Louis Gueuze Fond Tradition is a pure traditional gueuze, a real connoisseur's beer, neither sweetened nor filtered. This gueuze contains a blend of young and old lambic, a spontaneously fermented beer. When the wort for the lambic cools down in the open 'koelschip' or cooling basin, it is permeated by the ambient wild yeasts. Besides St-Louis Gueuze Fond Tradition there is a fruit beer, St-Louis Kriek Fond Tradition, which is also unfiltered, unpasteurised and unsweetened. In contrast, the classic St-Louis Premium Gueuze is traditionally sweetened in keeping with the regional habit of adding sugar to slightly sour beers such as gueuze.

St-Louis Gueuze Fond Tradition has the pure taste of a real gueuze based on young and old lambic. The fruity aromas of young apple stand out here. The slightly sour touches, characteristic for lambic beers, are noticeably present in the taste. Very dry finish.

www.vanhonsebrouck.be

'Old (oude) gueuze'

'Old (oude) gueuze' contains 100% lambic. Old and young lambic are cut (blended) to achieve a perfect mix. A typical blend will contain 60% one-year old lambic, 30% lambic that has aged for two years and 10% three-year old lambic. The old lambic emanates a distinctive aroma and provides plenty of depth whereas the younger lambic lends a sour touch to the beer.

Dead and superfluous yeast cells are removed from the lambic. The residual yeast ensures that the beer re-ferments in the bottle.

An old gueuze will keep for dozens of years. Horal, the High Council for Artisan Lambic Beers (Hoge Raad voor Ambachtelijke Lambicbieren), unites most of the artisan lambic beers and 'gueuzestekerijen' from the Zenne Valley and the Pajottenland area around Brussels. Thanks to Horal, old gueuze is now a protected beer style (*source: http://www.horal.be/lambic-gueuze-kriek/juridische-bescherming*). Old gueuze now enjoys legal protection from the European Union. The term 'old gueuze' may only be used if the old lambic is at least three years old, has matured in wooden barrels and no artificial sweeteners are used. An artisan gueuze such as this can be recognised by its champagne bottle, the cork and the 'muselet': the wire cage that prevents the cork from popping out due to the pressure in the bottle.

3 Fonteinen Oude Gueuze (7%)

Painting with tastes

Lambic brewer and gueuzesteker Armand De Belder of the 3 Fonteinen brewery was taught all the ins and outs of his craft by his father Gaston. Armand pays attention to even the tiniest details and searches obsessively for natural ingredients and the most suitable methods. His efforts have paid off: his beers are highly rated around the world. Brussels, the nearby Valley of the Zenne and the Pajottenland area are the traditional birthplace of lambic beers such as gueuze. Between the two World Wars you would find one or more gueuzestekers in every village. If the beer was of a high quality, people would be crowding the bar. After World War II, however, the craft was in decline. Everyone was drinking pils and many gueuzestekers threw in the towel. Nevertheless, the municipality of Beersel counted no fewer than 14 gueuzestekers at the start of the 1950s. Amongst them was Gaston Debelder, who took over the 3 Fonteinen café-restaurant at that time. The village held its own. The rest is history.

———

3 Fonteinen Oude Gueuze has a sharp sourness, is earthy and complex, just like a real traditional gueuze ought to be, but with a champagne-like sparkle and refreshing taste.

www.3fonteinen.be

Lindemans Oude Gueuze Cuvée René (5,5%)

Back to the roots

Thanks to in-bottle re-fermentation, the Lindemans Oude Gueuze Cuvée René sparkles and froths in a natural way. This oude gueuze contains one third old lambic of at least two years old. Two thirds are made up of young lambic that is at least one year old and has matured in large oak barrels. The yeasts and sugars from the young lambic set the in-bottle re-fermentation in motion. Slowly but surely, the wild yeasts will convert all of the residual sugars into alcohol and carbon dioxide. After six months the result is a sparkling, mildly sour gueuze with a golden colour. This beer can be stored in a cool and dark chamber for a number of years, during which time its taste will continue to evolve. Lindemans is amongst eight lambic breweries that continue to brew authentic lambic beers in the Zenne Valley near Brussels.

———

This old gueuze is surprisingly complex. Its fruity aromas return in the taste of this sour-ish beer with its dry, freshly sour finish.

www.lindemans.be

Mort Subite Oude Gueuze (7%)

The game is over

This lambic brewery was founded in 1869 but uses modern technology. Bruno Reinders, the brewer: 'You learn how to brew a lambic by doing it. You have to take a number of factors into account: the effect of nature itself, of the seasons, varying degrees of fermentation and temperatures, all the while managing to deliver a stable and consistent product. Lambic brewers must not be allowed to stand still. We also use the advantages of technology. Just think of temperature control, not available in the old days. This is how we can produce a beer of consistent quality.' The beer only comes in contact with oxygen to start off the fermentation. Once that is done, the entire process will take place in closed tanks. They protect the beer from harmful micro-organisms and means that brewing can be done all the year around. 'We are limiting negative influences from the outside', Bruno assures us. 'This is why we do not use an open cooling basin. The air in the fermentation tanks contains plenty of wild yeasts and furthermore, we inject air from time to time to speed up the fermentation.'

———

A dry, sour gueuze with a fresh, zesty and citrusy character.

www.mort-subite.be

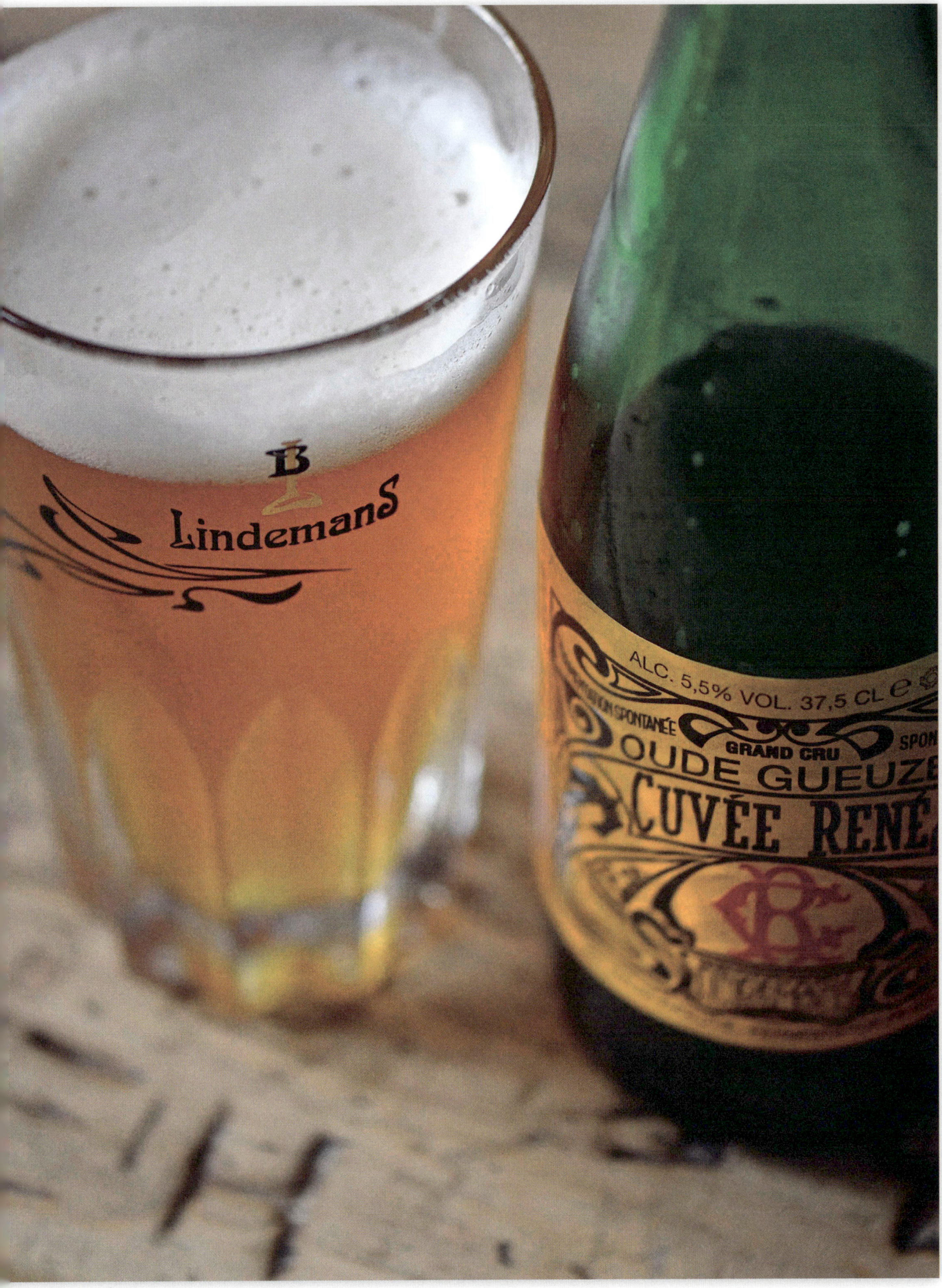
Lindemans
ALC. 5,5% VOL. 37,5 CL
GRAND CRU
OUDE GUEUZE
CUVÉE RENÉ

OUDE GEUZE VIEILLE
Oud Beersel

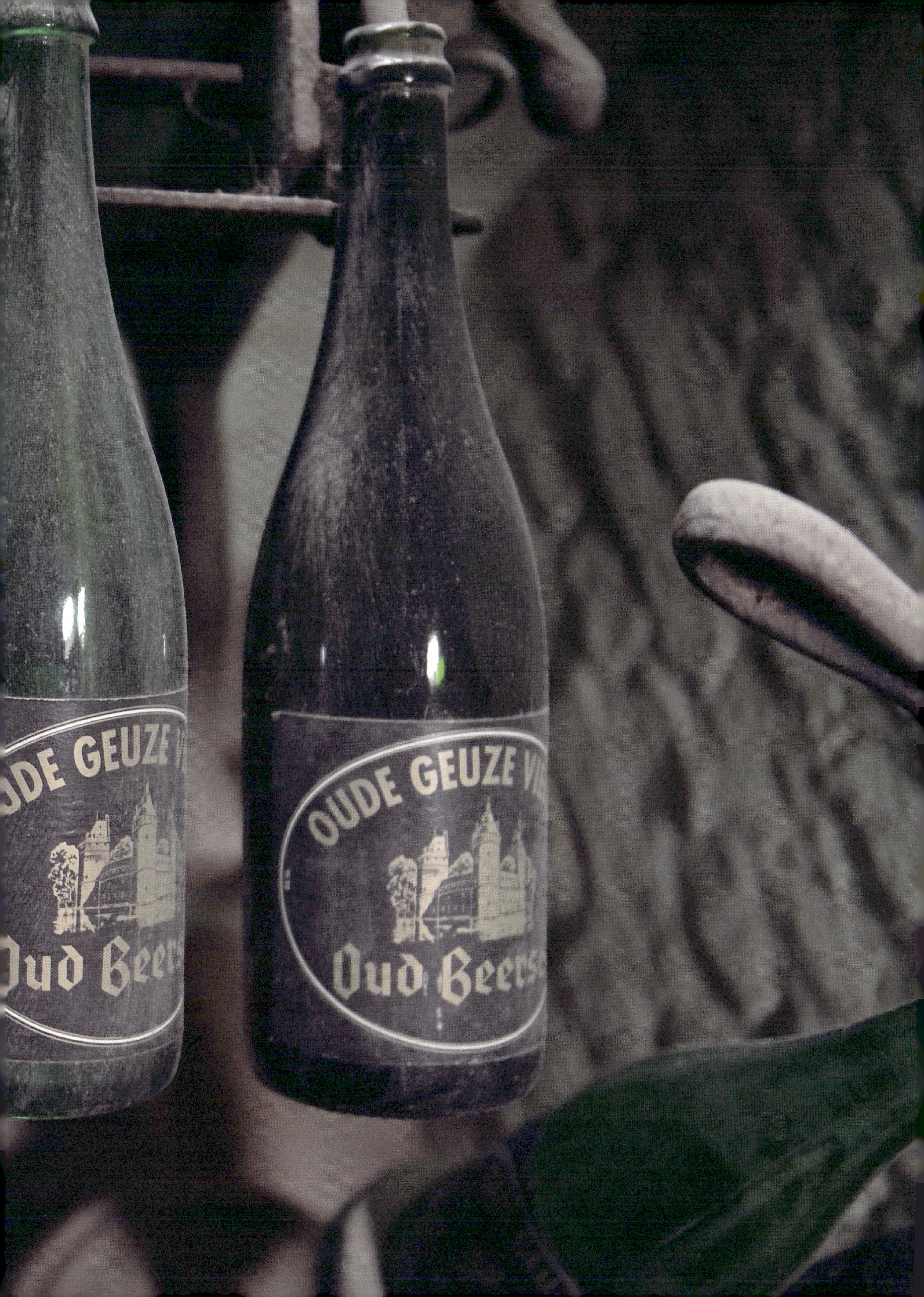
OUDE GEUZE VI
Oud Beers
ODE GEUZE VI
Oud Beers

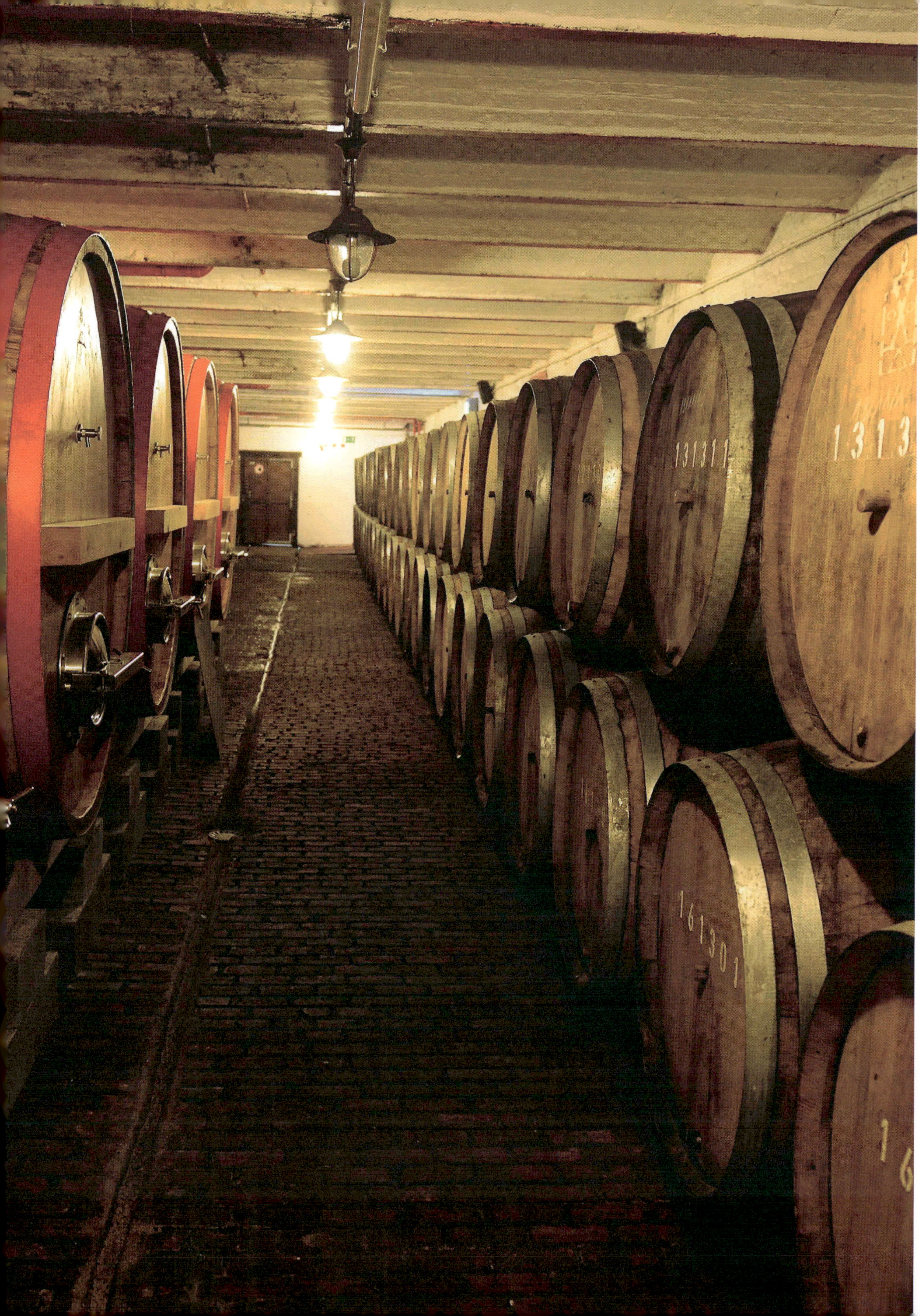
131311
161301

Oud Beersel Oude Gueuze (6%)

The art is in the blending

Oud Beersel is considered the bitterest lambic and gueuze thanks to its noticeable but light touches of hop. Gueuzesteker Gert Christiaens: 'I buy my lambic from Boon, where it is brewed to my own recipe. They pay a lot of attention to quality checks which makes the lambic more tender, pleasant and accessible. The recipe has remained unchanged. We are making a traditional lambic with a lot of taste and without acetic acid.' Brouwerij Oud Beersel closed its doors in 2002 for lack of a successor, but they had not counted on Gert Christiaens, one of their best customers. Once he found out that the brewer had thrown in the towel, he decided to take over the business. Gert served an apprenticeship with Henri Vandevelden, the grandson of the founder. He gave Oud Beersel a second lease of life and gueuze has been blended here once again since 2005. Gert Christiaens: 'That's how it goes sometimes. When I started out, it was said that lambic was for the older generation. The gueuze drinker died out some time around 2000. He was at least 40 years old. And now we come across lovers of lambic and gueuze of varying ages, youngsters included.'

―――――

A sharp, sour-ish oude gueuze reminiscent of champagne. Pleasantly bitter, mildly sour, subtle and complex at the same time.

www.oudbeersel.com

Timmermans Oude Gueuze (5,5%)

Crafted to perfection

The oldest lambic brewery in the world was founded in 1702. Eight generations on, the craft has remained unchanged. Lambic that has matured in oak barrels for up to three years is blended with young lambic. The wild yeasts carry on their work in the bottle until every last trace of residual sugars has vanished. This beer improves beautifully with age and will keep for years and years

―――――

Freshly sour, fruity aromas of lambic with accents of citrus also colour the taste. Not a trace of hop bitter.

www.anthonymartin.be

KRIEK AND FRUIT BEERS

Kriek is the most traditional fruit beer. 'Kriekenbier' has all the characteristics of an oude gueuze, complemented with a pleasantly fruity taste. Brewers add krieken cherries to lambic to enhance the aroma. The fruits also speed up fermentation. Several sources claim that in 1878 a farmer from Schepdaal wrote down the first recipe for kriek beer. Lambic beer from the Brussels region is naturally tart and not easy to drink. From 1878 onwards large quantities of krieken cherries (20 kilogram/100 litres) were added at the fermentation stage. The pulp residue would be filtered out at the end. Because krieken cherries, just like lambic, are naturally sour, the first artisan krieken beer was also very sour. This is why many people were used to adding liquid sugar to the beer. Oude kriek contains a blend of lambic beers with an average age of at least one year with added krieken cherries (10–25%), krieken juice or concentrate. It is important that the krieken ferment together with the beer and continue to mature for two months at least. These beers are usually quite sour, with a white to pale pink head of froth and the complex tartness of a lambic.

Boon Kriek Mariage Parfait (8%)

Tightrope walker

Kriek Boon Mariage Parfait is made with heavy one-year old lambic, flavoured with 400 grams overripe real krieken per litre. This beer's exceptional taste comes from the extra-long maturation in both large and small oak barrels. Well-made gueuze and kriek are ready to drink half a year after bottling and will keep for at least twenty years. 'Thanks to the wild yeasts, the beer undergoes a positive taste evolution in the bottle', lambic brewer Frank Boon assures us. He feels that kriek and gueuze are the most Belgian of all specialty beers made in our country. He prefers them after three years in the bottle or in the barrel. Brouwerij Boon supplies lambic to gueuzestekers and also produces a classic oude gueuze and oude kriek as well as a vibrant kriek on the basis of traditional lambic, a spontaneous fermentation beer. The lambic matures in oak barrels. The wood has to be old as new oak contains too many tannins which makes it unsuitable for beer. The oak lets in just enough oxygen to stimulate the development of the wild yeasts. This spontaneous fermentation produces the finest lambic. Each foeder, filled to the brim, has its own character and affects the taste in its own unique way.

Fresh and fruity, with a mild lambic aroma and a hint of almond. The wild yeasts give colour to the initial taste, swiftly followed by tart krieken cherries. The finish provides an undercurrent of mild bitter with touches of wood and almond. An accessible, mild oude kriek.

www.boon.be

Girardin Kriek (5%)

A good kriek will sell itself

Girardin Kriek is a well-kept secret. This complex kriek is well-known in connoisseur circles. Lambic brewer and gueuzesteker Armand Debelder of the 3 Fonteinen brewery calls Girardin the 'Château d'Yquem of lambic breweries'. This farm brewery enjoys a unique location. It can be spotted from afar, located on the crest of the Lindenberg hill, surrounded by fields. Girardin brews with grain that he has grown himself. He also uses two open cooling tanks kept at different temperatures so he can respond to weather conditions and juggle the best possible effects of the wild yeasts. This lambic brewery was founded in 1845 and formed part of an estate owned by the nobility. It was acquired in 1882 by the Girardin family. The fourth generation is now in charge.

A quite dark, slightly sparkling kriek with hardly any froth. Sour and fruity aromas. The taste is slightly sweet-and-sour and mildly bitter. A very balanced classic.

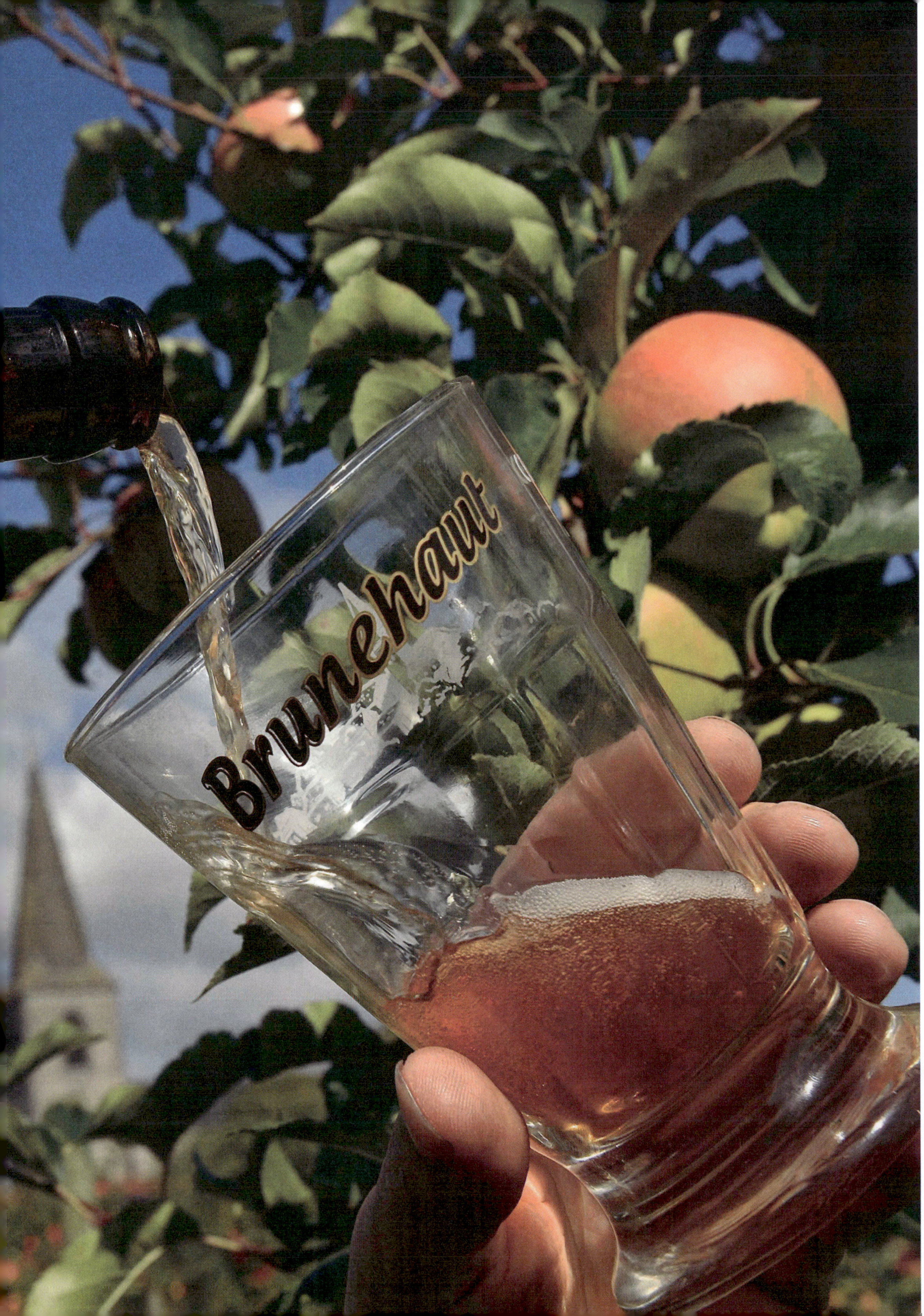
Brunehaut

Lou Pepe Kriek (5%)
Advanced only

Brewer Jean-Pierre Van Roy does not beat about the bush: 'We're not in the business of brewing syrup.' Lou Pepe gueuze is a blend of two-year old lambics fermented in recycled bordeaux wine barrels. The in-bottle re-fermentation is encouraged by adding liqueur. There is also a Lou Pepe Kriek and a Framboise, where the fruits mature in lambic in bordeaux barrels. The Cantillon brewery (1900) is a living museum. There, lambic is still brewed in the same way as one hundred years ago. The building itself plays an important role in the spontaneous fermentation. Microflora from the wild yeasts and other fermentation agents 'infect' the wort and multiply by feeding on the sugars it contains, after which alcohol and aromatic components are produced. This brewer likes his lambic very dry. The vintage editions contain hardly any carbon dioxide and are more like a fino sherry than a beer. Jean-Pierre Van Roy uses various types of wood and even recycled port barrels. He is proud of the fact that his beer ferments in a natural way, is unpasteurised and ages well. The famous micro-organisms *Brettanomyces bruxellensis* and *Brettanomyces lambicus* from the Zenne Valley remain active for years, giving the beer more character and structure. They also provide the typical toasted aromas, however, even after twenty or thirty years, the taste remains pure and fresh.

This ruby-red brew with a delicate level of carbon dioxide gives off an intense aroma of cherries and a fragrance of oak. It possesses a light body with a sharp sourness and solid taste of fruits with a noticeable undercurrent of wood. The beer as a whole flows into a mildly dry finish.

www.cantillon.be

Tilquin Oude Quetsche (6,4%)
A plum gueuze

Pierre Tilquin belongs to the new wave of gueuzestekers. He acquired his craft at the 3 Fonteinen and Cantillon breweries. Pierre's aim is to produce rounded beers that preserve the character and taste of each lambic used. His gueuze contains a minimum of 10% lambic from each brewery he works with. Pierre adds liquid sugar to kick off fermentation. The beer will then spend six months in the warm chamber (18 °C). His gueuze is on average two-and-a-half years old. Tilquin is opposed to the myths that have been created around gueuze. 'It is an accessible beer', he feels. 'I provide the best possible conditions for the lambic to mature. I fill the barrels to a level that suffices to limit the risk of oxidation.' His Oude Quetsche is made by steeping fresh plums with their stones removed for four months in a lambic aged between one and two years from Boon, Lindemans, Girardin and/or Cantillon.

Plum brandy aromas. The taste is slightly sour with fruit but rounded overall. The beer has the slight dryness of prune skins.

www.gueuzerietilquin.be

Modern fruit beers
....

Modern fruit beers often have sugar added before bottling as well as substances that enhance the taste and colour. Lambics are not the only beers to which fruit juice or syrup is added. A number of pils and white beers are also made with added fruit.

Brunehaut Pomfraiz' (5,5%)
Apple and strawberry

The Brunehaut name stands for organic – and gluten-free – beers brewed with natural ingredients. Their Brunehaut Pom'Fraiz is a light, natural, gluten-free, unsweetened fruit beer that is based on Brunehaut Blanche, a white beer, and re-ferments with the juices of strawberries and apples. This beer pays homage to the traditional fruit growers who ply their trade in the area surrounding the brewery. Brunehaut Blanche, the mother beer, is brewed with malts from millet and buckwheat, coriander, star anise and sweet as well as bitter orange peel. Brunehaut Pom'Fraiz is a refreshing thirstquencher, a successful marriage of beer and fruit.

The initial taste frees up the fresh, floral touches of the Brunehaut Blanche mother beer, enriched with strawberry aromas. The hop bitterness is always present in the background. This unsweetened fruit beer is refreshingly quaffable. At the re-fermentation stage, the yeast is fed by natural juices of strawberries and apples.

www.brunehaut.com

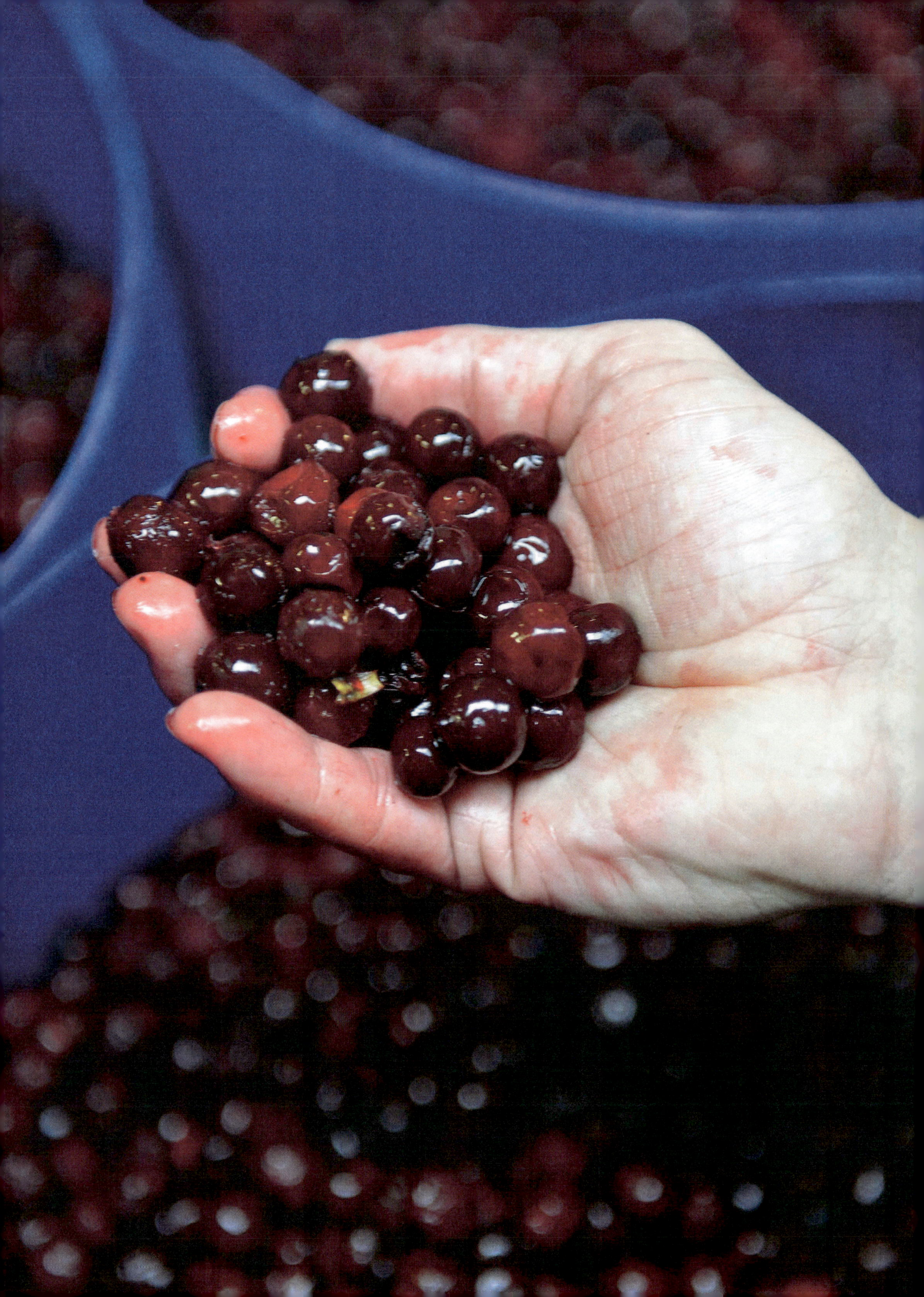

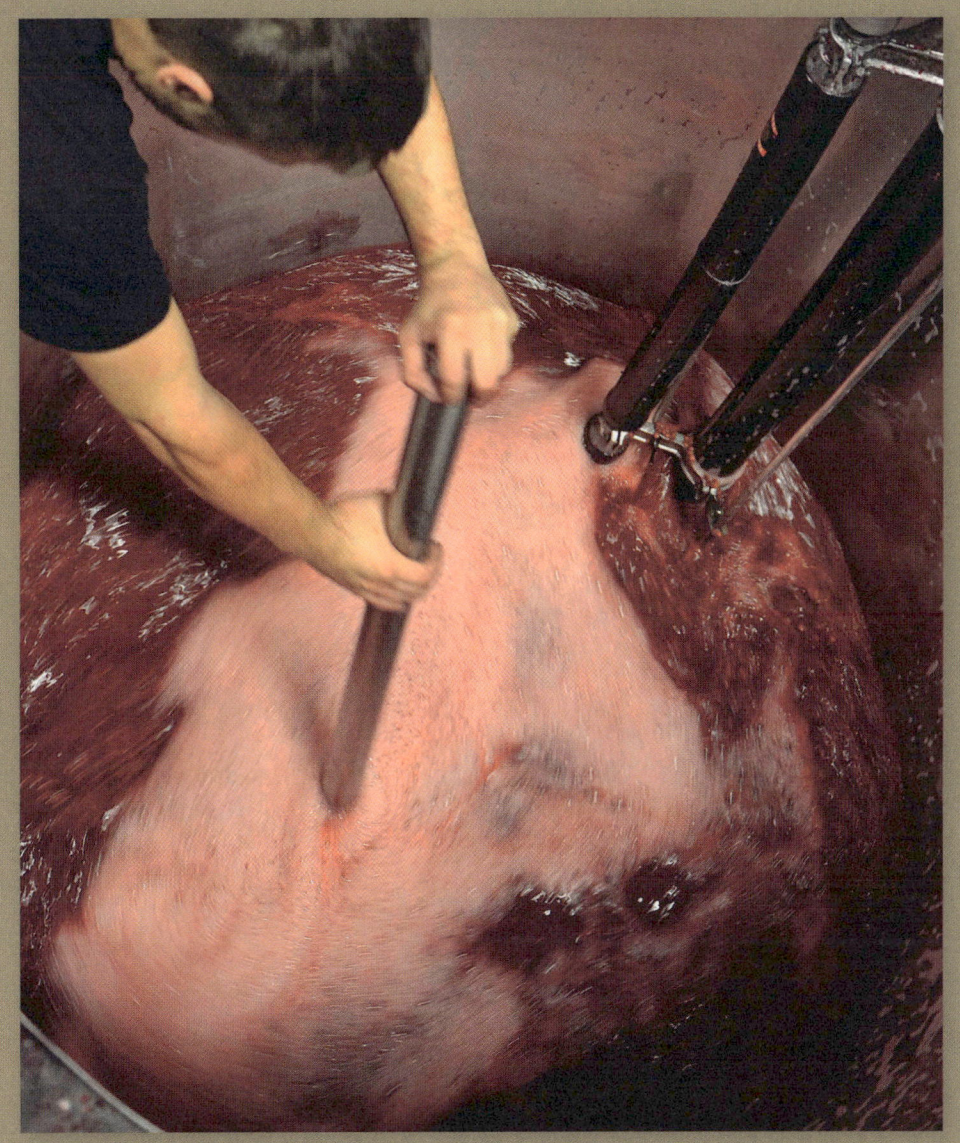

Adding fresh krieken cherries to the lambic at the Lindemans brewery.

Kasteel Rouge (8%)

Fruitbom

A strong fruit beer created by blending Kasteel Donker and a sweet cherry liqueur. From that point of view, this 'fruity' beer is different from other fruit beers based on lambic or white beer, the St-Louis fruit beers for example. The odd one out, definitely with a mind of its own, in the Kasteel range that also includes Kasteel Blond, Kasteel Donker, Kasteel Hoppy and Kasteel Triple.

―――――

You will taste alcohol, sweet cherries, fruit, chocolate and pepper. Slowly but surely, the complex character of this degustation beer gains the upper hand on the overwhelmingly sweet taste.

www.vanhonsebrouck.be

Kriek Max (3,5%)

Going for sweetness

Kriek Max is tailor-made for lovers of sweet and light fruit beers. Wood-matured foeder beers are its basis. At the Omer Vander Ghinste brewery, krieken cherries are fermenting, accompanied by lambic beers, in the oak foeders, causing the aromas and tastes to merge gradually. This sweet fruit beer is a hit with customers sunning themselves on a terrace. A thirstquencher that goes down easily without sending your head into a spin.

―――――

A very sweet kriek with fresh and fruity aromas of cherries, not unlike boiled sweets. The beer is made up of 25% krieken and krieken juice, which explains its overwhelming taste.

www.kriekmax.be

Lindemans Framboise (2,5%)

Raspberry lambic

We Belgians mastered the art of making fruit beers hundreds of years ago. The fruit lambic, for example. Lambic is a spontaneously fermented beer, produced without adding yeast. It starts to ferment at the cooling-down stage in open cooling basins. This allows the microflora (Brettanomyces) from the Pajottenland region and the Zenne Valley to get in contact with the wort. Lindemans introduced its Framboise in 1980. To make this fruit beer, 30% pure raspberry juice is added to one-year-old lambic, hence the dark pink colour. Fruit juice is blended with lambic which brings down the alcohol content of the beer. Framboise makes for an excellent aperitif and is also useful in the kitchen, as a basis for sauces for example.

―――――

The first aromas yield fruity raspberries with a sweet undercurrent. These carry on in the taste, together with the scintillating, sweetly sour touches of raspberry and lambic. In the finish you can detect gentle touches of wood.

www.lindemans.com

5 • BELGIAN BEER STYLES

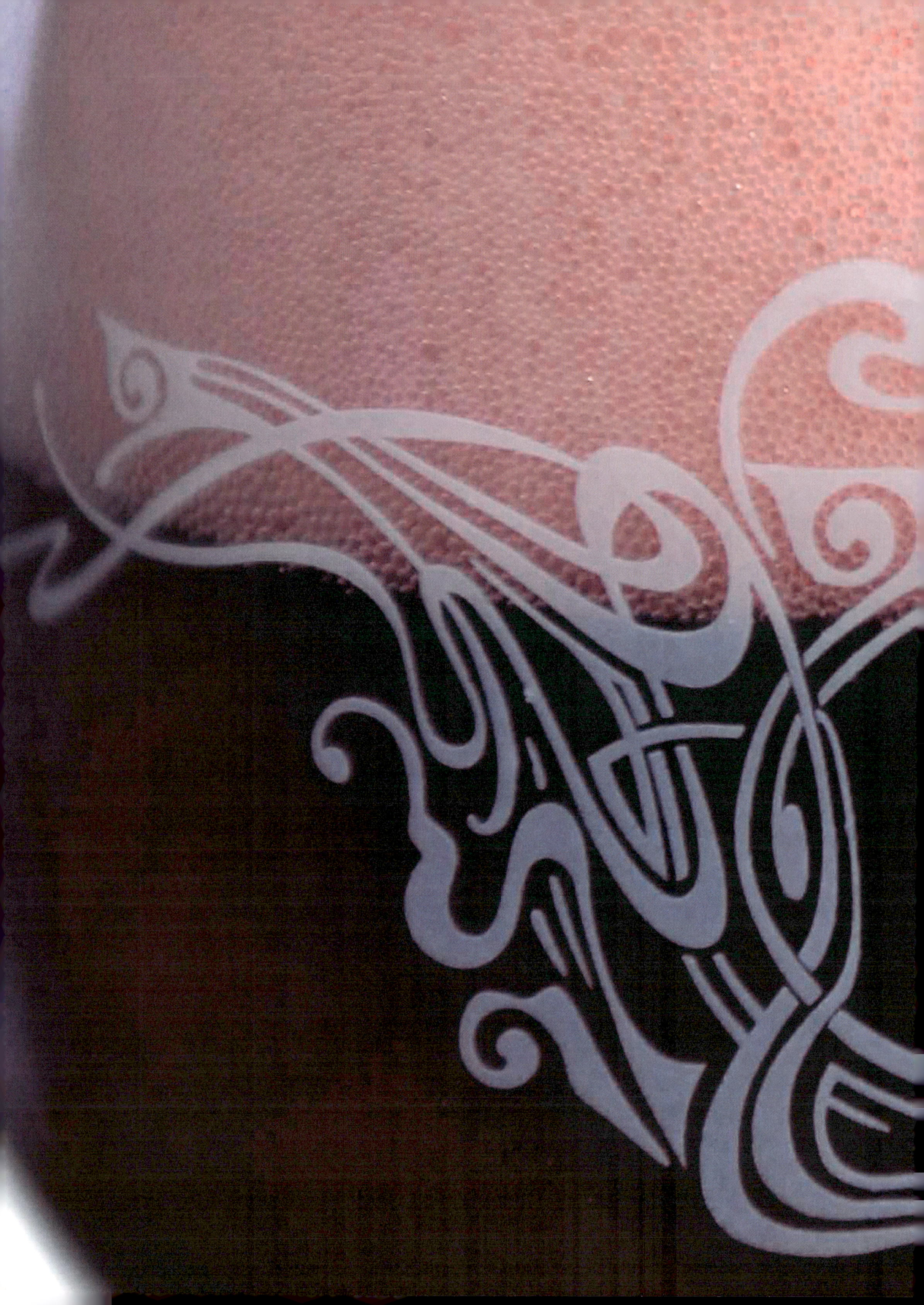

ANNO 1822

Lindemans

Lambic

PILS

❖

On a global scale, pils is the beer that is brewed the most. The word comes from the city of Plzen in the Czech Republic, where pils was produced for the first time in the year 1842. The basic ingredients of pils are water, malt, hops and yeast. These days breweries may add further ingredients such as sugar, maize or barley. Most of the taste of pils comes from the yeast. To brew a tasty pils you need soft water. Pils is a thirstquencher first and foremost. Above all, the beer has to be pure, with a particular finish that does not hang around, before reverting to a neutral taste. If pils is poured correctly from the tap or the bottle, it will be transparent. You can see straight away if it has been filtered properly. Pils is best drunk as fresh as possible.

Bavik Premium Pils (5,2%)

M stands for malt

Never call a pils… just a pils. Bavik Premium Pils is brewed in the traditional way, using aroma hops only. The beer is cold-stored over an extra-long period of thirty days, during which it clarifies in the natural way. Also, unusually for a pils, this beer is unpasteurised. This pils is leaning towards the German tradition. With the so-called *Green High Gravity* method, all the ingredients are added to the brewing water at the same time. No dilution occurs which explains the full taste. Thanks to the exclusive use of aroma hops (Saaz) the brewer obtains a delicately bitter taste and a refreshing aroma. A long fermentation (eight days) and a long cold storage (thirty days) result in a natural, clear beer with a consistent taste.

―――――

A malty pils with fruity aromas. Impressions of apricot and peach relegate the hop to the background. The malt is more pronounced in the taste, still with a subtle presence of hop bitter floating around. A refreshing thirstquencher.

www.brouwerijdebrabandere.be

Cristal (4,8%)

A pils with character

Cristal is one of the oldest pils beers in Belgium. The recipe dates back to 1928 and is still the basis for the quality and the taste of this pils, which is one of the bitterest pils beers in Belgium. The Alken brewery set out to quench the thirst of the miners in the 1920s and 1930s. At the time this was a revolutionary beer as not many Belgian breweries were capable of brewing bottom-fermented beers. The current brewery was founded in 1924 and was the first in the region to use the bottom fermentation process. Cristal is brewed with soft water, is free from calcium and minerals, is delicately hopped with Saaz from the Czech Republic and is easy to digest. This pils owes its mild taste and clear colour to the combination of malt and maize. 1988 saw the merger of Alken with Maes, the well-known pils brewery. Both are now owned by the Heineken group.

―――――

A refreshing pils with a bitter finish.

www.cristal.be

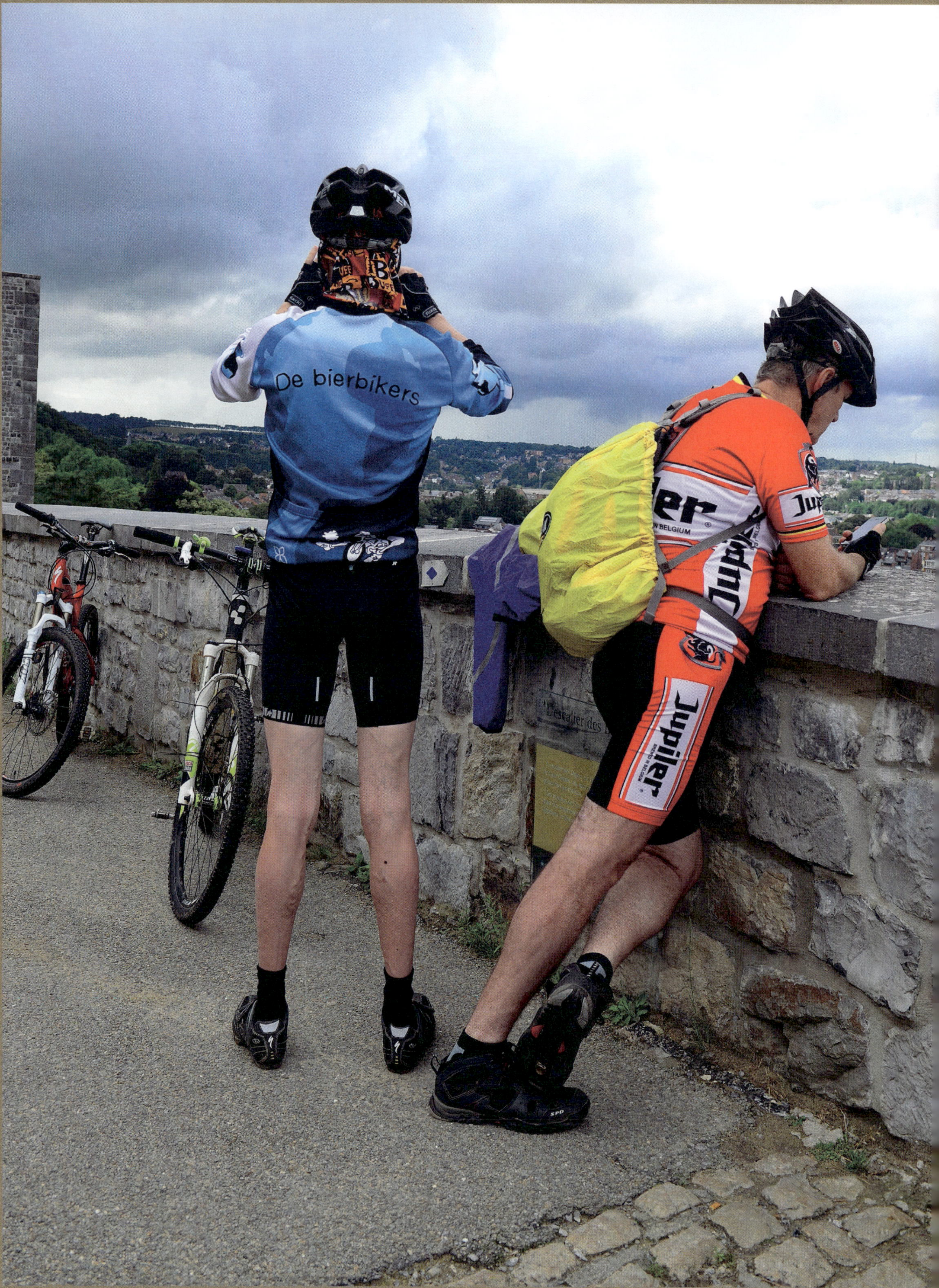
De bierbikers
Jupiler

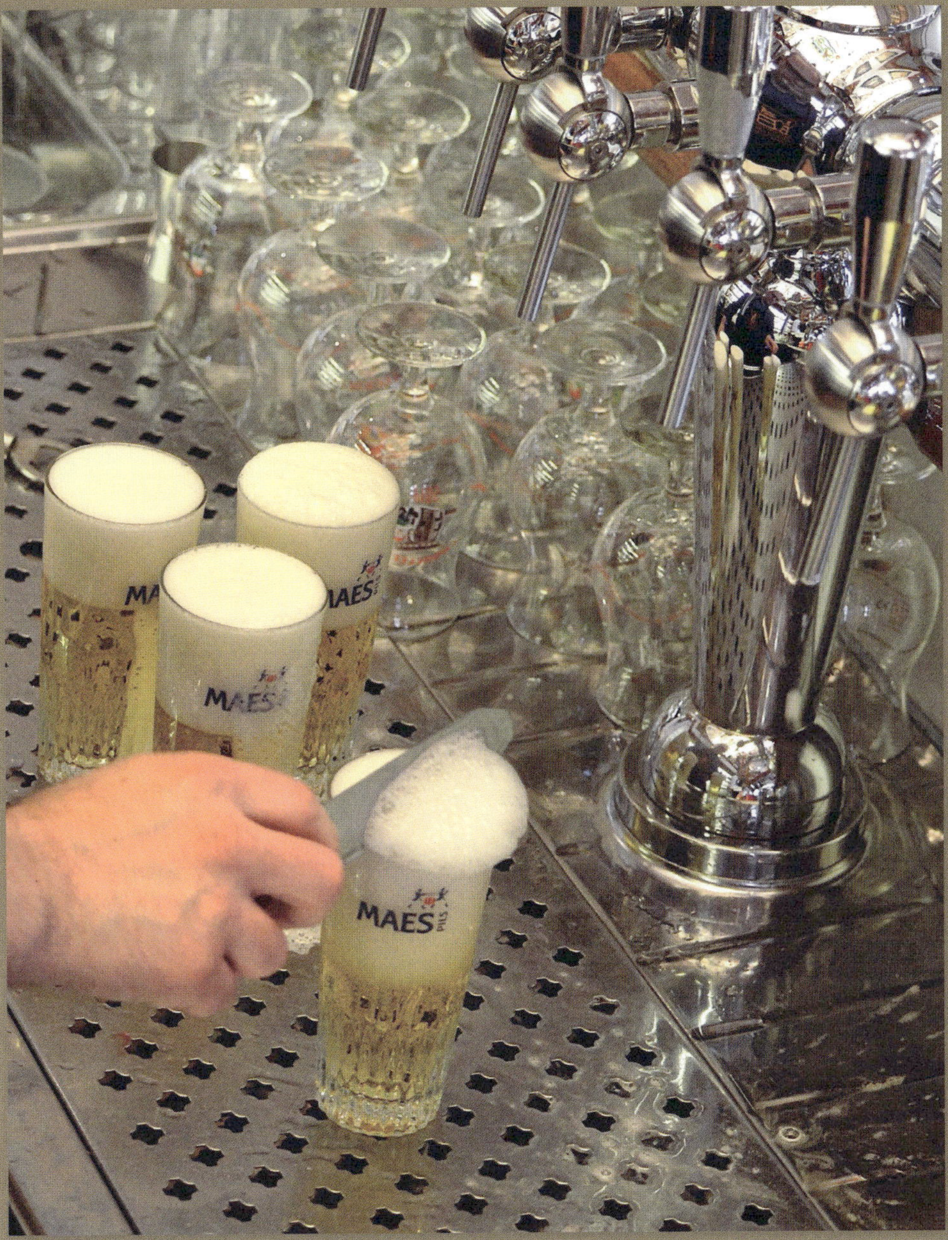
MAES

Jupiler (5,2%)

Men know why!

Jupiler is Belgium's most popular pils. It takes three weeks to produce. Quality checks and tastings are done throughout the process. 'Jupiler has taken pils to a higher level', in the brewer's opinion. All aspects of quality are considered, from start to finish: the ingredients, the water treatment, all the way down to how the beer is served in cafés and restaurants. This is a necessity rather than a luxury, as pils is a very delicate product. You can taste and smell any mistakes made during the brewing process and will also notice when the beer is not fresh enough or the tap is clogged. Jupiler is owned by AB Inbev. The roots of the brewery in Jupille go all the way back to 1853, when Piedboeuf introduced its light table beer. Jupiler pils was born in the 1960s under the name of Extra Pils. Jupiler '5' hit the market in 1966. This beer has conquered Belgian football and, in fact, the entire country. Every second pils consumed in Belgium is a Jupiler.

———

An extremely tender, mild pils, light, refreshing, fruity, malty and very mild in the finish. A pils for everyone.

www.jupiler.be

Primus (5,2%)

Ready to do battle

Brabant Duke Jan Primus (13th century) was keen on tournaments, songs about love performed by troubadours and loved a good knees-up. This knight is brought back to life on the label of this popular pils made by Haacht. Pop into 'het Brouwershof' just across from the brewery where you can taste the unfiltered and unpasteurised version. Haacht was founded at the end of the 19th century. Founder Eugène De Ro launched a bottom-fermented beer in 1902. It took only ten years for Haacht to join the top ranks of Belgian brewers. The splendid brewhall with elements of art nouveau was built in the 1920s and the current brewhall, still in use, saw the light in the 1930s. Haacht opened a bottling plant in 1950. One year afterwards, son-in-law Alfred Van der Kelen took over the management of the brewery, which is now in the hands of the fourth generation.

———

A light, sweet thirstquencher with an understated bitterness and a dry finish.

www.primus.be

Maes Pils (5,2%)

Say no to sweet

This classic has undergone a taste lift. Ever since 1946 Maes Pils has been a firm fixture in the Belgian beer landscape. This pils used to be brewed by Maes in Waarloos and now flows out of the tanks of Cristal in Alken. It has turned its back on the trend for ever-sweeter pils beers. The 'new' Maes came onto the market in 2009. The new edition has a higher malt content, no longer contains wheat but benefits from the use of Saaz aroma hops. The result is a beer that tastes fuller in the mouth and comes with a refined bitterness.

———

The initial taste has remained unchanged from the olden days, fresh and slightly sweet. The beer tastes very full in the mouth and benefits from a noticeably zesty and dry finish

www.maes.be

Stella Artois (5,2%)

Leuven conquers the world

Stella Artois is the main ambassador for Belgian beer. This pils that forms part of the AB Inbev range travels around the world. Its birthplace is the main brewery in Leuven but this beer is now brewed all around the globe. In the 1970s Stella Artois significantly increased its market share in its own country with the 'Stop de tijd. Neem een Stella!' campaign ('Stop time. Have a Stella!'), featuring a satisfied customer enjoying his pint at a table in a busy railway station. Later on, Stella Artois was to become 'het bier van het land van het bier' ('the beer of the country of beer'). In the United Kingdom, Stella Artois is said to be 'reassuringly expensive'. Stella Artois was first brewed in 1926 as a 'Christmas beer' and was consequently given the name Stella (Latin for 'star'). The history of the Artois brewery, now called AB Inbev, goes all the way back to 1366, the year that is incorporated in the logo. Tax records from the archives of the city of Leuven demonstrate that the inn cum brewery named Den Hoorn was already in existence. On 13 June 1708 Sebastian Artois acquired the highly coveted title of master-brewer. Ever since, the Artois name has been inextricably linked to beer.

———

A mild pils with aromas of flowers and herbs contributed by the Saaz hop. A gently bitter and hoppy taste.

www.stellaartois.com

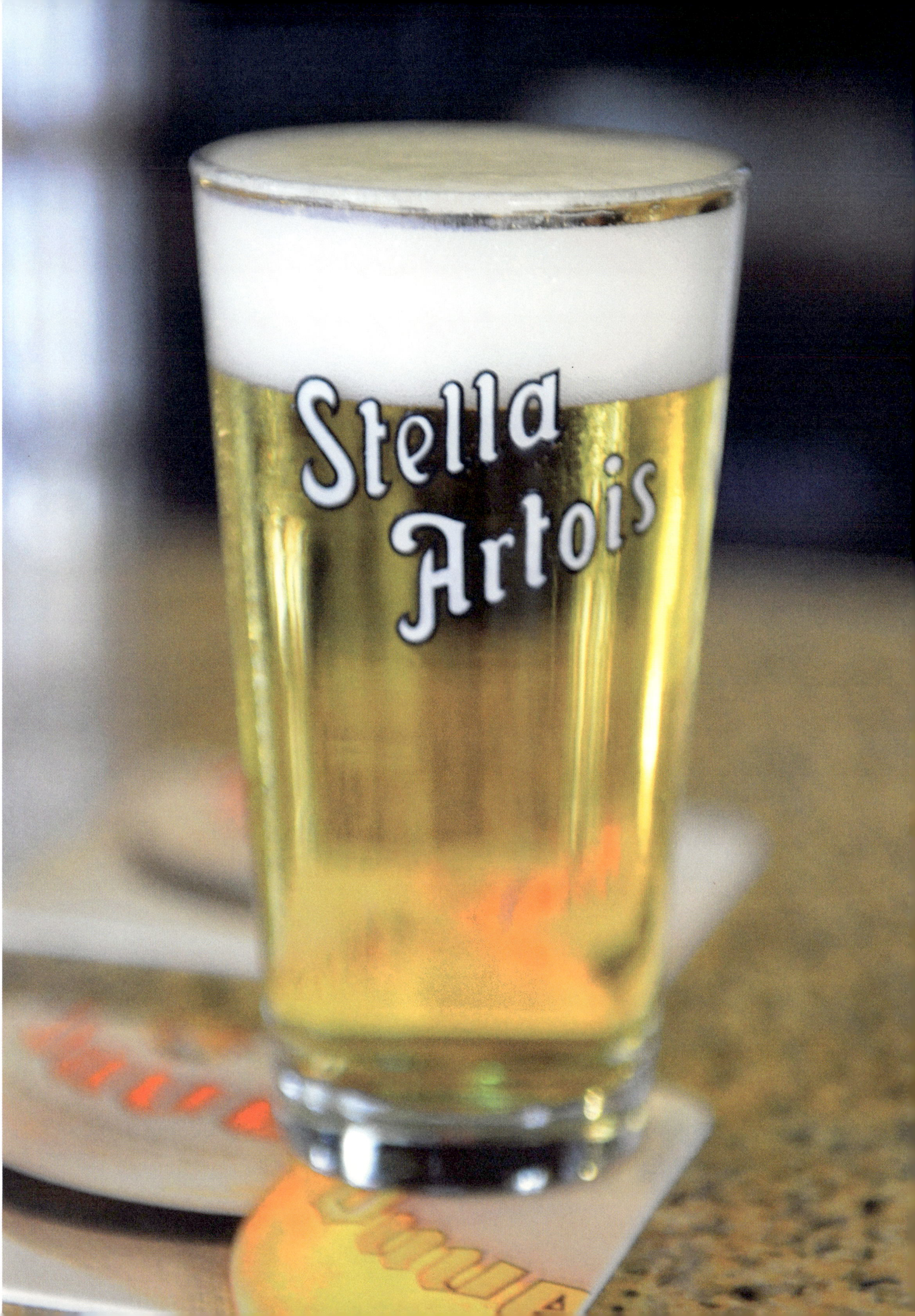
Stella
Artois

SAISON

The traditional saison is a light, slightly sour, dry, zesty and fruity beer that was brewed during the winter for drinking the following summer. The law used to impose a brewing period of up to 29 March to avoid contamination by wild yeasts that should not form part of the beer. Saisons are now produced all the year around. The roots of this slightly sour thirstquencher lie in the area of Bergen (Mons) and Doornik (Tournai). The oldest sources go back to the 17th century, when most saisons were brewed with spelt. Nowadays a saison tends to be quite strong, orange in colour and very sparkly. Saisons have a lovely head of froth due to the in-bottle re-fermentation. Their aroma is usually very fruity with a strong presence of hop, often thanks to the use of dry hopping. The latest saisons also contain exotic aroma hops. Who'd ever have thought that the dusty old saison would turn übertrendy overnight? In the 1980s this beer was only popular with a local, often elderly, customer base. The tide turned with late British beer guru Michael Jackson, who described the saison in his Great Beers of Belgium. In the early 1990s the first American importers jumped on the bandwagon and ever since then the flow has been unstoppable. There are over seven hundred saisons in the USA. In common with oude gueuze, the traditional Belgian saison is increasingly popular with beer lovers abroad in search of the real stuff.

Moinette Bio (7,5%)

Saison Turbo

In 1955 Sylva Rosier, the grandfather of current brewer Olivier Dedeycker, introduced a stronger version of the Saison Dupont and called it Moinette. This beer contains the same ingredients and is brewed using artisan methods. However, it has a higher density of ingredients. Consequently, the fermentation process is not quite the same, leading to the production of different esters. This makes the Moinette more tender and fruity compared to a classic saison. It is a degustation beer that stores well. In 1990 Olivier started brewing organic beers at the request of the Malterie de Beloeil, a malt works in the same region. This is how the Moinette Bio and the Saison Dupont Bio were created. The Moinette Bio differs from the classic Moinette through its use of different hop varieties. To brew an organic beer requires a hefty dose of discipline, but a brewery like Dupont, with its strict adherence to tradition, has discipline in spades.

A fruity beer with delicate aromas of malt and hops and impressions of citrus. A tender, well-hopped thirstquencher that owes its complex character to the long re-fermentation in the bottle.

www.brasserie-dupont.com

IV Saison (6,5%)

Aroma-hoppy

'I dream of well-hopped, quaffable beers brewed with Belgian know-how.' Alexandre Dumont de Chassart of Brasserie Jandrain Jandrenouille feels that the taste of your average beer drinker is too limited. He is also an importer and as such, he discovered the variety of American aroma hops that he is keen to use in his beers. The number in his IV Saison is a reference to the four basic elements in this beer, inspired by the traditional saison. The drawing depicting the 'IV' towering over the hop fields was created by well-known Brussels cartoonist François Schuiten. Alexandre brews an artisan, unfiltered beer that uses dry hopping and re-ferments in the bottle. This engineer is keen on balance. He is not aiming to produce a niche beer, rather he is after one with hop bitter that goes down smoothly. His beers stand out thanks to their rich hop aromas. 'The hop lies at the basis,' Alexandre confirms. 'We want to taste what we have put in. A quaffable beer with a great finish.'

A dry beer with fresh and fruity aromas, impressions of citrus and herbs and a delicate bitterness that continues to vibrate in the long finish.

www.brasseriedejandrainjandrenouille.com

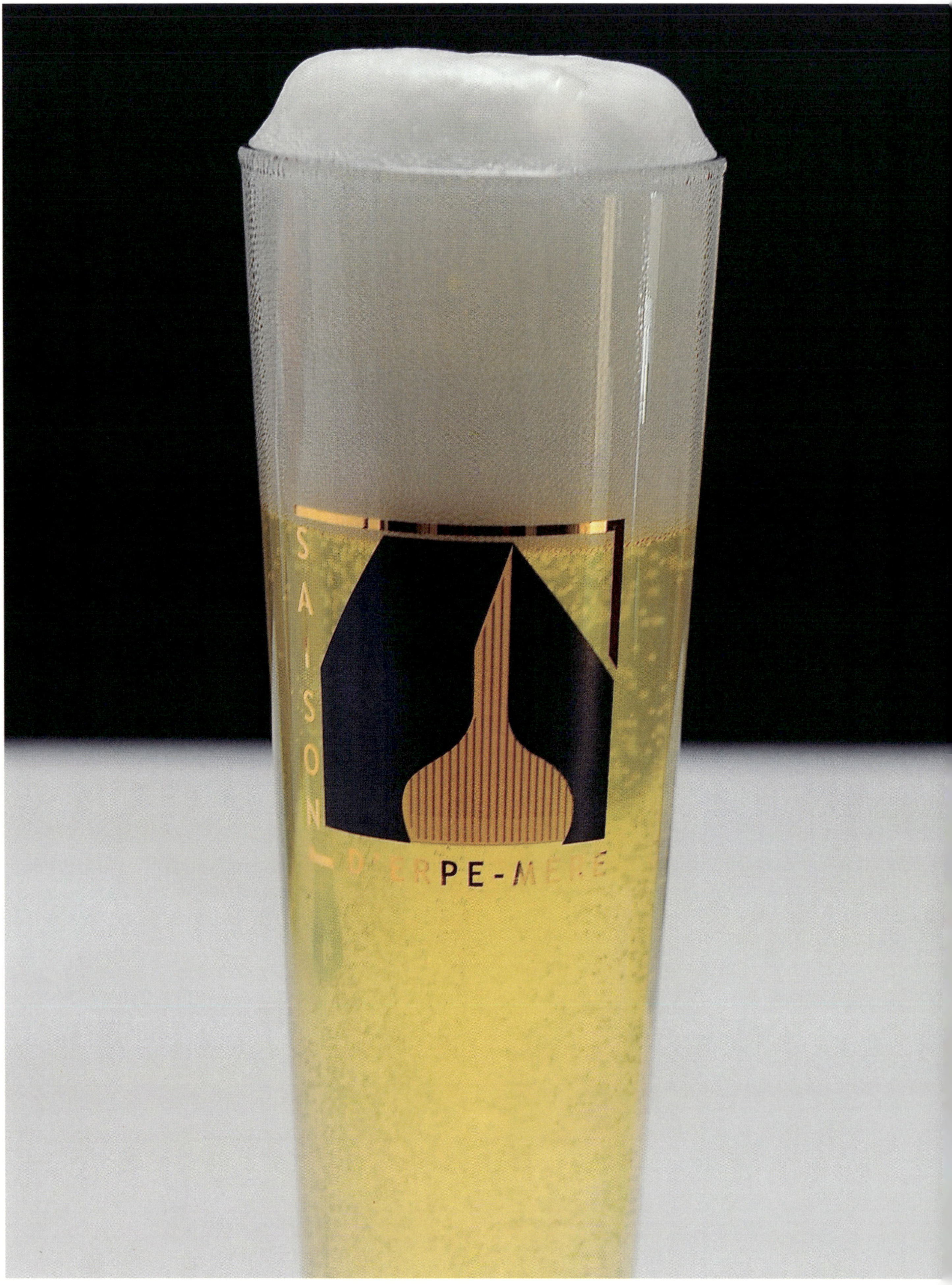
SAISON
D'ERPE-MERE

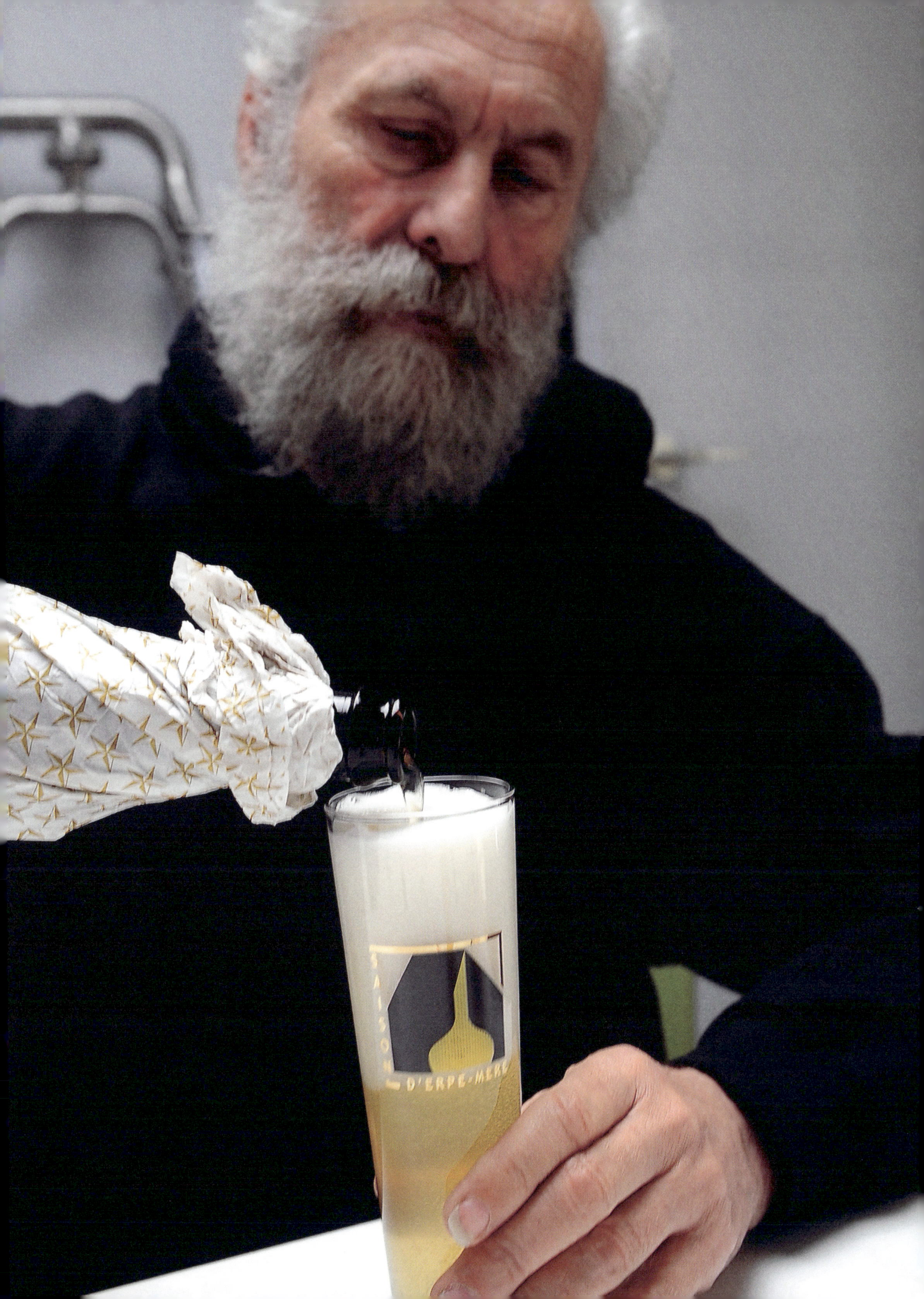
SAISON
D'ERPE-MERE

Saison d'Erpe Mere (6,9%)

A refined beer for the people

Jef Van den Steen, beer author and brewer, re-interprets existing beer styles without betraying their original character. His Saison d'Erpe Mere makes for a good thirstquencher, the way it was meant to be. This dry, hoppy saison was brewed at the farms of the Hainaut during the winter to quench the thirst of the land workers the following summer. Large quantities of hops were used so the beer could be stored for longer, as hops act as a natural preservation agent. Saison d'Erpe Mere is a genuine saison using three different hop varieties: Spalt for its aroma, Magnum to promote bitterness and Hallertau Mittelfrüh from Aalst for the late hopping. At De Glazen Toren they brew in the traditional manner but with modern-day equipment. For example, the kettle is heated by the flame from the gas burner, giving a full-bodied taste. The temperature is increased by adding boiling water. The brewer prepares a thick mash. This intensifies the conversion of the malts resulting in drier beers.

―――――

Aromas of herbs and citrus with an undercurrent of hop and malt. The taste offers even more herbs and fruit. Well-saturated thirstquencher with strong pearlisation.

www.glazentoren.be

Saison Dupont (6,5%)

Staying true to tradition

Amongst the saisons from the Hainaut, Saison Dupont is the one and only reference beer. Thirty years ago, this typical farm beer was in danger of dying out. There are now around twenty Belgian saisons on the market and what is more, this traditional beer style is also inspiring brewers from abroad. The main fermentation is followed by a long maturation in the warm chambers. Hops are also added. The in-bottle re-fermentation provides a higher carbon dioxide content, giving the beer its refreshing and zesty taste. Saison Dupont is a classic from 1844. This copper-blond beer has surprisingly delicate aromas and a pronounced hop bitterness. An important role is played by the houseyeast and the hard well water used in brewing. The in-bottle re-fermentation leads to the development of a complex, exceptionally aromatic beer. This unfiltered saison sticks to the tradition of the original farm beer, which explains its cloudy veil. However, it is stronger and fuller in body than the saisons of old. These were more like a light table beer with an alcohol volume of 2% to 3%.

―――――

This refreshing thirstquencher is quite sharp at the outset, with fruity aromas of citrus (lime, lemon, orange), wet grass and hay, typical of this type of traditional farm beers. The beer is slightly sour and quite dry with a pronounced hop bitterness, prominent in the long finish.

www.brasserie-dupont.com

Surfine (6,5%)

Boisterous

One that is hard to tame in the glass. All we can recommend is to pour it slowly… Surfine is a hidden pearl from the rich assortment of the oldest brewery in Wallonia. A trawl through the archives of the Dubuisson brewery turned up a 'hidden' brand, older even than the iconic Bush Ambrée from 1933. Surfine — its name means 'extra fine' and is a pun on a well-known bubbly drink — was born as an amber-coloured Spéciale Belge and remained on the market until the 1950s. The brand was re-born in 2014 as a typical saison from the Hainaut. For Dubuisson this is an instant introduction into the world of more strongly hopped beers. Surfine is brewed with three varieties of malt and three Belgian hops. Dubuisson is emphasising the Belgian origins of this beer as the brewery strongly supports its local 'terroir'. Surfine owed its balanced character to the alchemy between its various ingredients. Finally, another new aspect is that the Surfine undergoes three fermentation stages. A different yeast is used each time. At the last fermentation stage, the 'wild' yeasts convert the last remaining sugars into carbon dioxide, hence the dry character.

———

The nose picks up surprisingly fruity, zesty and floral aromas with impressions of citrus and pepper. In the tasting, the pleasant dry-bitter taste comes to the fore. The wild yeasts from the final fermentation provide a hint of sourness, making this newcomer refreshing and thirstquenching and easily digestible.

www.dubuisson.com

Waterloo Récolte (6%)

A harvest beer

Breweries grew out of farms. Harvest beers such as the Waterloo Récolte are imbibed with this farming history, just like a saison or a white beer. All the ingredients are readily available from the rich Brabant farmland surrounding the brand new microbrewery located at the Ferme de Mont Saint-Jean. Besides the Waterloo Récolte, the range includes the Triple Blond, Strong Dark and Cuvée Impériale. The Ferme de Mont Saint-Jean is a historic, square-shaped farmhouse, located on the edge of the battlefield of Waterloo, where Napoleon was defeated in 1815. The farm served as a field hospital for English soldiers. The brewer found his inspiration in a recipe for soldiers' beer dating back to 1815.

———

This very quaffable beer comes with impressively refreshing and fruity aromas. A striking, slightly sour touch of wheat complements the malt and the delicate hop bitterness.

www.waterloo-brewery.com

Grisette

....

Grisette is a forgotten beer style that originated in the areas of Bergen (Mons), Charleroi and Doornik (Tournai). This type of beer was created at the end of the 19th century as a response to the wave of pils beers that flooded the old continent. Not only did the brewers launch the amber-coloured Spéciale Belge (Palm, De Koninck), they also came up with the Grisette. In those days, the classic and better-known saison beers often had a sour taste thanks to the influence of the wild yeasts of the Brettanomyces type. A grisette can be defined as a rather strong saison with a robust dosage of hops, in other words, a luxury version or an upgrade to a saison. The best and most noble hops were selected to make a grisette. This beer was especially popular with the local labour force, working on the land or in the factories. The St-Feuillien brewery patented the Grisette name for some of its beers.

Brasserie de Waterloo is found at the Ferme de Mont St Jean close to the battlefield.
In 1815 English solders were nursed here, now there is beer flowing from the tanks.
The Waterloo Récolte is a farm beer inspired by saison.

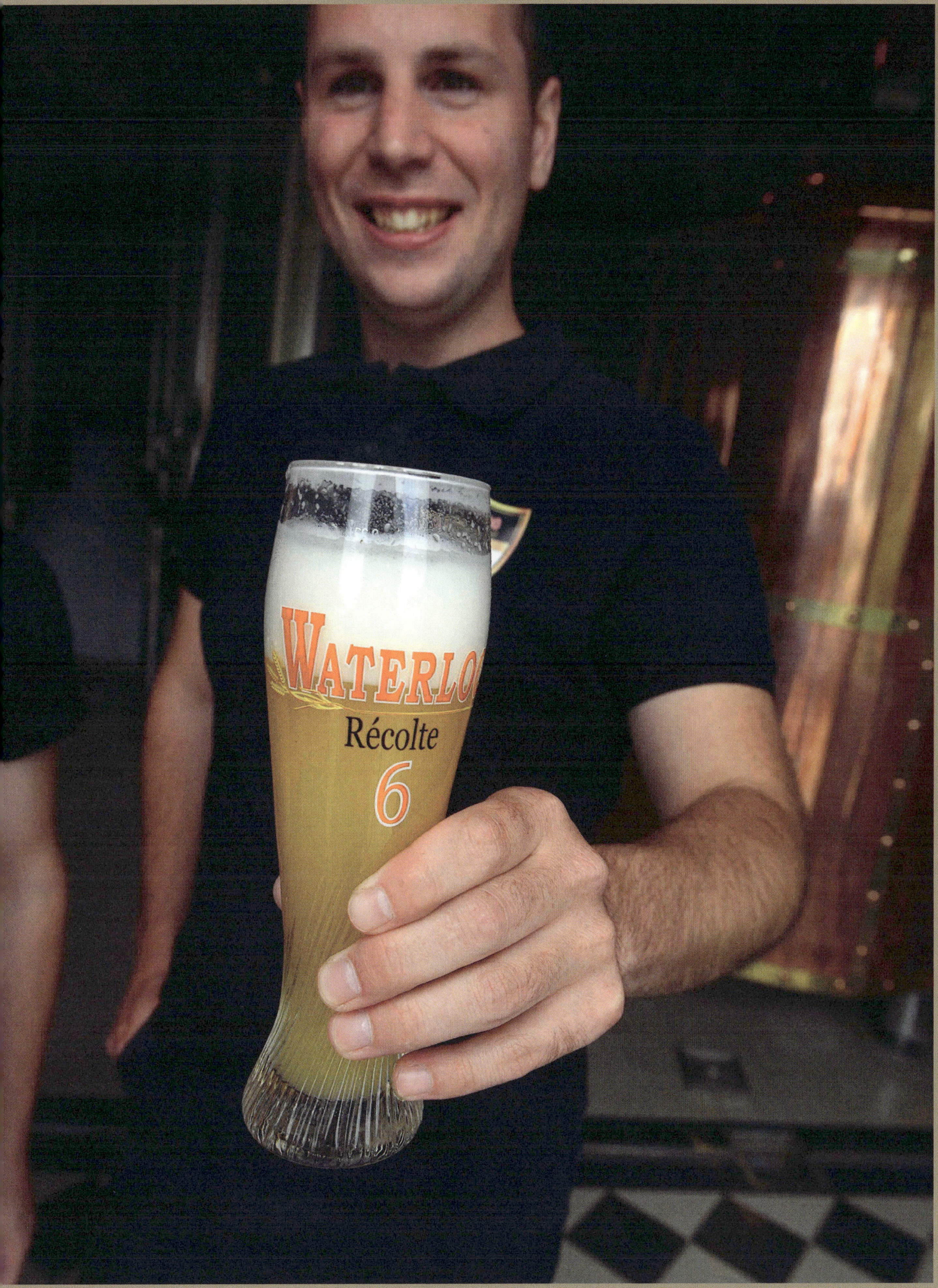
Récolte
6

FLEMISH RED-BROWN

Sweet and sour. That is the overriding taste of a Flemish red-brown beer. It goes down easily and makes for an ideal thirstquencher. All well and good, but this beer is really the outcome of an ancient preservation method. A herbal mixture called gruit, or gruut, was used in the early Middle Ages to increase the storage period of a beer and give it taste. Hops were not yet known in our region. Red-brown beer contains lactic and acetic acids which aids its storage period. The Flemish red-brown beers are mixed fermentation beers. Following the main fermentation stage the beers mature – or sour – in oak 'foeders'. This process accounts for their mildly sour taste and complex fruitiness. The 'mixed fermentation' process means that the brewer blends – or cuts – recently fermented beer with old, mature beer. A range of micro-organisms ensure the fermentation of the beer during its maturation in wooden foeders and are largely responsible for the taste. Each red-brown beer is a unique blend. This method is used in the area surrounding Kortrijk and Roeselare. The Flemish red-brown beers go all the way back to the Middle Ages, when beer was stored without the use of hops. A beer that contains lactic and acetic acids will store for longer. This gave rise to the tradition of 'soured beers', where a proportion of recently fermented beer is blended, or 'cut, with old mature beer. You cannot taste hop bitter in this beer.

Bacchus Oud Bruin (4,5%)

Many shades of sweet and sour

Bacchus fits into the tradition of the Flemish red-brown beers. It is made by allowing a top-fermented beer to be injected with wild yeasts from the St-Louis-gueuze made by the Van Honsebrouck brewery. This creates a slightly sour beer with a strong aroma and a 'wine taste'. Bacchus was introduced in 1954 and owes its name to the ancient Greek god of Dyonisos — Bacchus in Latin — who has come to symbolise wine and feasting. Bacchus is an excellent thirstquencher. Besides a prominent sourness, you can detect the slight touch of caramel coming from the roasted malts. Bacchus also serves as the mother beer for Bacchus Frambozenbier (raspberries) and the Bacchus Kriekenbier.

Bacchus Oud Bruin yields fruity and flowery aromas. The taste of this red-brown beer is not dissimilar to wine. The sourness, with hints of balsamic vinegar, is not as pronounced as that of other Flemish red-brown beers. Very refreshing with a pleasant finish.

www.vanhonsebrouck.be

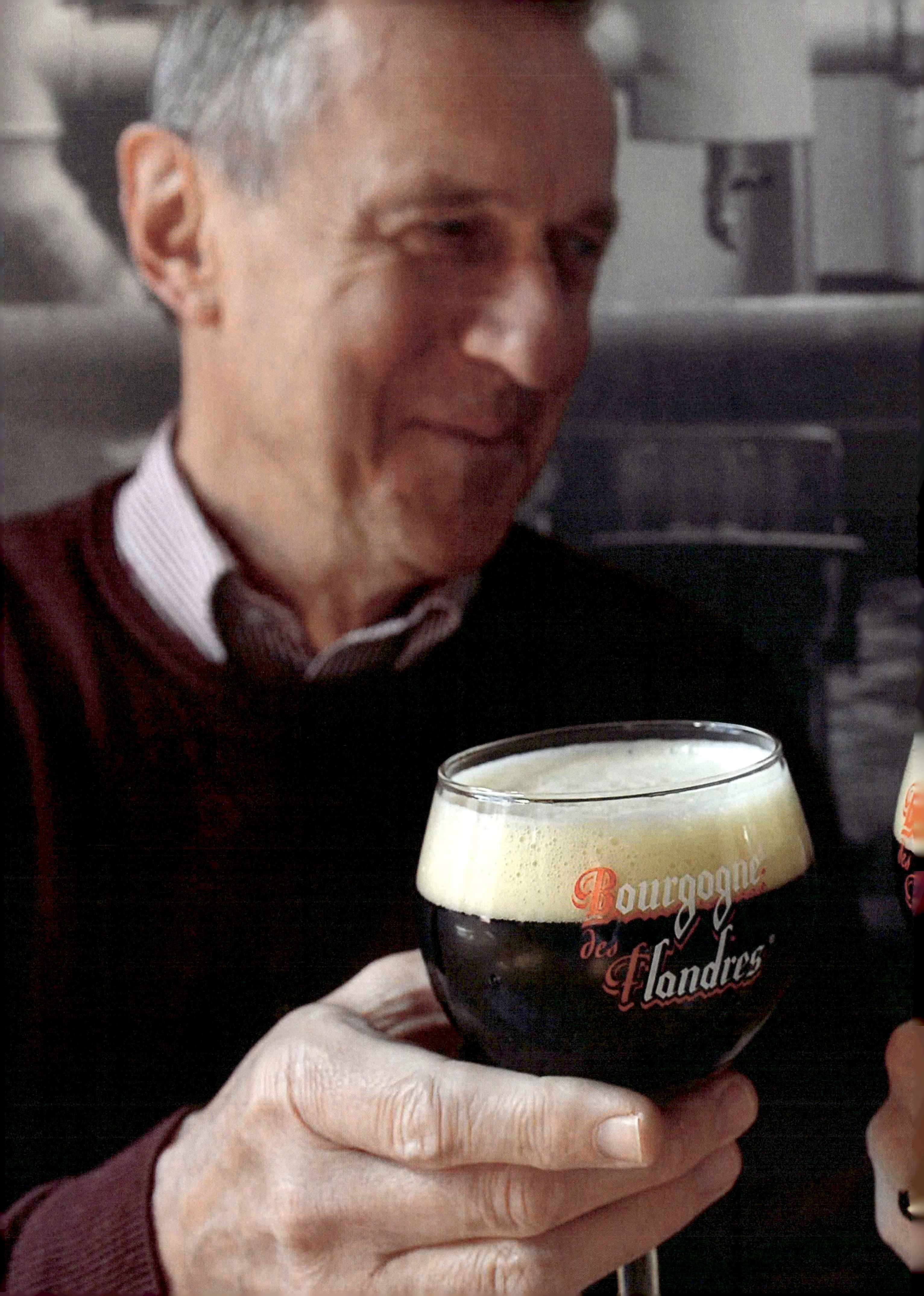
Bourgogne
des Flandres

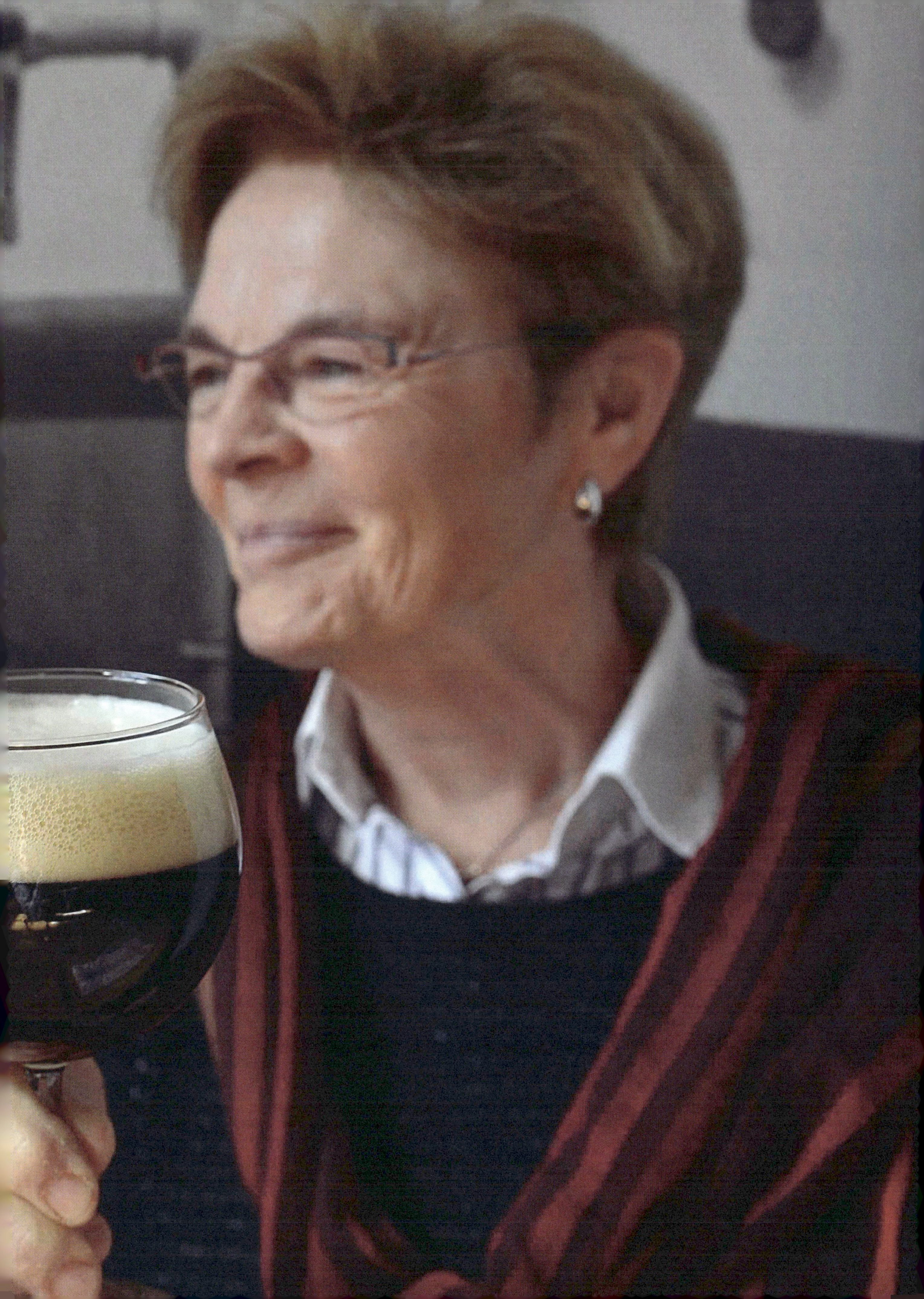

Bourgogne des Flandres (5%)

Burgundian Bruges

Bourgogne des Flandres is a blend of a top-fermented brown beer and a lambic matured in wooden barrels. This beer, characteristic of Bruges, was brewed in the city by the Van Houtryve family between 1910 and 1957. Production was later moved to the Verhaeghe-Vichte brewery before being taken over by the Timmermans lambic brewery. Since 2016 this beer is brewed once again in Bruges in a brand new microbrewery.

———

This red-brown beer owes its full-bodied, creamy taste to the well-judged blend of brown top-fermented beer with spontaneously fermented lambic followed by months of maturation on oak barrels. Malty, slightly toasted aroma. The taste is gently sweet and sour with a finish of roast malt.

www.bourgognedesflandres.be

Cuvée des Jacobins (5,5%)

Foeder lambic

This uncut lambic has spent eighteen months maturing on oak foeders. The beer's name is a reference to the famous French Dominican monastery, the Hospice Saint Jacques (1218), that provided an overnight stay to pilgrims travelling to Compostela. During the First World War, Omer Rémi, brewer at Omer Vander Ghinste, spent some time in the Rue des Jacobins in Paris. This is where, in 1789, the heart of the French Revolution was beating strongly.

———

This red-brown beer has an aroma of lactic acid and fruits (krieken) with touches of wood. A complex but very balanced sour beer that culminates in a finish of vanilla and red fruits. Quite a creamy mouth feel.

www.omer.be

Duchesse de Bourgogne (6,2%)

In homage to the Duchess

In Vichte, Mary of Burgundy still lives in the memory after many centuries. This Duchess, born in Brussels, married Maximilian I. 'She bestowed many rights on the citizens and supported the brewers,' Karl Verhaeghe of the Verhaeghe-Vichte brewery, tells us. Here they are still brewing the regional beers from the times when the brewery was founded in 1885. These are Flemish red-brown beers, a blend of young, top-fermented beer and spontaneously fermented beer matured on oak foeders, of the lambic type. Tradition is more than an empty slogan. After all, what else can you say if you have been brewing Flemish red-brown for four generations, from great-grandfather to great-grandchild? For Karl and his brother Peter, the story began with the Vichtenaar. The Duchesse de Bourgogne has now become their star beer.

———

A typical Flemish red-brown beer. Vinous aromas and a sharp sourness are tempered by the sweetish character of the malt.

www.brouwerijverhaeghe.be

Petrus Oud Bruin (5,5%)

oak-matured

Petrus Oud Bruin is a traditional Flemish-red brown beer. This beer, with its deep dark-red colour, matures in oak foeders for eighteen months. And this is how the Petrus Original — called Petrus Oud Bruin in Belgium — with its slightly sour taste that is not dissimilar to wine, is born. This relatively light beer makes for a perfect thirstquencher, a great aperitif beer or a companion for a meal. Petrus Oud Bruin is a blend of 33% Petrus Aged Pale, a pure foeder beer that has matured for two years in oak foeders, and 67% young brown beer. A 'cut beer' such as this harks back to the tradition of blending young and soured beers to increase its 'shelf life'. The young, darker beer provides the colour and the Petrus Aged Pale provides the sour touch. Ever since the 1970s, De Brabandere has focused on foeder beers and gradually expanded its range.

———

Aromas of candied fruits, figs with fruity accents coming from cherry, peach, malt, butter and caramel. The overall taste is slightly sour (lactic acid).

www.brouwerijdebrabandere.be

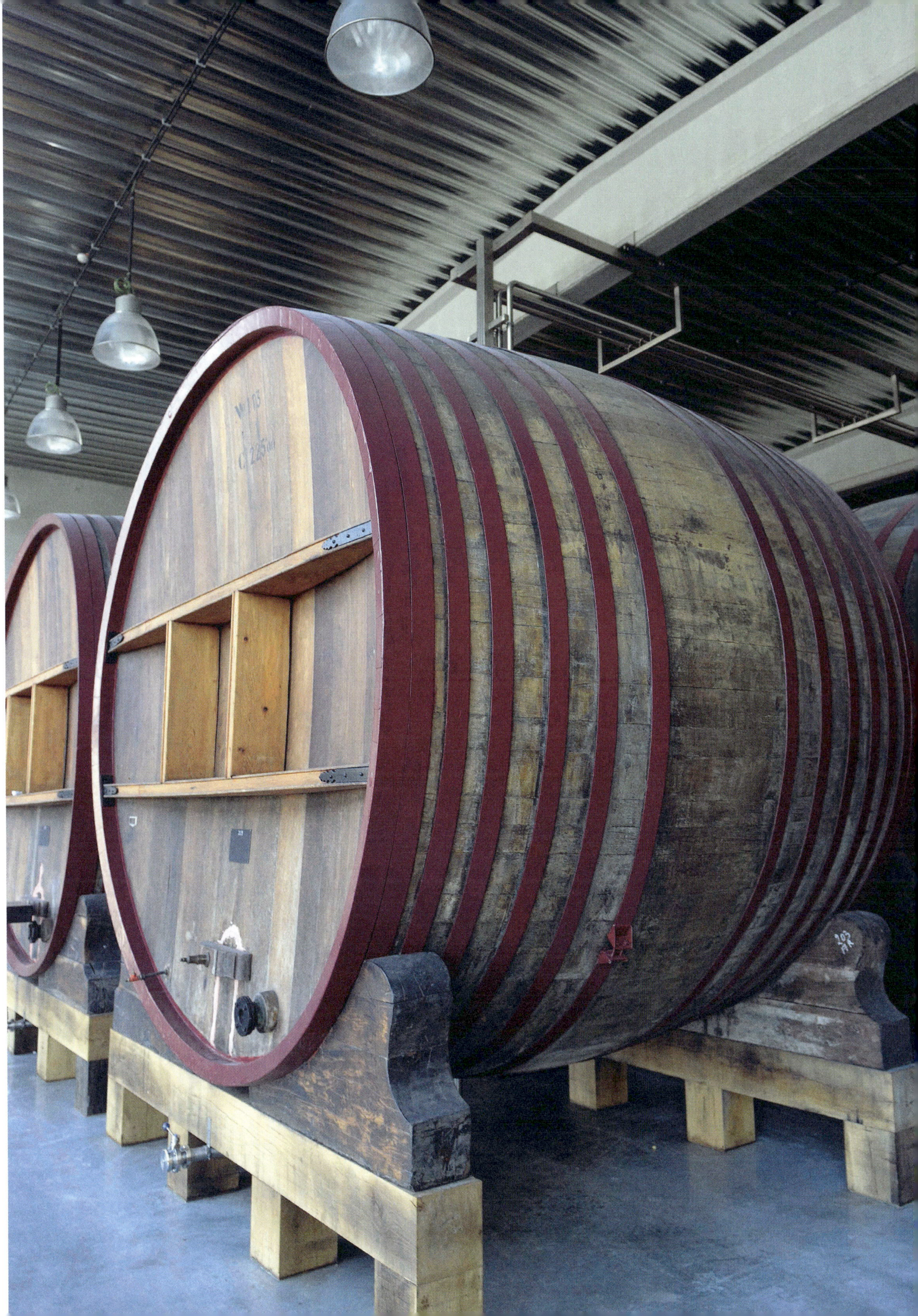

Reninge Oud Bruin (6%)

A cut beer

Beer archaealogist Chris Vandewalle is unearthing the pre-war beers from the Westhoek region. His Reninge Oud Bruin is a Flemish red-brown beer, cut with a brown beer that has matured on oak for eight months, brewed using Magnum hops from Poperinge. The maturation in oak barrels and the in-bottle re-fermentation ensure a complex, intense and delicately sour taste. Chris is in charge of the archives of the city of Diksmuide. Pre-war newspapers taught him that: *'Het oud bruin bier was sinds jaren in geheel de streke van Veurne-Ambacht door en door gekend voor 't fijnste, 't vroomste en 't lekkerste aller bieren.'* In other words, the brown beer of the region was considered the finest around. The brown colour of this beer and its caramel-bitter or sour taste were attributed to the calcium and iron contained in the water of Reninge. Chris takes all the time in the world to 'educate' his beers. He is not forcing them to grow up. Chris is a scion from a brewing family. 'I blend my own yeast. The water comes from the Blankaart reservoir.' Chris is captivated by the history of the brewers in his region and is the author of several publications on breweries that were around between 1760 and 1960. 'I am following the tradition of cut beers (a young beer blended with a beer that is one year old). Reninge Oud Bruin continues to mature in wooden foeders. Brewers used to be 'cutters' (blenders) first and foremost. Just look at the gueuzestekers who were blending different vintages of lambic. Until the 1950s my family produced lambic in the Yser Valley that they cut into a gueuze.'

A mild aroma of lactic acid with a slight touch of wood. Very gently sour with a delicately sweet accent and just a hint of wood. The finish is dry with a hint of sweetness.

www.seizoensbrouwerij.be

Rodenbach Grand Cru (6%)

Fifty shades of sour

Rodenbach Grand Cru is a reference beer for the Flemish red-brown beer style. Each and every red-brown beer is a unique blend. A Rodenbach Grand Cru owes its typical, gently sour taste to its two fermentation stages. During the so-called 'mixed fermentation', the top-fermenting yeasts are sharing a home with the lactic acid flora. Afterwards, the Rodenbach Grand Cru will mature in oak foeders over a period of two years, providing the unique complex fruitiness that makes the beer come close to a wine. The Rodenbach mother beers contain, on average, a quarter of old, mature beer and three quarters of young beer. The Rodenbach Grand Cru is made with two thirds of old, mature beer and one third young beer.

The Rodenbach Grand Cru stands out through its aromas of red fruits, vanilla, wood, cheese, chocolate and caramel. The taste is mild and beautifully balanced between lactic acids and acetic acids. This beer is not unlike wine, cider and calvados.

www.rodenbach.be

Oerbier (9%)

Wet but packs a great punch

Oerbier heralded the new wave of microbreweries in 1980. This now classic beer is made with a variety of malts, Kent Golding hop cones and a house yeast that gives a sharpness to the beer when it ages. This beer develops aromas of wine after a few years' ageing. The Oerbierman or 'ancient beer man' adorns the label on the bottle. He stands for work and science, keeps a firm hold on the mashing stick and peers into the glass. The Dolle Brouwers are experimenting with natural ingredients. Their beers are unfiltered, unpasteurised and produced without any colouring agents. 't Oerisme has now become a popular activity in the Diksmuide area. (Pun on tourism, let me know if I need to elaborate) This brewer is also an architect and painter, specialising in water colours. His creative devils are unleashed in his beer.

Full in the mouth, gentle and creamy beer with impressions of hop and malt. Mild and slightly sour thanks to the lactic acid bacteria contained in the yeast. Aromas of freshly baked pastry, dark fruits, vanilla and caramel as well as alcohol. A complex beer providing a long finish.
www.dedollebrouwers.be

Oudenaards Bruin

Similar to an Oude Gueuze, the beer style known as Oudenaards Bruin is also a blend of different beers. The mother beer undergoes a first fermentation to which the house yeast is added. Tradition dictates that a second beer is brewed. Both beers are cut (blended) and bottled after sugars and yeast are added. The beer is mild but with a pleasant sourness, dry and complex. Discover its aroma to meet touches of caramel contributed by the malt, but also hints of nuts and cherries that provide the link with wine. The malt is dried or oasted for a slightly longer period and at a slightly higher temperature, which makes the beer take on a darker colour. Oudenaards Bruin is distinguished from a Vlaams Roodbruin by the slightly salty water used in brewing and the very long boiling time.

The baseline 'nat en straf' (wet and strong) describes it to a tee: not a beer for wimps.

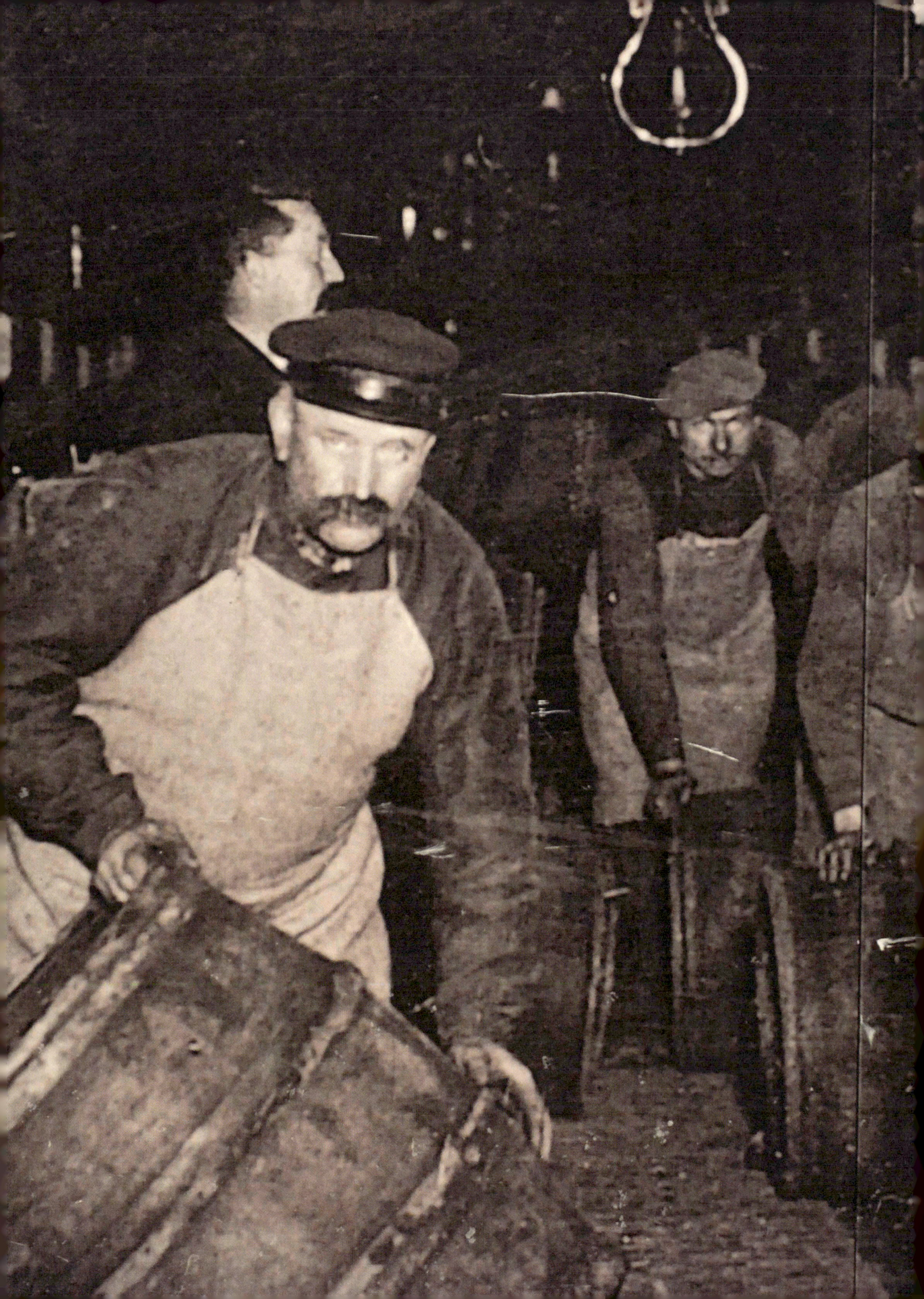

At Rodenbach's, beer is souring in oak foeders. It will later be 'cut' (blended) with young beer. The uncut foeder beer, 'vin de céréales', is reminiscent of sherry.

Brewer carrying out checks in the brewhall at Roman's.

Adriaen Brouwer Dark Gold (8,5%)

The five senses

We are making our way to Oudenaarde, home to the oldest brewery in the country. The Roman brewery (1545) has been owned by fourteen generations of 'Romans'. Their Roman Oudenaards beer was re-launched in 2003 under the name of Adriaen Brouwer. This name is a reference to the painter-artist from Oudenaarde (17th century) who immortalised the five senses and was generally known as a 'bon vivant'. The Adriaen Brouwer beer is different from other brown beers from Oudenaarde as it is brewed with hard spring water from the Flemish Ardennes. In addition, a pure yeast is used in brewing and the beer does not undergo a spontaneous fermentation process (using wild yeasts) which is different to the process used by breweries in other parts of the region. Finally, this brewery does not 'cut' (blend) young beer with old beer.

The Adriaen Brouwer Dark Gold is a degustation beer based on an Adriaen Brouwer that re-ferments in the bottle. You will immediately notice the intense aromas of roast malt and caramel. Far from a coincidence. The malt is dried or 'oasted' for a slightly longer period and at a higher temperature, resulting in a darker colour and a stronger taste that remains for longer.

A whiff of sour in the nose. Creamy and bitter with a bitter-sweet finish. The alcohol makes its presence felt. A great balance between caramel, roast malt and dried fruits.

www.roman.be

Liefmans Goudenband (8%)

Improves with age

One that is happy to be left alone for a while. Liefmans Goudenband is a 'provisiebier', in other words, one that is suitable for laying down. It is the stronger version of the Liefmans Oud Bruin, matured in the bottle at the brewery. This festive beer used to be served on special occasions. It is not usual to allow such a strong beer to turn sour as the alcohol restrains the work of the bacteria. However, the longer maturation period results in a very fruity and beautiful balance. The Liefmans Goudenband is a feast for the senses. The beer colours a deep brown in the glass and on tasting you discover a wide range of aromas and tastes. Thanks to the mixed fermentation, the beer has a complex aroma that tends towards wood. At Liefmans an open cooling basin is used. The yeasts and bacteria that have made their home in the pores of the copper equipment are responsible for the typical lactic acid taste. The mother beer is top-fermented and cools down in the 'koelschip' where it will ferment spontaneously as it comes in contact with the microflora in the ambient air. The beers are lagered for up to three years in chilled metal tanks. Older beer is blended with younger, fresher and sweeter beer to renew the taste. The beer will re-ferment after the cutting (blending).

Exceptionally zesty with a dry and slightly caramelised taste of malt, enriched by fruity touches of nuts and dried raisins. Mildly sour and slightly sweet. The complex finish provides rich aromas.

www.liefmans.be

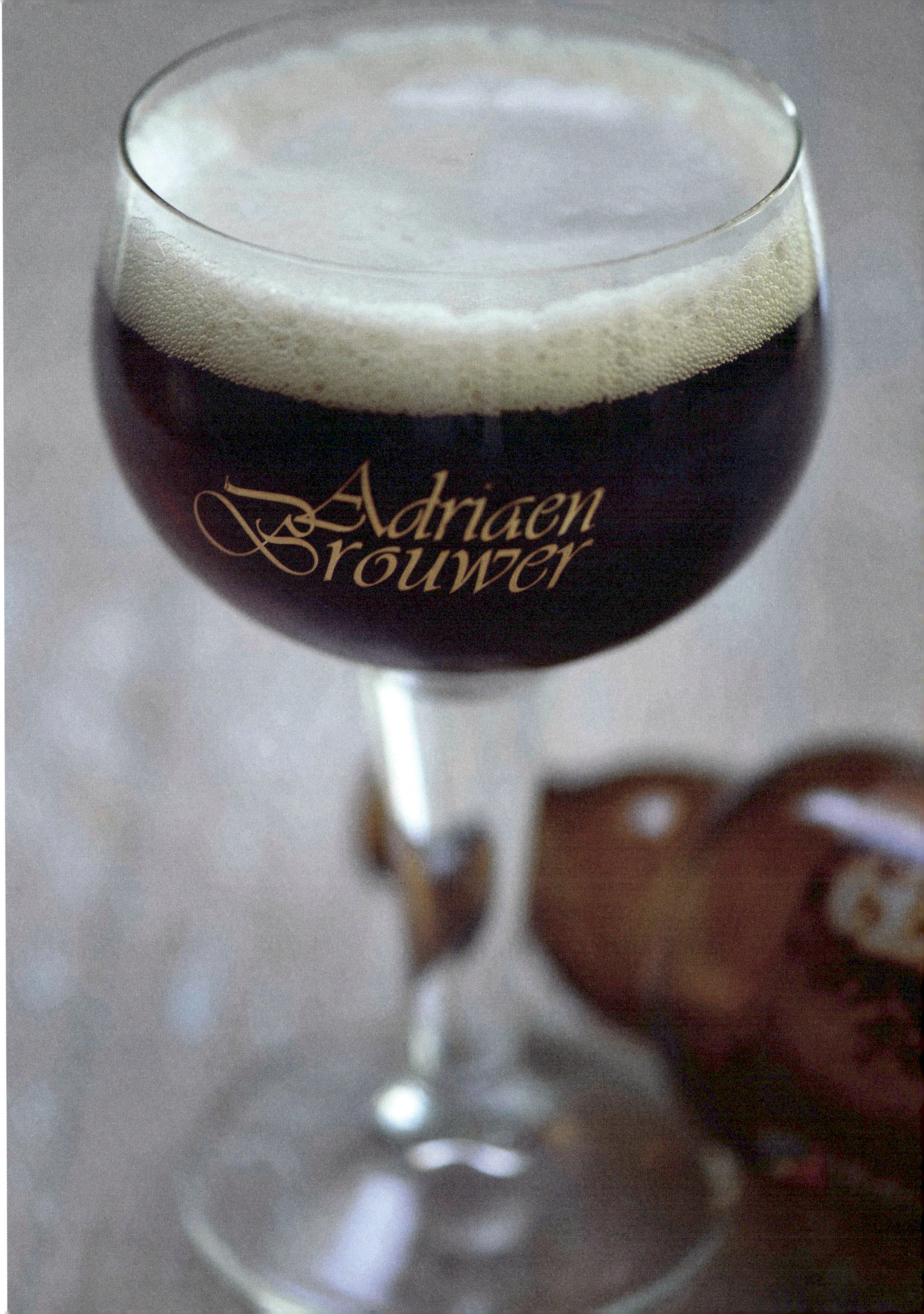
Adriaen
Brouwer

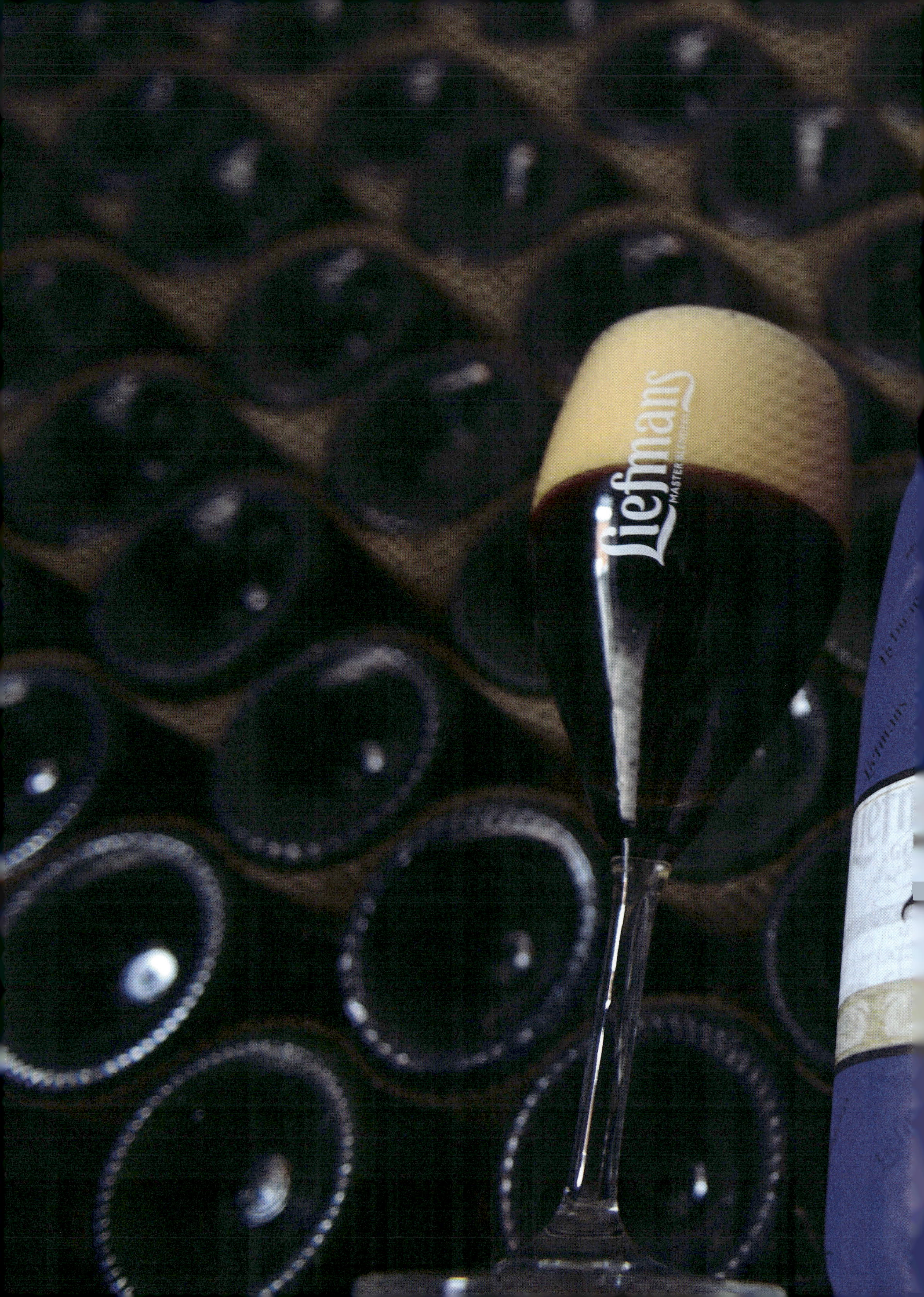
Liefmans

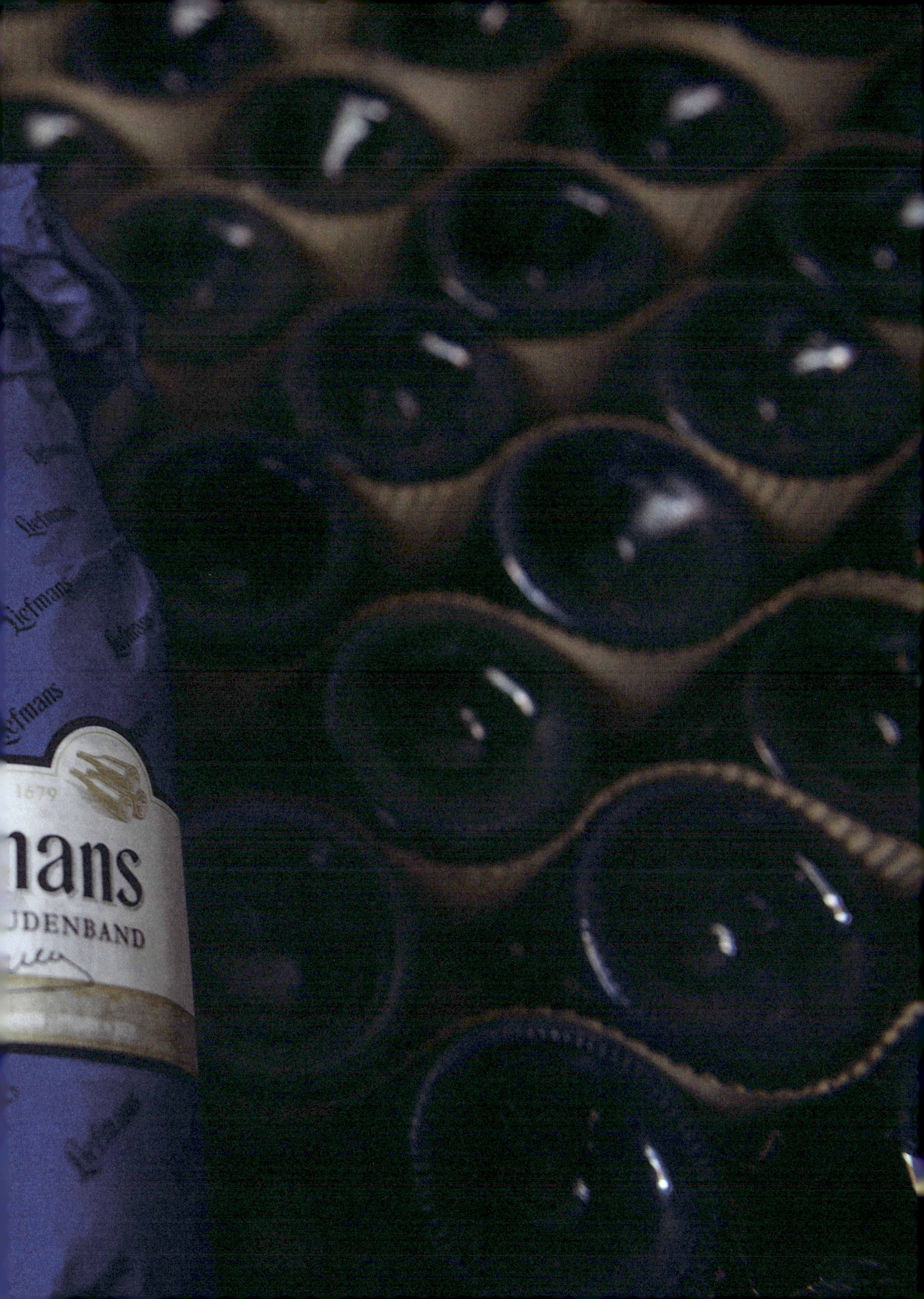
Liefmans
1679
mans
UDENBAND

WITBIER (WHITE BEER)

―――――◆―――――

White beer is a top-fermented, unfiltered beer. To produce a white beer the brewer will use a minimum of 30% unmalted wheat. The use of herbs such as coriander and orange peel is typical of Belgian white beer. They provide its pleasantly refreshing aroma. White beer re-ferments in the bottle and is unfiltered. This results in a cloudy beer in your glass with a pleasantly mild taste and a slightly sour touch.

Hoegaarden (4,8%)

Place a bet on white

The white beer of Hoegaarden lays at the foundation of the revival of specialty beers. In 1966 Pierre Celis started brewing witbier in Hoegaarden once again. He would also introduce it to the USA later on under the name of Celis White. This unfiltered beer with its natural 'look' was an instant hit with the youth market. Thanks to mouth-to-mouth advertising this 'witte van Hoegaarden' grew into a phenomenon. Ever since the wildly popular beer mat campaign Hoegaarden is synonymous with a culture of self-depreciation and adventure. Let's go back in time for a moment. Malt, wheat, hop, coriander, dried orange peel and water. These are the ingredients used to brew white beer in Hoegaarden since records began. The first written sources date back to 1318. Even then, beer drinkers had a taste for white beer as the number of breweries was increasing steadily. Hoegaarden numbered over thirty breweries in the 18th century. With the increased popularity of pils the old-fashioned, almost corny white beer lost much ground in the 20th century. The last white beer brewery closed its doors in 1957. Fortunately Pierre Celis re-launched this traditional brew and ensured its survival.

The nose detects aromas of citrus, apple, wheat and spices. The taste is somewhere in between wheat, honey and citrus, not unlike cider, with an undercurrent of hop and coriander. Citrus and spices dominate the finish.

www.hoegaarden.com

Limburgse Witte (5%)

A beer to enjoy on a terrace

Brouwerij Cornelissen introduced its Limburgse Witte in 1993. Malt, unmalted wheat, hop, coriander, dried orange peel and water. These are the ingredients used to brew white beer since records began and the Limburgse Witte is no exception. The white beer epoch started around 1445 when monks divided their time between prayer, worship, wine making and beer brewing. They discovered the recipe for the slightly sour white beer. Exotic herbs and spices became popular in later years. This prompted the addition of coriander and orange peel. White beer was produced in large quantities as wheat was plentiful. When pils grew in popularity the white beer came under threat. The revival of Belgian specialty beers proved to be to the advantage of white beer. And this is how Limburg acquired its 'witte'.

Excellent for quenching your thirst on a sunny terrace. The wheat gives the beer a slightly bitter taste. The coriander lends a spicy touch and the orange peel provides the fruitiness.

www.brouwerijcornelissen.be

Imperial White

Imperial White is an American beer style inspired by white beer. You recognise the basic recipe of this tried and trusted wheat beer with its touches of coriander and orange peel. However, the beer is stronger than the standard 'witte' and has a more pronounced and often zestier character.

Arthur's Legacy White Widow (7,1%)

Spices, fruit, hops or wood?

This white widow is the first-born of a new generation of niche beers created by Palm Belgian Craft Brewers, brewed in the new microbrewery De Hoorn at the Palm brewery site in Steenhuffel. Spurred on by the *craft brewers* this established brewery is now marketing innovative beers made with spices or fruit, hoppy beers and beers with a woody aroma, the Cornet for example. There are four brewmasters, each of whom develops new beers in 'their' section: fruit, hop, herbs and spices or wood. White Widow is brewed with pale malt and unmalted wheat. It is a rather strong white beer. Its name, Arthur's Legacy, is a reference to Arthur Van Roy. He is one of the former owners of the brewery and a true visionary. Arthur resolutely chose to produce top-fermented beers, rowing against the tide of the upcoming pils beers.

An unfiltered, golden-blonde white beer with a cloudy veil. Well-rounded and quite dry with impressions of coriander and curaçao (orange peel). Quite bitter in the finish.

www.palm.be

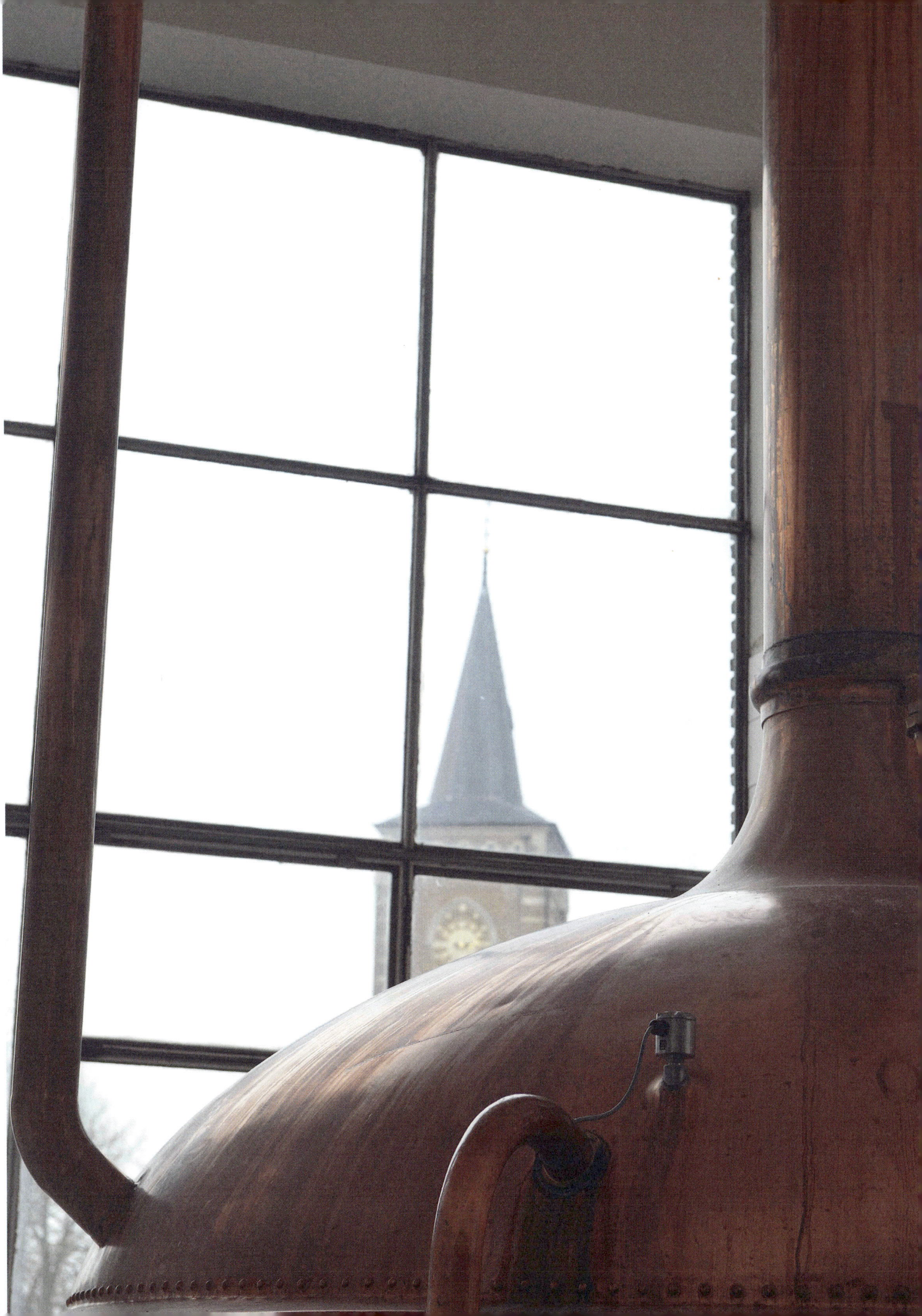

ARTHUR'S LEGACY
BROUWERIJ DE HOORN
LIMITED EDITIONS
WHITE WIDOW
HOPS
SPICES
WOOD
FRUIT
OTHER
brew date 20/01/2015
release date 06/03/2015
bottle number 5307 / 8000

ARTHUR'S LEGACY

LIMITED EDITION

SCOTCH

British beer styles were immensely popular between the two World Wars and just after the Second World War. They lost some ground owing to the revival of the Belgian specialty beers from the 1960s onwards. Scotch ales are dark brown, top-fermented beers based on caramel malts and roasted malt. A Scotch tastes full in the mouth with a balanced character and a slight aftertaste. In terms of beer styles, you can place a Scotch between double and dark brown beers and stout. During the interbellum practically all of the Belgian breweries included a scotch in their range. The beer gained its wings after the Allied victory in the First World War but this style had to give ground to Belgian specialty beers from the 1970s onwards. The scotch held its ground in Wallonia thanks to the persistence of fans from the Liège and Charleroi regions. Scotch Ale is the name that was originally given to the strong ales from Edinburgh (Scotland). These beers have a malty character and a smoky taste palette. They tend to be powerful but on the tongue, they can be mild, sweet or a combination of the two. Their nickname in the United Kingdom is 'Wee Heavy', a reference to a 19th century measuring scale used in Britain, that tied the price of beer to its alcohol content. Beer containing over 6° vol. – really quite high for the Brits – was more expensive. The colour can be anything between amber yellow with reflections of gold, to a deep brown. The malt tends to be roasted or caramelised. The thoroughly smoky touches usually come from whisky malt. The heating process of Scotch Ales is traditionally quite long, leading to caramelisation of the wort. These beers contain a relatively low quantity of hops; the malt and the alcohol are dominant. In our country, Scotch Ales have been relegated to the far background. The large brewing conglomerates treat it as their Cinderella.

McChouffe (8%)
A sKotch from the Ardennes

La Chouffe (1982), the famous blond gnome beer, acquired a dark sibling in 1987. The McChouffe hesitates between a traditional, dark abbey beer of the 'double' type and a, usually maltier, scotch beer. The term used at Brasserie d'Achouffe is an 'Ardennes sKotch'. Bearing in mind that this is a re-fermented dark beer, the McChouffe has a rather neutral taste. In contrast with the La Chouffe, no herbs and spices are added during the brewing process. However, when you taste this beer, your nose is filled with zesty aromas pushed along by the alcohol. The starring role is claimed by aniseed and liquorice, complemented with caramel. However challenging the aroma of this beer, the taste is surprisingly mild, with impressions of tree fruits, especially pears. The McChouffe does not have a pronounced bitter taste and provides a long, warming finish.

———

A full-mouthed beer with the fruity aromas of peaches and apricots and touches of caramel. McChouffe provides a pleasant surprise thanks to its fruity bouquet and the slightly bitter finish.

www.achouffe.be

Scotch de Silly (7,5%)
With thanks to Jack Peyne

With this scotch we are making a leap back to the First World War. After his wanderings Scottish soldier Jack Peyne ended up at Brasserie de Silly. He taught the brewers the ins and outs of making scotch using Kent Golding hops. Scotch was popular up to the 1950s but has faded into the background ever since. Scotch de Silly owes its sweet taste to the candi sugar. The hops are barely discernible. A limited edition has been launched every year since 2012, matured in recycled barrels used for red bordeaux and port, amongst others.

———

Sweet aromas of toffee, candi sugar, caramel and maple syrup with impressions of hazelnut that permeate the taste.

www.silly-beer.com

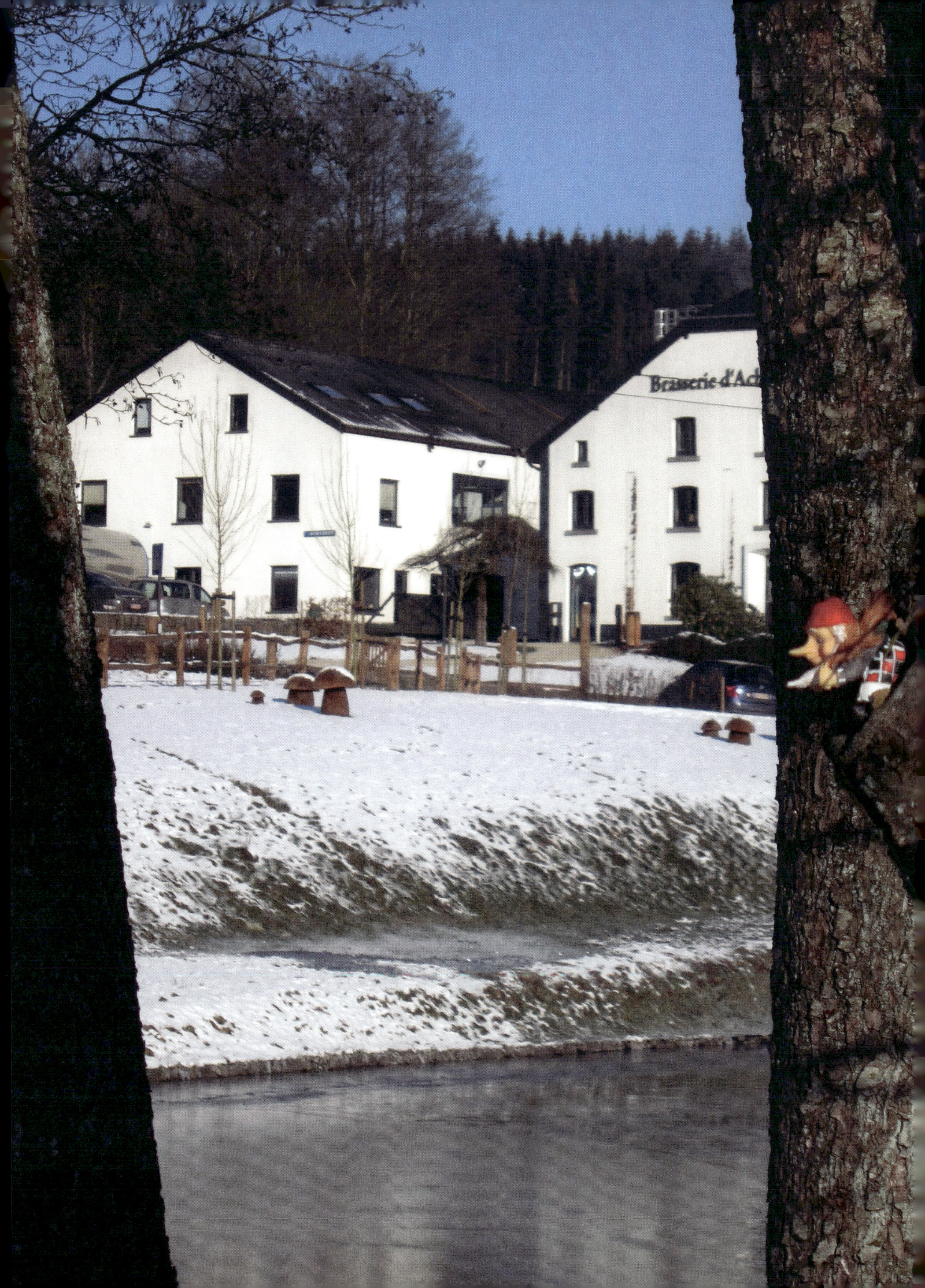
Brasserie d'Ach

BRASSERIE D'ACHOUFFE

STOUT

Stout is brewed with roasted or burned malt that gives it its dark colour. The beer tastes of roast coffee and/or chocolate and is quite bitter. Variations on this theme include the strong 'Russian imperial stout' and the 'sweet stout' or 'milk stout'. Guinness, the most famous stout of all, is classed as a 'bitter stout' or 'dry stout'. The Russian imperial stout is popular with American craft brewers and is also offered by a handful of Belgian microbreweries.

Ominous symbols on the bottle of this ink-black stout from De Struise Brouwers. Drink at your own risk?

Ardenne Stout (8%)

Stout with malt

Stout, once very popular in Belgium, has faded into the background in recent years. Stout is a usually quite bitter and dark beer, brewed with roast or burnt malt. One of its varieties is this strong Russian imperial stout, of which this Ardenne Stout is an example. We are dealing with a full-mouthed, pure malt beer. An Ardenne Stout is brewed with roast and burnt barley and spelt malts, with the addition of three aroma hops, followed by dry hopping. This stout is drier than the typical stout from England and includes fewer hops than American stout. Philippe Minne, its brewer, achieved the right balance between the rounded mildness and bitterness from the malt, the hop bitterness and aromas – with fresh hop cones used in dry hopping – and the slightly tart taste provided by the spelt malt.

———

In the initial tasting the aromas are dominated by roast and burnt malt, chocolate, coffee, whisky and fruits of the forest. Impressions of wine, wood and roasty touches give colour to the taste palette. Thanks to the use of several malts the beer develops a rounded character in addition to the clearly distinguishable hop bitter.

www.brasseriedebastogne.be

Black Damnation (13%)

Black magic

We cannot even begin to list the endless variety of beers produced by De Struise Brouwers. Their niche beers find an eager audience in the world of beer geeks. 'We are really quite lucky to be based in the Westhoek region', smiles Carlo Grootaers, the right-hand man to Urbain, one of the Struise Brouwers. 'The very first beer I ever drank was a Westvleteren. I could have done a lot worse.' In 2008 the Struise Brouwers were awarded the title of 'best brewers in the world' on www.ratebeer.com. 'We are aiming for an international niche market of people who primarily go for taste', Carlo Grootaers tells us. This former wine trader has been converted to beer. Why this turn-around? 'I blame our fantastic brewer Urbain Coutteau', he laughs. 'Also, beer has a far broader taste spectrum. That also goes for the alcohol content. You come across beers ranging from 2% to 13%. A great playground for brewers.' The Struise Brouwers have vowed to never avoid new developments in the beer world. They don't want to be even more extreme, they just want to do even better. Black Damnation is the name given to a project rather than to a range. This is the flag that covers a co-brewing project with colleagues from abroad. Sparks may fly.

———

A heavy, jet-black Russian imperial stout with roast touches of espresso and chocolate, complex, with a very long finish accented by a slight sweetness.

www.struise.com

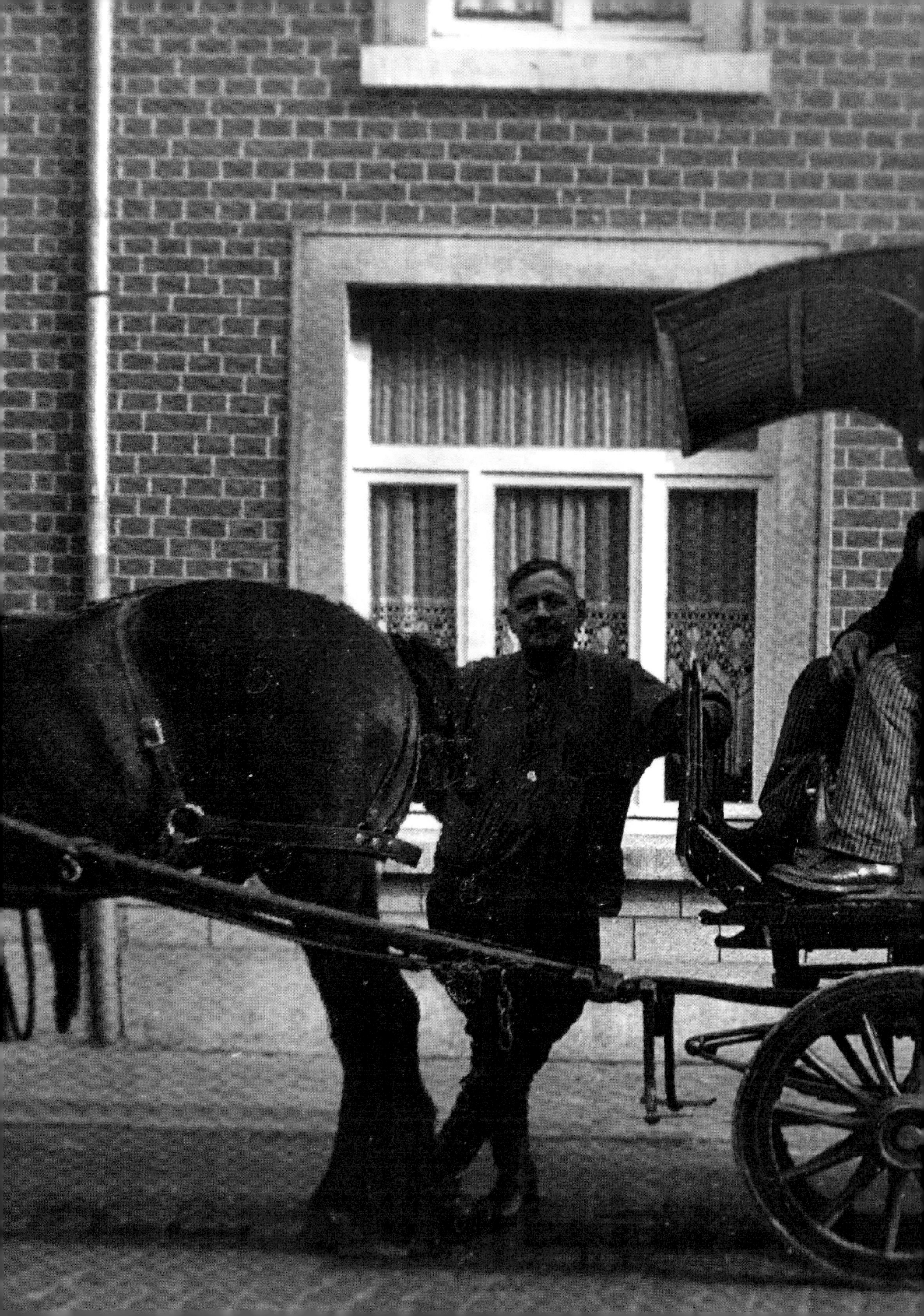

BRASSERIE BECO
J. MINNE   Succ.
VAL-St-LAMBERT   Tél. 300.27

Buffalo Stout (6%)

Left to burn

In 1907 the legendary Buffalo Bill set up camp in Ghent. The Van den Bossche brewing crew paid a visit to the circus and left the beer to boil. They paid an urchin to keep an eye on the fire that was stoking up the brewing kettle. The boy took good care of the fire but did not stir the wort often enough, so a sediment slowly formed on the bottom of the kettle. Even so, this burnt wort was used in the production of this beer, giving rise to a heavier beer with touches of caramel. The Buffalo Stout beer is now brewed with roasted malts and caramel malts. Buffalo Stout is a dark, top-fermented beer that veers between a sweet scotch and a bitter stout. The Buffalo Belgian Stout is a variety of this beer that has matured in barrels formerly used for Bordeaux, a vinous beer that re-ferments in the bottle. Bruno Van den Bossche: 'You smell the red wine and you taste the oak.'

———

A dark brown beer, zesty, with impressions of coffee and roast malt. You taste the dark chocolate, strongly supported by the coffee.

www.paterlieven.be

Pol Ghekiere of Inter-Pol pours a Zwarte Pol. His portrait adorns the bottle.

Oesterstout (8,5%)

A sea of tastes

Oesterstout, or 'Oyster Stout', is a beer that you would expect to come from Ireland. At the Scheldebrouwerij, with its roots in the nearby province of Zeeland in the Netherlands, the sea is never far away. Their range also includes a Zeezuiper and Strandgaper. Their Oesterstout is filtered on a bed of oyster shells, hence the distinctive mineral touch. This microbrewery uses natural ingredients only and their beers are unfiltered and unpasteurised. They are brewing hoppy beers, both dark and blonde, as well as a triple and a white beer. "We like to raise the bar as high as we can. Brew less but better. We'll have you know that our beers spend at least three weeks in cold storage. Quality takes time.' We are in complete agreement.

———

A mild, black stout forming a successful marriage between a mild caramel malt, a bitter roast malt and a hint of oyster that is hard to define, with a long and bitter finish.

www.scheldebrouwerij.com

Zwarte Pol (6,5%)

In the company of Pol and Tine

A sculptor from Dadizele brews a stout in the heart of the Ardennes. His ambitions are really rather modest. 'I have a passion for brewing but I am only brewing for fun. I am not really looking to expand,' confesses Pol Ghekiere. Together with his wife Tine, this sculptor is managing a bed & breakfast in an ancient smithy in the village of Mont, only a stone's throw away from the Achouffe brewery. This could well be the smallest brewery in Belgium. You drink the beer in Pol's own café. And for the connoisseurs, Zwarte Pol is a milk stout with cocoa powder added.

———

Aromas of chocolate and wood that persist in the taste and the slightly bitter, dry finish.

www.vieilleforge.freehostia.com

5 · BELGIAN BEER STYLES

BARREL AGED

♦

When it comes to barrel ageing brewers let their beers mature in barrels previously used for wine, cognac, port or whisky, allowing the aromas and tastes of the drink previously stored in these barrels to merge with the young beer. This is a quest for a deeper taste, primarily using strong amber-coloured or dark beers that do not have a predominant taste of hops. There is an art to barrel aging: allowing the beer to mature to the point where it absorbs the aromas and tastes of the wine or spirit that was previously stored in the barrel without betraying its own individual character.

Chefs Jean-Baptiste and Christophe Thomaes of Le Château du Mylord are tasting Dubuisson's Bush de Charmes.

Bush de Charmes (10,5%)

Beer or bourgogne?

Ever since it launched its wood-matured Bush de Nuits and Bush Prestige, Dubuisson has been following the path of gastronomic beers. Its Bush de Charmes has now joined the range. To produce this particular beer, owner and brewer Hugues Dubuisson allowed his Bush Blonde to mature for four months in oak barrels that were previously home to the well-known Charmes Meursault, a white burgundy wine. So, unusually, this Bush Blonde has not spent any time in cold storage tanks at a temperature of 0°C as is normally the way. This Bush de Charmes has a surprisingly complex character and a rich taste palette. As to its production process, a small dosis of sugar and yeast is added during bottling. The beer will then re-ferment for three weeks in a warm chamber at a temperature that is maintained around 25 °C. The re-fermentation saturates the beer with carbon dioxide and encourages the formation of a naturally cloudy veil and a frothy collar.

In the first instance the aromas of yellow and white fruits come to the fore, accompanied by floral and citrusy touches and the vinous impressions of the Chardonnay grape. This is a well-balanced, tender beer with a delicate bitterness and a subtly sour touch from which it derives its lively character. A beer that is not far removed from wine.

www.dubuisson.com

Embrasse Oak Aged (9%)

Smoky

There are niche beers and cult beers. In the latter category fall the creations of Ronald Mengerink, brewer at Dochter van de Korenaar. His 'thing' is wood-matured beers. For example, his heavy and dark Embrasse will spend three months resting in previously used peat whisky barrels, giving the beer a smoky touch. 'With this type of beer, the art is in bottling it at exactly the right moment,' Ronald finds. This brewer does not confine himself to the Belgian beer landscape. America is another source of inspiration. 'Take a stout matured on bourbon… just lovely!'

———

The jet-black Embrasse veers between a dark abbey beer, a stout and a malty and hoppy, dark English porter. Besides the roast malt, coffee and chocolate you sniff the aromas of dried fruits. This full-mouthed, malty and hoppy Belgian Imperial Stout comes with a lovely, bitter-sweet taste.

www.dedochtervandekorenaar.be

Trignac XII (12%)

Where beer meets cognac

Beer and cognac meet one another in the Trignac XII. This is a Kasteel Triple matured on barrels previously used for cognac and re-fermented in the bottle. Its taste is different every year. Eventually, nature, the ingredients, the barrels, the interaction between all of these elements added to the brewer's expertise determine the outcome. The brewer has mastered the art to allow the beer to mature long enough – but not too long – in wooden barrels, making sure that the taste of cognac never becomes dominant. The Trignac name is a reference both to the use of the Kasteel Triple and to the name of the village of Trignac in the French Cognac area.

———

Sweet grapes, wine and alcohol dominate the nose and also make an imprint on the taste, with cognac being the overriding taste. The alcohol completely fills the mouth and gives a warm feeling that continues to glow for a long time.

www.vanhonsebrouck.be

XO La Binchoise (12%)

Between beer and Armagnac

Wood-matured degustation beers are 'hot'. These beers mature in previously used wine, whisky or cognac barrels and absorb the aromas and tastes of the drink previously stored in these barrels, thus gaining in complexity. Bruno Deghorain , brewer at La Binchoise, launched his XO at the beginning of 2008. He was inspired by viniculture and ended up selecting wood barrels from the French Landes region that had been used to store Armagnac. His La Binchoise XO is now fermenting and maturing in horizontal barrels before going into cold storage and undergoing a light *dry hopping* using fresh hop cones, before re-fermenting in the bottle. The primary influence on the taste is the lengthy maturation on wood. This gives rise to a degustation beer that remains true to its beery character but, at the same time, is permeated by the full aromas and rich taste of an armagnac. XO stands for Exceptionally Old: in other words, at least six years old.

———

Initally, striking aromas of apple, raspberry and vanilla. A sweet and slightly bitter taste, with impressions of roast malt and wood. The alcohol glow presents itself when the beer is warming up in the glass. Thanks to its slightly sparkly character, this complex beer is reminiscent of a liqueur, with an aftertaste of vieil armagnac and a slightly sweet finish.

www.brasserielabinchoise.be

KASTEEL
- 2013 -
TRIGNAC
n° 14403/30000
- 2013 -
TRIGNAC
KASTEEL TRIPEL AGED IN COGNAC CASKS
XII

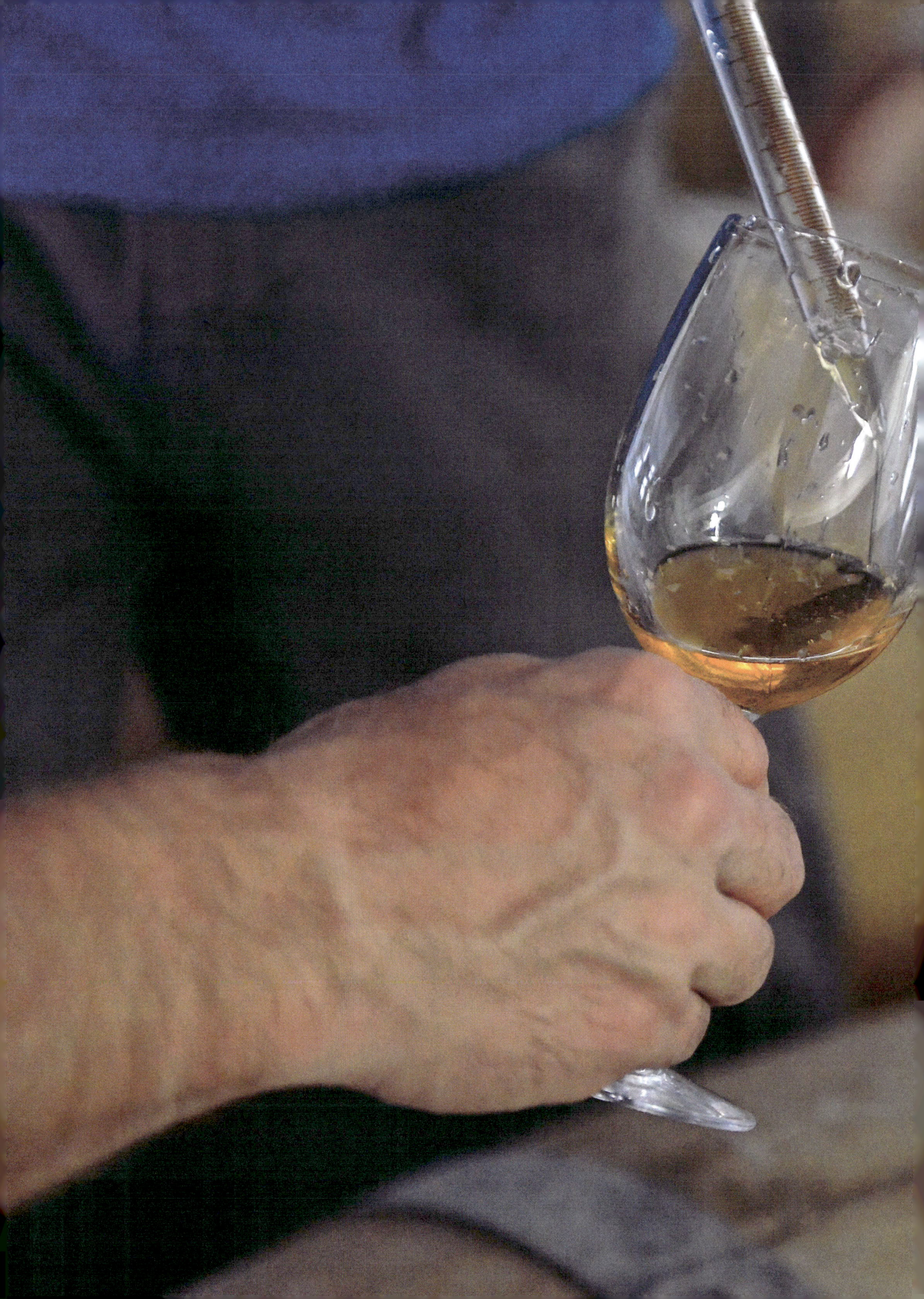

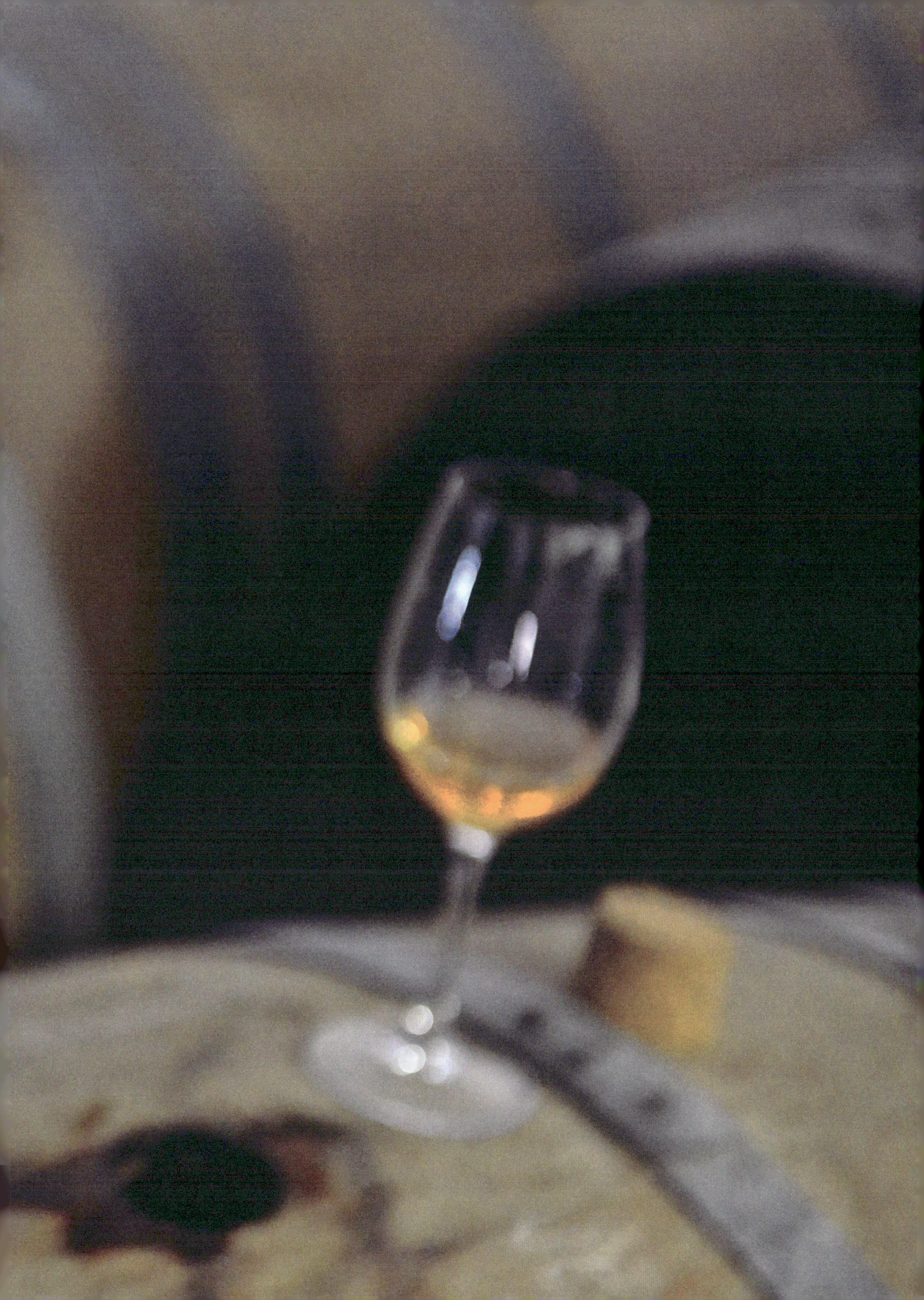

WOOD-LAGERED BEER

♦

It is perfectly possible for wood to act as a taste agent on its own. The wall of an oak barrel consists of insoluble as well as soluble substances. Certain substances contained within the wood affect the taste of the beer. In that sense, wood qualifies as a separate ingredient. The taste of Cornet from Palm Belgian Craft Brewers, a strong blond wood-matured beer, is heavily influenced by wood.

5 · BELGIAN BEER STYLES

In a Cornet the wood contributes mild vanilla touches.

Cornet (8,5%)

Wood in the glass

In 2014 the De Hoorn microbrewery was set up by Palm Belgian Craft Brewers at their Steenhuffel site. Cornet has joined the tradition of oaked beers where oak wood produces the taste. The beer has a surprisingly subtle, idiosyncratic and refined taste of wood and a velvety mouth feel. You can taste the successful balance between the fruity yeast and the vanilla-sweet wood. The long finish is warming with a mild bitterness. The beer was named after Theodoor Cornet, a 17th-century inn keeper, brewer and stoker with Afspanning De Hoorn, a coaching inn at Steenhuffel. At the request of the Count of Maldeghem-Steenhuffel, Lord of Diepensteyn, he brewed a provision beer. This beer matured in oak barrels in the cellars of Diepensteyn Castle, now owned by the brewery.

This strong blond beer, lagered with oak, keeps the balance between the fruitiness of the yeast and the mild vanilla touches from the wood. It has a strikingly full, warm finish on a background of mild bitter. The typical velouté mouthfeel rivals that of oak-matured wine.

www.palm.be

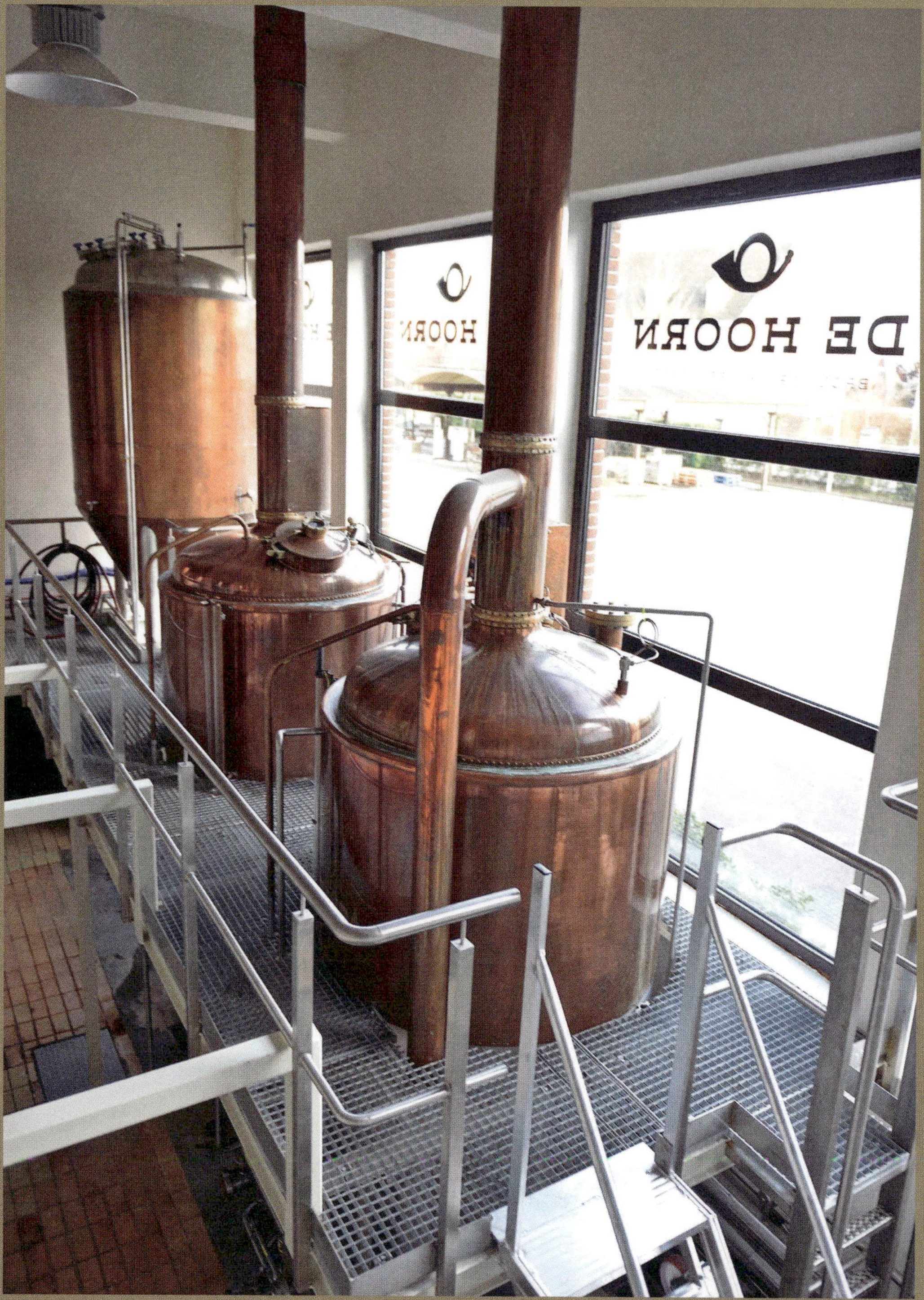
DE HOORN

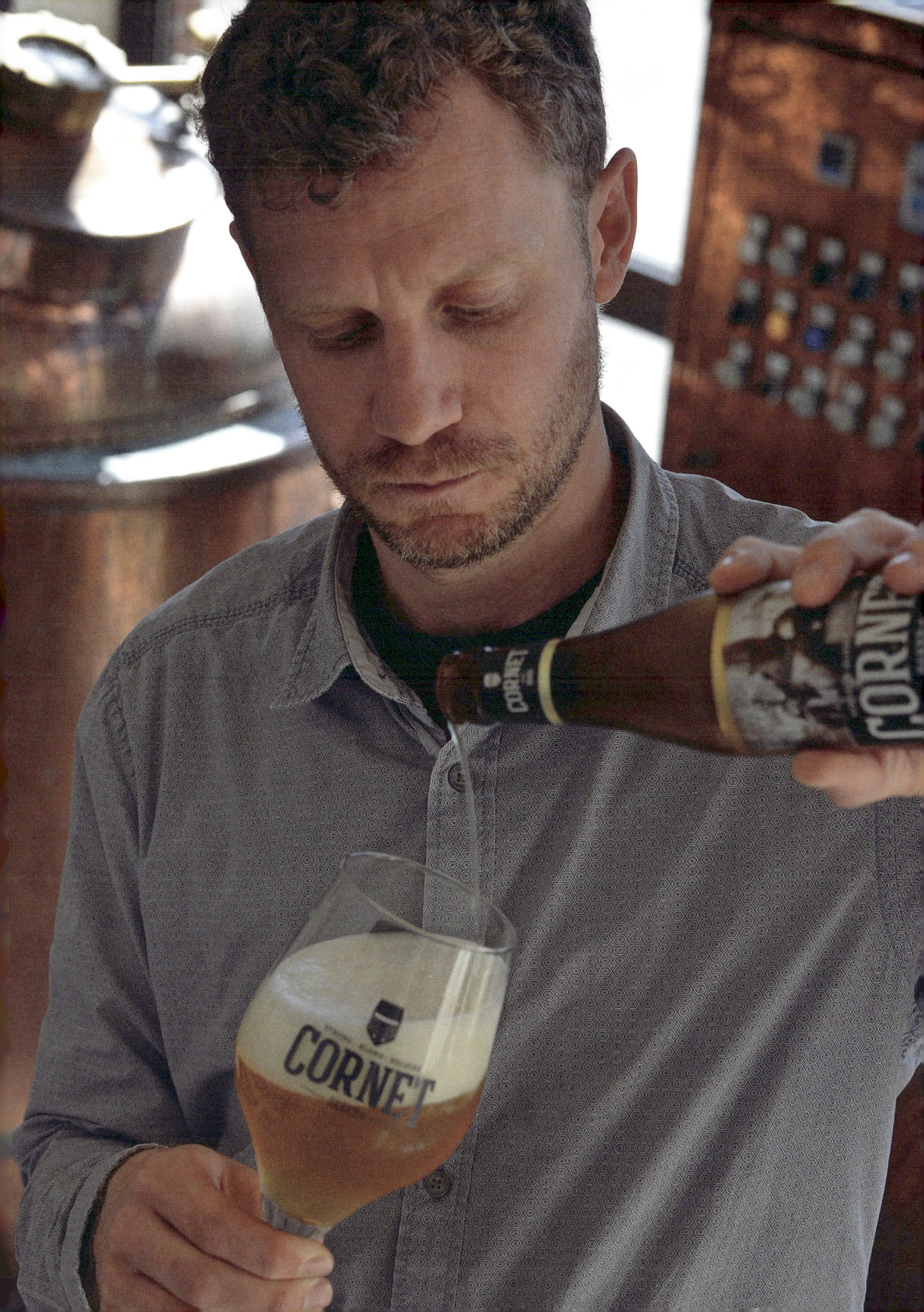
CORNET

IPA (INDIA PALE ALE)

IPAs exemplify the new bitter. This beer style is wildly popular with artisan brewers. An IPA (India Pale Ale) is a very hoppy beer. IPAs may include beers that are bitter to extremely bitter as well as very aromatic beers. This beer style originates in England. The beer brewed there did not withstand the lengthy transport by boat to India. This gave the English brewers the idea to add more hops so the beer would keep for longer. Later on, this beer style would be the starting shot for the race for bitterness. It inspires Belgian brewers to produce well-hopped, quite bitter or aromatic but usually also balanced beers.

Catherine Minne of Brasserie de Bastogne is proud of Bastogne Pale Ale, their response to an IPA.

Bastogne Pale Ale (5,5%)

IPA à l'ardennaise

The Bastogne Pale Ale is the Ardennes answer to the India Pale Ale (IPA), albeit with a less pronounced bitterness. This Belgian Pale Ale (BPA) is made with the Warrior, Hallertau Hersbrucker and Cascade aroma hops. Thanks to the *dry hopping* with hop cones from Cascade and Hallertau at the end of the brewing process, the beer develops surprising floral and zesty touches to complement the bitterness. The roast malt adds impressions of caramel. The Bastogne Pale joins the ranks of light, quaffable beers with plenty of character. The beer takes on a typical Ardennes character through the use of spelt, an ancient grain variety that thrives in the hard, rocky soil of the region. Its rustic nature is emphasised by the wild boar depicted on the label. This animal is the symbol of the forests of the Ardennes and is found in large numbers in the area around Bastogne.

———

The beer is fragrant with aromas of grass, honey, flowers and grains. The hop bitter is toned down by the mild touches of caramel coming from the roast malt. The finish is light and dry.

www.brasseriedebastogne.be

Delta IPA (6,5%)

Playground

You know where you're at straight away. Brussels Beer Project does not follow tradition, quite the opposite. This microbrewery in the heart of Brussels is focused on co-creation and crowdfunding. You can feel the vite of this multicultural metropole. Belgian brewers always experimented to their heart's content with aromas and taste. Brussels Beer Project carries on the experiment and wants to take large steps. 'We want to brew twenty new beers every year!'. Duly noted. Delta IPA has now been added to the standard range. 850 Brusselians selected this beer out of four prototypes that were introduced on Facebook.

———

Travel through the tropics of Brussels on a current of lychee and passion fruit. Enjoy the fresh bitterness of this thirstquencher.

www.beerproject.be

Duvel Tripel Hop (9,5%)

Third time hoppy

One Duvel is not like another ever since... a bet was won in 2010. Wanne Madelijns of the beer lovers' society Lambicstoempers posed a challenge to Duvel Moortgat. If their club managed to collect nine thousand signatures on Facebook, the brewery would agree to brew the Duvel Triple Hop, an occasional beer, once again. The initiative was supported by twelve thousand followers and, as a result, Duvel Triple Hop is now a standard part of the range. In contrast to the regular Duvel, the Duvel Triple Hop is made with its two usual hop varieties plus a third aroma hop that is different every year. In 2012 Citra was used, in 2013 it was Sorachi Ace, in 2014 came the turn of Mosaic and in 2015 Equinox was selected... In *dry hopping* the aromatic hop cones are not only added during boiling but also at the maturation stage. This results in a hoppier beer with more aromas and a richer taste palette. Duvel's younger brother is also stronger. Beer lovers always look forward to the latest edition. The taste is different every year and depends on the third hop used.

www.duvel.com

Green Killer IPA (6,5%)

A hop kick

The Pink Killer is fragrant with grapefruit; the Green Killer IPA is bursting with hops. This blonde impresses with her beautiful balance between aromas and tastes from the malt and powerful hops. The *dry hopping* at the end of the brewing process gives an extra hop boost to the Green Killer IPA. In this beer's strong aromas, touches of citrus and pepper dominate. Green Killer IPA has a robust bitterness, particularly towards the end. The dry finish makes a perfect fit with the malty taste. This is a degustation beer for people who love a bitter taste. Nevertheless, this full-in-the-mouth IPA is very balanced. The bitterness is sufficiently powerful without ever becoming aggressive.

The hop provides powerful aromas of citrus and hints of pepper in the beer. Green Killer IPA is deliciously bitter with a dry finish that flows imperceptibly into the taste of malt.

www.silly-beer.com

Gulden Spoor IPA (7%)

This blond packs a punch

In 1302 the French occupier was defeated at the Battle of the Golden Spurs (Dutch: Guldensporenslag) near Kortrijk. Gulden Spoor beers are now flowing out of the tanks not far from the battlefield. Het Gulden Spoor is the house brewery of beer restaurant 't Rusteel. All of their beers are tasted by resident chef Domien Plouvier, beer sommelier Peter Koopman and Björn Desmadryl, the brewer. Brief beer pairing tips are printed on the bottle label. This IPA (India Pale Ale) is a well-hopped beer inspired by the original British tradition. It turned out to be a quaffable, zesty beer with a vibrant blonde colour and a rubust collar of froth. This IPA is made with a number of Belgian hop varieties. Its rich palette of aromas and tastes varies between mildly fruity and strong bitter. The bitterness is toned down by the aroma hops.

The hop aromas in this IPA span the range from fruity mango and citrus to zesty, with a hint of pepper. The alcohol serves to re-enforce the pronounced hoppiness. Its bitterness is toned town by the residual sugars from the beer.

www.guldenspoor.be

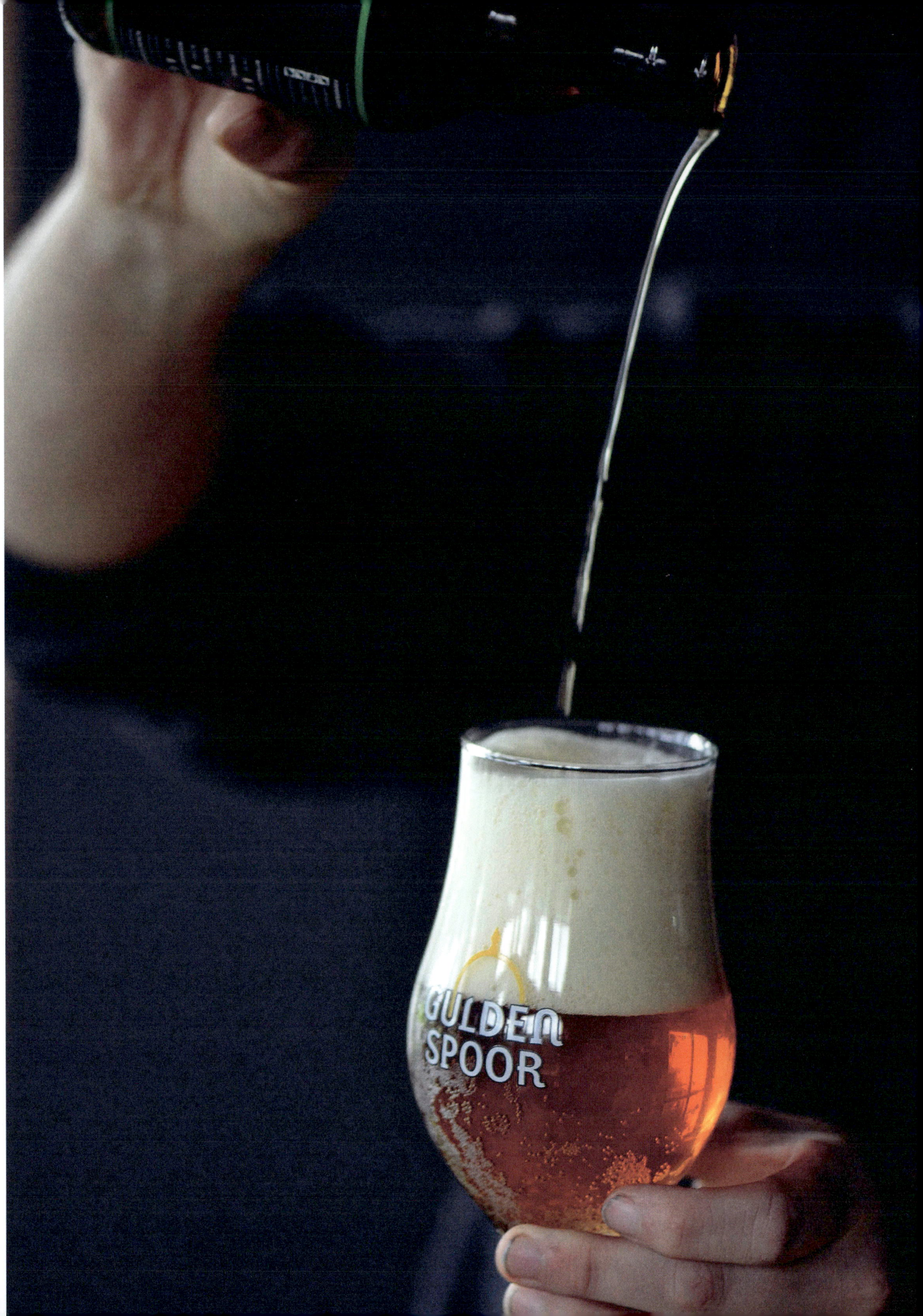
GULDEN
SPOOR

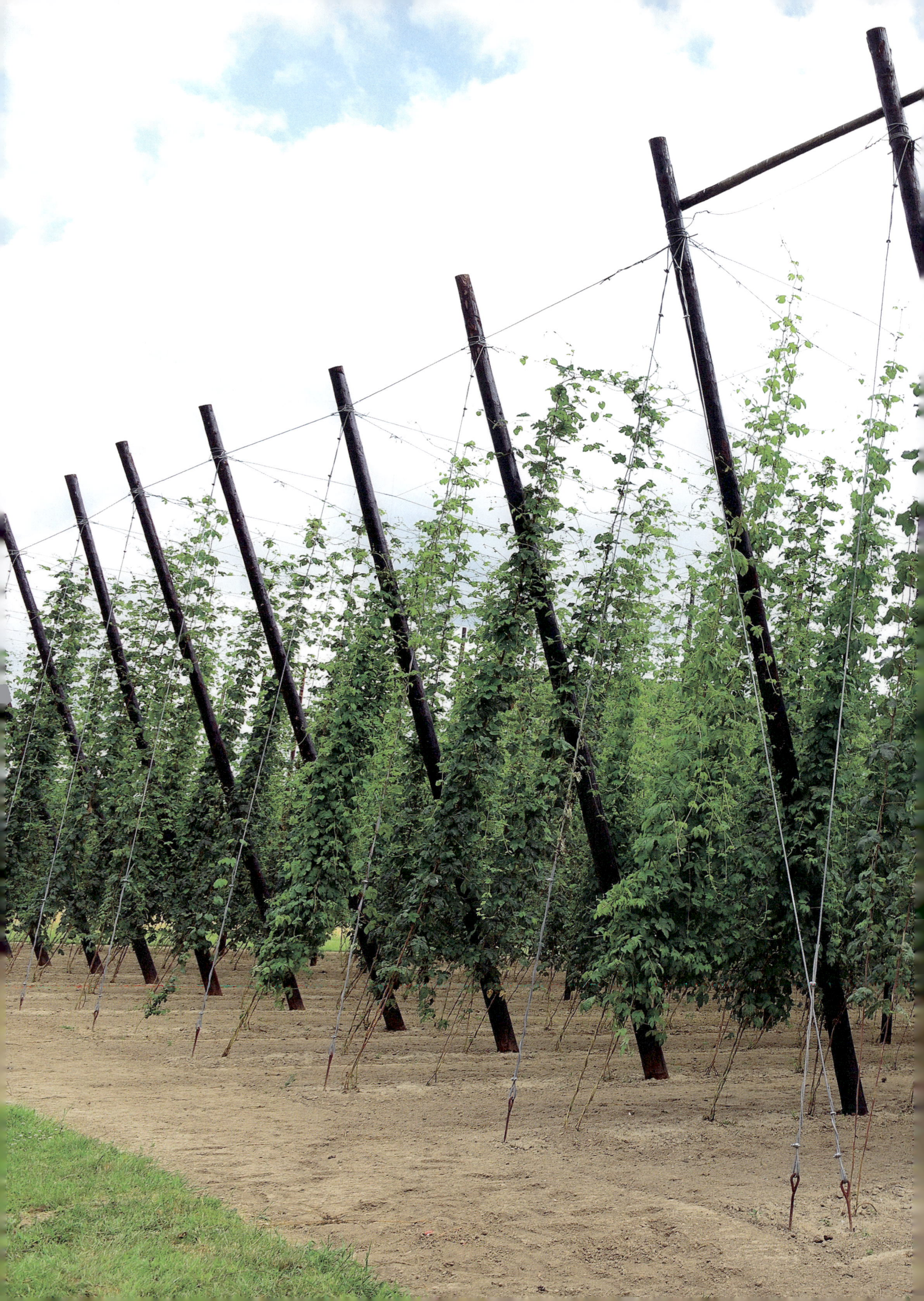

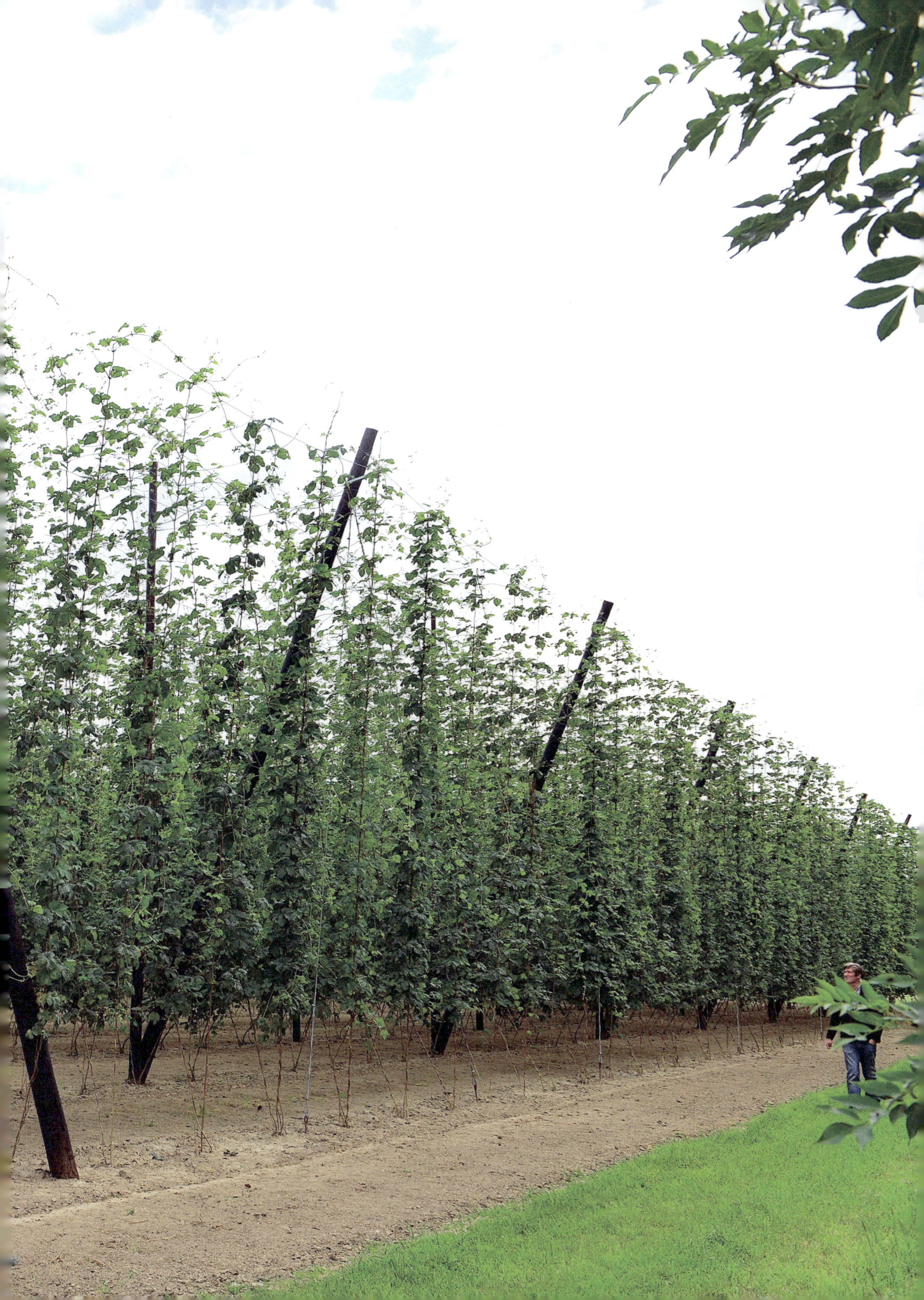

Houblon Chouffe (9%)

Belgium Pale Ale (BPA)

One of the first Belgian IPAs (India Pale Ale) or, rather, BPAs (Belgium Pale Ale). Launched in 2006, the Houblon Chouffe is three times as bitter as La Chouffe. This is a beer with intense hop aromas. It has striking impressions of citrus (grapefruit) that complement its zesty, green hoppy character.

―――――

The Houblon Chouffe gives off surprisingly pronounced hop aromas with touches of citrus including grapefruit. This beer has a rich and complex hoppy taste with touches of citrus thanks to the American aroma hops and fruity impressions contributed by the Achouffe yeast. The higher alcohol percentage makes for a fine balance.

www.achouffe.be

Vedett IPA (5,5%)

Game, set and match to aromas

The IPA (India Pale Ale) beer style is focused on aroma rather than hop bitter. Duvel Moortgat has proved this three times over with its Houblon Chouffe, Duvel Triple Hop and Vedett IPA. The latter is an unfiltered top-fermented beer that re-ferments in the bottle. The brewer will add two different American hop varieties during boiling and two more for the dry hopping. This process results in a fresh, hoppy and complex beer with fruity, flowery and green aromas on a background of citrus (grapefruit), with a mildly bitter taste and a long, dry finish.

―――――

Fruity aromas of citrus and flowers. A mildly bitter taste that increases in intensity, with impressions of grapefruit backed by malt and caramel, followed by a dry fisnish.

www.vedett.be

XX Bitter (6,2%)

Bitter just like a beer

De Ranke is proud to produce bitter beers 'with a real beer taste'. The brewer uses fresh hop cones and neither filters nor pasteurises his beer. Its beers are robust, rich in aromas and very hoppy. Thanks to the Rodenbach yeast they take on an 'Orvallian' character'. The XX Bitter, introduced in 1996, was the bitterest beer in our country at the time. 'We do not set out to brew the bitterest beer,' brewer Nino Bacelle explains. 'That is not our main target. Above all, it has to be balanced.' XX Bitter is brewed with pale malt, Brewers Gold and Hallertau hop cones and dry Fermentis yeast. It is fully fermented, hence its dry character. A reference for the new wave of bitter Belgian beers. De Ranke is a source of inspiration for Brasserie de la Senne, Brouwers Verzet and others. Nino Bacelle refers to the XX Bitter as a 'bitter pale ale'. This particular beer was developed before the IPA conquered Belgium.

―――――

Bitterness reigns all around, in the aromas, the taste as well as the finish. An ode to hop flowing on an earthy undercurrent of yeast.

www.deranke.be

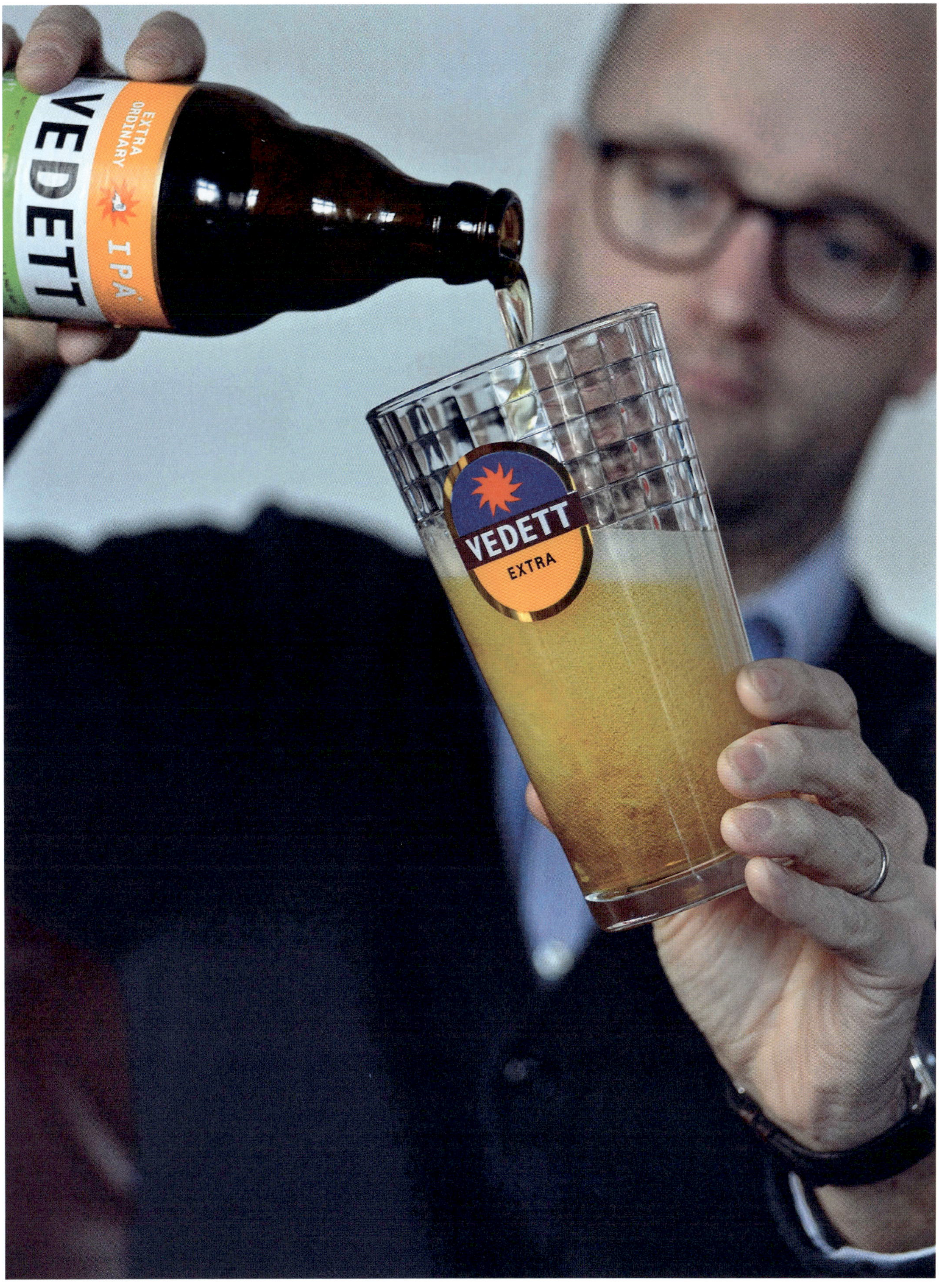
VEDETT
EXTRA ORDINARY
IPA
VEDETT
EXTRA

THE NEW 'SOUR'

New top-fermented beers are frequently coming onto the market. These are produced by adding wild yeasts (Brettanomyces) just before bottling. These wild yeasts cause the beer to re-ferment in the bottle and give it a sour taste. This trend can be placed in the context of the increased popularity of 'sour ales' ('sour is the new bitter').

With Wild Jo spontaneous fermentation (Brettanomyces) makes a breakthrough at De Koninck's.

Morpheus Undressed (6,9%)

Yeasty

At Alvinne's they like to go off the beaten track, even though they draw their inspiration from our rich tradition. Morpheus Undressed is a slightly sour, thirst-quenching Flemish red-brown beer. The beer is initially brewed with very few hops to give free rein to the lactic acid bacteria. The beer will then spend several months maturing in a 75hl foeder prior to being bottled. The yeast is the soul of the beer, lending it structure and body. Alvinne is proud of its Morpheus house yeast. It is a blended culture of two beer yeasts (*Saccharomyces cerevisiae*) and lactic acid bacteria (*Lactobacillus*), cultivated from yeast strains originating in the French Auvergne region. 'It all came down to the selection, separating the good yeast strains from the bad ones, trying out what works with heavy beers without producing any off flavours', Davy Spiessens explains. Alvinne is a niche brewer well aware of international trends. 'We are not following the classic beer styles. Instead, we just brew what we feel like brewing.' Are they managing to come up with a taste that is consistent? 'We like you to taste the season, just as you do with wine', is Davy's response. 'Brewing conditions are always different and this also goes for the quality of the raw ingredients. Therefore, the taste of the beer will vary unless you carry out a manual intervention.'

Aromas of wine, wood and krieken cherries. A slightly sour taste with impressions of citrus and wood. Tannins in the finish.

www.acbf.be

Wild Jo (5,8%)

Rock-'n-roll in a bottle

With their Wild Jo, the De Koninck brewers have swapped their tried and trusted top-fermented beers for a tempestuous Belgian Wild Ale, re-fermented with the use of wild yeasts (*Brettanomyces*). The beer becomes wilder and its taste more intense. *Dry hopping* with two varieties of European hops delivers an intensely hoppy aroma. The 'Wild Jo' name was not plucked out of thin air. The 'Jo' name is a reference to a former brewmaster, Joseph Van den Bogaert, who oversaw the resurrection of the brewery after the First World War. The launch of the Wild Jo in 2015 coincided with the opening of this completely refurbished Antwerp city brewery.

Earthy and floral aromas of stone fruits (apricot, peach) and citrus (orange). The first taste is slightly sweet with a hint of grapefruit on a slightly sour undercurrent, followed by a bitter finish.

www.dekoninck.be

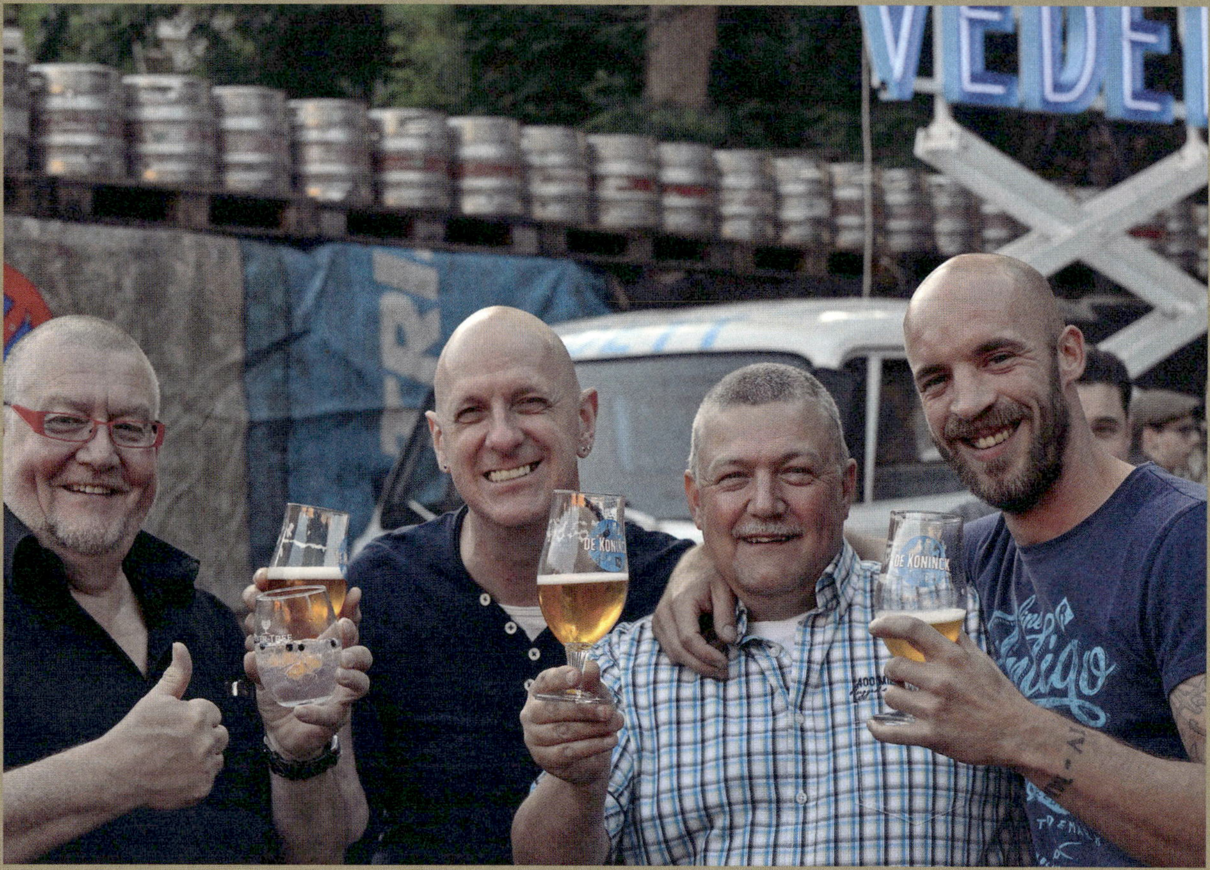

DE KONINCK

A MIX OF BEER STYLES

◆

If you like to steer away from the well-trodden path, you will explore the boundaries of existing beer styles and beer types. Your quest for the best of two worlds will lead you to exciting combinations that yield a surprisingly wide range of aromas and tastes.

Rulquin (7%)

Where stout meets gueuze

Rulquin is an unfiltered blend of wood-matured La Rulles Brune and a lambic from Tilquin, re-fermented in the bottle. Its name establishes the link between the La Rulles brewery in the Gaume region and Tilquin, the only 'gueuzestekerij' located in Wallonia. At Brasserie de Rulles, Grégory Verhelst is brewing traditional Belgian blonde and brown beers as well as a triple. He is also the power behind the international Brassigaume festival for microbrewers, that takes place every year in Marbehan during the third weekend in October. Spring water with a low mineral salt content, the Orval yeast and very aromatic hops account for the distinctive taste of the Rulles beers. Here, the wort ferments in open basins (open fermentation) which means that it is continuously in contact with oxygen. The brewer is of the opinion that the yeast in the open and shallow basins is less susceptible to stress which leads it to produce more fruity esters. As a result the aromas are more delicate and appealing. The Rulles beers are quite dry and rather mild. 'Here, we can smell and see everything that goes on', he explains. 'From experience and a 'gut feel', we know exactly when the beer is ready to go into cold storage. The beer is pumped across to the lager tanks at exactly the right moment. The greatest thing is that, as a brewer, you are in sensory contact with the yeast .' He is using a sieving spoon to extract the yeast that is floating on the top of the brew. 'This is the start of the next brew', he laughs.

Rulquin from Brasserie de Rulles is a blend of a top-fermented beer and a gueuze from Tilquin.

Slightly sour aromas with a mild character of Brettanomyces and hints of wet wood that flow into the taste with just a little sweetness in the distance. Pleasantly sweet and sour, with a finish that does not tend to cling to the palate.

www.larulles.be

www.gueuzerietilquin.be

Tuverbol (10,6%)

Blond meets lambic

Tuverbol (2006) is a blended beer. It mixes the top-fermented beer that goes by the name of Loterbol from the eponymous brewery in Diest, with a lambic from 3 Fonteinen, an unfiltered beer that has spontaneously re-fermented in the bottle. 'Tuveren' is dialect for 'toveren', in other words, 'performing magic' and refers to the alchemy that is conjured up by the blend of both beers. This strong bastard gueuze may be nothing less than blasphemy for the purists amongst lambic lovers. Did they intend it to be this sour or did the Devil have a hand in it?

———

Freshly sour, fruity lambic aromas with additional malt. The delicately sour taste of a lambic flows into that of a malty triple with a sharp, bitter-sour finish.

www.loterbol.be

Vicaris Generaal (8,5%)

Triple meets gueuze

Vicaris Generaal is a blend of Vicaris Tipel and Boon Oude Gueuze (formerly Girardin). You taste and smell the gueuze and enjoy the mild elements of a triple as a bonus. Both Anne-Cathérine Dilewyns, the brewer, and her father Vincent go for a pure taste. This is why they do not filter or pasteurise their brews. Vincent: 'I am brewing in the traditional way but with the use of modern-day equipment. I allow one week for the 'warm' fermentation, three weeks for the cold storage, two weeks for the re-fermentation and then another two weeks to let my beers rest and mature. My beers are completely fermented out. You will not find residual sugars in any of them.'

———

The sweet initial aromas of this triple soon give way to the mildly sour accents provided by the old gueuze. A fresh and fruity thirst-quencher.

www.vicaris.be

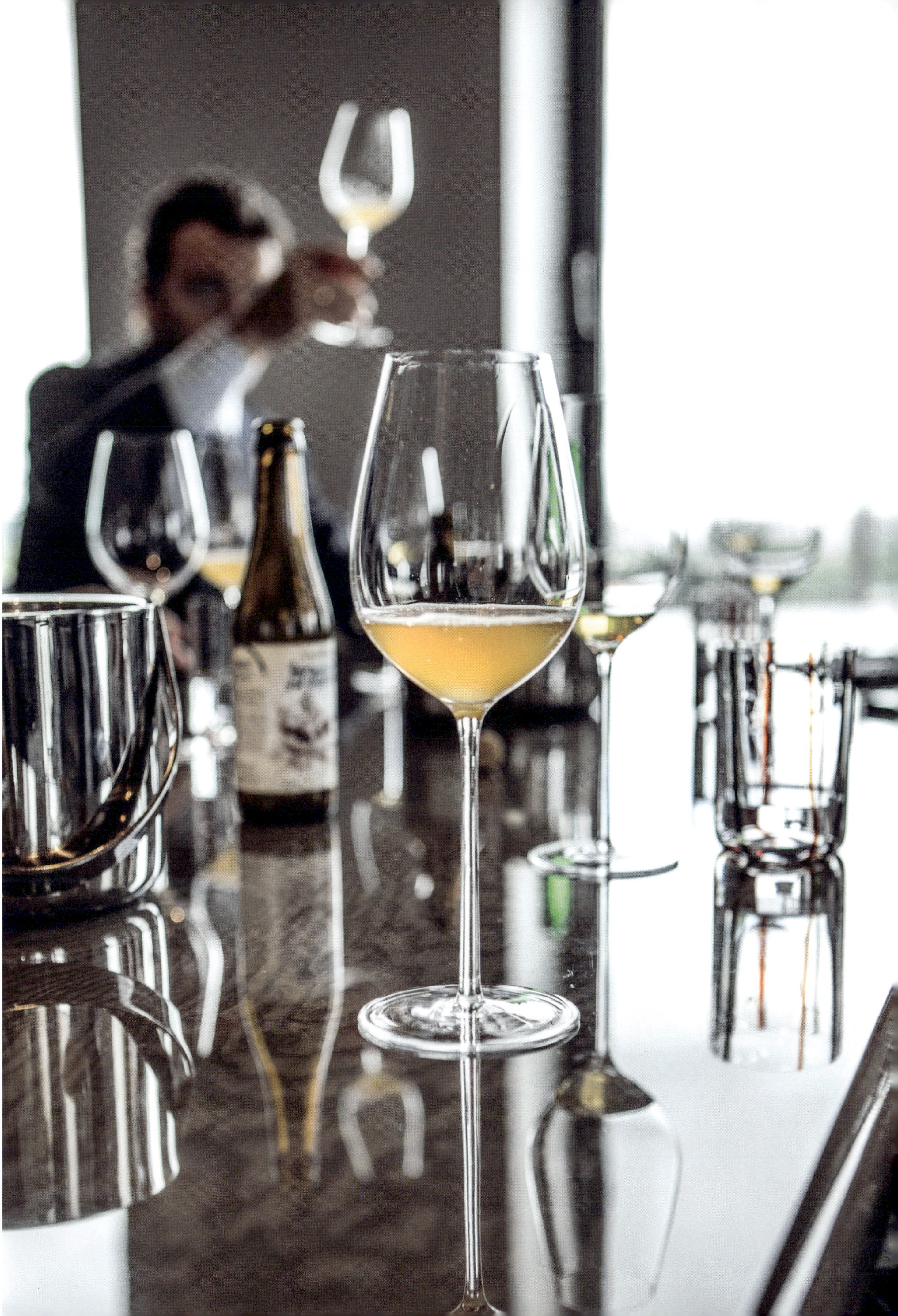

KASTEEL
HOPPY
BELGIUM
BIERE DES TRAPPISTES
8
Cat.S
ROCHEFORT
Duvel
TRIPEL HOP
ANNO 1871

CHIMAY
BRASSERIE D'ACHOUFFE
BELGIUM
BELGIUM
SPECIAAL MOUT EN BESTE HOP MAKEN HET GOED BIER
VEDETT
EXTRA ORDINARY
IPA

EXTREME BEERS

♦

The trend for extreme beers has made its way across to us from the USA. These beers are often extremely strong ('barley wine'), extremely bitter, hoppy ('Double IPA') or sour or else contain a hefty dose of exotic ingredients such as pilipili. This is where the brewer is leaving the tried and trusted paths. Brewing with heather and lavender, with a double or triple dose of hops and malt or an even higher dosage... or else using chocolate, peanut butter or espresso, oysters or seaweed... the possibilities are legion. This trend is the complete opposite of the Belgian brewing tradition that strives for precision and balance. Especially the micro-breweries, with a lot of their produce going to exports, like to choose the path of the extreme. For example, the Struise Brewers have hit the market with a beer with an alcohol content of 26%. To produce this, they use ice distillation. When a beer cools down, the water will freeze before the alcohol does. You separate the frozen water and you are left with a concentrate with a more intense taste and a higher alcohol content. The process takes six months and 70% of the volume will be lost. But, is this still a beer?

Cuvée Delphine (11%)
Koninklijk

The Struise Brouwers started up in 2001 a stone's throw away from the very well known Abbey of Sint-Sixtus in Westvleteren. They quickly made a name for themselves, not only in their own country but also in Scandinavia and the USA. Their love of women shows in the affectionate nicknames they have given their beers, such as Roste Jeanne or Shark Pants. They also choose their beer styles in a light-hearted manner. The Black Albert for example (type stout, alc.vol. 7%) is made in the style of a Russian Imperial Stout. In its own country it soon acquired the name of Belgian Royal Stout. You're with us so far, but the lads went one step further. Black Albert absolutely had to have a daughter beer. To invent the name and design the label they got in touch with artist Delphine Boël, the illegitimate daughter of former Belgian King Albert II. He never officially recognised her and to this day Delphine remains angry about this. She made her art work, or at least a reproduction, available free of charge. It depicts a Belgian flag and the text *'Truth can set you free'*. Belgian irony at its finest. The Cuvée Delphine is quite a special beer. It is a Black Albert matured in bourbon barrels used for Kentucky Four Roses. For a year. And what is the effect of maturation on this strong beer…?

This beer, black through and through, unveils a very complex aroma of roast malt, chocolate, yeast and whisky (a.k.a. Bourbon) of course. The taste is replete with toasty aromas, chocolate, vanilla… Beautifully resplendent and we could even call it royal, why not? You will also discover touches of wood.

www.struise.com

The label of Cuvée Delphine is an amusing reference to artist Delphine Boël, the illegitimate daughter of former Belgian King Albert II.

Extase (8,5%)

Fourteen is your lucky number

Emperor Charles V (1500–1588) once proclaimed: 'I prefer the juice of the ear of the corn ('de dochter van de korenaar') better than the blood of grapes', hinting that he preferred beer to wine. This statement provided the name for this brewery that opened its doors in 2007 in Baarle-Hertog, the Belgian enclave in the Netherlands. The brewer, Ronald Mengerink, initially wanted to start up a brewery in the Dutch part of Baarle-Nassau. However, in the Netherlands a small-scale brewery (producing 15,000 litres per month) is classified as heavy industry, he established himself in the Belgian part of the village of Baarle. The Mengerink family spent a number of years living in Brittany and the French influence shines through in the names of their beers: Noblesse, Bravoure (one of the few Belgian smoke beers), Embrasse, Courage and Finesse, their standard beer. This is a genuine family brewery with a love for beer at the centre of everything they do. Ronald has recently created the Extase beer, a Double IPA that blends fourteen different hop varieties (Cascade, Millenium, Simcoe, Chinook, Cluster, Columbus, Centennial, Summit, Crystal, Bramling Cross, Aurora, Styrian Golding, Perlé and Saaz).

With its extreme hoppiness of over 100 IBU, Extase lives up to its name. Daily fare for an American beer geek, but in our little triangular country on the North Sea, Extase is rated a very extreme beer. 'To boldly go where no taster has gone before'.

Well over 1000 beers at Geers'
. . . .

Beer lovers need no introduction to Dranken Geers in Oostakker, a village in the vicinity of Ghent. At Geers' you will find all of the Belgian classics, including many Lambic beers and Trappists as well as 'limited editions' and rare beers from microbreweries. Most of the beers featured in this book are available here.

Dranken Geers, Ledergemstraat 7
B-9040 Oostakker-Gent, België, +32 (0)9 251 05 83
info@drankengeers.be, www.drankengeers.be

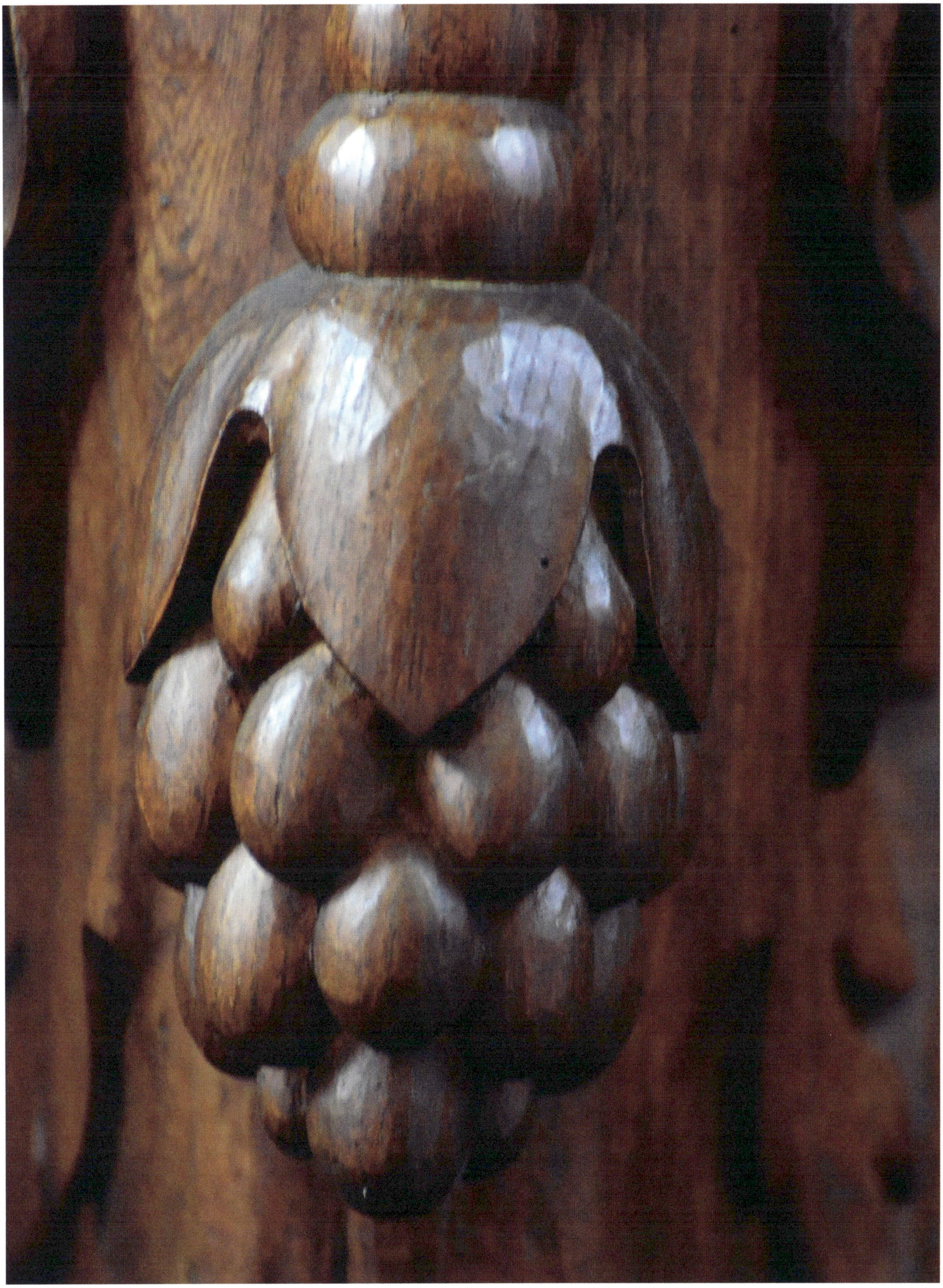

THE RITUAL
Step N° 3 · The Liquid Alchemy
Windows 7
BEST MUSICAL
IN THE HEIGHTS
2008 TONY AWA
BEST MUSIC
STELLA ARTOIS
PERFECTION HAS ITS PRICE.
www.stellaartois.com
Always enjoy responsibly.

FROM THE LARGEST MICRO-BREWERY IN THE WORLD, BELGIUM

Stella Artois

Bloesem kriek
Sweet cherry

PETRUS

BUFFALO STOUT 9%
PRIMUS
Duvel
BEER

DE KONINCK

Duvel

Geuze
Boon

Duvel
ZBF 2016

Westmalle
TRAPPIST

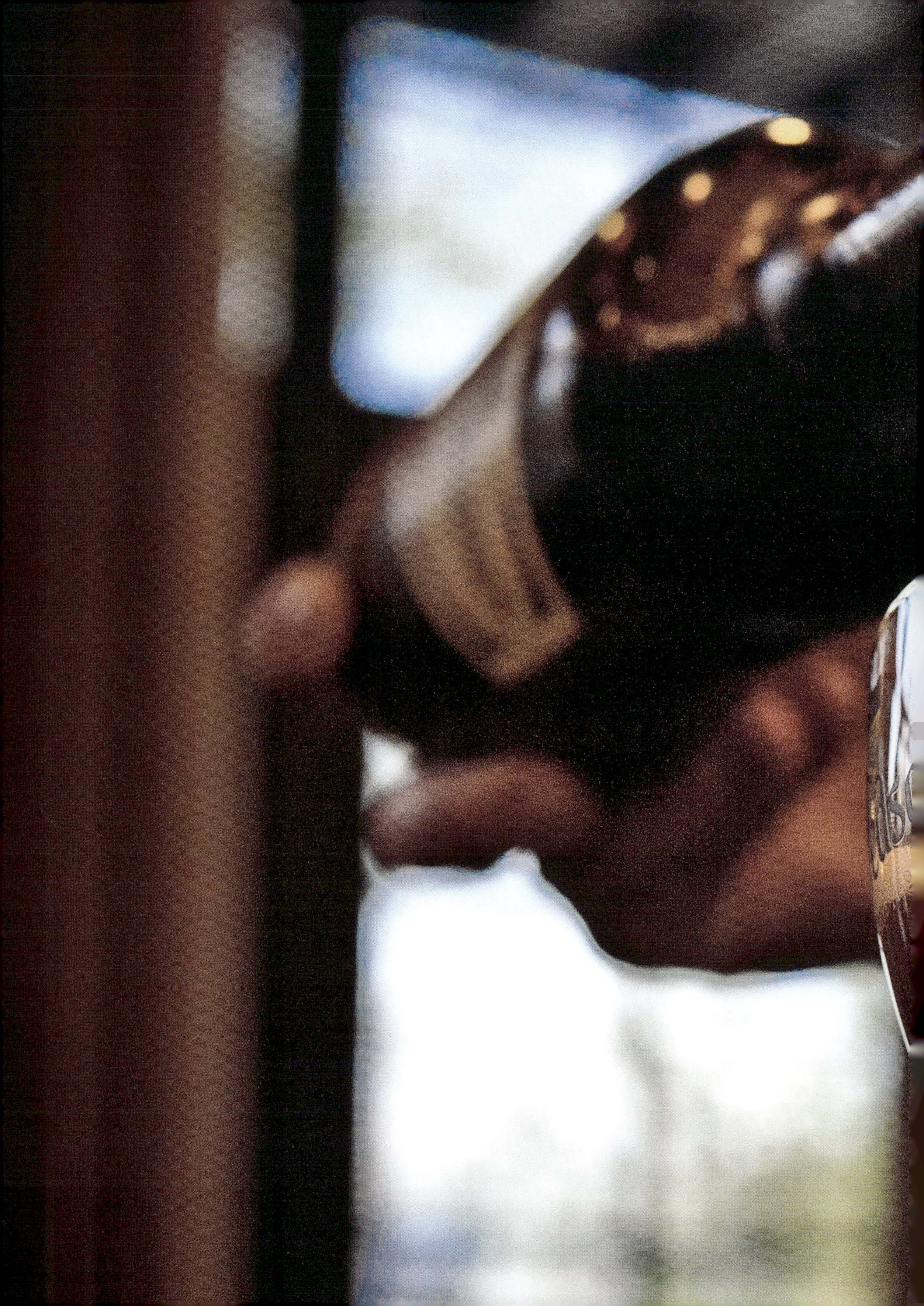

6

HOW TO TAP, POUR, TASTE AND STORE

HOW TO TAP, POUR, POUR TASTE AND STORE

Your beer did not come straight from the brewer but from a café or restaurant or you may have bought it from a shop. After this initiation in tapping and pouring, you are the judge. Does the café owner, waiter or sommelier serve your beer in the way it should be presented? It takes a bit of time to acquire the art of beer tasting. Here you will find helpful hints and tips about basic beer tasting techniques. Finally, you will also find the answer to the much-asked question: 'Does beer really get better over time'?

6 · HOW TO TAP, POUR, TASTE AND STORE

411

BEER TAPPING

Drawing a beer from the tap is an art in itself. Just take a look at the international World Draught Master competition staged by Stella Artois. Dozens of countries from around the world delegate their national draught champion to take part. The winner will travel around the world to teach the art of 'draughtsmanship'. Observe the spectacle and you will soon realise that it is fiendishly difficult to deliver two perfectly poured pints in what amounts to no time at all. The pouring ritual follows the requisite nine steps (see diagram). Former National Champion of Belgium, Yves Van Roy of Antwerp café De Vismijn, is in complete agreement: 'The most difficult thing is to produce exactly the same result twice over. Both heads have to be completely identical. You should not be able to tell them apart.' Café owner Tommy Goukens was crowned Stella Artois World Draught Master 2008. What, for him, is a well-tapped pint? 'Ideally, the barrel has to be emptied within 24 hours (72 hours at the most). Disconnect it overnight, flush the pipes and fill it with water. The main requirements are: clean glasses, well-maintained pipes, glasses without any traces of detergent and to rinse the glasses in cold water once more. Duly noted.

Clean glasses

So, when you pop into a café, how do you know that your beer is served as it should be?
- A beautiful aroma, a pleasant finish, no off-flavours.
- Carbon dioxide does not gather in a small cloud below the head.
- No pearls of carbon dioxide on the side of the glass (dirty glass!).
- A beautiful, robust and consistent head of froth, at least 2 centimetres thick

To achieve a perfectly tapped glass of beer, the glasses need to be more than just clean. They have to be 'beer clean', as the head on the beer is extremely sensitive to impurities. Grease is especially bad in terms of affecting froth. When you drink from a 'beer clean' glass, every mouthful leaves 'circles of froth' that cling to the inside of the glass.

For glass that is perfectly clean, do the following:
- Use a beer glass for beer only.
- Rinse the glasses straight after use.
- Use your rinsing basin for beer glasses only.
- Add fresh cold water to the rinsing basin on a continuous basis.
- Use cleaning agents specifically formulated for beer glasses, Becharein for example.
- Preferably, use a brush with three parts that will clean both the inside and the outside of the beer glass.
- Rinse the glasses in cold water.
- Don't drain the glasses on a tea towel (it may leave lint).
- Dry with a lint-free tea towel, e.g. Vileda.
- Regularly wash the glasses in warm water with bicarbonate of soda.

Serving a perfectly tapped beer

To serve a beer from the tap you need the utmost care. The first requirement is the very best tap installation with just the right pressure on the tap. As in so many other areas, the old adage applies here too: practice makes perfect.
https://www.youtube.com/watch?v=TVox1FR2M1o

6 · HOW TO TAP, POUR, TASTE AND STORE

1
Purification
De-grease, clean and rinse the glass holding it by the stem. The final particles of dust disappear and the glass reaches the right temperature. The glass is draining. Now take the glass by the stem.

2
The offering
Open the tap with one fluid movement and allow the first drops of beer to flow away.

3
The boiling alchemy
Hold the glass by its stem at a 45° angle just below the tap

4
The head
Lower the glass to allow the head of froth to form in a natural way.

5
The removal
Quickly close the tap and remove the glass from underneath. No further beer should dribble into the glass.

6
The decapitation
Carefully remove the froth that sticks out from the top of the glass with a beer spatula.

7
The verdict
The ideal head is two fingers' thick (3 centimetres).

8
The last cleanse
Rinse the foot and the sides of the glass with water.

9
The presentation
Serve the beer on a clean beer mat with the logo pointing towards the drinker

POURING THE BEER FROM THE BOTTLE

Serving a perfect glass of beer from the bottle is nothing less than a ritual.
- It is up to you whether or not to rinse the glass in advance. Remove the last few particles of dust and allow the glass to reach room temperature.
- Only use a clean towel to clean the glasses for a degustation beer.
- Use a good bottle opener to prevent breakages.
- Use both hands when pouring:
  One for the glass
  One for the bottle
- Handle the glass at the top.
- Hold it at a slight angle.
- Calmly pour out the beer above the glass and allow it to spiral down the inside of the glass.
- Don't swirl the beer around the neck of the bottle.
- When the glass is almost full, slowly turn it into an upright position.
- Put glass and bottle on separate beer mats to present to the guest. Place the bottle on the right-hand side behind the glass and make sure the logo on the glass and the bottle label are turned towards the client.

Correct serving temperature

A simple rule of thumb: the higher the alcohol percentage, the warmer the beer is drunk. No two beers are poured in the same way. What's more, one and the same beer can be served at different moments at a different temperature to do it justice. The ideal serving temperature of a beer primarily depends on personal preference. Other factors also play a major role:
- Outside temperature
- As a thirst-quenching moment (quite chilled)
- Served at the table with a gastronomic dish (a little warmer)

If in doubt, serve the beer on the chilled side rather than on the warm side.

Beer type	Serving temperature
• Pils, light, alcohol free	3–5 °C (these beers are served increasingly chilled, even at 0 °C)
• Luxe (premium) pils	4–5 °C
• White beer	3–5 °C
• Weizen	6–8 °C
• Amber (Spéciale Belge)	6–8 °C
• Spontaneous fermentation	4–7 °C
• Stout	6–8 °C
• Strong blond beers	5–10 °C
• Strong dark beers	8–13 °C

PETRUS
AGED PALE
PETRUS
AGED RED
PETRUS
PALE
11.2 FL.OZ.
100%
SOUR SCALE
PETRUS
PRODUCT OF BELGIUM

BEER TASTING

All senses at the ready

No-one treats a glass of beer with as much love as the brewer, who is unable to hide his pride. Rightly so, as he knows better than anyone else how much work and know-how are required to produce a good brew. Judging a beer turns out to be a challenge for all of the senses. It starts off with feeling. Do I have the right glass in my hand? Does this glass suit the beer type? You wouldn't drink a Trappist from a flute or a plastic beaker, would you? The thickness of the glass also plays a role. Drinking from an elegant, fragile chalice on a tall stem is different from holding a robust glass used for gueuze. Besides, the glass has to seduce you. It has to look so attractive that you cannot wait to taste what's inside. Then we are pouring into the glass. It sounds fabulous in French: '*voir une bière*'. An entire world is hidden in the glass. What does the colour tell you? Does it suit a particular beer style or is the brewer staying away from the well-trodden path? Is the beer clear – strongly filtered, in other words – or does it present a cloudy veil? Do you see a powerful pearlisation or is there hardly any sparkle? And what does the head tell us? Is this a moon landscape full or craters or are we seeing a smooth cream? Does the froth disappear straight away? Or do we first have to drink our way through a collar that is as solid as a rock? The glass plays an important role here too. Some glasses are designed especially to preserve the head for as long as possible. If the beer does not form a head at all, this could be down to the beer or to a badly cleaned glass. However, it is inherent to several beer types that they produce very little froth.

Let's take a look at the practice. When we uncork the beer we can hear it come to life. If we don't hear a 'ssst', there may be something wrong with the beer. The froth should not rise quickly and then vanish straight away, as is the case with champagne. The head forms a natural lid that protects the beer from oxygen. Is the head coarse or delicate, are the carbon dioxide bubbles large or small? For the experienced taster, the nose provides a lot of information about the beer. You register the aromas *nasally* by smelling them, but also a second time when these same aromatic substances enter the nose through the mouth cavity (*retronasally*). If you allow the beer to flush around your mouth, less volatile compounds are released. Consequently, the aroma when swallowing will be different from that perceived when smelling. Then follows the taste. Don't forget to taste the head of the beer as well. The froth also has a flavour, as it is formed from proteins from the beer and carbon dioxide. Is the taste of the beer well-balanced? Is it mature/immature or just old/young? Is this a quality beer? This is the type of thing we want to find out. In the worst case, the head is the harbinger of bad news as it could denote a colourless or contaminated beer. In contrast to wine, beer is swallowed during tasting as, on swallowing, you receive a confirmation of the aromas you have already perceived. Another tip: to taste properly you require a lot of training, during which you learn to recognise and name the various aromas and tastes. We wish you lots of patience and lots of success! And above all, don't forget to enjoy the learning process.

To drink or to taste?

There is a huge difference between drinking a beer and tasting it professionally. Above all, drinking stands for quenching your thirst and enjoyment. Personal preference and circumstances play a major role. With friends, at the bar of a busy and noisy café it is less important which beer you are drinking. The social interaction is what matters here. If you are looking for a specific beer, enjoyment is your priority. This is when you go in search of a specialty beer café with a suitable atmosphere. When you are tasting a beer you want to describe it objectively. Personal values do not come into it.

TASTING

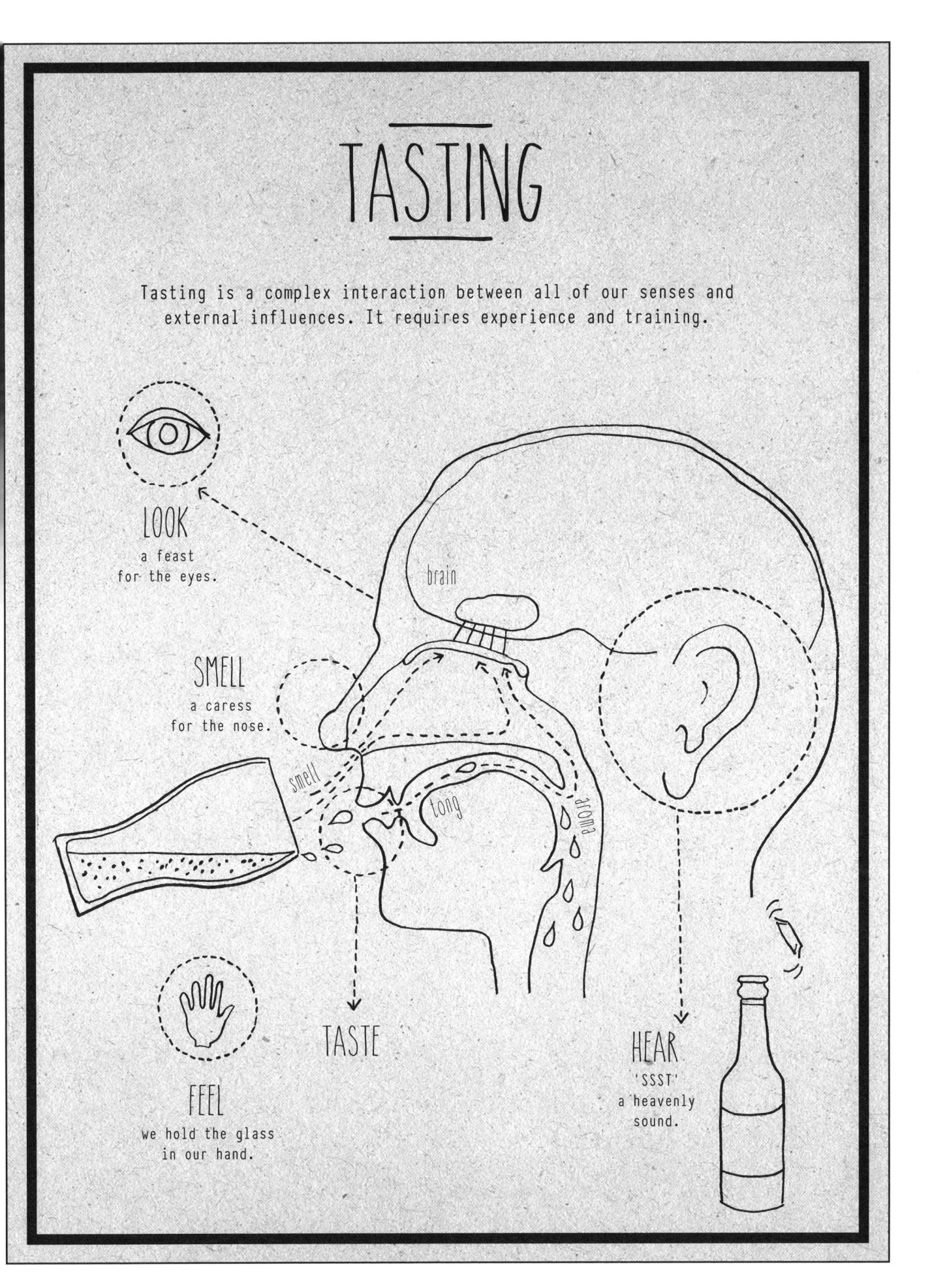

Tasting is a complex interaction between all of our senses and external influences. It requires experience and training.

LOOK
a feast for the eyes.

SMELL
a caress for the nose.

brain

smell

tong

aroma

FEEL
we hold the glass in our hand.

TASTE

HEAR
'SSST'
a heavenly sound.

THE FLAVOUR WHEEL

The taste and aromas found in beer are exceptionally complex and are produced by different substances. Over one hundred active substances have been discovered in beer and the end is not yet in sight.
Based on Meilgaard's Flavor Wheel, the findings of Mark Dregde and Lindsay Barr's Beer Flavor Map, we are bringing you our own vision. Simple, easy to use and complete.

fruity ◆ floral ◆ zesty ◆ grassy ◆ earthy ◆ wood
nutty ◆ grainy ◆ roast ◆ phenolic ◆ creamy ◆ vegetal ◆ medicinal
chemical ◆ metallic (mineral) ◆ alcoholic

AROMA

TASTE

BASIC TASTE

MOUTH FEEL

sweet ◆ sour
salt ◆ bitte ◆ umami

body
irritation ◆ temperature
finish

This requires knowledge, training and experience. Learning how to taste is not something you do alone as almost every taster, whether amateur or professional, has his or her 'blind spot'.

Flavour

The word 'flavour' refers to the total impression made by a food product. In reality, the taste buds on the tongue can only distinguish the following flavours: salt, sweet, sour, bitter, 'umami' (the taste-enhancing, bouillon/stock-like effect of glutamate, known as 'vetsin' in Chinese cuisine).

Taste, in the narrower sense of the word, is called **gustation**. The recognition of the taste of a product is not done by the tongue, but by the olfactory epithelium in the nose: the aroma. The English word *flavour* (*flavor* in the USA) means gustation and **olfaction** (aroma) together. Without the nose you will not recognise the taste of a product. You can see for yourself when you pinch your nose whilst taking a mouthful of beer. Only when you open your nose again, will the aroma reach the **olfactory epithelium** and we can notice the taste (that we may or may not recognise). People with a heavy cold can't 'taste' anything as their nose is blocked. The perception of taste in the mouth is very complex. The nerve ends of the **trigeminus**, the largest cranial nerve, register the temperature and the mouthfeel. Gustation and aroma are freed and, during chewing and blending with saliva, the structure is gradually broken down and diluted. The workings of the enzymes also play a role in this dynamic phenomenon. Then follows the crucial moment: like it or lump it. Or just spit it out: will you absorb the product or not?

Source: Leonard Schutte: 'Slikken of brok in de keel'

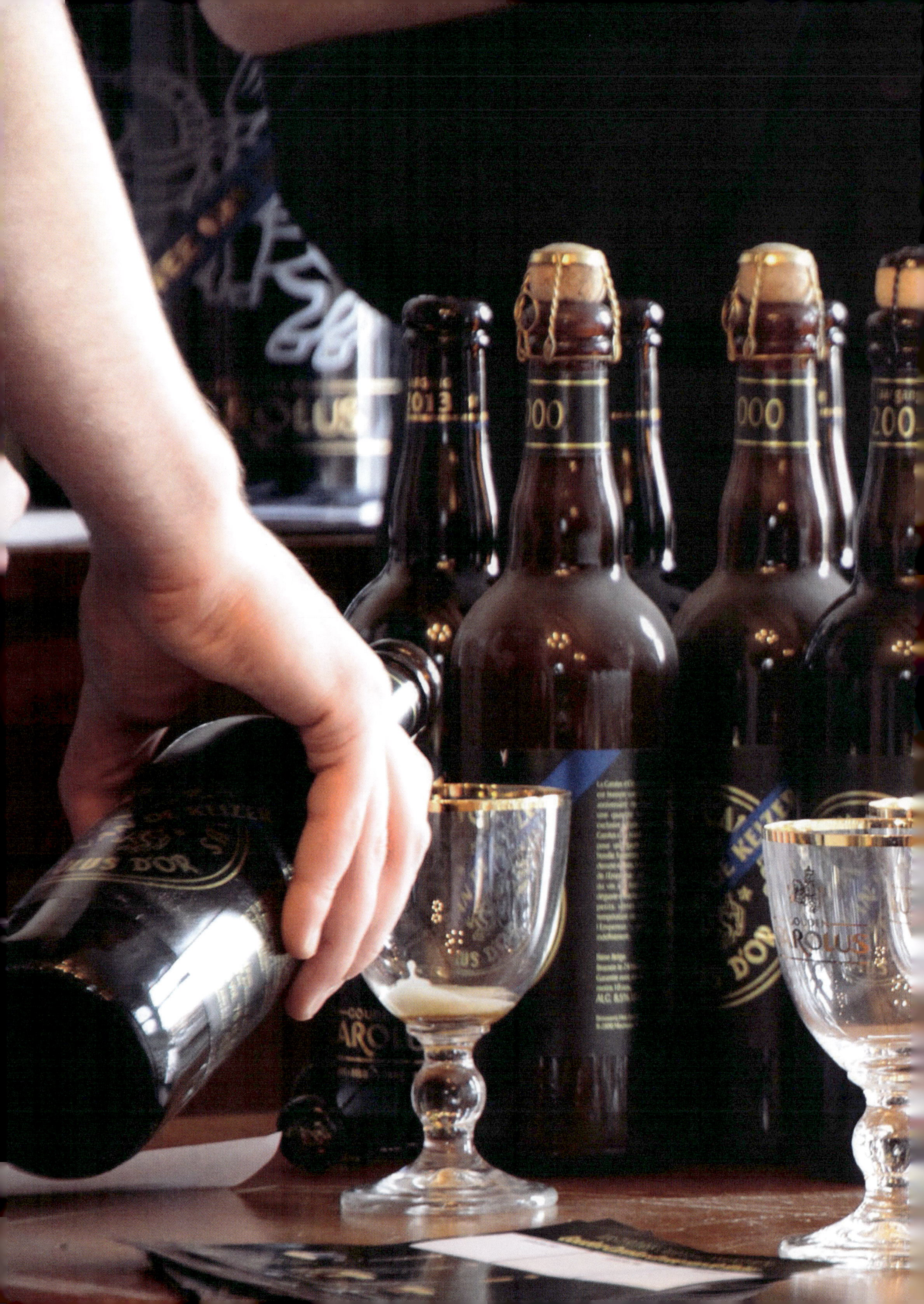
2013

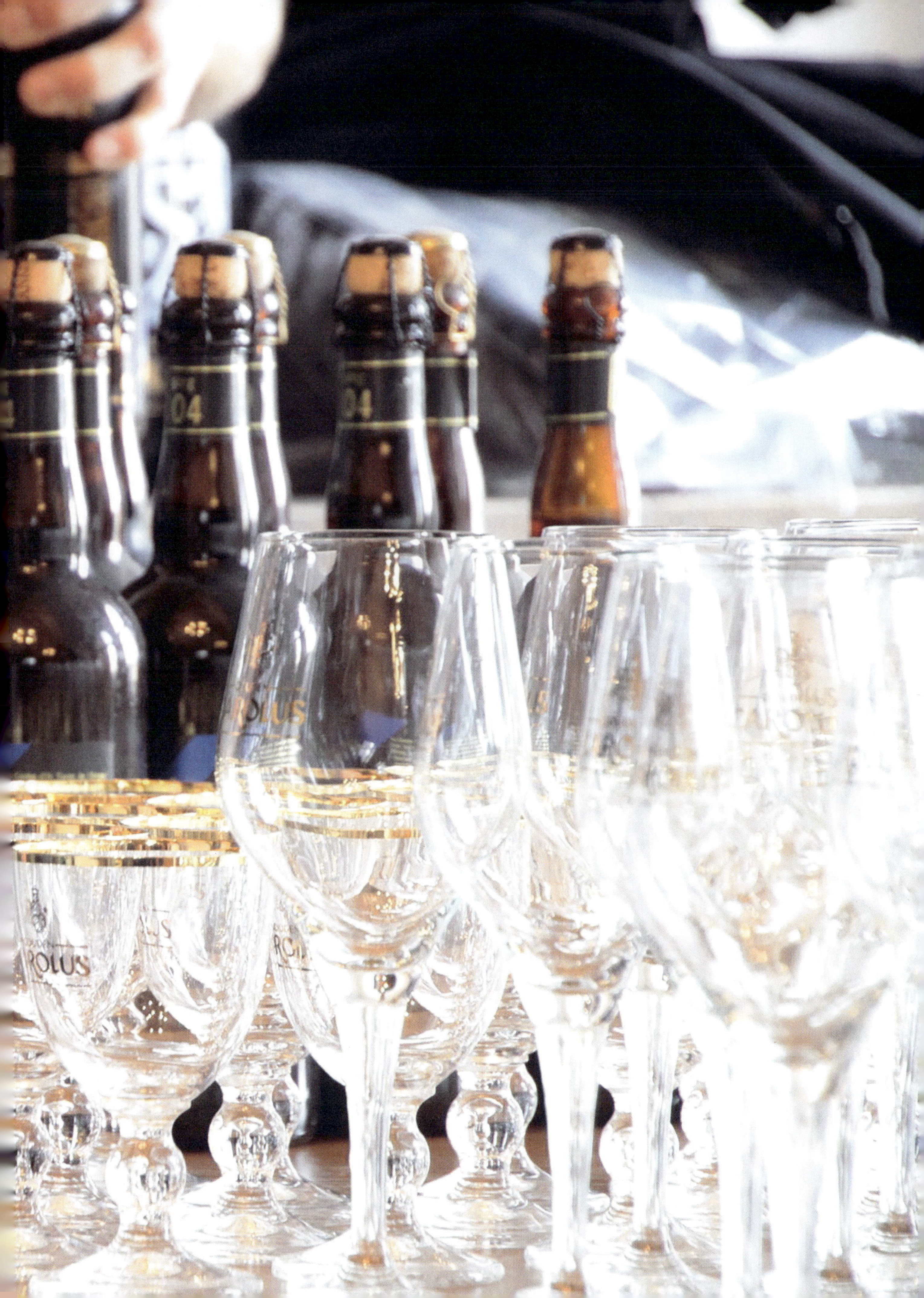

Basic tastes

German physician Adolph Fick described the four basic tastes in 1864. Japanese scientist Kikunae Ikeda discovered the fifth basic taste, 'umami', in 1908. Each basic taste corresponds to a specific need of the body. Sweet indicates food that is rich in calories. Salt indicates sodium whereas umami points at the presence of protein in the food. Sour often serves as a warning signal: it allows you to tell ripe fruit apart from immature fruit or fresh milk from that which is spoilt. Bitter also serves as a warning. Many toxic herbs and plants are bitter. Consequently, human beings are equipped with around thirty receptors for bitter and only one for sweet. This allows us to spot the bitter taste so we avoid eating the plant we have just picked and dying a painful death. From the third month of pregnancy the unborn child can taste what is in the amniotic fluid. A coffee brand from the Philippines is using this in its marketing: they have developed sweets with the taste of their coffee and hand them out to pregnant women. In this way, they hope to create an in-born demand for their coffee.

All of the senses are on high alert during the degustation. All that remains is to record your findings correctly.

Salt

First and foremost, salt re-enforces the taste. It naturally elevates the taste quotient. Salt allows other flavours to come to the fore. In other words, the taste of many preparations, ingredients and products is improved by adding salt. As always, there is such a thing as too much. An overload of salt makes us less receptive to other basic tastes.
Sweet tastes weaken salty tastes.
Bitter and umami strengthen a salty taste.
A touch of sour emphasises a salty taste but will also neutralise the salty touch when a sweet and sour ingredient is used.

Sweet

'*Wie zoet is krijgt lekkers*' ('sweet children get sweets', a Dutch St. Nicholas song), the sweet mother's milk ... Sweet is a reward. It is an accessible taste. We have a hankering for sweet that comes from our need for carbohydrates. Sweet is masking both bitter and sour. This is why food producers, including breweries, like to use sweet. Everything becomes less sharp and pronounced but also more boring and flat. The experience is different for everyone and moreover, you get used to a sweet taste. Sweet is addictive: before you know it, you need more and more sugar as your perception threshold has gone up.

Sour

The basic taste of acidic is found in all sour ingredients. Sour contributes freshness and is dynamic. Each sour has a different taste with considerable variations in strength. From the freshly sour taste of a ripe apple to the tartly sour taste of rhubarb. Lemon sour is sharper than apple sour and apple sour has a sharper taste than the mild lactic acid (in yoghurt, for example).

Acids affect mouthfeel: the sourer the taste, the tighter the mouthfeel. Acids may oxidise quickly to produce a bitter taste (e.g. hop) but they can also lend a lively touch to products. The art lies in finding the right balance with the other tastes: sweet, salt, bitter and umami. Sour and sour add up very quickly. It won't be long before a product tastes too sour.

Bitter

We have a natural dislike of bitter. A bitter taste serves as a natural warning of toxic substances. Unsurprisingly, bitter is an 'adult' taste that you have to learn to appreciate. Just remember how your offspring reacts when you put endives or Brussels sprouts in front of them. Or think back to your very first mouthful of beer. However, there is more than one side to this story. Coffee, tea, beer and chocolate are regarded as the most popular food and drink in the world. What do they have in common? Bitterness.
Bitter plays an important role in digestibility. It makes the beer go down more easily. Also, bitter sharpens the appetite.
Sour lessens our perception of bitter.
Salt and umami re-enforce a sweet taste already present in a bitter ingredient.

Umami

Umami is not a separate taste but a taste-enhancing, stock-like effect of glutamate (glutamic acid). Umami increases the flavour content and enhances other tastes. The meaning of the Japanese word Umami is 'delicious'. In English, the term *glutamic taste* is used. The discoverer of umami, Kikunae Ikeda, took out a patent and developed a synthetic glutamate: monosodium glutamate (E621), popular in Chinese restaurants as a taste enhancer.

In 1913 Shintaro Komada was able to isolate sodium inosinate (E631) and in 1957 Akira Kuninaka was able to separate sodium guanylate (E627) in shiitake mushrooms. These three amino acids form the basis of umami.

More than eighty years before the discovery of umami, Frenchman Jean-Anthelme Brillat-Savarin included a description of a substance that is strongly reminiscent of umami in his tome *Physiologie du goût*. He gave it the name of *osmazôme*, 'that exceptionally tasty part of the meat that dissolves in cold water and distinguishes itself from the extracted part that can only be dissolved in boiling water'. This *osmazôme* 'determines the taste of the most delicious soups.'

Taste

Taste is a sensory function of the central nervous system, created by receptors on the tongue, the palate and uvula. Three types of taste buds, or papillae, on the tongue discern all of the basic tastes:
- Fungiform papillae
- Circumvallate papillae
- Foliate papillae

Older books or training courses often contain a 'map of the tongue' that depicts the areas where various tastes are based. It is said that sweet is primarily tasted at the front of the tongue, sour is tasted on the sides and bitterness is mainly discerned at the back of the mouth. However, it is not true that the various parts of the tongue are exclusively responsible for the registration of a specific taste. The work of German scientist David Hänig (1901) has been interpreted incorrectly. Hänig's report did include *taste belts*, but he never suggested the existence of exclusive taste zones on the tongue.

In fact, all taste sensations are found on every part of the tongue, although some parts are more sensitive to particular tastes than others. The surface of the tongue is covered in numerous papillae. Embedded here are the so-called taste buds. Each taste bud contains between just a few to 250 taste papillae. Most papillae are sensitive to sweet, sour, bitter, salty and umami tastes, although there are slightly more sweet-sensitive papillae at the front. At the back of the tongue there is a row of large papillae that are especially sensitive to bitter.

Internal smell

During masticating and swallowing, volatile, aromatic substances are released which, from within the mouth (retronasally) reach the olfactory receptors just above the nose. In fact, there is an open channel between the cavities of the oral and nasal cavities. The system responsible for smell produces independent observations and reports back to the brain. This system is so closely linked to the **gustatory system** that we are incapable of separating the two elements. 80% of what we taste comes from the olfactory receptors.

In flavour three aspects play a role: taste, smell and mouthfeel.

Besides, we have to take **extrinsic and intrinsic components** into account. Extrinsic components relate to the properties of a product that we can judge without really taking the product into the mouth (the way it looks, sounds, feels and smells). Gustation, smell (internal), sound (internal) and feel (internal) are the senses that are directly related to tasting.

Sense

The fourth type of taste bud is receptive to sensation rather than taste. There are three types of taste receptors:
- Mechanoreceptors: registering hard and soft
- Thermoreceptors: registering warm and cold
- Pain receptors: detecting painful substances and irritants

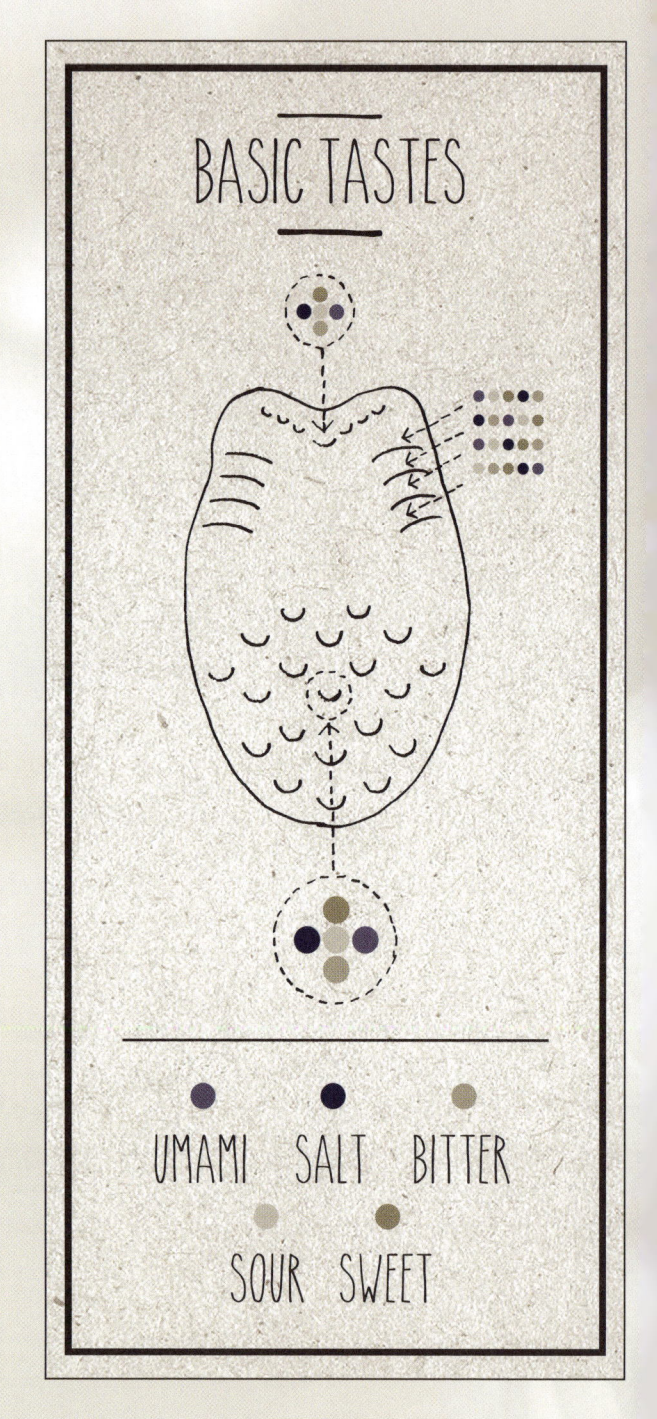

BASIC TASTES

UMAMI SALT BITTER

SOUR SWEET

Footnote 1: Klosse, P. Het Proefboek. P. 36-77.

How to taste

To increase objectivity we are tasting in a structured fashion, step by step, and pay attention to the following aspects:

A lovely sound

When we taste beer we do not immediately think of sound. However, sound can be an important indicator. Listen well when the bottle is opened. If you hear 'fttt' or 'pop', you can confidently assume that the beer is sparkling. If you hear nothing, the beer contains only little carbon dioxide, either intentionally or unintentionally.

A feast for the eyes

EBC is a measurement for the colour of beer. The abbreviation stands for European Brewery Convention (an organisation of large European breweries). A look at the beer reveals much about the beer style. Colour, clarity, formation of carbon dioxide and froth – all of these provide much information about the beer itself and the beer type or style. A powerful torch makes for a handy tool.

Colours may vary from blond, amber, red, brown to black; with fruit beers, they range from pale pink via dark red to burgundy. Except in the case of fruit beers, the colour is derived from the varieties of malt used.

Additives such as caramel, candi sugar and extracts can also affect the colour.

Colour does not affect the strength or taste intensity of the beer.

Clarity

Is the beer clear or cloudy? Clarity depends on filtration and the age of the beer. Clarity can vary between brilliant to cloudy with lumps. If a beer is served at too low a temperature, a cold cloud will form. This cloudiness will disappear spontaneously at a beer temperature of 10 °C and above.

Head

Delicate or large bubbles? Does the head remain stable or does it collapse? Does it cling to the inside of the glass, or not? The typical colour varies between snowy white, via light beige to red/pink in the case of some fruit beers.

Pearlisation

Rising bubbles, semi-strong or no pearlisation at all. Some brewers use *nucleation sites*, indentations deliberately applied to the bottom of the glass (e.g. Duvel) so the beer produces more bubbles.

A feast for the nose

Aromas are freed up by briefly swirling the beer in the glass. In the same way as a wine tasting, there is a specific jargon used for naming the different beer aromas (*also see page 418*).

Three main groups:
An additional tasting sensation is created by retronasal olfaction. Inhale air during swallowing and the taste sensation will be heightened. This method is also used in wine tasting.
- Hop aromas and herbs: The volatile compounds from hop bells and herbs
- Malt aromas: Sweet caramel and honey-like aromas
- Fermentation aromas: Fruity ester aromas (apple, beer, banana), phenolic aromas or sulphuric compounds

Source: Quality can be tasted (leaflet from Dutch beer club)

Aah, we're having a drink of beer

See P.422-425 for all the delicious details.

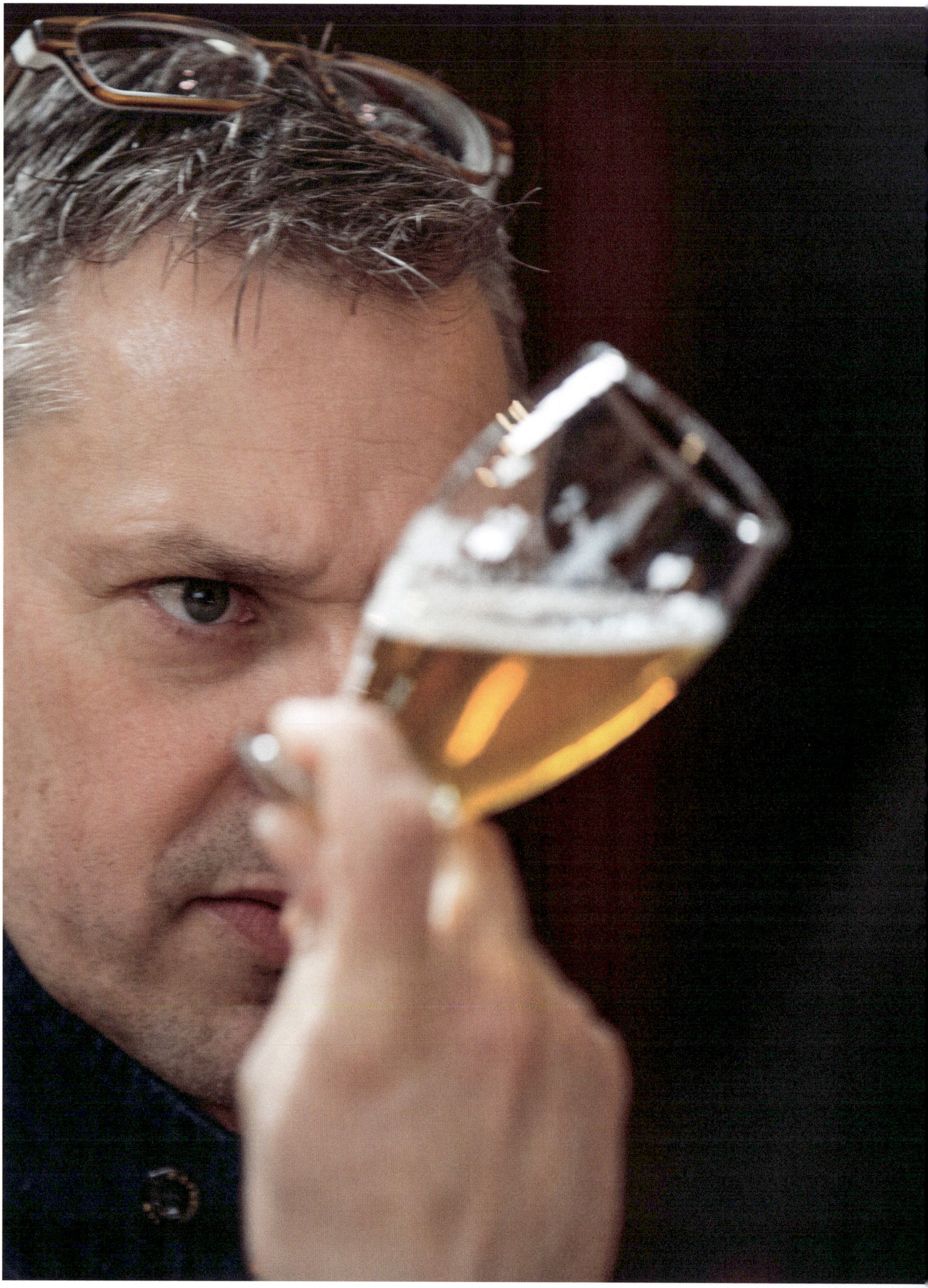

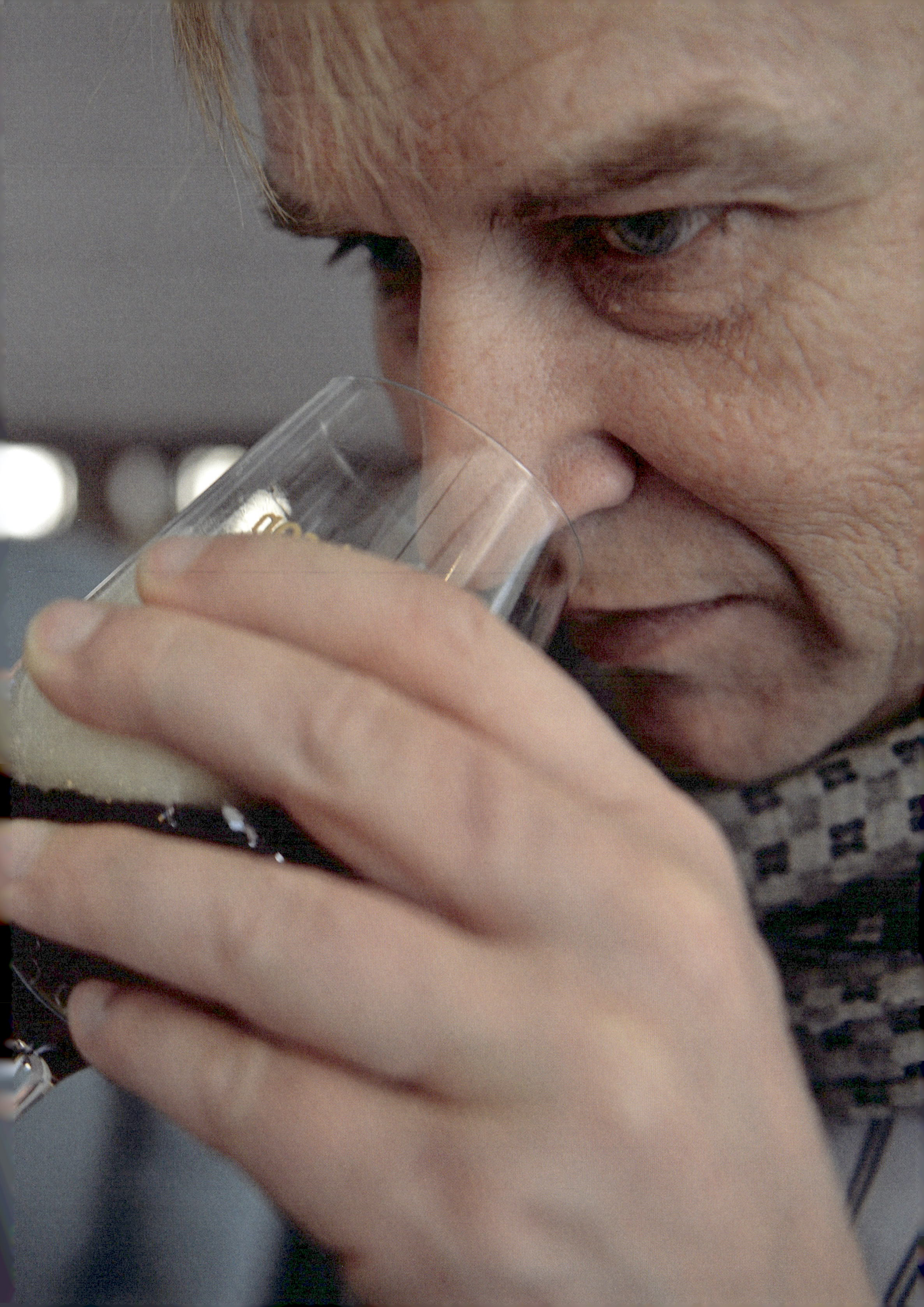

Tasting in the right order

After listening, watching and smelling the time for tasting has come. When you are tasting a range of beers, the order of serving is of the greatest importance. We use the following basic rules:
- From low in alcohol to high in alcohol
- From low bitterness to high bitterness
- From light in colour to dark in colour

Desirable and undesirable substances / taste deviations in beer

Desirable / necessary	Desirable / necessary in small amounts	Desirable / necessary in specialty beers	Not necessary for the taste of the beer. Taste deviation if too strong a presence	Undesirable / taste deviation
Bitter	Caprylic	Honey	Other esters	Like mould
Alcoholic	Dimethyl sulphide	Like liquorice	Rose-like	Like metal
Carbon dioxide	Hydrogen sulphide	Cheese-like	Other flowers	Like wort
Hoppy	Mercaptan	Like cloves	Perfumed	Like grain
Malty	Diacetyl	Woodruff (Gallium Odoratum)	Resinous	Like straw
Caramel	Sweet	Other herbs	Yeasty	Woody
Astringent	Salt	Cherries	Acetaldehyde	Like bread
Banana esters	Warming	Other fruit	Sulphide	Like paper
Apple esters	Cooling	Vinegar	Gaseous	Chloride phenol
Sour	Vinous	Phenolic	Burnt	Rank
Body	Nutty	Smoky		Oily
				Lightstruck
				Stale

Source: Kwaliteit is te proeven (quality can be tasted) (folder produced by Dutch beer club)

Beer tasting is an acquired art

The Gruut home brewery in Ghent is a particularly lovely melting pot of the art of brewing beer and the art of serving it. Annick Desplenter, the brewer, specialises in beers containing herbs. She is inspired by recipes from the early Middle Ages, an era when the hop plant was still unknown in Belgium. In those days, brewing was done using a mixture of herbs called gruit (or 'gruut'). The current 'gruit' beers, made without hops, are consequently less bitter and are popular with women. It is said that herbs increase the libido whereas hops are ascribed the opposite effect… Annick points out the importance of the senses in the beer experience. Far too often, people impose their own limits when it comes to developing their sense of taste. Annick herself wants to smell everything beforehand, even when she visits a restaurant. Beer tasting is an art that has to be taught, she finds. This is how you notice particular tastes and learn to filter out certain negative tastes, the off flavours.

Women and beer

It is a myth that beer was exclusively brewed by men, for men. History teaches us that, throughout the ages, brewing was also women's work. It was part of household management, just like bread baking. We even find out about witches' trials where the female brewer was accused of using the wrong herbs (usually those that heightened the libido). When it came to the science of brewing, women proved themselves at least the equals of men. As early as the 13th century, German abbess Hildegard von Bingen described the qualities of the hop plant. She played an important role in the spread of this beer ingredient. Returning to the Belgian beer world, we have to highlight the iconic role played by Rosa Merckx. It is still her signature that adorns the silk wrappers covering the bottles of Liefmans Goudenband and Kriek Brut. Rosa was involved in brewing this beer for forty years and, to a large extent, is responsible for the current sweet-and-sour taste of this brown beer from Oudenaarde. Rosa Merckx started her career as a secretary. It soon became apparent that she had a great talent for beer tasting. Rosa acquired her brewing skills along the way. When she found that the taste of the Liefmans beers was just a little too sharp, she fine-tuned the recipe. Rosa Merckx now looks back upon these times with justified pride. 'Beer is definitely alive. It has a soul. If I'd had to work with a product without a soul, or just in an admin office, I would never have lasted so long. If you are a brewer, your work gives you satisfaction. You are proud of your product and you bring joy to people', Rosa finds. 'Partly thanks to me, Liefmans has evolved from an extremely sharp or sour beer towards a milder, slightly sour beer. I have contributed to this evolution. This has nothing to do with sweetening the beers. Rather, it is related to an increased awareness of hygiene in production that allowed us to get a grip on the local sour fermentation.'

Beer does not mean bitter

Passion burst into full flower with gueuze connoisseur Yves Panneels after he received a gift from colleagues: a beer case containing several bottles of good kriek and gueuze. 'I got a taste for it. I wanted to try some more and was happy to discover that I could find these beers close to where I lived.' Fast-forward a number of years. Yves has been running, together with his brother Kurt, their village café every Sunday morning. It is based in Eizeringen, goes under the name of In de Verzekering tegen de Grote Dorst ('Insure yourself against the Great Thirst') and has been crowned the best beer café in the world several times over. They are also in charge of online beer store 'Het Huis van de Geuze'.
In addition, Yves organises the 'Dag van de Lambic'

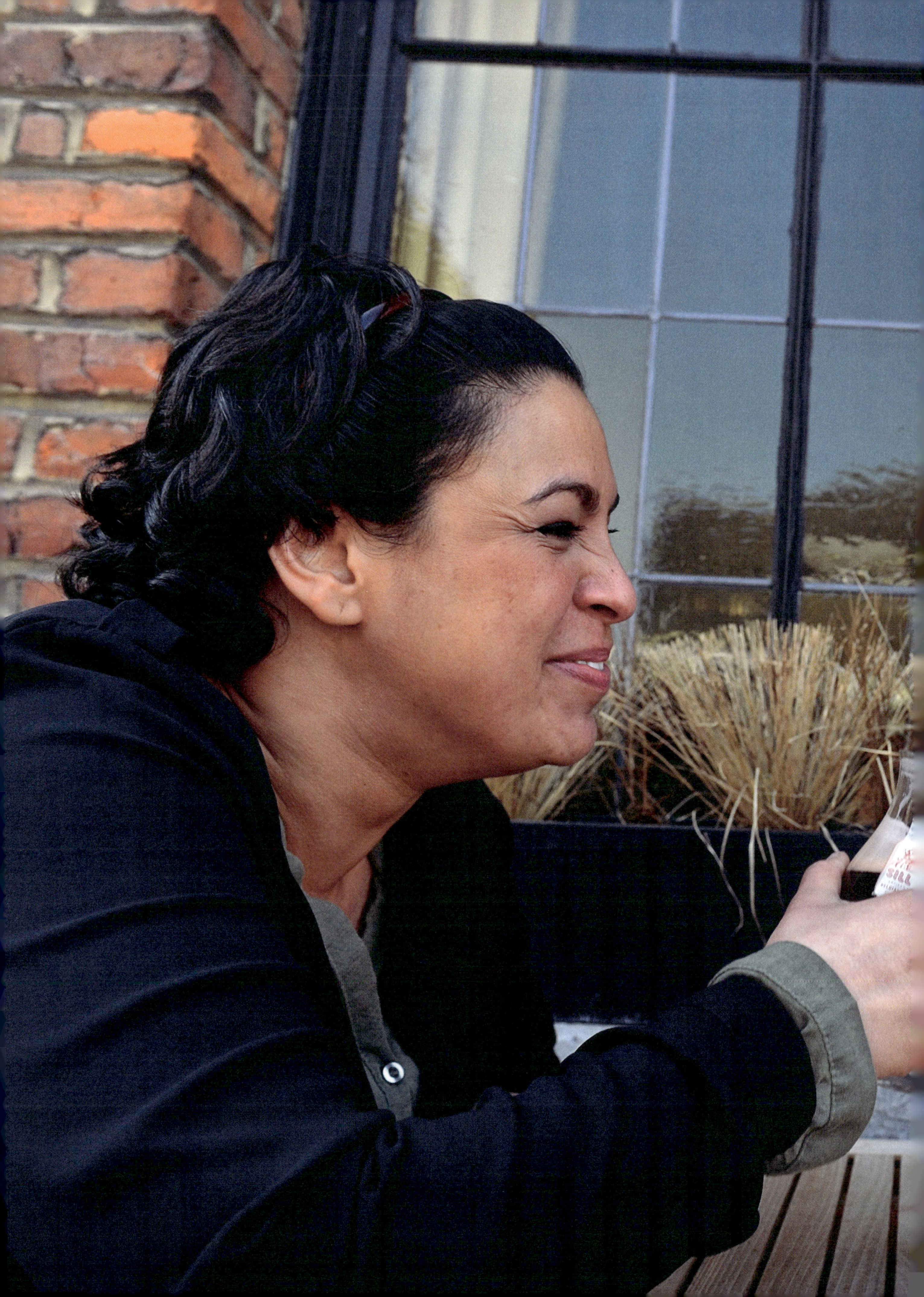

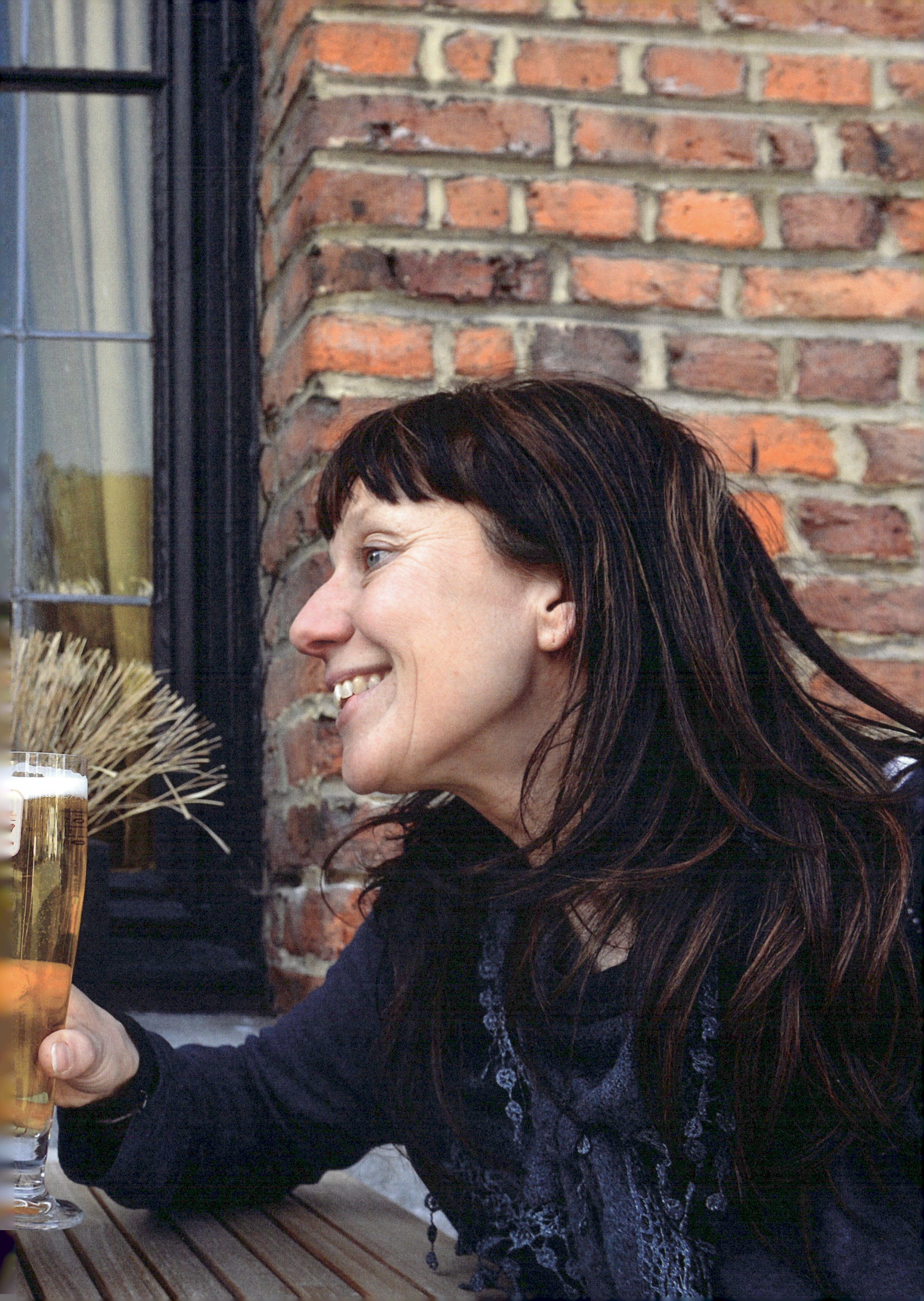

and the 'Dag van de Kriek' on an annual basis. Every other year he stages the 'Nacht van de Grote Dorst' (the Night of the Great Thirst), the Pajottenland's international gueuze and kriek festival. 'There are still plenty of prejudices when it comes to beer, but they are not based in fact. Beer does not always have to be bitter and is far more than a thirst-quencher. Compare beer with wine and you'll be amazed at the variety. Just like one Bordeaux can be different from another, a kriek can vary depending on the producer, the year and the way it is made. You may not like a particular beer but that does not mean that you don't like any of the beers in that beer style.'

STORING BEER

Beer is a sensitive drink that deserves to be treated with the utmost care. It is a natural product. This means that, over time, the taste and appearance of a beer will be affected by its environment. Oxygen, light and temperature all have an effect on the taste. This evolution in the taste can be intentional (occurring during maturation and cold storage) or unintentional. Beer has a best-before date and cannot be stored indefinitely. A number of guidelines:

- Store the beer in a cool and dark environment, at a constant temperature between 10 °C and 15 °C.
- A cellar or dark cupboard protects from sunlight. Dark brown or dark green bottles do this as well.
- The best-before date is a guideline for sustainability.
- Pils beers and light beers can be stored for six months.
- Other session beers are best consumed within twelve months.
- Beers that re-ferment in the bottle can be stored for twelve months or longer in the right conditions.
- Bottles topped with a crown cap must be stored vertically.
- Just like wine bottles, beer bottles with a cork stopper are best stored horizontally to prevent the cork from drying out.
- Before drinking a beer that has re-fermented in the bottle, place it in a vertical position a few days before drinking to allow the yeast to float to the bottom.

The enemies of beer

Oxygen and beer are arch-enemies. When beer is exposed to oxygen it will start to oxidise. Also, it gives bacteria an opportunity to convert alcohol into acetic acid. The contact with oxygen gives the beer a so-called bread taste (oxidation higher alcohol). There is a reason why the advice to 'store in a cool and dark environment' is printed on the label. Packaging made from metal, such as barrels and cans, is impervious to light and will extend the 'shelf life' of a beer. The effect of light is, however, noticeable in glass bottles and causes the isohumulone from the hop to change its character. The beer starts to smell like 'cats' pee', the so-called *'LSF' Light Struck Flavour*. This is why most beer bottles are made out of green or brown glass, with the latter offering the most protection. Conduct your own test. Take two bottles of pils, place one in the fridge for a week and the other one in the sun. The results will speak for themselves.

Temperature also affects the sustainability of the beer. The lower the temperature (without freezing the beer), the longer the beer can be stored. Besides undesirable taste evolutions, which deviate from the usual taste, there are also evolutions in taste that are highly coveted. Just bring to mind an old Orval, in which the wild yeasts (the *Brettanomyces*, typical for spontaneously fermented lambic beers) are gaining the upper hand. Or think of an old Chimay Bleue, dominated by its touches of port and Madeira. Oude gueuze is another example of a beer that can be stored almost indefinitely.

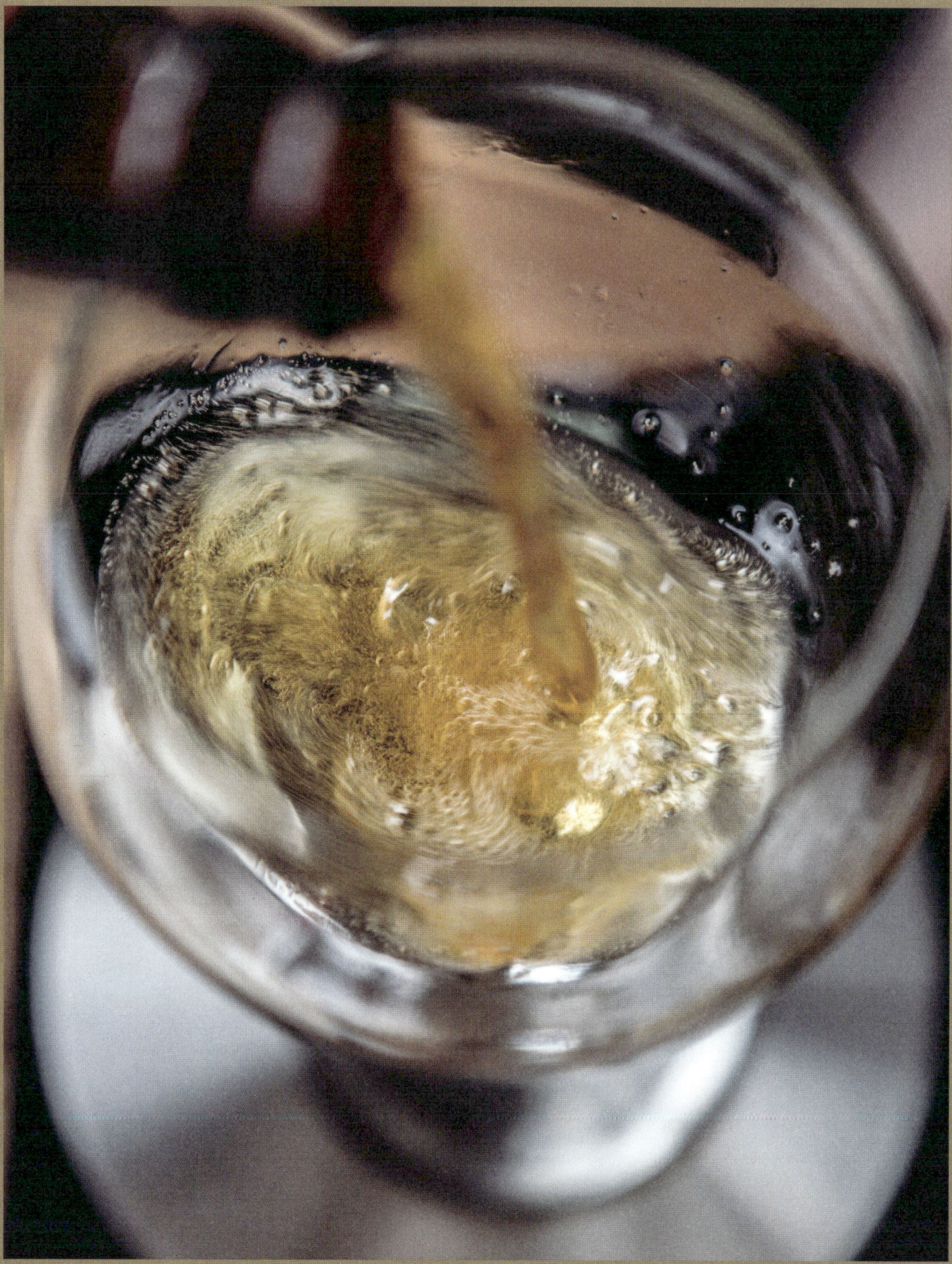

WHAT LIGHT IS TO THE EYES, WHAT AIR IS TO THE LUNGS, WHAT LOVE IS TO THE HEART, BEER IS TO THE SOUL OF MAN

Robert Green Ingersoll

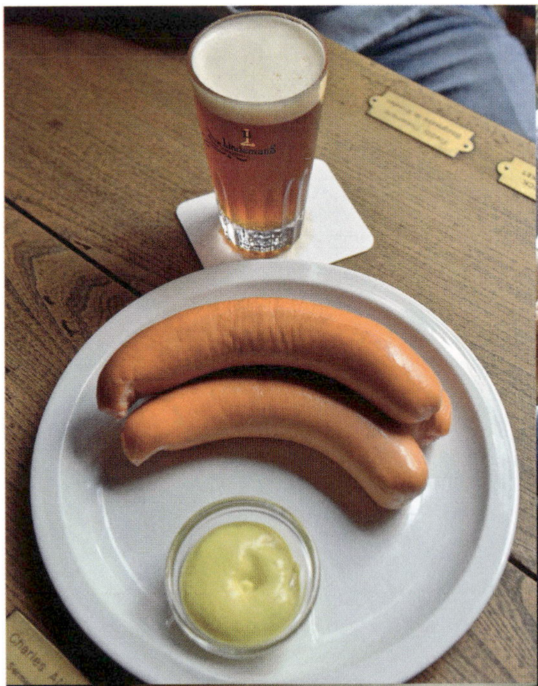
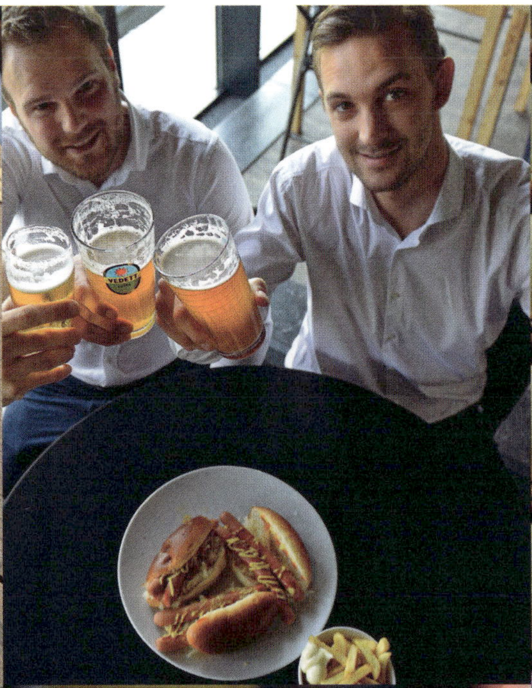
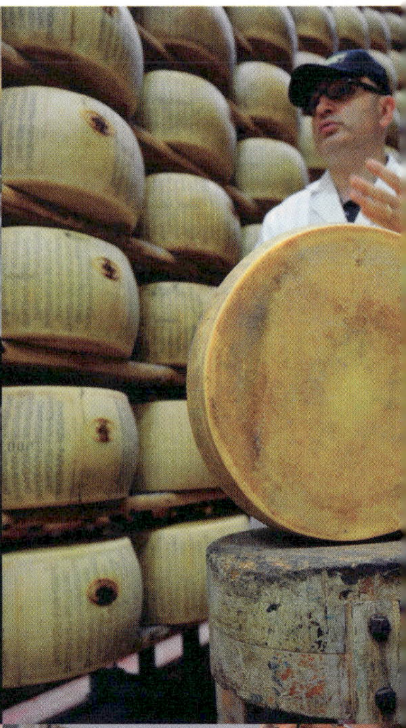
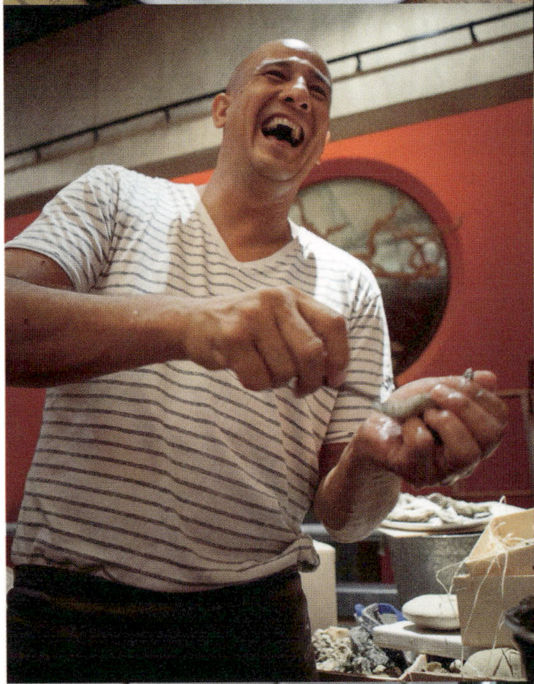
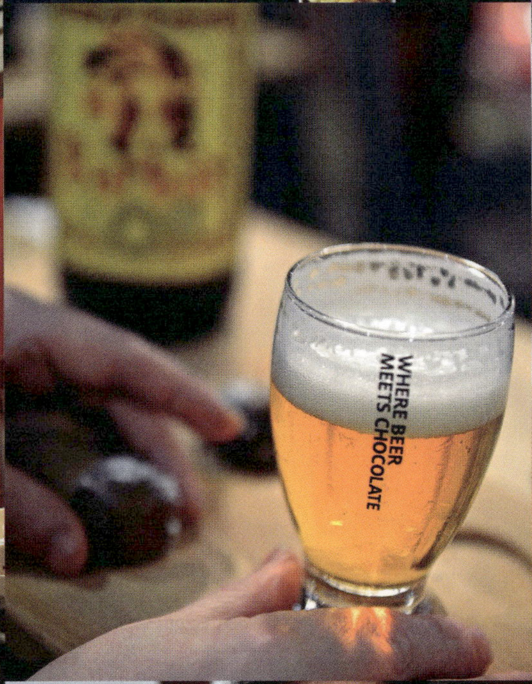
WHERE BEER
MEETS CHOCOLATE
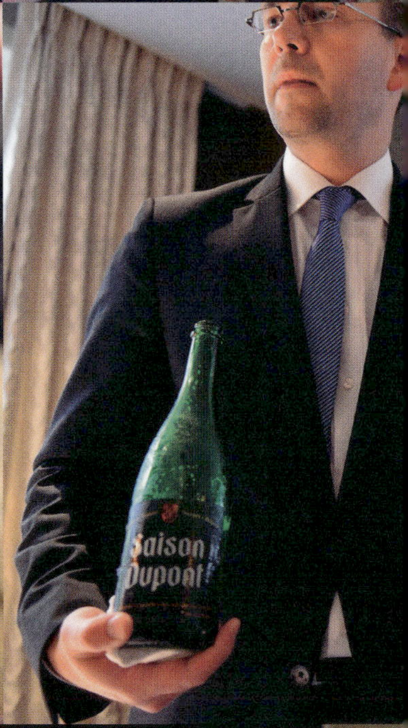
Saison
Dupont
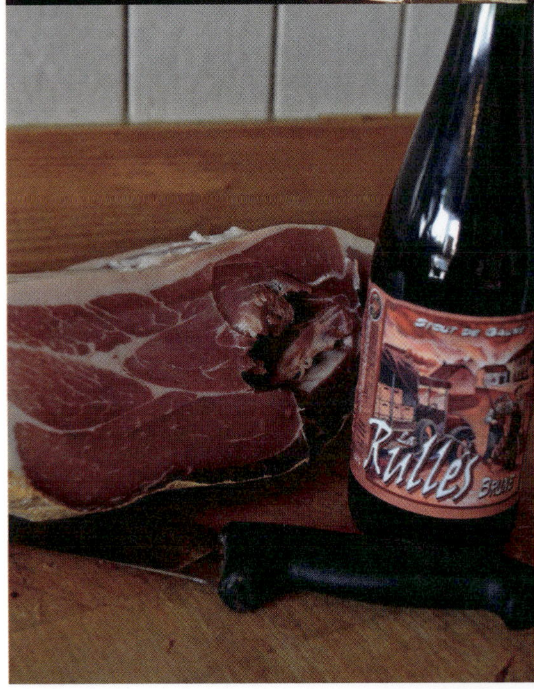
Rulles
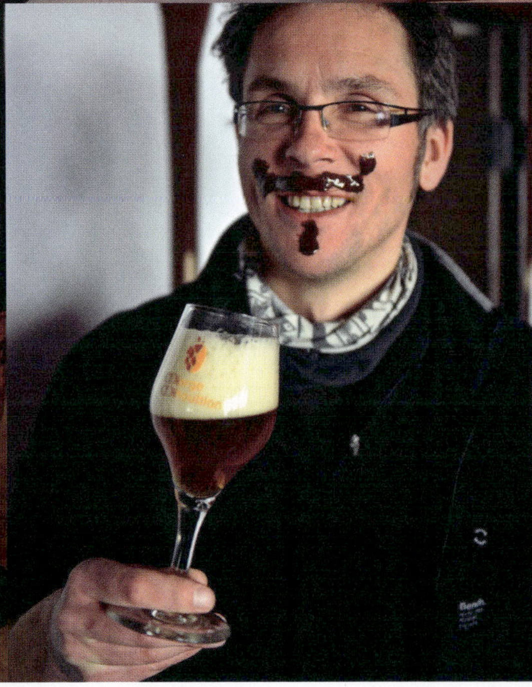
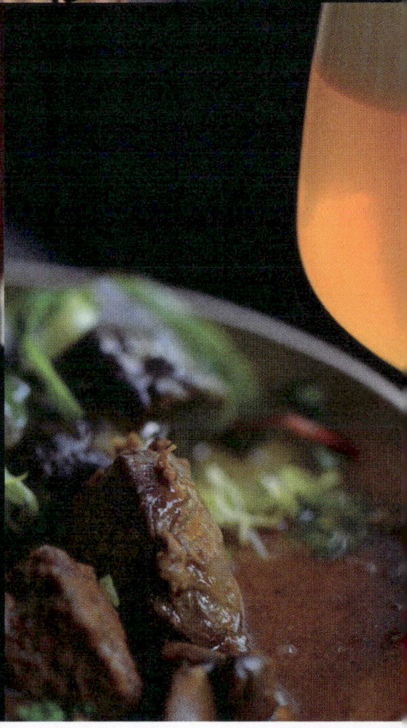

BRUSSELS
BEER
PROJECT
DELTA
IPA
IBU 45
EBC 18

1

BEER WINE
BATTLE

MONS
AVEC LES
Bons Vœux
DE LA BRASSERIE DUPONT

Bush
Prestige

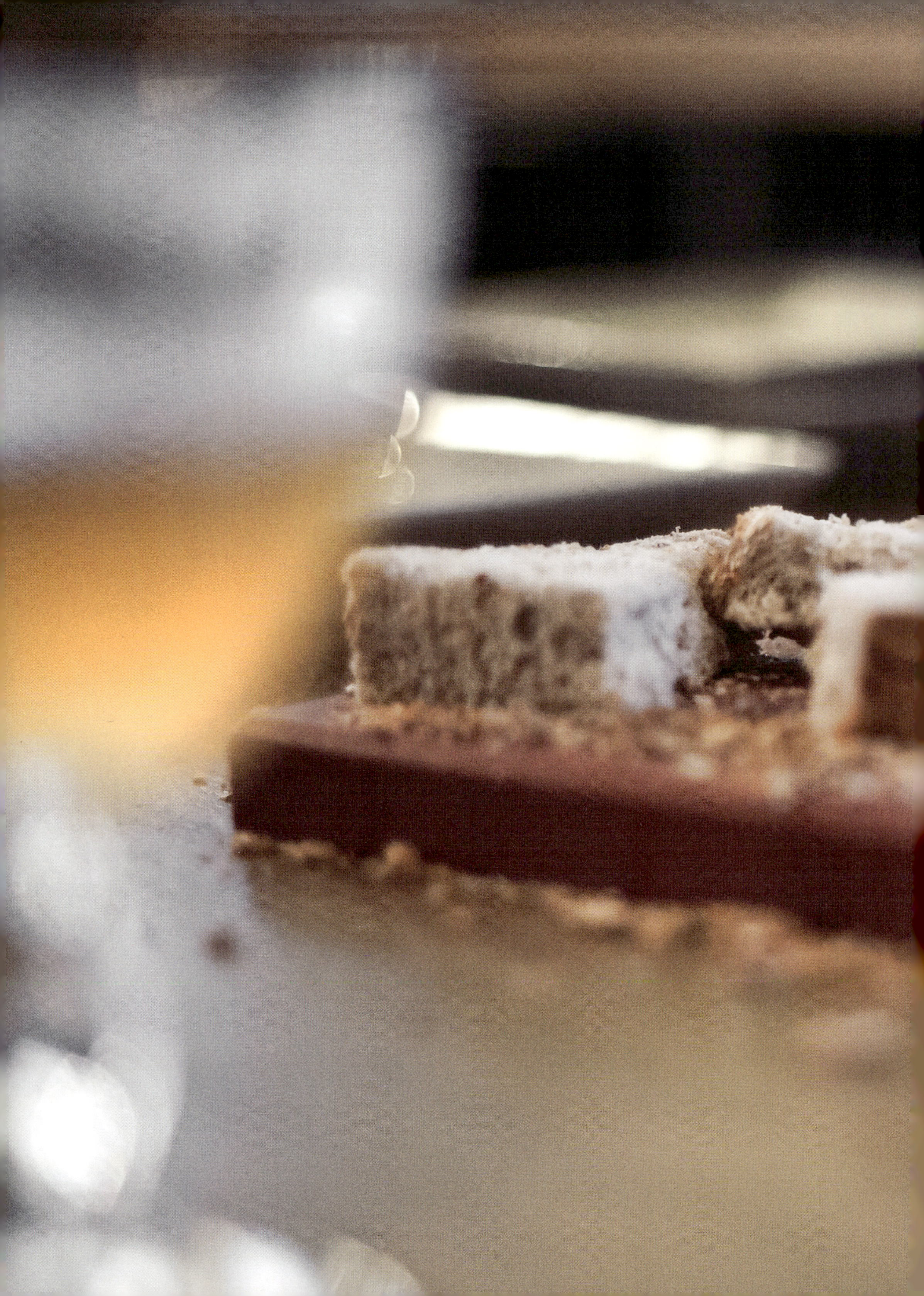

7

BEER KITCHEN AND FOOD PAIRING

BEER KITCHEN AND FOOD PAIRING

The ability to digest alcohol is in our genes; we have been doing it for hundreds of thousands of years. We have now also mastered the art of brewing beer. The general term of 'beer' covers a wide range of aromas and tastes. Chefs and sommeliers are discovering the culinary riches offered by beer. In this chapter, we are handing the microphone over to them. You will find inspiration for pairings with fish, shellfish, seafood, burgers, game, chocolate, cheese, pasta, bread, pizzas and Eastern cuisine. Finally, we will act as your guide and take you to the best Belgian beer restaurants.

Alcohol Habituation

We have been drinking alcohol for hundreds of thousands of years. We are able to digest alcohol thanks to the enzymes contained in our bodies. Since when have we had this ability? The answer is not clear-cut by any means. Some scientists state that alcohol became part of our diet when we started fermenting food, around 9,000 years ago. Others are convinced that primates were able to absorb alcohol from fruit 80 million years ago. Matthew Carrigan of Santa Fe College in the USA and his colleagues studied the ADH4-enzyme that plays an important part in processing alcohol. His analysis shows that mankind started fermenting alcohol around 10 million years ago. This era saw the forests of East Africa make way for grasslands and savannahs. Primates descended from the trees to start life on the ground. Fruit that has fallen on soil ferments far more quickly. This fermentation creates alcohol. Individuals with the enhanced ADH4-enzyme were more able to cope with alcohol. Professor Frank Wiens and his team at Bayreuth University observed the pen-tailed tree shrew in Malaysia. This small animal often feasts on palm flower nectar, which contains alcohol. However, it shows no signs of inebriation. The alcohol only serves as a source of food and energy. Amongst all of the living beings, the pen-tailed tree shrew most closely resembles the common ancestor of simians. Ancient humans too were able to obtain their portion of alcohol from rotting fruit. We were born with the capacity to break down alcohol. However, we humans do get drunk when we absorb alcohol over and above the quantity our ancestors derived from rotting fruit.

Hop shoots from the Westhoek

Think of beer and hops spring to mind. However, hops are more than a basic ingredient of beer. Hop shoots are also a culinary delicacy. We make our way to 't Hoppecruyt, a hop farm in Proven near Poperinge. The majority of Belgian hops are produced in this region, the so-called 'Westhoek', also known as 'Flanders Fields' as it is the location of the frontline during the First World War. It is no coincidence that so many hops are grown around here. The mild maritime climate and the fertile soil made up of sand and loam have proved to be very suitable for hop cultivation. 't Hoppecruyt is a mixed agricultural business with around a hundred Blue Belgian cattle grazing its fields. The hop field covers 6.5 hectare. Benedikte Desmyter, the flamboyant farmer, is happy to provide an explanation. "People mainly used to grow bitter hops for pils," Benedikte tells us. "Aromatic varieties, like the Cascade, Safir, Tettnanger or Kent Golding are now in high demand. We supply directly to the breweries. They prefer Belgian hops for some of their beers and they like to use that in their promotion." Thinking of hops, the hop cones, harvested in September, are foremost on our minds. The female hop cones contain an agent called lupuline, which helps to extend the storage period of the beer. But gourmets are also keen on hops. The hop shoots that are picked in the spring are a veritable delicacy. They can be found on the menu of several Westhoek restaurants during the first four months of the year. 't Hoppecruyt only harvests hop shoots from bitter hops, Magnum and Mercure for example. The hop plant produces hop cones on an annual basis and continues to do so for many years. Hop plants are cut back to the ground post-harvest whereupon, in the spring, the plant once again starts to produce underground shoots. "Before the hop starts to shoot, we remove the roots of plants that are about fifteen years old," Benedikte tells us. "After all, the older the plant, the lower the yield." The farmer heads for her barns and we follow in her wake. This is where the roots are 'tabled', or ensconced in square shapes underneath a layer of earth around ten centimetres thick. The floor is heated and the roots are watered regularly. As soon as the thick white shoots start to grow, there is no stopping them. You can start picking in two weeks' time. "During picking we remove the fibrous parts," Benedikte shows us whilst cutting the shoots with a potato peeler. "You can only learn to pick hop shoots by doing it. We only keep the crunchy part of the shoot." The freshly picked shoots are delivered daily to local restaurants.

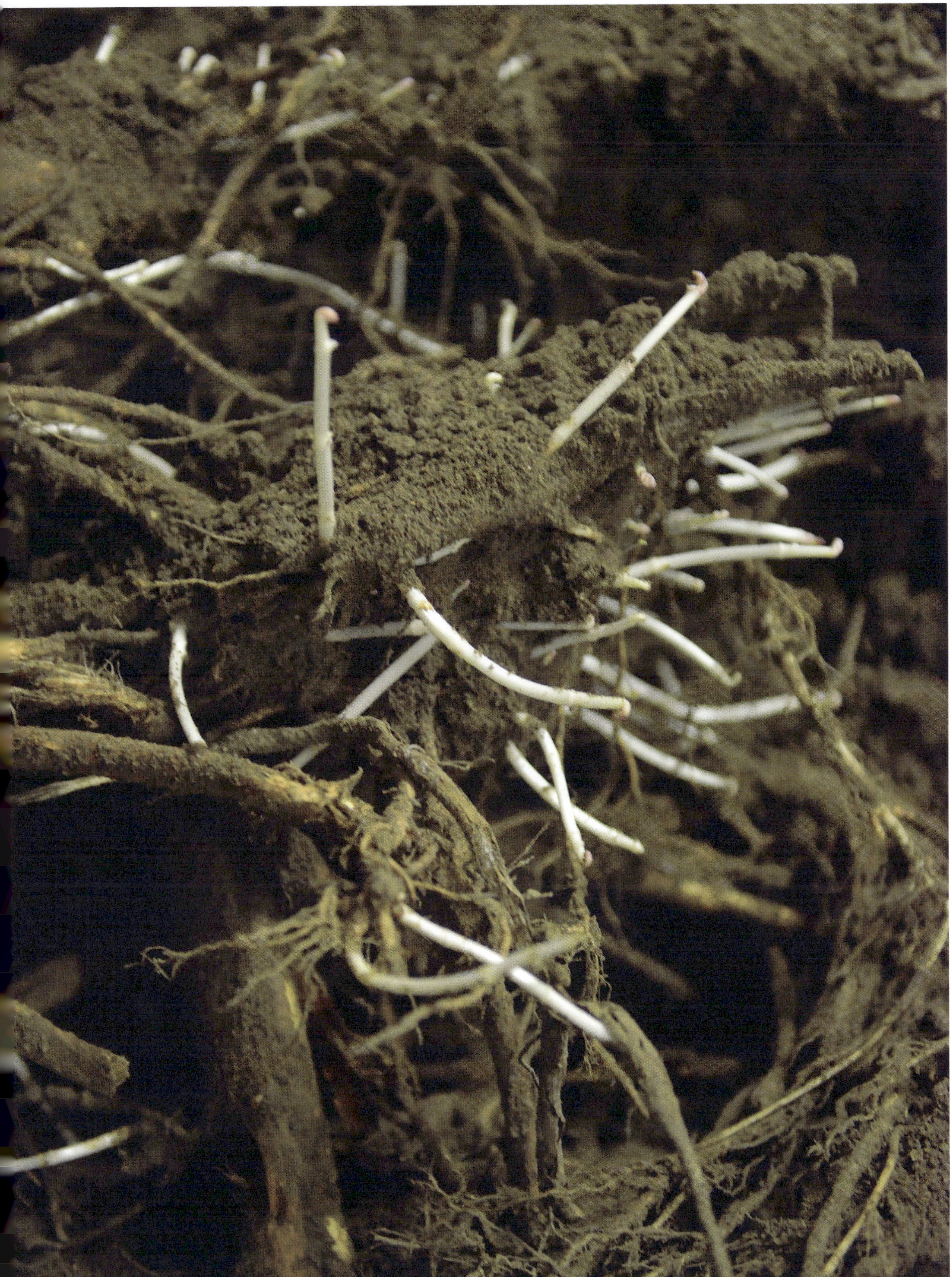

Beer with your meal

"Nobody puts beer in a corner." The good life. That means enjoying food and drink, especially in the right combination. Give some thought to the drinks you are serving at the table as this can have a positive effect on the atmosphere. Make intelligent choices. Beer and gastronomy are 'a match made in heaven'. Your taste buds will be in ecstasy. Compared with wine, beer covers more 'taste extremes': sour, sweet and bitter. Therefore, beer offers a wider range of possibilities in the kitchen and at the table. For example, beer works better with zesty and spicy Asian recipes. Recipes with a roast and/or caramel-like character, roast beef for example, also provide a better match with beer. This is no coincidence as you could pair it with a beer that is brewed with toasted malt, yielding touches of toasted caramel. Compared to the winemaker, the brewer has far more ingredients at his disposal to 'grow' a taste. Malt, water, hops and yeast are the basic ingredients of beer, but the brewer can also use herbs and spices, fruit, coffee, chocolate and even foils such as wood shavings to produce his beer.

A champion of taste

Indeed, the combinations verge on the endless. All of the basic tastes are found in beer. Some beers are on the 'dry' side (old gueuze, Orval, saison), others veer towards the syrupy (quadruples, double bock, barley wines). In this case, the unfermented malt sugars provide the sweetness. The other basic taste, salt, comes from the minerals in the brewing water. Famous examples include the pale ales from the English town of Burton-On-Trent. The "Mor Braz" brewery from Brittany is unique in that is uses sea water for brewing, giving a very different taste sensation. Basic taste number three, sour, is created by specific varieties of yeast. Examples include the "Brettanomyces Bruxellensis" and "Brettanomyces Lambicus", coveted for their earthy, animal-like sourness and characteristic of lambic and oude gueuze. Other types of yeast create a mild lactic acid sourness in a Vlaams roodbruin or Oudenaards bruin to name but two. And yes, the bitter touch is also present. Hops and some malts account for the bitterness. Some beers don't have a hoppy character at all (wheat beers, some lagers, fruit beers...) whereas others are extremely bitter. Malt bitterness is derived from toasted malt varieties. This bitterness gives a hard mouth feel that verges on burning (like you get with an Irish Dry Stout). We are going one step further: beer is no stranger to 'umami'. Umami is neither salt, sweet, bitter nor sour but it elevates flavours. Umami comes from yeast and malt chromosomes and is created by breaking down proteins (through ageing and/or heating). Examples include Parmesan cheese, soy sauce, oysters, green tea and Guinness. In addition to these basic tastes, beer also includes alcohol – what else? – and carbon dioxide. Alcohol carries the taste and brings sweetness, warmth and fullness. Carbon dioxide cleans the palate and provides dryness and an astringent feeling in the mouth. You have to admit it, which other drink has so much going for it?

Beer ambassadors

We make the best beers in the world. The entire world agrees with us. So why do we, the Belgians, not drink more beer at the table? The Germans, Americans and English value a delicious beer at the gastronomic table as highly as a glass of wine. Why don't we? Undoubtedly, the boundless chauvinism of our neighbours from the south, the French, comes into play here. Under the guise of: 'the best cuisine in the world with the best wines in the world', the wine & food combination dominates haute cuisine. The term wine & dine expresses this perfectly. Beer has been an integral part of the rich Belgian popular cuisine for years and years. You will find no end of recipes for stews and marinades… with beer. But, until recently, wine was king of the refined kitchen. In a restaurant it was usually 'not done' to order a suitable beer with your meal. The tide is turning, slowly but surely. Chefs of star-awarded restaurants have recently been experimenting with beer. American chef-brewmaster Garret Oliver of Brooklyn Brewery gave the impetus to this 'revolution'. In his book *The Brewmaster's Table* he combines a large range of beers with suitable recipes. Oliver enjoys the good life and is a real foodie. Trained as both a chef and a brewmaster he is very well placed to pair each beer with a dish that fits it to a tee.

Closer to home we also see attempts to give beer a place in quality dining. And why not? Our Belgian cuisine is one of the best in the world. 'French cuisine with German quantities', is how visitors from abroad express it. Yannick Boes, formerly Managing Director of the Alken brewery, published a book in the 1990s: *Bier als drank bij gastronomische gerechten* (*Beer as a drink with gastronomic dishes*), in collaboration with the Herk-de-Stad hotel school. Wine gurus Herwig Van Hove (*Bier & Bord – Beer & Plate*) and Frank Van der Auwera (*Hop in het bord – Hop on your plate*) also gave their backing to this beer project. Each year, the Biergenootschap der Lage Landen – Beer Society of the Low Countries (Belgium and the Netherlands) awards the title of 'Beer & Gastronomy Ambassador' to a promoter of beer and gastronomy. And a few years ago, the 'hoppas' were born. Hoppas are tapas made with Belgian regional products, served with Belgian beer. Their name has now been changed to 'bapas'. The 'bapas' books written by Sven Gatz and Karl Van Malderen contain a number of recipes with beers to suit.

Scientific

Despite ferocious efforts by a number of pioneers, our chefs are not yet sufficiently familiar with beer & food pairing. Neither is the general population. This is why brewers are having their beers analysed. They want to find the best pairings based on this scientific analysis. 'Sense for taste' is a great initiative. Results are represented in the form of a food pairing tree. Beer is shown with all its possible combinations. The beer or product selected is in the centre, surrounded by the ingredients that suit it best. The closer to the centre, the stronger the pairing.

http://www.sensefortaste.com/

Julie Herz of the US Brewers Association uses, as her starting point, the 'Beer Characteristics Chart' and 'Pairing Interactions' where the most important elements are:

1. *Complement*
   When specific elements in food and drink complement one another.
2. *Counter/Contrast*
   When specific elements reinforce or neutralise one another. The sweetness of malt tones down the sweet touch of certain dishes.
3. *Cut*
   Touches of hop bitter and a high carbon dioxide content will cut through the 'fatty' character of some foodstuffs (beer and cheese, for example) and cleanse the palate. Under certain conditions, sour also offers this quality.
4. *Home run*
   The whole is better than the sum of the individual parts; forget about mathematics. $1 + 1 = 3$. The perfect pairing.
5. *Train wreck*
   A disaster, the flavours are clashing and fighting one another. Just think of toothpaste and orange juice. $1 + 1 = -1$. Definitely one to avoid.
6. *Rest*
   A place of rest. A neutral combination with beer to restore the palate. The Trou Normand (sorbet) in the middle of the meal performs the same function.
7. *Bridge*
   When there is a meeting of taste after taste, beer provides the hook or the link. The road to harmony and perfection.
8. *Echo*
   When the taste sensations succeed and repeat one another.
9. *Harmony*
   When all the elements are in synergy.

On the home front

A scientific approach such as this is valuable as it brings new, often surprising insights. Granted, this type of formula doesn't always work when all you want is a good glass of beer with your everyday meal. But why throw the baby out with the bathwater? Below are ten useful tips:

1. Choose your food before choosing the beer.
2. Intensity: Beer and dish have to have an equally strong taste. A light beer with a light dish, a more complex beer with a dish that is stronger in taste.
3. Aim for a balance between sour, sweet and bitter, both in the food and the beer. Repeat the flavours of the dish by serving a beer with a similar taste profile and reinforce the taste. Or else you could go for contrast, sweet versus sour. Use bitter, carbon dioxide and sour to cleanse your palate. Always make sure that the whole is larger than the sum of the parts.
4. In case of doubt, play safe. Fall back on the classics such as a dark beer with a beef stew or a gueuze with fish.
5. As well as the ingredients, the preparation method (baking, grilling, stewing, boiling, etc.) affects the choice of beer.
6. The sauce and complements also influence the beer choice. Add a dried tomato and the dish will taste different, requiring a different beer.
7. Bear the seasons in mind. A light dish and a light beer are ideal for summer. In winter, a robust game dish and a heavier beer are more likely to hit the spot.
8. Within a menu, we recommend you serve beers in this order:
   sparse before creamy;
   uncomplicated tastes before complex ones;
   thin before robust;
   light before high alcohol content.
9. Avoid a cold shower: in other words, don't serve the beers too chilled.
10. And the most important rule of all: enjoy.

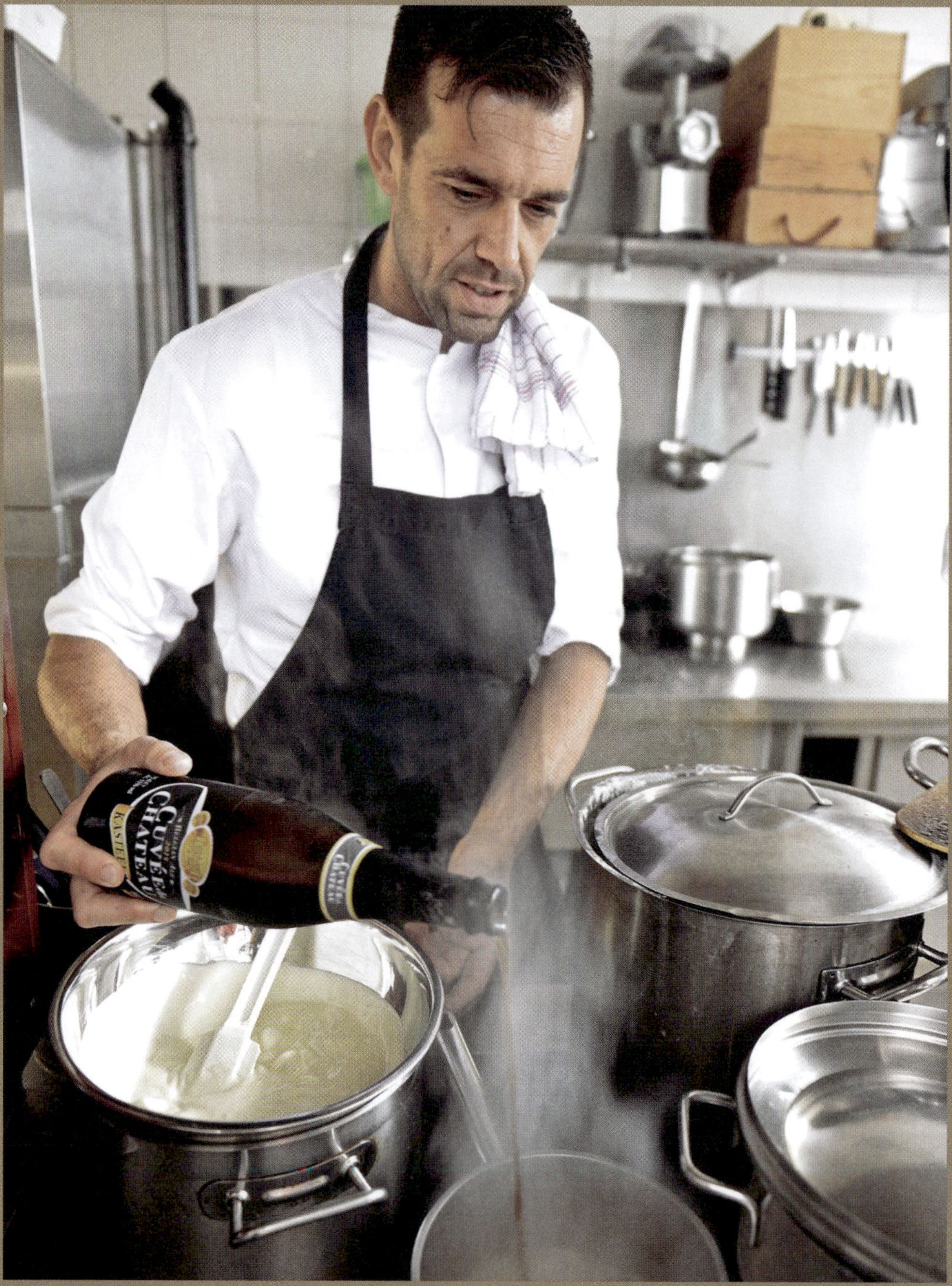
CUVÉE
CHATEAU

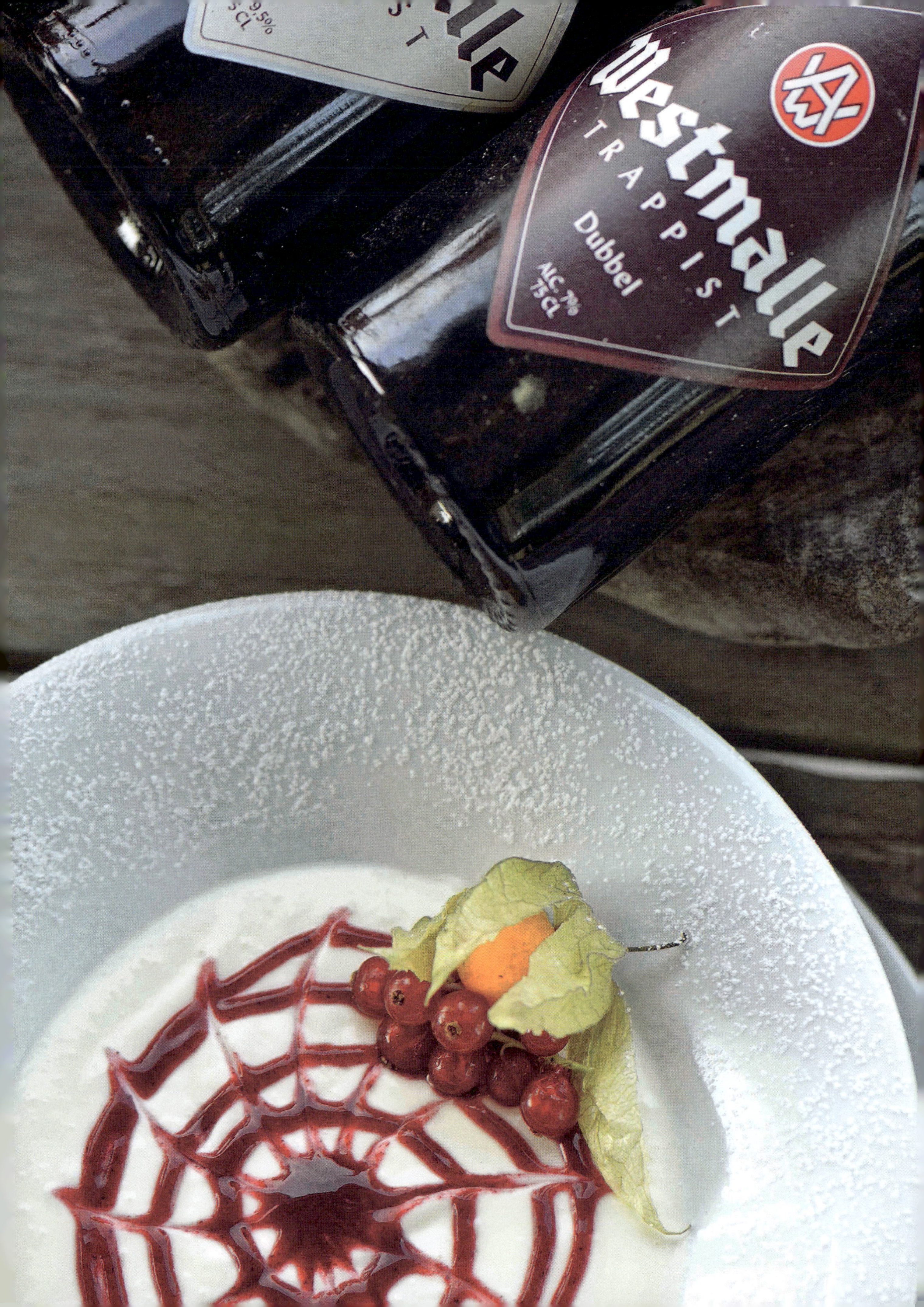
Westmalle
TRAPPIST
Dubbel
ALC. 7%
75 CL

Brewing is cooking

Hildegard Van Ostaden is the chef at beer restaurant De Hoppeschuur in Knesselare where she serves twelve beers, brewed in-house, that you cannot taste anywhere else. Hildegard is a qualified brewing engineer and divides her time between brewing and cooking. "I don't view these two as separate," she tells us. "At the end of the day, it is about developing and combining flavours. Now that I am only serving my own beers I own the whole process. Beer is a versatile product and offers a huge range of possibilities when it comes to taste. We are now seeing an explosion of creativity, with the hoppy IPAs (India Pale Ale), Russian Imperial Stout, sour beers with wild fermentation, and so on." At De Hoppeschuur you can choose from tapped beers that include triple, spelt beer, coffee beer, wood-matured beer and gueuze. During the summer months you will find Hefeweizen white beer inspired by Germany. Dark beers are served during the winter months. Hildegard uses beer as a starting point and creates a lovely recipe to suit. There is a rib-eye of Duroc pork with a robust beer on the side. Or a salmon trout paired with a spelt beer containing citrusy touches. "My beers are quite dry", Hildegard states. "If you want a sweet beer, you might be better off going elsewhere." She does not shy away from experimenting. For Sergio Herman, chef of The Jane, a star-awarded restaurant in Antwerp, she is brewing a buckthorn beer. The chef uses this very acidic berry in a coulis or vinaigrette. The beer is fermenting in wooden barrels previously used for lambic. The buckthorn merges with the lactic acid that resides in the barrels. At De Hoppeschuur, beer is an integral part of everything they do. Hildegard is using her beer in the production of beer vinegar and vinaigrettes. "You will also find the ingredients of the beer in the gin, whisky, vermouth and liqueur that we offer here," her husband Bas explains. "This story really appeals to people." Each dish is accompanied by a beer tip. "We aim for complementary aromas and tastes or else we are seeking contrast," Hildegard explains. "Although some pairings may be far-fetched, when you combine the two, the result is usually a pleasant surprise."

Hildegard and Bas are experienced guides, well qualified to take their guests on a culinary journey of discovery. Hildegard: "We are taking time to build up the menu, without forcing it." The main focus is on enjoying textures, colours, aromas and tastes. It turns out that cooking and brewing is all about building bridges.

www.hoppeschuur.be

Beer tastings

Gather several chefs and brewers around a table, give them a few beers to taste and before long, the discussion heats up. Jean-Baptiste and Christophe Thomaes of Le Château du Mylord, a restaurant awarded with two Michelin stars, and sommelier Bart Lamon also of Le Château du Mylord, hosted a beer tasting and invited some of their colleagues. The invitation was accepted by Eric Martin from Lemonnier in Lavaux Ste-Anne, Laurent Martin from La Frairie in Perwez and Eric Fernez from the two-star-winning Eugénie à Emilie, brasserie Le Faitout and café La Marelle in Baudour. Three brewers also followed suit: Marc Lemay from Brasserie Dubuisson and Charles and Bruno Delroisse from La Frasnoise. Catherine and Antoine Malingret of Ca Brasse Pour Moi in Boussu own a beer shop but they have plans to start up their own brewing operation. Muriel Lombard and Marjorie Elich speak for women with their La Bière des Femmes. The gathering was completed by Edmée Hooghe, a fruit farmer who supplies to Christophe Thomaes, amongst others. She has caused a revival of ancient fruit varieties in her splendid garden just around the corner from Le Château du Mylord. So many people, so many opinions. The company is unanimous on certain points but disagrees on others. Chef Jean-Baptiste Thomaes finds that beer quality has come along in leaps and bounds in recent years. Quite a few beers now deserve their place in gastronomy. With beer, you get a surprising range of new aromas and tastes. Also, there is now a wider range of techniques allowing chefs to work beer into a recipe, gels for example.

Enjoyment at the table

At the table, most chefs prefer heavier beers with a degree of complexity. They prefer these beers to be served in small glasses. All chefs agree that, when designing a beer menu, the lighter beers should come first and the more outspoken ones, that pack more of a punch, should be kept till last. If an IPA or a heavy stout is served at the start of a meal, the taste of these dominantly bitter beers will stay with you throughout the meal. Bart Lamon, sommelier at Le Château du Mylord, feels that beer can accompany every course of a gastronomic menu. However, the chefs are not won over straight away. They also feel that their average customer is not ready for this. Chef Jean-Baptiste Thomaes likes to serve beer and wine and lets it depend on what is better suited to the

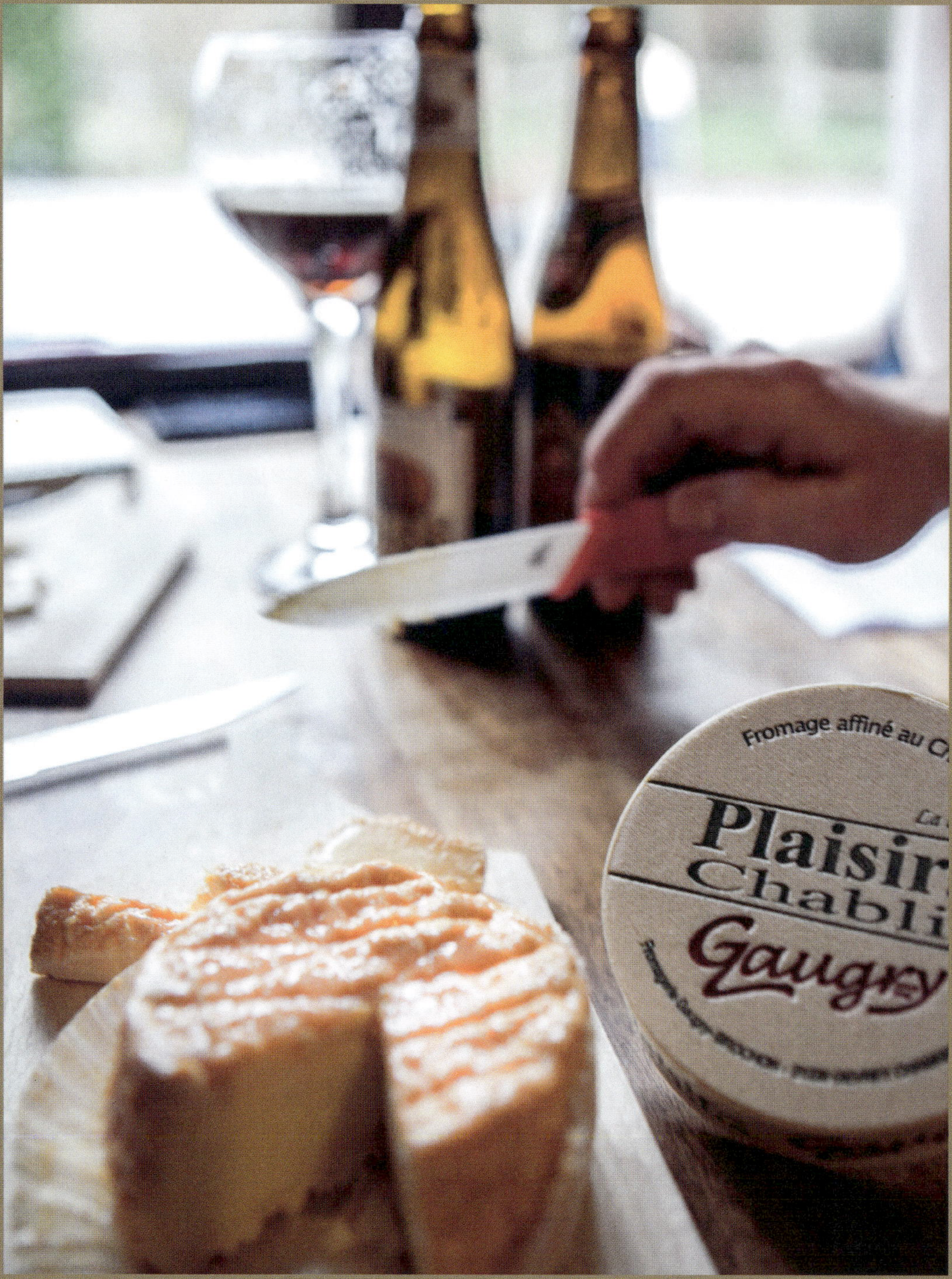
Fromage affiné au
Gaugry

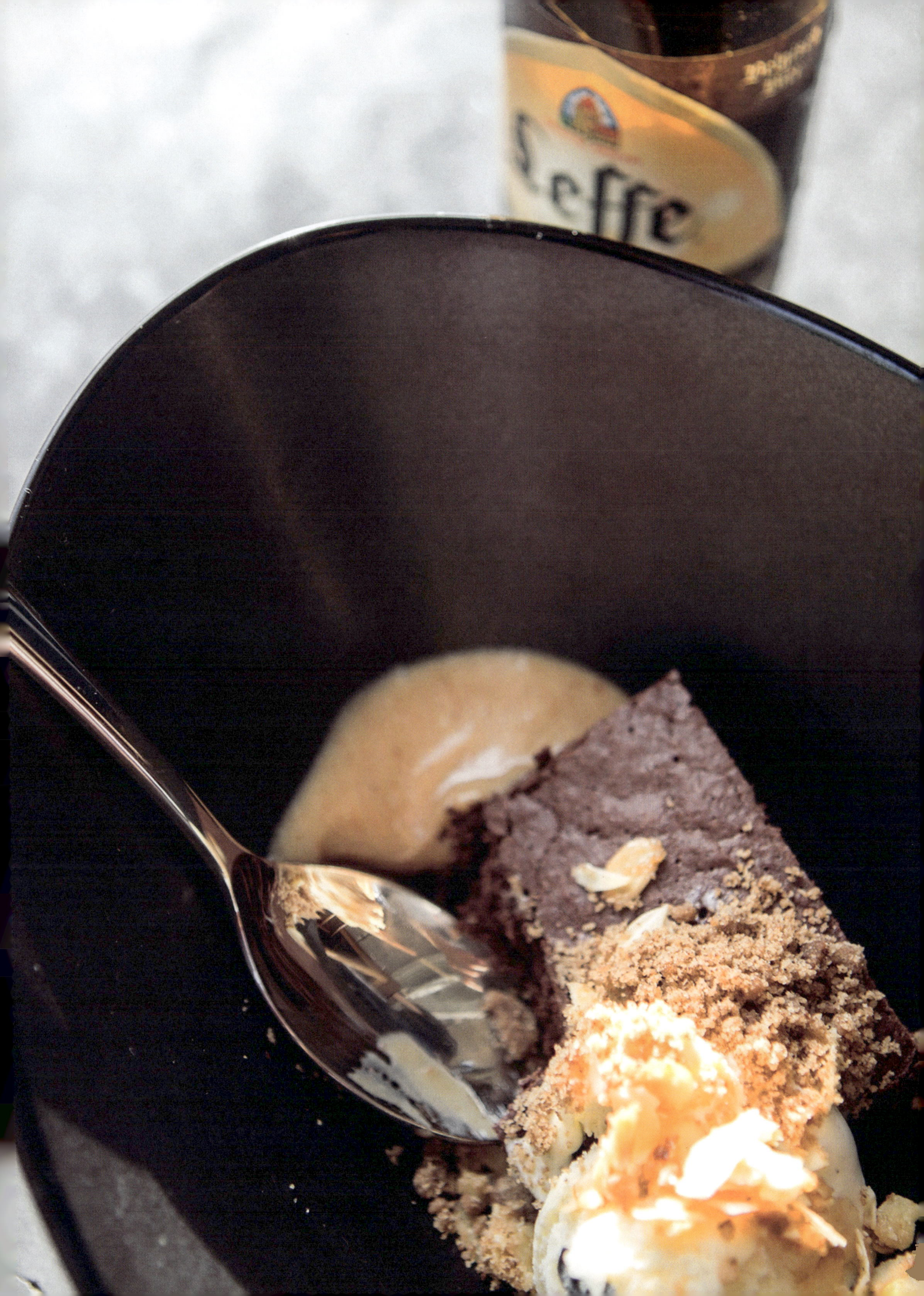
Leffe

meal. "It's all about enjoying yourself when you go out to dinner," Marc Lemay, the brewer, states. "You can do that with beer as well as wine." According to his colleague Bruno Delroisse you have to surprise your guests and introduce them to new aromas and tastes. But your guests need to be guided by professionals to make the best choice. In response to this statement, Marjorie Elich feels that the hotel, restaurant and café trade in general is lacking in beer knowledge. Education and training has a primary focus on wine. Here lies a task for brewers. They can play an important role by organising guided tours where they can tell the story of their brewery and beers. And so, 'the man in the street' can discover the amount of professional know-how hidden in his glass.

To boldly go where no man has gone before

The chefs feel that not every beer is suited to gastronomy. Lighter 'session beers' are generally not to their taste. Also, we discover that some beers can accompany entirely different dishes. Pair a dry 'saison' with an oily fish like mackerel, or serve it with an apple pie for a great contrast with the sweet flavour of the pie. A zesty blonde Lupulus brewed by Les 3 Fourquets makes a great pairing with sweetbreads or it can be served with white meat enhanced by thyme and rosemary. Flemish red-brown beers, the Reninge Oud Bruin from Seizoensbrouwerij Vandewalle for example, go very well with blood sausage and foie gras. The sour flavours cut through the greasy meat. Some degustation beers are just born for gastronomy. The wood-matured Bush De Charmes from Dubuisson makes for an excellent companion to raw fish recipes, steamed couscous or else cheeses made from goat's or sheep's milk. Also try it with a dessert made with peach, raspberry or chocolate. The Extase from Dochter van de Korenaar, a Double IPA with a blend of no fewer than fourteen hop varieties, concludes our tasting. This beer has overpowering aromas and will bowl over the average Belgian beer lover who, after all, is not used to extreme beers such as this. The chefs are confident this beer has plenty of gastronomic potential. They recommend it in pairing with a very mature cheese. Or else with a sweet dessert made with fruits...? "The occasion determines the beer," Marc Lemay concludes. "Meet friends at the bar and you will choose a pils. When you want to enjoy fine dining you are after a little more depth and want to discover a bit more. But when all is said and done, people will decide for themselves what suits them best at that particular moment or what they feel like drinking at that time." The message couldn't be clearer: take pleasure where you find it. Discover. And, most of all... enjoy!

A concentration of flavours

We are meeting at 't Zilte restaurant. It boasts two Michelin stars and towers over Antwerp. We are tasting beers in the company of chef Viki Geunes and Aaron Moeraert, his sommelier; Mieke Dockx of Antwerp restaurant Marie; Piet Vannieuwenhuyse who used to manage the Brasserie Dock's Café in Antwerp; Thomas Debelder from the 3 Fonteinen restaurant in Beersel (the restaurant associated with the lambic brewery that bears the same name) and Cas Goossens and Hans Lachi, both from De Rooden Hoed in Antwerp. This particular tasting shows us that some beers can almost literally blow you away. Also, we learn that there is only a very fine line between some beers and a sherry. Viki Geunes helped to develop both the Rodenbach Caractère Rouge and Vintage and created the Arthur's Legacy by Viki, brewed by the De Hoorn microbrewery. We are talking about a zesty triple based on a Cornet. Does Viki agree with the majority of his colleagues, who feel that beer has to be powerful both in the kitchen and at the table? Viki: "Yes, I do. The trend is towards a lighter and more delicate kitchen which prompts us to seek out concentrated tastes. Alcohol can play its part in this development." We are enjoying a tasting of the blonde Strandgaper made by the Scheldebrouwerij. This blonde is amazingly complex with a sweet aroma, rounded flavours and a refreshingly bitter finish. It makes a beautiful pairing with shrimps and potatoes in a sour cream dressing or, with any type of seafood, according to the chefs.

Hype into vision

The Tuverbol was created in 2007 but has stood the test of time. It blends a blonde top-fermented beer from the Loterbol brewery with a lambic made by 3 Fonteinen. This lambic has spontaneously re-fermented in the bottle and is unfiltered. You can taste the refreshingly sour and fruity aromas from the lambic with a higher dosage of malt. The finish of the Tuverbol veers between tart, bitter and sour. "A hare that has been hanged and re-buried", is Viki's description of this particular brew. The panel detects aromas of rhubarb, orange peel and apple blossom with a touch of honey and impressions of sherry. Aaron, the sommelier, feels this beer is close to 'orange wines'. The culinary experts are now discussing aromas of mushrooms, green olives and poultry. We are aware that the taste of lambic beers quite often deepens with age. And consequently, the verdict on the young Vicaris triple gueuze is that it is a bit on the light side. The Hopsinjoor, made by Het Anker,

Chef Viki Geunes (left) and Cas Goossens (right) are swirling, smelling and tasting at the degustation in 't Zilte restaurant in Antwerp.

is heavily hopped to Belgian taste, even though the aromas of the European hops never jump out. The chefs are not keen on heavily hyped beer experiments. Their advice is not to search too far. Learn from the great classics like Orval. These beers have survived many years. The Achel Blond is a fine example. This Trappist gives aromas of banana, pear syrup and even a whiff of cognac. We close our eyes and an ancient vision appears. We see and smell a range of poultry with silverskin onions and lardons in a chasseur sauce, or caramelised endives.

Enjoyment at the table

The Millevertus brewery likes to go off the beaten track now and again. The peppery aroma of La Poivrote will surprise you. This beer also comes with sweet touches that especially stand out at the start and the finish. This blonde is perfect for use as a hare marinade. La Fumette, an amber beer with smoky tones, evokes the aromas of smoked ham and bacon from the Ardennes. Makes an ideal pairing with autumnal dishes containing dried morels and mushrooms. The slightly bitter MacVertus occupies the middle ground between a scotch and a stout. The chefs' pairing suggestions include a sweet tagine, a Pastilla or a dish made with tripe accompanied by an apple puree. Dochter van de Korenaar's Enfant Terrible, made with spontaneous fermentation using wild yeasts (Brettanomyces)

was not very popular with the chefs as the yeast smell was felt to be overpowering. The chefs also judged that this beer was lacking in complexity. The Rodenbach Vin de Céréales was far better received. This is a Flemish red-brown beer that has spent three years maturing in a single foeder. Sherry territory is not far away. Viki Geunes uses this beer as an ingredient for a sorbet and recommends a pairing with a mature cheddar or Comté — with salt crystals — to create a splendid contrast between sour and salt. This one also makes a perfect pairing with a tartare of raw langoustines.

We conclude our tasting with a beautifully complex old gueuze from Girardin. This is the perfect accompaniment with a hard cheese or a young, slightly sour goat's cheese. So, does beer have a place in gastronomy? "Yes, definitely, but don't forget the ritual at the table," Cas Goossens recommends. "We always use elegant wine glasses to serve beer. It is part of the experience." Piet feels that both beer and wine have a place at the table. It is not an 'either/or' story, rather one of 'and/and'. The carbon dioxide content in the beer makes it refreshing. Beer makes for an ideal aperitif and can also provide a lovely finish to a meal. Beer is also a great thirstquencher, a quality that can be appreciated in its own right and should not be disregarded. Mieke highlights the convivial atmosphere that naturally comes when beer is consumed. Finally, beer is relatively low-priced — totting up a few more points in its favour. The world-class beers of Belgium are really quite affordable.

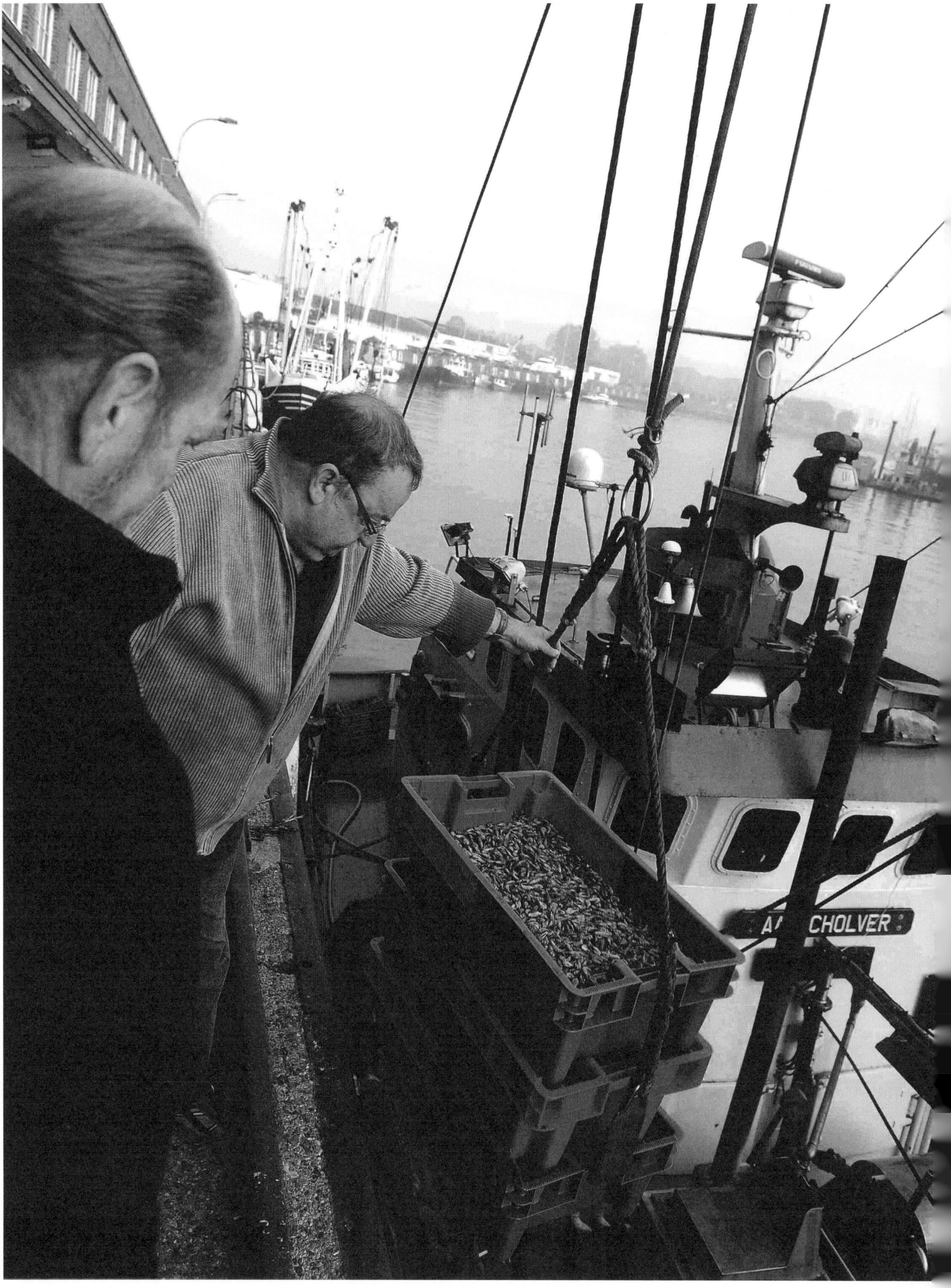
CHOLVER

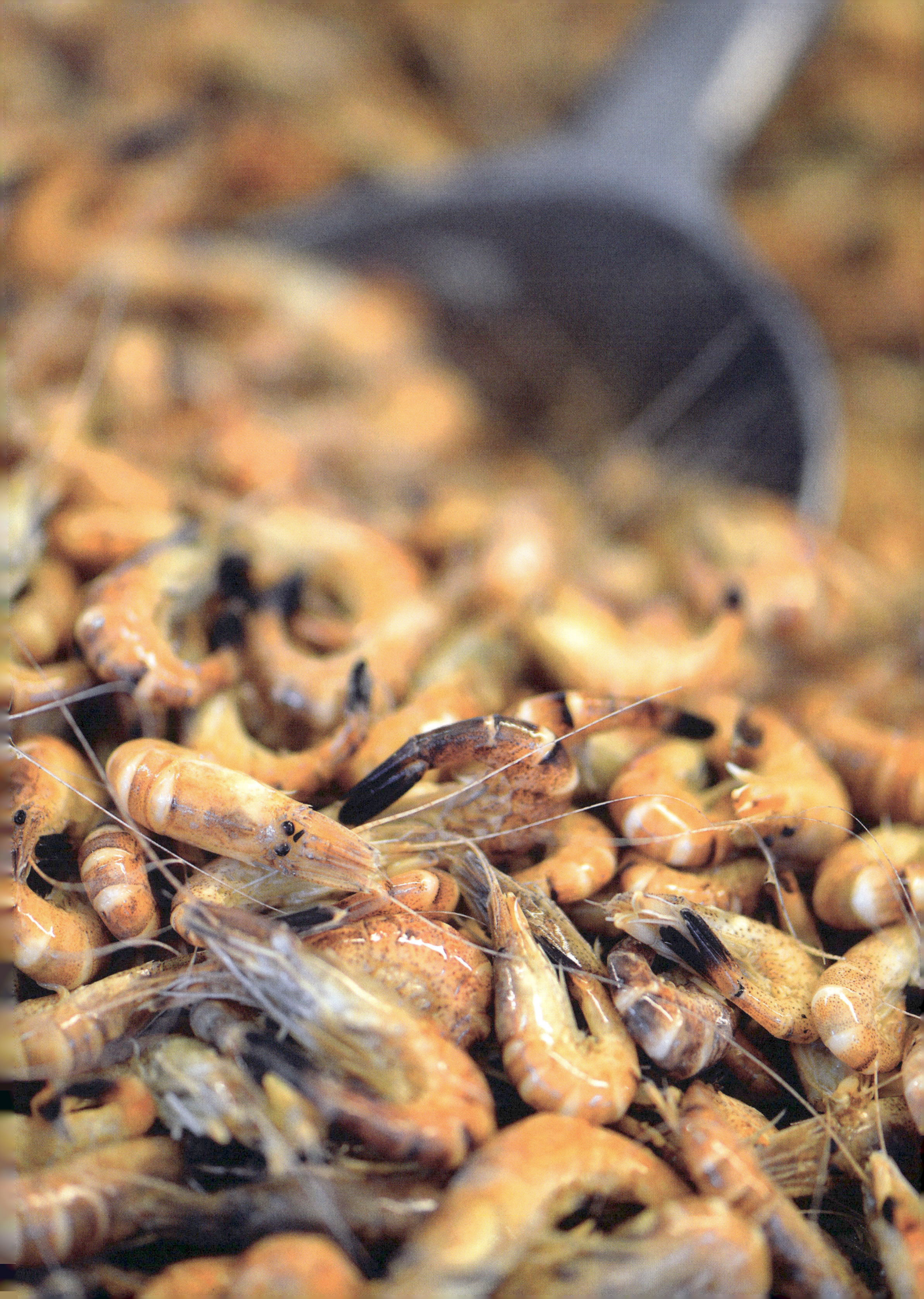

BEER WITH FISH, CRUSTACEANS AND SEAFOOD

A Rodenbach enjoyed with grey shrimps from the Belgian coast, mussels with white beer, fried sole with a triple, 'maatjes' herring with a glass of pils, oysters with an ink-black stout or the quintessentially English fish and chips with a pale ale... all of these are great pairings based in popular cuisine. However, beer also forms a great combination with gastronomic recipes using turbot, brill or lemon sole. People used to adhere to the rule that 'blond beers go with white fish'. But, in our search for the ultimate taste experience, we have found many more possible combinations.

Carpaccio of fish

A Flemish red-brown beer fits a carpaccio of salmon to a tee. The slightly sour touches from the beer form a harmonious combination with the acidic touch of lemon. The malty and sweet touches from the beer provide a great interaction with the fish. With a carpaccio of white fish (cod, for example) we will opt for a calming, slightly sour white beer.

Fish terrine

A luscious, creamy fish terrine is begging for a full-mouthed triple. The power of the triple matches that of the terrine. The carbon dioxide and the bitter agents in the beer 'slice through' the oiliness of the dish. Another option is an old gueuze, which works well thanks to the acid in the beer.

Smoked fish

Smoked herring, smoked mackerel... both oily fish with a strong flavour. They are made for an amber 'spéciale belge'. The malts rein in the fish whereas the touches of caramel will embrace it.

Oysters

Our Belgian spontaneously fermented beers love oysters, as do our white beers. 'Oud bruin' and 'oud rood' suit certain varieties particularly well thanks to their sour character. And of course, we should not overlook our brut beers, which can stand a comparison with the best champagnes. Many people enthuse about the pairing of raw oysters with beers of the stout or porter type. The salty taste of oysters forms a great combination with the often savoury, strongly tasted malts contained in a stout or porter. An oyster dish made with different ingredients will suit a variety of beer types.

Grey shrimp

No doubt whatsoever: Rodenbach is the one. The salty/sweet taste of these shrimps is a gift from God to this sour and sweet beer. You could not be more Belgian if you tried.

Fish fried in batter (fish and chips)

A robust beer of the IPA type is perfectly suited to the fried fish, which packs quite a punch. The bitterness from the hops counteracts the grease. But bear in mind the texture of the fish. Popular television chef Jeroen Meus is treating us to a 'salmon burger with a salad of cucumber and salsa verde'. We are pairing it with a Belle-Fleur IPA from Dochter van de Korenaar. The touches of bitter and fruit from the beer perfectly complement the amazing flavours from the salmon burger. The bitterness and carbon dioxide content in the beer flush away the oiliness of the salmon. And, this beer's floral touches make a perfect complement to the piquant sauce.

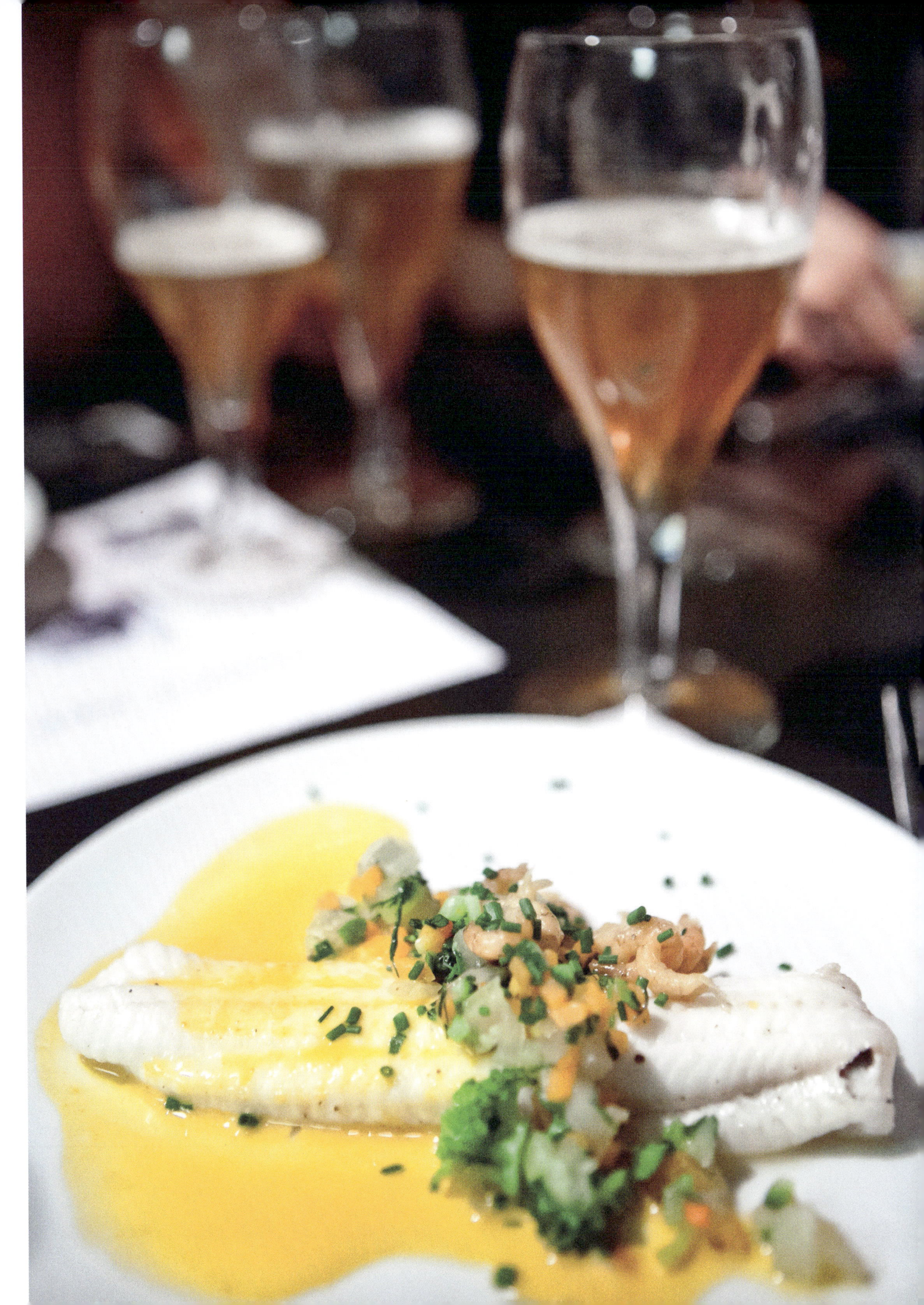

BEER AND BURGERS

By a long way, the hamburger is the most popular sandwich in the world. And mankind's most popular drink is beer. The match between these two is evident. We could upgrade to a Samurai Salmon burger: fillet of wild salmon, Chuka Kuki wakamé, ginger confit, toasted sesame seed and a wasabi mayonnaise. Perfect in combination with a Westmalle Tripel. The complexity of this beer stands up to the rich and varied flavours of this dish. The malty touches of the beer flow into that of the bread roll whereas the hop bitterness emphasises the mild zestiness of the Eastern ingredients. Gourmet burgers are 'hot' right now. We are giving the Royal Fred a go: made with melted Emmentaler and blue-veined cheese, stewed apple with paprika, a salad of rucola and a sweet honey dressing. On the side, a strong Bush Ambrée made by Dubuisson. Both burger and beer have an intense flavour, they reinforce one another and provide the necessary complement.

7 • BEER KITCHEN AND FOOD PAIRING

BEER AND GAME

Nowadays, anyone is 'game' for a degustation beer. Even in star-awarded restaurants like Le Château du Mylord, gastronomic recipes are increasingly paired with high-quality beers. Game dishes and beer form a superb combination. But which beers are best for serving with game recipes? Take your cue from the seasons and the answer is obvious. When the sun is high in the sky and the temperature is high, light, quaffable beers and thirst-quenchers are the answer. These go very well with dishes served in a summery setting: salads and light meals. In autumn and winter we abandon our taste for lighter flavours. This is the time to wheel out the heavy artillery, triples for example, to run along with the game season. So how can we pair beer with game? Yes, you got it spot-on: autumn, game, triple: the tried and trusted marriage. This stands to reason. Autumn is when the leaves are falling from the trees. On the humid soil, they are producing a layer of humus, which you can smell particularly well in the forest. These earthy aromas are found in forest-reared game and in tripels. Doubles and quadruples also make a perfect pairing with rich game dishes. Their sweet, powerful tastes and occasionally high alcohol percentages pack a punch and stand up to the overpowering aromas and complex flavours of the game recipes.

And now let's talk about wood-matured beers. These are complex, often refreshingly acidic and well capable of standing up to any game dish. Here we could even draw a parallel with the combination of game and Burgundy wines. The Rodenbach Grand Cru, Bourgogne des Flanders or a Liefmans Goudenband spring to mind... As an exception to the rule, several fruit beers are also suitable to pair with game. How about an 'oude kriek' with a paté of wild boar of a fillet of duck breast?

Pairings

Below are some pairings that are close to our heart and are guaranteed to make you drool:

Partridge

Its meat veers between pink and pale yellow-brown and has quite a dry taste. We recommend that you lard this meat, in other words, lace it with fat, to make it juicier. A robust triple or a full blonde beer make for an excellent pairing.

Pheasant

The delicate, aromatic flavour of wild pheasant is perfectly suited to zesty and fruity blond beers or triples. Enjoy a saison with a roast pheasant with sauerkraut.

Wild boar

Wild boar is an ancestor to the pig. Its meat is denser and leaner than pork. The meat of a young boar is tenderer and less pronounced in taste compared to that of a more mature animal. The meat is darker in colour and covered with a thin layer of fat. Boar is consumed slightly rosé, or pink. Delicious with herbs such as thyme or rosemary and in combination with sweet flavours, confit of onions or apple and cranberry for example. Perfect vegetable accompaniments include celeriac, endives, red or white cabbage. Generally, powerful brown beers with a sweet touch do very well in the company of wild boar. A great suggestion: a ragout of wild boar with winter vegetables accompanied by a Rochefort 8.

Roebuck and doe

This classic venison gives beautiful cuts of meat: chops, fillet and steak. The remainders are used to make a ragout. Meat from fawns and does tends to have a more delicate taste and structure than that of a roebuck. You will therefore opt for a more refined beer type, a Rodenbach Grand Cru or Liefmans Goudenband for example. To accompany a roebuck with its stronger taste, we prefer a powerful brown beer.

Roe deer

The meat has a very delicate and less pronounced gamey taste. Roe deer meat is eaten red to pink (rosé). Winter vegetables such as turnip, carrots, celeriac, green cabbage and Brussels sprouts go very well with this delicate meat. A beautifully fruity and yeasty triple rounds it off to perfection.

Charcuterie

Autumn cuisine would not be complete without a game paté. A unctuous boar paté with a salad of endives makes a lovely pairing with an Orval. The bitter and sour touches from the Orval cleanse the mouth and the hop bitterness from the beer provides a hook with the bitter endives. An old 'kriek' also performs very well with a paté.
A smoked fillet of boar goes very well with a zesty blonde beer in the vein of Brugse Zot or Goliath blond.

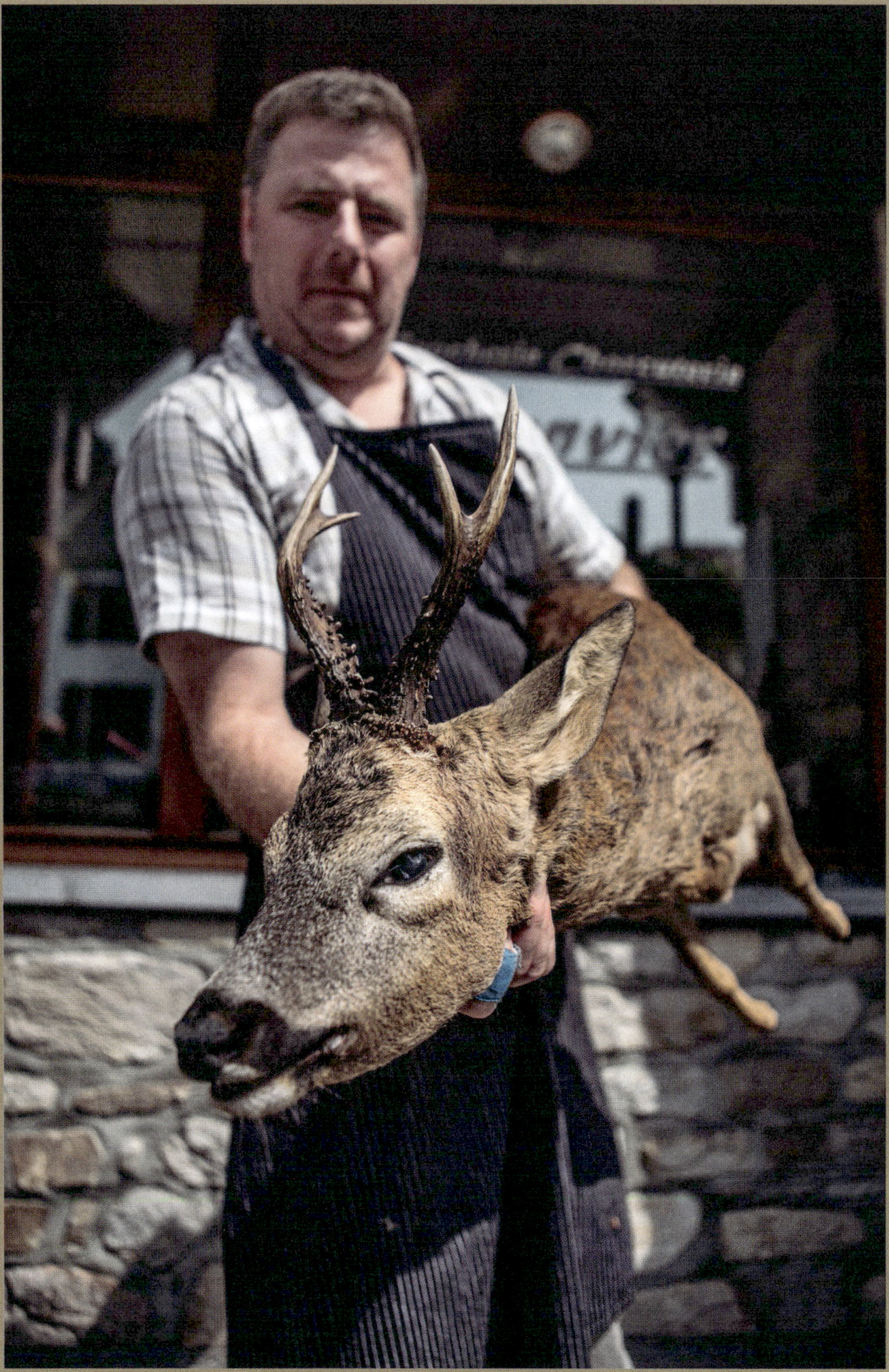

Ardenne Saison
Bière Sauvage

BEER AND CHOCOLATE

The Belgian Connection

'Heureux chocolat, qui après avoir couru le monde, à travers le sourire des femmes, trouve la mort dans un baiser savoureux et fondant de leur bouche.' (Anthelme Brillat-Savarin).

"Belgium? That's beer and chocolate!" You can hear tourists say this all the time. Even Barack Obama sang the praise of these quintessentially Belgian products. These two wonderfully delicious products travelled thousands of miles and took many centuries to reach Belgium. And then to meet and find one another... beer and chocolate make for a great couple. Beer and chocolate, a successful marriage between partners from far-away regions. A passionate relationship that flourishes to perfection on Belgian soil.

What is chocolate?

The main ingredient of chocolate is the cocoa bean. Its basic shape is that of a rugby ball. As part of the chocolate production process, the beans are crushed, fermented, dried and then toasted or burnt. The producer grinds the beans before pressing them into cocoa butter, cocoa mass or powder. Pure chocolate is a blend of cocoa butter and cocoa mass with added sugars, flavourings (vanilla for example) and thickening agents such as lecithin.

The following ingredients are mixed depending on the desired colour:
Dark chocolate: cocoa mass, cocoa butter, sugar;
Milk chocolate: cocoa mass, cocoa butter, sugar, milk powder;
White chocolate: cocoa butter, sugar, milk powder.

In Belgium there are two chocolate giants responsible for import and production. Callebaut and Belcolade arrange an ideal and stable blend of cocoa beans from different plantations, ensuring consistent quality and flavour. There are at least 800 different types of 'couverture' or luxury chocolates: white chocolate with subtle touches of vanilla, milk chocolate with hints of caramel and/or coffee... With a pure 'fondant' chocolate, bitterness takes centre stage. The quantity of cocoa mass is of prime importance to the taste. A plain chocolate has a very dry and bitter flavour whereas a white chocolate is sweet and cloying. A 'single origin chocolate' is made with chocolate beans originating from one single region or plantation.

Types of chocolate

The mixture is flattened into microscopically small particles. This process gives the chocolate its typically smooth texture. The chocolate is then heated to a temperature of 45 °C when it reaches its most liquid form. The chocolatier then 'tempers' the liquid mass. The chocolate now cools down to 30 °C. Cocoa butter contains several types of crystals that affect the shine, the bite and the fragility of the chocolate. A correctly 'tempered' chocolate hardens (crystallises) in five minutes. As to fillings, the possibilities are endless:

Praliné or nut cream is a Belgian classic. The nuts are ground until they release their oils and a dough is formed. By adding the correct flavourings the chocolatier creates his or her desired praliné.
Ganache or chocolate cream. Cream, chocolate and the chosen flavouring are the basis of this filling. Alcohol is a favourite flavouring. It also serves as a preservation agent. Naturally, beer is getting a look-in here.
Cream pralines or Manons. These are based on fats (butter) and sugar dough. The filling is given the desired taste with a flavouring. *Marzipan* is also often used as an ingredient.

The quotation 'Everything you can imagine is real' (Pablo Picasso) suits the Belgian chocolatiers. They are often launching creations that are bordering on the genius.

'I CAN RESIST EVERYTHING BUT TEMPTATION.'

OSCAR WILDE

Chocolatier Dominique Persoone disguised as a surrealist.

The ultimate seduction

A successful marriage, as it turns out. 'Beer'. This word alone makes many men drool. 'Chocolate' has the same effect on women. Or, at least, so the cliche has it. Beer as well as chocolate are said to be the ultimate seduction, although many foodies are of the opinion that it is difficult to find a pairing between chocolate and fermented alcoholic drinks. However, in a country like Belgium which, after all, is a beer and chocolate heaven, many harmonious combinations can still be found. Thanks to the large variety of tastes and structures, it is possible to pair chocolate with beer or else to use beer to lend flavour to a recipe. In classic gastronomy, traditional 'chocolate beers' like a Chimay Bleue, Rochefort 10 or Gouden Carolus are usually paired with dark chocolate. The roast, bitter, coffee-like touches from the toasted malts form the perfect complement to dark, fondant chocolate. These beers are also suited to chocolate with a dark, bitter filling. Praliné with a powerful flavour of nuts goes well with amber beers of the Spéciale Belge type. These beers have a subtly nutty taste complemented by touches of caramel and malts. Honey beers are the perfect complement to chocolate with a honey filling but nougat also yields fine results. We are in search of harmony. Thanks to its creamy taste, a St Bernardus Tripel goes hand in hand with a buttery truffle. And the sour character of a 'Manon Blueberry' performs a perfect symbiotic dance with a Rodenbach.

We could follow a different path and aim for contrast. Try this same Rodenbach with a 'Coconut'. The praline provides a sweet and exotic touch whereas the Rodenbach adds a subtly sour taste — a classic example where the whole is more than the sum of its parts. Less evident is the combination of 'chocolate and hoppy beers'. However, a Palm Hop Select and an ice praline made with vanilla ice cream give a playful whole. A great IPA suits a milk chocolate. In some cases, the citrusy touches of the IPA are reinforced by the chocolate. Savoury chocolate dishes and beer also make for a successful match. A chicken with a zesty Molle Poblano sauce from Mexico suits a white beer. The refreshing, calming beer tones down the 'hot' sauce. The fullness from the wheat stands up to the intense taste of the chocolate sauce.

Jean Le Chocolatier: "A great beer paired with a delicious chocolate. You won't find anything more Belgian. Two lovely products that reinforce one another or melt in the mouth to make a beautiful whole. A pleasure to work with!"

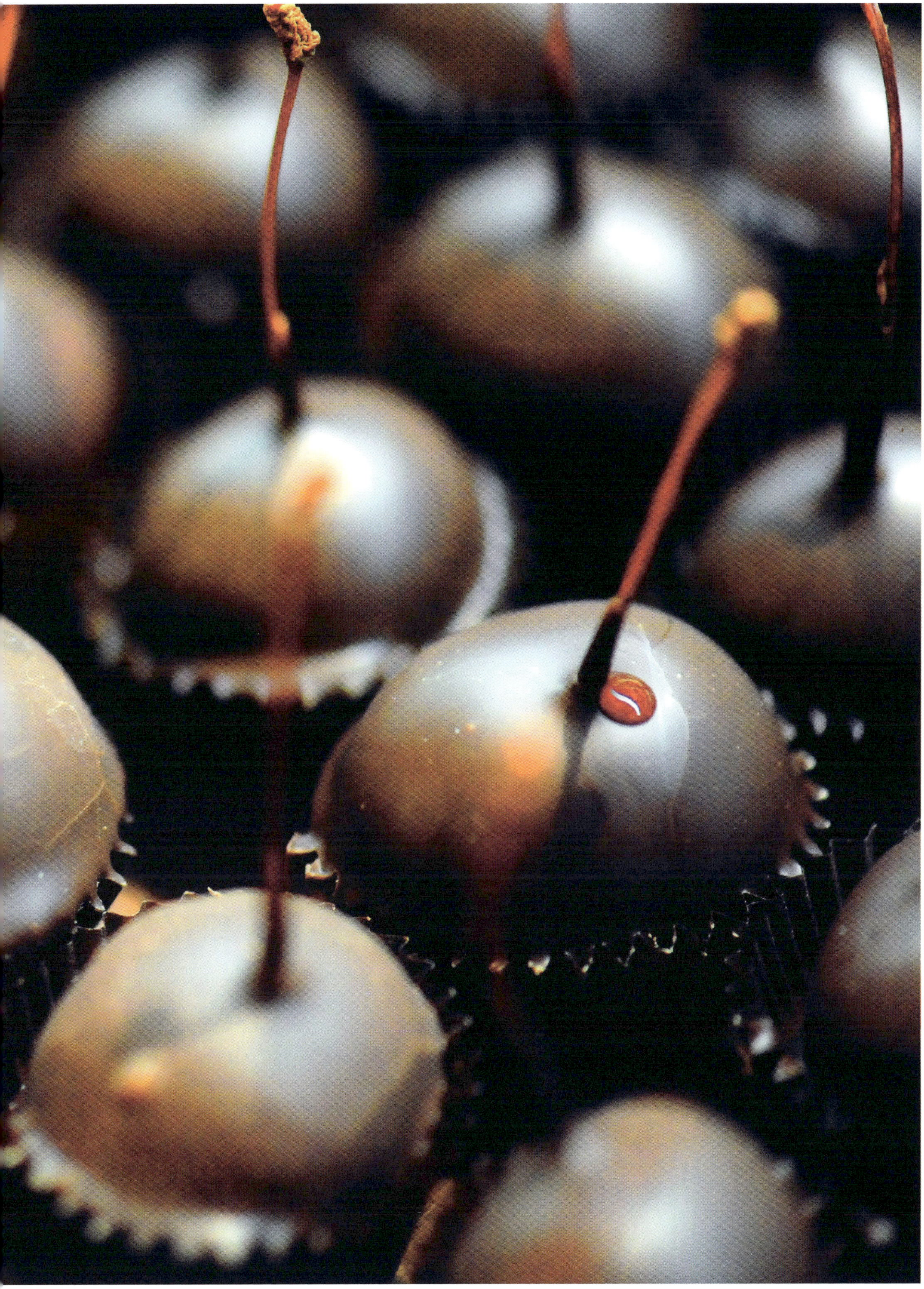

BEER AND CHEESE

Beer and cheese go hand in hand. It is no coincidence that many Belgian abbeys produce beer as well as cheese. A Chimay or a Westmalle is equally delicious in the glass as it is on the plate. The monks are aware that, thanks to its higher alcohol content, the rich taste of their beers makes for a lovely balance with a creamy cheese with a high fat content. The cheese forms a film to cover the taste buds. To free up your taste buds, you need a slightly sour and bitter drink. This can only be beer, as it is drunk in larger mouthfuls and in this way, provokes a unique taste reaction. Chefs have discovered this principle as well. Several restaurants and trendy brasseries are offering their guests a range of cheeses as well as a beer menu to finish off their meal.

Hemelse combinaties

Brie with Oude Kriek
'Plattekaas' (cottage cheese) with Oude Gueuze
Pas de Rouge with Orval
Sable de Wisant with Chimay Bleue
Maroilles with Chimay Rouge
Keiemse witte with Rochefort 10
Pas de Bleu with Achel Extra
Pavé de Soignies with Embrasse

Cheese making and beer brewing are two traditional crafts still practised in abbeys.

A few guidelines

Beer type	Cheese type
White beer	Hard cheese with a slightly sour touch. Avoid strong mature cheeses
Pils	Hard cheese but avoid red or blue-veined cheeses or those with a strong aftertaste
Spéciale Belge	Cheese with a crust, lightly rinsed, a bit stronger in taste
Double	Hard cheese, possibly blue-veined cheese
Triple	Hard cheese, quite mature
Strong blonde	Hard cheese, quite mature
Strong bitter	Blue veined
Gueuzes & lambics	'Plattekaas' (cottage cheese)

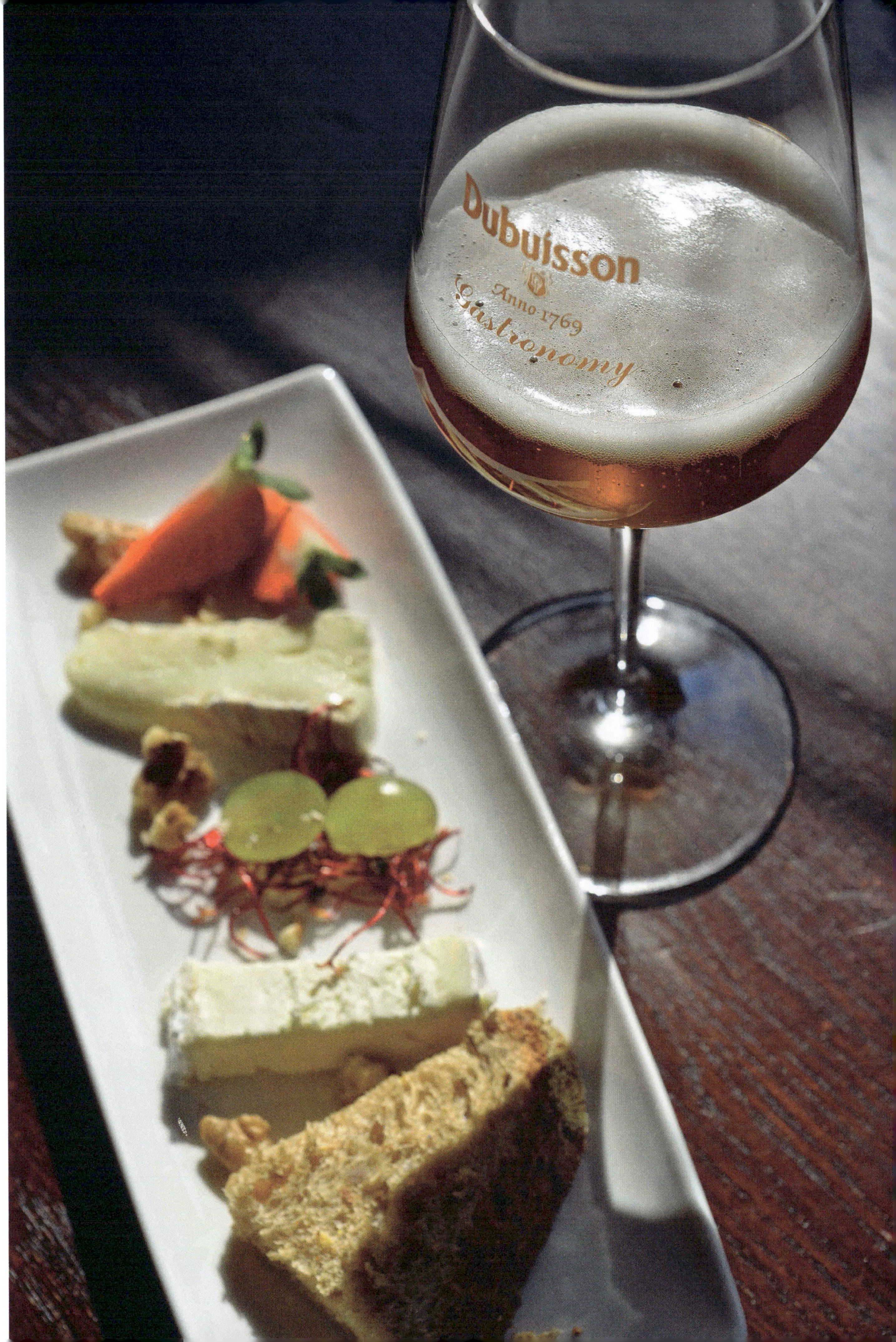
Dubuisson
Anno 1769
Gastronomy

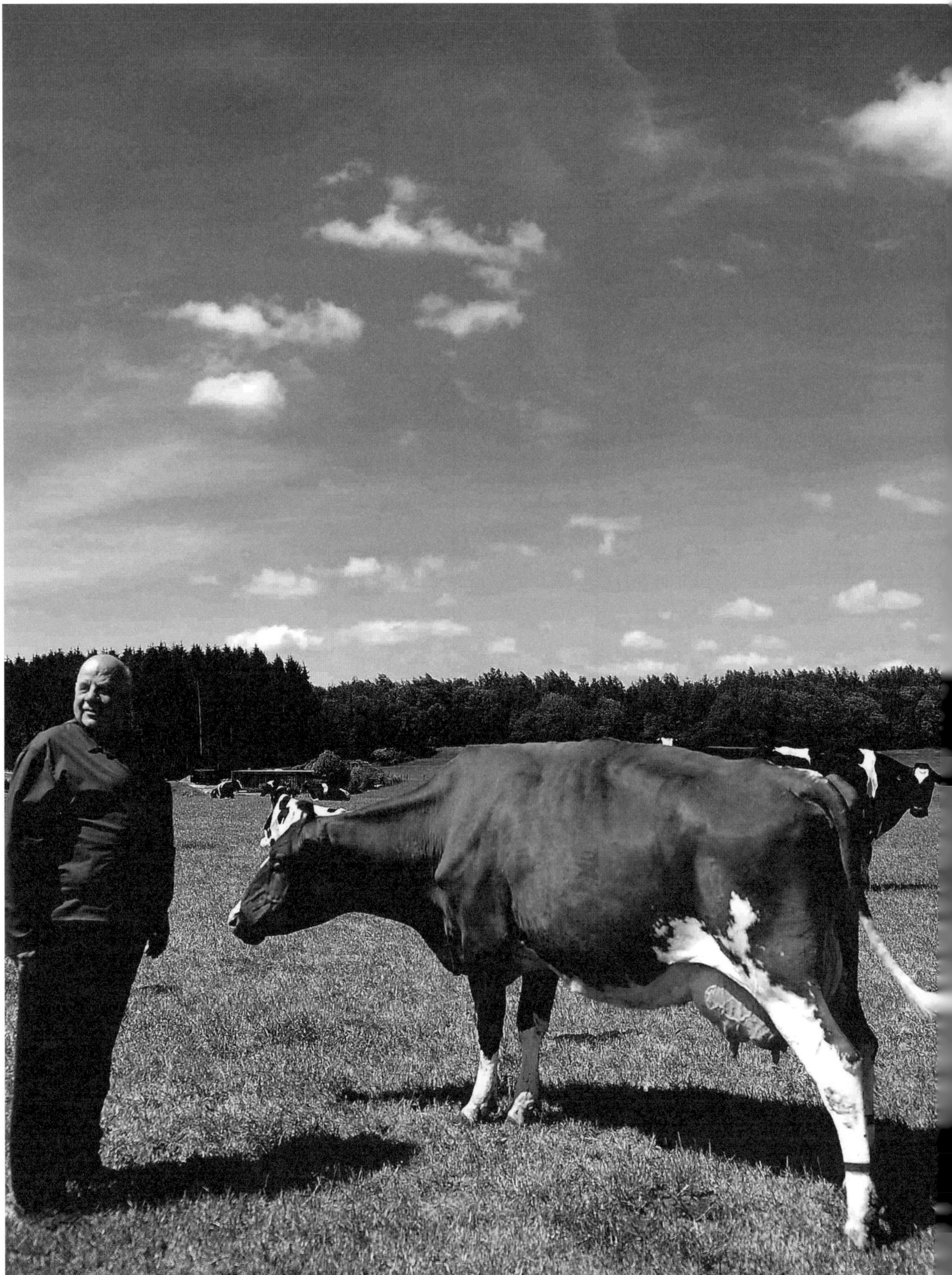

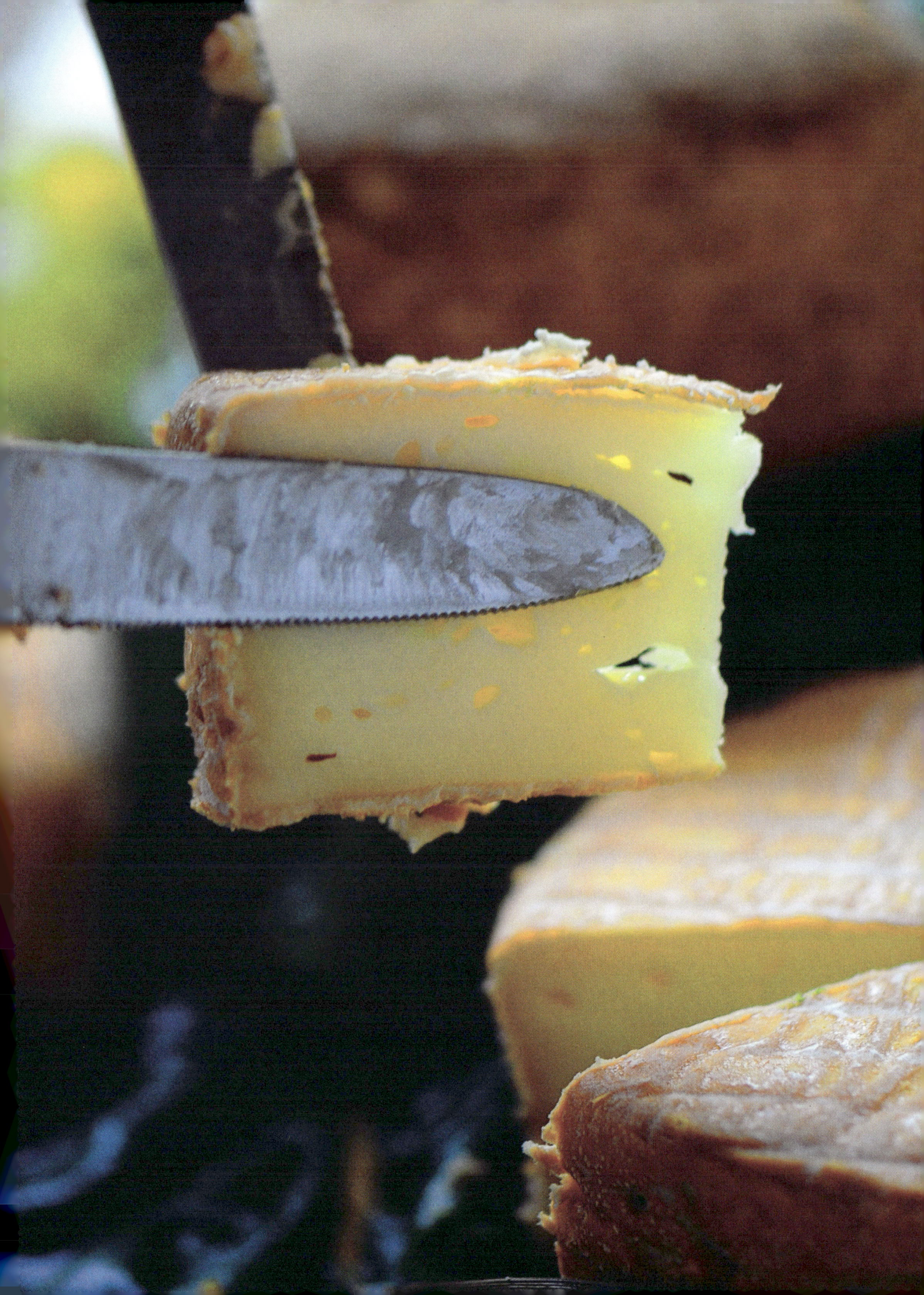

Beer with cheese

In the culinary world, the marriage between cheese and red wine appears to be signed, sealed and delivered. We always hear that they form a 'perfect partnership'. However, appearances may deceive. Red wine has a tannin content that is too high. In combination with tannins, cheese produces a tart feeling in the mouth. A successful pairing allows space to each of the partners. As we all know, one plus one has to add up to more than two, certainly not less. This is why the French prefer to pair their cheese with white wines. This is a great idea: the fresh acids make a far better combination with the greasy cheese. We can be grateful – or perhaps not - to our Southern neighbours and their unbridled chauvinism for the popular 'cheese and wine' evenings. These were held under the banner of 'the best cuisine in the world with the best wines in the world'. And 'les petits Belges' took this as gospel without ever doubting it. We even forgot about our own cheese and beer heritage. Fortunately the tide is now turning and we are increasingly pairing cheese with beer. Thanks to the initiative of a number of top chefs and also the book *Kaas & bier: 50 speelse bier & kaas combinaties met Vinken en Van Tricht* (*Cheese & beer: 50 playful beer & cheese combinations with Vinken en Van Tricht*) the Belgians, when serving cheese, are now serving it with beer. This is not a complete novelty. It has been done before. The venerable English 'Ploughman's lunch' – beer, bread and cheese – used to be popular in our regions as well. Drinking water was polluted, coffee and tea had not yet made inroads and the common man was unable to afford wine and meat. All that remained were bread, cheese and beer. It was no coincidence that many abbeys produced these. Maredsous, Orval and Chimay taste as good in the glass as they do on the plate. The monks knew that the rich taste of the beer provided a fine contrast with the creamy cheese with a high fat content. However, this pairing was also popular away from the abbey. De Vierhoekhoeve in Gijzenzele near Ghent provides a great example.

Beer cheese

De Vierhoekhoeve farm has been owned by the De Sutter family for many years. Its name, Vierhoekhoeve or 'four-cornered farm' is a reference to the four elements of life: water, wind, sun and earth, all essential for humans, animals and plants. In 2006 the family set up a farm shop called 'Bella Boe' and an on-site cheese dairy was founded in the same year. One year later, they idea of creating their own beer cheese took hold after a visit to the Huyghe brewery in nearby Melle. Cheese making is traditional but, at the same time, quite simple, in theory at least. The rule of thumb: for a good cheese, you need a good milk. The cheese maker chooses between cattle, goats and sheep and considers the breed, the food they need and the season. De Vierhoekhoeve only uses raw cow's milk. The cows here are fed with bostel from the Huyghe brewery.

Rennet and souring agents are added to the milk. The souring agent helps the milk to congeal, ensures it keeps for longer and also improves the taste. The rennet is often derived from a calf's stomach, the abomasum in particular. The rennet ensures that the solid components from the milk – fat and proteins – congeal to form a gelatinous mass: the curds. The curds are stirred or chopped into small bits to separate the solid components from the liquids, also called the whey. The point in time (temperature) when the curds are cut is the most important decision in the cheese dairy. The consistency of the cheese depends on it. The grainy curds are transferred to moulds before being pressed. The cheese will be pressed into the mould and take on a homogenous shape. The cheeses are now plunged into a brine bath. This allows salt to permeate the cheese, solidify it and ensure a longer storage period. The brine forms a crust and contributes to the taste. The last stage in cheese production is the maturation, or 'affinage', in the ripening chambers. This allows the cheese to firm up and acquire its final taste and aroma.

It takes several specific steps to make a beer cheese. You can rinse the cheese in beer, inject it with beer or add beer to the curds. De Vierhoekhoeve has chosen the third option. They use 0.22 litres of beer per kilogram of cheese. Pieter Taelman from De Vierhoekhoeve asked cheese affineur Michel Van Tricht for advice. Thanks to Michel's tips.

Pieter is now producing beer cheeses with Duvel, Liefmans Kriek, Tripel Karmeliet, Ommegang, Amburon, Gruut, Delirium Tremens and Hopus. This is how Pieter advertises his cheeses: "In our cheeses you taste the love of our craft, but first of all the full taste of raw milk. In the morning we fill up the cheese tub with the freshly produced milk from our cows and just before noon the cheese is already resting underneath the press. We check on our cheeses every day during the weeks-long maturation period. This patience shines through in the taste... Each recipe is the fruit of craftsmanship, our creations are original and set the trend." Still not convinced?

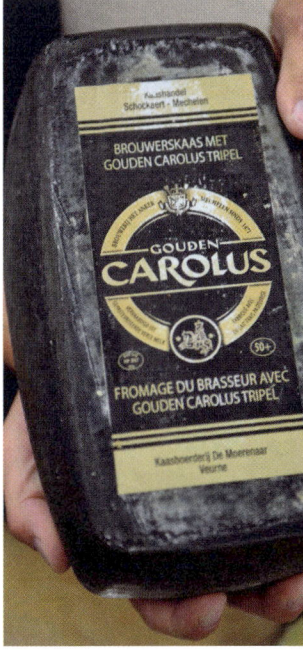

Witkap Stimulo from the Slaghmuylder brewery with a goat's cheese covered in an ash crust (left). Gouden Carolus beer cheese (right).

BEER AND PASTA

Ravioli, basil pasta, several types of pesto, fresh tomato sauce... gluten-free pasta even. The 'Pastaman' Stijn Jasperse has been part of the Antwerp food landscape for over twenty years. Stijn Jasperse, a.k.a. 'Pastaman', is preparing fresh pastas, pestos and related dishes every day. His 'hoppasta' is a ravioli filled with a slightly bitter mixture of white cheese and hops. It will delight hardened 'hopheads', especially in a pairing with a Westmalle Tripel. The 'hoppasta' with orange peel is even more subtly flavoured. The bitter taste of hops is reinforced by the bitterness of the orange peel, but at the same time it is countered and softened by the fruity touch. Look out for the Pastaman at the Antwerp Saturday market.

http://www.pastaman.eu

BEER AND BREAD

Bakkerij Goossens

Bakkerij Goossens is the Antwerp baker par excellence. Just ask for a 'roggeverdommeke' and you will understand why people are queueing around the block. Its sugar and raisin bread is very moreish. You just cannot help picking at it. Even after a few days, it tastes lovely from the toaster or as a French toast. But beer lovers pop in here to pick up a 'Keuninckske', a loaf of bread prepared with Antwerp's city beer, De Koninck. Take the bread to your lips and sniff the aroma. You will smell a warm cloud of malt and yeast, just like in the brewery. From the first bite, your mouth will be filled with tender, crispy and moist textures. As you would expect from a beer bread, the Keuninckske gives off all the delightful aromas of a tasty beer: caramel, malt and yeast... But this is a beer that can be chewed.

Korte Gasthuisstraat 31 — Antwerpen

BEER AND PIZZA

Just like the first brewer or brewster, the first 'pizzaiolo' is equally unknown but revered all the same. Pizza has its origins around the Mediterranean. The population of ancient Egypt, Persia, Greece and the Roman Empire had one thing in common: they were very fond of flatbreads that bear a strong resemblance to pizza. The origin of the word 'pizza' itself is also shrouded in the mists of time. Opinions are divided. Some state that the term is derived from the Latin 'picea', indicating a type of bread that takes on a darker colour in the oven. Our modern Italian pizza has a crusty base that is covered in gooey, melted cheese, a zesty tomato sauce, delicate vegetables, fish or meat. A Turkish pizza is a small 'boat' made from dough, filled with vegetables and savoury ingredients. This snack is served with a refreshing yoghurt sauce. Italians, without fail, will have a beer with their pizza. We often don't realise this in our country. The Italians are wont to have an industrial pils with this delicacy, served in one of the many inexpensive eateries. Refreshing and quite tasty, but we can and should do better. We can recommend the following beer and pizza combinations:

Pizza Margherita: Spéciale Belge
Pizza Primavera: a hoppy pils or a slightly hopped blonde
Pizza Pepperoni: white beer
Pizza Diavolo: IPA
Pizza Frutti di Mare: strong blonde
Pizza Capricciosa: a yeasty triple
Pizza Pepperoni: pale ale
Pizza: Bolognese: double
Pizza Spinaci: old lambic

Bread and pizza contain grain and yeast, just like beer.

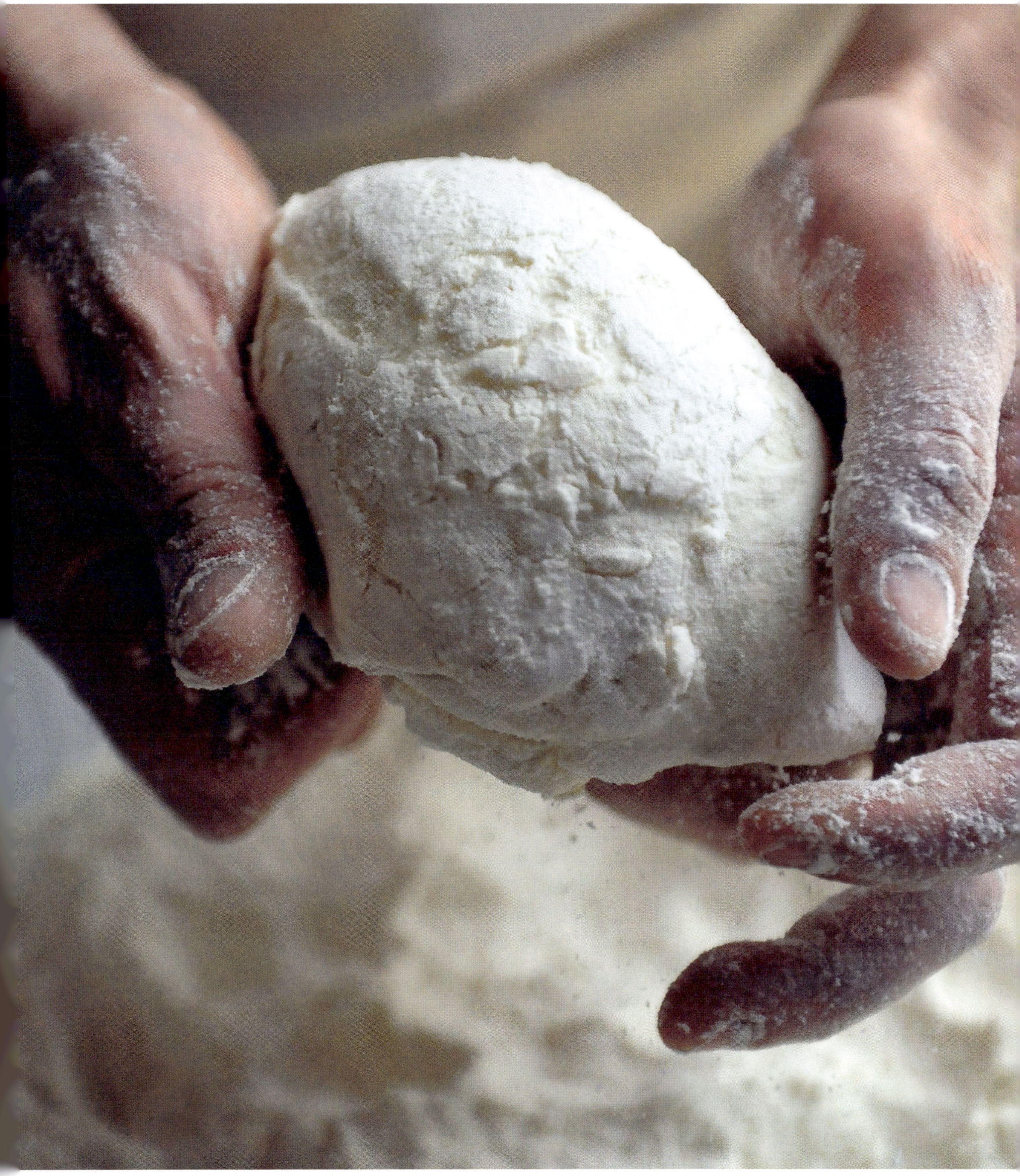

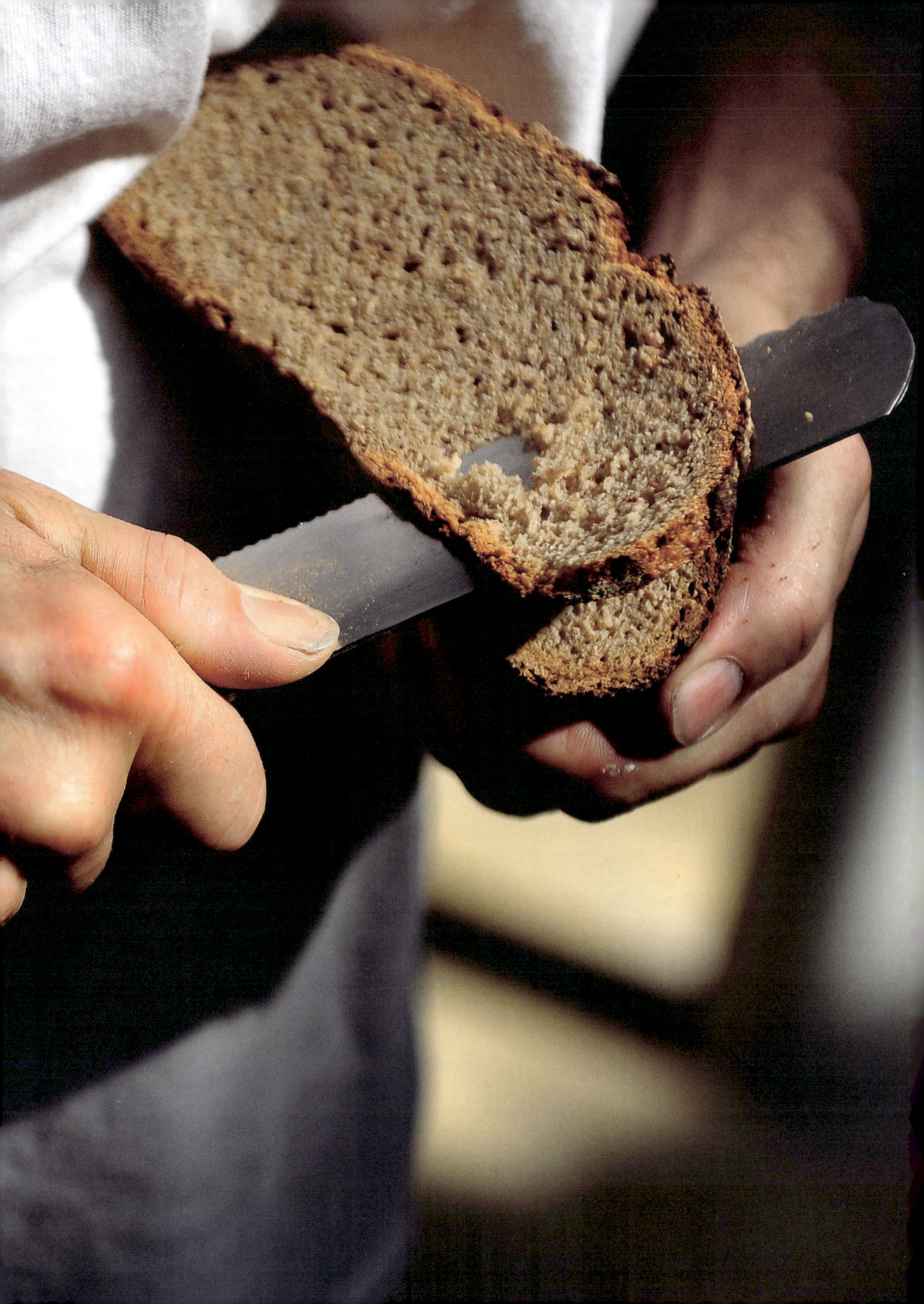

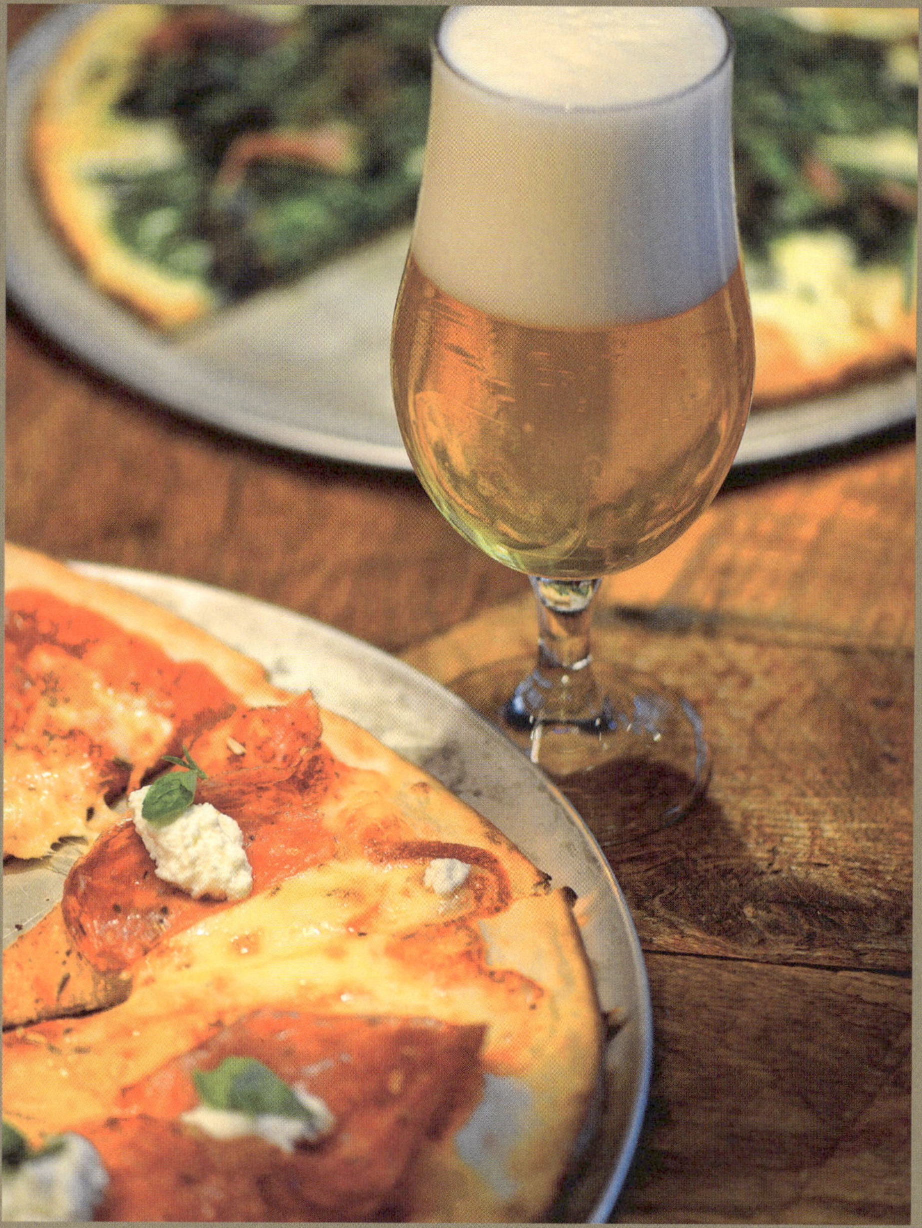

BEER AND THE EASTERN CUISINE

When we talk about the Eastern kitchen, we could mean anything from the Middle East to China. Below we are describing only a few of these classic cuisines. Which Belgian beers are best suited to these dishes? A brief overview.

The Middle East

The Arabic kitchen is famous for its delicious mezzes: a large offering of small dishes with surprising flavours, made with a wide variety of ingredients. The most important ones are listed below:

Hummus: a thick paste or spread made from boiled and pureed chickpeas blended with tahini (sesame paste), garlic, olive oil and lemon. This dip is traditionally served with a thin flatbread baked on a hot stone. A malty and slightly bitter SpécialeBelge goes very well with hummus.

Kubba: fried cones filled with a blend of bulgur (cracked wheat), ground beef and onion. A fresh, hoppy IPA will provide the necessary counter-ammunition and refresh our taste palette.

Waraq Dawa sage: steamed vine leaves filled with rice and meat. This dish is done full justice by a blond abbey beer with a beautiful balance between sweet and bitter and a fruity touch.

Baklava: filo pastry filled with nuts and drenched in honey. This is a no-brainer: a Barbar Blonde by Lefèbvre or a sweet barley wine.

India

India is a patchwork of regional cuisines. What they have in common is that all the dishes are subtly spiced. The soul of Indian gastronomy is 'masala', a blend of herbs and spices that can vary greatly between regions. Think of curcuma, coriander, cloves, mustard seed, poppy seed, mace... The general denomination of 'rice' includes white rice as well as aromatic basmati rice served with fragrant curries, simmered vegetables, legumes and powerful stews. The menu often includes mutton and lamb. The cooks will simmer the meat in a 'korma', a type of yoghurt, or roast it. Other well-known Indian dishes include curries, tandooris, tikkas and koftas, eaten with rice or fresh bread. We recommend zesty saisons, smooth and zesty white beers or powerful triples to accompany Indian cuisine. Some lamb recipes are simply begging for a zesty dark abbey beer of the St-Feuillien type. A match made in heaven.

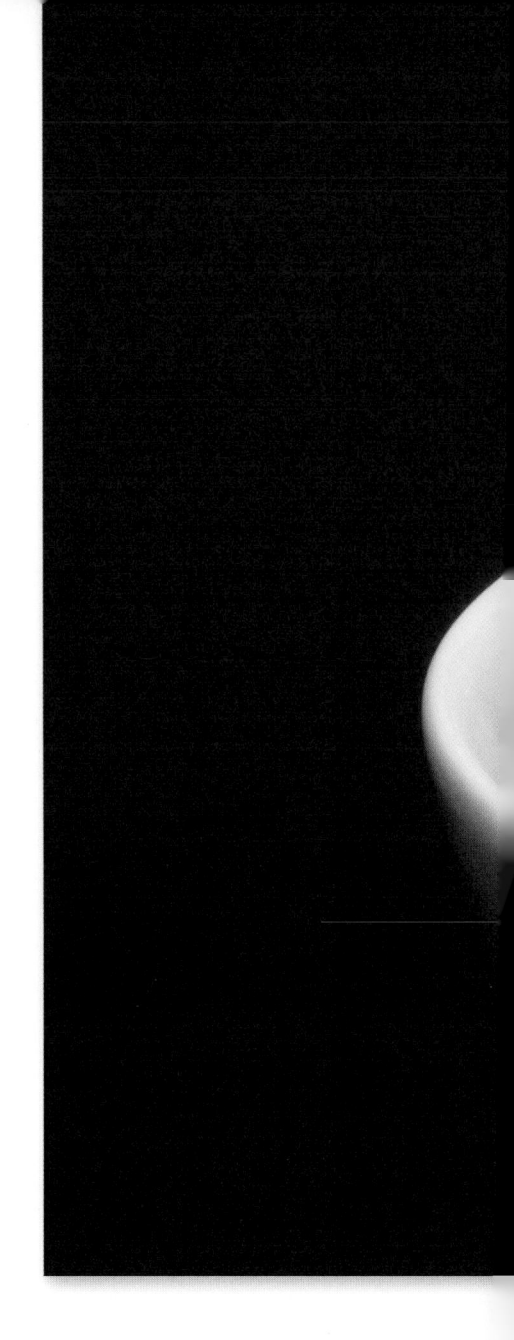

China

In China we distinguish four main cuisines: Guangdong (Canton), Shanghai, Peking (Beijing) and Sichuan, in other words the south, east, north and south-west. These cuisines are then sub-divided into local variants. Rice and mie (noodles) form the basis of Chinese cuisine and are served with a wide variety of vegetables, meat and fish. Condiments often used to give taste to the food often include soy sauce, oyster sauce, fish sauce and hoisin sauce, fresh gin-

Balanced beers with a pure taste go well with sushi and sashimi.

ger, star anise and five spice powder. Stir-frying is a popular and ancient technique. The chopped ingredients are quickly fried in a wok and are done within three to four minutes. The choice of beer depends on the intensity of the dish and the products used, but as a general rule, we can use the recommendations for the Indian kitchen. A dry pils can serve as a passe-partout and is a good choice as all the dishes appear on the plate at almost the same time.

Japan

The Land of the Rising Sun is blessed with an elegant, sober and healthy cuisine. The essence of a natural and pure taste is highly valued. The use of fats (oil and butter) is frowned upon and proteins are mainly derived from fish, seafood and crustaceans. Soy products, such as tofu and miso, and fresh vegetables are characteristic for Japanese cuisine. A typical meal consists of rice, fish, seaweed or soy beans. Little meat is consumed. Nevertheless, Japanese Kobe beef is regarded as the best in the world. The cattle are massaged every day and are served a portion of beer from time to time. The stars of the Japanese cuisine are sushi and sashimi: raw fish served with soy sauce, sea weed, rice and wasabi. For Japanese dishes the choice of beer is different from that in other regions as Japanese cuisine is more sober, less exuberant and, you could also say, more balanced. We are therefore opting for beers that are perfectly balanced and have a pure taste, from pils via light blonde to hoppy IPAs. Dry, toasted stouts also do fabulously with certain fish recipes.

BIERRESTAURANTS

ANTWERPEN

't Zilte

Chef Viki Geunes of Antwerp restaurant "t Zilte', the proud bearer of two Michelin stars, cooks with feeling and knows how to combine flavours and textures perfectly. He is not shying away from experiments, rather, he embraces them. "It starts off with an idea", Viki Geunes explains. "I 'taste' the flavours in my head and then I think about the composition as an interaction of contrasts. I will always look for structures that give the best result. I start off with one basic product that I pair with three other ingredients prepared in different ways: raw, cooked, hot-cold, sweet-sour... A recipe becomes captivating and exciting thanks to the contrasts between flavours and preparation." The chef feels that Belgian products are undervalued. Viki Geunes: "'We are not chauvinistic enough. This is why I will also integrate quality regional produce into my recipes wherever I can." He has plenty of experience with using beer in the kitchen. 't Zilte uses beer for one of its breads, in sauces with meat, paired with asparagus or hop shoots for example but equally well with Coquilles St. Jacques, langoustines or lobster. "Beer allows for unique taste pairings," Viki Geunes states. "If, for example, you are drinking a blonde beer with 'maatjes' herring, you will have a taste experience that wine simply cannot provide." Personally I support 'acids' in food and that is also where beer has a powerful advantage. There has to be acidity, also when it comes to desserts, otherwise a dish becomes boring very quickly."

The chef has been involved in the development of the Flemish red-brown beers made by the Rodenbach brewery, including its Caractère Rouge.

Hanzestedenplaats 5 – +32(0)3/283 40 40
info@tzilte.be – www.tzilte.be

Brasserie Dock's Café

Brasserie Dock's Café is held in high regard in Antwerp. It serves as a 'canteen' for the big bosses in charge of the port and the captains of industry but extends its welcome to ordinary citizens like you and me. This restaurant's appeal can partly be explained by its exceptional décor designed by Portuguese architect/designer/cook Antonio Pinto. The buffet with seafood and crustaceans is a particular draw. The oyster bar has a phenomenal offering of seafood and oysters, caught fresh every day. No fewer than ten different varieties of oyster are on display, including two types that carry the signature of the Brasserie. To complement all of this, chef Yannick Frooninckx dishes up a high-quality brasserie cuisine. All these delicacies deserve a high-quality beer. The beer menu at Dock's is comprehensive and includes two excellent house beers: Principale Tripel and Bruin.

Jordaenskaai 7 – +32(0)3/226 63 30
info@docks.be – www.docks.be

Grand Café De Rooden Hoed

Grand Café De Rooden Hoed is Antwerp's oldest restaurant with an exceptionally rich history. Painter and artist Quinten Matsys is reputed to have lived in the building. The Grand Café went through a difficult time and, at one point, was even declared insolvent. Emerging from this difficult period, the business underwent a through renovation and re-opened in 2013. Here, you can not only enjoy seafood and fish specialties, but tuck into all the classics that have been on the menu for dozens of years: Choucroute d'Alsace (sauerkraut), steak tartare, escargots (snails), rabbit, a 'waterzooi' or 'stoofvlees' (a beef stew). All of these dishes are served with Belgian beers. All of the staff has enjoyed excellent training and will explain, with a smile, why beer X make a good pairing with dish Y. Just one example: Crab Bellevue paired with a Koninck. And by all means, ask owner-chef Cas to prepare a sabayon with Liefmans at the table. You will enjoy his showmanship.

Oude Koornmarkt 25 – +32(0)3/289 09 09
info@deroodenhoed.be – www.deroodenhoed.be

Bacchus Framboos from brouwerij Van Honsebrouck with the tiramisu, in De Rooden Hoed in Antwerp.

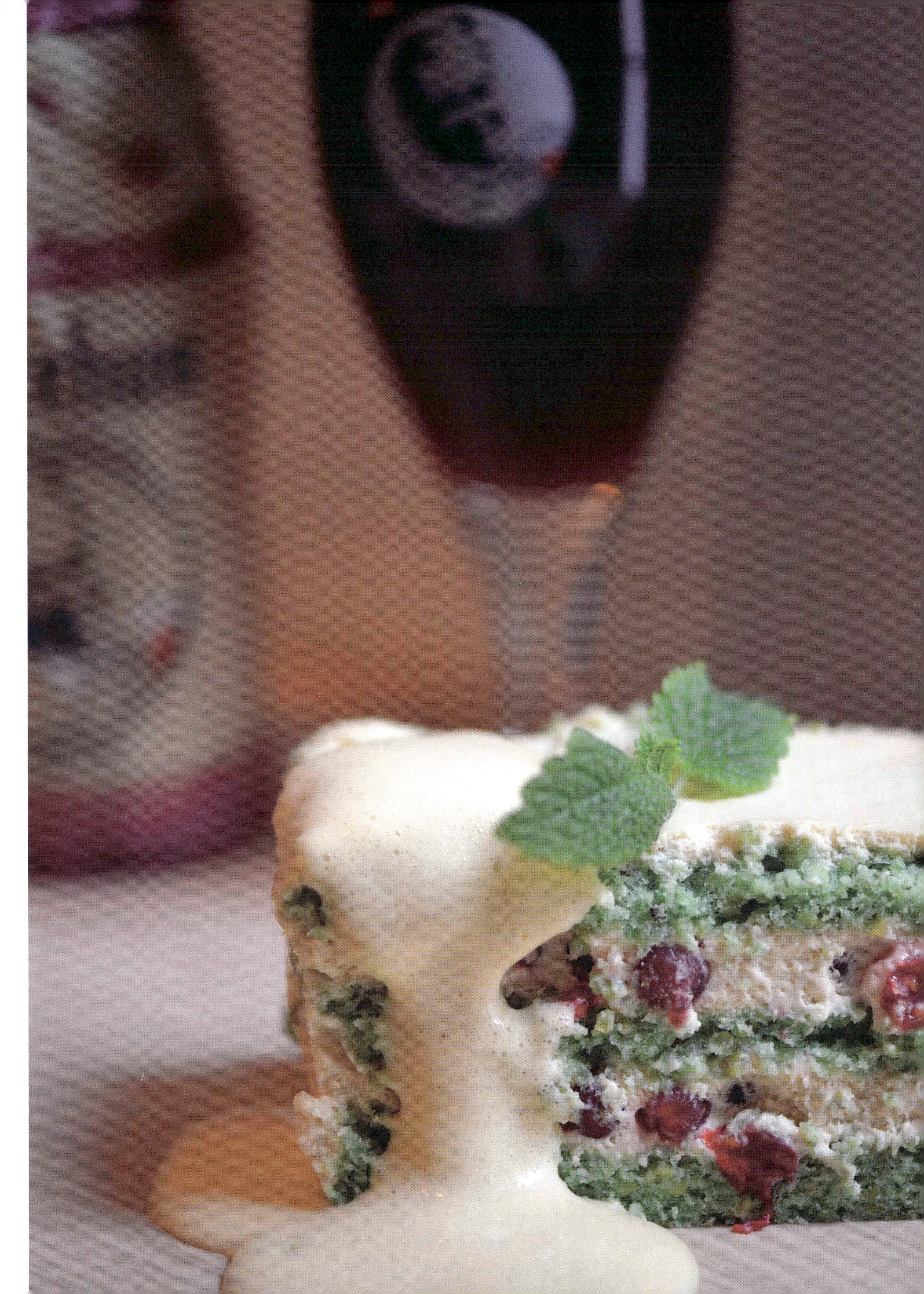

Food pairing with house beer Principale Bruin in Dock's Café in Antwerp.

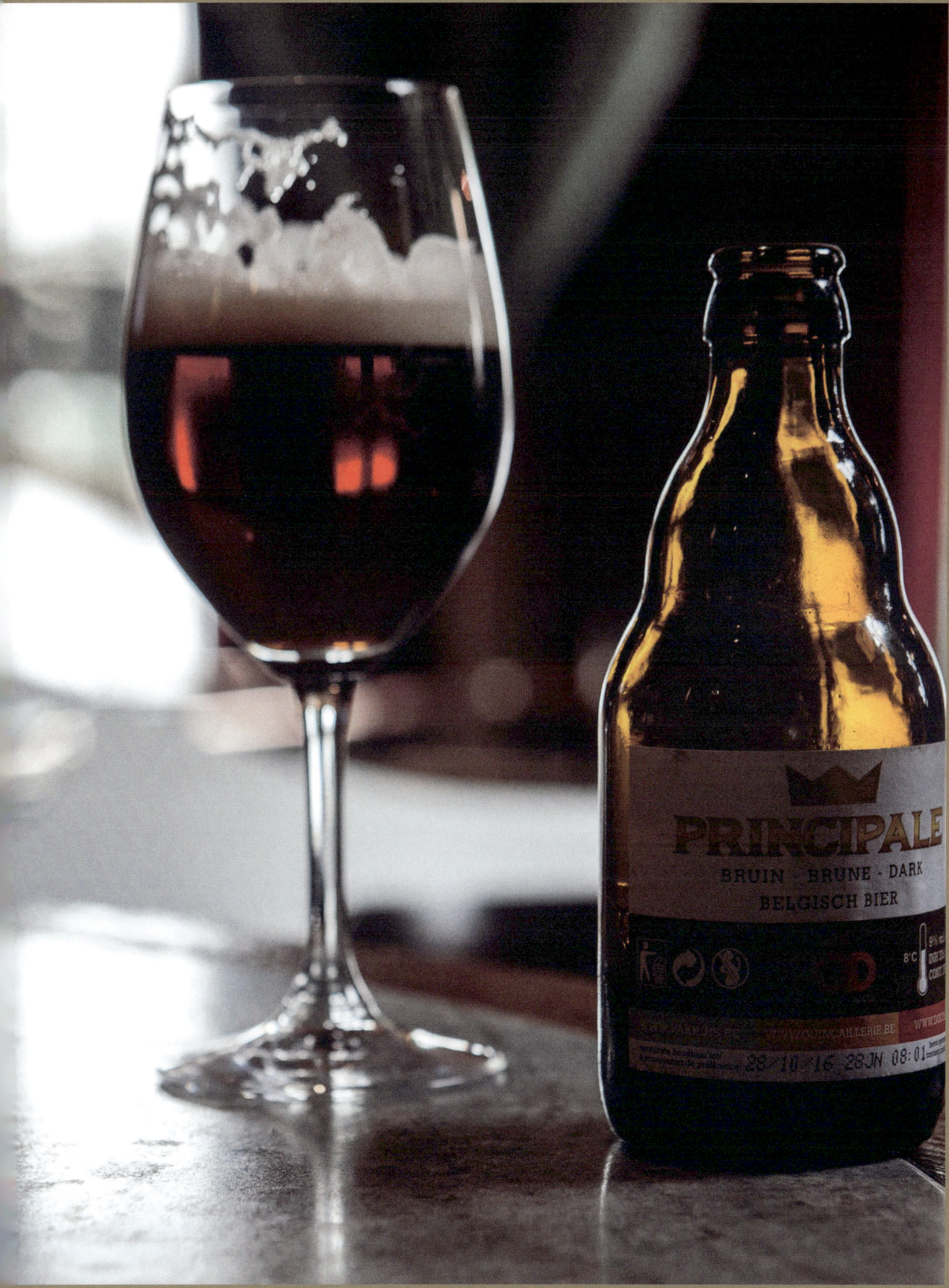
PRINCIPALE
BRUIN - BRUNE - DARK
BELGISCH BIER

PAJOTTENLAND

3 Fonteinen

In the early 1950s, the village of Beersel had as many as fourteen gueuzestekers. Gaston Debelder was amongst their ranks. He took over the 3 Fonteinen café restaurant. Gaston then taught his son Armand all he needed to know about the gueuzesteker trade. At that time, Armand, who was trained as a chef, still spent his time at the cooking range, but he was to make a firm decision to become a lambic brewer and gueuzesteker. The restaurant was passed on to his brother Guido, sister-in-law Trees and cousin Thomas. 3 Fonteinen specialises in traditional Belgian popular cuisine and has made its name with regional dishes based on gueuze, faro and kriek. Examples include mussels, eel in a green sauce, rabbit with gueuze, guinea fowl with kriek, beef stew or rooster in a faro sauce. We can also go back to basics and order a simple slice of bread with real 'pottekaas': a mixture of Brussels 'schepkaas' (spoonable cheese), commonly known as 'stinky cheese' — and 'mandjeskaas', a Pajottenland specialty. A great combination with a glass of gueuze and also rumoured to be a great hangover remedy. The menu used to only include the traditional lambic, gueuze and kriek but now comprises other styles of beer.

Herman Teirlinckplein 3 — +32(0)2/331 06 52
info@3fonteinenrestaurant.com — www.3fonteinenrestaurant.com

BRUSSELS

Nüetnigenough

Translated literally, the name of this restaurant beautifully summarises the soul of the 'Brusseleir', who could always 'pack in a little bit more'. The ideal place to go for gourmands, perfectionists and gueuze lovers alike. This description is a perfect reflection of the concept and the soul of this establishment: good food and drink enjoyed in a convivial, easy-going atmosphere. The meals on offer here make you lick your lips and the large portions ensure that you feel that yes, you really have eaten enough! In addition to typically Belgian cuisine, the menu also includes a number of vegetarian dishes. The beer menu can only be called impressive and, besides several Belgian evergreens, mainly lists beers from smaller craft breweries. The service is helpful and attentive. The waiters have a fair amount of beer knowledge. Julien, one of the waiters, is even studying to be a zythologue.

Lombardstraat 25 — +32(0)2/513 78 84
info@nuetnigenough.be — www.nuetnigenough.be

Les Brigittines

Les Brigittines is located in the centre of Brussels not far from the colourful Marolles area. The restaurant is oozing class and sophistication. Master chef Dirk Myny introduces his 'fun kitchen' which uses local produce. This is high-quality brasserie cuisine. Dirk is Brussels born and bred. His father is Flemish, his mother is from Wallonia. This shines through in the kitchen. One of Dirk's creations is the famous ZennePot: cabbage boiled in gueuze from Cantillon, 'Bloedpanch' (a traditional black sausage from Brussels), dry sausage and whelks, with the chef's talent thrown in. The menu proudly presents several gueuzes, lambics and craft beers, including those from Brasserie de la Senne

Kapellemarkt 5 — +32(0)2/512 41 30
info@lesbrigittines.com — www.lesbrigittines.com

AB Café & Resto

The 'Ancienne Belgique' is found in a historic location in the heart of Brussels. It is one of the best concert venues in the Low Countries. The AB brings you contemporary music from major and lesser-known performers. Its stage has seen many great names in the music business. Are you a beer lover as well as a music lover? Don't forget to pop into the AB Café & Resto. A world kitchen awaits you, complemented by a splendid, ever-changing range of Belgian beers. The spotlight is on a different beer every month. Large, smaller and small breweries keep each other company on the menu in a brotherly fashion. The venue organised a beer & food pairing once a month. On offer: beer & cheese, beer & chocolate, beer & North Sea fish, bapas and much more.

Steenstraat 23 — www.abconcerts.be

7 • BEER KITCHEN AND FOOD PAIRING

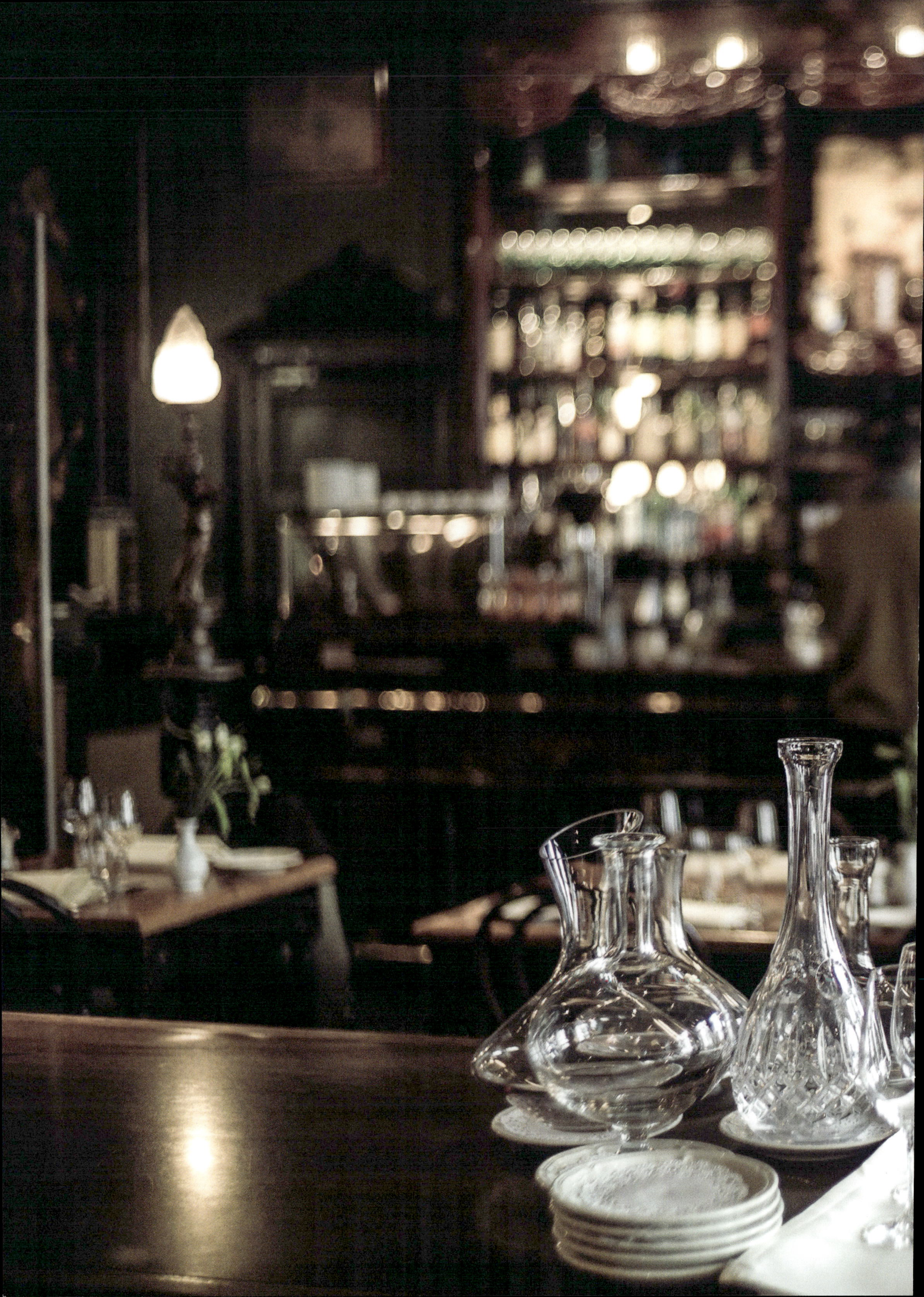

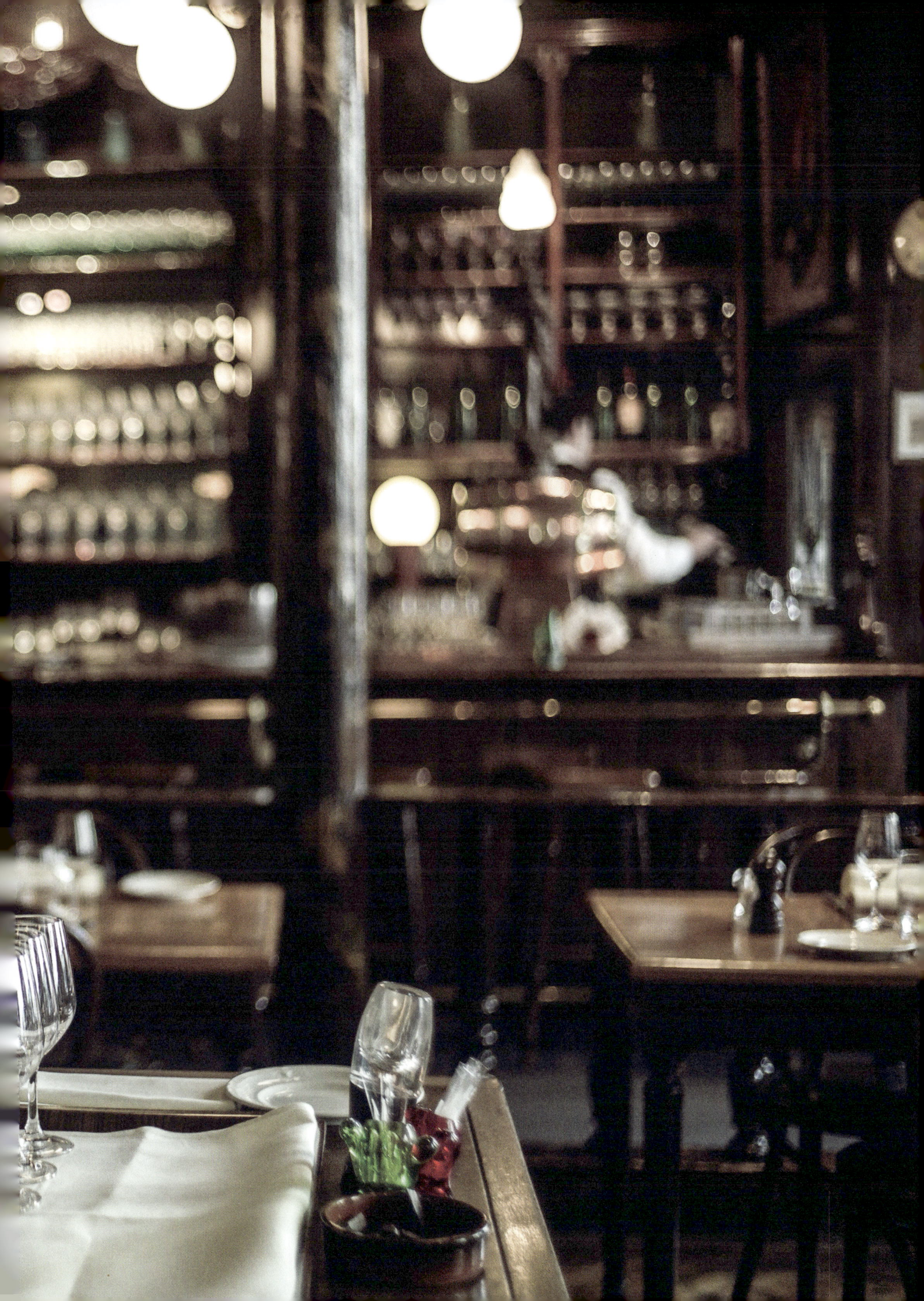

CHIMAY

L'Eau Blanche

On the banks of 'L'Eau Blanche' – from which this establishment derives its name – and with a view towards a rock that is colossal in Belgian terms, you can enjoy the local specialties. The owner serves trout fried in good butter with fresh, home-made fries and the local 'escavèche' delicacy. For the uninitiated, this is a cold dish based on river fish and onions. The fish and onions are 'cooked' cold in a mixture of vinegar and white wine. The dish was inspired by Spanish cuisine. The steak américain also comes highly recommended here. Strictly speaking, L'Eau Blanche is not a specialty beer restaurant. However, the beers from Wallonia and especially the Trappist from nearby Chimay are served here with love and skill.

27, rue Gustave Joaris – +32(0)60/21 18 64

DENDERLEEUW

De Heeren van Liedekercke

Crowned the best beer restaurant in the world, no fewer than five years in a row... De Heeren van Liedekercke in Denderleeuw near Brussels is a veritable icon amongst beer lovers. A place of pilgrimage for beer geeks. When they make their reservation they want to know straight away which vintage beers are kept in the cellar. "Gueuze fans in particular know where to find us," Joost Du Four laughs. "They know that we are serving unique blends. We also stock all of the Belgian Trappists, older vintages included". Beer is treated here with all the respect it deserves. If you order an Orval, it will be at least six months old. "At that stage, it has ripened to perfection," finds Orval ambassador cum laude Joost Du Four. A visit to the beer cellar is no less than a revelation. I ask for the oldest Orval. Joost dives into the cellar and comes back with a handful of bottles. "Older than I am", smiles Joost, who is in his forties. It is doubtful whether the oldest Orval is still drinkable. "We are also commissioning house beers on the basis of our own recipe," Joost tells us. Het Heerenbier, brewed by Boelens, is a dark beer with dry hopping. Sodalitas is a bitter blonde that De Herberg has produced for us and we also have a house gueuze made by Cantillon." De Heeren have always been in support of small breweries. They like to surprise their guests. Does anyone know the herbal beers from La Botteresse?

Pralines shaped like a brewing kettle in beer restaurant De Heeren van Liedekercke.

Joost was barely twelve years old when he was bitten by the beer bug. A few years on he started to visit breweries. In the meantime, he was an avid reader of any book to do with beer. Joost: "When I set up my café here, I wanted to offer all the beers from lambic brewers and gueuzestekers. With one of them, it didn't work. Armand Debelder, the brewer at 3 Fonteinen, would only sell me his lambic, oude gueuze and kriek on the condition that I did an apprenticeship with him. I will be forever grateful. If anything, my love for lambic beers has only grown since then." The 'gentlemen' (Heeren) are now hosting beer lovers from the USA, Italy, Scandinavia, Great Britain and Canada, amongst others. They take their pick from the well-stocked beer menu. If you are looking for extreme beers, you are looking in vain. "Belgian brewers are after balance in the glass, that is our tradition," Joost assures us. "They make beers that go down easily or beers that you like when you taste them for the first time."

Even though beer is said to be 'a sandwich in a glass', you still expect something on your plate when you go to a restaurant. De Heeren van Liedekercke go over and above this by offering a tasting menu that changes every month. This includes between five and seven courses with two complementary beers for each course, poured into small tasting glasses. "We are aiming for harmony as well as contrast," finds Tom Du Four, the beer chef. The preference is for regional products that are freshly supplied on a daily basis. The restaurant gets its produce from a local artisan butcher and a local farmer. The chef is also in tune with the seasons and will put asparagus on the menu in the spring, strawberries when summer is around the corner, and so on. This higher quality brasserie kitchen translates into classics such as steak, mussels, beef stew or cockerel in a beer sauce, accompanied by frites or bread. But culinary inspiration is equally drawn from across the borders with a lasagna or recipes with the Italian burrata cheese, not unlike mozzarella. The beer ensures that you land on familiar Belgian soil every single time. "I'm glad that beer is now finally taking up its rightful place in gastronomy," Tom remarks. He is placing a box of 'pralines from the house' in front of us. The 'brewing kettle' confectionary contains hop jenever, the other six pralines comprise two beer ganaches, using sweet and sour kriek respectively, each one of the house beers and Orval and Tripel Karmeliet. This also demonstrates the art of beer pairing with a different chocolate jacket every single time. Beer and chocolate, 'this must be Belgium!'

Kasteelstraat 33 — +32(0)53/68 08 88
info@heerenvanliedekercke.be — www.heerenvanliedekercke.be

ELLEZELLES

Le Château du Mylord

Le Château du Mylord is a prestigious restaurant founded in 1981 by chief cook Jean-Baptiste Thomaes. His brother Christophe has now joined the establishment as a patissier. The restaurant was awarded its first Michelin star in 1987. Another star was added in 2002. The restaurant is housed in a classic English-style mansion surrounded by its own park. The menu is geared to French cuisine prepared in a rather traditional vein. Sommelier Bart Lamon often serves beers with the menu. This establishment often collaborates with Brasserie Dubuisson, a brewery from the Hainaut region. One of the most popular items on the menu, therefore, is 'tartare of oyster gel of Bush de Nuits with an espuma of smoked butter'. Ask Bart for his knowledgeable advice to help you choose your beer.

Rue Saint-Mortier, 35 — +32(0)6854 26 02
info@mylord.be — www.mylord.be

MECHELEN

Als ik mijn ogen toe doe ben ik in Honoloeloe

At the end of last year, the city of Mechelen saw the opening of a bar with probably the funniest and longest name in Belgium. The owners derived this rather unusual name from a poem by Dutch poet and performer Jules Deelder. You can enjoy lunch here with real pistolets, linger over an afternoon tea with tea or coffee, where the sweet sinful delicacies are provided by BAKED from Antwerp. The bar has a surprising range of lesser-known beers from Belgium and abroad. The highlights are the beers from Danish Gypsy brewery To Øl. However, these beers are brewed by the Lochristi Proefbrouwerij (tasting brewery), which does not detract from their quality in any way, quite the contrary in fact. This is the 'place to lunch' thanks to its original beer menu, the excellent food, the striking interior and the splendid terrace located at the Grote Markt, the main market square.

Grote Markt 11 — +32(0)468/25 06 10
info@honoloeloe.com — www.honoloeloe.com

7 • BEER KITCHEN AND FOOD PAIRING

RETIE

Postel ter Heyde

At a stone's throw from the Dutch border and not far from Postel Abbey, you will find hotel-restaurant Postel Ter Heyde surrounded by the forests of the Kempen region. This establishment is well known for its excellent meat dishes and its splendid beer menu. The meat is transferred straight from the grill onto your plate and is reared sustainably, managed by the owners. The cattle is of the French 'Salers' breed. Its meat rates amongst the highest in the world. Besides the usual suspects, the beer menu comprises a plethora of regional beers, which includes the entire range of De Dochter van de Korenaar from the nearby municipality of Baarle-Hertog. At Postel ter Heyde, there is much to enjoy for meat lovers and beer geeks alike. Burgundian enjoyment surrounded by nature.

Postelsebaan 74 — +32(0)14/37 23 21
www.postelterheyde.be

WESTHOEK

In De Zon

The owner-chef of this rustic eatery used to be a competitive cyclist. The menu is small and traditional with a regional feel. Its paté or rillettes 'maison' make for the perfect starter. Marrow bones, eel in a green sauce, osso bucco, veal kidneys and other regional dishes make up the menu. The unadulterated 'esprit flandrien', or the Flemish spirit, is kept alive at a stone's throw from the French border. Just think of all the possible beer pairings.

Dikkebusstraat 80, De Klijte — +32(0)57/21 26 26
info@indezon.be — www.indezon.be

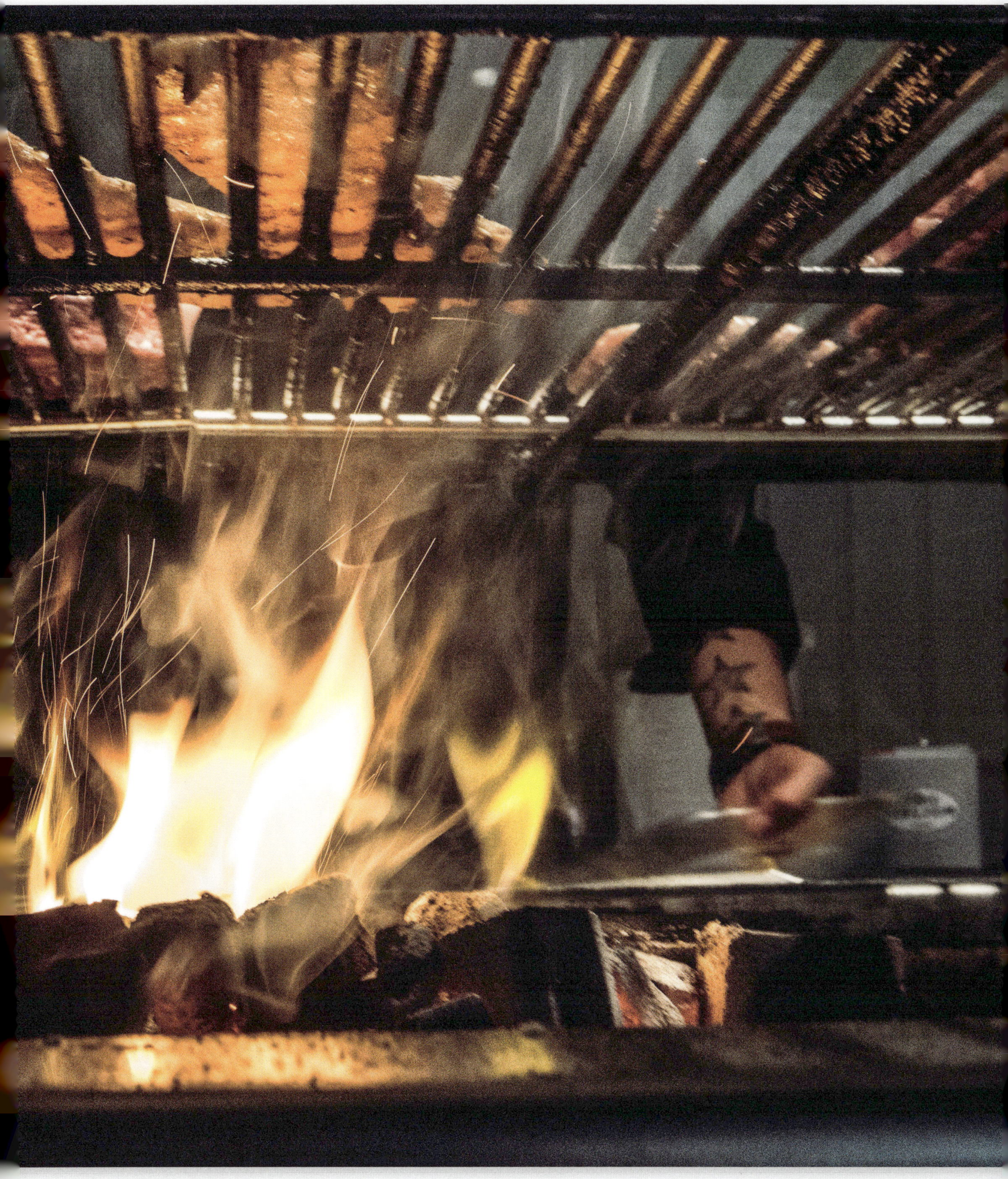

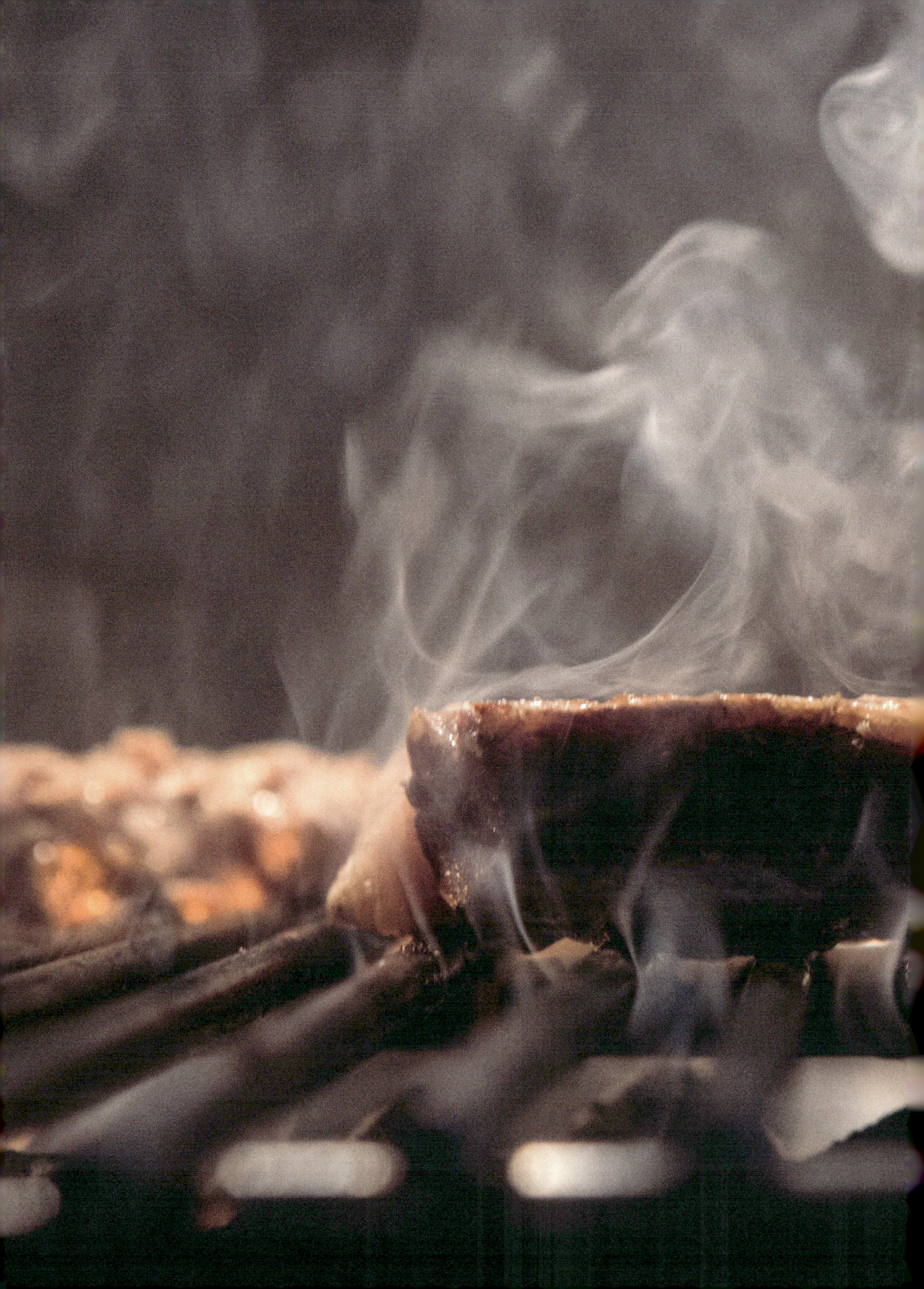

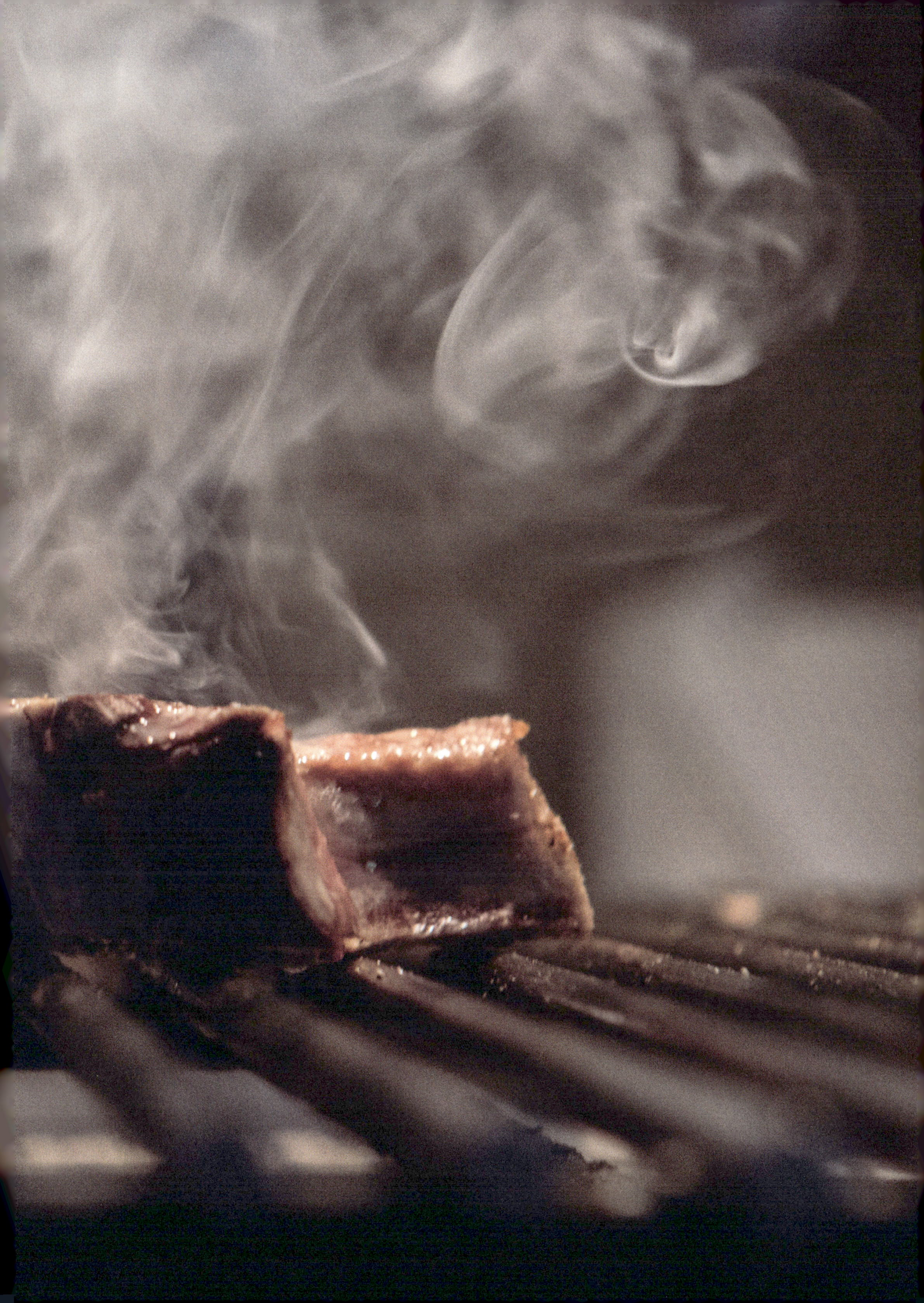

't Hommelhof

Honour where it's due. Stefaan Couttenye is a beer kitchen pioneer. Whilst enjoying the house aperitif of Watou white beer enriched with Kapittel Abt, he tells me: 'When I established myself here in the Westhoek region, there were two brewers producing thirteen beers between them. I wanted to take advantage straight away of this local 'terroir'. But in those days, serving beer with a meal or using it in cooking could not be further from people's minds.' I am enjoying the fillet of veal and tuna mayonnaise with a salad of asparagus, marinated in raspberry beer, with a Boon raspberry beer on the side, making for a perfect complement. My main course consists of a fillet of guinea fowl with dune asparagus from Ghyvelde and a 'parmentier' silverside steak in St-Bernardus Prior with Kapittel Watou. After the rhubarb crumble with pistachio ice cream and a glass of St-Bernardus Prior I can barely lift myself up from the table. Beer tourists get excited about 't Hommelhof. The table next to me is hosting a group of Americans who are eagerly searching for the roots of 'Belgian beers'. 'Times have changed', Stefaan laughs. 'When brewers were dining in my restaurant, they used to drink wine. Ordering a beer to go with your meal was a no-no in those days.' I ask Stefaan what to look out for if you are cooking with beer. 'Beer turns bitter when it's heated up so it's important to dose it carefully', Stefaan recommends. He is delighted to see that many brewers have abandoned the trend towards sweet beers and have started to produce beers that are more markedly sour or bitter. He is not too happy about the current trend for beer sommeliers. 'You shouldn't try to turn beer into wine,' he finds. 'It is a different product with a different culture.' The convivial atmosphere that surrounds beer is certainly still around. Everybody feels at home in 't Hommelhof, even though its photo gallery testifies to a parade of famous guests, from famous Belgian artist Panamarenko to premiers or even Presidents.

't Hommelhof (Watou), Watouplein 17 – +32(0)57/38 80 24
www.hommelhof.be

Cheese making at Chimay Abbey, under the watchful eye of a monk. >

7 • BEER KITCHEN AND FOOD PAIRING

Halté !
BLOND
AZIO
THINK BEFORE YOU DRINK BEFORE YOU DRIVE
DE PANNE

YOU CAN'T BE A REAL COUNTRY UNLESS YOU HAVE A BEER AND AN AIRLINE

Frank Zappa

Taverne
Chouffe Shop
Départ VISITES
WC

LIEFHEBBERS VAN GOED BIER
DRINKT UIT NIEUWSGIERIGHEID
EEN
EXTRA MARS
VAN DE BROUWERIJ
VAN HONSEBROUCK. GEBRS

BROUWERIJ BOON
Nr.116
LEMBEEK

MORT SUBITE
Het bier voor Bons Vivants.
MORT SUBITE

E KONINCK
1833
ENZINNIG LEKKER

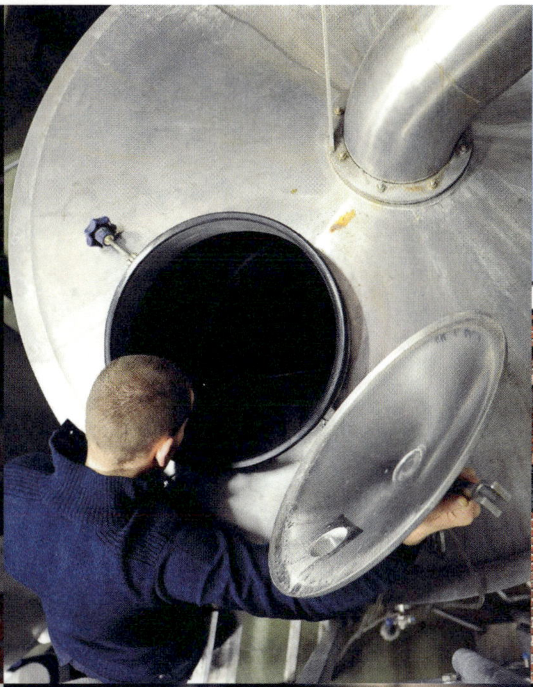

BRASSERIE FRIART

DE GEUZE VIEILLE
d Beersel
EER TRADITIONS REBORN

Lindemans

501
CHM

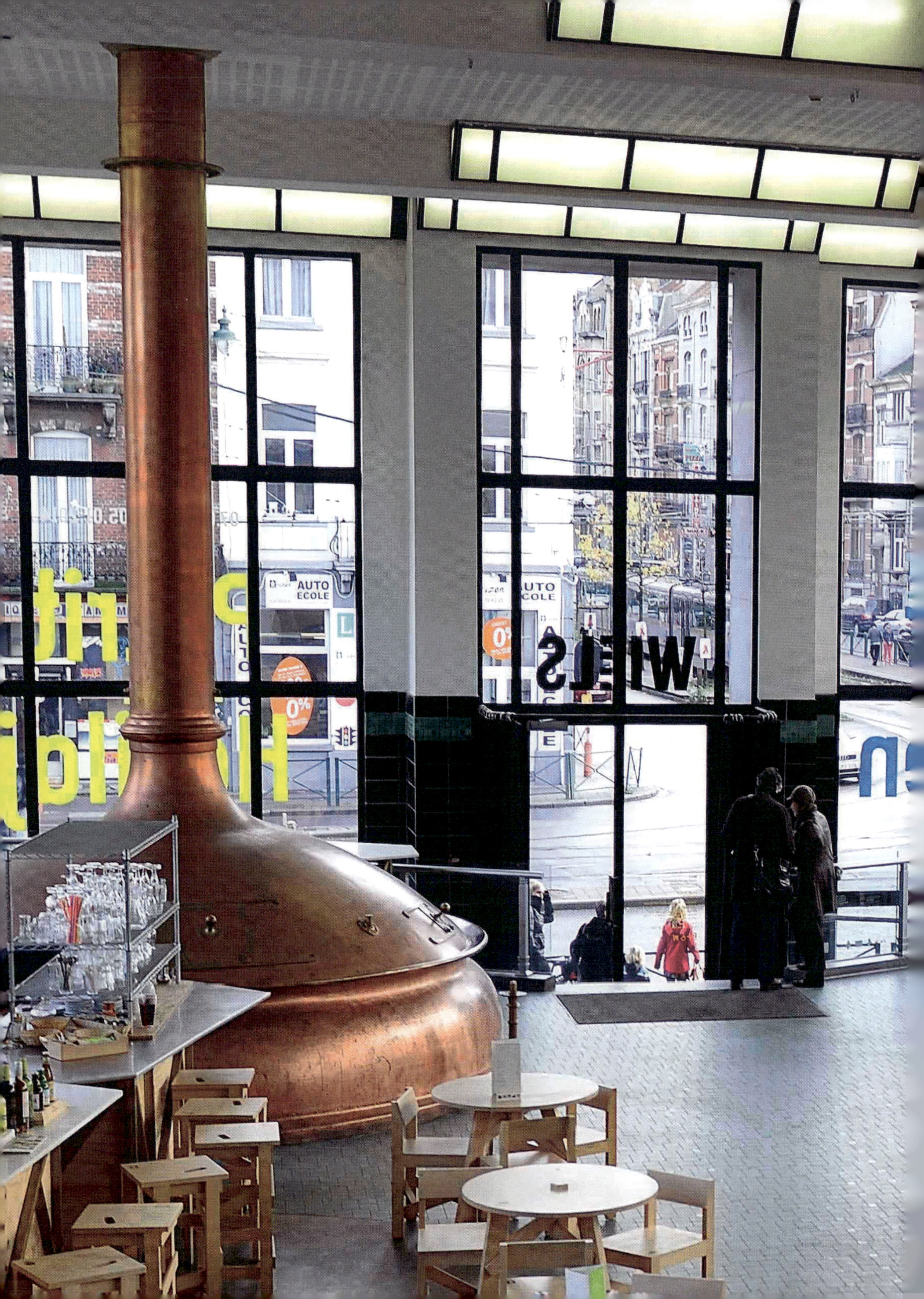
AUTO ECOLE

8

BEER TOURISM

BEER TOURISM

Brewing runs through the veins of every Belgian. Spread across the length and breadth of our country you will find breweries that vary in size from tiny to huge. We are making beer in a garage, an empty warehouse, on a brand new site using the latest technology or within ancient abbey walls. Each brewer and every single brewery tells their own story. Discover the brewing country of Belgium. This chapter provides you with all the guidance you need.

BREWERY VISITS

Monuments

'Once you've seen one brewery, you've seen them all,' you often hear. However, it is just when you have been to several breweries that you start to notice the differences. The details make it twice as interesting. Many abbeys are sited in extraordinary places. This stands to reason as the monks were invariably in search of an oasis of peace and quiet. If there is a brewery within the abbey walls, the monks want to keep the noise down. This is why you often find yourself in front of a closed door. If there is a visitors' centre or a café, in Westvleteren, Westmalle, Chimay and Orval for example, this is tidily tucked away outside the abbey walls. In Orval you visit the ruins of the medieval abbey whilst enjoying the view of the monumental 'new' abbey, as if you were making a leap through one thousand years of history. The splendid historic brew halls of Westmalle and Rochefort are closed to the public. If you do want to sample the atmosphere of an abbey and tour an active brewery within the abbey walls, the abbey ruins of Abbaye d'Aulne are the place to go, with its idyllic location on the banks of the Sambre to the south of Charleroi. Another destination is Val-Dieu in the Green Land of Herve in the vicinity of Liège. We also recommend De Kluis in Achel, where you can see the brewer at work behind a glass wall.

Bière
Abbaye d'Aulne
A.D.A.

BENEDICTUS-

ABBAYE

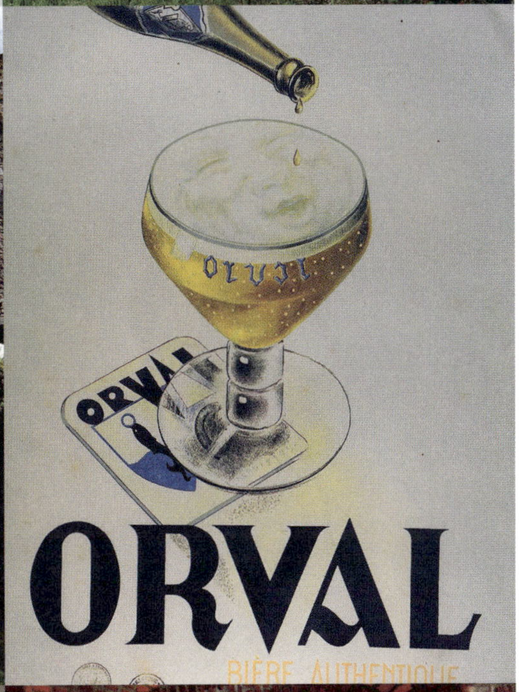
ORVAL
ORVAL

Abbaye d'Aulne
ADA 8
SELECTION

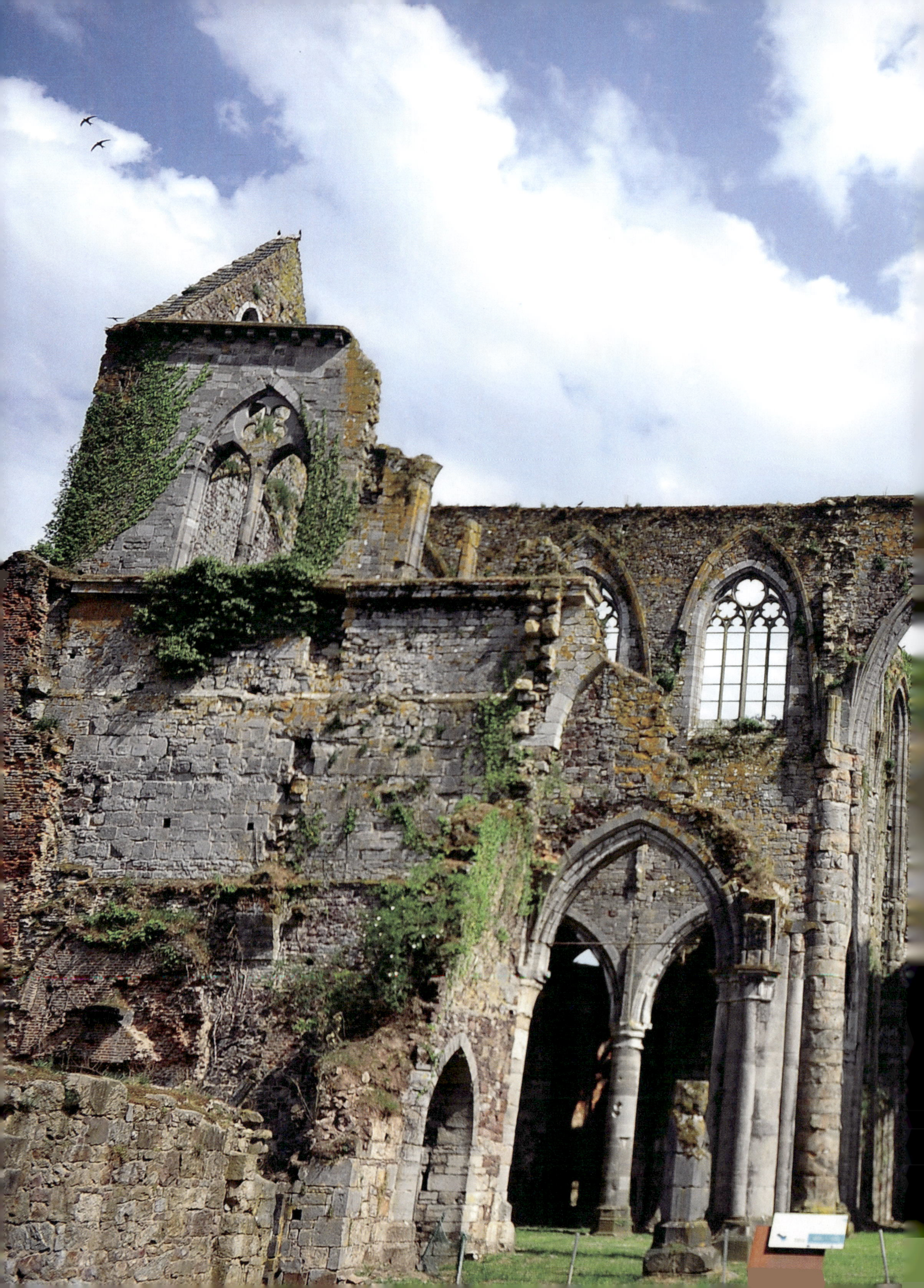

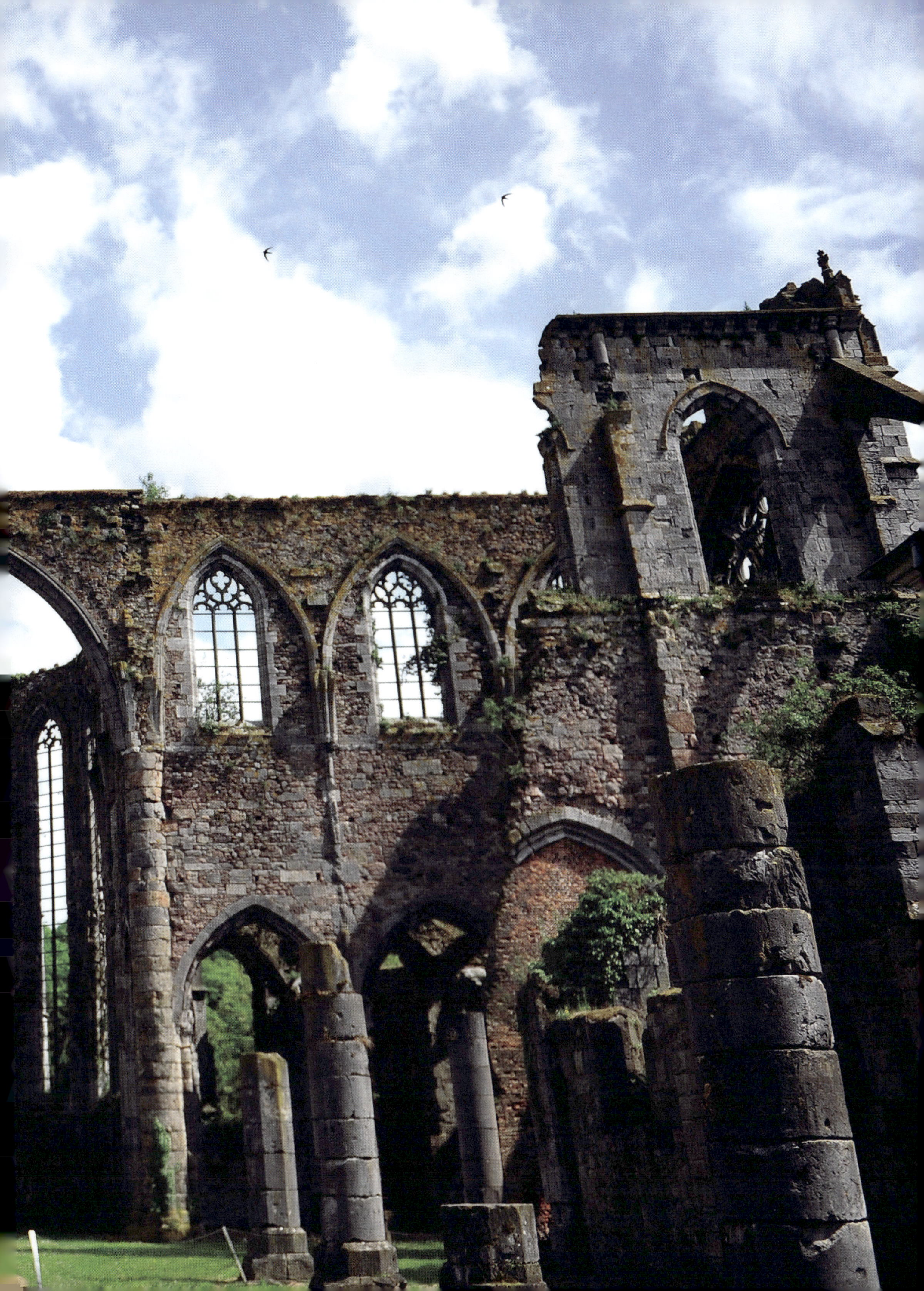

In the city

Every town or city used to have several breweries. People travelled less than they do today and their lives were lived within the small world of their own local area. Houses were often smaller, with fewer modern conveniences, and so people used to meet up in the café. Such a brewery would supply a number of local cafés. Het Anker in Mechelen is a typical city brewery, located in the historic beguinage. De Koninck in Antwerp has undergone an extensive face-lift. You find yourself in a comprehensive experience centre with an interactive exhibition with a spotlight on the city, the brewery and its beers. The site also includes artisan food stores with a bakery, cheese affineur, butcher's shop, chocolaterie and restaurant all on-site. Taste is the common denominator. Everything is prepared on the premises and you can see the artisans at work. Cantillon in Brussels is an authentic lambic brewery founded in 1900. This living museum is a tourist attraction and draws in lovers of lambic, oude gueuze, kriek and faro. Slaghmuylder in Ninove has also preserved its character. Here you can see a steam machine in operation. De Halve Maan in the heart of Bruges pairs its unique location with modern production facilities. A tour of the brewery museum affords a splendid panorama of the historic inner city. At Rodenbach's in Roeselare you will find an amazing round 'oast house', used for drying the malt, and the foeder halls where the Flemish red-brown beer is maturing in hundreds of giant wooden barrels. La Binchoise is another city brewery worth a visit. This is a former malt house in the shadow of Binche's city walls. We should not forget Louvain, the birthplace of AB Inbev, the world's largest brewery. Admire the splendidly restored Stella Artois brewhall, now called De Hoorn. A few streets further on, you come across the largest brewery in Europe. A tour of the brewhall brings home the principle of economies of scale. But, small is also beautiful. Just take a look at Gruut in Ghent and Brasserie C (Curtius) right in the heart of Liège, at the bottom of the Montagne de Bueren step-stairway.

In the village

Many villages are proud of 'their' brewery and beers. Cristal (1928) is one of the oldest pils beers in Belgium and to this day is brewed in Alken, although the brewery has outgrown its original premises many times over. At first sight,

The prestigious brewer's house at Bosteels illustrates the status formerly accorded to brewers.

Martens in Bocholt is sticking to village proportions. But its façade hides one of the largest pils breweries in the country, as there is now a second Martens facility a few streets down. Its brewery museum gives an overview of brewing technology throughout the ages. The handsome brewer's house at Bosteels in Buggenhout is an illustration of the former status of the brewer as a dignitary. Huyghe in Melle near Ghent will surprise you with its stark contrast between the old and the new. Completely authentic is the Cnudde village brewery in Eine (Oudenaarde) with its 1950s brewhall. Brouwerij Vandenbossche at Sint-Lievens-Esse village square has the look of a pre-war still life. Dupont in Leuze, known for its saison, blends the old with the new. Their boiling kettle is still heated by gas. Brasserie à Vapeur in the adjacent village of Pipaix goes back even further in time: the brewer is using 19th century steam equipment. Both De Brabandere in Bavikhove and Omer VanderGhinste in Bellegem are modern breweries where the Flemish red-brown beers are produced in the traditional way. The beers mature in wooden barrels. Many village and city breweries are fighting for space once they start suffering growing pains. This is why Van Honsebrouck, known for its Kasteel beers, commissioned an entirely new brewery. Ingelmunster was swapped for Izegem. Their new building with its twin towers has the look of a fortress. Village breweries proliferate in the Valley of the Zenne to the west of Brussels. This is 'gueuze country' where lambic beers undergo their traditional 'wild' or 'spontaneous' fermentation during the cooling-down period in the open cooling basin or 'koelschip'. Boon in Halle is brewing lambic in the traditional way, albeit with the use of modern production equipment. Timmermans in Dilbeek is the oldest lambic brewery in the country with a brewery museum attached. Modern lambic breweries include Lindemans and Mort Subite. Traditional 'gueuzestekerijen' are well worth a visit. These are not involved in brewing, rather, they blend lambic beers to obtain an oude gueuze. Visitors are welcome at De Cam in Gooik, De Troch in Ternat, Oud Beersel and 3 Fonteinen in Beersel. De Struise Brouwers in Oostvleteren take a different approach. Their brewery is set up in the former village school. Their story is written in chalk on the blackboard and you taste the beers sitting on a school bench in the classroom.

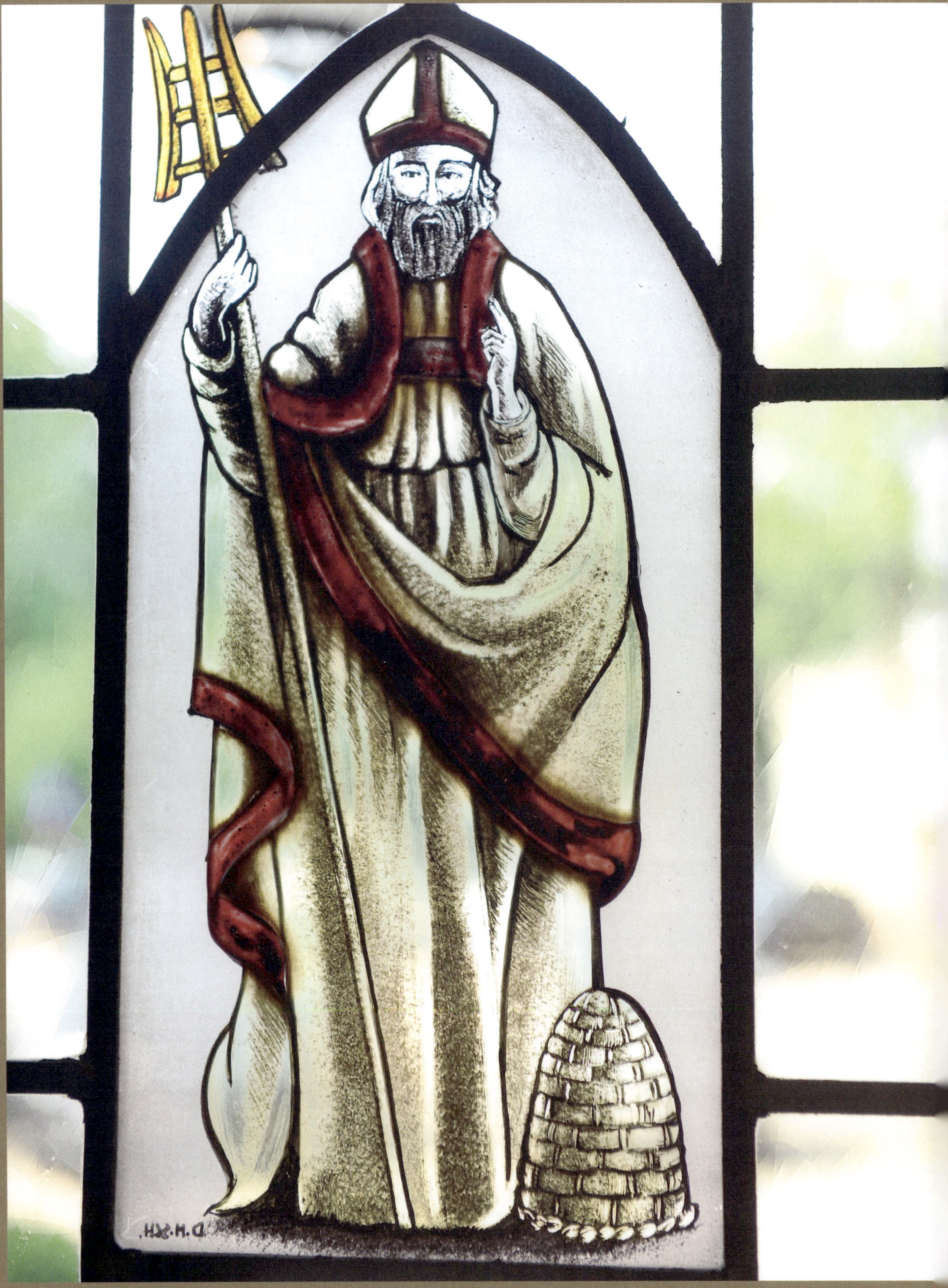

Records show that Brouwerij Die Maene (De Maan) in Bruges dates all the way back to 1564. De Halve Maan is now a tourist attraction.

On the farm

Brewing used to be closely intertwined with farming. Traditional beers, lambic and saison for example, were brewed during the winter for consumption in the following spring and summer. Large breweries such as Palm Belgian Craft Brewers and Duvel Moortgat also have agricultural origins but now there are not many traces left of their past. At Palm's, the brewery's own hop field and the stud farm for Belgian draft horses are a lasting reminder of their agricultural roots. Roman in Oudenaarde dates back to the 16th century. The brewery has occupied the same site since its conception and has always been owned by the Roman family. Agriculture played a significant part throughout the ages. The Haacht brewery in Boortmeerbeek used to be an industrial dairy farm. This impressive brewery site has a strikingly uniform look and is built on a large scale. In other words, with room for growth. Dubuisson in Pipaix is another brewery that began as a farm, as evidenced by the hop field next to the brewery. Brasserie des Légendes in Ellezelles farms its own barley whereas Jessenhofke in Hasselt has outsourced the cultivation of organic barley to a local farmer. Brasserie de Cazeau in Templeuve and Jandrain-Jandrenouille in the eponymous hamlet are both housed in traditional square farms, characteristic for the region. The Cazeau farm has a historic character that has remained virtually unchanged throughout the ages. Microbrewery Jandrain-Jandrenouille is in danger of getting lost in the monumental barn. A textbook example of a farm brewery is Hof Ten Dormaal in Tildonk near Leuven. This brewery, known for its endives beer and wood-matured brews, lies in the middle of the fields. Its brewer is also a farmer. He grows his own barley and hops. Wilderen in Sint-Truiden used to be a self-sufficient farm enterprise with its own distillery. After a truly spectacular renovation, a brand new brewery and distillery now take pride of place next to the historic distillery. The monumental timber-framed barn houses the brewery tavern. In a former life, Ter Dolen in Houthalen was the summer residence for Sint-Truiden abbey. This brewery, resident in a barn, also offers an experience of outdoor life. Another classic farm brewery is Saint-Monon in the Ardennes, not far from Nassogne. The brewers here are also keen to safeguard the pedigree of the Ardennes draft horse. The countryside is never far away in Brasserie d'Achouffe (Houffalize) and the tiny, tiny Inter-Pol in nearby Mont, both in the heart of the Ardennes. Finally, wood is the future at Caracole in Anseremme (Dinant). Their kettles are wood-fired.

Before the Second World War, brewers used carts such as these to transport 'tonnekensbier' (beer from wooden barrels). Nowadays these carts are only seen during parades.

Visiting breweries

When you are touring a large brewery, it soon looks too 'technical' and you are in danger of getting lost in-between the maze of pipes. You are bombarded by numbers right, left and centre but, to give the brewers their due, they are also doing their very best to explain the brewing process to you. Far from simple as, when you are walking from one building to the next, you may well lose the thread. Leaving breadcrumbs to mark the trail is not really an option as these are flushed away almost immediately. Just take a look. Brewers are flushing as if their lives depended on it, hence the wet floors everywhere. Things become even more complicated when a brewery is expanding… another cold storage tank here, another buffer tank there… This is typical for village breweries that are bursting out of the seams of a jacket that has grown too small. Consequently, breweries that are enjoying a growth spurt will outsource part of their activities, bottling and logistics for example. You can tour the production area but the other part of the story is played out elsewhere. However, there is a huge variety in brewing methods. Take a look at the artisan lambic brewers. They allow the wort to cool down in open cooling basins before transferring it to wooden barrels where the wort will continue to ferment. Visit their cellars to get the feel of a wine Château and enter a different world.

On a small scale

Microbreweries come in all shapes and sizes, from your common 'home and garden' brewer all the way up to the professionals. On the smallest scale, you will come across a brewer who, every week, produces just enough for his own little café. Gone is gone. Pop in and enjoy the experience. The brewer tells his tale in the same room where he does his brewing and pours his beer at the same time. This 'first-hand education' is inspirational. It makes you want to roll up your sleeves and start brewing. It seems so simple until the first question marks arise. Why does my beer taste different from last week's batch? What have I done wrong? And this takes us to the essential process of analysis. The major brewers invest heavily in analysis as, after all, the consumer expects to find the same beer in his glass every single time from their trusty waiter. "Same again please!" This fires up the microbrewer – I am generalising here – to discuss natural ingredients and seasonal influences. "After all, wines vary depending on their vintage. Should this difference not be recognised in a natural product such as beer?" If the brewer is not available to show you around, there is bound to be a guide whose enthusiasm is infectious. He or she will afford you a glimpse behind the scenes and into the glass. And so, every brewery visit turns into an experience that you will remember with fondness whenever your eye happens to rest on that one single beer, well hidden in the cellar. What was its name again?

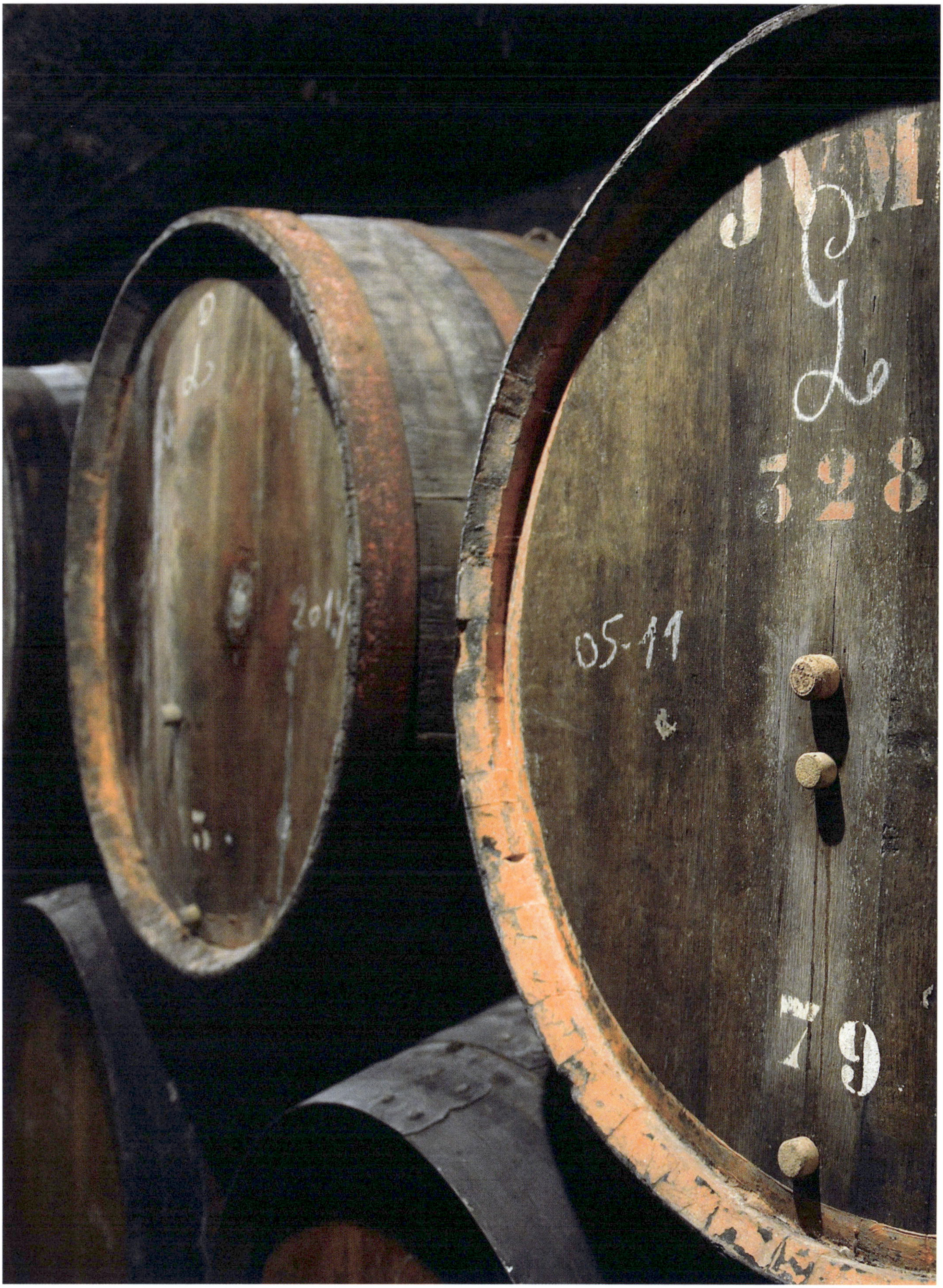
328
05-11
2014
79

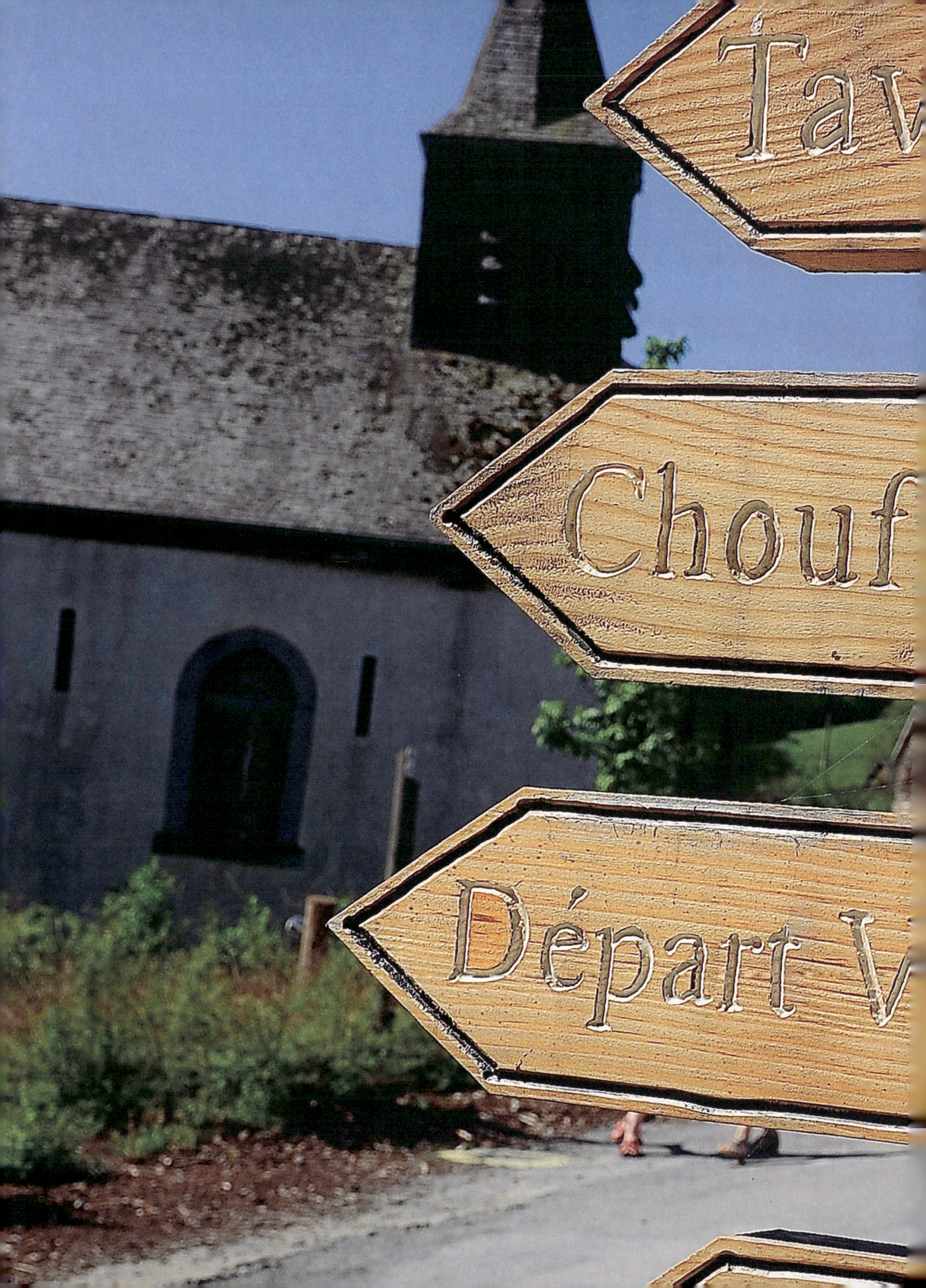
Tav
Chouf
Départ V

...rne

...Shop

...ITES

REGIONAL BEER TOURISM

AARLEN
BASTENAKEN
LA ROCHE
BOUILLON

Achouffe (Brasserie d')

Chouffe Soleil, La Chouffe, McChouffe, Houblon Chouffe, N'Ice Chouffe

———

Achouffe lies in the heart of the Ardennes. It is picture-postcard pretty with only a handful of houses embraced by a sea of green. A guided brewery tour must be arranged in advance. Don't forget to pop into the brewery tavern and adjacent shop and by all means, sample what the local hostelries have to offer. Guided tours: book in advance for groups of a maximum of 25 per guide. Individual visitors are welcome on specific dates and times. There is plenty here to enjoy for walkers, cyclists, horse riders and anyone else who is fond of the good life. Pop into Houffalize Tourist Office (www.houffalize.be) for a detailed map of all the walking trails in the area. Tip: keep your eye on the calendar to keep track of events such as the annual Choufferie in August.

Achouffe 32, Wibrin (Houffalize), +32(0)61/23 04 44
visitebrasserie@achouffe.be, www.achouffe.be

Bastogne (Brasserie de)

Ardenne Saison, Ardenne Spirit Old Ale, Ardenne Stout, Bastogne Pale Ale, Trouffette-gamma

———

Microbrewery attached to an Ardennes farmhouse. May soon be moving to new premises near Marche-en-Famenne. Visits by appointment.

BelleEau 3, Vaux-sur-Sûre, +32(0)478/59 51 13
info@brasseriedebastogne.be, www.brasseriedebastogne.be

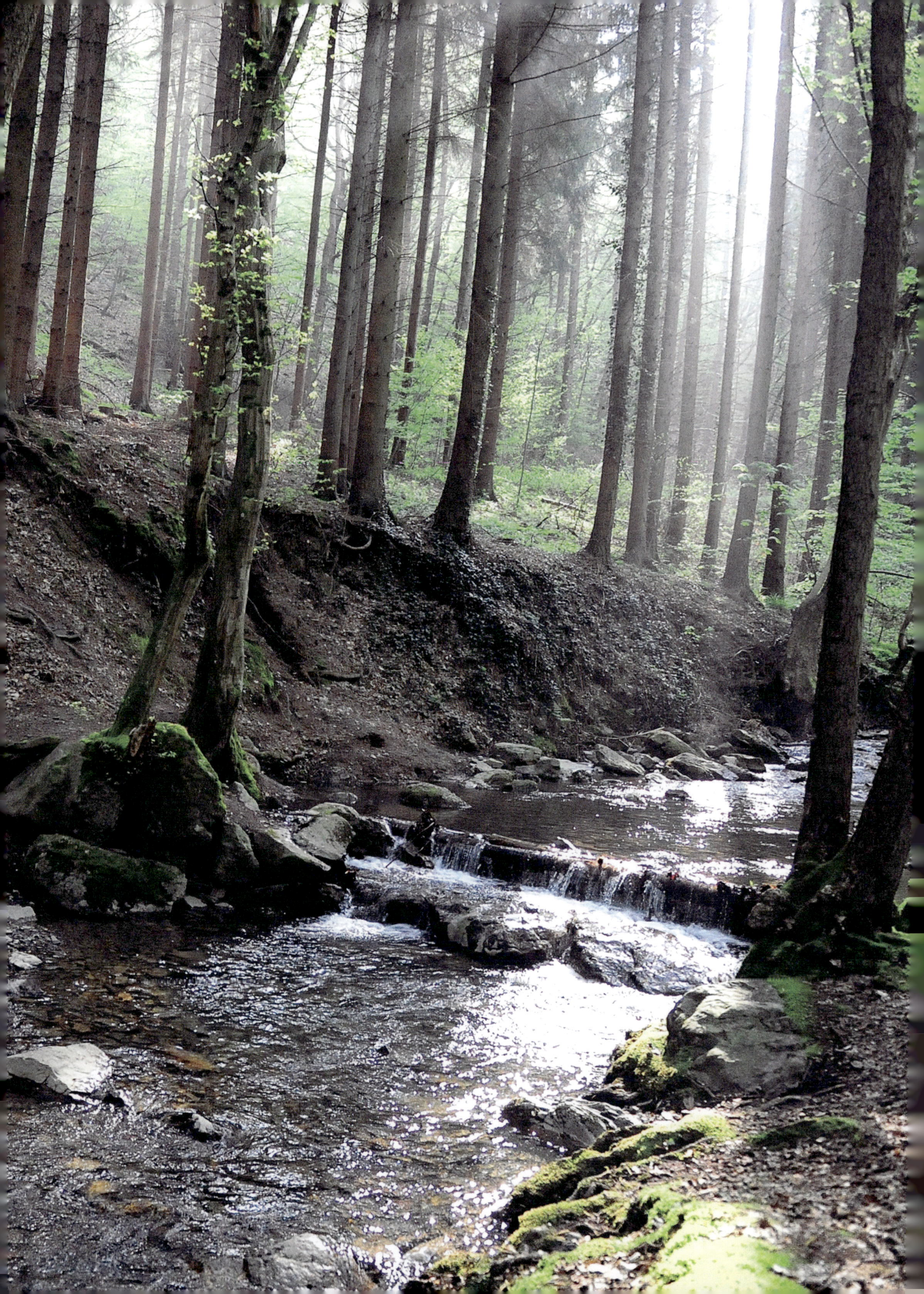

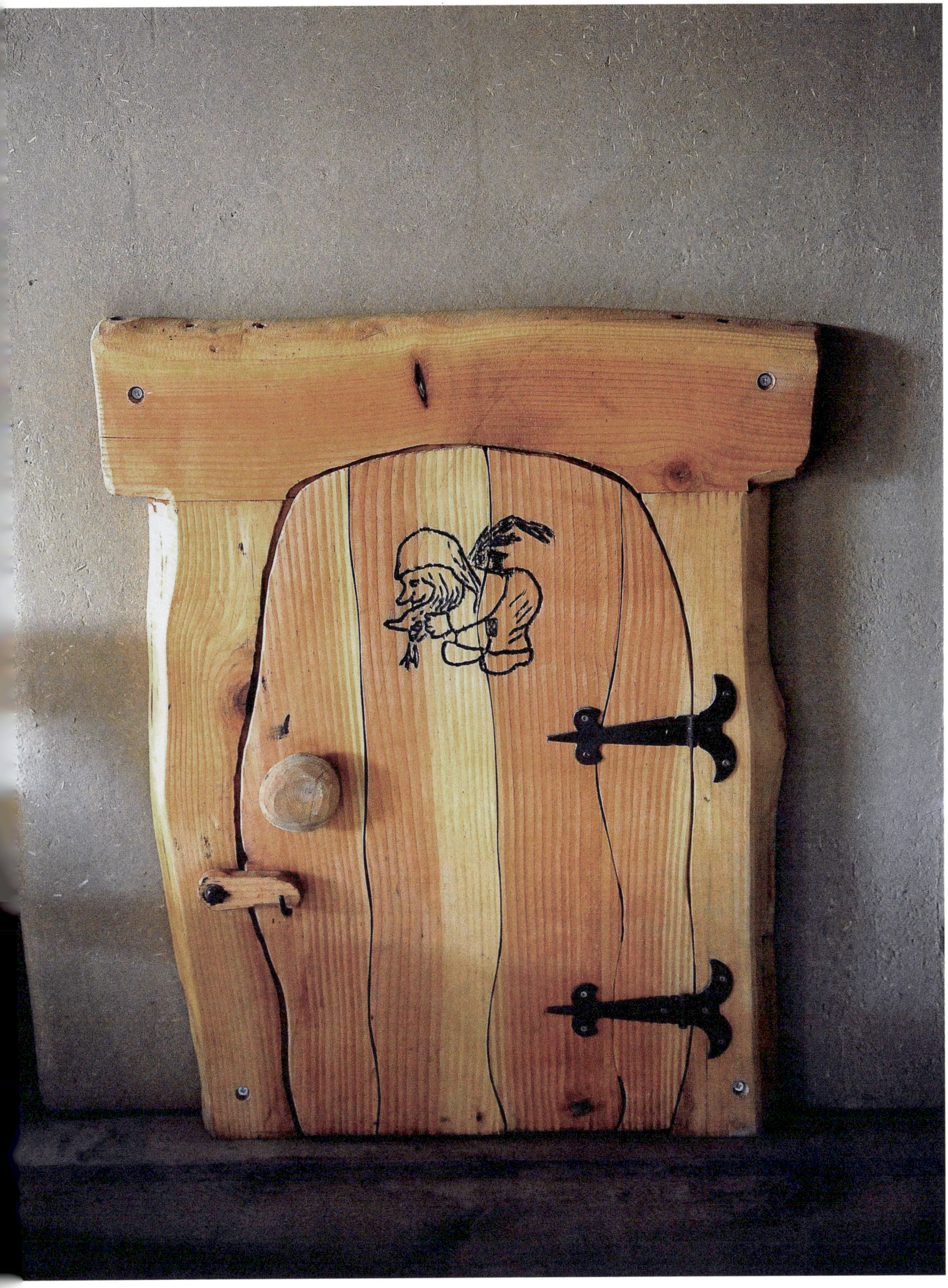

Bouillon (Brasserie de)

Blanche de Bouillon, Bouillonnaise, Cuvée de Bouillon, Médiévale

---

Microbrewery with tasting room on the edge of Bouillon. Has ties with Le Marché de Nathalie beer shop close to Bouillon Castle. Book in advance for a guided tour and a meal.

Rue de la Girafe 76, Sensenruth (Bouillon), +32(0)61/46 89 40, info@brasseriedebouillon.be, www.brasseriedebouillon.be

Le Marché de Nathalie, Grand'Rue 22

Demanez (Brasserie)

B.R. Blonde bio

Microbrewery in the heart of the Ardennes. Visits by prior arrangement.

Magerotte 7, Sainte-Ode, +32(0)61/21 95 74, sebastien@demanez.be, www.demanez.be

Fantôme (Brasserie de)

Fantôme, Saison d'Erezée

A village brewery in the heart of the Ardennes. Guided tours by appointment for groups of 15 and over. Tasting facilities. Tavern open during weekends and school holidays and by prior arrangement for groups.

Rue Préal 8, Soy (Erezée), +32(0)86/47 70 44, contact@fantome.be, www.fantome.be

GenGoulf (Brasserie)

GenGoulf

Microbrewery not a million miles away from Orval Abbey, set up by a laboratory worker from the Orval Brewery. Visits by appointment only.

Rue des Hawys 24, Villers-devant-Orval (Florenville), +32(0)61/29 22 39, contact@Gengoulf.be, www.gengoulf.be

Inter-Pol

Witte Pol, Zwarte Pol

Tiny Microbrewery set up in the café of B&B La Vieille Forge at a stone's throw from Brasserie d'Achouffe. Visits by appointment only.

Mont 33, Mont (Houffalize), +32(0)61/28 96 39, www.la-vieilleforge.be

Millevertus (Brasserie de)

Douce Vertus, Fumette, Papesse, Poivrote, Safranaise

Microbrewery located near Orval. For lovers of beers made with herbs and spices. Visits by prior arrangement for groups of 25 and over. With its own cafeteria and shop.

Chemin de l'Eau Vive 3 (rue du Pont 53), Breuvanne (Tintigny), +32(0)63/22 34 97, info@millevertus.be, www.millevertus.be

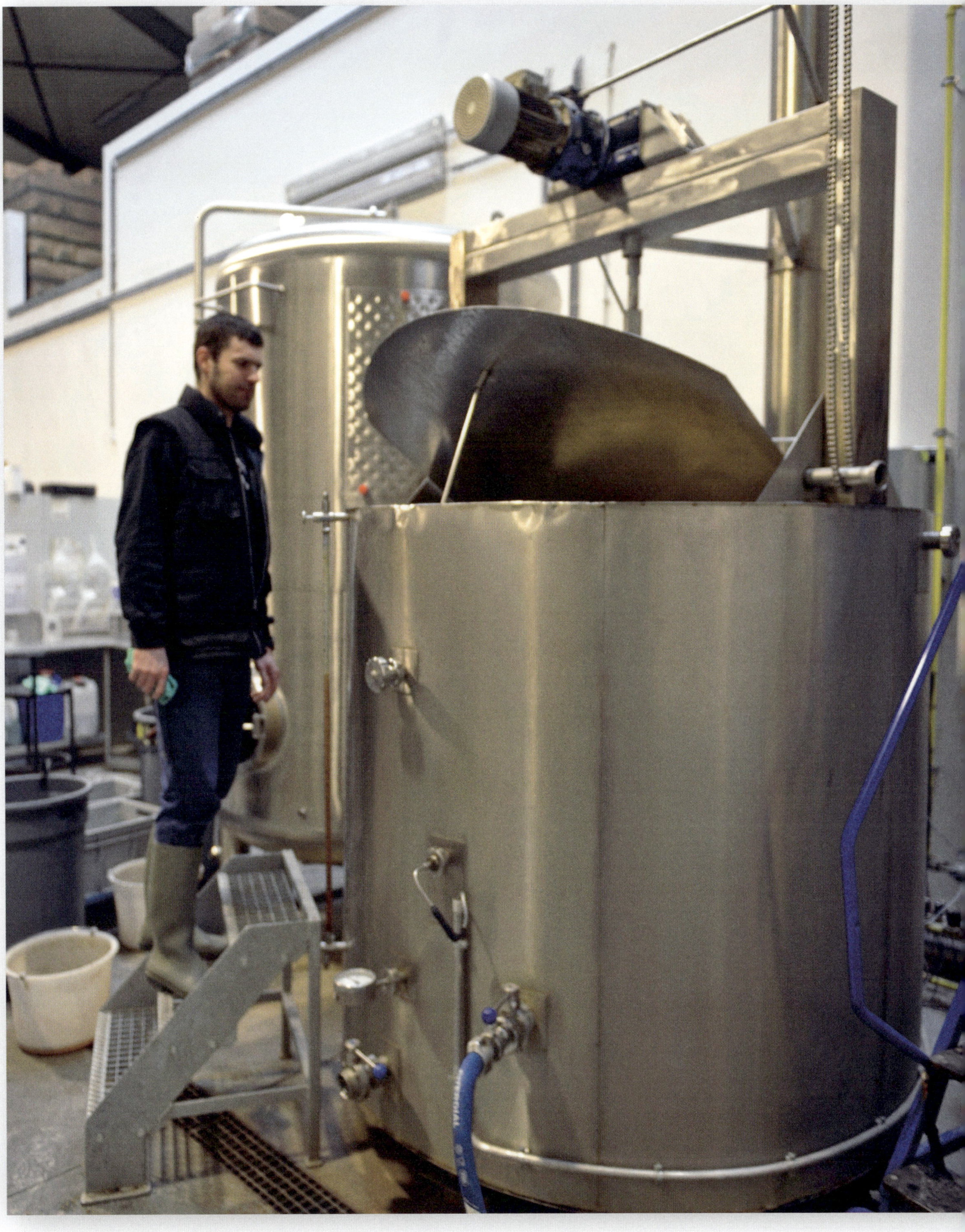

Mathilde, who was a widow, accidentally dropped her wedding ring into the well of the valley. She begged God for help and, before long, a trout came to the surface, holding the precious ring in its mouth. Whereupon Mathilde exclaimed: "This really is a valley of gold!" (Orval, "val d'or" means "valley of gold") and out of gratitude, she decided to found an abbey on this blessed site. And, according to legend, this is how Orval Abbey was born.

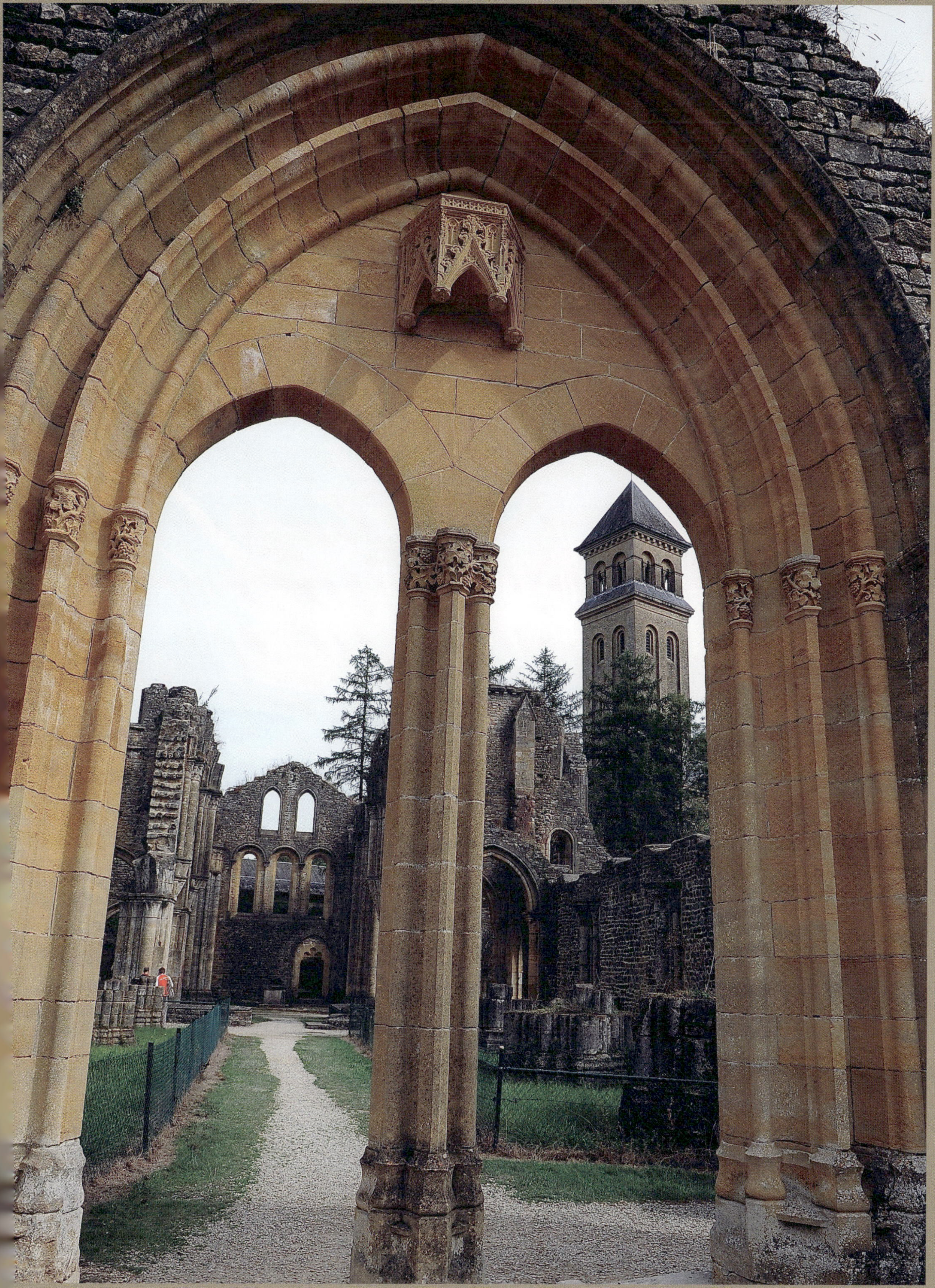

Orval (Abbaye d')

Orval

The brewery itself is only open to the public on Open Doors days. The ruins of the medieval abbey, the abbey church and the museum are accessible every day. Taste the beers in L'Ange Gardien, the abbey tavern. Try the light 'green' Orval, the monks' refectory beer. The abbey is a great starting point for exploring the Ardennes and the Gaume by bike or on foot.

Abbaye Notre Dame d'Orval, Villers-devant-Orval (Florenville), +32(0)61/31 10 60, www.orval.be

Rulles (Brasserie de)

Rulles

Microbrewery in the heart of the Gaume region, where the beer still ferments in open cooling basins. Book your tour in advance (including a tasting session) for a minimum of ten participants.

Rue Maurice Grévisse 36, Rulles, +32(0)63/41 18 38 info@larulles.be, www.larulles.be

Saint-Monon (Brasserie de)

Saint-Monon

Microbrewery located at a farm with a permanent stable of Ardennes draft horses. Group visits by appointment. Has a tasting room.

Rue Principale 45, Ambly (Nassogne), +32(0)84/21 46 32 info@saintmonon.be, www.saintmonon.be

Sainte-Hélène (Brasserie)

Mistinguett, Lily Blue, Gypsy Rose, Grognarde, Prime, Barley Wine

Village brewery near Virton. Brewery visits by appointment for groups of five or more.

Rue de la Colline 21, Ethe (Virton), +32(0)63/43 48 64 info@sainte-helene.be, www.sainte-helene.be

3 Fourquets (Les)

Lupulus

At five kilometres from the Luxembourg border Les 3 Fourquets has set up a microbrewery with tasting room in a converted Ardennes farmhouse. Pierre Gobron is the heart and soul behind the project. With Chris Bauweraerts he is the original founder of Brasserie d'Achouffe. Visits by prior arrangement for groups of 10 and over. Try their Lupulus cheese.

Courtil 50, Courtil (Gouvy), +32(0)80/64 38 39, +32(0)497/46 03 21 of +32(0)499/38 21 55, julien@lupulus.be, dgrtrt@gmail.com, www.les3fourquets.be

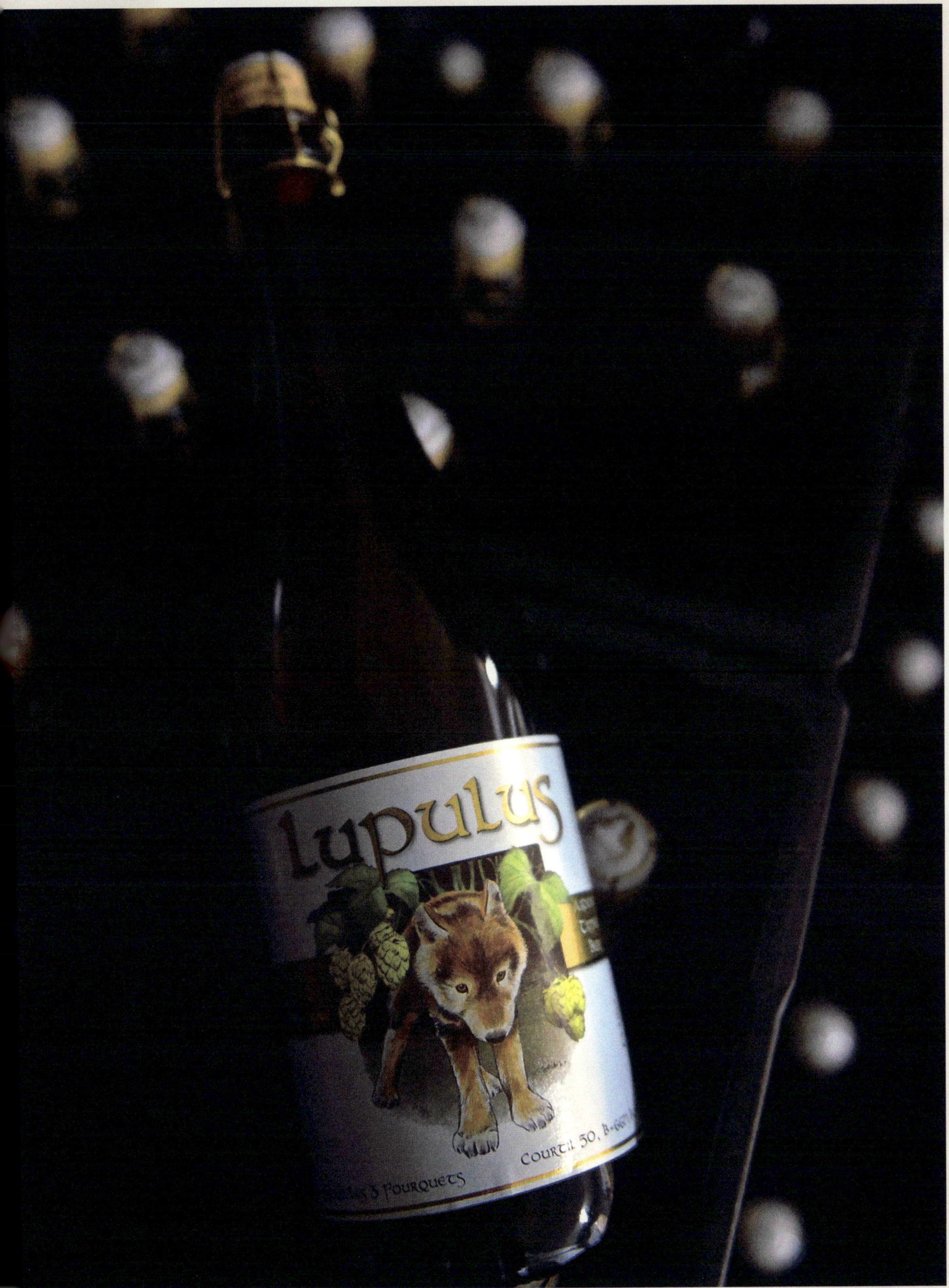
lupulus

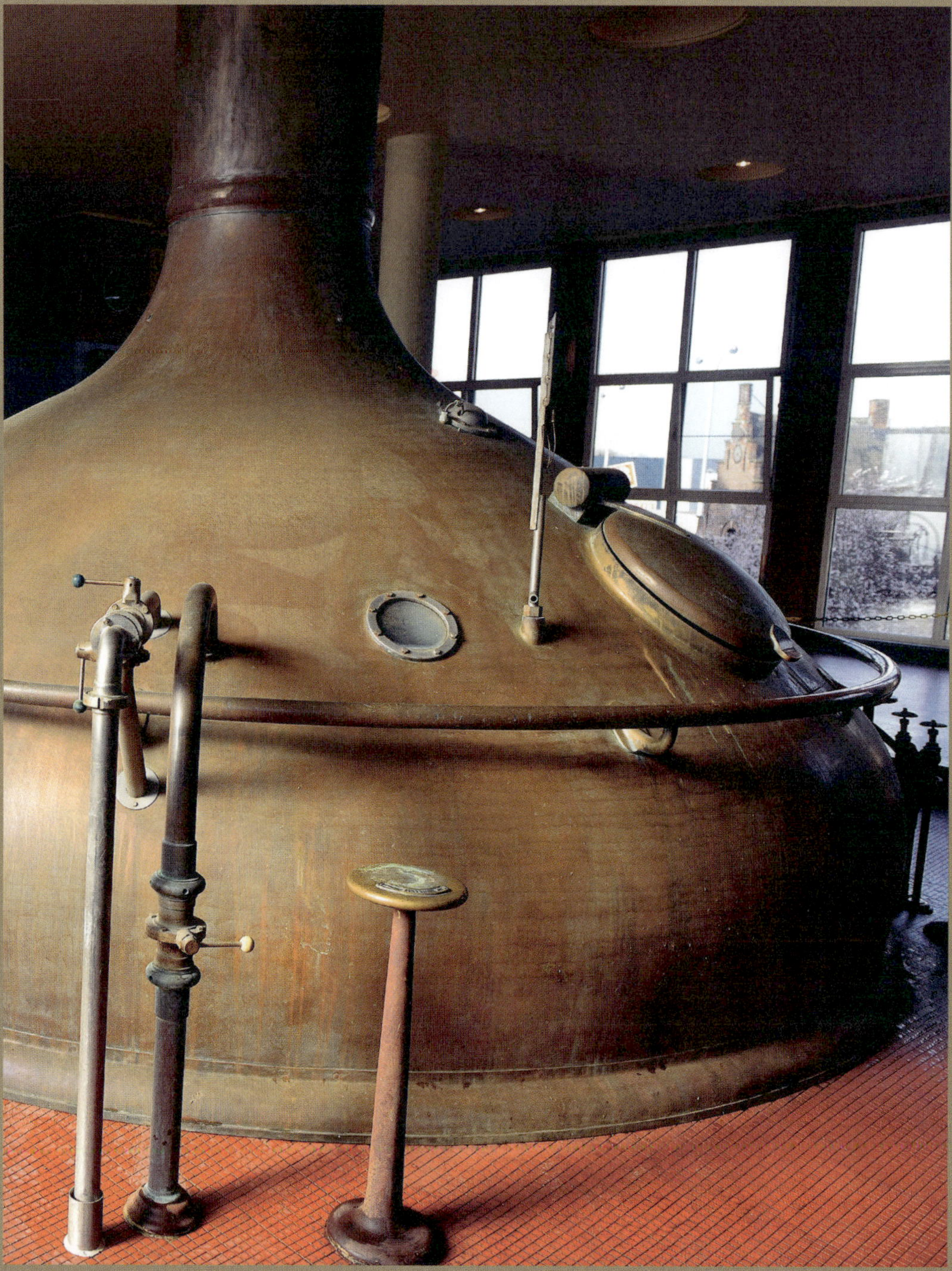

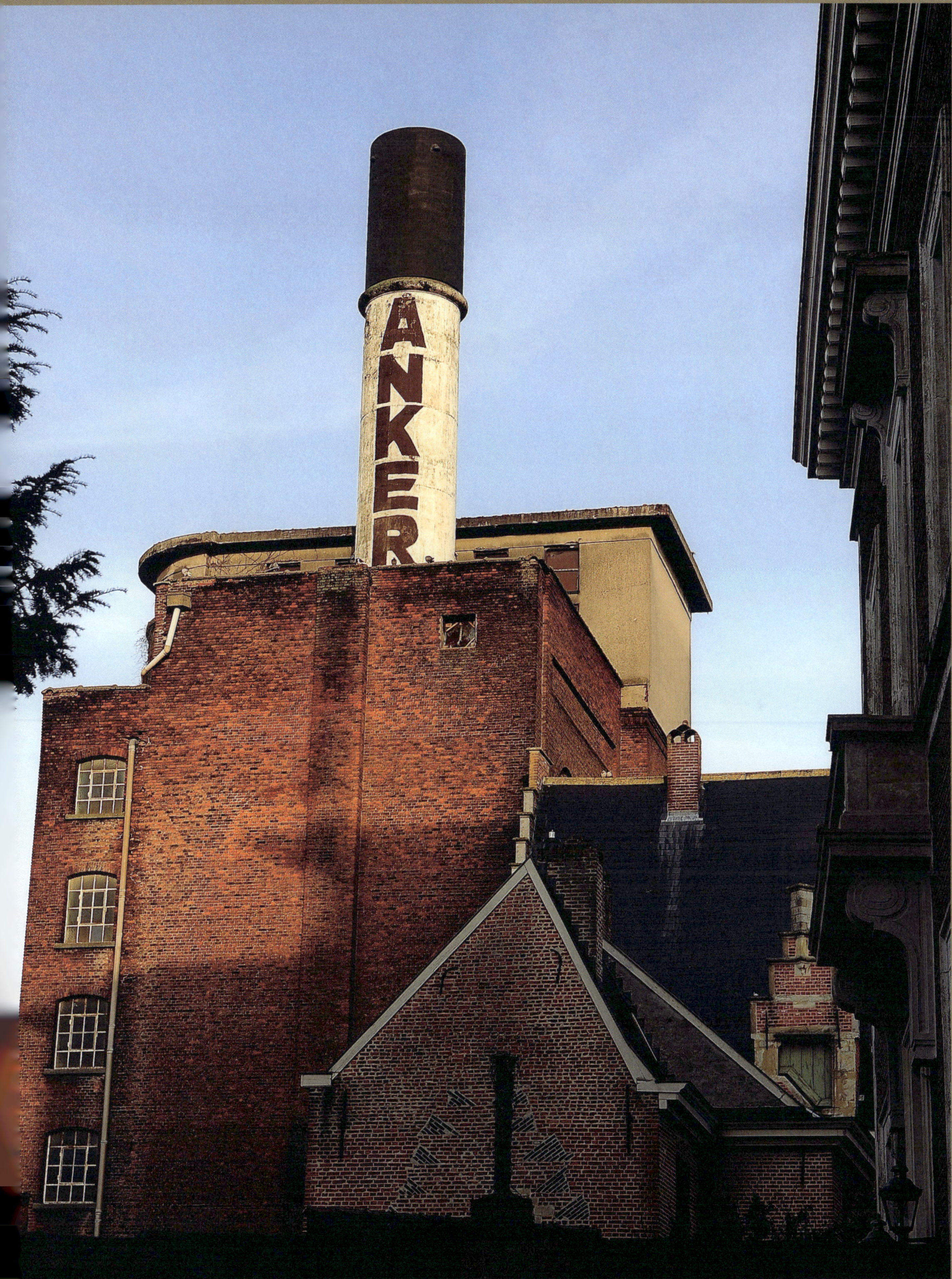
ANKER

REGIONAL BEER TOURISM

ANTWERP MECHELEN TURNHOUT

Anker (Het)

Boscoli, Cuvée van de Keizer, Gouden Carolus, Lucifer, Maneblusser

———

Het Anker offers the complete beer experience with its historic brewery-maltings in the city, a brasserie and hotel. You will also visit the chambers used for maturing the Gouden Carolus Single Malt brewery whisky. You can visit the brewery as a group or on an individual basis. Groups (between 10 and 25) need to make a reservation. Visitors not attached to a group are invited to join a guided tour every Friday, Saturday and Sunday at 11:00. The brasserie always offers a range of house beers on tap and offers several dishes prepared with one of the beers. Reserve your table at brasserie-hotel@hetanker.be or via +32(0)15/28 71 41. Combine with a visit to house distillery De Molenberg where the Gouden Carolus Single Malt whisky is produced. Located seven kilometres away from the brewery.

Guido Gezellelaan 49, Mechelen, +32(0)15/28 71 47 info@hetanker.be, www.hetanker.be

De Molenberg, Klaterstraat 1, Blaasveld, +32(0)3/501 82 12 www.stokerijdemolenberg.be

Brouwershuis ('t)

Bossiebier

———

Microbrewery with café and terrace close to the expansive Kalmthout nature reserve. Visits by arrangement.

Noordeind 31, Dorp-Heuvel (Kalmthout), +32(0)497/47 99 94, info@hetbrouwershuis.com, www.hetbrouwershuis.com

DijkWaert

Eeuwige Liefde, Fruitig Bierreke, Goeie Koffe, McThals, Thals, Thuiske, Vurig Bierreke, Xmas in Thals

———

Microbrewery and shop selling regional produce in Herentals. Visits or guided tours including tasting available by appointment.

Olmenlaan 7A, Herentals, +32(0)14/73 40 31 of +32(0)478/94 65 64 – info@dijkwaert.be, www.dijkwaert.be

Dochter van de Korenaar (De)

Belle Fleur, Bravoure, Charbon, Crime Passionel, Embrasse, Finesse, Noblesse

———

Microbrewery offering wood-matured niche beers. Tours available for groups comprising 8-25 people. The brewer himself explains the brewing process in detail. There is an opportunity to taste the beers once you have done the rounds. Tasting room open Saturdays between 13:00 and 17:00.

Pastoor de Katerstraat 24, Baarle-Hertog, +32(0)14/69 98 00, brouwerij@dedochtervandekorenaar.be, www.dedochtervandekorenaar.be

Brewer Ronald Mengerink of De Dochter van de Korenaar was a chef in a previous life. With his niche beers he is exploring the boundaries of taste.

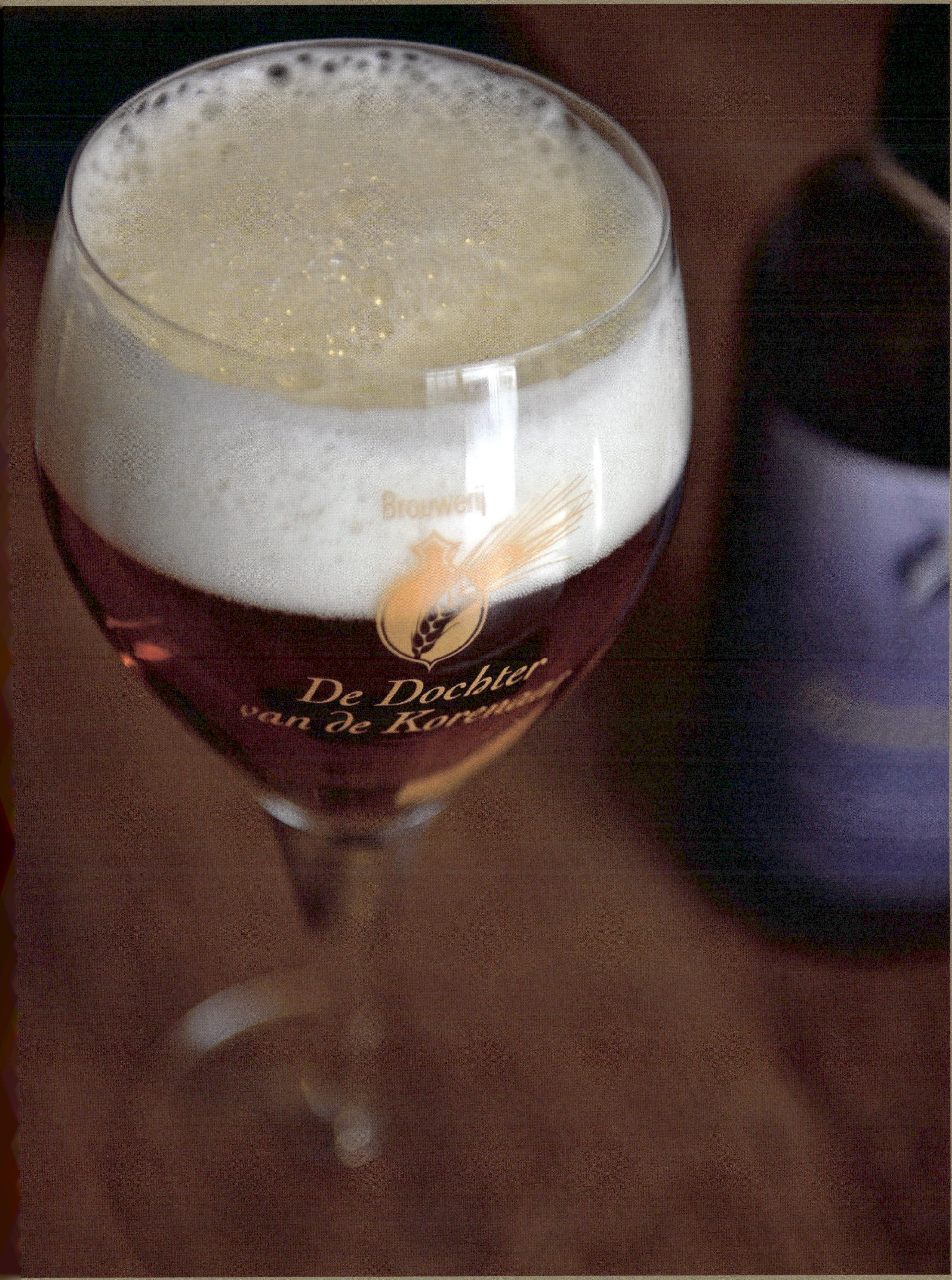
Brouwerij
De Dochter
van de

MB
MOORTGAT

MB

Lonck.

XTRA

ortgat

Dorpsbrouwerij Humulus

Arendonker

———

Visits: book in advance for groups of 8 to 15 participants.

Pelgrimsplein 19, Arendonk, +32(0)476/25 44 20, info@dorpsbrouwerijhumulus.be, www.dorpsbrouwerijhumulus.be, www.arendonker.com

Duvel Moortgat

Bel Pils, Duvel, Duvel Tripel Hop, Maredsous, Vedett

———

This is the birthplace of Duvel, Maredsous and Vedett. The guided tour provides an insight into the history of the brewery and the entire brewing process. The tour starts and finishes in Den Depot visitors' centre which is also the brewery café. A standard visit (15-70 people) or a beer tasting (up to 20) conducted by a beer sommelier are available by appointment.

Breendonkdorp 58, Breendonk-Puurs, +32(0)3/886 71 21, www.duvel.be

Hofbrouwerijke ('t)

Blondelle, Bosprotter, Hofblues, Hofelf, Hofpint, Hoftrol

———

Microbrewery. Book your visit in advance.

Hoogstraat 151, Beerzel, +32(0)15/75 77 07, info@thofbrouwerijke.be, www.thofbrouwerijke.be

Hopperd (Den)

Cannabier, Kameleon-gamma

———

The tasting room, a small café on the Laak- and Netepad cycling route, opens its doors every Sunday between 13:00 and 18:00. With terrace. Taste one of the organic beers or visit the brewery. Groups of a minimum of 15 are encouraged to make arrangements for their visit beforehand.

Netestraat 67, Westmeerbeek (Hulshout), +32(0)16/68 09 78 of +32(0)495/25 82 23, denhopperd@telenet.be

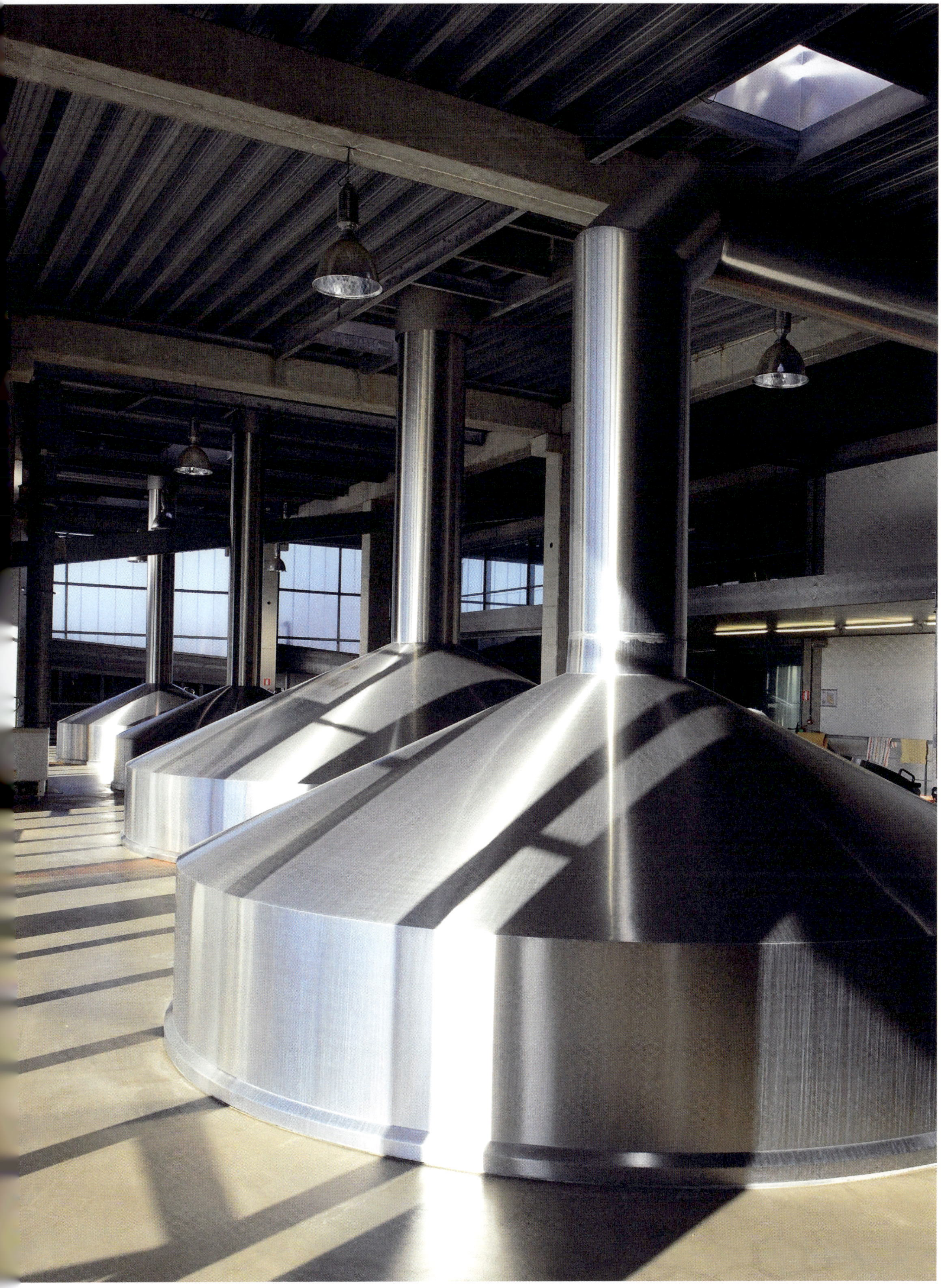

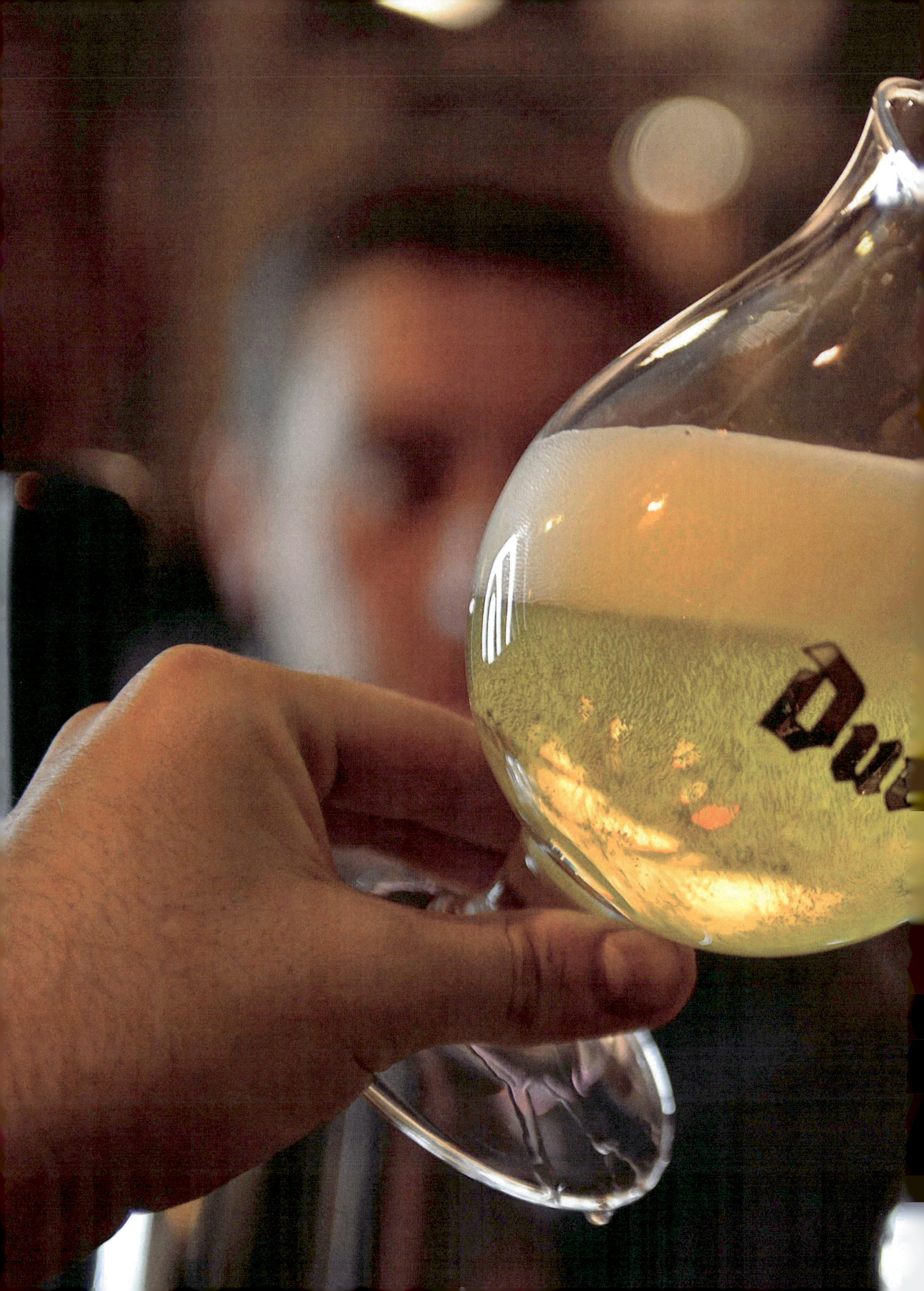

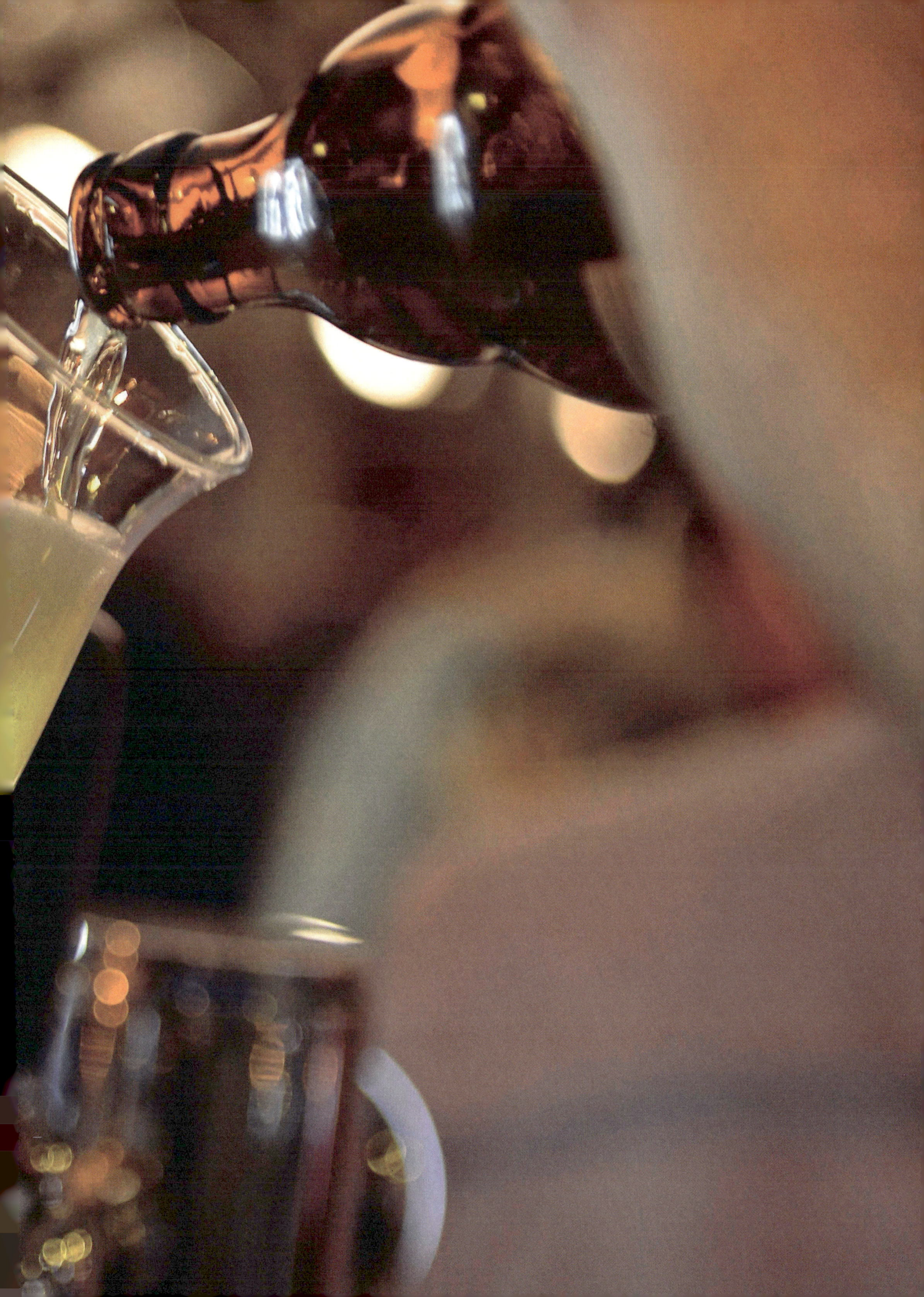

DE KONINCK

1833

EIGENZINNIG LEKKER

Michel Moortgat, CEO of Duvel Moortgat, and brewer Dennis De Potter raise a glass to the Antwerp city beer.

Koninck (De)

De Koninck, Triple d'Anvers, Wild Jo

Koninck city brewery. Find out everything you want to know about Antwerp, Belgian beers and the brewing process. Get the full 360° experience thanks to the many interactive displays and audio-visual effects. Follow the visitors' itinerary before tasting De Koninck beers in the former brewhall, now converted into a bar. If you want to come as a group, make your reservation in advance. The site also includes a cheese shop, a butcher's, a baker's and a chocolaterie where there is produce crafted on the premises. The house restaurant uses all these products and pairs them with the beers of Duvel Moortgat.

Mechelsesteenweg 291, Antwerpen, +32(0)3/218 40 48, www.dekoninck.be

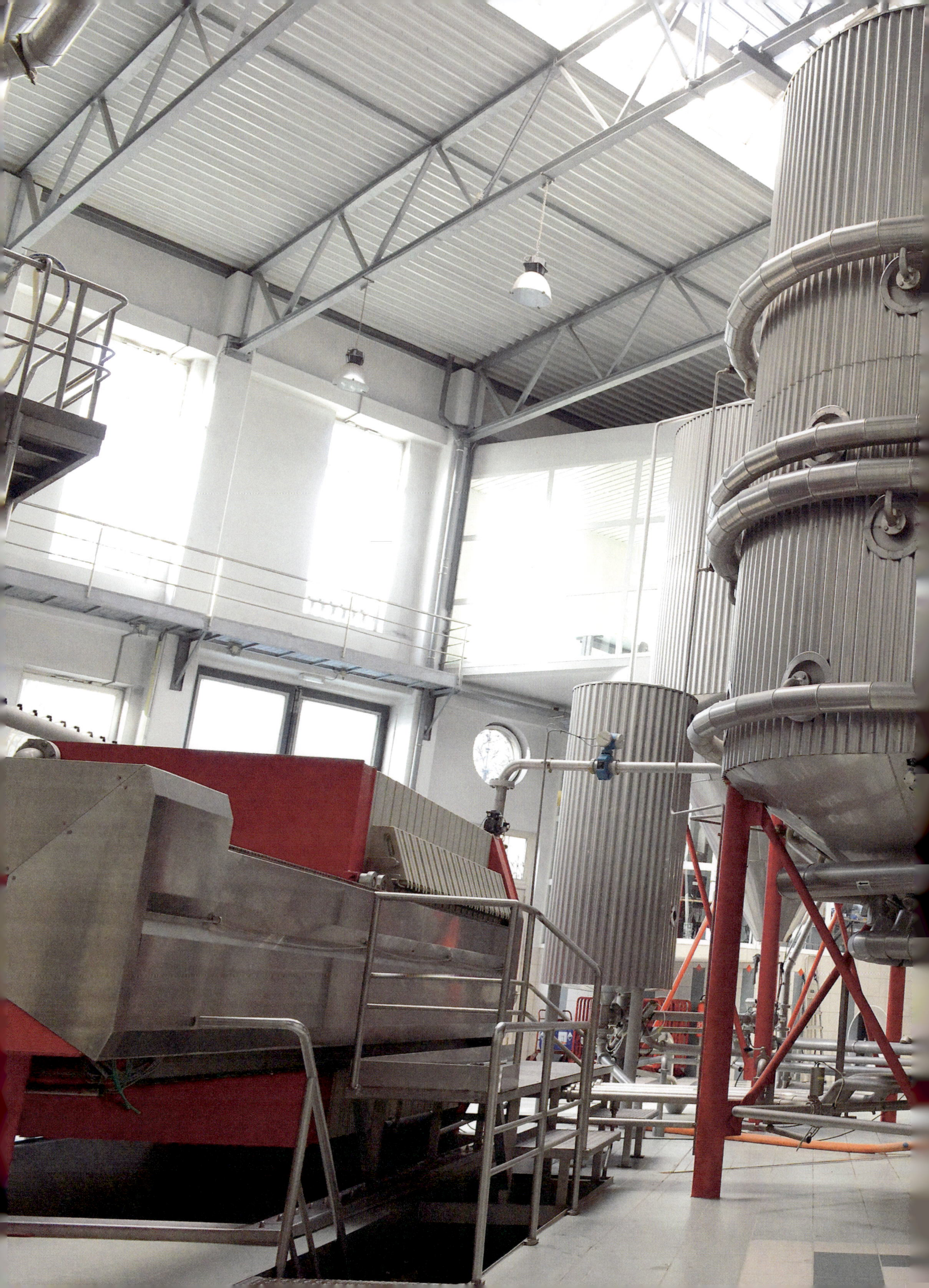

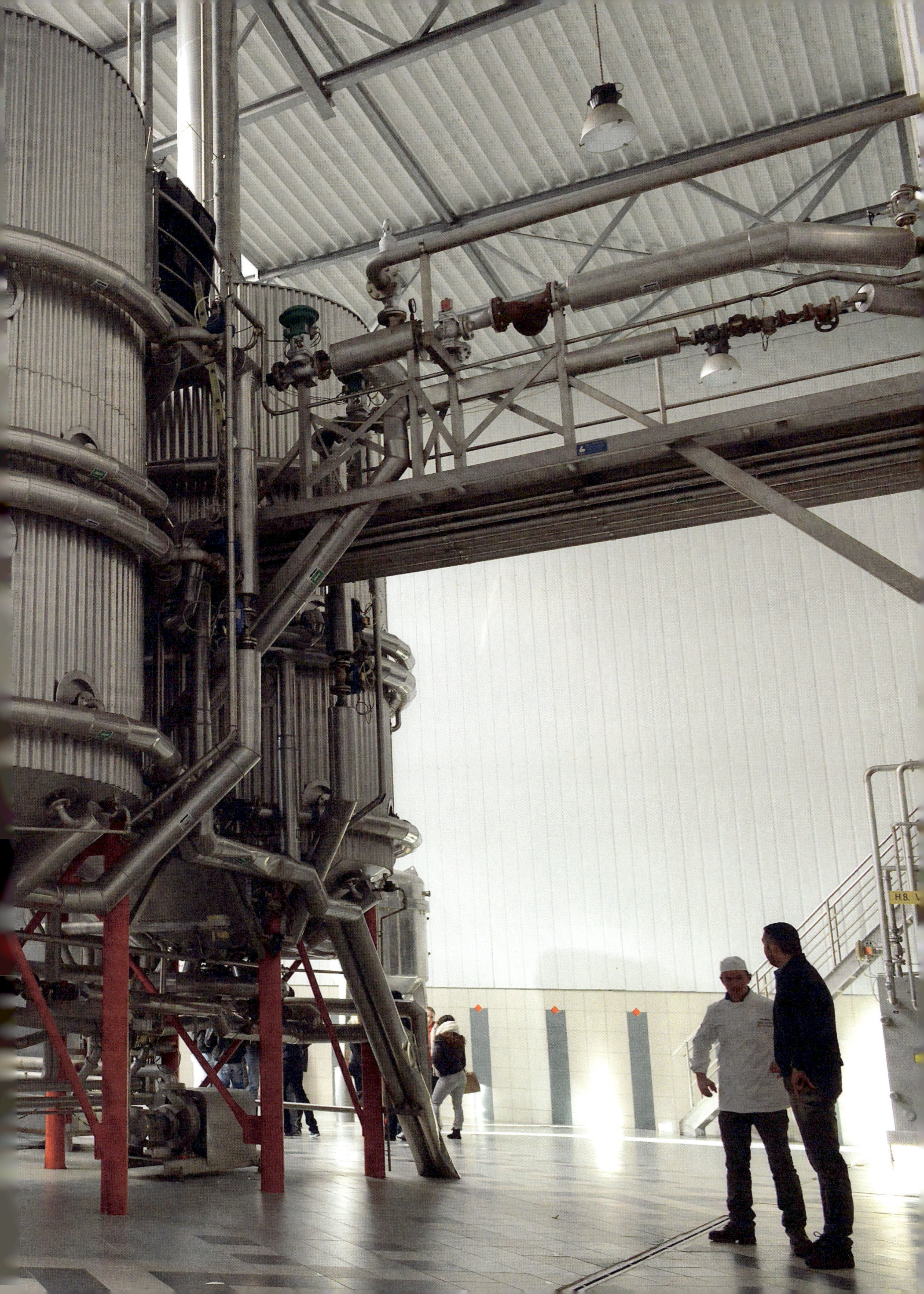

BROUWERIJ DE KONINCK
Kaasaffineurs
Van Tricht
RIJPINGSKAMERS
DE KONINCK
DE KONINCK
DE KONINCK
BOOMGAARD

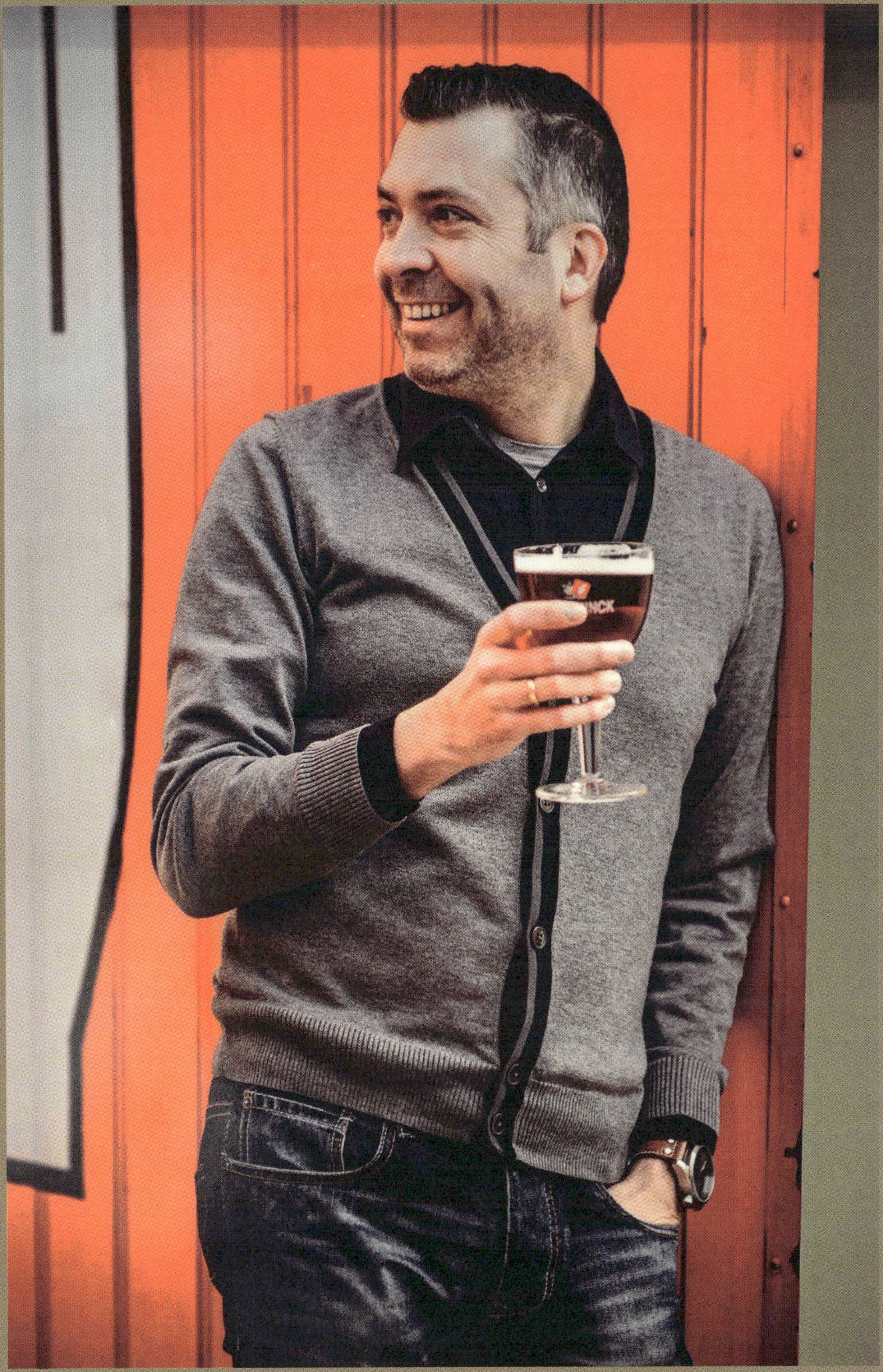

Nest (Het)

KlevereTien, SchuppenBoer, KoekeDam, HertenHeer, SchuppenAas, Turnhoutse Patriot, Dead Man's Hand

―――

This brand new microbrewery in Turnhout is the trump card of a city that is world-famous for the production of playing cards. It comprises tasting room and shop. Open Saturday afternoons, free entry. For group visits, book in advance.

Beyntel 17 (bedrijvenzone), Oud-Turnhout, +32(0)491/50 73 80, www.brouwerijhetnest.be

Pakhuis ('t)

Antwerps Blond, Antwerps Bruin, Den Bangelijke

―――

The 1,000 litre mashing kettle basin and the filtration tank take pride of place right in the centre of this brewery. From behind a glass wall you can keep an eye on the brewing process. Visits by appointment for groups of 15 and over. Taste the beers in the brewery tavern.

Vlaamse Kaai 76, Antwerpen, +32(0)3/238 12 40, info@pakhuis.info, www.huisbrouwerijpakhuis.be

Pirlot – Kempisch Vuur

Hoppergod, Kempisch Vuur, Jeneverbier, Haverstout

―――

Microbrewery and distillery in converted longhouse farm typical of the Kempen region. Tavern and terrace. To visit, book in advance for groups between 10 and 25. Situated at the cycling node network and the Gouverneur Kinsbergen and Conscience cycle trails.

Heistraat 3, Zandhoven, +32(0)475/42 61 95, info@kempisch-vuur.be, www.kempisch-vuur.be

Weldebrouck

Weldebrouck Tripel

―――

Microbrewery in the heart of Willebroek. Visits by appointment.

Gezondheidsstraat 37, Willebroek, +32(0)484/40 38 00, info@weldebrouck, www.weldebrouck.be

8 · BEER TOURISM

Brewing in a closed circuit in a modern, stainless steel brewhall.

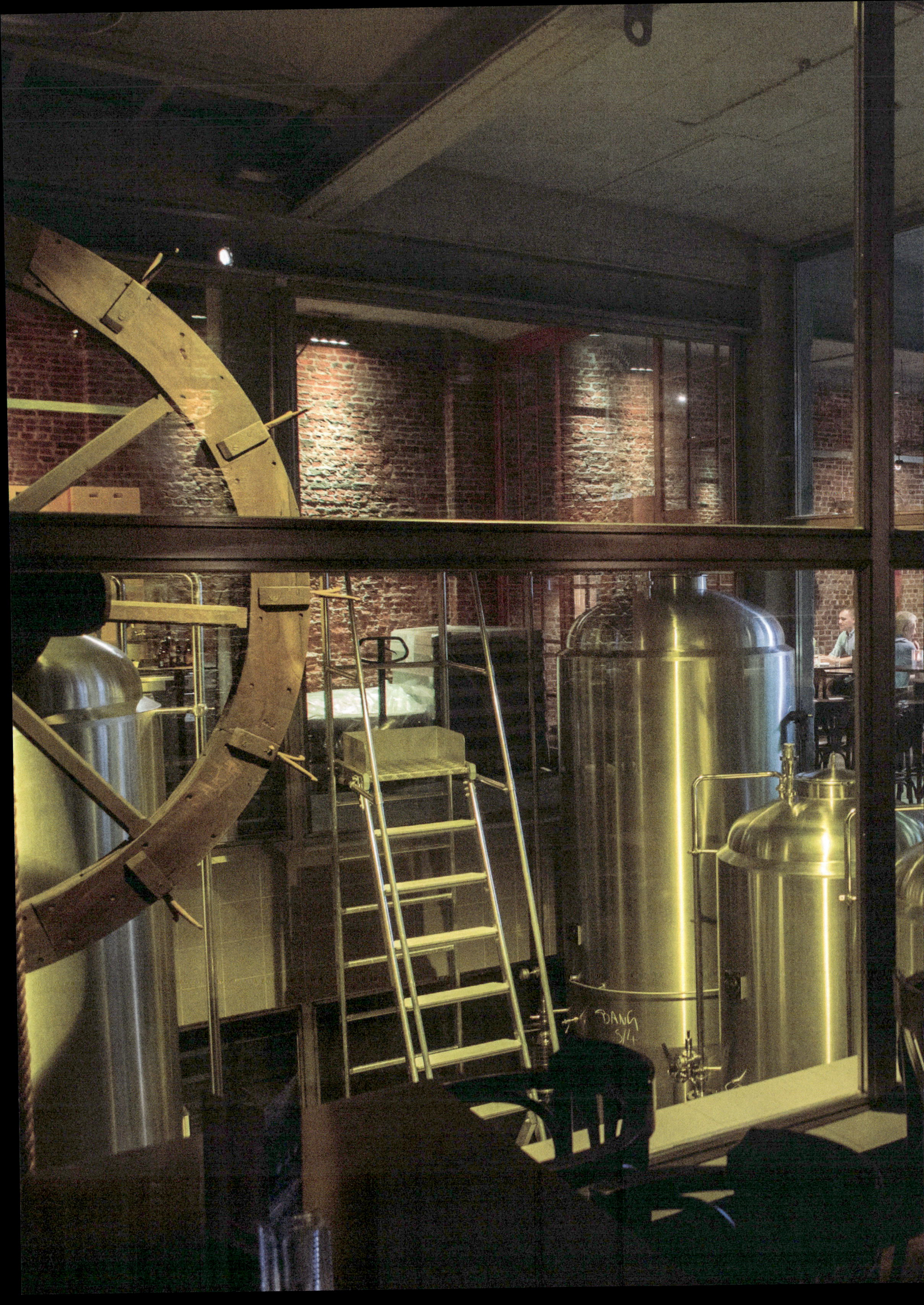

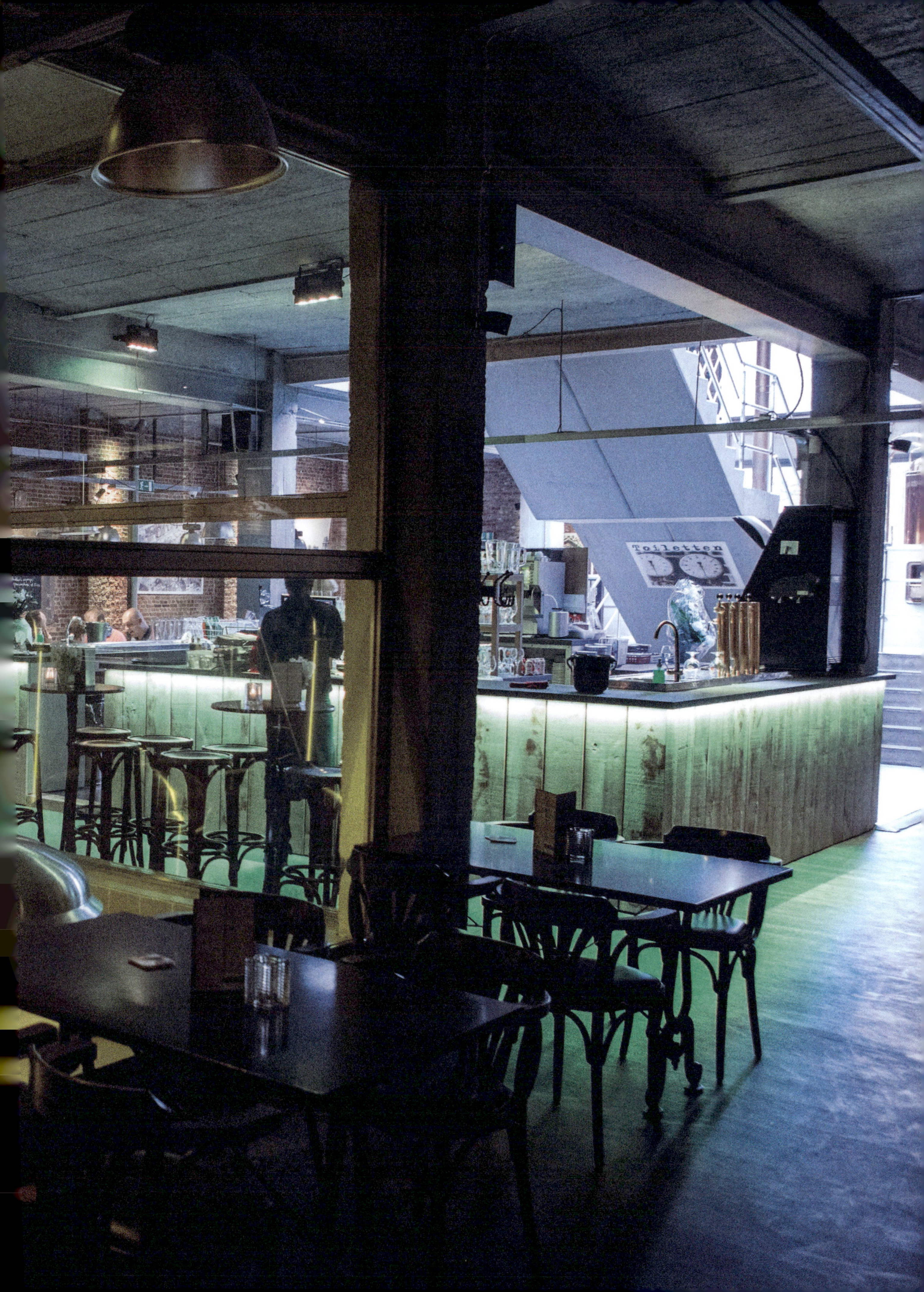
Toiletten

Westmalle (Abdij)

Westmalle Dubbel en Tripel

This Trappist abbey and brewery are not open to visitors. Have a drink or a bite to eat at the De Trappisten abbey tavern and see a video showing life and work in an abbey. Order a 'half and half' (half triple, half double), try the light monks' beer called Extra and sample the Westmalle cheese. This abbey makes a great starting point for hikes on foot or by bike in the green Kempen region.

Antwerpsesteenweg 487, Westmalle, +32(0)3/312 05 02, www.trappisten.be

8 • BEER TOURISM

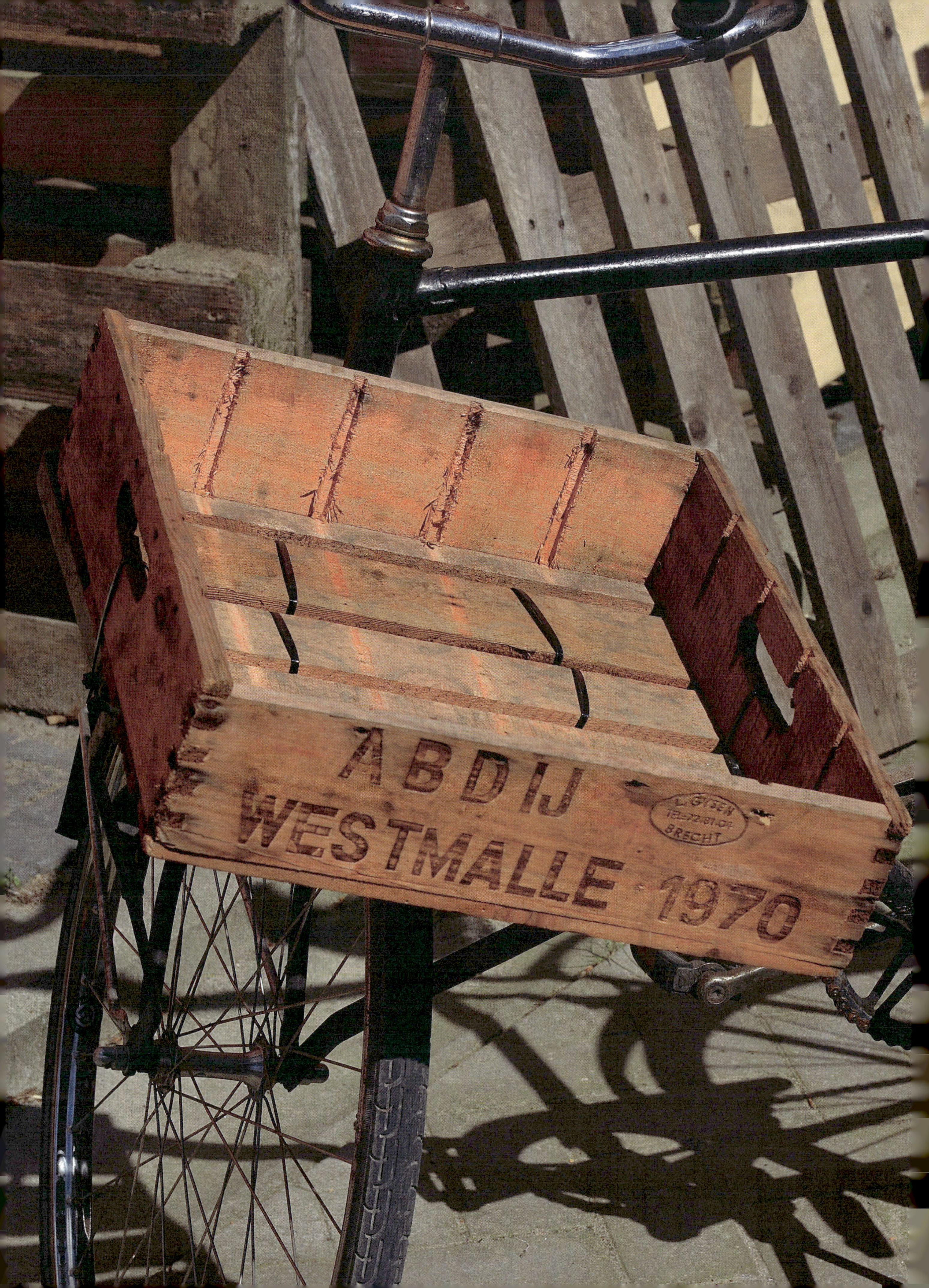
ABDIJ
WESTMALLE 1970
L. GIJSEN
TEL. 72.87.04
BRECHT

Looking over the wall at Westmalle Abbey.

WORTH SEEING

Biermuseum Olen Beer Museum

This beer museum, housed in Onze-Lieve-Vrouw-Olen railway station, displays paraphernalia related to almost 5,000 different brands of beer and jenever. You can taste around 175 different types. Admire hundreds of beer glasses, tins and bottles, toys and stoneware mugs. Collector Eddy Bosmans has assembled over 100,000 beer labels from across the world, 17,000 from Belgium alone, all classed by brewery, province, town, community and country. For his collection of crown corks he uses a special bottle opener that does not leave a dent in the cork. Eddy also collects advertising posters and enamel signs. Taste a Straffe Charel in a convivial ambiance.

Open daily between 10:00 and 22:00. +32(0)14/22 10 50
www.hemelvagevuurhel.be

Grand Café Lamot

Grand Café Lamot forms part of Lamot, a conference and heritage centre now occupying the restored and modernised buildings that were once a pils brewery.

Van Beethovenstraat 8/10, Mechelen, +32(0)15/20 95 30
www.grandcafelamot.be

BIÈRE BELGE
FALEAU
Dégustez
UN STOUT "ALLIANCE"
VENDU AU VERRE
VENDU AU LITRE
ALLIANCE STOUT ALLIANCE
meilleure
BIÈRE BELGE
CRISTAL-CITRON
a l'eau de
CRISTAL
CHAUDFONTAINE
Eau de Villée
DISTILLERIE de BIERCEE
DEPUIS 1946
PHEBUS
EXPORT
LABOR
MONS
WIEZE
WIEZE
BUVEZ
PRIMA
LE PALE ALE
BELGE
PRIMA
BRASSERIE DUSSART
GILLY
BIÈRES
CHASSE
ROYALE

REGIONAL BEER TOURISM

BERGEN
DOORNIK
ATH

Abbaye des Rocs (Brasserie d')

Abbaye des Rocs, Montagnarde, Blanche des Honnelles

———

Village brewery. Guided tours by appointment, for groups and single visitors. Whilst you are here, pay a visit to the water mill and bee-keeping centre.

Chaussée de Brunehault 14, Audregnies, +32(0)65/75 59 99 of +32(0)476/41 91 03, www.abbaye-des-rocs.com

Art d'en brasser (L')

Belle de Saison, Fougueuse, Gourmande, Lunatique

———

Microbrewery with arts centre. Visit the brewery and its art exhibitions. By appointment only.

Chaussée de Lessines 361, Horrues (Zinnik), +32(0)478/38 73 16 info@lartdenbrasser.be, www.lartdenbrasser.be

Augrenoise

Augrenelle, Augrenette, Augrenoise

———

This microbrewery forms part of a community project. Some of its staff members have a disability. Once a month, when brewing is in progress, the brewery is open to the public. For dates, visit the website.

Home Saint Alfred, chaussée de Bruxelles 184, +32(0)65/72 82 66 — saint-alfred-cateau@acis-group.org, www.augrenoise.com

Authentique Brasserie

Authentique-gamma, Cuvée de la Grande Bruyère, Pils des 3 Canaux, Saison, Stout

———

Microbrewery. Group visits by appointment.

Rue de Condé 5, Blaton, +32(0)69/58 07 78 www.authentiquebrasserie.be

La Binchoise (left) quenches the thirst of the Gilles (right) during Binche Carnival, now elevated to Unesco World Heritage status.

Barbiot

Barbiot-gamma

Microbrewery set up by a vegetable grower. Book in advance.

Rue du Coron 27, Ville-sur-Haine, +32(0)65/87 37 23 of +32(0)476/80 87 36, brasserie-la-barbiot@hotmail.com, http://brasserie-la-barbiot.wikeo.be

Binchoise (La)

Bière des Ours, Binchoise, Organic' Brune Bio, Rose des Remparts, XO

Microbrewery set up in a former maltings in the shadow of the city walls. Visits by appointment only. Its highlight is the beautiful brewery tavern with a fine collection of enamel signs displayed on its industrial-looking walls. Shop attached. Tip: open all day during Binche Carnival, now Unesco World Heritage.

Faubourg Saint-Paul 38, Binche,: +32(0)64/33 61 86 www.brasserielabinchoise.be

Ook via vvv Binche: +32(0)64/33 67 27, tourisme@binche.be, www.binche.be

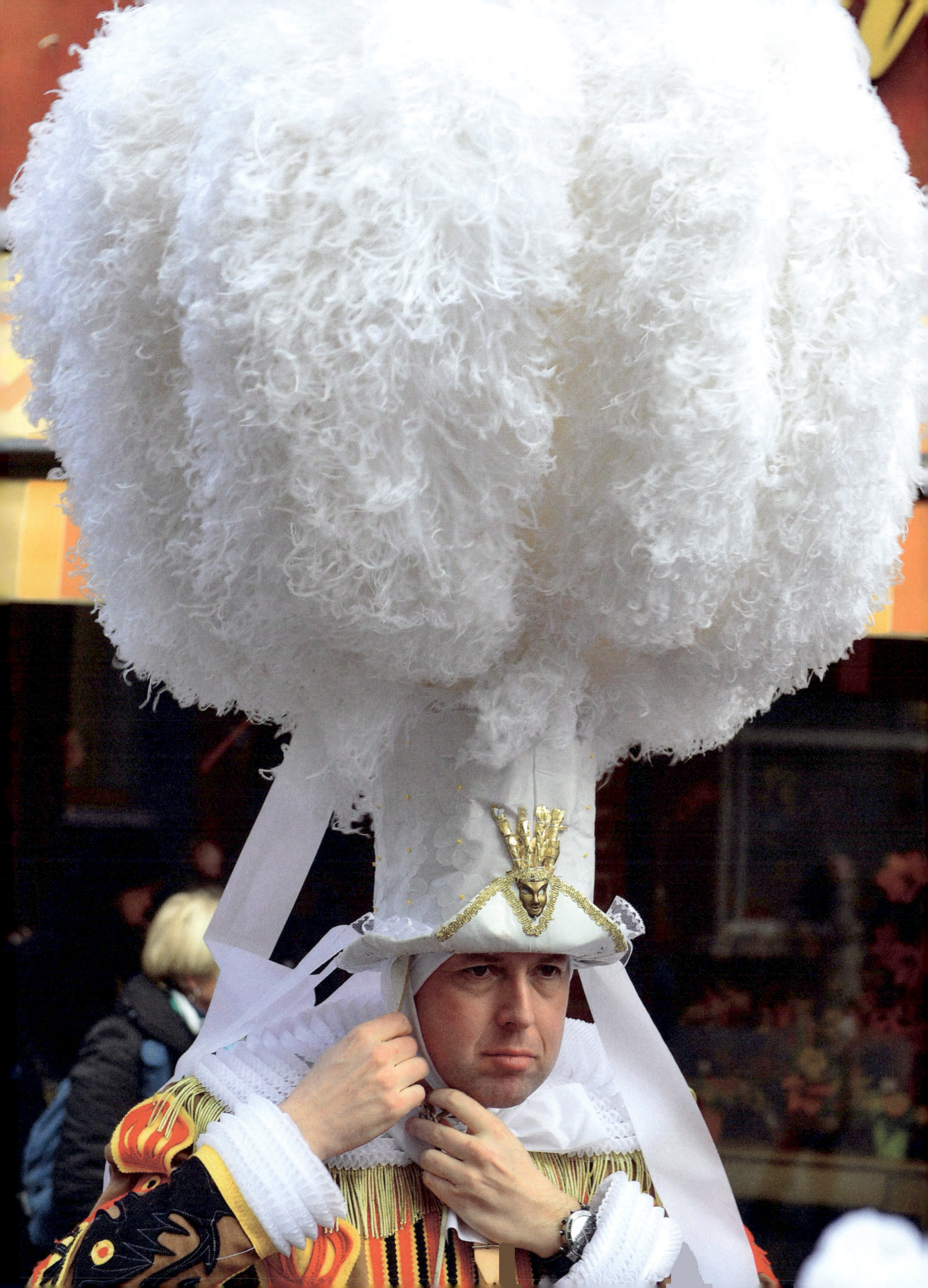

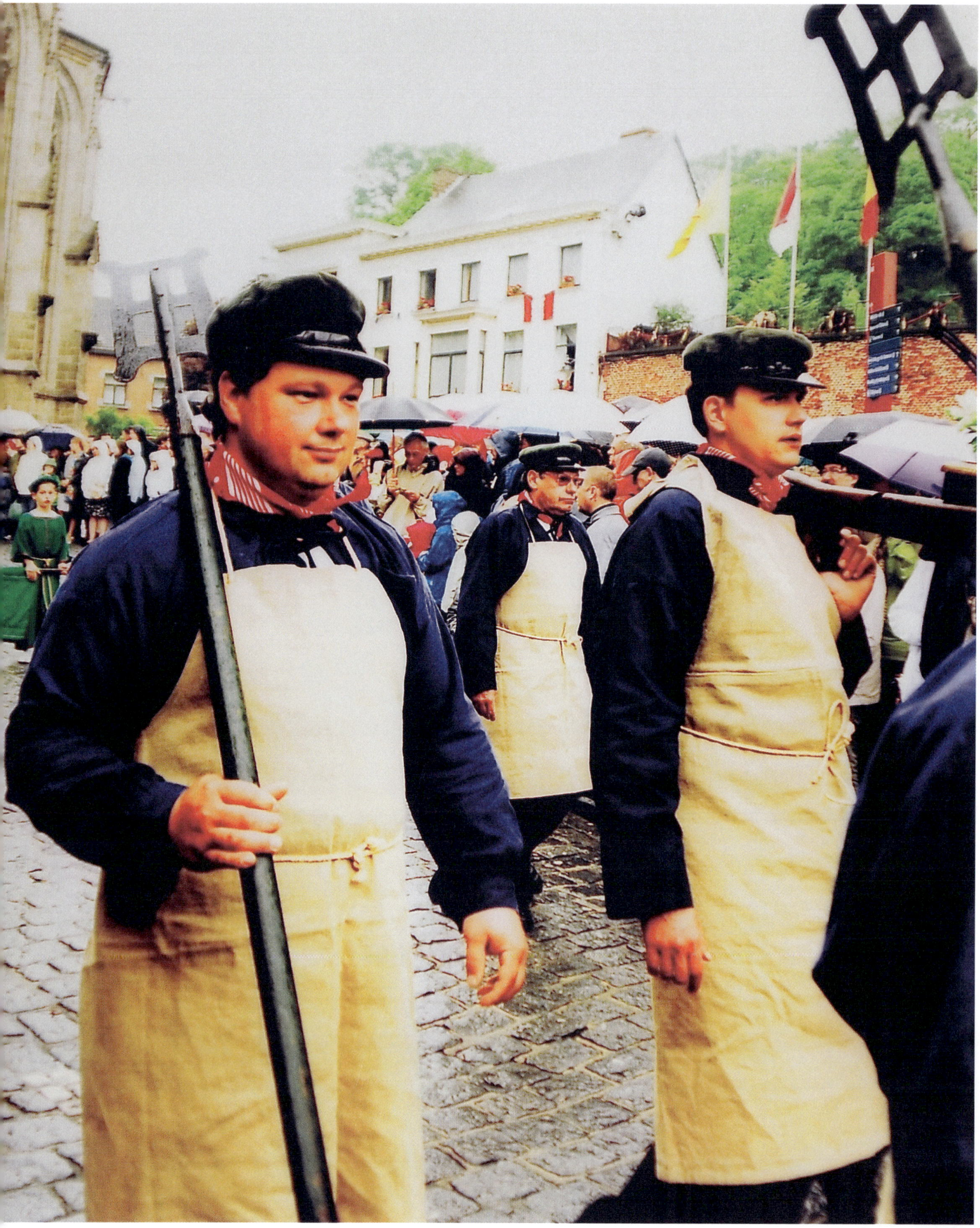

Blaugies (Brasserie de)

Bière Darbyste, Moneuse, Saison d'Epeautre, Vermontoise

———

Microbrewery. Visits by appointment. Grill restaurant and local 'terroir' cuisine at the Le Fourquet brewery tavern.

Rue de la Frontière 435, Blaugies (Dour), +32(0)65/65 03 60, info@brasseriedeblaugies.com, www.brasseriedeblaugies.be

Brasserie à Vapeur

La Saison de Pipaix, La Vapeur en Folie, Vapeur Cochonne

———

The Steam Brewery. A 19th century workshop shows you how brewing was once powered up by steam. Unique steam equipment. Guided tours: every Sunday from April to October at 11:00; book in advance. Brewing is usually done on the last Saturday of the month. Contact the brewery to make lunch reservations.

Rue du Maréchal 1, Pipaix, +32(0)69/66 20 47 of +32(0)495/25 94 52 – bav@euphony.be, www.vapeur.com

Brasserie des Géants (Brasserie des Légendes)

Ambiorix, Ducasse, Goliath, Gouyasse, Saison Voisin, Rondeau des Géants

———

Microbrewery with a particular fondness for the giants of Ath. Located in a traditional square farm. Guided group tours available from Monday to Friday.

Rue du Castel 19, Irchonwelz (Ath), +32(0)68/28 79 36 of +32(0)499/03 96 28 – info@brasseriedeslegendes.be, www.brasseriedeslegendes.be

Brasserie Ellezelloise (Brasserie des Légendes)

Quintine, Hercule

———

Plenty of witches are flying around this microbrewery with visitors' centre and playground in the green heart of the 'Pays des Collines'. Brasserie Ellezelloise dishes up regional products, jams, cheeses, snacks and of course its own beers. Get in touch with the brewery to arrange a group visit for a minimum of 20 participants.

Rue Guinaumont 75, Ellezelles, +32(0)68/54 31 60 www.brasseriedeslegendes.be

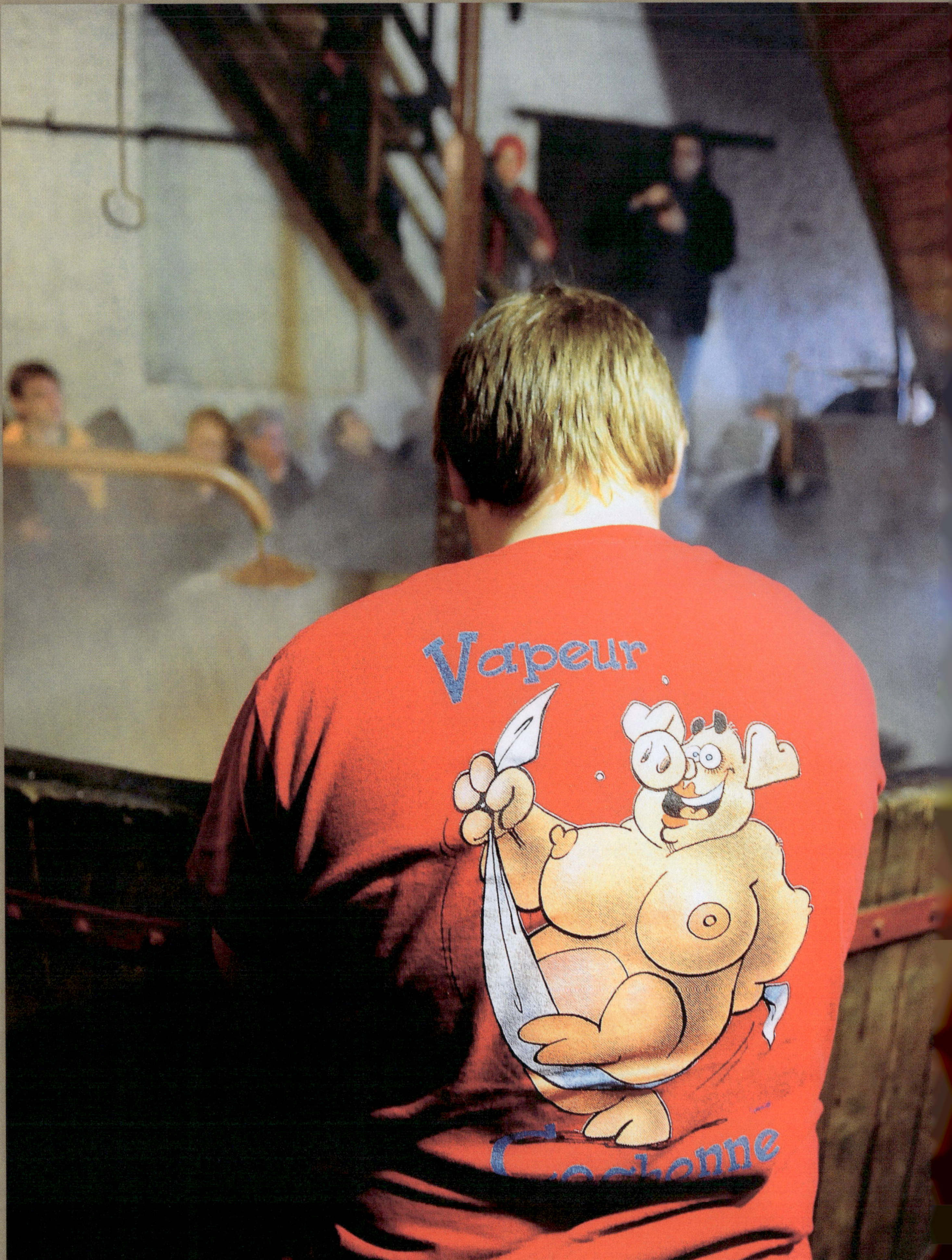
Vapeur

Brewing with 19th century steam equipment at Brasserie à Vapeur (left).
Fermentation and cold storage at Caulier (right).

Brasse-Temps (Le)

Ambrasse-Temps, Blanche de Ste Waudru, Brasse-Temps, Bush-gamma, Cuvée des Trolls, Surfine

———

Café brewery with tavern on the outskirts of the City of Mons. Groups of five or more welcome to visit between 11:00 and 17:00 Monday to Friday. The tavern serves all of the Brasserie Dubuisson beers as well as the freshly brewed house beers. Have a meal in the tavern or on the terrace.

Complexe Imagix – Site des Grands Prés, boulevard André Delvaux 1, +32(0)65/84 94 14 – mons@brassetemps.be, www.brassetemps.be

Brunehaut

Brunehaut bio, St-Martin

———

Microbrewery at a stone's throw from Tournai (Doornik). Guided tours Monday-Friday – book in advance. Also visit the Domaine de Graux, a traditional square-built farm owned by the brewery, with its orchard and cheese dairy.

Rue des Panneries 17, Rongy, +32(0)69/34 64 11, info@brunehaut.com, www.brunehaut.com

Carrières (Brasserie des)

Diôle

———

Microbrewery housed in former sawmill. See the brewers at work every Saturday.

Rue de Condé (Bas) 62, Basècles (Beloeil), +32(0)471/78 44 39, brasseriedescarrieres@skynet.be, www.diole.be

Caulier

Bon Secours, Paix-Dieu Pleine Lune, Blonde de Noël

———

Family brewery in the centre of Péruwelz. Group visits: book in advance. Taste the beers in the brewery tavern.

Brasserie Caulier, rue de Sondeville 134, Péruwelz, +32(0)69/36 26 10 – www.brasseriecaulier.com

Cazeau (Brasserie de)

Tournay, Saison Cazeau

Microbrewery set up in historic square farmhouse surrounded by fields. Visits by prior arrangement for groups of 10 to 50.

Rue de Cazeau 67, Templeuve, +32(0)69/35 25 53 of +32(0)472/97 09 53 – info@brasseriedecazeau.be, www.brasseriedecazeau.be

Chimay (Abbaye de)

Chimay

Abbey and brewery are not open to the public. Visitors will receive a warm reception in the Espace Chimay Visitors' Centre, at a short distance from the abbey, and in the nearby Auberge de Poteaupré with its restaurant and several guest rooms. Find out all you want to know about the abbey and its beers and cheeses. Tip: when in the area, visit the town of Chimay, the lake of Virelles and the lovely village of Lompret.

Rue de Poteaupré 5, Bourlers (Chimay), +32(0)60/21 14 33, poteaupre@chimay.com, www.chimay.com

Brother Théodore isolated a new yeast strain and developed the current Chimay Bleue in 1948.

Dubuisson (Brasserie)

Bush, Cuvée des Trolls, Surfine

The headquarters of the oldest brewery in the South of Belgium has come a long way from its farming roots. This brewery now uses state-of-the-art technology and the former brewhall has been converted into a brewery museum. In its cellars the gastronomic Bush Prestige, Bush de Nuits and Bush de Charmes are maturing in oak wine barrels. The brewery is surrounded by its own hop fields. Group visits by appointment from Tuesday-Saturday. Come along in a smaller group or on your own, every Saturday at 15:00. Taste the beers and sample regional cuisine in the Troll & Bush brewery tavern.

Chaussée de Mons 28, Pipaix, +32(0)69/67 22 22
info@br-dubuisson.com, www.br-dubuisson.com

Dupont (Brasserie)

Bière de Beloeil, Bière de Miel, Biolégère, Bons Voeux, Moinette, Monk's Stout, Redor Pils, Saison Dupont, Triomfbier Vooruit

---

At this village brewery, known for its saison, you can see how craft brewing techniques form a perfect blend with modern technology. It has its own cheese workshop. Visits by appointment for groups with 35-50 participants.

Rue Basse 5, Tourpes (Leuze),
+32(0)69/67 10 66, contact@brasserie-dupont.com,
www.brasserie-dupont.com

Erquelinnes (Brasserie d')

Angelus, Sambresse

Village brewery with educational hop field. Feel free to come along on a Saturday. Group tours available during the week on request (maximum of 50 participants).

Rue de Maubeuge 197, Erquelinnes, +32(0)479 88 78 35,
angelus.br@swing.be, www.bierenaturelle.be

Frasnoise (La)

Givrée, Rétro, Tijézu

Village brewery with tasting room. Visits on request.

Rue Basse 5, Frasnes, +32(0)495/42 60 38
lafrasnoise@hotmail.com, www.brasserie-frasnoise.be

Pairi Daiza

Cambron

Pairi Daiza is an experience centre with a focus on animals from around the world. This estate also comprises the ruins of a Benedictine abbey. The monks used to brew with water from the Saint Bernard well. These days the blonde and brown Cambron abbey beers are produced by an on-site microbrewery.

Domaine de Cambron (Brugelette), +32(0)68/45 54 05
www.pairidaiza.eu

Ranke (De)

Cuvée De Ranke, Guldenberg, Kriek De Ranke, Noir de Dottignies, XX Bitter

---

Discover the hoppy beers of De Ranke at this microbrewery set up in a former textile factory. Arrange to view the brewery and taste its beers on a Saturday afternoon. By appointment only.

Rue du Petit Tourcoing 1a, Dottignies, +32(0)56/41 82 41
www.deranke.be

St-Feuillien (Brasserie de)

Car d'Or, Grisette, Léon 1893, St-Feuillien

Hop vines accord a warm embrace to those who visit the beautifully restored interior court of this brewery complex (1893) with its splendid vintage brewhall. The new brewing hall with all its modern facilities then takes its turn in the spotlight. Group visits: daily on request for groups of ten and over. Smaller groups and individual visits: every Saturday at 14:00 – just turn up – or at 10:30 on a Sunday by prior arrangement.

Rue d'Houdeng 20, Le Roeulx, +32(0)64/31 18 18 of +32(0)498/86 41 82 – visite.st-feuillien@gmail.com, www.st-feuillien.com

Scassènes (Brasserie de)

1830

The former Brasserie d'Ecaussinnes has been resurrected and now bears the name of Scassènes. Make an appointment to visit this microbrewery that is located in a restored farmhouse.

Rue de Restaumont 118, Ecaussinnes-d'Enghien, +32(0)474 82 35 29 – info@brasseriescassenes.be, www.brasseriescassenes.be

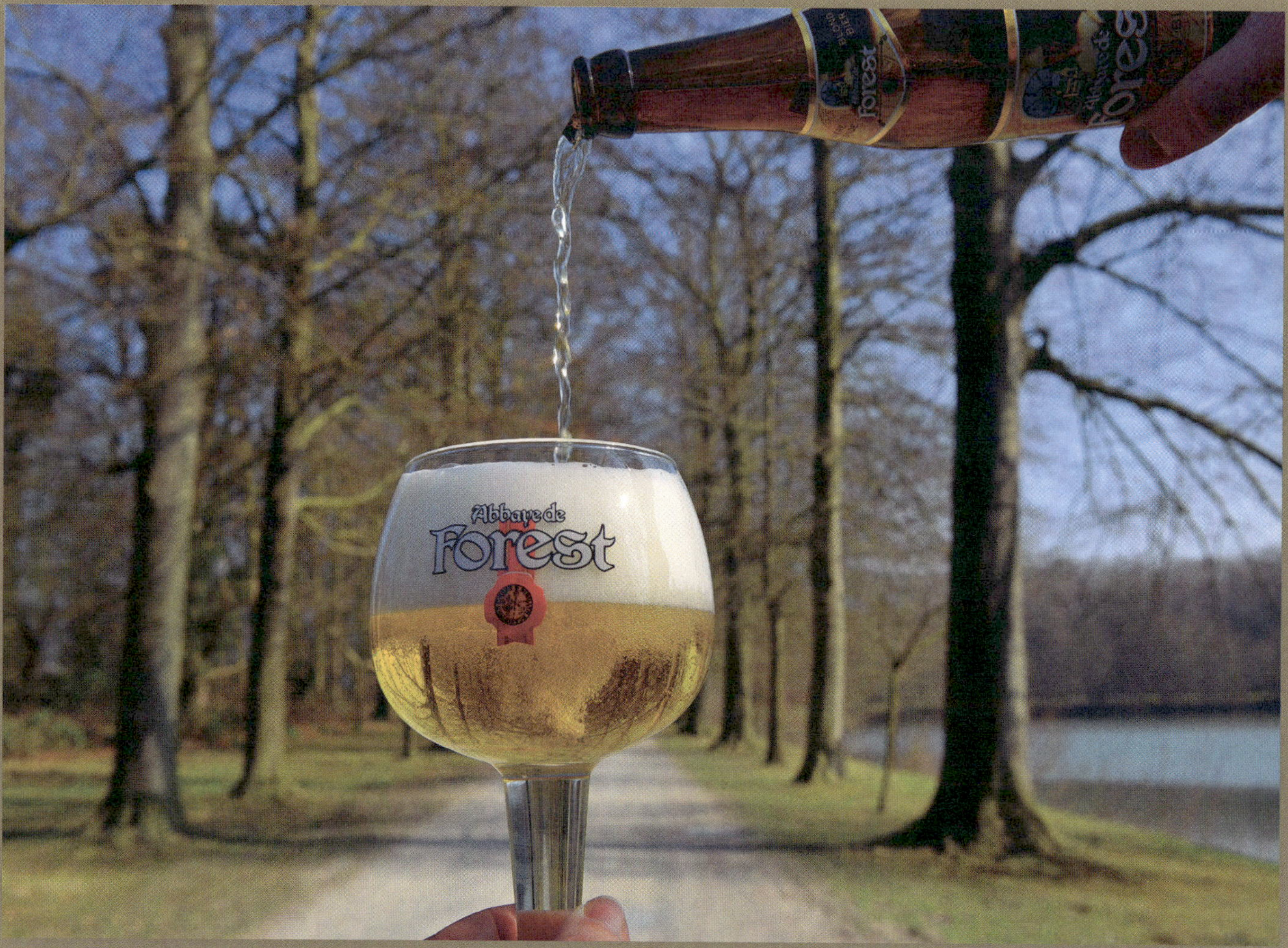
Abbaye de
Forest

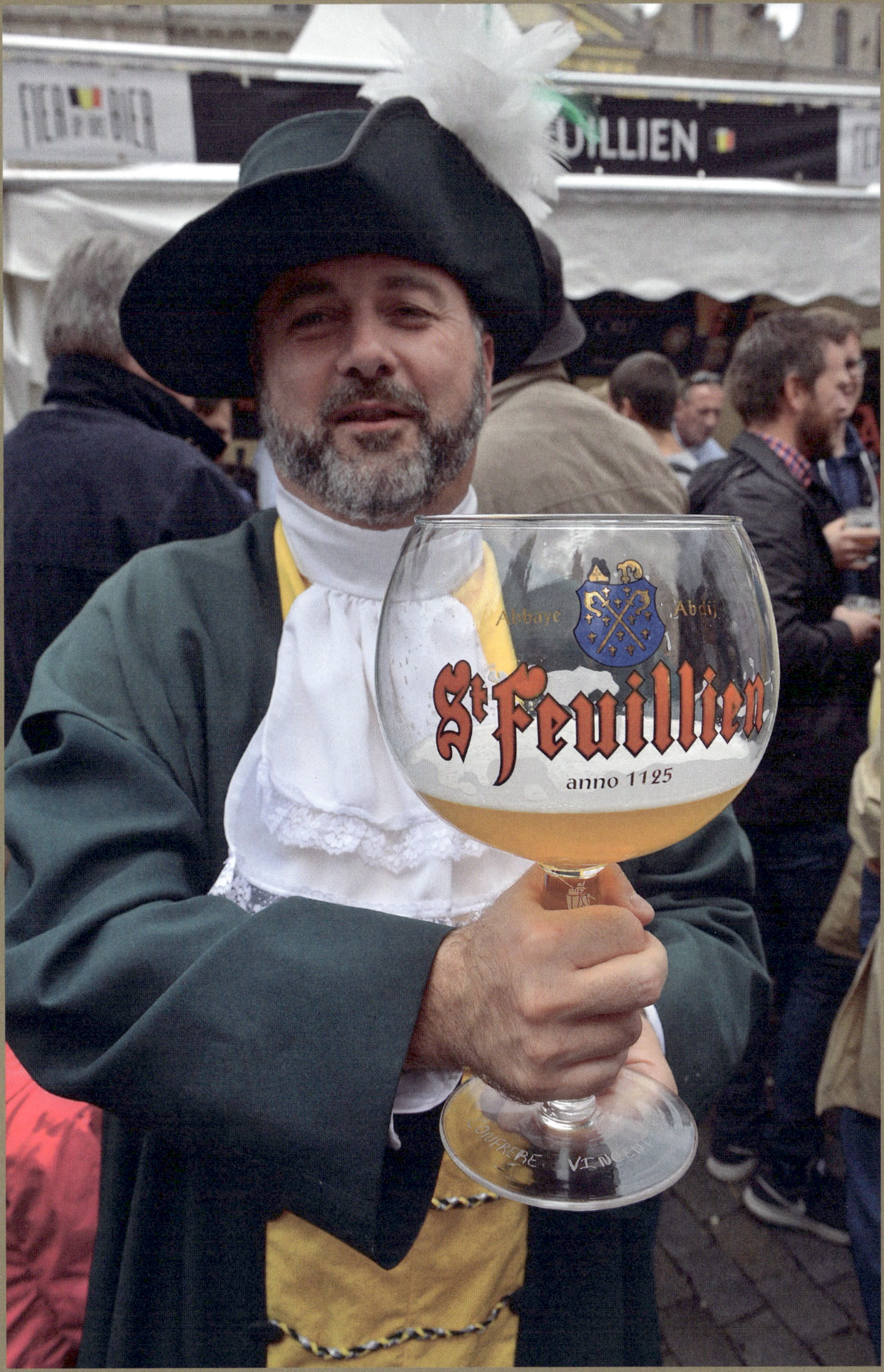
Abbaye
Abdij
St Feuillien
anno 1125

Silly (Brasserie de)

Abbaye de Forest, Blanche de Silly, Divine, Double Enghien, Green Killer, Pink Killer, Saison de Silly, Scotch de Silly, Silly Pils, Super 64

―――――

Village brewery in the Ath region. Group visits by arrangement for 15-40 participants.

Rue Ville Basse 2, Silly, +32(0)68/25 04 81
www.silly-beer.com

Val de Sambre (Brasserie du)

Abbaye d'Aulne, Abbaye d'Heylissem, Blanche de Charleroi, Chérie, Jazz Beer

―――――

The ruins of the abbey of Aulne on the banks of the Sambre attract over 200,000 visitors each year. This site is also home to a microbrewery where you can taste the beers. Visit by request for groups with a maximum of 50 participants.

Rue Emile Vandervelde 273, Gozée, +32(0)71/56 20 73,
contact@valdesambre.be, www.valdesambre.be

Brewing at Val de Sambre in Aulne Abbey.

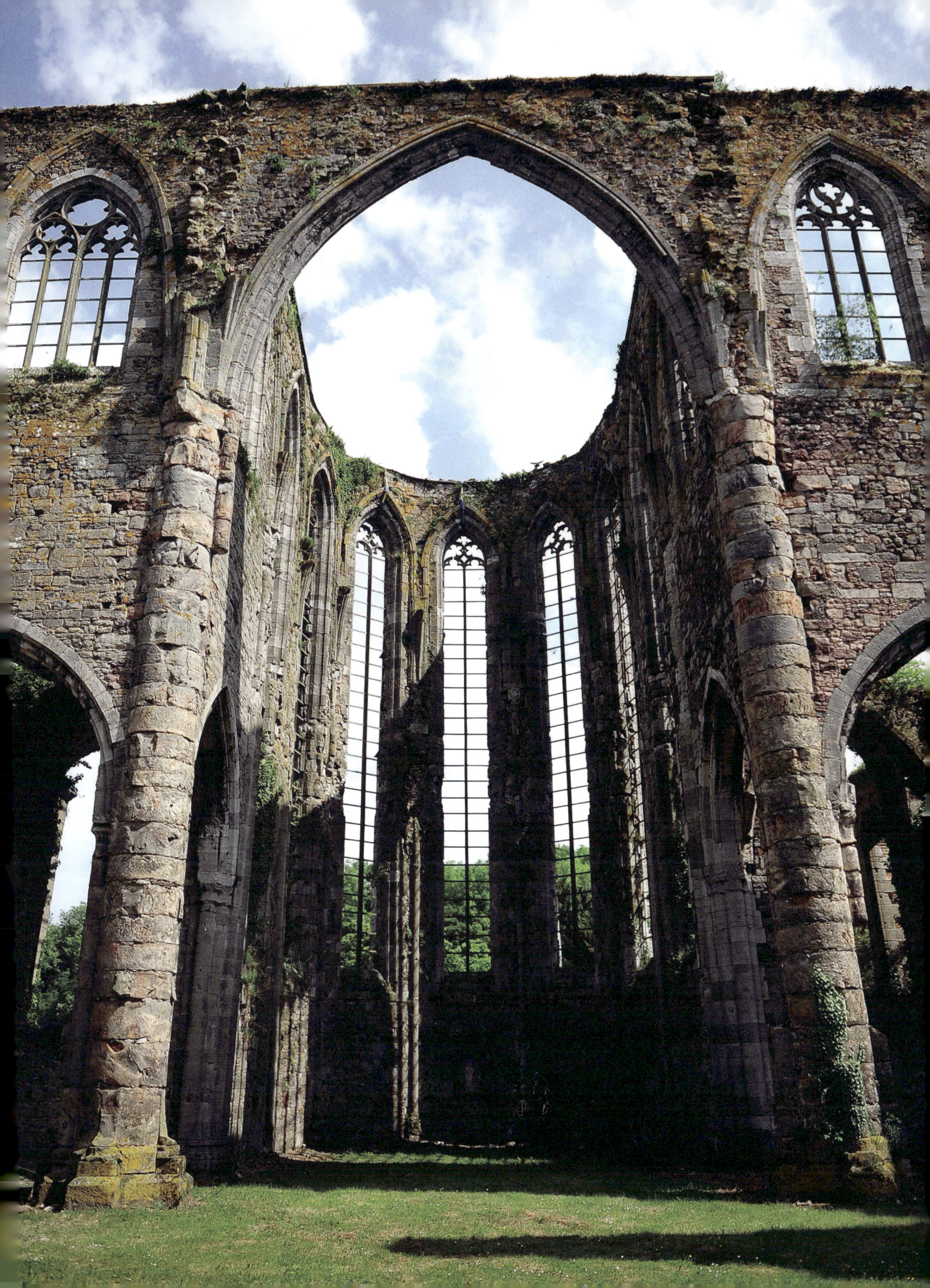

REGIONAL BEER TOURISM

BRUGES
KORTRIJK
ROESELARE
OSTEND

Alvinne

Base Beers, Chain Reaction, Land van Mortagne, Morpheus, Mano Negra, Omega, Pays d'Erpigny, Phi, Sigma, Undressed Foederbier, Ich bin ein Berliner Ryesse

---

This microbrewery loves to experiment. You can taste its beers next to the beer tanks and you can buy them in the Alvinne shop. Visits (20-50 participants) by appointment only. Keep an eye on the calendar to find out when the annual Alvinne Beer Festival is being held.

Vaartstraat 4a, Moen (Zwevegem), +32(0)496/35 96 19
info@alvinne.be, www.alvinne.be

Bie (De)

De Bie, Hellekapelle, Helleketelbier

Get in touch with this brewery with its own hop fields on the banks of the River Leie to arrange a visit. Complete with tasting café, small hop museum and butcher's shop. Stock up on Limousin beef or try their paté made with beer, ham and cheese. The café welcomes bikers and hikers.

Vijvestraat 47, Wakken (Dentergem), +32(0)475/23 47 95
info@brouwerijdebie.be, www.brouwerijdebie.be

Bourgogne des Flandres

Bourgogne des Flandres-gamma

A traditional Bruges beer is flowing out of the tanks of this microbrewery located in the heart of this ancient city. Book your visit in advance. With restaurant and terrace with view on the canals.

Kartuizerinnenstraat 8, Brugge, +32(0)50/33 54 26
info@bourgognedesflandres.be, www.bourgognedesflandres.be

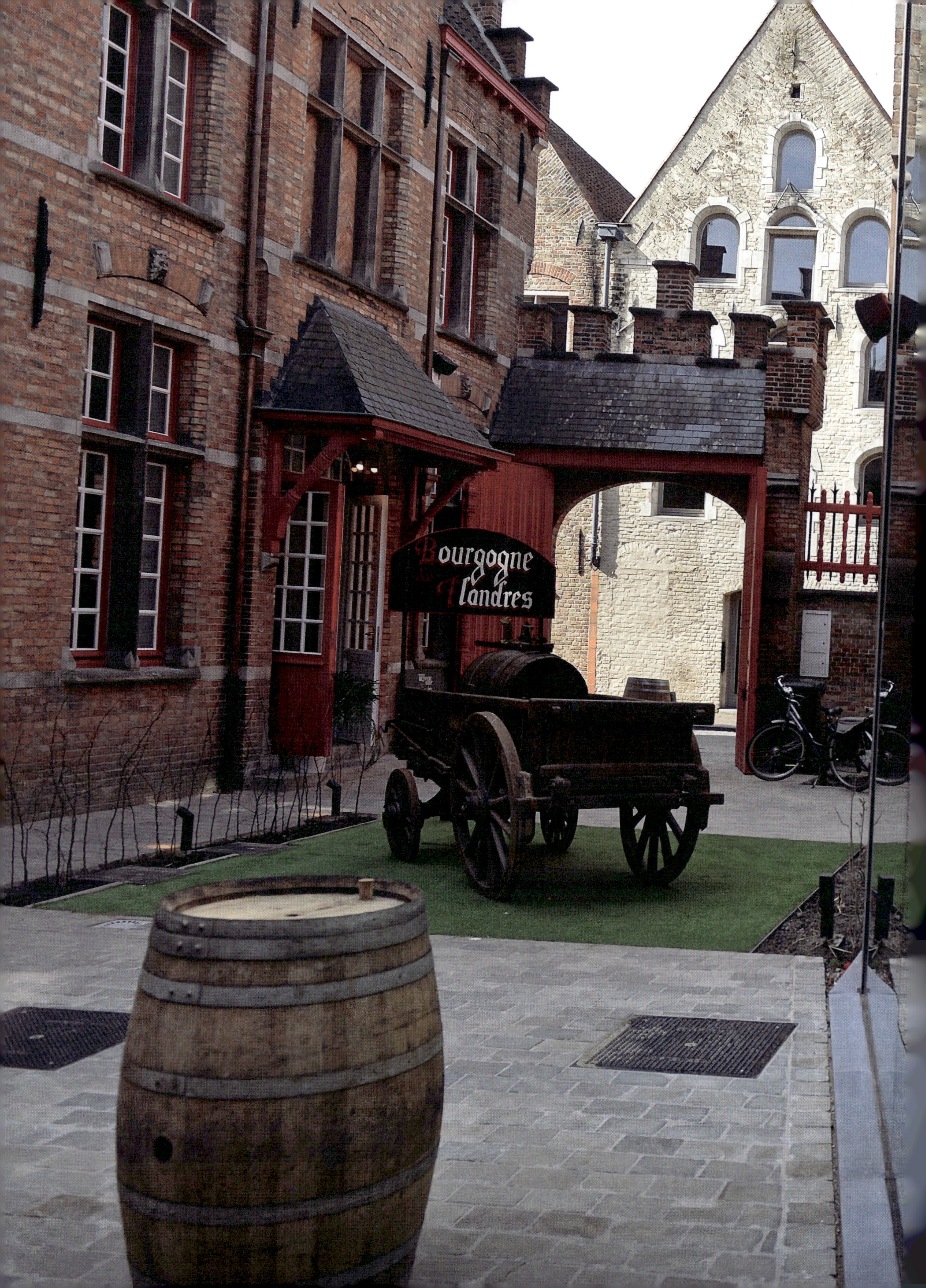
Bourgogne
Flandres

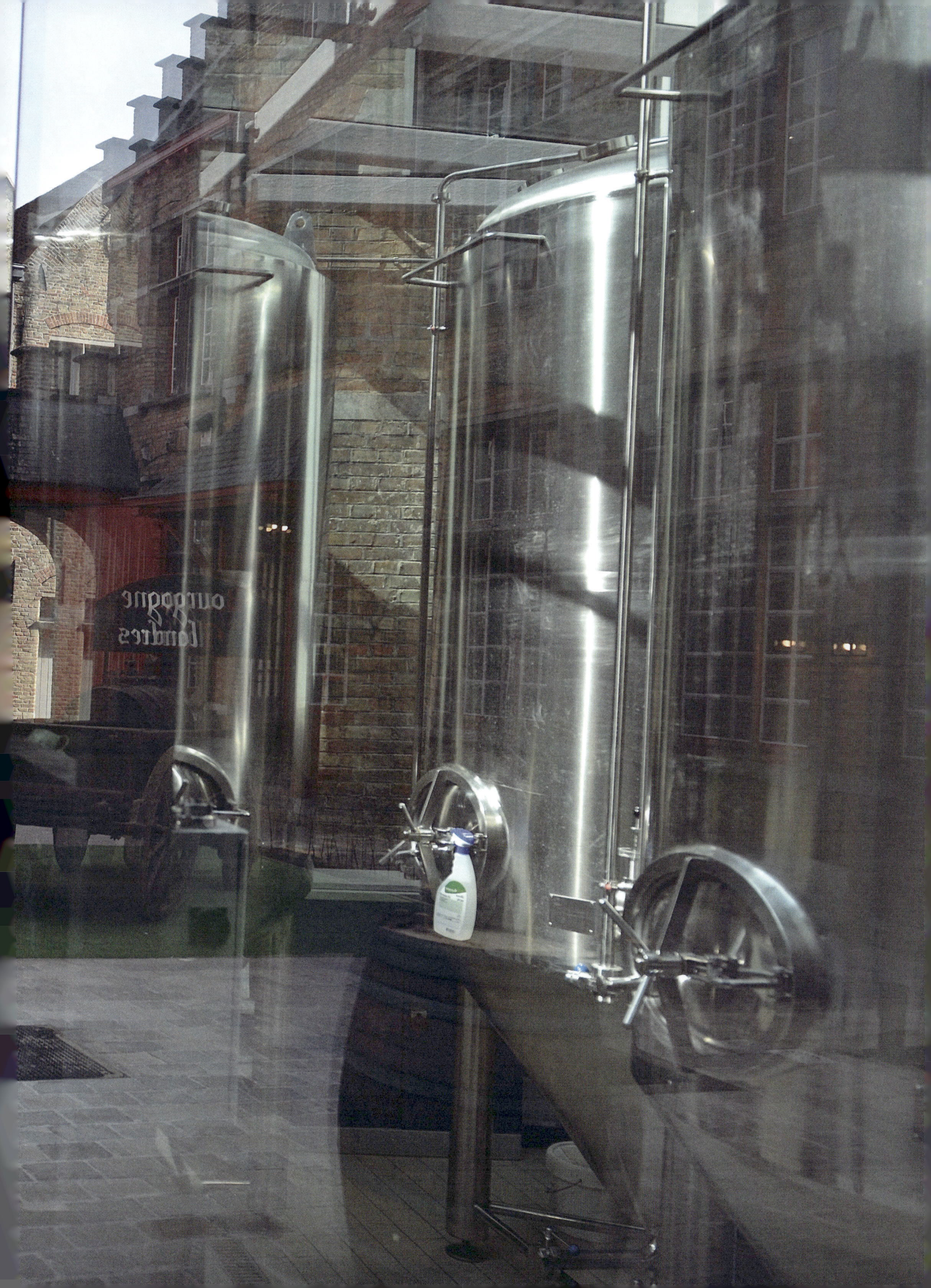

Bryggja Brewery

Amuse, Bryggja, Triple B

Microbrewery in the picturesque village of Damme in the vicinity of Bruges. Book your visit in advance.

Moerkerkebrug 3, Damme, +32(0)479/22 01 13, www.bryggjabrewery.be

De Brabandere

Bavik, Wittekerke, Ezel, Petrus, Pilaarbijter, Kwaremont

Family brewery known for its traditional Flemish red-brown beers as well as the Kwaremont 'koersbier' or cycling beer, named after a classic bike race. With foeder hall and tasting room. Open to the public by appointment from 2017.

Rijksweg 33, Bavikhove, +32(0)56/71 90 91 www.brouwerijdebrabandere.be

Dolle Brouwers (De)

Arabier, Boskeun, Dulle Teve, Oerbier, Stille Nacht, Stout

Brewery with historic brewhall from 1840, tasting room and café (weekends only). Visit by prior arrangement for groups with a minimum of 30 participants. The brewery welcomes smaller groups and single visitors every Sunday afternoon at 15:00.

Roeselarestraat 12b, Esen (Diksmuide), +32(0)51/50 27 81 of +32(0)498/10 29 35, info@dedollebrouwers.be, www.dedollebrouwers.be

Fort Lapin

Fort Lapin

A Bruges microbrewery with café. Visits by appointment.

Koolkerksesteenweg 32, Brugge, +32(0)495/50 26 70 www.fortlapin.com

Gaverhopke ('t)

Bitter Sweet Symphony, Blondje, Branding Hopke, Bruintje, Den 12, Koerseklakske, Kriek, Spring Tipple, Stasegemse Loper, Zingende Blondine

---

Family brewery on the site of a castle farm with tavern, terrace and playground.

Platanendreef 16, Nieuwenhove (Waregem), +32(0)497/76 04 12, info@tgaverhopke.be www.tgaverhopke.be

Gulden Spoor (Het)

Gulden Spoor, Netebuk

A newly opened brewhall next to 't Rusteel beer restaurant. Visits by appointment. Combine your trip with Kortrijk or the Westhoek region. Explore the Heulebeek nature reserve in the heart of the Leie region on foot or by bike.

Heulestraat 168 (Gullegem), +32(0)497/54 88 80
info@brouwkot.be, www.brouwkot.be

Halve Maan (De)

Brugse Zot, Straffe Hendrik

One of Bruges' main tourist attractions. The centuries-old tradition of this Bruges brewery is documented in a museum. Guided tours are held daily. Enjoy a splendid panorama of Bruges from the roof of the brewery. The tavern specialises in regional dishes and brewery cuisine. The terrace is located in the interior court and the beer shop sells beers and merchandise.

Walplein 26, Brugge, +32(0)50/33 26 97, www.halvemaan.be

The rotating blades of an open cooling basin displayed at De Halve Maan's brewery museum.

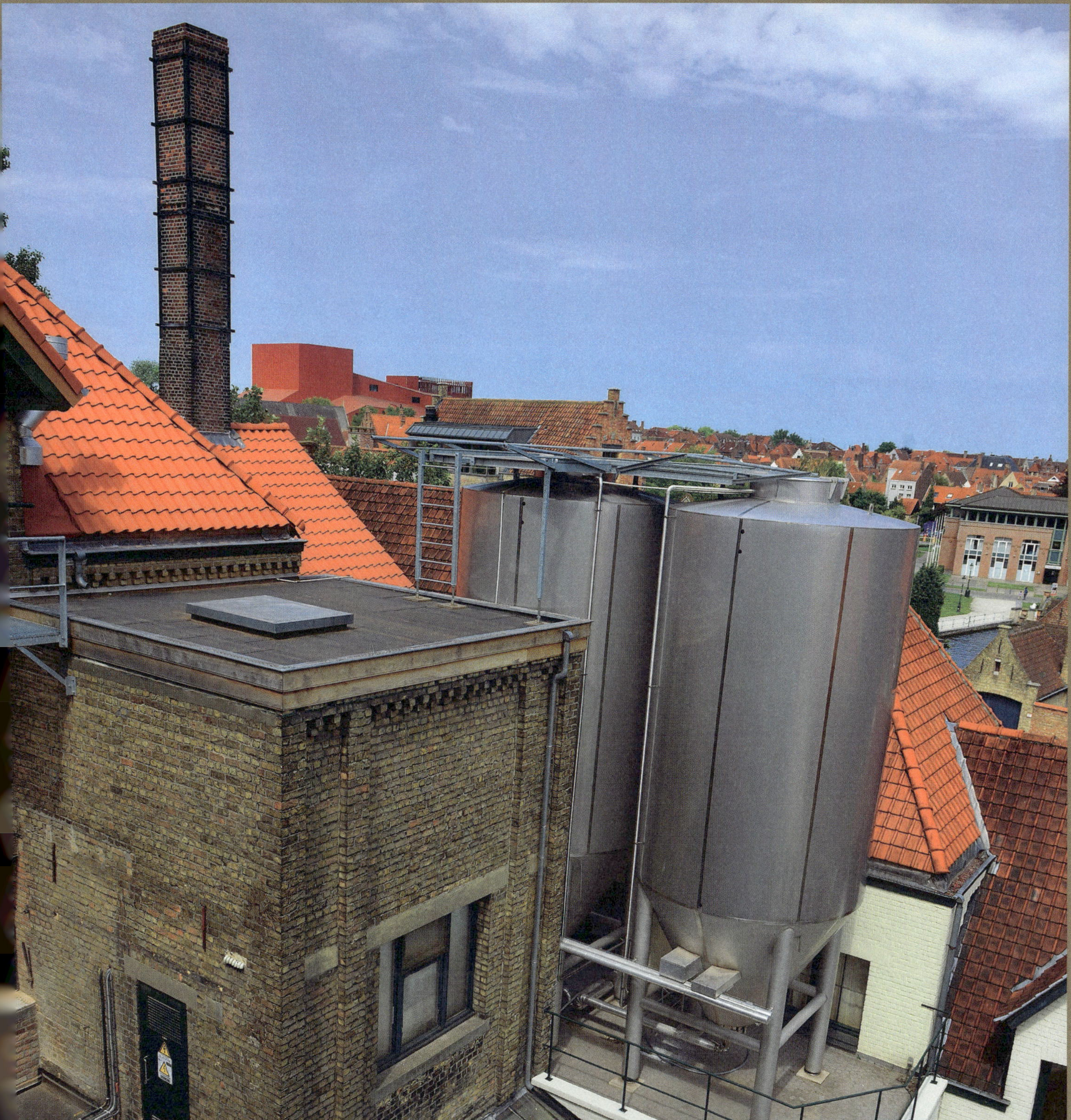

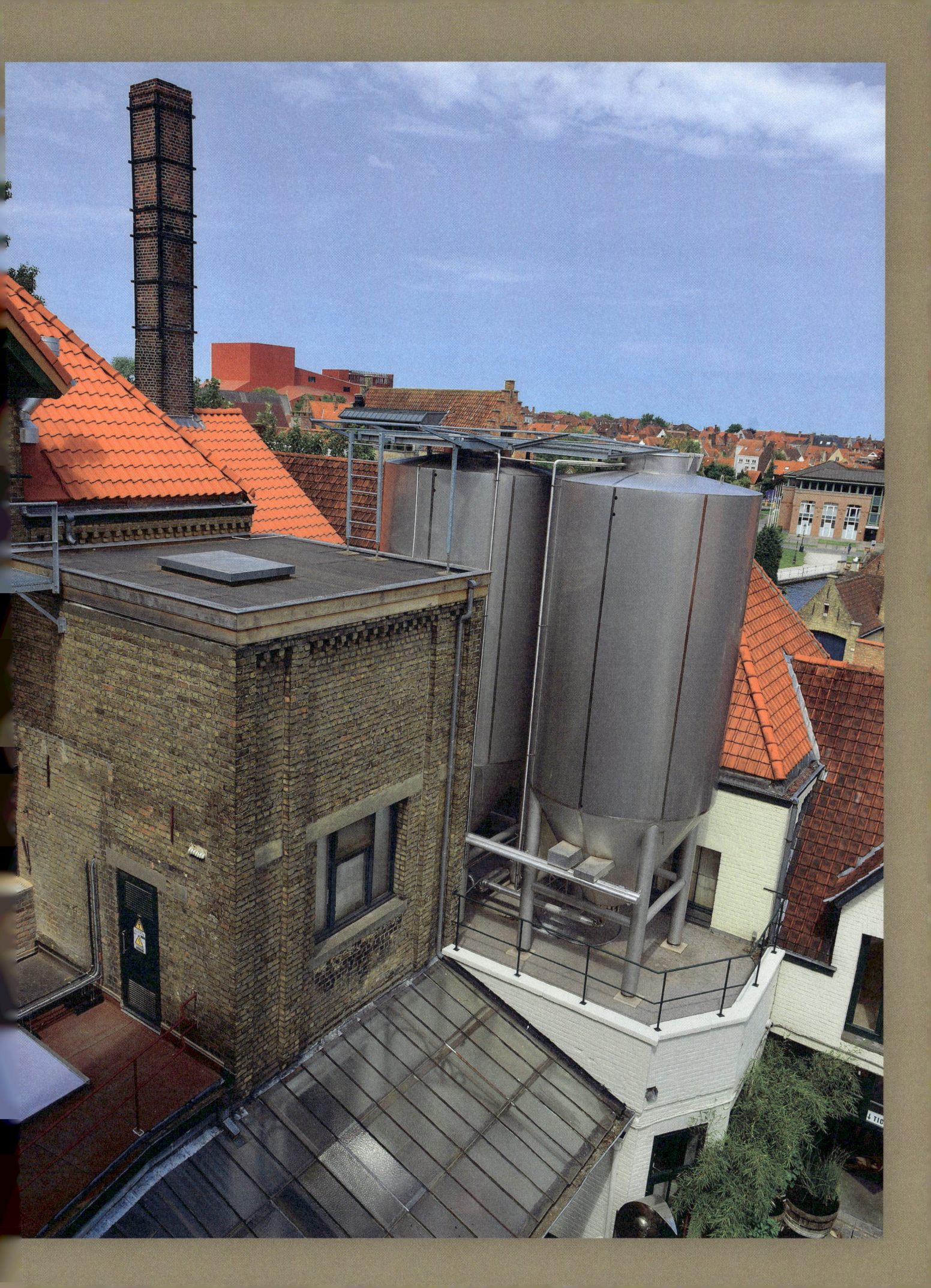

Brewer Luc Vermeersch keeps an eye on the boiling kettle at De Leite.

Kazematten (De)

The Wipers Times 14, Grotten Santé

There is a microbrewery tucked away in Ypres' former casemats. This is where, during the First World War, the British army printed its newspaper for soldiers, The Wipers Times. You can now taste a beer with the same name. A beer rooted in the heritage of the Grottenbier, formulated by the late Pierre Celis, the spiritual father of Hoegaarden witbier, is also flowing out of the tanks.

Houten Paard 1, Ieper, +32(0)57/38 80 21
info@kazematten.be, www.kazematten.be

Leite (De)

Bon Homme, Cuvée Jeun homme, Cuvée Mam' zelle, Cuvée Soeur' Ise, Enfant Terriple, Femme Fatale, Fils à Papa, Ma Mère Spéciale, Merci Maman

---

A hobby project transformed into a microbrewery. Groups with a minimum of 20 participants are welcome by appointment.

De Leiteweg 32, Ruddervoorde, +32(0)50/25 07 96,
luc.vermeersch@deleite.be, www.deleite.be

Maenhout

Blinde Mol, Ferre Quadrupel, Hoppa Hontas, Koeketiene

Microbrewery with tasting room. Open every Saturday between 14:00 and 18:00. Tours by appointment.

Brugsesteenweg 157, Pittem, +32(0)477/75 00 20,
info@brouwerijmaenhout.be, www.brouwerijmaenhout.be

Omer Vander Ghinste

Blauw, Bellegems Witbier, Bockor, Brasserie Le Fort, Cuvée des Jacobins, Gueuze Jacobins, Geuze Max, Kriek des Jacobins, Kriek Max, Omer

---

Village brewery with historic brewing tower, brewhall, cooling basin and foeder hall. Known for its sour Flemish red-brown foeder beers. With café in retro style. Visits by appointment.

Kwabrugstraat 5, Bellegem, +32(0)56/23 51 71,
visit@omer.be, www.omervanderghinste.be

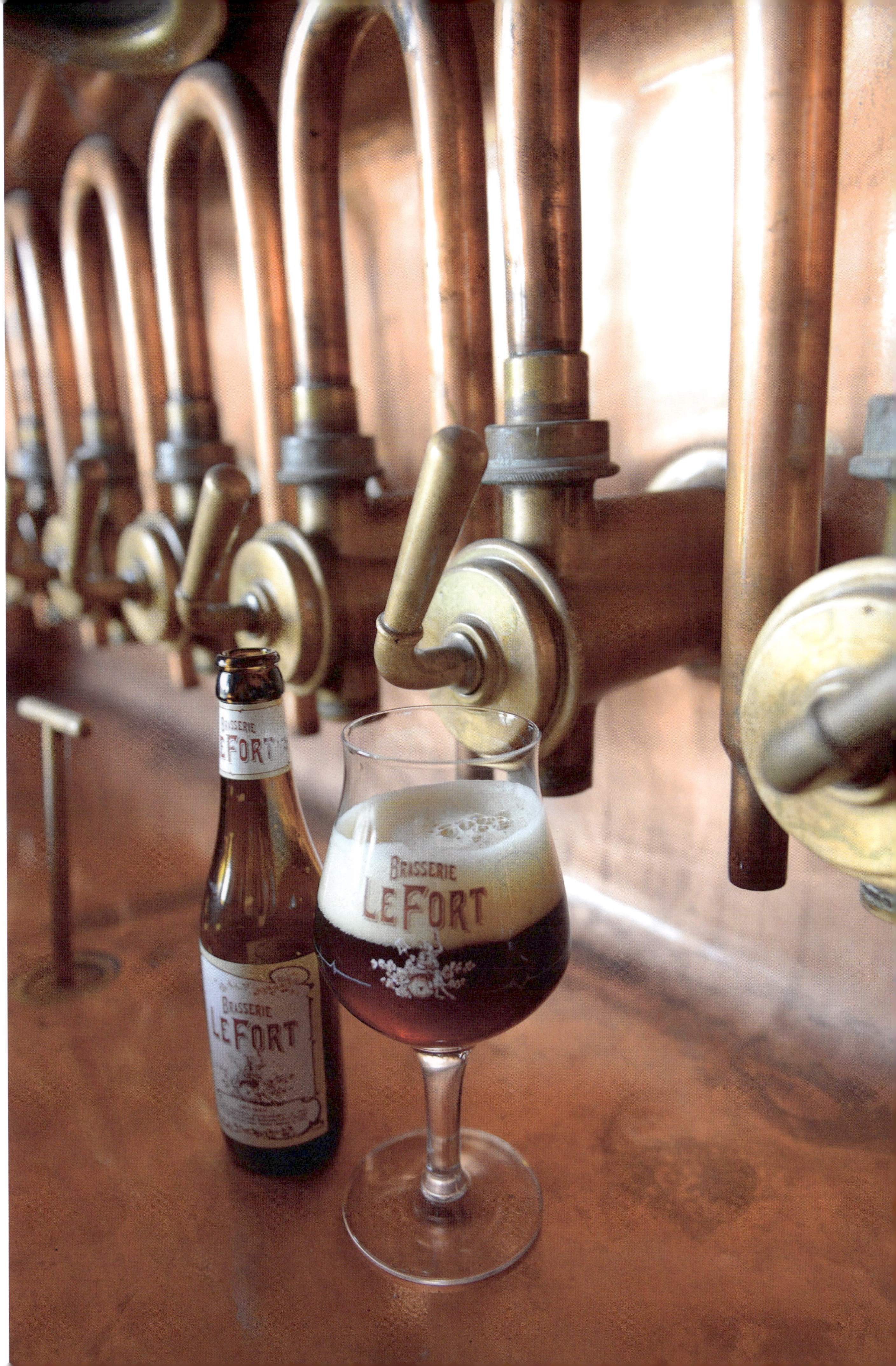
BRASSERIE
LEFORT
BRASSERIE
LEFORT
BRASSERIE
LEFORT

BOCKO
ANNO

BIER
OMER. VAN
STOUT

TOM BOONEN
LAZER
QUICK·STEP

KWABRUGSTRAAT

Oude Maalderij (Brouwerij d')

Qantelaar, Redenaar, Hop De Brewer, Deo, Optimo, Maximo, Leviathan vs The Kraken, Farang

---

Microbrewery with cafe and shop. In addition to the home-brewed beers on tap, try the vintage beers. Visits by appointment.

Ardooiestraat 130, Izegem
doudemaalderij@hotmail.com, www.doudemaalderij.com

Plukker (De)

Keikop

Grower of organic hops started up a microbrewery in the middle of the hop fields. Guided group visits by appointment. Single visits on Saturday afternoons.

Elverdingseweg 14a, Proven (Poperinge), +32(0)475/57 36 85,
brouwerij@plukker.be, www.plukker.be

Rodenbach

Rodenbach, Caractère Rouge, Grand Cru, Rosso, Vintage

A monument of the Belgian beer world. Your visit follows a circuit, interspersed with viewpoints that allow you to observe the brewing process from beginning to end. Follow the trail and admire the stainless steel brewing kettles in the glass-enclosed brewing hall, the original 'moutast' or malt drying floor, an authentic steam-driven kettle and much more. Above all, you cannot fail to be impressed by the foeder halls where close to three hundred foeders, each with a capacity of 10,000 to 65,000 litres are standing proud. Some of these are one hundred and fifty years old. Your visit concludes with a tasting. Group visits can be arranged from Monday-Thursday for 15-50 participants. The visitors' centre offers a Rodenbach menu to enjoy either before or after your visit.

Spanjestraat 133, Roeselare, +32(0)51/22 34 00
www.palm.be, www.rodenbach.be

Dienst bezoeken, Steenhuffeldorp 3, Steenhuffel,
+32(0)52/31 74 14, events@palmbreweries.com,
www.palmbreweries.com

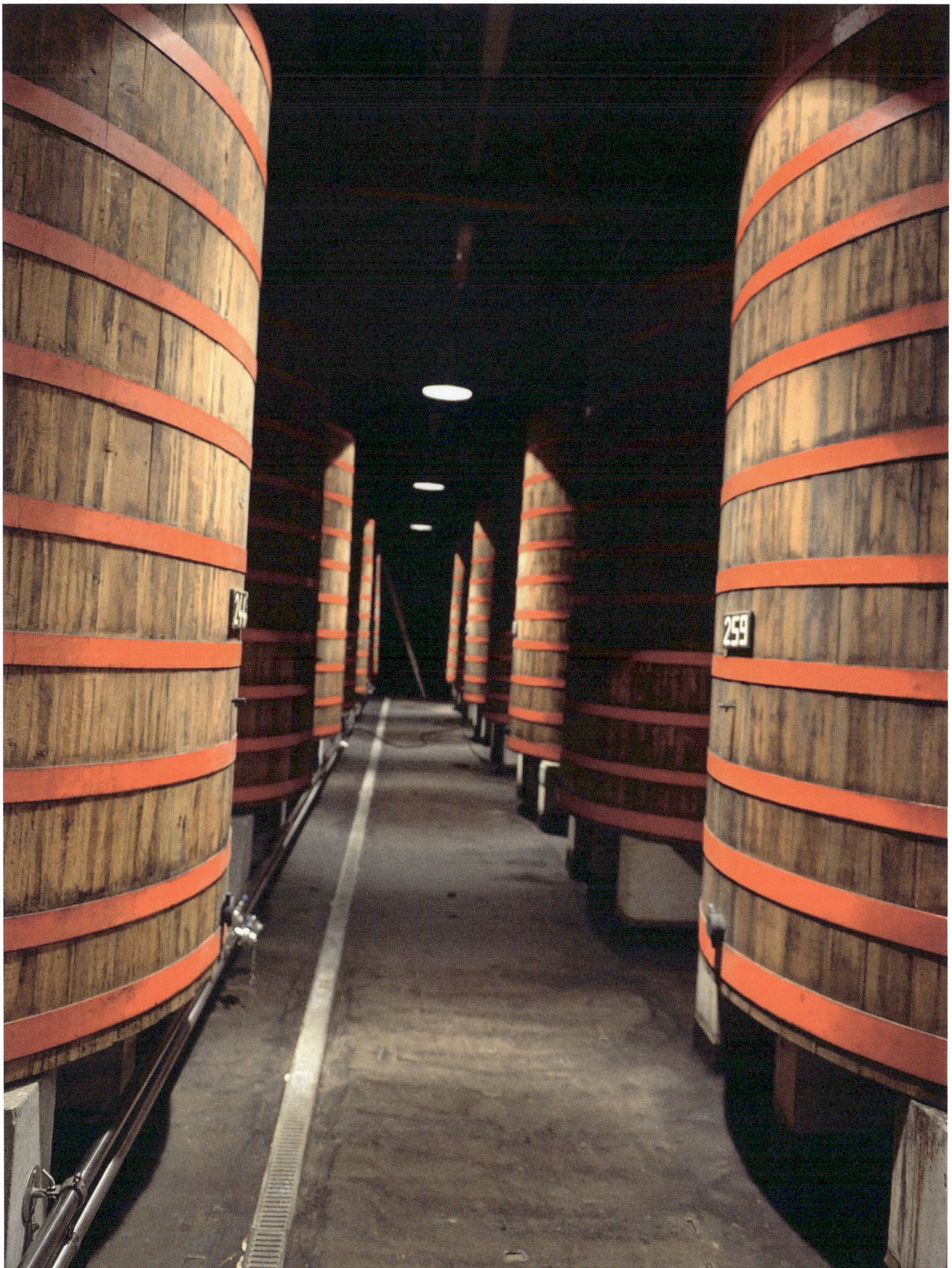
259

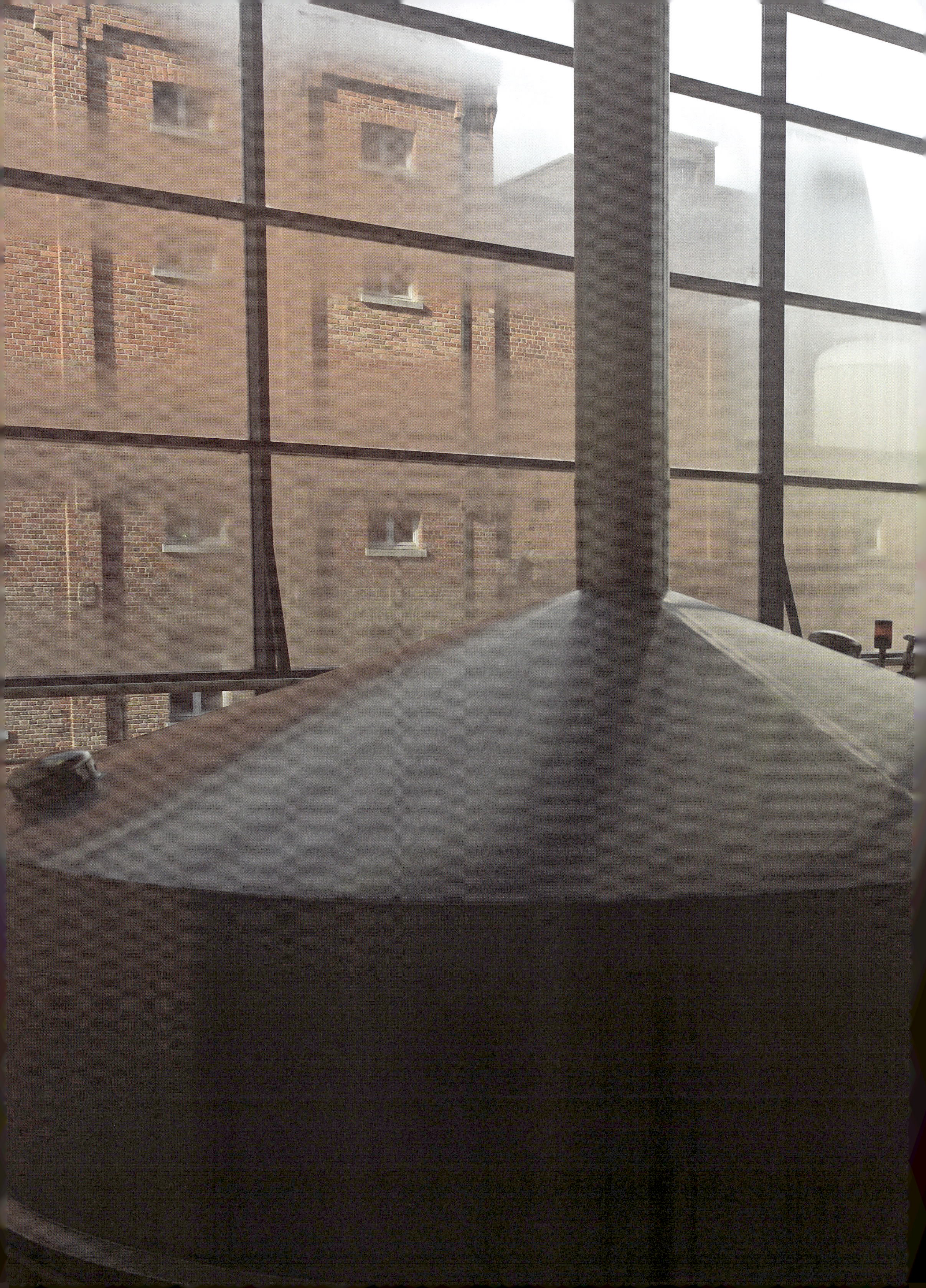

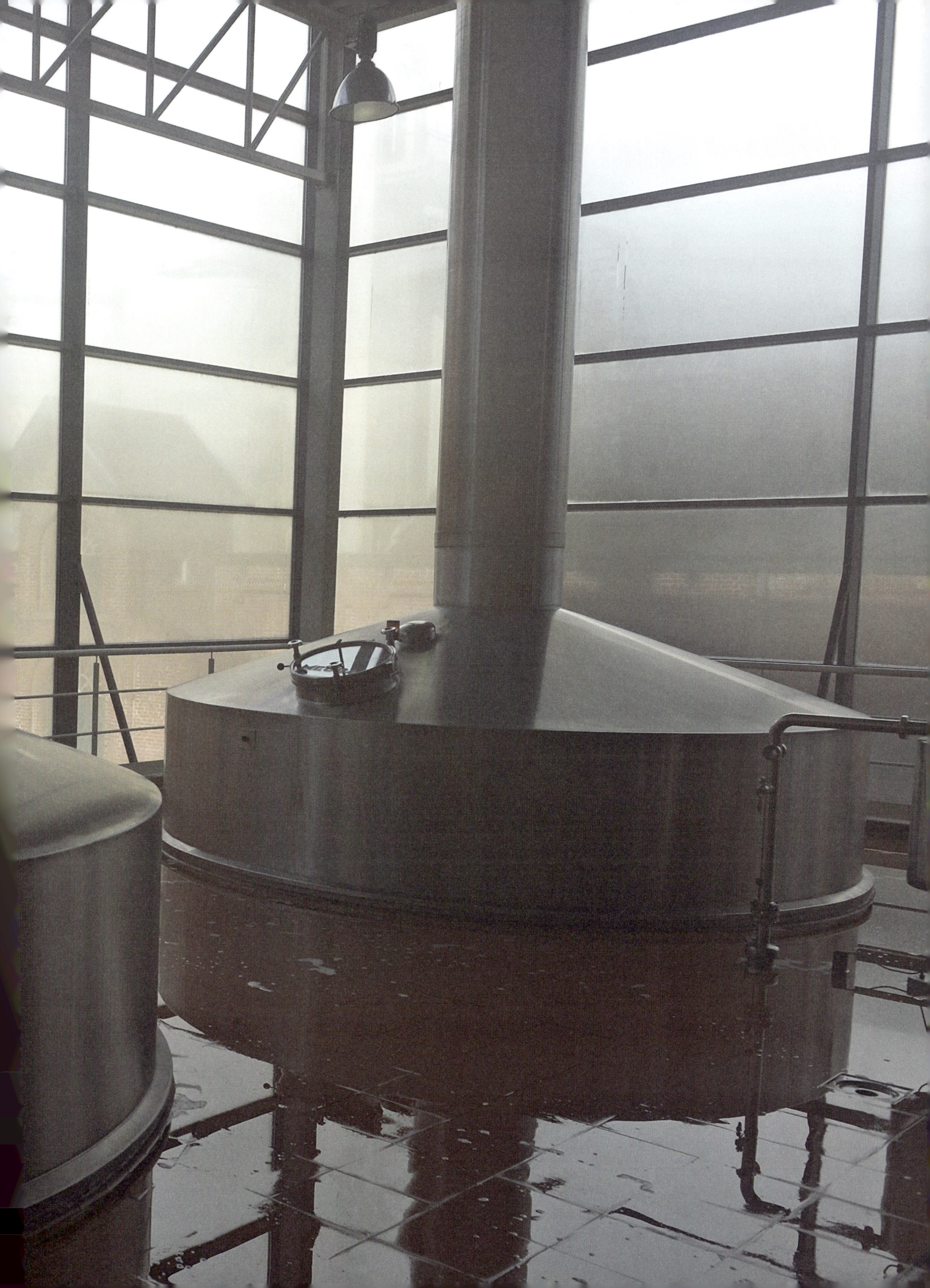

Seizoensbrouwerij Vandewalle

Reninge Bitter Blond (à lambiek), Reninge Krieken Rood, Reninge Oud Bruin

———

Chris Vandewalle, keeper of the archives of the City of Diksmuide, is breathing new life into beers that had all but disappeared from the Westhoek region. Visits by appointment only – maximum of five guests. Beer tasting.

Zwartestraat 43, Reninge, +32(0)497/54 95 85
info@seizoensbrouwerij.be, www.seizoensbrouwerij.be

St. Bernardus

St. Bernardus-gamma, Watou Tripel

———

Not far from the French border you come across this brewery with its own hop field. Guided tours available during the week or at weekends but on request only. Spend the night 'at the brewery' in the 'Brouwershuis' B&B. Get in touch with the Poperinge Tourism Association to request a guided tour by bike with a 'hop and beer' theme, including a visit to the brewery.

Trappistenweg 23, Watou, +32(0)57/38 80 21
visit@sintbernardus.be, www.sintbernardus.be

Brewer Urbain Coutteau of De Struise Brouwers.

Strubbe

De Couckelaerschen Doedel, Dikke Mathile, Edel-Brau, Ichtegem's Oud Bruin, Houten Kop, Keyte, Kriekenbier, Oud Bier, Strubbe Pils, Vlas Kop, Wittoen

———

A traditional family brewery 'just below the church spire', known for its Flemish red-brown sour beers. Visits on request.

Markt 1, Ichtegem, +32(0)51/58 81 16
www.brouwerij-strubbe.be

Struise Brouwers (De)

AJ, Black Albert, Black Damnation, Cuvée Delphine, Elliot, Five Squared, Havic, Imperialist, Kabert, Macadame, Our Nastiest Effort, Pannepot, Struise Witte, Tjeeses, Ypres

———

Familiarise yourself with the new beer alphabet in this former village school-cum-brewery close to Westvleteren abbey. You are welcome to visit every Saturday afternoon. A beer tasting class is also on the menu.

Kasteelstraat 50, Oostvleteren, +32(0)495/28 86 23
struisesales@gmail.com, www.struise.com

Toye (Brouwerij)

Goedendag

———

Microbrewery. Phone ahead to arrange your visit.

Rekkemsestraat 64, Marke (Kortrijk), +32(0)498/39 37 11
info@goedendagbier.be, www.goedendagbier.be

hommelbier

Het Kapittel Watou

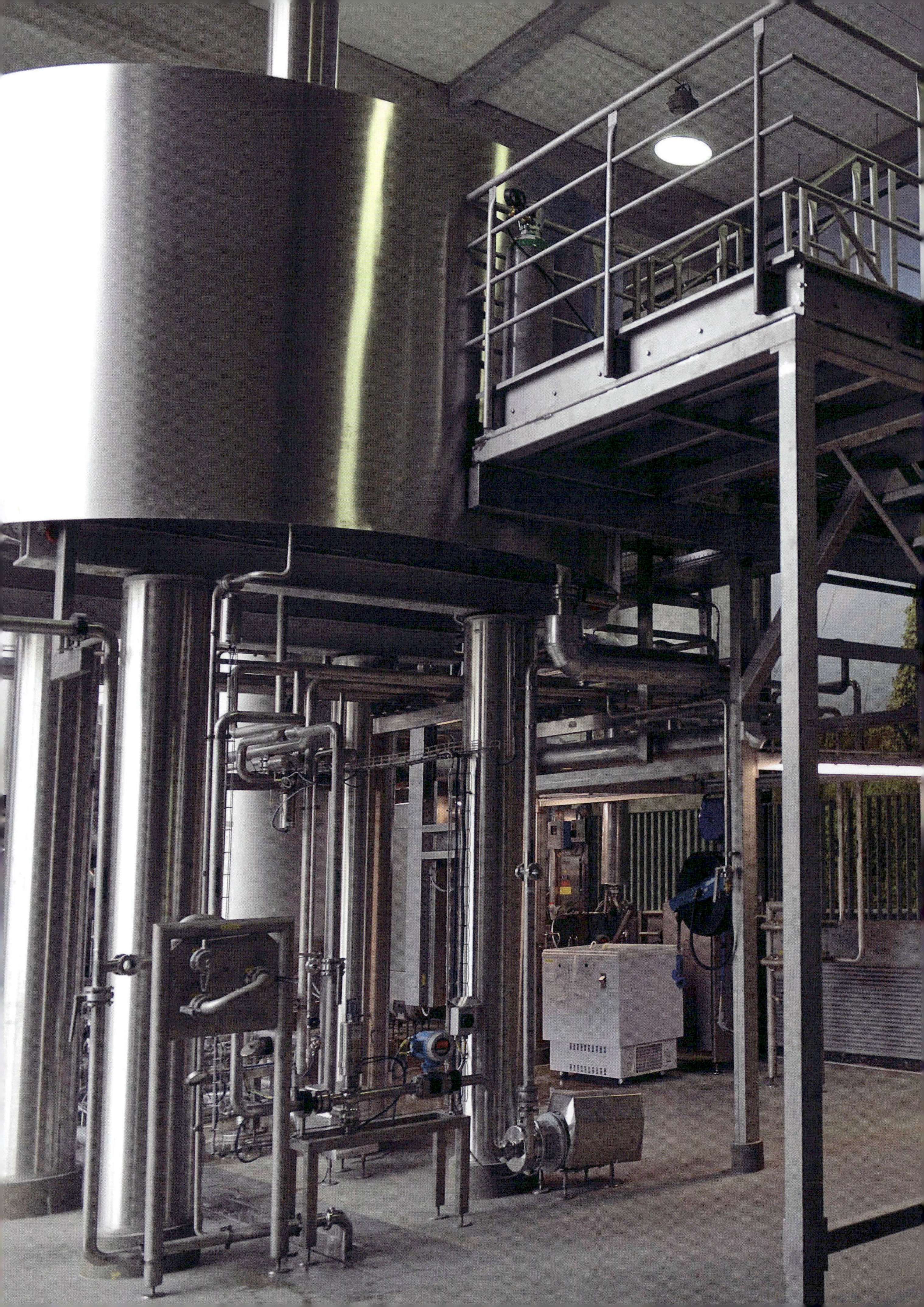

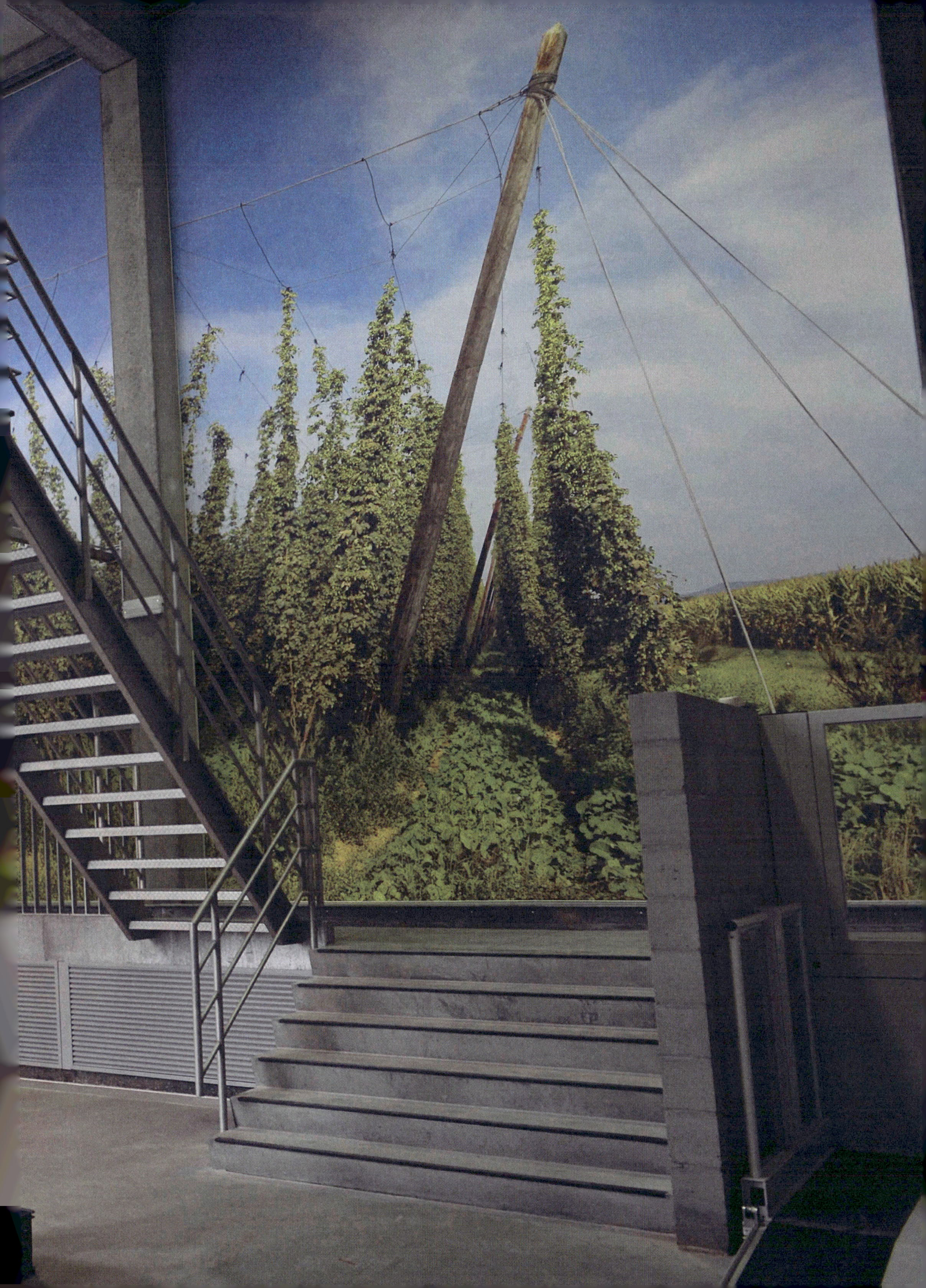

Van Eecke

Hommelbier, Kapittel, Leroy Christmas, Watou's Wit

Get in touch with this village brewery in the heart of the Westhoek region to arrange your visit. This brewery's beers can be tasted in Het Brouwershof adjacent to the brewery.

Douvieweg 2, Watou,
+32(0)457/38 80 30 of +32(0)57/42 20 05
info@brouwerijvaneecke.be, wwww.hommelbier.be
of www.tkapittelwatou.be

Van Honsebrouck (Kasteelbrouwerij)

Bacchus, Brigand, Cuvée du Chateau, Filou, Kasteel-gamma, St-Louis-gamma, Slurfke, Trignac XII

Castle Brewery Van Honsebrouck decamped lock, stock and barrel from Ingelmunster to the nearby town of Izegem where it established a brand new, 'state of the art' brewery with a particular focus on specialty beers. Izegem has something for everyone. Enjoy the food and drink on offer. Visit the impressive brewhall, bottle line and the chambers where the Van Honsebrouck beers are maturing in oak barrels. The brewery provides all the facilities you need to host your conferences, meetings and celebrations.

Ingelmunstersestraat 80, Emelgem (Izegem),
+32(0)51/33 51 60, www.vanhonsebrouck.be

Verhaeghe-Vichte

Duchesse de Bourgogne, Echt Kriekenbier, Barbe, Vichtenaar, Verhaeghe Pils, Cambrinus, Christmas Verhaeghe

Duchesse de Bourgogne, Echt Kriekenbier, Barbe, Vichtenaar, Verhaeghe Pils, Cambrinus, Christmas Verhaeghe The brewery was founded in 1885. Its buildings are listed based on its industrial-archaeological merits as a typical example of a 19th century maltings-brewery. Over the years a bottling plant was added as well as a cold storage building for bottom-fermented beers. The equipment and associated buildings, such as the malting tower with malt floor, the steeping basins and sprouting floor, the storage lofts and the free-standing factory chimney all date from the late 19th century. Visits by pre-arrangement.

Sint-Dierikserf 1, Vichte, +32(0)56 77 70 32
www.brouwerijverhaeghe.be

Verzet (Brouwers)

Oakey Moakey Whisky Stout, Super NoAH, Moose Blues, Oud Bruin, Rebel Local

Plenty of room for experiments in this microbrewery. On top of the standard range they frequently launch one-off, quirky 'bootlegs'. Discover the taste of an old brown or 'oudbruin' beer, enriched with infusions of fruit. Visit by appointment only.

Grote Leiestraat 117, Anzegem
+32(0)470/17 06 34, info@brouwersverzet.be
www.brouwersverzet.be

Westvleteren (Sint-Sixtusabdij)

Westvleteren 6, 8 en 12

Neither the brewery nor the abbey are open to visitors. However, you can find out more about the abbey at Het Claustrum, an interactive information centre just down the road. For a drink and a bite to eat, pop into the In De Vrede abbey tavern. Make the most of your visit by walking the Sint-Sixtus walk (7 or 10km) or visit one of over 200 war cemeteries from the First World War. Also: the Flanders Fields museum in Ypres and the Hop Museum in Poperinge are well worth a visit.

Donkerstraat 13, Westvleteren
+32(0)57/40 03 77, info@indevrede.be, www.indevrede.be

Trappist Westvleteren
bevat gerstemout
BIER 8% VOL.
8

STEEN
BRUGES
BEER
EXPERIENCE
needed
love
LIFE
NAMIBIA
FREEDOM
PEACE
LOVE
BRUGES
BEER
EXPERIENCE
BRUGES
BEER
EXPERIENCE
Samen zullen
we dit overleven.
We zullen hier
Samen sterker
uitkomen!

WELL WORTH A VISIT

Poperinge Hop Museum

The Hop Museum is housed in the former 'Stadsschaal' or Municipal Weighing House. This is where hops were weighed, rated and stacked. Hops used to be dried just below the roof of the farm before being 'sacked' and reduced in size by the 'stomper'. Home to an extensive collection of vintage hop growing equipment complemented by fragments of audio-visual footage and quiz modules. This contemporary museum explains the history and life cycle of the hop plant. Many visitors are not aware of the importance and the benefits of hops and are in for a surprise. The brewers use the unfertilised — female — hop cones that contain the lupuline agent that helps to preserve the beer. Hops are also used to add bitterness and aroma. The local soil, made of loam and sand with a sub-strata of clay, has proved excellent for the cultivation of hops. During the Middle Ages, Ypres and Poperinge were engaged in a battle for the linen trade. The Count of Flanders, under pressure from Ypres, forbade any linen being grown or traded in Poperinge. In later years, thanks to an intervention by the Count of Saint-Omer in Northern France, the cultivation of hops was to provide an alternative.

Gasthuisstraat 71, 8970 Poperinge, +32(0)57/33 79 22, hopmuseum@poperinge.be, www.hopmuseum.be

Brouwerijmuseum De Snoek

Het Mout- en Brouwhuis De Snoek is een uniek museum dat volgens het authentieke cascadesysteem is gebouwd. Van zolder tot kelder maken de bezoekers uitgebreid kennis met het volledige mout- en brouwproces uit begin 19de eeuw. Dat gebeurt aan de hand van koperen brouwketels, een gietijzeren roerkuip, eeuwenoude gistingskuipen en -tonnen, een intact gebleven mouteest, een antieke gasmotor enzovoort. De rondleiding eindigt in de gerestaureerde oude herberg Het Brouwershof, waar je het Snoekbier kunt proeven. Je hoort het verhaal van de dorst in de Groote Oorlog en treedt in het spoor van de frontsoldaten. Frank Becuwe, bezieler van het museum: 'Soldaten zochten troost in alcohol. Maar om bier te brouwen heb je gist, mout en hop nodig en in bezet België was dat een groot probleem. De brouwers moesten hun koperen installaties ontmantelen. Veel brouwerijen gingen op de fles en deden dienst als schuilkelder, onderdak voor zieken, ontluizingscentrum, wasserij en een enkele keer zelfs als gevangenis. In onbezet België daarentegen verhoogden de brouwerijen hun capaciteit en zochten hun toevlucht in mechanisatie. Door de aanwezigheid van soldaten en vluchtelingen nam de vraag naar bier sterk toe. Het bier was vaak niet te drinken door de slechte kwaliteit van het water uit de putten in de IJzerstreek. De brouwers lieten het niet aan hun hart komen en de cafébazen deden gouden zaken.'

Fortem 40, Alveringem, +32(0)58/28 96 74, infomuseum@desnoek.be, www.desnoek.be

Beer Museum

In this beer museum, located in the shadow of the belfry, you discover the rich beer history of Bruges and Belgium, iPad in hand. Click on the QR code displayed with an object and you will find out all there is to know about several major topics: beer and health, women and beer, beer types... You test your own beer knowledge with a quiz. There is a separate 'kids tour', illustrated with beautiful pictures. On the top floor you will find brewers' 'alaam' or equipment on display. The brewing process and ingredients are explained in large oak foeders where you also discover the secret of the Trappist beers. Before, during or after your visit you can taste typical beers from Bruges or else beers made by Palm Belgian Craft Brewers including the unfiltered Palm and the foeder beers made by Rodenbach and the Boon lambic brewery. Ask if there is anything 'special' available on the day. They may let you taste a test brew.

Breidelstraat 3, Brugge, +32(0)50/69 92 29, info@brugesbeermuseum.com, www.brugesbeermuseum.com

REGIONAL BEER TOURISM

BRUSSELS LOUVAIN

AB Inbev (Stella Artois)

Stella Artois, Leffe

Europe's largest brewery, soon to account for an annual production of 12,000,000 hectolitres of beer. Groups of fifteen participants and over are welcome from Tuesday – Sunday, make your reservation via www.breweryvisits.com.

Brouwerijplein 1, Leuven, +32(0)16/24 71 11
www.ab-inbev.com

Brouwerij De Hoorn was founded in 1923 and is the cradle of Stella Artois. This listed building owes its special character mainly to the monumental Artois brewhall and the special way in which it is constructed. Stella Artois was brewed here for the first time in 1926. State-of-the-art displays throughout the building take visitors on a journey of discovery of the history and importance of De Hoorn, which also has its very own Stella Artois Flagship Café.

Sluisstraat 79, Leuven, +32(0)4585/16 90 24
www.dehoorn.eu

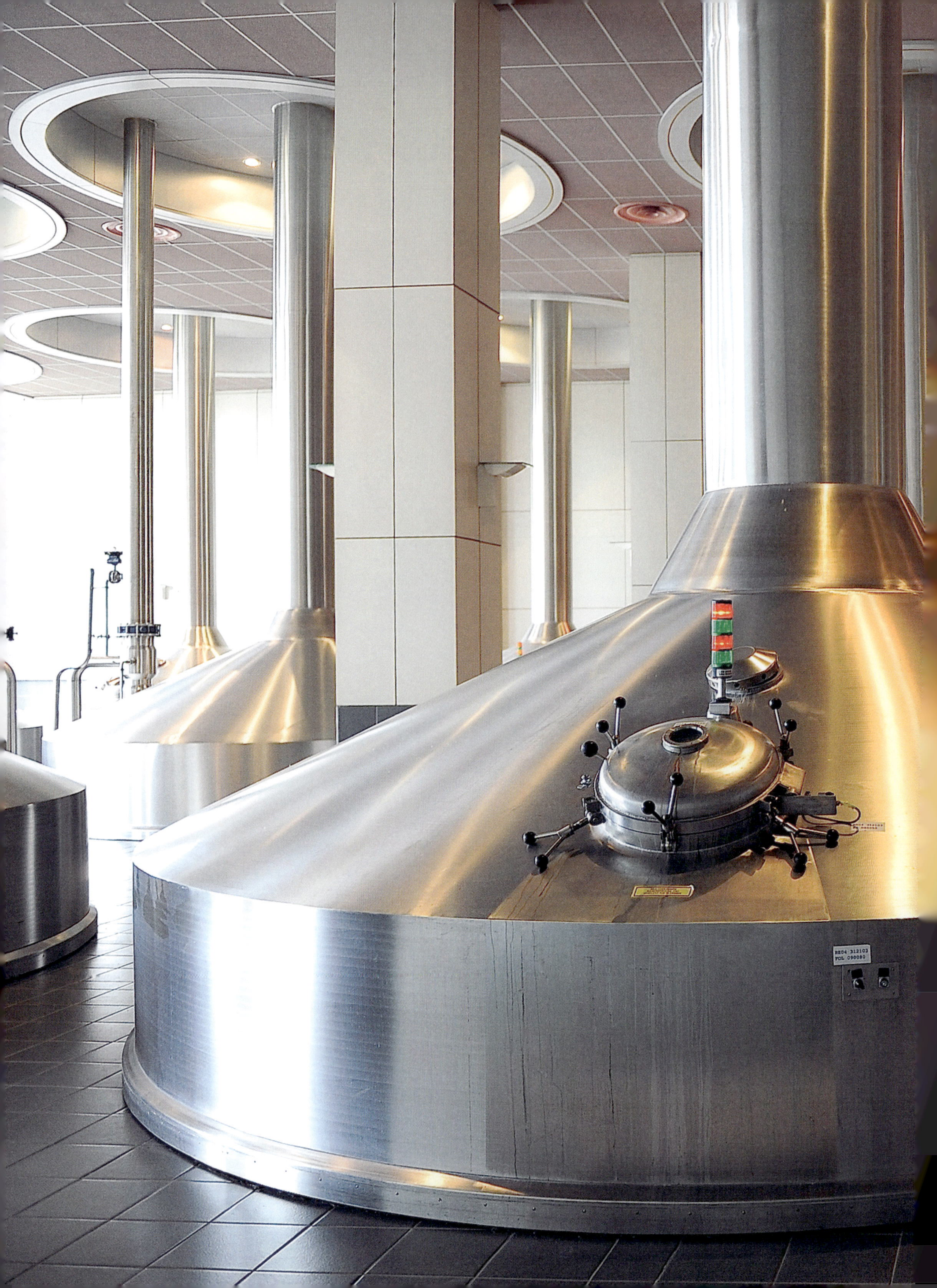

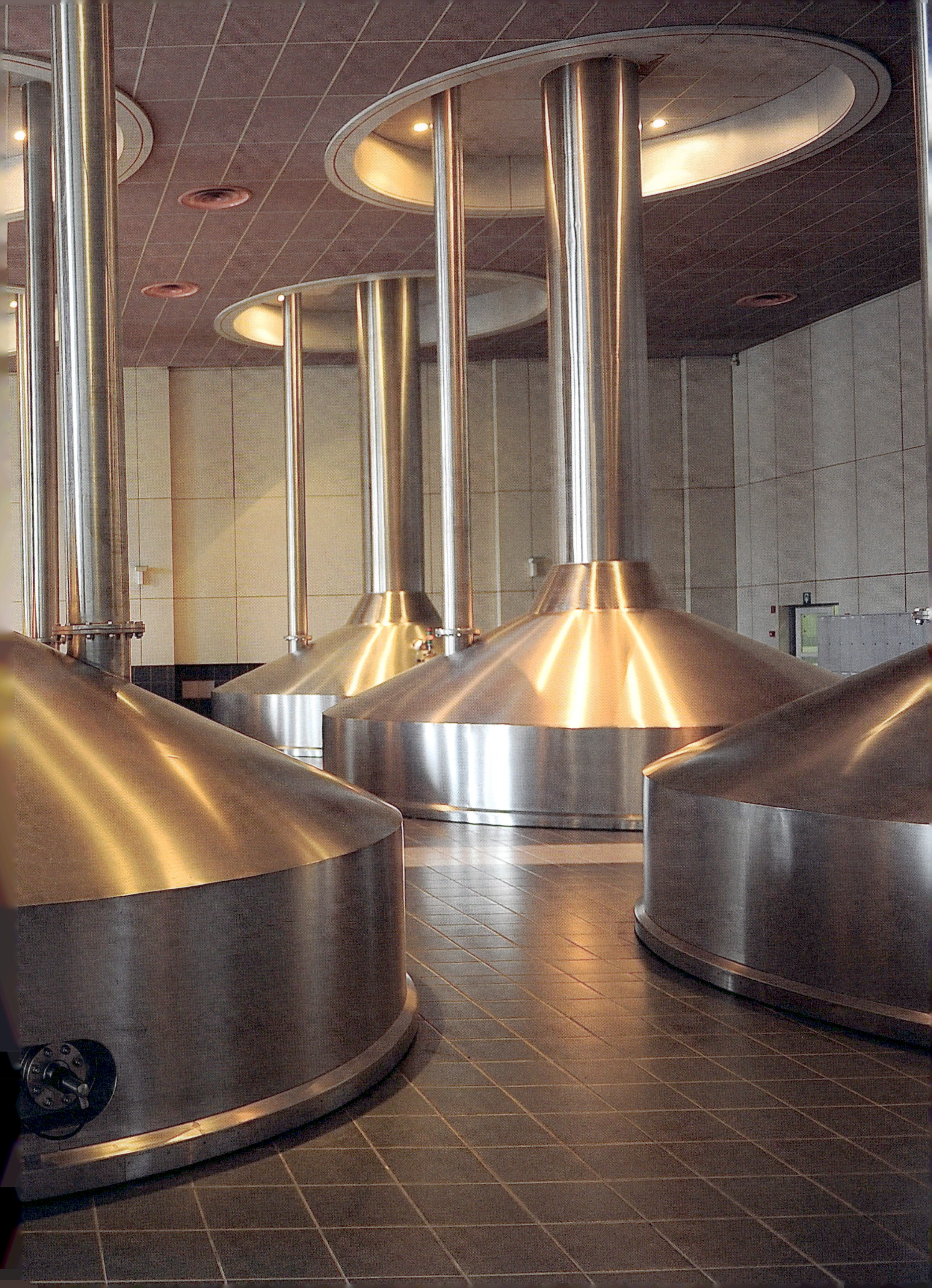

Angerik

Dilleke

Microbrewery.
Visits on Saturdays between 12.00 and 16.00.

Snakkaertstraat 30, Dilbeek, +32(0)477/37 15 86, info@angerik.be

Averbode

Averbode, Momentum

Averbode abbey is home to a microbrewery. Taste the home-brewed abbey beer either before or after a guided visit to the abbey. The Averbode abbey beer is only served in this location and is different from the bottled beer that is brewed by Huyghe.

Abdijstraat 1 (Herseltsebaan 2), Averbode, +32(0)13 78 04 40, abdij@abdijaverbode.be, www.averbodia.be

Boon

Oude Geuze Boon, Geuze Mariage Parfait, Kriek Boon, Oude Kriek Boon, Kriek Mariage Parfait, Framboise Boon, Faro Boon

---

The very best reference for lambic beers. Get in touch with the tourism office for the Pajottenland & Zennevallei-Halle regions to visit this brewery with its imposing foeders. Groups and single visitors both welcome. Contact Halle Tourism: tel. +32(0)2/356 42 59 – www.toerisme-halle.be.

Fonteinstraat 65, Lembeek (Halle), +32(0)2/356 66 44, info@boon.be, www.boon.be

Brasse-Temps (Le)

Ambrasse-Temps, Blanche de Ste Waudru, Brasse-Temps, Bush, Cuvée des Trolls, Surfine

---

Café brewery, very popular with students. Visits by appointment. Plenty of drinks on offer but the choice of meals is limited. Taste the Brasserie Dubuisson beers as well as the beers of the house.

Place des Brabançons 4, Louvain-la-Neuve, +32(0)10/45 70 27, www.brassetemps.be

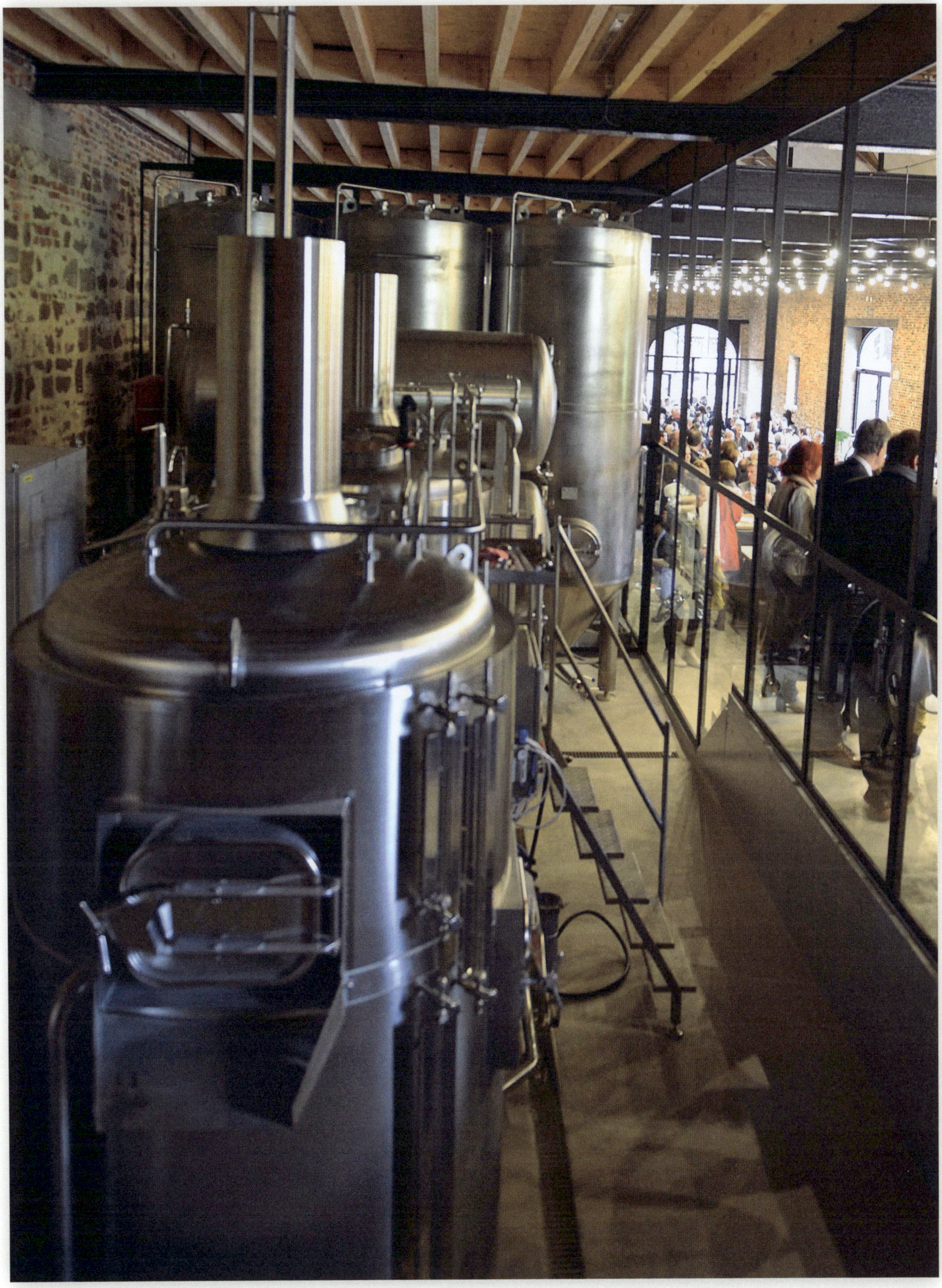

Brussels Beer Project

Babylone, Dark Sister, Delta, Grosse Bertha

Microbrewery in the heart of Brussels. The young brewers are keen on experimenting. They aim to conjure up twenty surprising brews each year from their amazing cauldron. Taste them all in the brewery café. Pop in for a visit every Thursday, Friday and Saturday between 14:00 and 22:00.

Dansaertstraat 188, keepintouch@beerproject.be, www.beerproject.be

Cantillon

100% Bio, Belgische vlag, Geuze, Grand Cru Bruocsella, Iris, Kriek, Rosé de Gambrinus, Vigneronne, Sint-Lamvinus, Fou' Foune, Lou Pepe

---

The one and only lambic brewery and 'gueuzestekerij' in Brussels, a short walk from the Brussels-Midi railway station. The brewer aims to re-acquaint people with real gueuze which is why he founded the Brussels Gueuze Museum. Open every day during brewing hours. Groups are welcome by prior arrangement.

Gheudestraat 56, Brussel, +32(0)2/521 49 28
info@cantillon.be, www.cantillon.be

De Block

Dendermonde, Kastaar, Réservée De Block, Satan, Sint-Timotheus

―――――

Microbrewery with brewery museum located in ancient farm. Discover a range of vintage brewing tools. Group visits by appointment.

Nieuwbaan 92, Peizegem-Merchtem, +32(0)52/37 21 59 www.satanbeer.com

De Cam

De Cam Frambozenbier, Oude Geuze, Kriekenlambiek, Oude Kriek

―――――

Gueuzestekerij De Cam is part of a community centre with a café open to all. Enjoy regional cooking and discover traditional family games. The first floor is home to a museum of musical instruments. Open every Sunday between 14:00 and 17:00, except bank holidays. Get in touch to arrange a guided tour or a visit at other times. You can also visit the gueuzestekerij by prior arrangement. Highly recommended to cyclists and mountain bikers. All the facilities for cyclist are available.

Dorpsstraat 67A, Gooik, +32(0)2/532 21 32 of +32(0)476/81 68 06, www.decam.be

Den Triest

Bruut'n Triest, De Neus, Den Triest Blond, Dubbel, Kesse, Kriek & Tripel, Greenhopping

―――――

Microbrewery with café where you are steeped in vintage beer advertising. The brewery and café are open every first Sunday of the month from 13:00 – 18:00. Marc, the brewer, is happy to share his secrets. Groups with 15 participants are welcome every day, reservations are recommended.

Trieststraat 24, Kapelle-Op-Den-Bos, +32(0)475/74 38 05 info@dentriest.be, www.dentriest.be

De Troch

Chapeau Apricot, Banana, Exotic, Faro, Fraise, Framboise, Gueuze, Kriek, Lemon & Peche, Cuvée Oude Gueuze

―――――

Lambic brewery turned into a living museum with authentic, historic brewhall in a majestic historic farmhouse. Tasting facilities at 200 metres from the brewery. Group or tours for smaller groups are available on request.

Langestraat 20, Wambeek (Ternat), +32(0)2/582 10 27, info@detroch.be, www.detroch.be

Domus (Huisbrouwerij)

Con Domus, Nen Engel, Nostra Domus

―――――

Taste its home-brewed beers in a typical brown café. A beer menu is also on offer. This brewery can be visited every day except Monday between 10:00 and 20:00 on requests only. For groups of eight participants and over.

Tiensestraat 8, Leuven, +32(0)16/20 14 49, info@domusleuven.be, www.domusleuven.be

3 Fonteinen

3 Fonteinen

An artisan gueuzestekerij for years, now also a lambic brewery. Oozing with tradition. Tours available on Friday and Saturday for groups between 10 and 30. Single visits one Saturday of every month (see website for details). Taste the beers and sample the cuisine in house restaurant 3 Fonteinen. A fully-fledged beer experience centre will open early 2017 in the nearby village of Lot. It will tell you all you need to know about kriek and Lambic.

Hoogstraat 2a, Beersel, +32(0)2/306 71 03 of +32(0)495/54 06 52, info@3fonteinen.be, www.3fonteinen.be

This is how they serve lambic beers from the tap in the house restaurant of 3 Fonteinen.

En Stoemelings

Curieuse Neus, En Stoemelings

Brussels has acquired a new, truly local brewery where you can see the brewer at work. Visit from Tuesday to Saturday between 11:00 and 18:00. Tip: spend a bit longer in the area and take a stroll around the daily 'brocante' market at Vossenplein.

Spiegelstraat 1, Brussel, +32(0)489 49 59 24, www.enstoemelings.be

Haacht

Adler, Export, Gildenbier, Keizer Karel, Mystic, Ommegang, Primus, Spéciale 1900, Star, Tongerlo, White by Mystic

A monumental brewery with humble dairy farm origins. Modern equipment was integrated seamlessly into a collection of buildings steeped in history without affecting the overall look. With original brewhall, barrel chamber and bottling plant. The majestic central building used to be a power station. The former hop oast (1898) has been converted into a brewery museum. The Brouwershof tavern opposite the brewery is furnished in the Belle Époque style (1910). It serves all of the Haacht beers and enjoy a cuisine that goes with the beers. Ask to see the beer menu. This is the only place where you can taste the unfiltered Primus with yeast. For group visits with 15 – 50 participants it is necessary to book in advance. Every brewery visit finishes with a beer tasting in Het Brouwershof.

Brouwerij Haacht, Provinciesteenweg 28, Boortmeerbeek, +32(0)16/60 15 01, visit@haacht.com, www.haacht.com

②

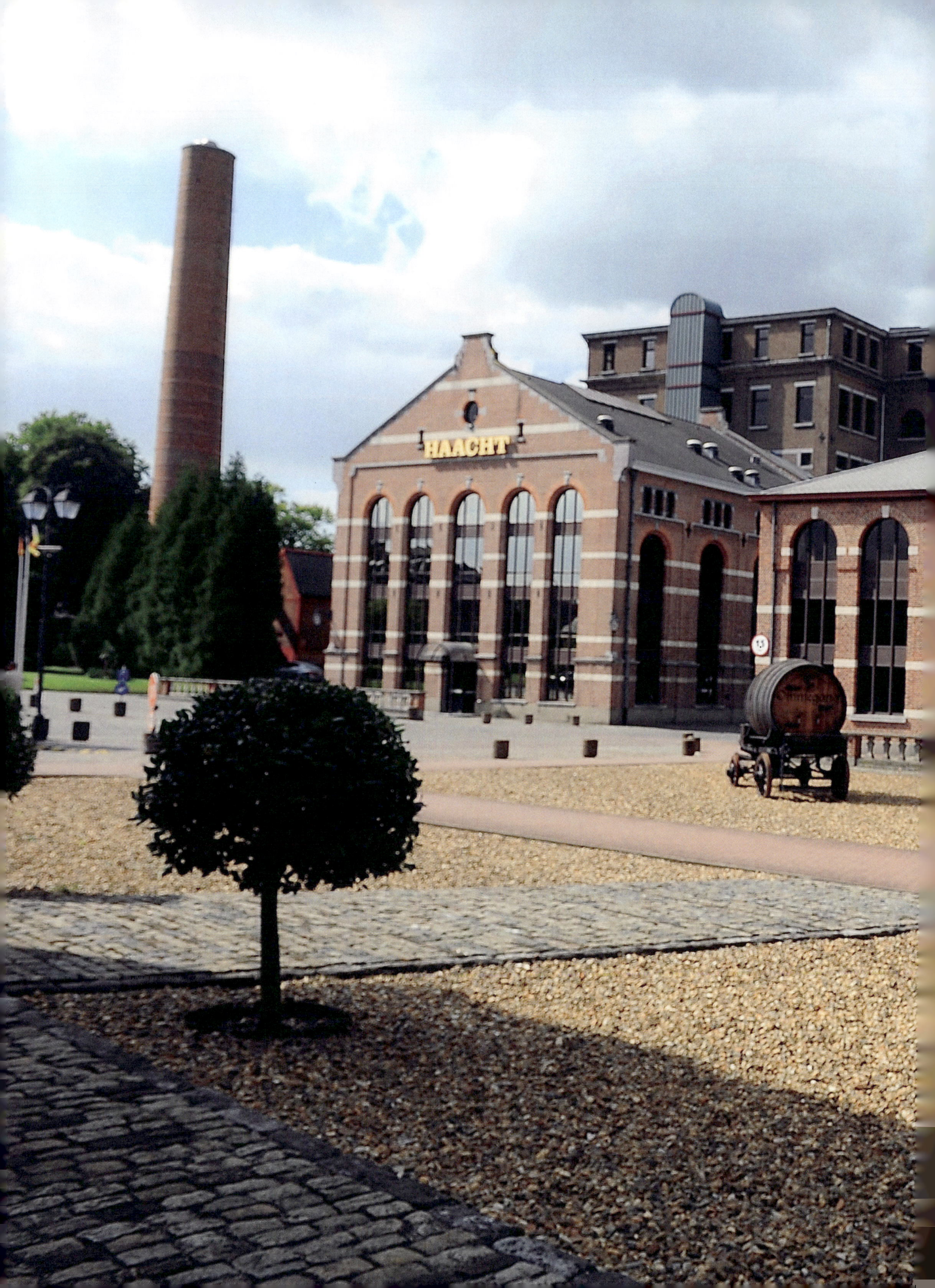
HAACHT

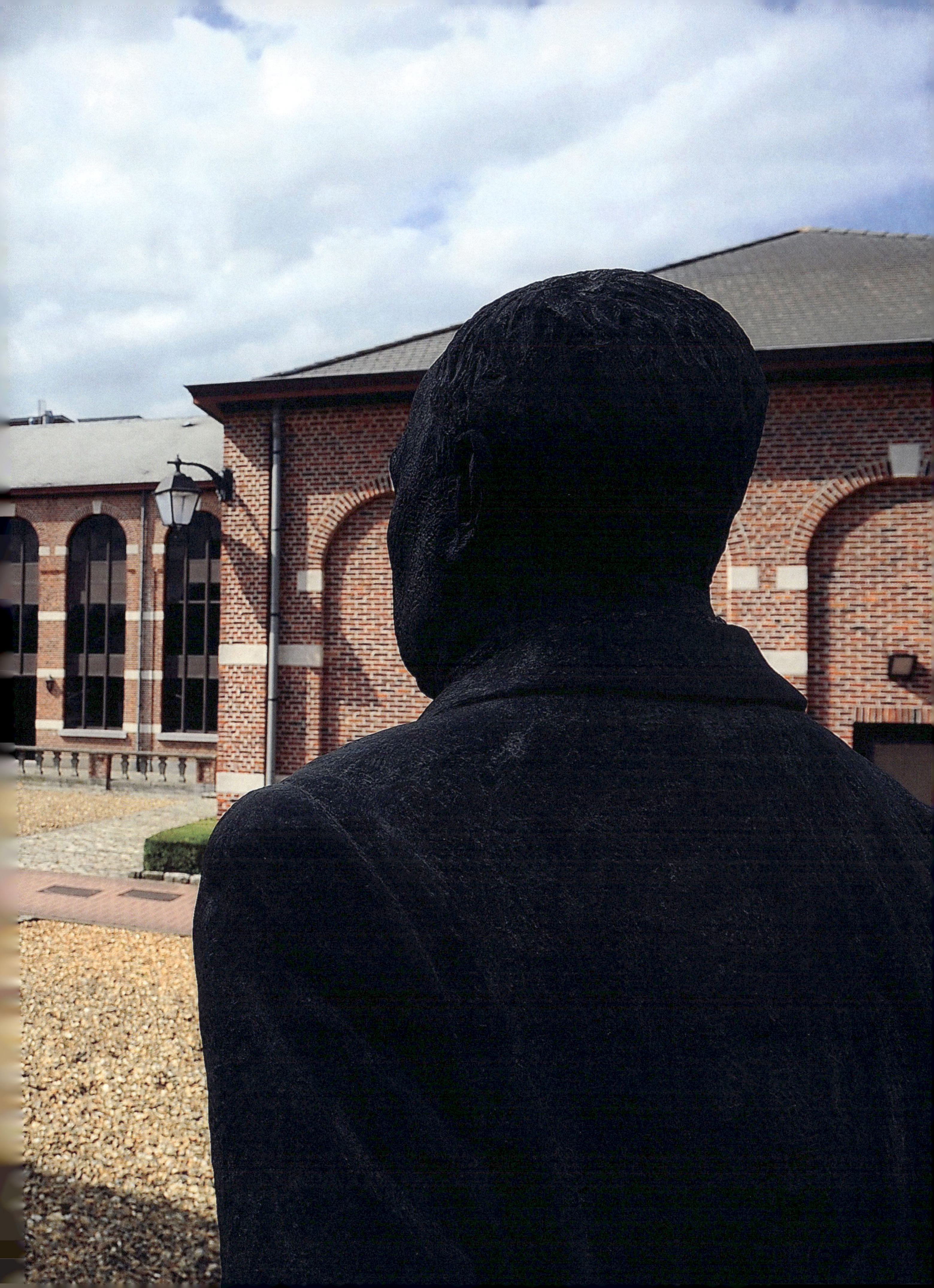

Hanssens Artisanaal

Hanssens Artisanaal Oude Geuze, Oude Kriek, Oud Beitje

Authentic gueuzestekerij with vintage equipment. Visits by appointment.

Vroenenbosstraat 15, Dworp, +32(0)2/380 31 33

Herberg (Den)

Den Herberg Amber, Blond, Bruin Tarwe

A genuine café brewery where brewing is done in the open, just behind the bar. For night owls and early birds. Open Mondays, Tuesdays, Wednesdays, Thursdays and Sundays from 11:00 – 01:00; Fridays and Saturdays 11:00 – 03:00.

Octave De Kerckhove d'Exaerdestraat 16, Buizingen, +32(0)2/305 36 56 of +32(0)476/41 92 67, www.denherberg.be

Hoegaarden

Hoegaarden, Grand Cru, Rosée, Spéciale, Verboden Vrucht, Witbier

---

Visit the birthplace of the most famous white beer in the world. Tours are held every Wednesday and Thursday. You don't need to book in advance for the 13:00 brewery tour. Group visits take place at 10:30 and 14:30 by prior application only. Find out about the history of this brewery, the ingredients used and how brewing is done and discover a host of trivia that may well surprise you. Tip: combine this brewery tour with a visit to the sugar city of Tienen and hop on your bike to explore this rural area.

Stoopkensstraat 24a, Hoegaarden, +32(0)16/76 98 11, info@breweryvisits.com, www.breweryvisits.com

Hof Ten Dormaal

Dormaal, Inferno, Kriek, Oak Aged Extra Strong Blond & Dark, Zure van Tildonk

---

Located at an authentic, operational brewery-farm amongst the fields. Brewhall with café is open to the public every Saturday from 14:00 to 17:00. Guided tours can be arranged. You can see Brabant draft horses grazing quietly. Now and again these splendid horses are used for carriage rides. Location: between cycle nodes 27 and 28.

Caubergstraat 2, Tildonk, +32(0)477/51 59 91, www.hoftendormaal.com

Jandrain-Jandrenouille

Big Mama, IV Saison, V Cense, VI Wheat

———

Microbrewery sited at handsome square farmhouse surrounded by fields. Guided tours by arrangement for groups of a minimum of 10. Taste their classic beers with a modern twist from American aroma hops.

Rue de la Féculerie 34, Jandrain-Jandrenouille (Orp-Jauche), +32(0)19/51 42 98 of +32(0)475/71 45 35, alexandre.dumont@skynet.be, www.brasseriedejandrainjandrenouille.com

Kortrijk-Dutsel

Kortrijk-dUtsel

———

Microbrewery. Visits available on request. Open evenings and weekends. Beer tasting facilities available.

Lindestraat 21, Kortrijk-Dutsel (Holsbeek), +32(0)16/43 47 60, brouwerijkortrijkdutsel@gmail.com

Kroon (De)

Delvaux, Job, Superkroon

Microbrewery and brewery museum on the site of a former brewery. Visits on request. Pop into the brewery tavern to taste the home-brewed beers and enjoy its brasserie cuisine.

Beekstraat 20, Neerijse, +32(0)16/43 94 72, info@brouwerijdekroon.be, www.brouwerijdekroon.be

Lindemans

Cuvée René Oude Gueuze & Oude Kriek, Lindemans Kriek, Gueuze, Faro, Pecheresse, Framboise, Cassis & Apple, SpontanBasil, BlossomGueuze

---

A lambic brewery that started off as a farm brewery but saw significant expansion throughout the years. Visits available Monday to Friday from 08:00 to 18:00. Guided tours by appointment only for groups comprising up to 25 participants.

Lenniksebaan 297, Vlezenbeek (St.-Pieters Leeuw), +32(0)2/569 03 90, info@lindemans.be, www.lindemans.be

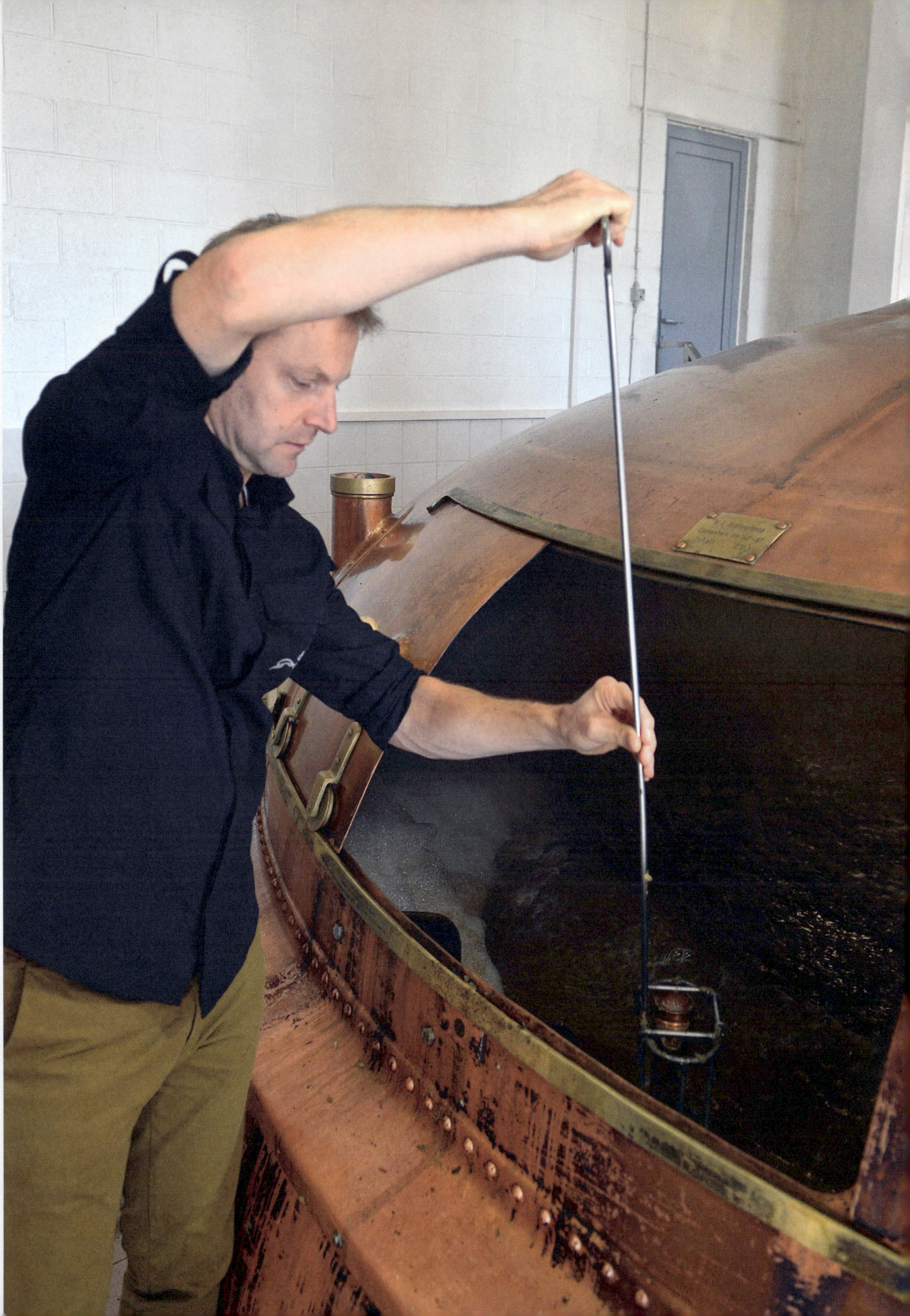

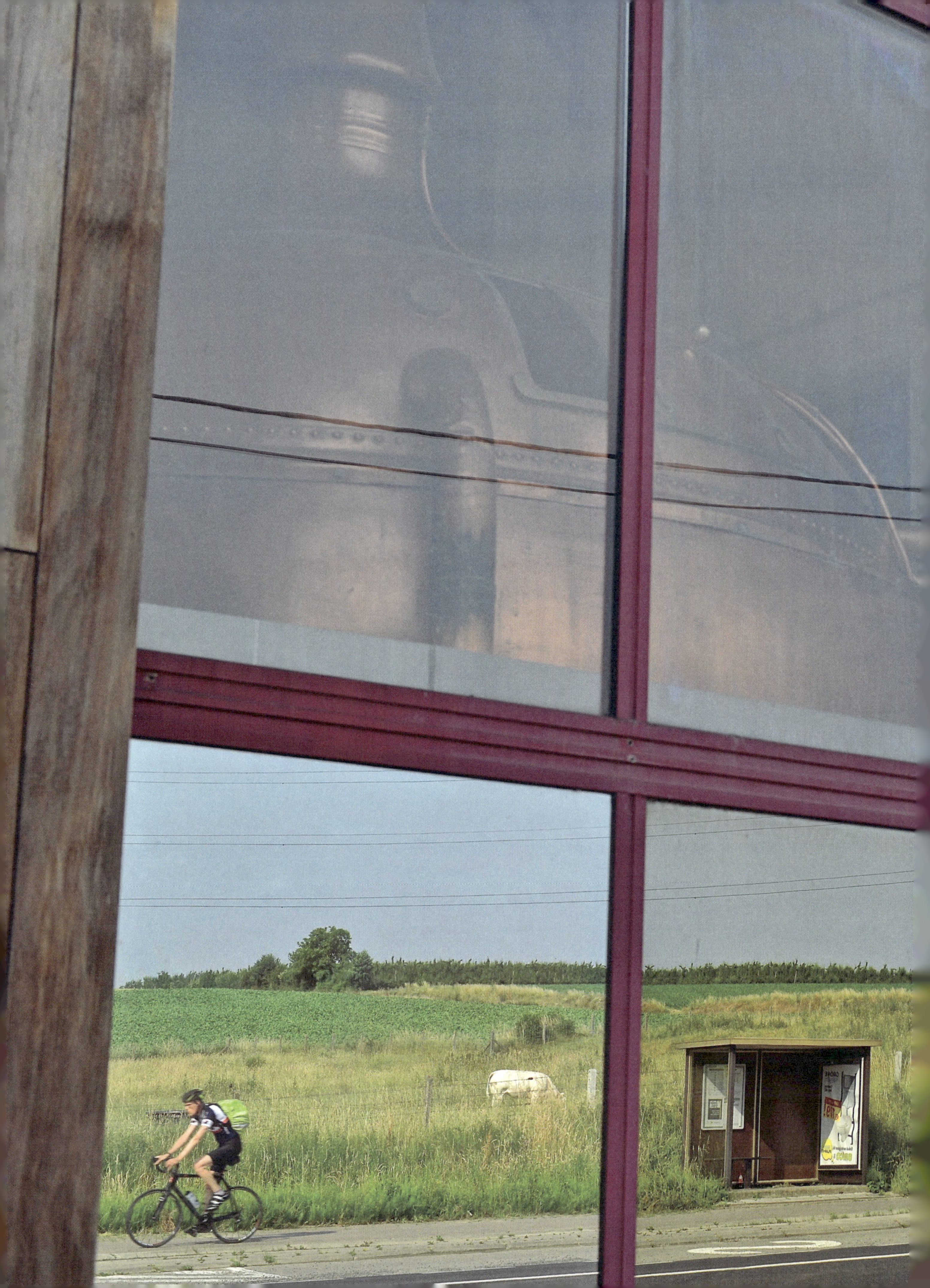

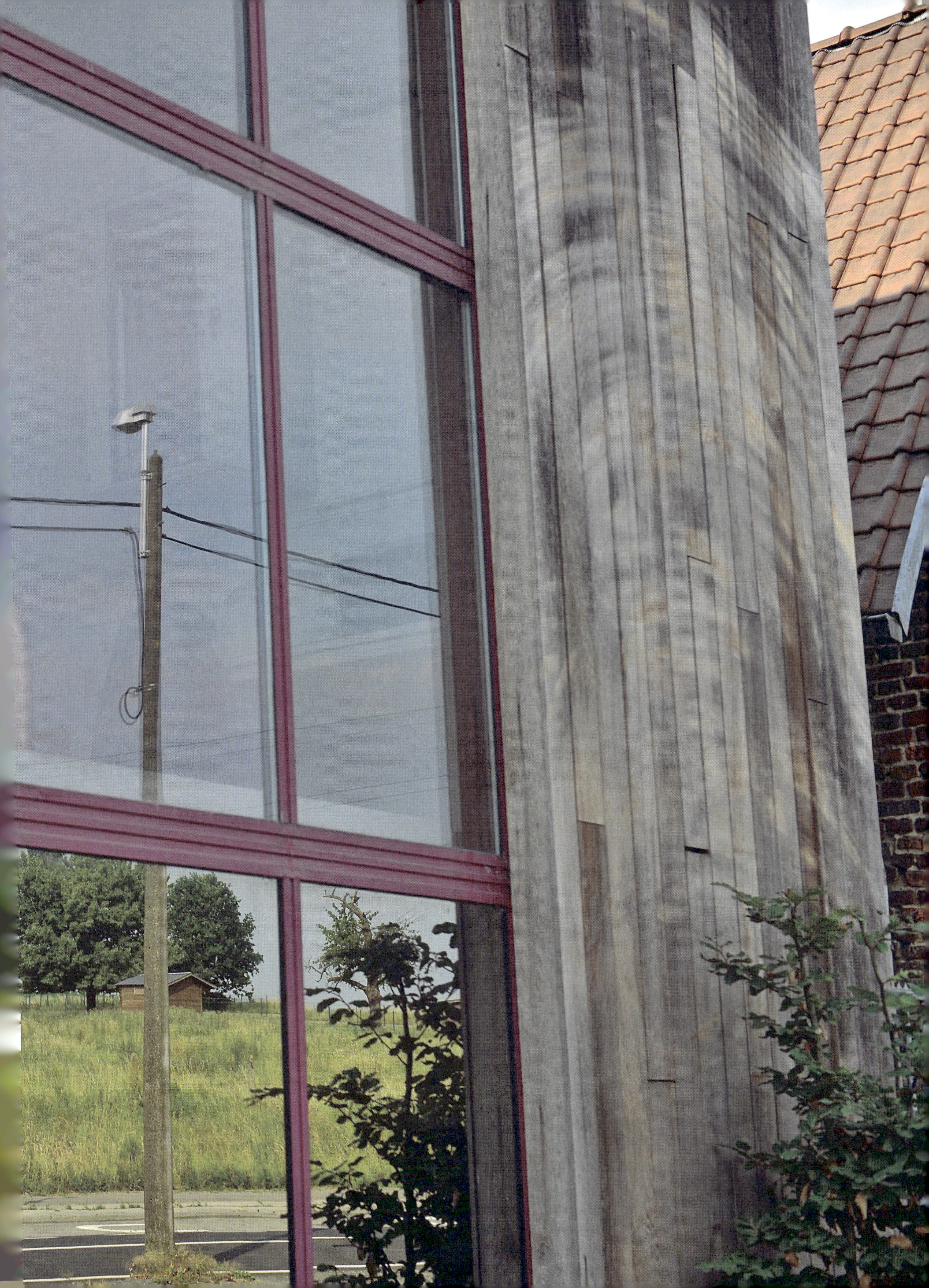

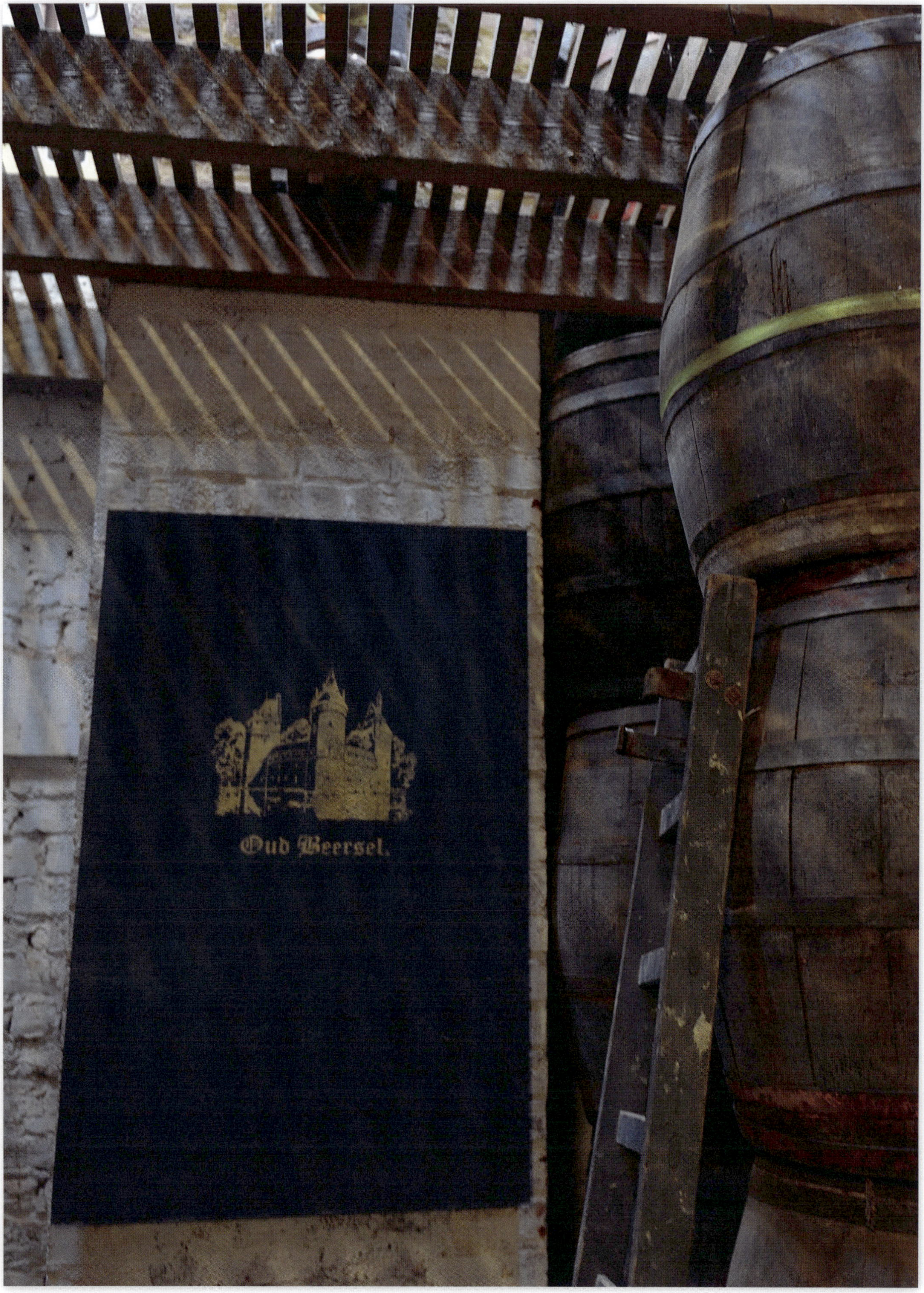
Oud Beersel.

Loterbol

Loterbol, Tuverbol

Every first Saturday of the month this listed 18th century brewery opens its doors to the public from 16:00 to midnight. Guided tours are available on request.

Michel Theysstraat 58a, Diest, +32(0)13/77 10 07
www.loterbol.be

Mort Subite

Mort Subite Kriek Lambic (Tradition), (Oude) Gueuze Lambic, Oude Kriek Lambic, Witte Lambic

---

Lambic brewery with splendid vintage brewhall and foeder hall. Guided tours by appointment on working days only for groups between 10 and 50. Make your reservation through 'Toerisme Brabantse Kouters', +32(0)2/270 99 30, www.brabantsekouters.be.

Lierput 1, Kobbegem (Asse), +32(0)2/454 11 11
infomortsubite@alken-maes.com, www.mort-subite.be

Nieuwhuys

Alpaïde, Cuvée van de Generaal, Huardis, Rosdel

Despite its name, 'New House', this brewery is the oldest stone-built edifice in Hoegaarden. The brewery itself is not open to the public but the café that was once the home of the original brewery is still alive and kicking. It regularly hosts live performances; it pays to keep an eye on the diary. Open Thursday to Saturday from 17:00. Open from 11:30 on Sundays.

Ernest Ourystraat 2, +32(0)16/81 71 64, jan@nieuwhuys.be,
www.nieuwhuys.be

Oud Beersel

Bersalis, Bzart lambiek & kriekenlambiek, Oud Beersel, Oude Geuze, Oude Kriek & Framboise

---

Artisan gueuzestekerij within an ancient brewery with splendid foeder halls. Guided tour every first and third Saturday of the month at 11:00 and 12:30. Group visits on request.

Laarheidestraat 230, Beersel, +32(0)486/69 36 29,
visit@degeuzenvanoudbeersel.be, www.degeuzenvanoudbeersel.be

Palm Belgian Craft Brewers/De Hoorn

Arthur's Legacy, Brugge Tripel, Estaminet, Cornet, Dobbel Palm, Palm, Palm Hop Select, Palm Royale, Palm Sauvin, Steenbrugge

———

Both Palm Belgian Craft Brewers as well as its new De Hoorn microbrewery are offering guided tours. You start at the visitors' centre De Oude Bottelarij, then then follow the tour which allows you to you to observe closely the entire production process of the top-fermented beers. Your first stop is the brewhall followed by the herbs storage area, the fermentation chambers, the bottling plant and the distribution hall. It goes without saying that your visit ends with a beer tasting. Guided tours for groups of 15-50 participants. If you wish you can visit the stud farm for Brabant draught horses in the grounds of Diepensteyn Castle.

Steenhuffeldorp 3, Steenhuffel, +32(0)52/31 74 14
www.palmbreweries.com

Tilquin (Gueuzerie)

Oude Gueuze Tilquin, Oude Quetsche Tilquin, Gueuze Tilquin van 't vat

———

Welcome to the youngest 'gueuzestekerij' in the country. Pierre Tilquin learnt his craft from the lambic brewers from whom he orders his lambic. It has a splendid foeder hall. Visits on request for groups of ten or more, Monday – Saturday. Free visit every Saturday between 10:30 and 13:00, when the shop is open.

Chaussée Maïeur Habils 110, Bierges, +32(0)472/91 82 91
info@gueuzerietilquin.be, www.gueuzerietilquin.be

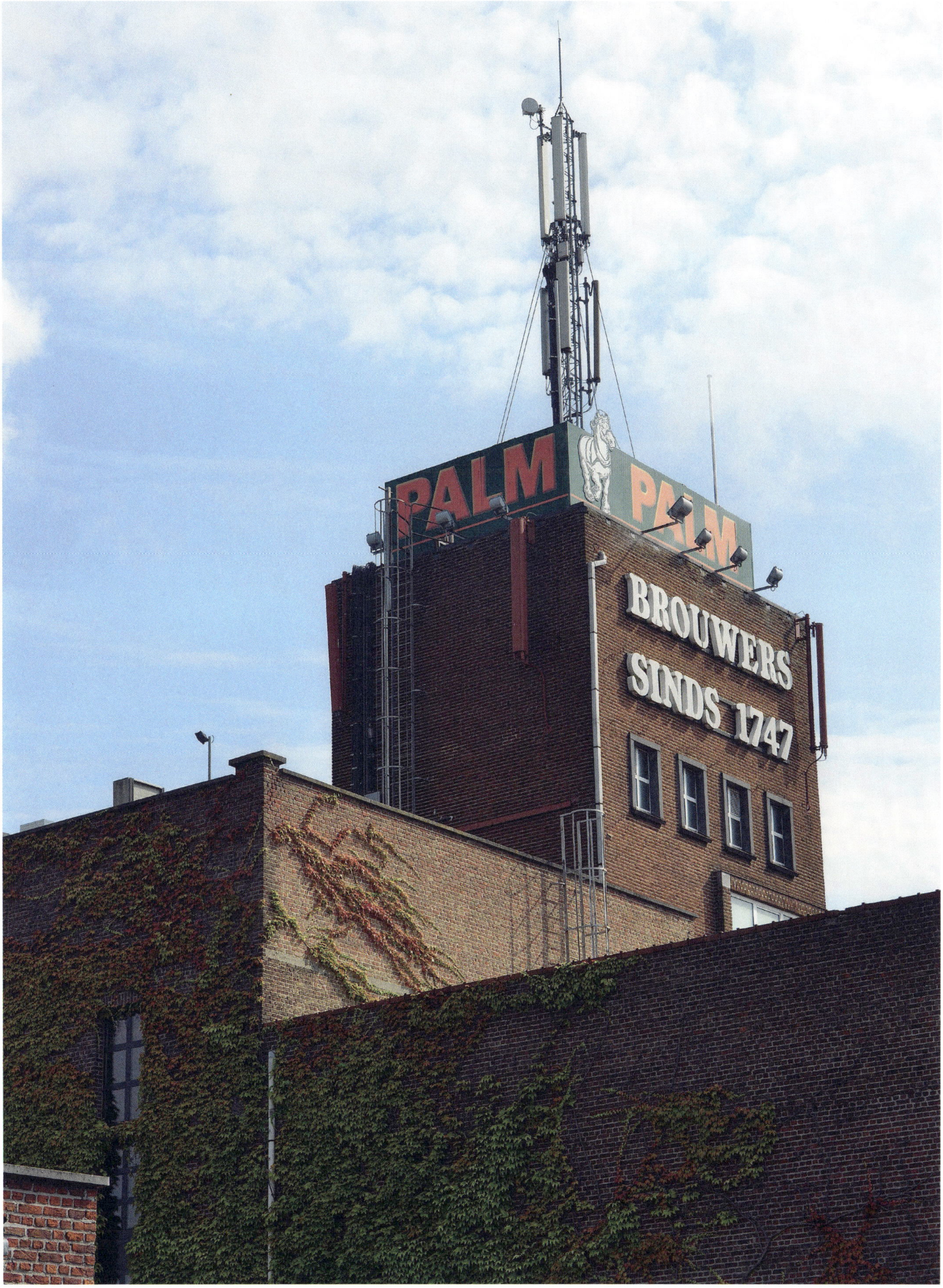
PALM
PALM
BROUWERS
SINDS 1747

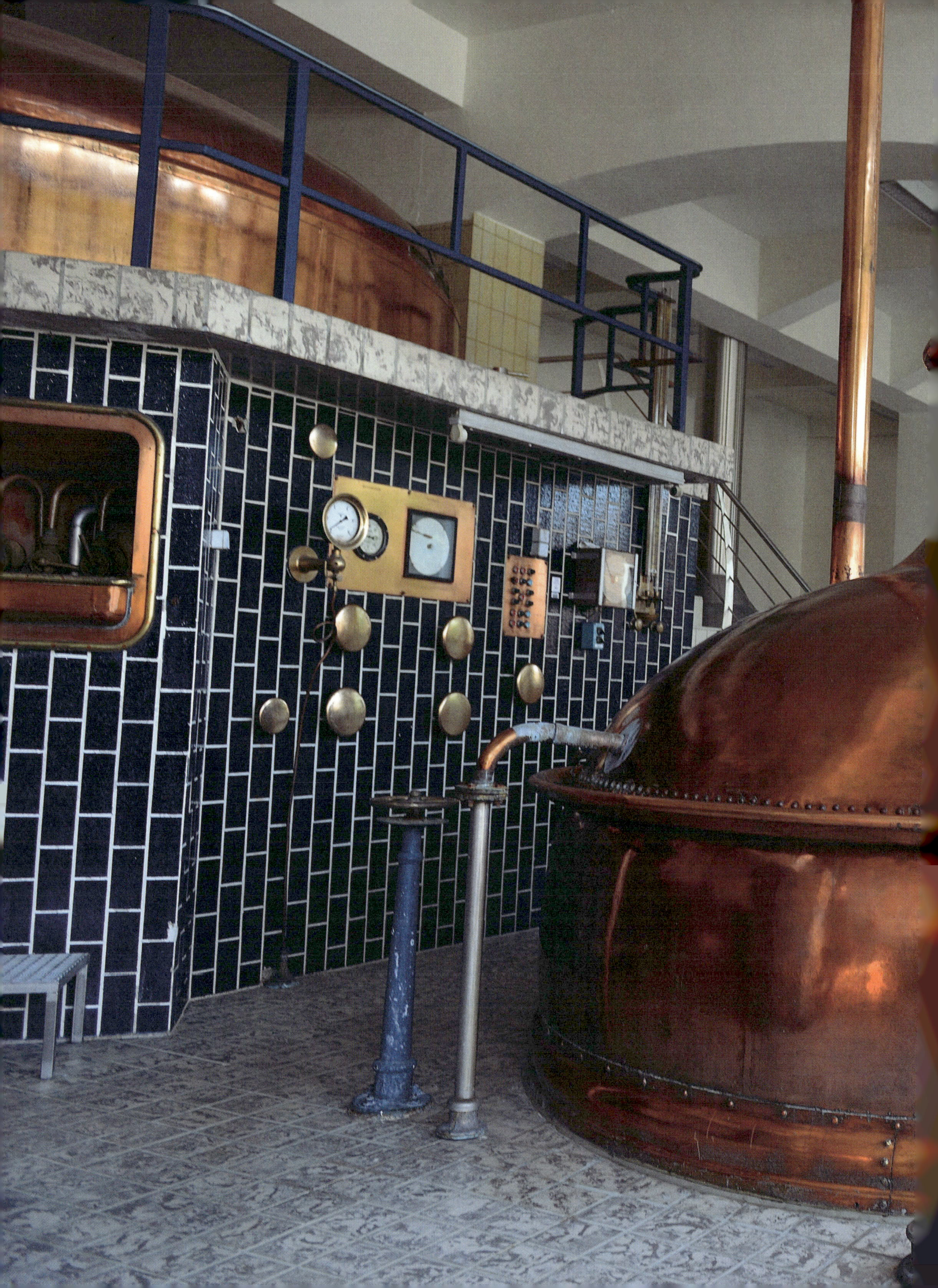

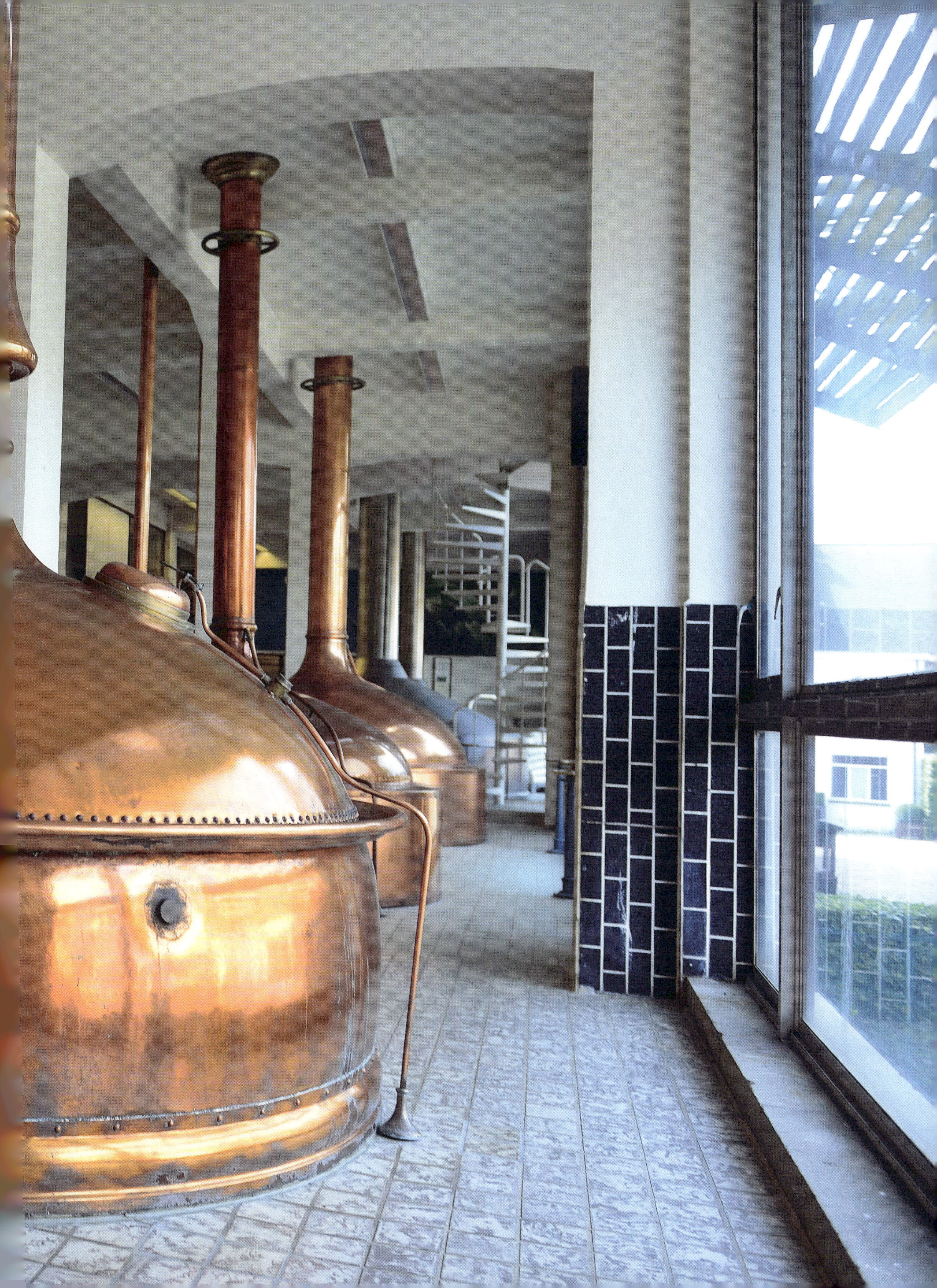

Mashing in the historic brewhall of the Timmermans lambic brewery.

Timmermans

Timmermans Blanche Lambicus, Faro Lambicus, Framboise Lambicus, Kriek Retro Lambicus, Oude Gueuze Lambicus, Oude Kriek Lambicus, Pêche Lambicus, Pumpkin Lambicus, Strawberry Lambicus

---

The oldest lambic brewery still operating in the world complete with its original infrastructure. The brewery museum documents three hundred years of Belgian brewing history. The brewery is open daily, including weekends, but by appointment only. Guided tours are available. The brewery is on the route of a Breughel walk and several cycling trails (www.dilbeek.be).

Kerkstraat 11, Itterbeek (Dilbeek), +32(0)2/569 03 57
www.anthonymartin.be/timmermans

Tubize (Brasserie de)

Abbaye de Boneffe, Betchard

Jean Rodriguez, the 'patron' of Brussels beer restaurant In 't Spinnekopke, set up this brewery on the banks of the Zenne. The bistro's fixtures and fittings were once part of the Falstaff Gourmand in Brussels. Visits including a tasting are on offer during the weekend.

Rue de la Filature 2, Tubize, +32(0)475/24 63 37
brasseriedetubize@gmail.com

In 't Spinnekopke, Bloementuinplein 1, Brussel, +32(0)2/511 86 95,
www.spinnekopke.be

The brand new microbrewery in the grounds of the former Abbey of Villers-la-Ville.

Van Campenhout

Witlov

This microbrewery can be visited every first Sunday of the month at 15:00. Taste the beers and enjoy the brasserie kitchen in the Labo Café that regularly plays host to live performances.

Brouwerijstraat 23F, Kampenhout, +32(0)16/22 64 66, info@brouwerijvancampenhout.be, www.brouwerijvancampenhout.be

Villers-la-Ville (Abbaye de)

Abbaye de Villers Blond & Tripel

On this imposing abbey site the ruins of a brewery can be found. Where a hostelry once stood, beer was brewed in later years. And now this site houses a brand new brewery. The organic abbey beers show the hand of Bruno Deghorain, brewer at La Binchoise. Visits to the site and the brewery by prior arrangement.

Rue de l'Abbaye 55, Villers-la-Ville, +32(0)71/88 09 80 info@villers.be, www.villers.be

Vissenaken

De Nacht, Fasso, Meetsel, Himelein

Home brewery that can be visited on request. Groups of between seven and 12 participants.

Metselstraat 74, Vissenaken (Tienen), +32(0)16/82 13 77, brouwerij.vissenaken@skynet.be, www.brouwerijvissenaken.net

Vlier (De)

Brut, De Vlier-gamma, Ferme Framboos, Gulden Delle, Holsbeekse Lentetripel, Onbekende Soldaat, Smokin' Elder, Xmas Spicy, Winter Stout

---

This detached home with spacious basement was turned into a brewery with tasting room. This is where Marc Andries unleashes his creative spirits. Open every second and third Saturday of the month from 16:00 – 20:00. Guided tour at 15:00. Groups with a maximum of 12 participants by prior arrangement.

Leuvensebaan 219, Holsbeek, +32(0)473/83 94 63, info@brouwerijdevlier.com, www.brouwerij-devlier.com

Waterloo (Brasserie de)

Waterloo, Récolte, Tripel Blond, Strong Oak, Cuvée Impériale, Kriek

---

The Ferme de Mont Saint-Jean close to the battlefield and the Lion of Waterloo statue is steeped in Grand History. This is where the English soldiers were treated for their injuries sustained in battle. The majestic square farm is now owned by Anthony Martin's Finest Drinks. You recognise the farm, the barns and stables, the pigsty, the oven, well and chapel. A brand new microbrewery was installed in one of the wings. Not only is there a brewery, you will also find a restaurant on this site: L'Orangerie du Prince and a museum about the Battle at Waterloo.

Chaussée de Charleroi 591, Waterloo, +32(0)2 38 50 103, www.waterloo-beer.com

Senne (Brasserie de la)

Brussels Calling, Crianza, Equinox, Jambe-de-Bois, Saison de la Senne, Schieve Tabarnak, Stouterik, Taras Boulba, Zinnebir, Zwarte Piet

---

You visit a microbrewery housed in a former industrial bakery in a popular area of Brussels. This brewery is keen on hops and loves to experiment. Visits by appointment for groups of 15 and over. The brewer will be moving to a new location near Tour & Taxis at the port of Brussels in the near future.

Steenweg op Gent 565, Brussel, +32(0)2/465 07 51, info@brasseriedelasenne.be, www.brasseriedelasenne.be

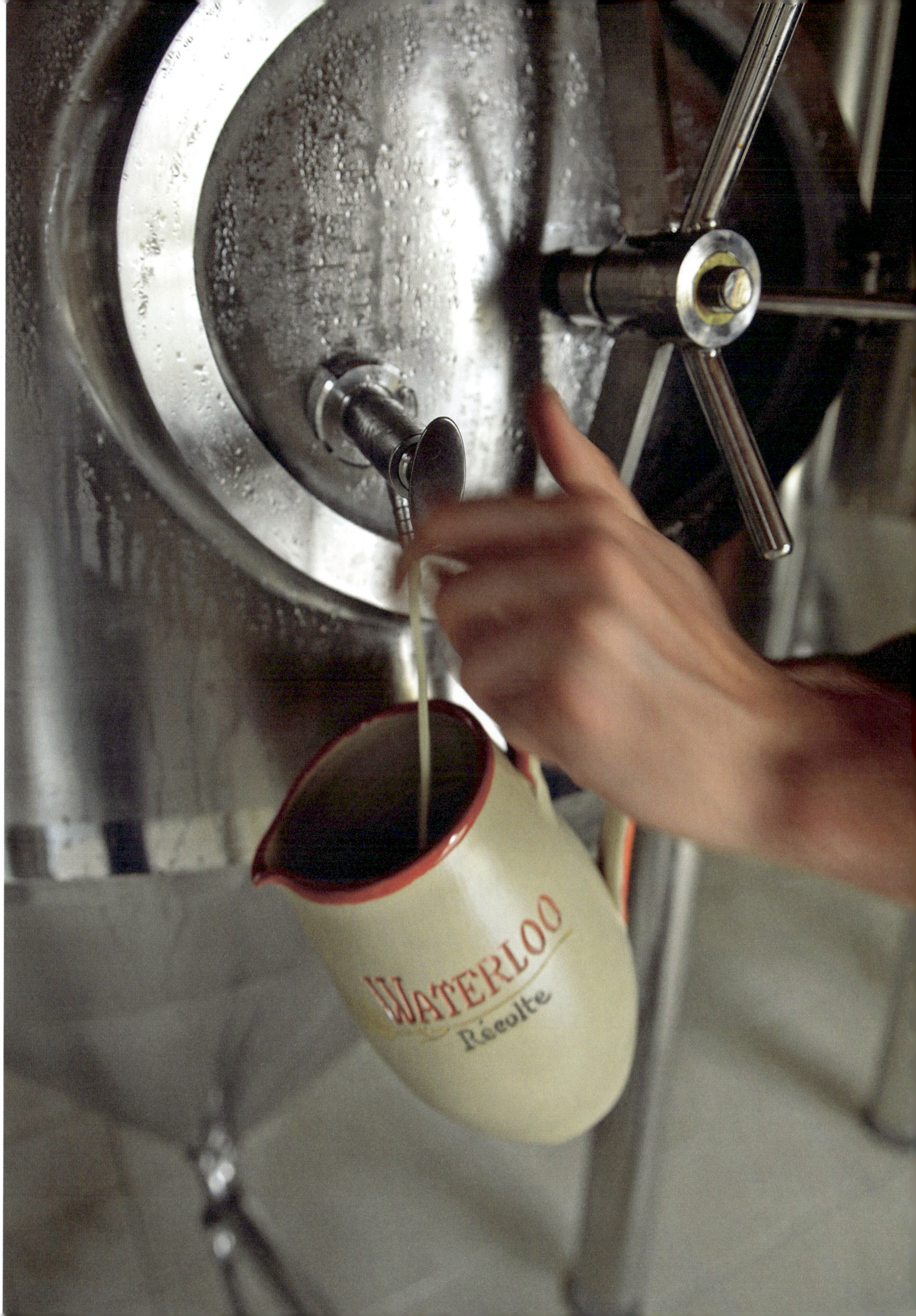
WATERLOO
Récolte

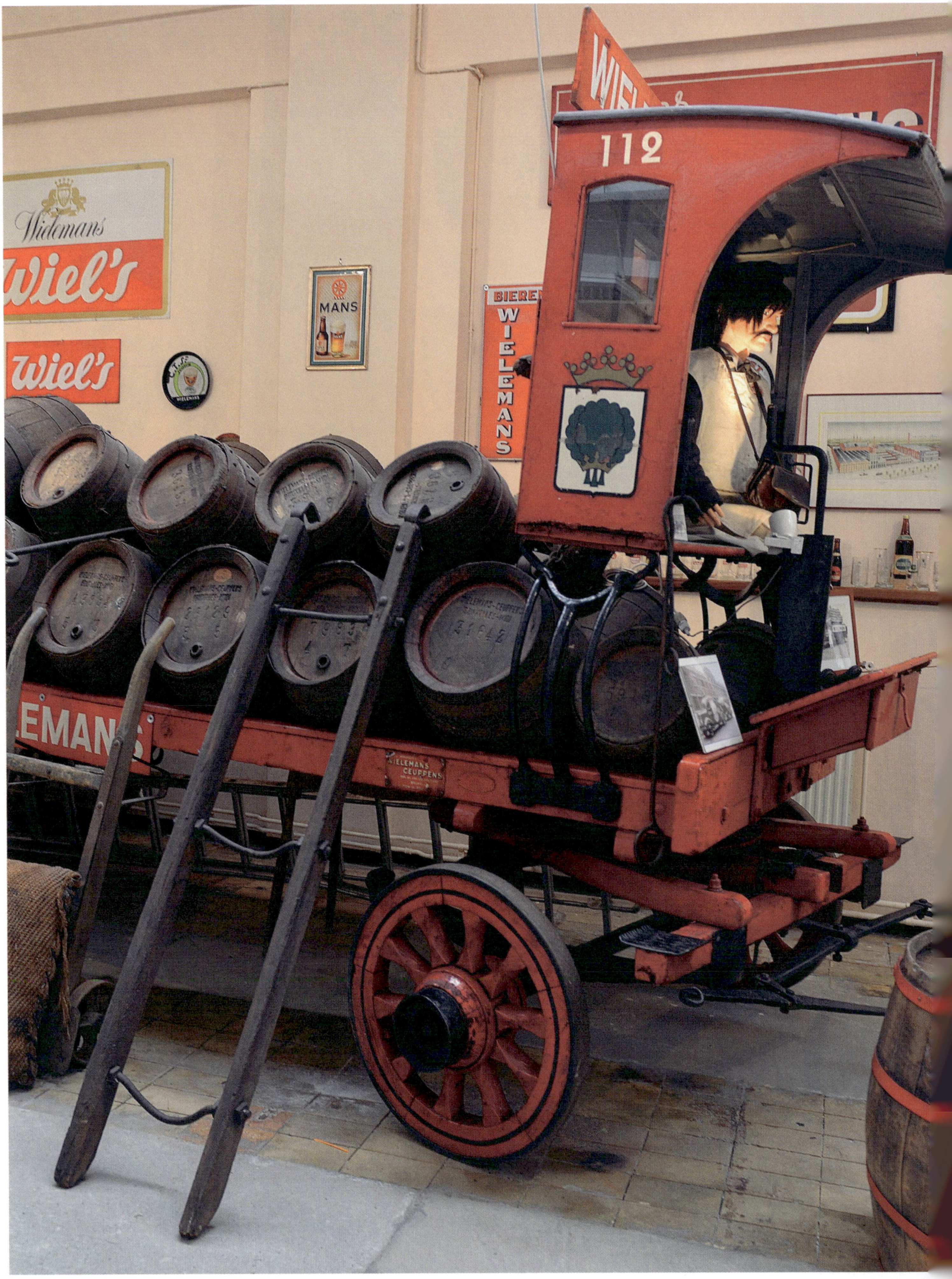
Wielemans
Wiel's
Wiel's
MANS
BIEREN
WIELEMANS
112

WORTH SEEING

Visitors' centre De Lambiek

This visitors' centre focuses on experience and discovery. Visitors are immersed in the tastes, aromas, sounds and texture of lambic beer. The Centre makes an excellent starting point for a journey of discovery of several lambic breweries in the Pajottenland region and the Zenne Valley. Regional attractions include Beersel Castle, the old paper mill at Herisem and many lambic breweries and 'gueuzestekerijen'. A brewery walk departs from the Centre and takes you to a number of breweries. The route is dotted with information boards and vintage equipment once used in the lambic breweries, such as the barrel cleaner that now takes pride of place at a roundabout in Lot. The walk is detailed in a brochure.

Gemeenveldstraat 1, Alsemberg, +32(0)2/359 16 36
toerisme@beersel.be, www.beersel.be

Dilbeek Hop Museum

The Land van Aalst, the countryside surrounding the city of Aalst, used to be the main area for hop cultivation in Belgium. This glorious heritage is carried on by only two or three companies, one of which is in Sint-Martens-Bodegem. In the barn attached to Huis Mostinckx the visitor gains an overview of the various aspects of local hop culture with a focus on the trellis fields and the hop oasts. The hop barn is open to the public on several Sundays between April and October (see www.toerismedilbeek.be). Seize your chance to taste one or more specialty beers. Guided tours on request.

Dorpsplein 5, St.-Martens-Bodegem (Dilbeek),
+32(0)2/451 69 34 – toerisme@dilbeek.be,
www.toerismedilbeek.be

Schaerbeek Museum Of Beer

Beer connoisseurs know that the best krieken lambic is made with krieken cherries from Schaarbeek. The name denotes the variety of cherries rather than their origin, as these days they are cultivated in the area around Sint-Truiden in the Haspengouw region. Schaarbeek is a highly populated community that forms part of Brussels. Looking a little out of place, the Schaarbeeks Bier Museum is found in the Louis Bertrandlaan (Avenue Louis Bertrand) where we are transported in a flash to the Belle Époque at the start of the 20th century. The museum occupies the workshops of a former vocational college and provides a brief initiation into the history of Belgian beer. Brewing equipment is used to explain the process. The primary focus is on traditional Belgian beer styles, mainly lambic, faro, gueuze and kriek, typical for Brussels and its surroundings. The museum's walls are clad in vintage enamel advertising boards. Over 1,500 Belgian beer bottles and glasses are displayed in alphabetical order by brewery. This collection comprises items from existing breweries and also covers brands and breweries that have disappeared. You will discover, for example, that Duvel has not always been served in its current iconic glass. At one time, it was poured into a flute. The furnishings of its small café take you back to the era between 1900 and 1930. After all, a museum without a café is like a sea without water. In this 'estaminet', below the watchful eye of Saint Arnold, the patron saint of brewers, you enjoy the Schaerbeekoise house beer, brewed by Abbaye des Rocs. If you have really been gripped by the beer history fever, you can trawl the library. For bargain hunters there is a range of collectors' items: the museum's own beer glasses, bottle openers, ballpoint pens carrying beer advertising, etc. The museum opens its doors every Wednesday and Saturday between 14:00 and 18:00. Group visits by prior arrangement. Tip: if you are still thirsty, turn left when you leave the museum. On the very first corner you will find a beer shop and café selling an extensive range of lesser-known beers.

Schaarbeeks Bier Museum, Louis Bertrandlaan 33, Brussel,
+32(0)2/241 56 27 – muschaerbiere@yahoo.fr,
users.skynet.be/museedelabiere

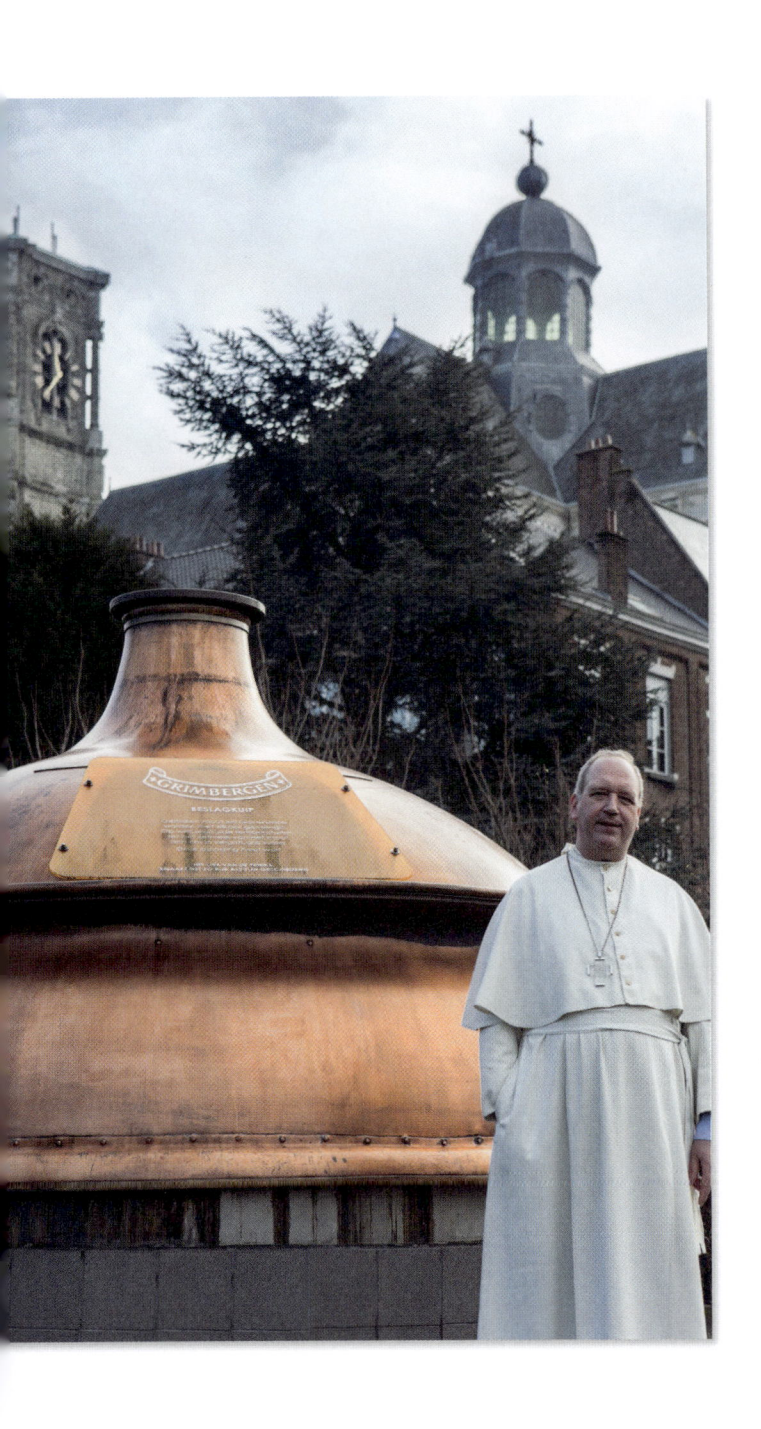

Grimbergen

Grimbergen is brewed at Alken-Maes. Access to the Basilica is every day from 07:00 – 19:00. The abbey itself is not open to the public, but there is an abbey beer museum that offers guided visits.

Abdijbiermuseum, Prinsenstraat 22, Grimbergen, +32(0)2/260 12 99, toerisme@grimbergen.be, www.abdijgrimbergen.be

Wiels (Kunstencentrum)

The former Wielemans-Ceuppens brewery in Vorst is now home to an arts centre. The listed building (1930) designed by Adrien Blomme unites stylistic elements of the art deco with those of industrial modernism. The building has the look of a freighter and is remarkable for its use of industrial building materials: re-enforced concrete, glass and steel. It once housed the brewhall where bottom-fermented beers were produced. The centre for contemporary arts opened its doors in 2007. The Wielemans-Ceuppens brewery, known for its Wiel's pils, ceased to exist in 1980. Free entry. Tip: don't forget to view the renovated machine hall and cooling equipment.

Van Volxemlaan 354, Brussel, +32(0)2/340 00 53, www.wiels.org

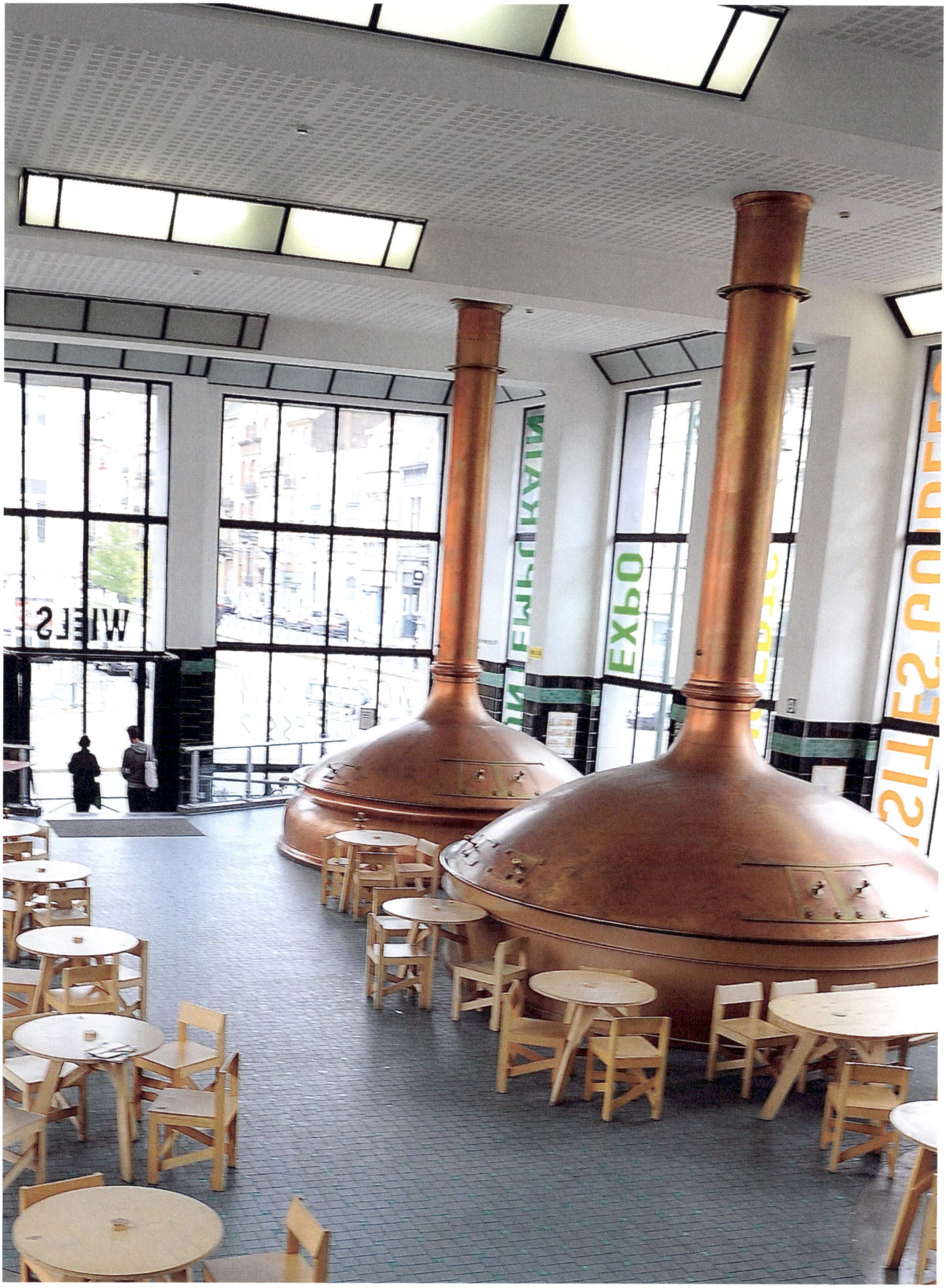

REGIONAL BEER TOURISM

GHENT
OUDENAARDE
ST-NIKLAAS
AALST

Boelens

Bieken, Dubbel Klok, Tripel Klok, Santa Bee, Waase Wolf, Waaslander

---

Village brewery known for its honey beer. Visit by prior arrangement for groups of 12 to 50 participants. Tips: church with beautiful wood carvings, park with lovely walks, plenty of village cafés serving Klok on tap.

Kerkstraat 7, Belsele (Sint-Niklaas), +32(0)3/772 32 00
info@brouwerijboelens.be, www.brouwerijboelens.be

Bosteels

DeuS Brut des Flandres, Pauwels Kwak, Tripel Karmeliet

Tradition and innovation go hand in hand at this brewery with its prestigious brewer's mansion, carriage collection and tasting room. Open to groups of 20 or more by prior arrangement, weekdays only. A ride on an authentic horse-drawn cart is available from time to time.

Kerkstraat 92, Buggenhout, +32(0)52/33 23 23
info@kwak.karmeliet.be, www.bestbelgianspecialbeers.be

CONTRERAS

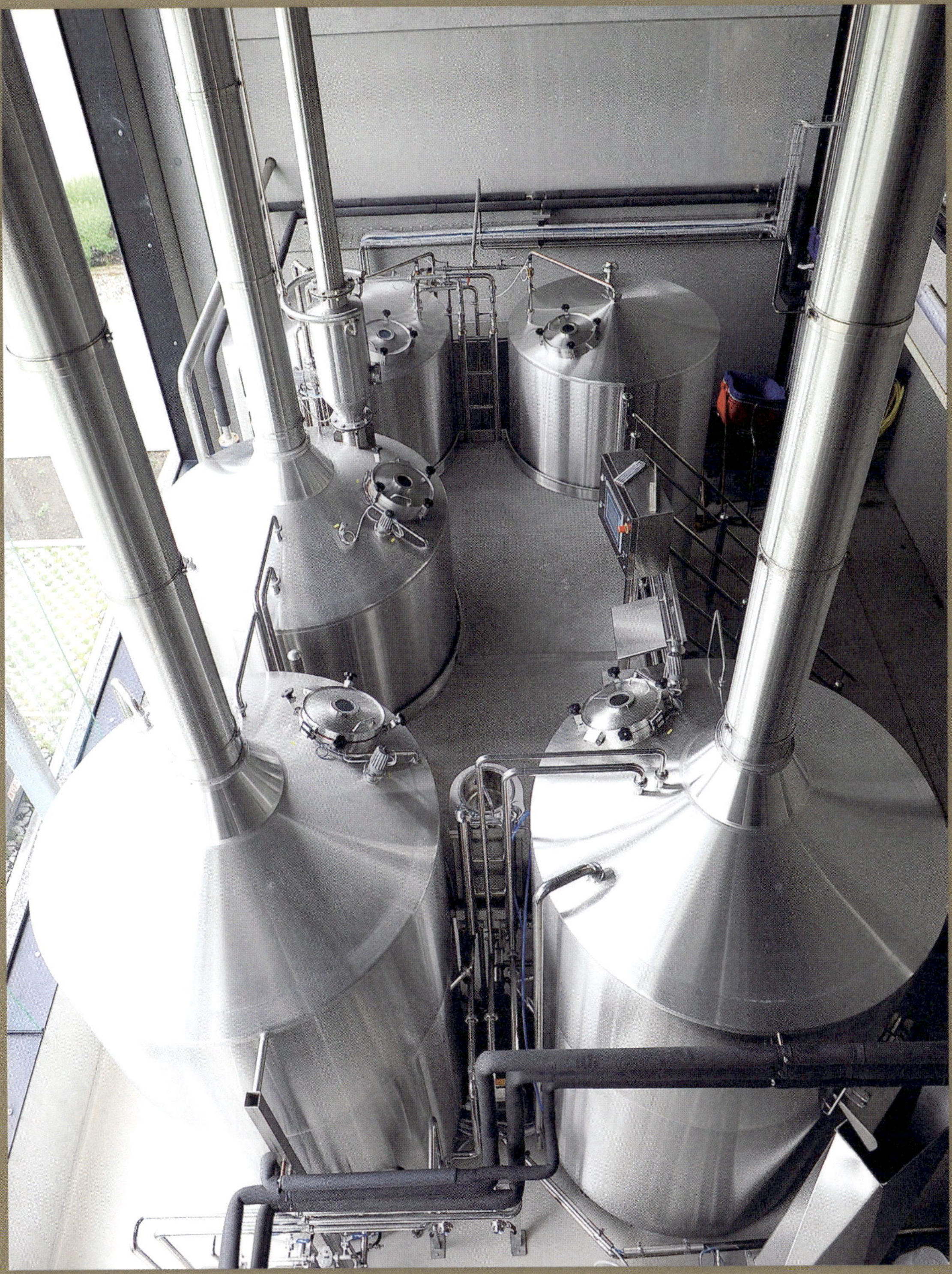

Cnudde

Bizonbier, Cnudde

Can you be any more authentic? This original village brewery from the 1950s takes reservations for groups of 15 or more.

Fabriekstraat 8, Eine (Oudenaarde), +32(0)55/31 18 34 cnudde.lieven@skynet.be

Contreras

Contrapils, Tonneke, Valeir

This village brewery, located close to the Flemish Ardennes, is a great blend of the old and the new. Open to groups of 20-50 participants by appointment. Walkers follow one of two trails: the 'Slag bij Gavere' or the 'Hasselkouter'. Bikers have the choice between the Valeir trail and the Scheldevallei trail, following the valley of the Scheldt.

Molenstraat 110, Gavere, +32(0)9/384 27 06, info@contreras.be, www.contreras.be

Danny

Kwibus

Village brewery. Get in touch to arrange your visit.

Kerkveldstraat 61, Erpe-Mere, +32(0)53/83 58 95, info@brdanny.be, www.brdanny.be

De Landtsheer (Malheur)

Malheur-gamma, Novic-gamma

Brewery known for its Brut party beers. Visits by prior arrangement on weekdays.

Mandekensstraat 179, Buggenhout, +32(0)52/33 39 11, info@malheur.be, www.malheur.be

Den Tseut

Belle Cies, Bras, Den Bi3r, Den Drupneuze, Den Mulder, Den Krulsteirt, Den Tseut, Hoppesnoet, 't Wijveke, 't Zeemken

This village brewery is dominated by the sign of the pig. Not surprising in a village of pig breeders. Group visits (up to 25 participants) on request. The small brewery café is open on Saturdays (14:00 – 21:30) and Sundays (16:00 – 21:30). Tip: bike routes Den Tseut (39.7 kilometres), Den Mulder (38.2km) and Den Bi3r (48.6km).

Oosteeklo-Dorp 40, Assenede, +32(0)485/37 20 11, den.tseut@skynet.be, www.huisbrouwerijdentseut.be

De Ryck

Arend, Blonde Bladelin, Gouden Arend, Special De Ryck, Steenuilke

Authentic village brewery with splendid interior court and reception area. Female brewer An De Ryck wields the mashing stick here. Visits by prior arrangement, for groups with 15-50 participants only. Tip: De Ryck has established the 'two breweries' route called Tussen Pot en Pint (44 or 13 kilometres) in collaboration with the Van den Bossche brewery.

Kerkstraat 24, Herzele, +32(0)53/62 23 02, info@brouwerijderyck.be, www.brouwerijderyck.be

Dilewyns

Vicaris-gamma

This young family brewery is run by Dad Vincent Dilewyns and his two daughters, Anne-Catherine and Claire. Visitors are welcome by prior arrangement from Tuesday to Saturday. For groups with 20 to 60 participants.

Vlassenhout 5, Dendermonde, +32(0)52/20 18 57 info@vicaris.be, www.vicaris.be

Donum Ignis

Noorderbierke, ZoemZoem, Zuiderbierke

A science teacher turned hobby brewer and one thing led to another. Arrange your visit in advance.

Leebrugstraat 55, Sinaai-Waas, +32(0)485/70 76 91 www.donumignis.be

Glazen Toren (De)

Saison d'Erpe Mere, Ondineke, Jan De Lichte, Cuvée Angélique, Canaster Winterscotch

---

Beer author Jef Van den Steen is one of the driving forces behind this microbrewery. De Glazen Toren promises its own, unique interpretation of 'beers of the people' and familiar beer styles. Visits by pre-arrangement only.

Glazentorenweg 11, Erpe-Mere, +32(0)53/83 03 80, +32(0)486/88 23 13, info@glazentoren.be, www.glazentoren.be

Brewing day at De Ryck in Herzele.

BROUWERY DE GOUDEN AREND

SPECIAL — DOBBEL

UITZET

DE RYCK
HERZELE

Gruut (Stadsbrouwerij)

Gruut

The Gruut city brewery has found a home in the historical heart of Ghent. Annick Desplenter brings the medieval 'gruut' beers – herbal beers brewed without hops – back to life. Free entry daily until 18:00. Groups of 8 and over by appointment only.

Rembert Dodoensdreef, Gent, +32(0)9/269 02 69,
www.gruut.be

Huyghe

Artevelde, Averbode, Blanche des Neiges, Campus, Delirium, Floris, La Guillotine, Mongozo, St. Idesbald, Villers

---

"You ask, we brew." This is the motto of the Huyghe brewery. Its best-known beer is Delirium Tremens but they are equally happy to magic up a coconut beer from their tanks. Group visits only, by prior arrangement, for 15 participants or more. The tour includes a brewery museum. The Huyghe brewery has established a chain of Delirium themed cafés, first of all at Getrouwheidsgang on Korte Beenhouwersstraat in Brussels but the concept has now spread far and wide. Just follow the pink elephant... The cafés stock three thousand beers. Over half of these are from Belgium.

Brusselsesteenweg 282, Melle, +32(0)9/252 15 01
jose.debock@telenet.be, www.delirium.be

Delirium Café, Getrouwheidsgang 4, Brussel,
+32(0)2/514 44 34, www.deliriumcafe.be

Kroontje ('t)

Rebelle

Microbrewery. Visits on request.

Hogebrug 62, Denderbelle, +32(0)495/43 33 25
www.tkroontje.be

Liefmans

Liefmans Fruitesse, Goudenband, Kriek Brut & Oud Bruin

Not many breweries can boast a history that goes all the way back to 1679. Liefmans has a monumental presence in the beer world and is best known for its traditional brown beers from Oudenaarde. A recently unveiled visitors' trail shows the brewing process through the ages, from the brewhall, cooling down, main fermentation in open basins, cold storage, souring, maturation of the krieken cherries on soured beer in the 'krieken tank' to produce the Liefmans Fruitesse and Kriek Brut all the way down to the maturation of the bottled Liefmans Goudenband in the 'caveaux' or cellars. The highlight of your visit is a tasting in the cosy brewery café. The guided tour takes approx. two hours and is available from Monday to Saturday at 10:00, 14:00 or 17:00. For groups comprising 15-35 participants.

Aalststraat 200, Oudenaarde, +32(0)3/860 94 00
brouwerijbezoek@liefmans.be, www.liefmans.be

8 • BEER TOURISM

Liefmans is reflected in the River Scheldt on the outskirts of the City of Oudenaarde. The slightly sour 'Oudenaards bruin bier' has been brewed here since time immemorial.

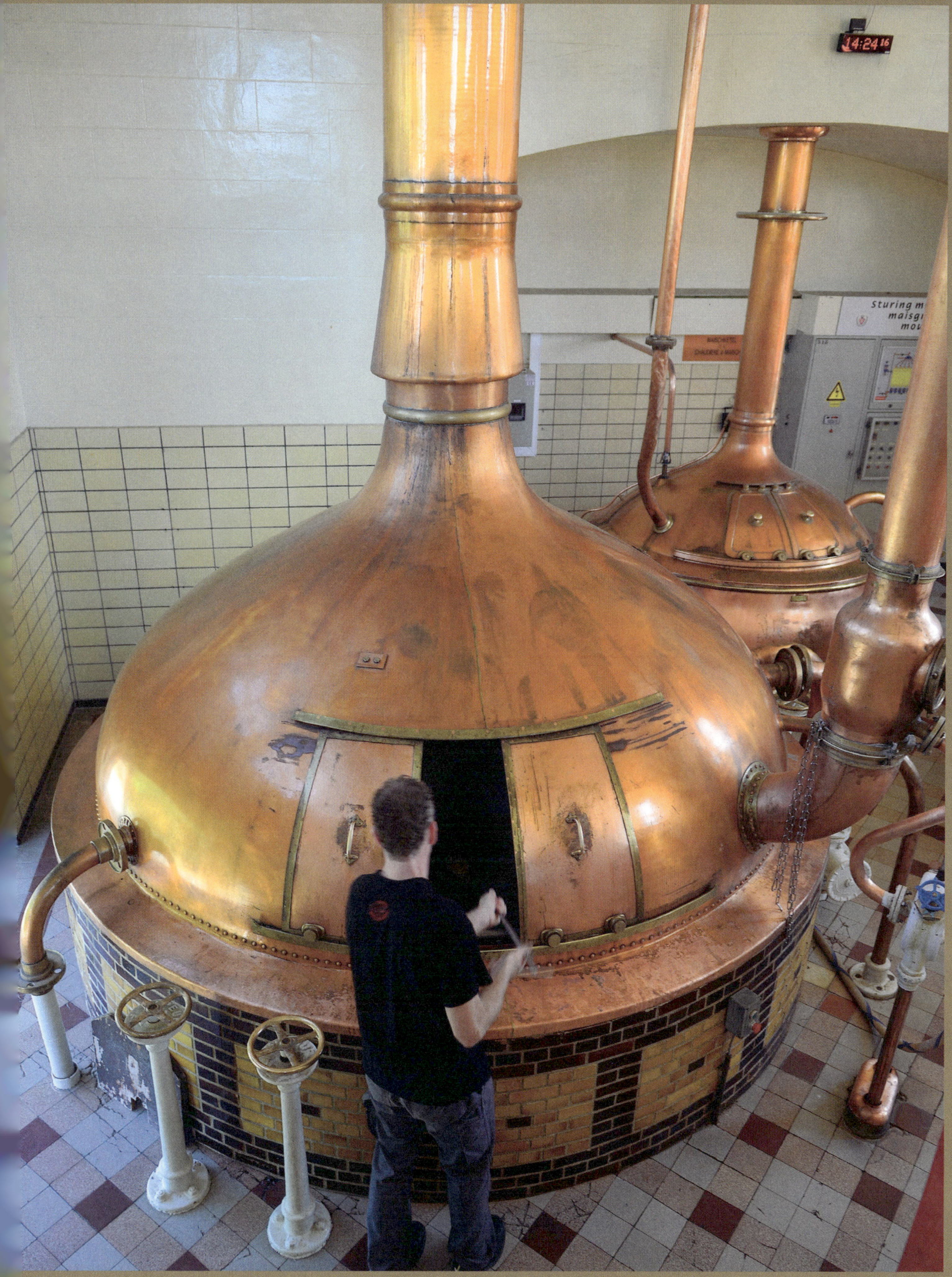
Sturing

Sint-Canarus

De Maeght van Gottem, Potteloerke, Sint Canarus Tripel

Small 'didactic' home brewery with tasting room attached. Attend a beer seminar conducted by Dr. Canarus or else get your order delivered to your home by beer tricycle. Open every Sunday from 11:00 – 21:00. Groups are advised to make prior reservations.

Polderweg 2, Gottem (Deinze), +32(0)51/63 69 31, info@sintcanarus.be, www.sintcanarus.be

Slaghmuylder

Ambiorix, Kerstbier, Paasbier, Slag Pils, Witkap-gamma, Wortelbier

---

Where time has stood still … A village brewery as well as a living museum, with an ancient mashing basin (1860) still in use as well as an open cooling basin, unique steam machine (1910), steam kettle (1926), vintage bottling machine, vintage tools, beer paraphernalia and advertising from days gone past. Visit on request for groups with 20 participants and more.

Denderhoutembaan 2, Ninove, +32(0)54/33 18 31, info@witkap.be, www.witkap.be

Roman

Adriaen Brouwer, Ename-gamma, Gentse Strop, Mater, Romy Pils, Sloeber

---

The majestic brewing tower at the oldest family brewery in Belgium boasts one of the most beautiful historic brewhalls, dating back to the 1930s. Vintage steam equipment is also on display. Visits by appointment for groups with a minimum of 15. Every Wednesday night in July, concerts are held in the spacious interior court.

Hauwaert 105, Mater (Oudenaarde), +32(0)55/45 54 01 info@roman.be, www.roman.be

Smisje

Big Bayou, Smiske

Johan Brands used to be a printer before he found his calling as a microbrewer. He set up his 'smithy' in a former lemonade factory. Call him to arrange your visit, groups of 20 or more, Monday to Friday. The brewery café is open every Sunday from May to October, between 15:00 and 19:00. Large garden terrace.

Driesleutelstraat 1, Mater (Oudenaarde), +32(0)475/36 44 89, visitsmisje@hotmail.com, www.smisje.be

Van den Bossche

Buffalo, Pater Lieven, Livinus & Lamoral

———

This truly original brewery, located in a village square, brings the past alive. Visit on request, only for groups of 20 and over. Tip: the Tussen Pot en Pint 'two breweries' walk was initiated by the De Ryck and Van den Bossche breweries. The Livinus trail is recommended for cyclists.

Sint-Lievensplein 16, Sint-Lievens-Esse (Herzele), +32(0)54/50 04 11, info@paterlieven.be, www.paterlieven.be

Van Steenberge

Augustijn, Bornem, Celis White, Gulden Draak, Leute Bokbier, Piraat, St. Stefanus

———

An authentic village brewery with an intriguing contrast between the old and the new. Nice visitors' centre, authentic brewery café. Visit on Monday, Tuesday and Wednesday by appointment only for groups with 8 to 30 participants. Tip: pay a visit to the Augustine abbey in Ghent that gave its name to the Augustijn abbey beers.

Lindenlaan 25, Ertvelde (Evergem), +32(0)9/344 50 71, info@vansteenberge.com, www.vansteenberge.com

REGIONAL BEER TOURISM

HASSELT
GENK
ST-TRUIDEN
TONGEREN

Achel (St.-Benedictusabdij)

Achel

———

Neither the abbey nor the brewery are open to the public. However, the abbey tavern and the interior court afford a view of the brewing kettles, with the brewing process being shielded by a glass wall. The Achelse Kluis abbey, set within a green oasis, is the only abbey where food and drink are served within the abbey walls. The abbey forms part of the cycling node network, lies on a tourist auto route, and is close to both the Leenderhei nature reserve and the forest of Hamont-Achel.

Kluis 1, Hamont-Achel, +32(0)11/80 07 60,
www.achelsekluis.org

Alken-Maes

Brugs Witbier, Ciney, Maes, Cristal, Grimbergen, Hapkin, Judas, Op-Ale, Postel

———

The birthplace of Cristal Pils has spawned a range of specialty beers. Phone or email ahead to arrange your visit. Afterwards, pop into village café Het Moment right next to the brewery.

Stationsstraat 2, Alken, +32(0)11/59 03 06,
www.alken-maes.be, www.cristal.be

Amai

Loemelaer

———

Microbrewery. Visits by appointment.

Konijnenpijp 11, Lommel, +32(0)472/17 02 20,
www.brouwerij-amai.be

Do you recognise the former tennis World Champion, Kim Clijsters, at the front of the picture? Kim lives in the village that is home to the Cornelissen brewery, which used to bear the name of St-Jozef.

Cornelissen (Dorpsbrouwerij)

Bokkereyer, Bosbier, Herkenrode, Kriekenbier, Limburgse Witte, Ops-Ale, Pax, Sint-Gummarus

---

Village brewery that used to be known as Sint-Jozef. Splendid historic brewhall. Tours available on request, on Tuesdays and Friday mornings, for groups of 10 and over. For food and drink, make your way to the village square. Included in several walking and cycling trails, close to the Kempisch Broek nature reserve.

Itterplein 19, Opitter (Bree), +32(0)89/86 47 11, info@brouwerijcornelissen.be, www.brouwerijcornelissen.be

Den Toeteler

Toeteler Amber Tripel, Echte Kriek, Speculaas, Special & Witbier

---

Microbrewery where everything revolves around the elderflower, known as 'toeteler' in local dialect. Groups welcome by prior arrangement, 6-25 participants.

Kleistraat 54, Hoeselt, +32(0)472/80 24 14, info@toeteler.be, www.toeteler.be

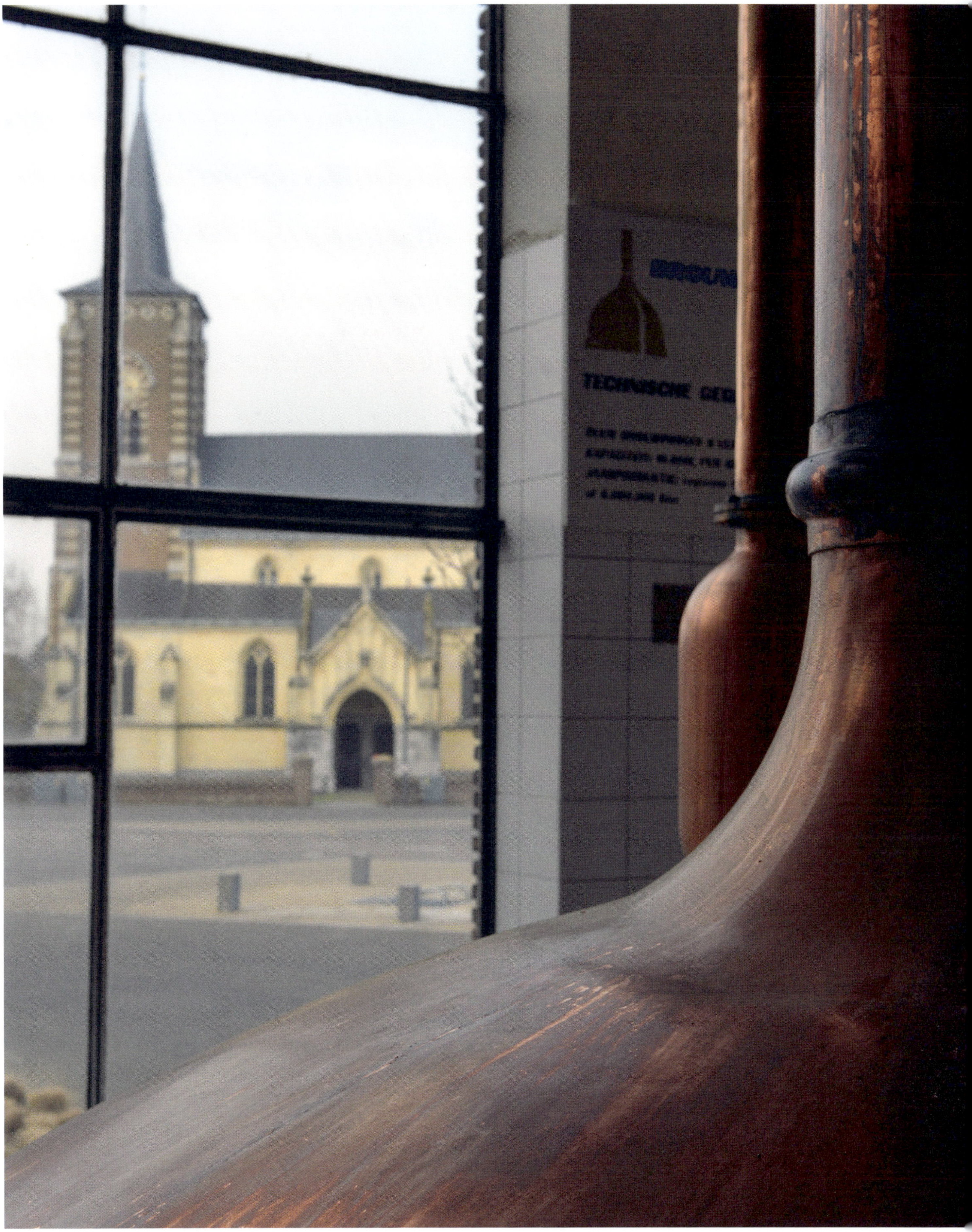
TECHNISCHE

Engilsen

Dief! Copper, Dief! Gold, Dief! Silver

———

Home brewery. Open every Thursday night from 19:00 to 21:00 or by appointment.

Lindenstraat 36, Tessenderlo, +32(0)13/29 58 21, info@brouwerijengilsen.be, www.brouwerijengilsen.be

Jessenhofke

Brown, Maya, Pimpernel, Regular, Reserva, Tripel

———

Home brewery known for its organic and short-chain beers brewed with local ingredients. Phone ahead to arrange a visit. Workshops are held regularly.

Simpernelstraat 17, Hasselt, +32(0)11/25 56 99, info@jessenhofke.be, www.jessenhofke.be

Kerkom

Adelardus, Bink, Bloesem Kriek, Hop Verdomme IPA, Kerckomse Triple, Winterkoninkske

———

Microbrewery in ancient square-shaped farm amongst the fields and orchards. With café unchanged from the old days (vintage bar, tiled floor, family pictures and stucco ceiling) and terrace in the spacious interior court. Open to single visitors 15:00 every Saturday afternoon from March to October. Groups of ten or more are welcome by pre-arrangement.

Naamsesteenweg 469, Kerkom (Sint-Truiden), +32(0)11/68 20 87, of +32(0)495/38 12 14, info@brouwerijkerkom, www.brouwerijkerkom.be

Perron Bieren

Boegetbier, Perron Blond Sorachi Ace, Saison Mandarina Bavaria

———

Microbrewery giving pride of place to beers containing exotic aroma hops. Book your visit in advance.

Houterstraat 72, Gellik (Lanaken), +32(0)468/20 82 86 info@perronbieren.be, www.perronbieren.be

Ter Dolen (Kasteelbrouwerij)

Armand, Ter Dolen Blond, Donker, Kriek, Tripel & Winter

———

This brewery is housed in a former sanctuary of the abbey of Sint-Truiden. From its tasting café you have access to its lovely, spacious courtyard with terrace. Very popular with hikers and bikers. Tours held every Saturday and Sunday at 15:00. Groups of 15 and over are welcome by prior arrangement.

Eikendreef 21, Helchteren-Houthalen, +32(0)11/60 69 99 info@terdolen.be, www.terdolen.be

Wilderen

Cuvée Clarisse, Wilderen Goud, Wilderen Kriek, Tripel Kanunnik

———

Wilderen has added a brand new distillery and brewery but has kept its vintage distillery. Enjoy the beers, gin, jenever and whisky, all produced on the premises, on the spacious terrace in the interior court or pop into the tavern that forms part of the impressive timber barn.
The playful guided tour of the alcohol distillery, the brewery and the industrial heritage is held on Saturdays, Sundays and bank holidays only at 15:00 and 16:00. Group visits by prior arrangement, to be booked online. Wilderen is on several cycling and walking trails in the Haspengouw region. Tip: highly recommended when the fruit trees are in bloom.

Wilderenlaan 8, Wilderen (Sint-Truiden), +32(0)11/58 06 80 info@brouwerijwilderen.be, www.brouwerijwilderen.be

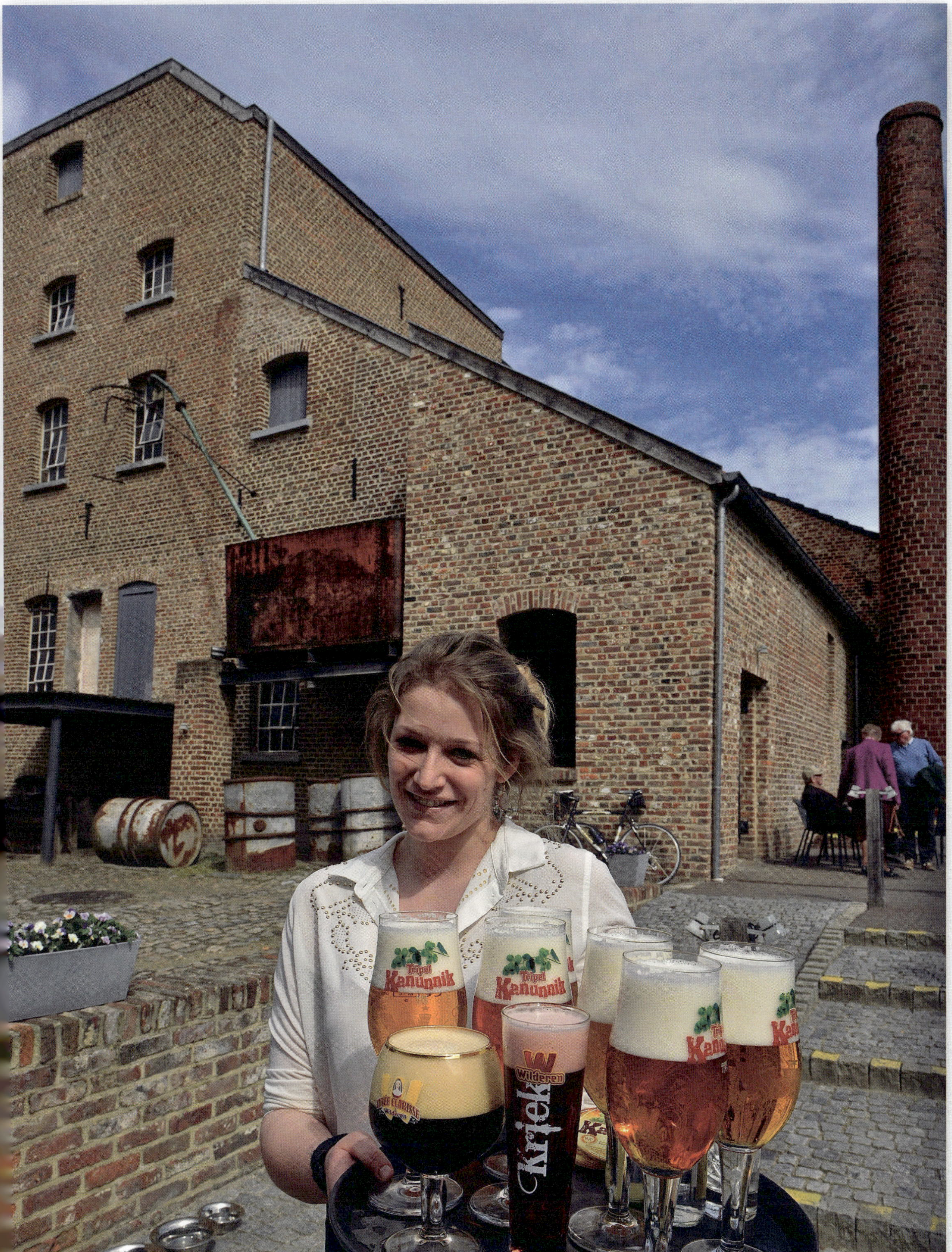
Tripel
Kanunnik
Wilderen
Kriek

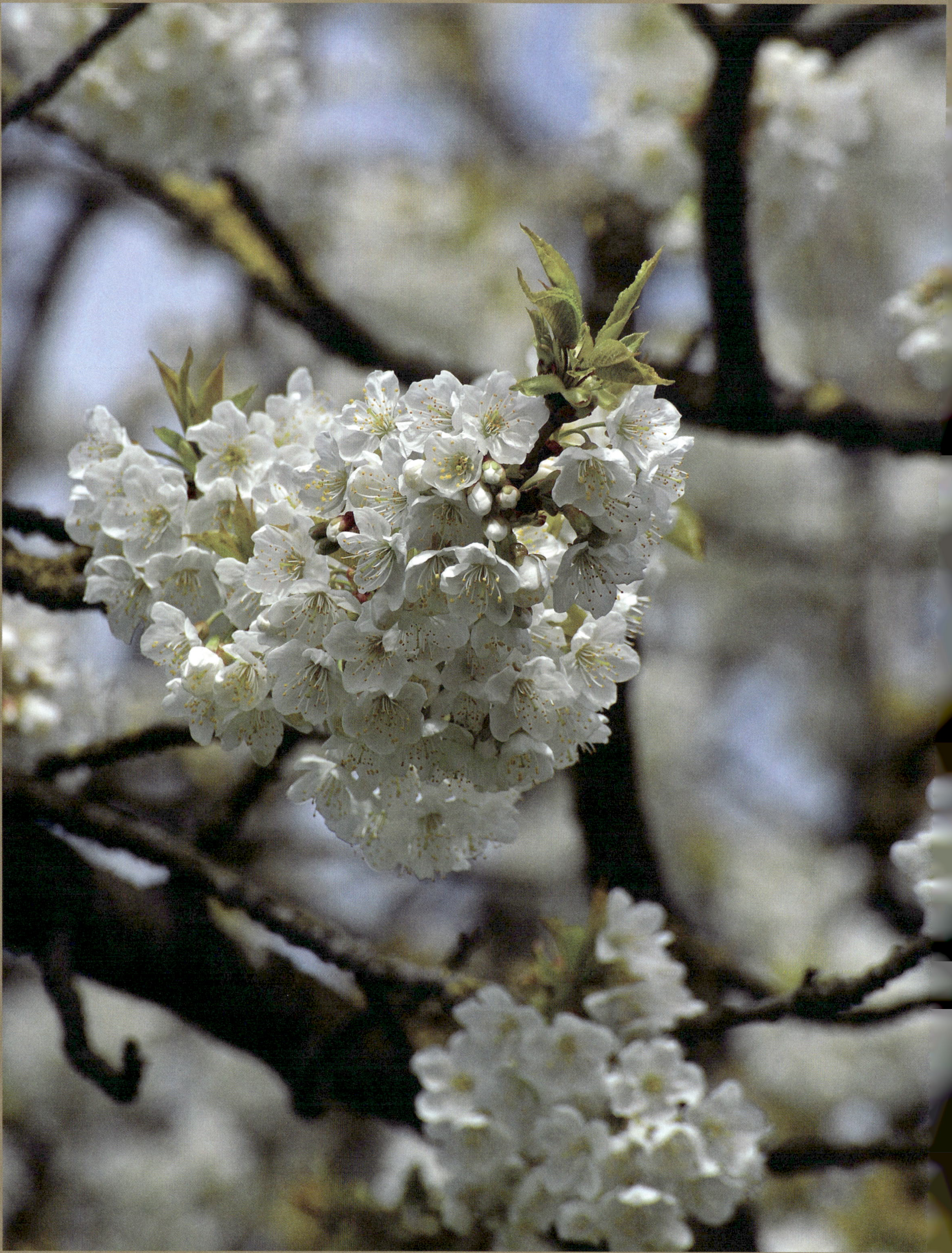

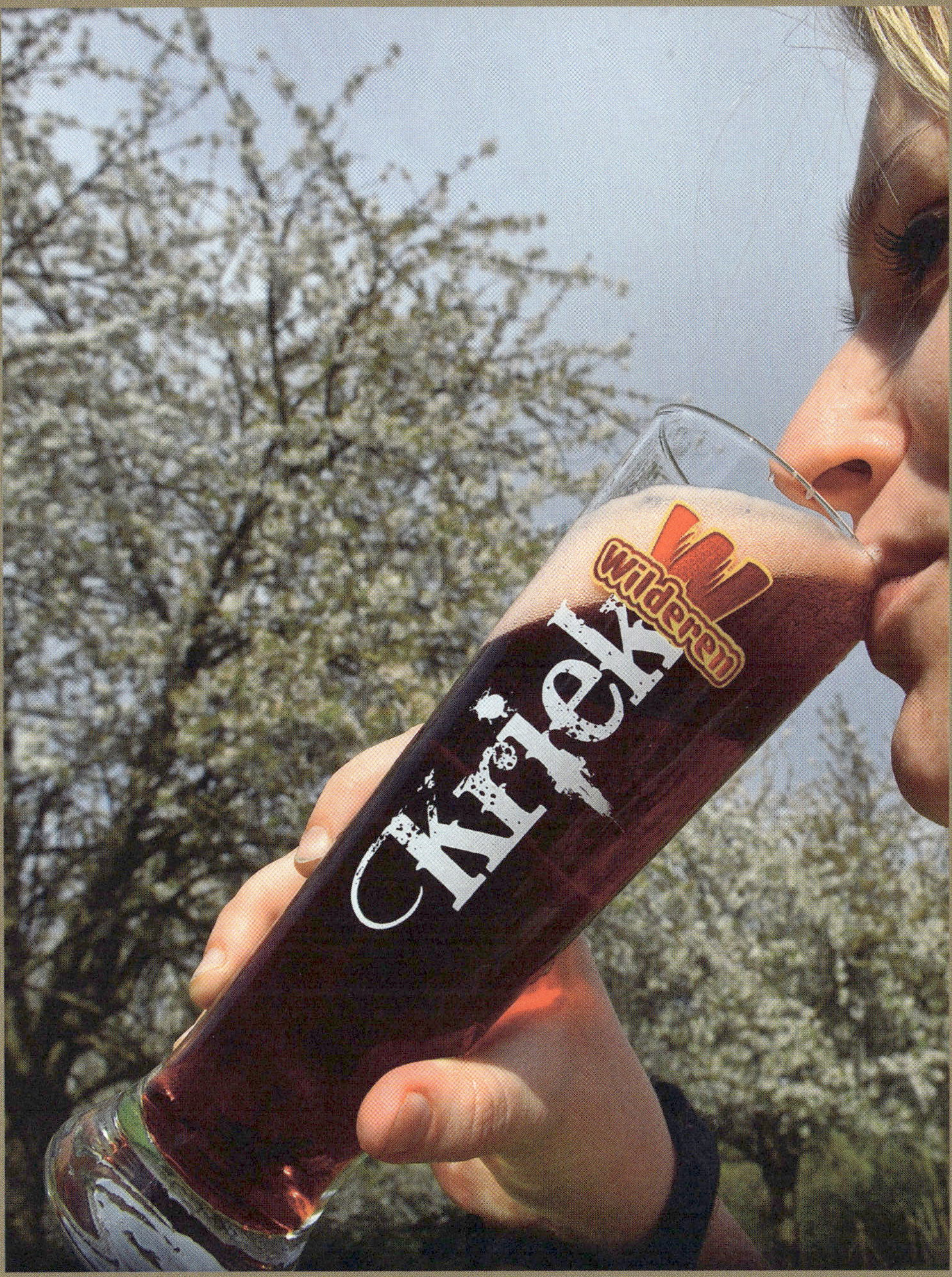
wilderen
Kriek

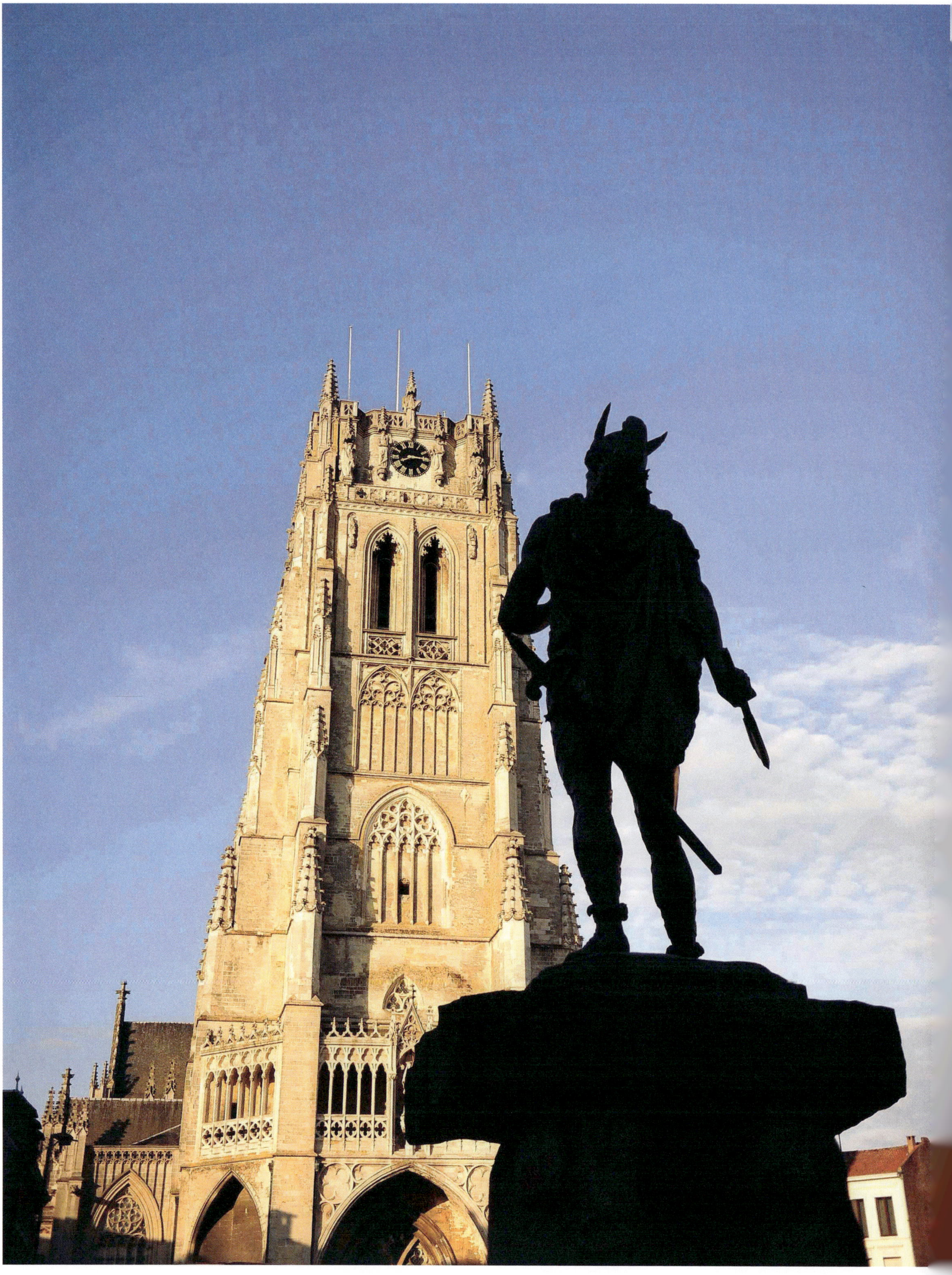

WORTH SEEING

Paenhuys – Bokrijk Open Air Museum

't Paenhuys is an authentic 17th century village brewery from Diepenbeek with fixtures and fittings from the Tomsin brewery that was once based in Hoegaarden. A hop field was established at the Abele farm on the museum site. You will also find a traditional 'hopast' – hop drying kiln – from Proven near Poperinge. Don't miss the Day of the Edible Landscape. Every third Sunday in September, Het Paenhuys is where 1,500 litres of beer are brewed in the artisan way. A truly unique evocation of a historic brewing process. The open air museum is open from 31 March up to and including 30 September, Tuesday to Sunday (10:00 – 18:00). Closed on Mondays with the exception of Easter and Pentecost.

Bokrijklaan 1, 3600 Genk, +32(0)11/26 53 00
infobokrijk@limburg.be, www.bokrijk.be

Bocholt Brewery Museum

The Bocholt Brewery Museum is located across the road from the Martens brewery. The museum collection began in 1919 and tells the story of the art of brewing beer from 1758 to modern times. Anything relating to malting is found in the attic. One floor lower down, in the brewhall, you are in danger of getting lost between the filtration basins, boiling kettles and draining basins. Once you have reached the basement you will come across bottling equipment as well as impressive wooden barrels used for cold-storing the beer. A collection of taps, beer pumps, pipework etc. is also on display. You find out the workings of many different types of equipment including steeping basins, malt ploughs, crate turners, boiling kettles, wort coolers, mash basins and barrel sealing equipment. We can highly recommend this museum to beer connoisseurs, hobby brewers and anyone with an interest in traditional brewing techniques. Your visit culminates in a degustation of Martens beers in a room where those with a nostalgic bent will lap up the vintage beer advertising decorating the walls. Group tours all year by pre-arrangement. Smaller groups and single visitors: July and August, from 13:00 to 18:00, guided tours at 13:30 and 15:30.

Dorpsstraat 53, B-3950 Bocholt, +32(0)89/48 16 76
www.bocholterbrouwerijmuseum.be of via VVV Bocholt,
+32(0)89/20 19 30, toerisme@bocholt.be

Herkenrode (Abdij)

Herkenrode Bruin and Tripel

From the Hasselt-West exit on the E313 motorway you can spot the impressive silhouette of the former abbey of Herkenrode. The most recent buildings date from the 17th century but the oldest traces of habitation go all the way back to 1182. Herkenrode lies at a mere five kilometres from Hasselt in a beautiful nature reserve where you can hike or bike to your heart's content. A shop sells local produce and a tavern serves local cuisine. You can visit the herb garden as part of a guided tour.

Herkenrodeabdij 4, +32(0)11/33 43 70
www.herkenrode.be, www.abdijsiteherkenrode.be

< *The statue of Ambiorix and Tongeren Basilica. With its Tungri beers, the Amburon brewery pays homage to the first inhabitants of this city.*

REGIONAL BEER TOURISM

LIÈGE
HERVE
HOEI
MALMEDY

Bellevaux (Brasserie de)

Bellevaux Black, Blanche, Blonde & Brune

———

On the edge of the Hoge Venen area there is a microbrewery located in a farmhouse. In the old stables you now find a tasting room. Its terrace looks out onto the copper kettles in the brewhall. The tasting room is open every weekend from 11:00 to 18:00 (closed in January). Guided tours every Saturday and Sunday at 16:00. Visits by groups of ten and over on request only. Tip: there are five walks named after the beers. They vary in length from 1.5 to 14.5 kilometres and depart from the brewery.

Bellevaux 5, Malmédy, +32(0)80/88 15 40
brasserie@brasseriedebellevaux.be, www.brasseriedebellevaux.be

Botteresse de Sur-les-Bois (La)

La Botteresse, Sur-les-Bois

———

A microbrewery installed in a former garage. With tasting room. Visits on request for groups of ten and over.

Rue Fond Méan 6, Saint-Georges, +32(0)475/78 23 51
info@labotteresse.be, www.labotteresse.be

Brasse & Vous

Esperluette, Legia

———

A microbrewery on the edge of Liège. Pure with occasionally surprising aromas and tastes. Enjoy the beers accompanied by regional cuisine in Le Réfectoire de la Brasserie. With a bit of luck you will see the brewer at work. Open on Thursday, Friday and Saturday nights. Visits by appointment.

Rue d'Alleur 27b, Luik, +32(0)4/384 84 78
lucky@brasse-et-vous.be, www.brasse-et-vous.be

Brasserie Artisanale du Flo

Bière du Flo, Cuvée du Flo, Cuvée Jolie Môme, Cuvée St-Antoine, L'Apicole, La Brune du Flo

———

Small village brewery in former town hall. With tasting room. Visits by appointment. Tasting room open every Sunday afternoon.

Rue du Château 2, Blehen (Hannuit), +32(0)19/51 70 57 of +32(0)495/59 57 59, www.brasserieduflo.be

< The Montagne de Bueren used to connect the elevated citadel with the city centre. Where the citadel once stood, there is now a hospital.

Brasserie C (Curtius)

Curtius, Torpah

―――

Microbrewery in the very centre of Liège, in a historic building forming part of the beguinage at the bottom of the famous Montagne de Bueren stepped road. The birthplace of elegant city beers. Visits by prior arrangement.

Impasse des Ursulines, +32(0)4/266 06 92
info@brasseriec.com, www.brasseriec.com

Elfique

La Redoutable, La Robuste

―――

Microbrewery in the heart of the Ardennes close to the La Heid des Gattes nature reserve and the Ninglingspo River, the only 'mountain river' in Belgium. For fans of fairy tales! Visit by prior arrangement.

Sur La Heid 23, Aywaille, +32(0)4/263 07 17
info@elfique.be, www.elfique.be

Brasserie de la Lienne

Grandgousier, Lienne

―――

Microbrewery set up in the barn of an Ardennes farmhouse. Taste the beers in the former stables. Visits by appointment. Tip: a great starting point for walks and mountain bike hikes. Close to Spa, Stavelot, Malmédy and Durbuy.

Reharmont 7, Lierneux, +32(0)80/39 99 06
info@brasseriedelalienne.be, www.brasseriedelalienne.be

Grain d'Orge

Aubel, Brice, Joup, Canaille, Grelotte

―――

Village brewery located on the 38 Ravel cycling trail, a converted railway that once ran between Liège and the German border. The beers' names are inspired by local folklore from the Land of Herve. Groups are welcome to tour the brewery and taste its beers throughout the year. Group size: between 10 and 50.

Grain d'Orge, rue Laschet 3, Hombourg (Plombières),
+32(0)87/78 77 84, brasserie@grain-dorge.com,
www.grain-dorge.com

{c} 2013
Curtius
LA BIÈRE LIÉGEOISE

LA BIERE LIEGEOIS[E]

BRASSERIE

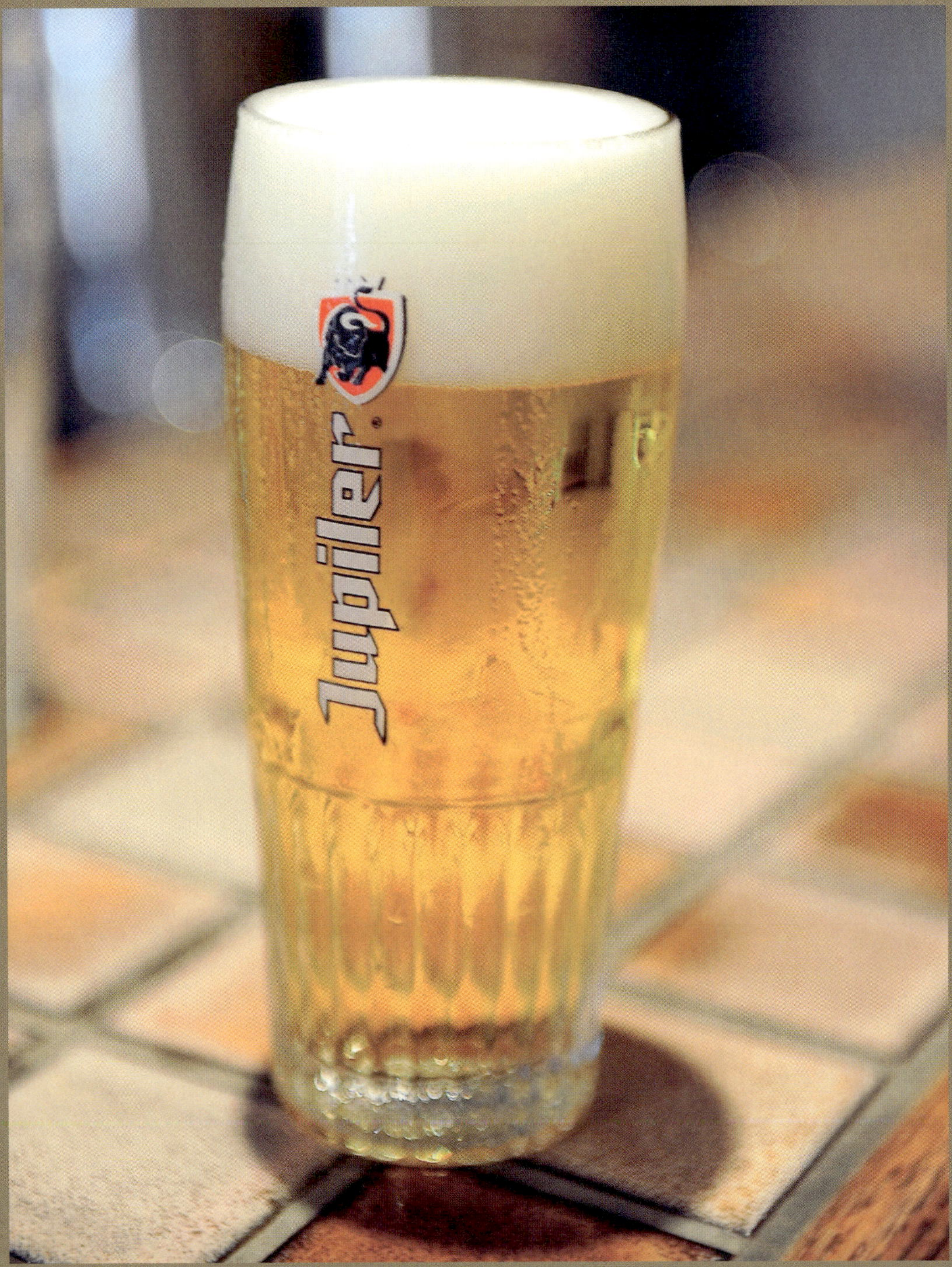
Jupiler

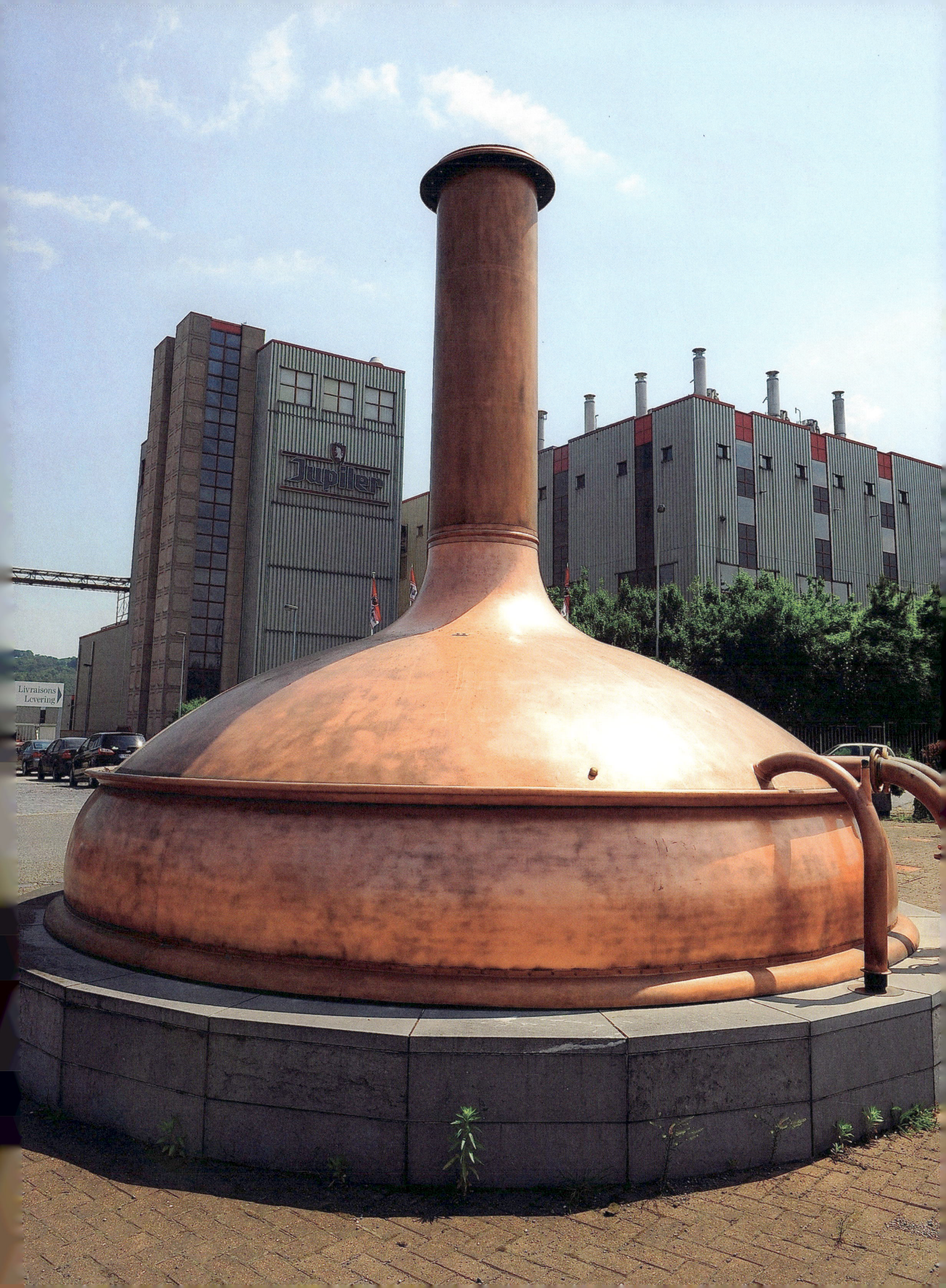
Jupiler
Livraisons
Levering

Marsinne

Léopold 7

Microbrewery in splendid castle farm brimming with royal charm. Visits by groups of ten or over by prior arrangement, on Monday, Thursday, Friday and Saturday.

Rue de la Médaille 17, Couthuin (Heron), +32(0)478/88 25 01
fannydominique@hotmail.com, www.leopold7.com

Jupille (Jupiler)

Jupiler

The second largest brewery in the country after Louvain, also owned by AB Inbev. Completely focused on the production of pils. Visit by prior arrangement for groups of 15 and over.

Rue des Anciennes Houblonnières 2, 4020 Jupille-sur-Meuse (Liège), +32(0)16/27 61 11, www.breweryvisits.com, www.ab-inbev.com

Sainte Nitouche (Brasserie de la Croix)

Sainte Nitouche

Microbrewery near Liège. Visits by appointment.

Rue des Cerisiers 48, Beyne Heusay, +32(0)476/37 20 06
info@saintenitouche.be, www.saintenitouche.be

Val-Dieu (Abbaye de)

Val-Dieu

An abbey with a history spanning eight centuries, with microbrewery set up in a former farm building in the Land of Herve. Free entry to the interior court, the Basilica and the gardens. Abbey and brewery tours on request for groups of 15 to 70 participants. Sample the beers and enjoy a meal in the abbey tavern or other cafés and restaurants in the vicinity.

Val-Dieu 225, Aubel, +32(0)87/69 28 28
infotourist@val-dieu.net, www.val-dieu.com

Warsage

Bière de Warsage

This microbrewery is keen on promoting 'terroir' and produces natural, unfiltered beers that re-ferment in the bottle. Get in touch with them to arrange a visit.

Rue de la Gare 17, Warsage (Dalhem), +32(0)474/06 04 34
info@brasseriewarsage.be, www.brasseriewarsage.be

Anno 1216
Val-Dieu
Het abdijbier

WORTH A VISIT

Anthisnes (Beer museum)

Anthisnes was turned into an ecclesiastic estate during the Middle Ages. However, the castle was seized by the judiciary powers as debts had not been paid. The main building, in the Maasland renaissance style, dates back to the 17th century. It is a massive square building with five floors and walls that are up to two metres thick. In 1897 the two Northern towers were destroyed by fire. Most of all, the 12th century castle tower fires the imagination. It now houses a beer museum with a fine collection of bottles and glasses. Your visit comprises a guided tour of the castle and the museum. Now what is the link between the castle and the beer? Ancient writings provide evidence of two village breweries around the year 1000. This is the age-old location where you sample regional beers in the splendidly vaulted cellars. The museum shop sells regional beers and produce.

Musée de la Bière et du Péket, Avouerie d'Anthisnes, avenue de l'Abbaye 19, +32(0)4/383 63 90 info@avouerie.be, www.avouerie.be

St Vith (Biermuseum)

In a chalet right at the top of the Tomberg ski run at Sankt-Vith, 4,500 bottles are awaiting the visitor. They are not meant for drinking but there is plenty to admire here. This is an exceptional collection of historic bottles that tourists have contributed to throughout the years.

Skihütte Verkehrsverein 'Wald und Tal' Rodt, Tomberg, Rodt 77, Sankt Vith, +32(0)80/22 63 01, info@biermuseum.be www.biermuseum.be

A beer degustation in the cellars of Avouerie d'Anthisnes.

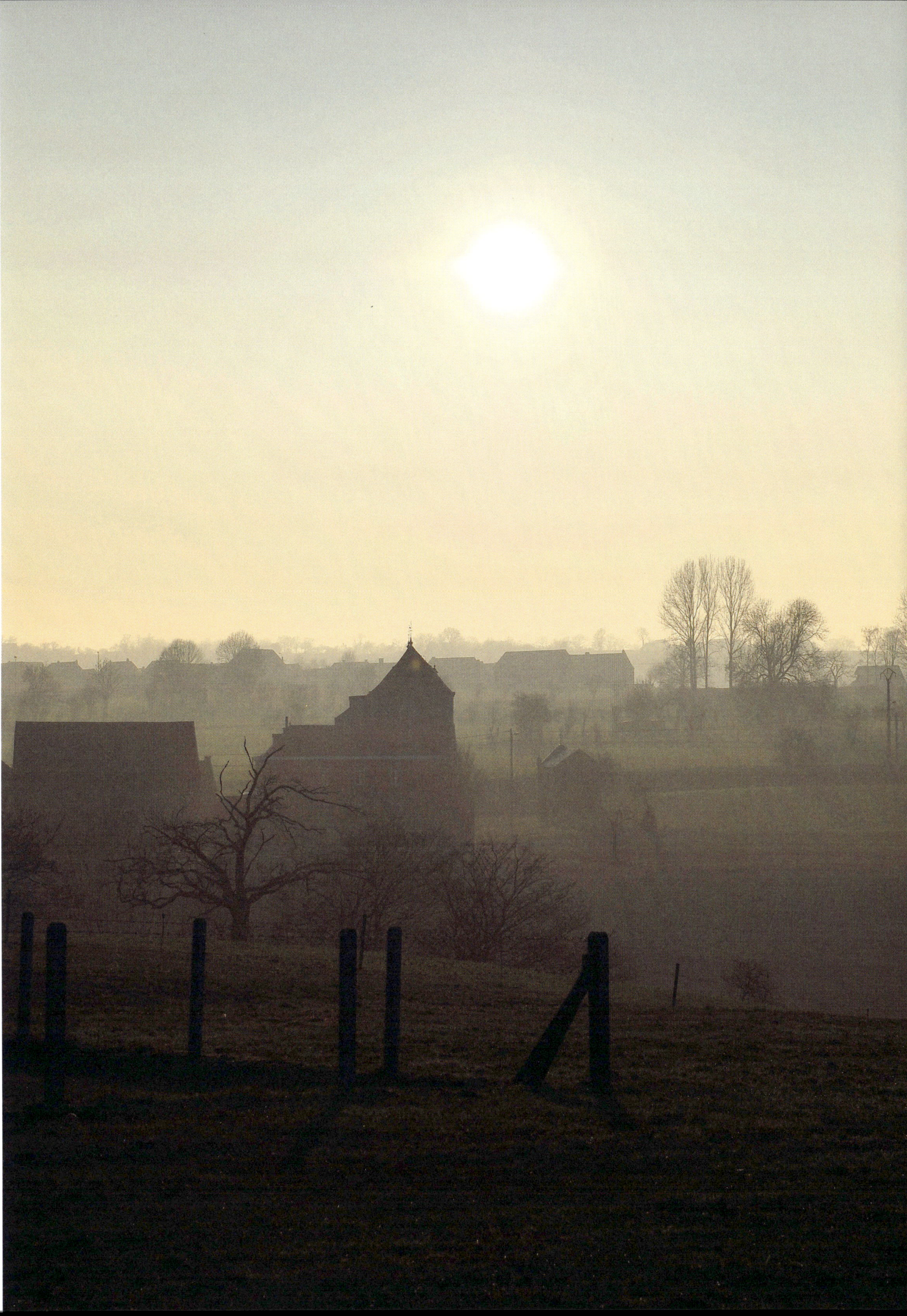

REGIONAL BEER TOURISM

NAMUR
DINANT

Brasserie du Bocq

Blanche de Namur, Corsendonck, Deugniet, Fruit Bocq, Gauloise, Saint Benoît, Saison 1858, Triple Moine

———

Traditional family brewery in the valley of the Bocq in the heart of the Condroz region. Visits, preferably by prior arrangement, throughout the year. No group tours without reservation.

Rue de la Brasserie 4, Purnode, +32(0)82/61 07 90
visite@bocq.be, www.bocq.be

Brogne (Abbaye Saint-Gérard de)

Abbaye de Brogne Blonde & Brune

———

A microbrewery in the former pilgrims' hall of the abbey. This is where Bruno Deghorain of La Binchoise brews his organic abbey beers. Visits by appointment but open brewing days are held regularly. Taste the beers and have a bite to eat in the abbey tavern.

Place de Brogne 3, Saint-Gérard (Mettet)
info@abbayedebrogne.com, www.abbayedebrogne.be

Bertinchamps (Ferme de)

Bertinchamps

———

A former brewer at Val-Dieu has set up a microbrewery in a majestic square farmhouse that is almost lost amongst the fields. Arrange your visit in advance. There's a tasting room, and on Thursday, Friday and Saturday evenings chef Stefan Jacobs prepares gastronomic meals.

Ferme de Bertinchamps 4, Grand-Manil (Gembloux),
+32(0)484/31 85 58, info@bertinchamps.be,
www.bertinchamps.be

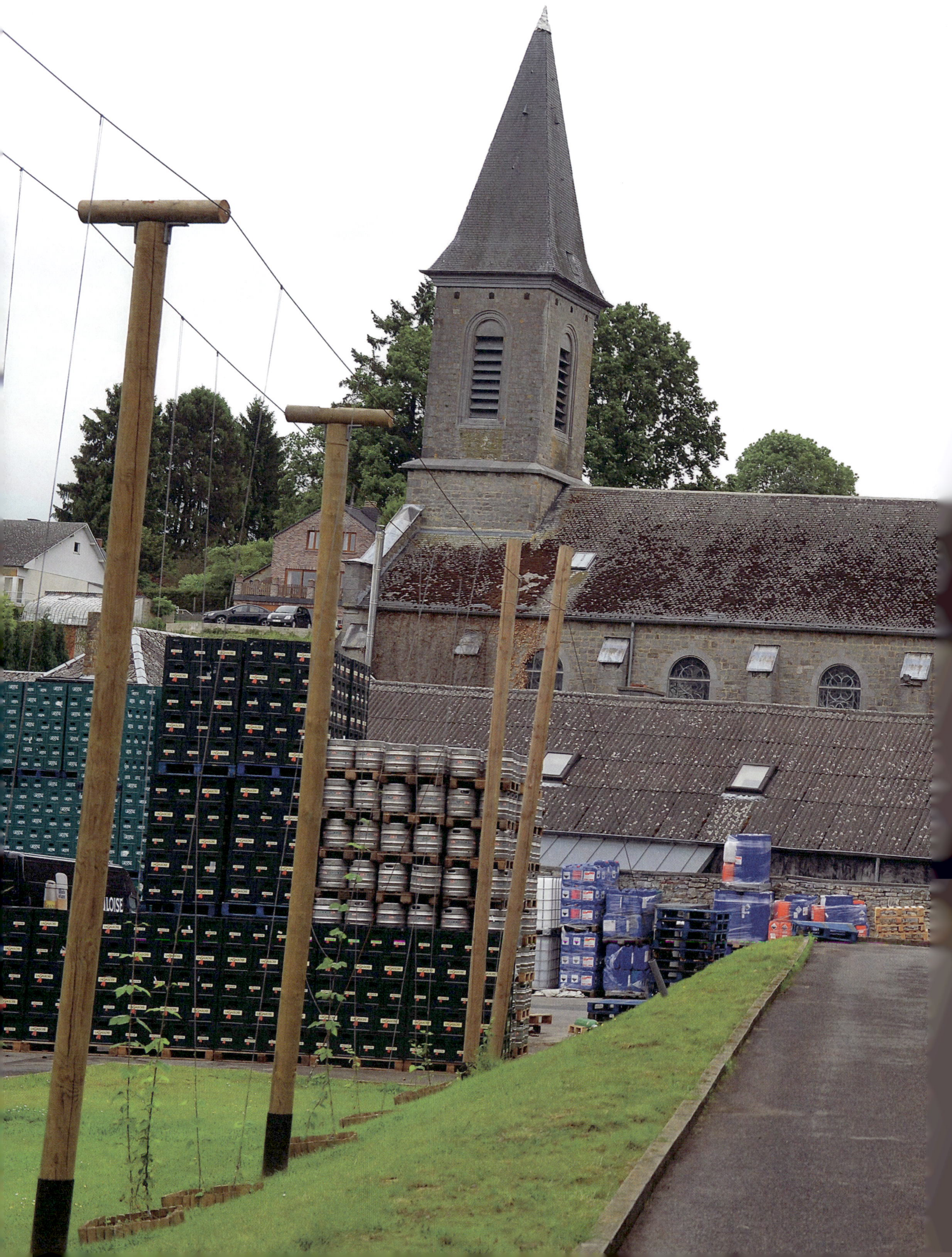

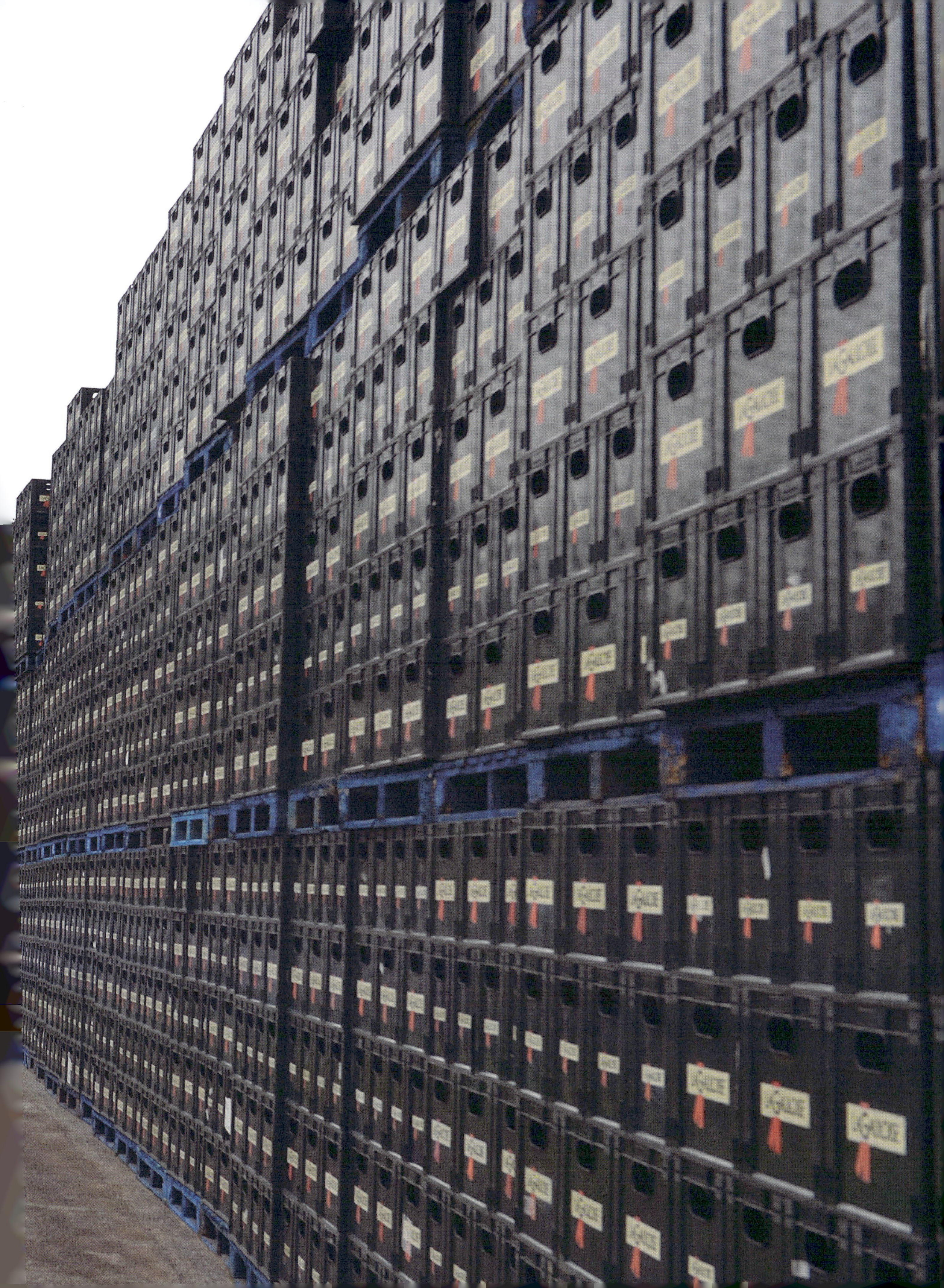

Caracole

Caracole, Les Bains d'Epices, Nostradamus, Saxo, Tournée Beaurinoise, Triek, Troublette

———

Time is given all the time it takes in this artisan brewery where the kettle is still stoked by wood. Discover this living museum just a stone's throw from Dinant. Free entry, group visits by pre-arrangement.

Côte Marie-Thérèse 86, Falmignoul (Dinant), +32(0)82/74 40 80 of +32(0)475/96 75 32 (gids)
brasserie.caracole@skynet.be

Fagnes (Brasserie des)

Super des Fagnes Blonde, Brune, Griottes, Scotch & Noël, Fagnes au Miel Biologique, Blanche, Cuvée Guillaume, Cuvée Junior, Cuvée Vigneronne, Fruits des Bois, Saison & Quatre Céréales

———

Take a seat in the café and watch the brewer at work. Pop into the brewery museum with its vintage equipment, advertising and photographs. From time to time the standard beer range is complemented with beers brewed on the spur of the moment, accompanied by regional food if you like. Brewing is done from Wednesday to Saturday and every brewing session is open to the public. Closed on Mondays (except July, August and public holidays). Closed on weekdays in January. Group visits by prior arrangement at any time.

Route de Nismes 26, Mariembourg (Couvin), +32(0)60/31 39 19 of +32(0)60/31 15 70, info@fagnes.be, www.brasseriedesfagnes.com

Floreffe (Abbaye de)

Floreffe

———

This abbey was founded in 1121 by Saint Norbert. Its church and gardens are open to the public. The wood-carved choir seats in the abbey church are well worth a visit. Have a drink and a bite to eat in the converted brewery mill (16th century). Around the year 1250 the Abbey inaugurated a 'brewery with its mill attached' within its walls and the first abbey beers saw the light of day soon afterwards. These abbey beers are now in the capable hands of the Lefèbvre brewery.

Rue Séminaire 7, +32(0)81/44 53 03, abbayefloreffe@skynet.be, www.abbaye-de-floreffe.be

Lesse (Brasserie de la)

Cambrée, Chinette, Hiveresse, Marie Blanche, Rouge-Croix

———

A group of friends joined hands to start up a village brewery. They set up shop in the former La Rochefortoise brewery with the blessing, and financial support, of the villagers. Visits on request for groups with 10 to 25 participants.

Rue du Treux 43B, Eprave (Rochefort), +32(0)84/45 75 25 of +32(0)471/51 06 34, www.brasseriedelalesse.be

Brasserie Lefèbvre has opted for a traditional flip-top bottle for its Floreffe abbey beers.

Maredsous (Abbaye de)

Maredsous

No, you will not find monks brewing on this site. Their beers now feel right at home at the Duvel Moortgat brewery. However, you can taste the abbey beers in the Saint-Joseph visitors' centre that also shows a video explaining the life and work of the monks. Phone ahead to arrange a visit to the abbey, the cheese workshop and the pottery.

Rue de Maredsous 11, Denée, +32(0)82/69 82 11
www.tourisme.maredsous.be

Silenrieux (Brasserie de)

Bière d'Autruche, Cuvée des Lacs de l'Eau d'Heure, Joseph, Kriek de Silenrieux, Noël de Silenrieux, Pavé de l'Ours, Sara

---

Traditional brewery in close proximity to the Eau d'Heure reservoirs. Brews organic beers made with the ancient grains of spelt and buckwheat. Sample the beers and local produce in the Chez l'Père Sarrasin tavern right next to the brewery. Groups welcome by prior arrangement.

Rue Noupré 1, Silenrieux (Cerfontaine), +32(0)71/63 32 01
brasserie.silenrieux@belgacom.net, www.brasseriedesilenrieux.be

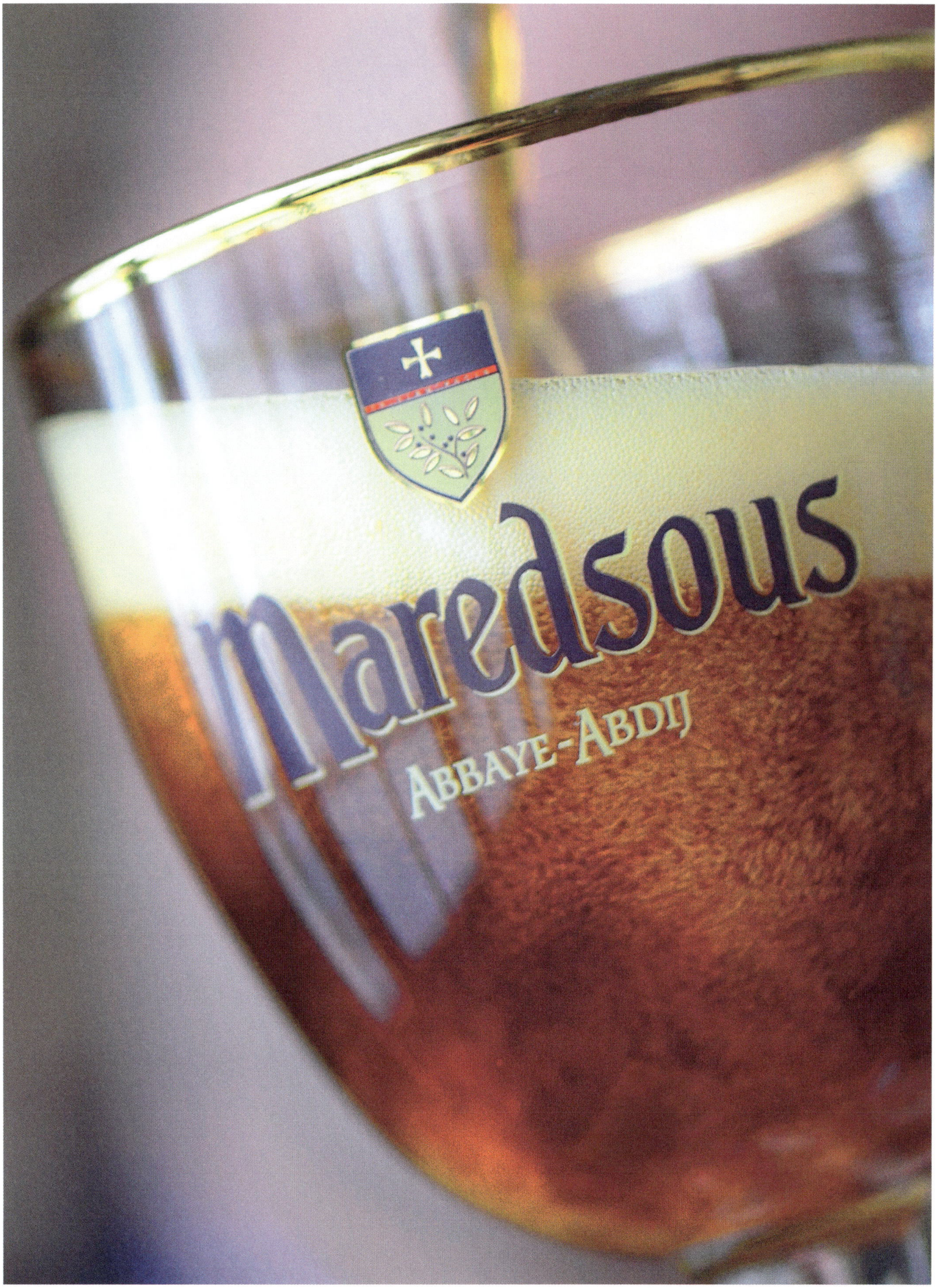
Maredsous
ABBAYE-ABDIJ

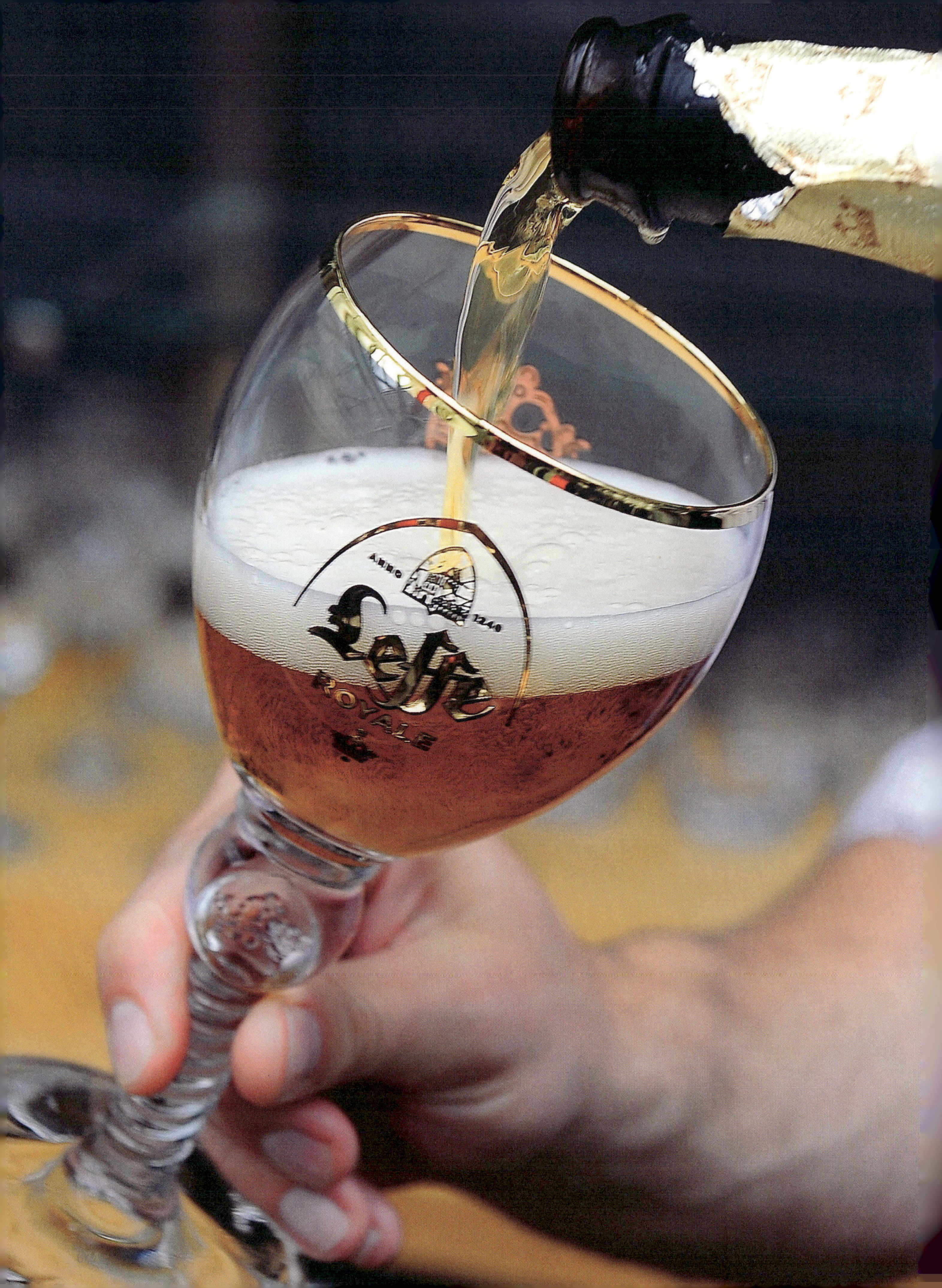
ANNO 1240
Leffe
ROYALE

WORTH A LOOK

Maison Leffe

Thanks to the powerful AB Inbev distribution network, the Leffe abbey beers are now available in over 60 countries around the globe. In Belgium they are brewed by AB Inbev's main brewery in Louvain. However, this beer has its roots in Leffe Abbey close to Dinant. The production of these abbey beers has been outsourced ever since 1952. In the meantime, beer lovers could do worse than visit Maison Leffe where they will be quickly brought up to speed with the history of abbey beers. Maison Leffe is a former abbey now converted into a wellness hotel. Make no mistakes – the Norbertine abbey that has given the beer its name is on the opposite side of the river Meuse and also at the other side of the city, where the Leffebeek joins the Meuse. Maison Leffe harbours cultural ambitions. Jam sessions are often held during the Leffe Jazz Nights in Dinant during the month of July.

La Maison Leffe, Charreau des Capucins 23,
+32(0)82/22 91 91, www.leffe.com

Lustin (beer museum)

Over 21,000 bottles, more than 20,000 beer glasses, ashtrays, umbrellas, posters and plenty of other paraphernalia with a focus on Belgian beer. 1,000 Belgian beers are available for tasting.… Welcome to Ali Baba's cave. Every single bottle or glass comes with its own story or anecdote. In the early 1980s when the beer world was swamped by mergers, take-overs and brewery closures, a handful of volunteers decided to provide a safe haven for bottles, glasses, mugs and advertising posters. And this is how the museum was born. The Lustin beer museum is a venue for 'brocante' flea markets and exchange fairs between Ascension Day and Pentecost and also on the first Sunday in October. The museum is open during weekends and public holidays from 11:00 to 19:30. Guided tours by prior arrangement. Tasting room available.

Rue de la Gare 19, Lustin (Profondeville), +32(0)81/41 11 02
musee.b.b@skynet.be, www.museebieresbelges.centerall.com

WAAR IS DAT FEESTJE?

BELGIAN BEERS & BREWS
RISTORANTE
DEL SUD CLASSICO
DRINKT
PAiSTe

BEER FESTIVALS IN BELGIUM

Just like music festivals, beer festivals are springing up everywhere in Belgium. They proliferate here, there and everywhere. Beer lovers congregate in towns and villages around the country. They exchange a rather modest amount of money for a handful of tokens, a tasting glass and the opportunity to excite their tastebuds, sampling the latest creations from Belgian brewers, either large or small. Far be it from us to list every single local beer festival (although you can find a diary of beer festivals at www.zythos.be). Here we are focusing on the main festivals that have put their names on the map. They draw in beer lovers from Belgium and abroad. Some are held in the open air, others take place in a large marquee or in an exhibition centre on the edge of the city. Their focus can also be vastly different. The smaller beer festivals are often happy to give a platform to the smaller market players. Come along and you will often have the opportunity to meet inspired microbrewers and taste their beers. Other beer festivals like to stick with the established medium large and large breweries. These large venues may still have something exclusive up their sleeves, however, Brewers often take advantage of these occasions to introduce a new brew and invite you to test it. Up to you to take up the gauntlet. Last but not least, there are plenty of niche festivals. The Christmas Beer Festival in Essen is a prime example. This is where you go for the largest selection of Christmas and winter beers. Schol!

Belgisch Bierweekend in Brussels

The first weekend in September is ringed in the diary of many a beer lover. This is when the Grand-Place in Brussels is turned into one giant bar. The Belgian Beer Weekend was initiated by the national brewing federation, Belgian Brewers for short. Around 100 breweries are members of this federation. Together they account for over 90% of the beer brewed in our country. At the seventeenth Belgian Beer Weekend, 400 beers from 44 breweries were available. At the Grand-Place the entire world unites around a good glass of beer. 'Tussen pot en pint' (between pot and pint), as we say in Belgium, you hear a multitude of languages. Beer loosens the tongue. At one booth friendships are made. A bit further on you will find members of a 'Confrérie' (brotherhood) promoting their St-Feuillien whereas members of 'L'Ordre du Faro' are singing the virtues of this traditional Brussels lambic beer. The message is simple: enjoy. This party is for the brewers. They use this opportunity to introduce their latest creations. 'Do people like my IPA, barrel aged scotch, lambic, triple or Trappist?' The beer drinker tries various brews and makes his choice. Connoisseurs are often in search of the exclusive or the extreme. Your average beer lover likes to stick to the tried and trusted paths but he may veer away from it, fired up by a stand worker who knows how to sell his wares or intrigued by what he has heard about a new beer.

www.belgianbrewers.be

Zythos Beer Festival in Louvain

Big, bigger, biggest... Even before official visitor numbers are known, it feels like the Zythos Beer Festival in Louvain, held during the last weekend in April, is bursting at the seams. Once it gets going, parts of it are so crowded that it is impossible to get through. You hear a cacophony of languages. The visitors come from all over Europe but also from the USA and Asia. The Zythos Beer Festival showcases a great range of Belgian specialty beers. .And all the brewers present are equal in the eyes of the law. Large or small, everyone is allocated the same size booth. In the meantime, the physical or virtual mouth-to-mouth advertising is in overdrive. 'Have you tried this 'limited edition'? Or that 'barrel aged' or 'brett'...? This is not the place to go if you are after a standard pils. So, what is on the menu? Around five hundred beers offered by 89 booths. Admittedly, there is no way they can cram in any more. With this extensive range Zythos measures up to the largest beer festivals in Europe and earns its place in the Belgian Top 3 next to the Brussels Beer Weekend and the BAB Bruges Beer Festival. Many visitors know that Belgium has more to offer than beer. Louvain is playing the beer card quite strongly. You can take part in many side events such as city tours, brewery visits and hotel packages with a cycling, walking or culinary theme. It so happens that beer is always included in the programme.

www.zythos.be

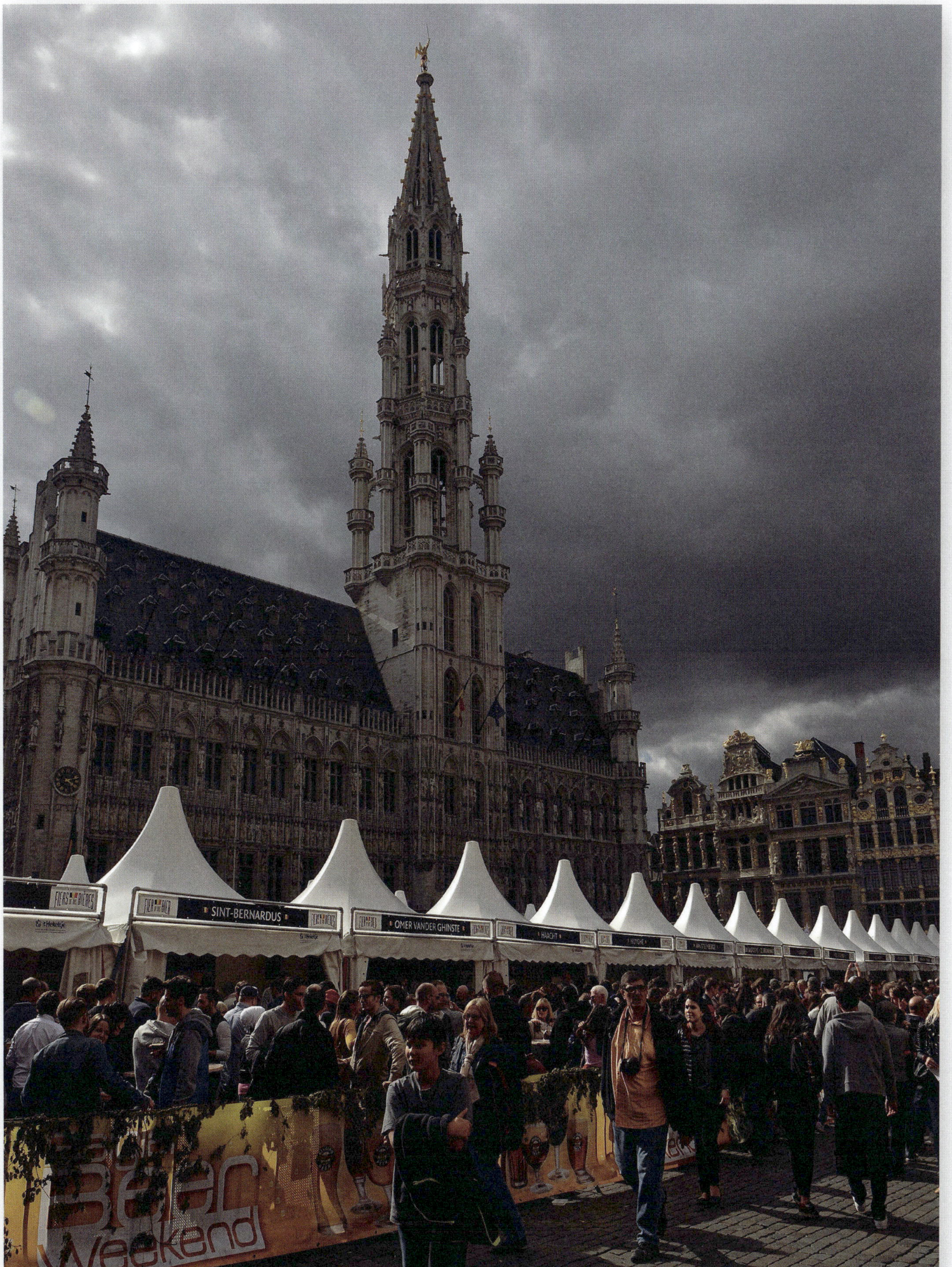
SINT-BERNARDUS
OMER VANDER GHINSTE
HAACHT
Beer
Weekend

BAB Brugs Bierfestival

The Brugs Bierfestival – the Bruges' beer festival – has been held every first weekend of February since 2007. It was set up by the BAB, a local association affiliated with the beer consumer association Zythos. As this festival grew year after year and threatened to outgrow its initial venue of the Linen Hall next to the belfry, it moved to the Beurshalle exhibition centre in 2014. Exhibitors include the main players such as Duvel Moortgat, Palm Craft Breweries and Huyghe as well as local heroes, De Halve Maan and Bourgogne de Flandres for example. You will also meet microbreweries: Den Triest and Brasserie des Carrières as well as beer firms, such as Vliegende Paard Brouwers and Beerdevelopment Viven. Many microbreweries and beer firms like to make their mark on the map with their lesser-known beer styles. There is also the increased popularity of the IPAs, imperial stout, porter and barley wine rooted in Belgian tradition but with the use of exotic aroma hops and techniques such as dry hopping. Blended styles such as a white beer triple or a triple using genuine krieken cherries also come to the fore. It is noticeable that 'sour ale' is growing in popularity now the 'IPA' hype seems to be fading. Other microbrewers are firmly in the 'terroir' camp with beer brewed with barley or hops from their own fields. You will hardly find any extreme beers – ultra-heavy, ultra-bitter, ultra-sour – at this Bruges festival.

www.brugsbierfestival.be

Ambiorix Bierfestival in Tongeren

Ambiorix Bierfestival is held in the city of Tongeren during the first weekend of August. For two days you will have the opportunity to talk to the brewers exhibiting here. At Ambiorix Bierfestival you will find 30 breweries showcasing over 100 beers. You can explore to your heart's content and at your own pace what is on offer in our Beer Country of Belgium. The focus here is on small-scale breweries including several players who are not very well known in the market. Connoisseurs and average beer lovers, all will find something they like. This beer festival aims to lower the threshold for new and unknown specialty beers. The success of the summer event was followed by a more intimate Christmas festival, first held at Tongeren's Veemarkt or Cattle Market on 8 December 2013. The Winter Festival provides an opportunity to taste Christmas beers and winter beers. Use your visit to discover one of the oldest cities in Belgium and don't miss out on the Sunday morning antiques market, the largest in the Benelux.

Beer Passion Weekend in Antwerp

The Beer Passion Weekend is traditionally held in a tented village at Groenplaats square in the heart of Antwerp. This is the rendezvous for the established medium-sized and large breweries in Belgium. Around thirty breweries are expected to attend this open air festival. The organiser is beer sommelier and editor Ben Vinken. His aim is to promote beer as a complex drink and the fruit of a craft that goes back centuries. The Beer Passion Weekend attracts a mixed audience including quite a few day tourists. Harmonic orchestras and jazz bands ensure a lively atmosphere. You may spot the odd Scotsman wearing his kilt. All of the Belgian beer styles are featured here: from white beer to Spéciale Belge, abbey and Trappist, gueuze lambic and kriek, heavy blond beers, brown and red beers, saisons, bière brut…. The brewers take advantage of the Weekend to present their new beers. It is also raining awards. The Michael Jackson Award is given to the individual who has made the most effort to promote the Belgian beer world. Who will be honoured this year?

www.beerpassion.com

North Sea Beer Festival in Ostend

A great ambiance and a relaxed atmosphere reign supreme at the North Sea Beer Festival held in Ostend during the last weekend in August. Happy faces all around. It is the dream finish to the tourist season. Under a cloudless blue sky, plenty of enjoyment is on offer in the romantic Leopoldpark, close to the beach. Over 150 beers are available to taste, providing a great overview of the beers on offer in Belgium. Ostend's best restaurants show off their culinary know-how. They are inspired by the salty sea breeze to create delicious tapas and snacks. Beer lovers stroll through the park, glass in hand. They enjoy the proceedings as part of a crowd, around a small table at one of the booths, on a park bench, by the pond, in the splendid kiosk or simply lying down under the trees. Hikers of any age have also discovered this beer festival. It is lovely to see how the entire world is united around a good glass of beer. Throats are lubricated and conversations are flowing. Amongst the stand holders you find large and medium-sized breweries as well as microbreweries and beer firms from every corner of Belgium.

www.northseabeerfestival.com

Modeste beer festival in Antwerp

The Modeste beer festival is held during the first weekend of October on the site of Antwerp city brewery De Koninck. Beer lovers soak up the sunshine in the spacious interior court or enjoy the shade provided by the large trees in the fine garden. Participants include microbreweries as well as the classics. The Modeste beer festival is named after the legendary former owner of the De Koninck brewery. 'Modeste', French for 'modest', also tells you something about the ambitions of this event.

In contrast to the BAB Brugs Bierfestival or Zythos in Louvain, you will not come across festival beers brewed specially for the occasion. The Modeste beer festival provides an overview of the art of artisan brewing throughout Belgium. While you're here, visit the interactive exhibition on Antwerp, brewing and beer in the De Koninck Antwerp City Brewery Experience Centre. De Koninck beers can be tasted in the brewery bar. The site also includes a cheese shop and affineur's, a chocolaterie, butcher's shop, bakery and restaurant. All of these shops sell their own produce made on the premises.

www.modestebierfestival.be

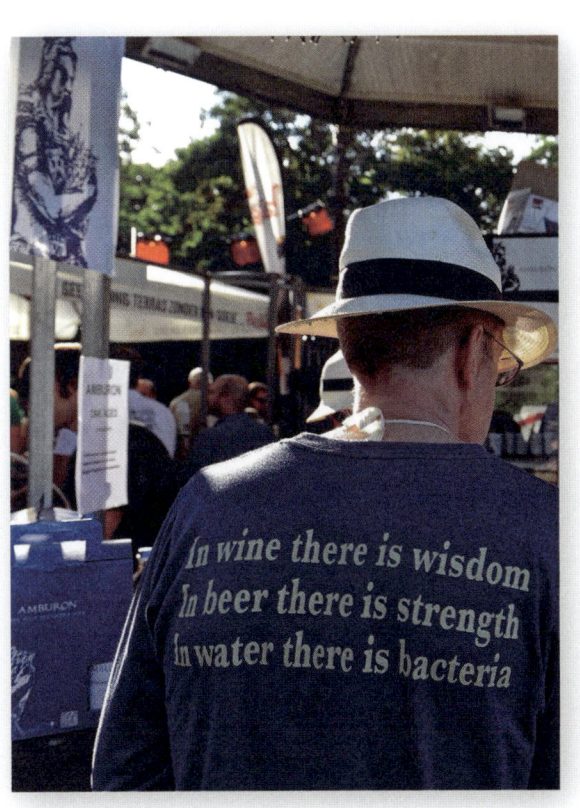

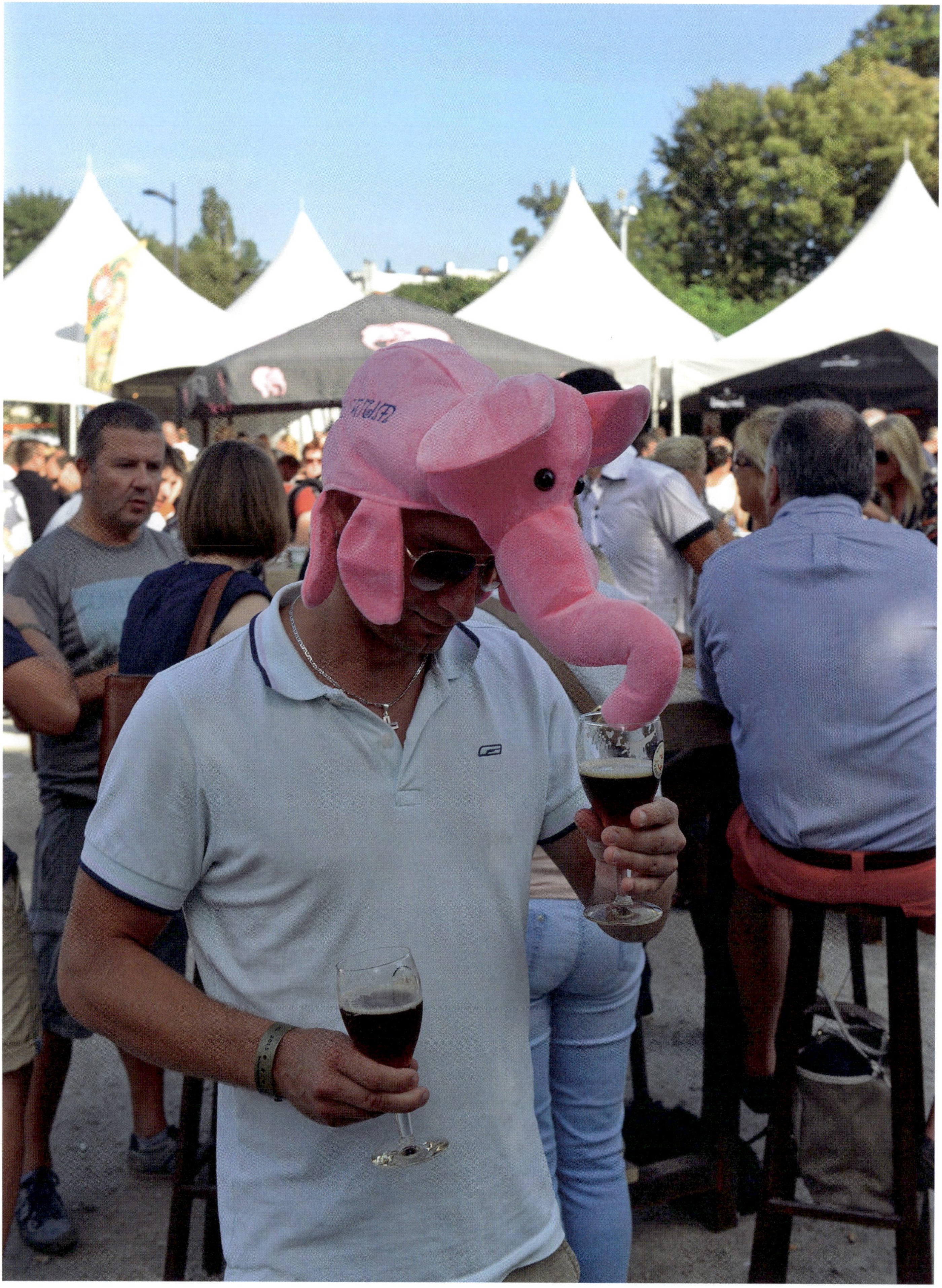

Brassigaume in Marbehan (Aarlen)

Brassigaume is the most important microbrewery festival in the South of Belgium, held in Marbehan, the village adjacent to Rulles. It is no coincidence that Grégory Verhelst, the owner of Brasserie de Rulles, is also the spiritual father of Brassigaume. His aim is to give a step-up to the 'craft brewers', of which he is one. In theory, you are a microbrewer when you are producing fewer than 4,000 hectolitres per annum. The reality is that several participating breweries produce more than that, thanks to exports. You will also come across a handful of local 'nanobreweries' and start-ups. Many breweries started off as a farm. This link is still tangible in the South of Belgium, where you can still find a number of farm breweries and a great sense of 'terroir'. Brewers will proudly state that they are using hops from their own fields or cultivate their own barley or else work with local growers. Sustainability is key. The 'short chain' is of paramount importance. When a brewery expands they often collaborate with local cheese dairies, artisan butchers, chocolatiers or chefs. Don't be surprised if you are offered a typical paté gaumais or a sausage, smoked or not, also from the Gaume to accompany your beer.

www.brassigaume.be

Christmas Beer Festival in Essen

If you want to know which Christmas beers were new to the market over the past year, pop into the international Christmas Beer Festival in the village of Essen just to the north of Antwerp. You will encounter hordes of enthusiastic beer lovers at work. They want to taste everything and are busy noting down their findings. So, what can you expect to see in your glass? Slanderous tongues will state that, at the last moment, the brewers throw together all the residues from their various tanks and name the result their Xmas Blend. Fortunately, reality is quite different. For the end-of-year festivities many breweries introduce a seasonal beer that tends to be a bit stronger. Amongst the abbey beers you will often find a Christmas version of the popular dark 'double'. Particularly in the South of the country, brewers have a more generous hand when it comes to adding herbs. The alcohol volume also tends to go up. After all, you tend to turn up the temperature in winter. Christmas beer is not a well-defined beer style. Precisely for that reason, an endless range of variations resonates to the familiar Christmas theme. In fact, too many to mention here. Now and again, you come across the odd one out. The Slaghmuylder brewery surprises its customers with an extra-hoppy, malty, blond bottom-fermented beer in the pils style, aiming squarely at the thirsty party-goer. There is a Christmas beer for everyone to be enjoyed at any moment. No-nonsense or complex. Usually less of a thirst-quencher and more of a degustation beer. A truly reviving beer, with a tad more alcohol thanks to the re-fermentation, strong aromas of caramel from the roast malt, a hint of fruitiness thanks to the yeast, a sufficient hop content to dam in the flow of sweetness and with often that one particular herb or spice that prompts you to order a second glass so you can find out exactly what has been used. Cloves? Or were they used in the warm Glühkriek I have just tasted? I cannot wait to see all the colours of winter that show up in the glass.

www.kerstbierfestival.be

BEER EVENTS

Toer de gueuze

The 'Toer de Gueuze' was staged for the first time in 1997. This open brewery day for the Pajottenland and the Zenne Valley is now held every two years. At the first event, Boon, De Cam, De Troch, 3 Fonteinen, Lindemans and Timmermans opened their doors to the public. Ever since, a number of members of the High Council for Artisan Lambic Beers (HORAL) have been opening their doors to the public, free of charge, with guided tours on offer. Enjoy a lambic, gueuze, kriek, framboise or another lambic beer where it is made. Entertainment is often added into the mix. Beware: entry is free so this event attracts a large crowd of visitors to the various lambic breweries and/or 'gueuzesteker' firms.

Toerisme Halle, +32(0)2/356 42 59,
www.toerismepajottenland.be, www.horal.be

Red-Brown Ale Trail

Four breweries: De Brabandere, Omer VanderGhinste, Rodenbach and Verhaeghe organise the beer event Rondje Roodbruin ('a round of red-brown') in co-operation with Toerisme Leiestreek (the tourism association of the Leiestreek area). Every two years, on the last Sunday in April these four breweries open their doors to the public. You can visit them free of charge, taste their Flemish red-brown beers and enjoy the varied entertainment available on the day.

www.toerisme-leiestreek.be, www.brouwerijdebrabandere.be,
www.brouwerijverhaeghe.be, www.omervanderghinste.be,
www.palmbreweries.com

Brew in Bokrijk

One weekend in September, the Bokrijk Open Air Museum invites you to discover all that is edible in the world of flora and fauna. Watch a demonstration of syrup distillation or beer brewing using the historic equipment at this open air museum. And there is a large market selling local produce from more than 60 stands. Het Paenhuys is an authentic 17th century village brewery from Diepenbeek near Hasselt. It allowed the 'Diepenbekenaren', or villagers of Diepenbeek, to brew their own beer on the site until the year 1700. This historic brewery has now been resurrected in Bokrijk. A hop field has been added to the Abele estate that forms part of the museum. Here you will also find a traditional 'hopast' – a drying kiln for hops - from Proven near Poperinge.

www.bokrijk.be

Exchange fair for beer items

The Hoegaarden exchange fair is one of the largest in Belgium and is held annually on the first weekend of November. An initiative from the Gambrinus collectors' club, which numbers 500 members including many from outside Belgium (also see chapter 3).

www.gambrinusclub.be

The European Beer Museum in Stenay

In the small town of Stenay in Northern France, half an hour's drive from Orval, you will find the Musée Européen de la Bière. This museum is housed in the former Governor's Palace (17th century) within what used to be the citadel. Later on, the building was also home to a malting works. The comprehensive collection numbers 55,000 objects, 20% of which are on display. The herb garden contains hops and herbs used in beer making. The collection provides an overview of universal beer history from the times beer was first brewed in former Mesopotamia (Iraq). Attention is paid to archaeology, science, brewing technology and art. So what can you admire here? An authentic brewhall with copper kettles, beer mats, bottle openers, lab equipment, vintage posters and enamel advertising signs from Belgian breweries and others. One of the eye-catching items on display is the stained glass window from the Palais de la Bière in Nancy depicting the miracle of St. Arnold, the patron saint of brewers. The visitor's itinerary comprises: the history of the museum and the building, the ingredients and brewing process, brewing beer then and now, beer and the imagination (advertising), beer consumption (sociology). From time to time themed exhibitions and tastings are held. The museum is open every day from 1 March to 1 December.

17, rue de la Citadelle, Stenay, Frankrijk, +33(0)3 29 80 68 78, musee.biere@meuse.fr, www.musee-de-la-biere.com

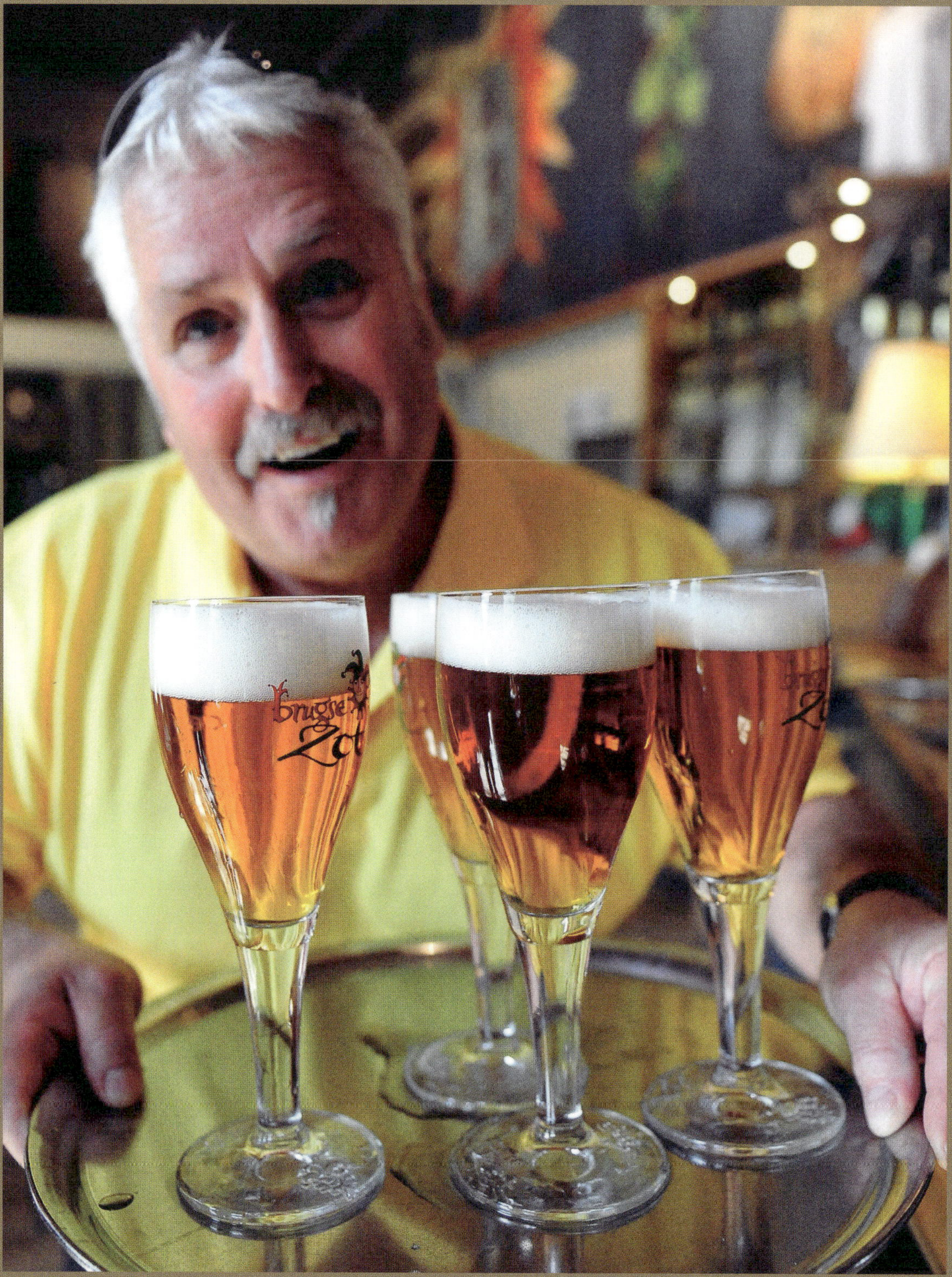
brugse

NEVER ASK FOR 'A BEER'

Michael Jackson, the Beer Hunter

BEER DICTIONARY

A

Abbey beer: beer brewed on behalf of an existing abbey or inspired by a former abbey
Acetic acid: an acid with a pungent smell, found in sour beers of the Flemish red-brown type
Acidity: the level of acid contained in the beer
Additive: substance added to the beer
Aftertaste: the taste that lingers after swallowing the beer
Alcohol percentage: a measure for the quantity of alcohol in a drink, expressed in percentage per volume
Amber beer: an amber-coloured beer, e.g. the Spéciale Belge beer style, De Koninck or Palm (see Chapter 5)
Aroma hop: a hop variety that is added at the end of the brewing process to increase the aroma
Aroma: comprises the fragrance, the taste, the mouthfeel and the aftertaste of the beer

B

Balance: the balance between aroma and taste
Barrel aged: beers matured in recycled wooden barrels that have been previously filled with other alcoholic drinks such as wine, whisky, Armagnac or cognac
Beer firm: a company that is involved in the marketing of beers without being involved in their brewing
Bitter hops: hop varieties selected for their bitterness
Bostel: the solid residue of the grain that is left behind once the liquids (the wort) have been removed from the mash by means of filtration; used as cattle feed
Bottling: filling the bottles at the bottle line
Bottom-fermented beer: beer that ferments at the bottom of the tank, ferments at a low temperature (-10 °C), e.g. pils
Bouquet: the whole of the fragrances given off by the beer
Brewhall: the heart of the brewery where the mash is produced and the wort is filtered and boiled after the hops are added
Brut bier: a clear and sparkling festive beer that, after brewing, is treated like champagne. Example: DeuS Brut des Flandres

C

Caramel: a beer colouring agent made with caramelised (slightly burnt) sugar
Caramelising: allowing sugar to burn slightly to give a caramel taste
Centrifuging: removing floating particles from the beer with the aid of a centrifuge - a piece of equipment that puts an object in rotation around a fixed axis
Coarse grinding: crushing or grinding the malt, allowing the enzymes to convert starch from the grain into sugars during the mashing process
Craft brewery: an artisan brewery

D

Degustation beer: a strong beer where the taste overrides the thirst-quenching character
Degustation: beer tasting
Density: the proportion of solid ingredients in the wort that ensure fermentation, also the basis for the calculation of excise duty on beer
Double: *dubbel*, refers to the greater proportion of malt added and the higher density of ingredients in comparison with a standard beer; originating in abbey breweries, now a generic term for a strong dark beer
Dry hopping: the addition of hop cones or extracts or oils derived from hops during the cold storage process to give the beer a stronger aroma of hops

E

EBC: European Brewery Convention, a colour scale for malt, wort and beer: the higher the EBC, the darker the beer
EBU: European Bitterness Unit, a unit of bitterness in beer
Ester: a compound between alcohol and acid; yields fruity aromas
Esterification: formation of esters by means of compounds between alcohol and acids during the maturation of the beer

F

Faro: a sweetened lambic
Fermentation: the process whereby yeast cells convert sugars into alcohol and carbon dioxide
Flavour: *flavor*, aroma, taste and mouth feel
Flemish red-brown beer: *Vlaams roodbruin bier*,

traditional mixed fermentation beer from the Kortrijk (Courtrai) and Roeselare areas, usually a blend of beer soured in oak barrels (foeders) with a young top-fermented beer, e.g. Rodenbach
Foeder: large wooden barrel used for the cold storage of beer, typically used to store lambic and Flemish red-brown beer

G

Geuzesteker: a brewer who blends, or 'cuts' gueuze, i.e. blends old and young lambic from several breweries to arrive at a unique gueuze (lambic re-ferments in the bottle)
Grisette: a hoppier version of a saison
Gruit: a mixture of herbs used in medieval brewing before the introduction of hops
Gueuze: or *geuze*, beer created by blending young and old lambics, cloudy with a matte to amber colour, slightly sour to bitter-sour, typical of the Zenne Valley and the Pajottenland near Brussels; usually sweetened

H

Hard water: contains a high proportion of calcium and magnesium salts
Head: collar of froth on top of the glass of beer, formed by proteins; protects the beer from oxygen
Home brewery: small brewery in a café or restaurant
Hop cone: the female hop flower, contains the lupuline agent that helps preserve the beer

I

IPA: India Pale Ale, a beer type that is English in origin, characterised by the addition of extra hops to improve the sustainability of the beer

K

Koelschip: flat open tray into which the hot wort is poured to cool down, after which it will ferment spontaneously after being 'infected' by the wild yeasts (microflora) that are present in the surrounding air; characteristic of artisan lambic beers
Kriek: fruit beer with sour cherries (krieken) made on the basis of lambic, white beer or top-fermented beer
Krieken lambic: lambic that has not fully finished the fermentation process, sour cherries (krieken) are added and the fruit sugars feed the wild yeasts in the beer to prompt the re-fermentation

L

Label beer: *etiket beer*, a beer sold under various names, a copy of an existing beer, applies to beers sold by various associations and supermarkets.
Lactic acid: an acid that gives soured milk its sour taste; is released during biological processes such as the fermentation of beer, characteristic of lambic beers and others
Lagering: cold storage; storage and maturation of beer in a cold environment
Lambic: *lambiek*, a spontaneously fermented beer, typical of the Zenne Valley and the Pajottenland near Brussels; contains 30% unmalted wheat and aged hop, is the mother beer for gueuze, kriek and a number of fruit beers, ferments spontaneously when it comes in touch with ambient 'wild' yeasts (microflora); the taste is mildly sour to distinctively sour, non-sparkling
Lightstruck: unwanted flavour caused by exposure to light
Lupuline: conserving agent present in the cones of the female hop plant

M

Main fermentation: the first fermentation stage

Malt (also see malting): grains of cereal grains – predominantly barley – that are first steeped to make them sprout and then dried to halt the sprouting process; with the aim of producing
enzymes that, during mashing, will convert the starch from the grain into sugars; malt varieties differ in colour from pale (pale malt) to very dark (roast malt); malt determines the colour and the taste of the beer

Malt beer: beer brewed using malt only, without unmalted grains

Malting: the process that prepares cereal grains (usually barley) for brewing. Barley grains cannot be used in their natural form. Using water, heat and air the barley grains are encouraged to sprout. As soon as the enzymes start to form, the malter will stop the sprouting by drying the grains. After malting we use the term malt (barley malt, wheat malt, oats malt...).

Mash: mixture of crushed and ground malt and water, prepared in the mashing basin, also known as *maischkuip*

Mashing: also called *maischen*; a stage in the brewing process during which enzymes from the malt convert starch into sugar

Maturation: aging

Mild: with a mild/not very distinctive taste

Mixed fermentation: characteristic of Flemish red-brown beers and the brown beers from Oudenaarde; in this case, top-fermented beer are subjected to an additional infection of lactic acid

O

Oasting: drying a green malt at a high temperature during the malting process, stops the malt from sprouting, also used in hop processing

Observation threshold: the minimum quantity of taste agents that can still be discerned

Off flavour: a deviation or abnormality in aroma and/or taste

Organoleptic: involving use of the sense organs

Oude geuze: old gueuze, created by blending 100% old, spontaneously fermented, lambic with a weighted average age of at least one year old, where the oldest lambic has fermented in wooden barrels for at least three years. The blend must undergo an in-bottle re-fermentation and, after a six-month maturation period in the bottle, must satisfy a number of biochemical criteria.

Oudenaards Bruin: a brown beer from the town of Oudenaarde; a slightly sour beer from Oudenaarde; (1) spontaneously fermented young top-fermented beer blended (cut) with older, soured beer of the Liefmans type; (2) uncut top-fermented beer with in-bottle re-fermentation, type Adriaen Brouwer

Oxidation: chemical process causing a stale 'old' taste in beer through exposure to oxygen

P

Pasteurisation: heating beer to a temperature of 60–75 °C to kill harmful micro-organisms

pH: degree of acidity/ measure of the degree in which a solution is acidic or alkaline

Plato: expresses the density of beer wort, more particularly the percentage by weight of substances (sugar especially) dissolved in the liquid prior to fermentation

Propagation: a technique for multiplying yeast

Q

Quadruple: *quadrupel*, a strong dark top-fermented beer with an alcohol volume of over 10%

R

Re-fermentation: re-fermentation in the bottle; as part of the bottling process extra sugar and yeast are added, prompting the beer to undergo a second fermentation in the bottle; deepens the taste and improves sustainability

Reinheitsgebot: German law stipulating that beer may only be brewed with water, malt, hop and yeast

Ring of froth: froth that clings to the side of the glass after each mouthful

S

Saint Arnold: the patron saint of brewers

Saison: a seasonal beer originating from farms in the Bergen (Mons) and Doornik (Tournai) areas, golden-blond to amber in colour, top-fermented beer, rather dry taste, Saison Dupont for example

Scotch: dark brown top-fermented beer on the basis of caramel malt and roast malt, example: Scotch de Silly

Single-cell culture: *'reincultuur'*, the cultivation of fresh yeast

Soft water: water with a low content of calcium salts and magnesium salts

Souring: to add acids or brewing salts to the mash

Spontaneous fermentation: a wild fermentation process during which no yeast is added and the wort ferments spontaneously after infection by wild yeasts (microflora), present in the ambient air, typical of artisan lambic beers
Stout: black top-fermented beer brewed with roast or burnt malts, example Guinness

T

Top-fermented beer: fermentation occurs at the top of the tank, the beer ferments at high temperatures (15–25 °C) with the yeast floating on the surface; applies to most Belgian specialty beers
Trappist beer: abbey beer brewed in a Trappist abbey under the supervision of monks belonging to the Cistercian order (Trappists); in Belgium, Trappist beer is brewed in Achel, Chimay, Orval, Rochefort, Westmalle and Westvleteren
Triple: *tripel*, strong blond top-fermented beer that re-ferments in the bottle, originally produced by abbey breweries and now a generic term, often the strongest beer in the brewery's range

V

Vinous: with a taste and aroma resembling wine
Viscous: syrupy, between solid and liquid, does not flow well

W

Wheat beer: beer containing unmalted wheat; gueuze or white beer for example
Whirlpool: piece of equipment used to clarify beer
White beer: witbier, unfiltered top-fermented beer brewed with malt, unmalted wheat, coriander and curaçao, e.g. Hoegaarden
Wort: name of brew prior to fermentation, only called beer post-fermentation

Z

Zythologue: beer connoisseur or beer sommelier (conform 'œnologue' for a wine connoisseur), term invented by Belgian beer lovers' association Zythos, combination of 'zythos', Greek for 'extract of barley' (beer) and knowledge

BEERS

A

Achel Blond (5%)	247
Abbaye de Brogne Brune (7,5%)	237
Adriaen Brouwer Dark Gold (8,5%)	352
Affligem Tripel (9,5%)	237
Ardenne Stout (8%)	367
Arend Tripel (8%)	291
Arthur's Legacy White Widow (7,1%)	358
Augustijn Blond (8%)	240
Averbode (7,5%)	240

B

Bacchus Oud Bruin (4,5%)	343
Barbar (8%)	275
Barista (11%)	299
Bastogne Pale Ale (5,5%)	383
Bavik Premium Pils (5,2%)	329
Bière Darbyste (5,8%)	267
Binchoise Blonde (6,2%)	267
Black Damnation (13%)	367
Boon Kriek Mariage Parfait (8%)	319
Bourgogne des Flandres (5%)	346
Brigand (9%)	275
Brugge Tripel (8,7%)	291
Brugse Zot Blond (6%)	271
Brunehaut Pomfraiz' (5,5%)	321
Bruut'n Triest (9%)	263
Buffalo (6%)	370
Bush Ambrée (12%)	259
Bush de Charmes (10,5%)	373

C

Caracole (7,5%)	259
Chapeau Faro (4,7%)	307
Cornet (8,5%)	379
Chimay Bleue (9%)	247
Cristal (4,8%)	329
Curtius (6,5%)	271
Cuvée Delphine (11%)	401
Cuvée des Jacobins (5,5%)	346

D

De Cam Oude Lambiek (5%)	307
De Koninck (5%)	255
Delirium Tremens (8,5%)	276
Delta IPA (6,5%)	383
DeuS Brut des Flandres (11,5%)	263
Diôle Brune (8,5%)	299
3 Fonteinen Oude Gueuze	312
Duchesse de Bourgogne (6,2%)	346
Duvel (8,5%)	278
Duvel Tripel Hop (9,5%)	384

E

Embrasse Oak Aged (9%)	374
Ename Pater (5,5%)	240
Extase (8,5%)	402

G

Gageleer (7,5%)	281
Gentse Strop (6,9%)	281
Girardin Kriek (5%)	319
Gouden Carolus Classic (8,5%)	300
Green Killer IPA (6,5%)	384
Grimbergen Blond (6,7%)	240
Gruut Inferno (9%)	281
Guillotine (La) (8,5%)	281
Gulden Draak (10,5%)	300
Gulden Spoor IPA (7%)	384

H

Herkenrode Bruin (7%)	243
Hoegaarden (4,8%)	357
Hof ten Dormaal Wit Goud (8%)	284
Hopus (8,3%)	285
HoublonChouffe (9%)	388

J

Jambe-de-Bois (8%)	294
Jupiler (5,2%)	332

K

Kasteel Rouge (8%)	324
Kriek Max (3,5%)	324
Kwaremont (6,6%)	271

L

La Chouffe (8%)	284
Leffe Blond (6,3%)	243
Liefmans Goudenband (8%)	352
Limburgse Witte (5%)	358
Lindemans Framboise (2,5%)	324
Lindemans Oude Gueuze Cuvée René (5,5%)	312
Lou Pepe Kriek (5%)	321
Lupulus Blonde (8,5%)	285

M

Maes Pils (5,2%)	332
Malheur Bière Brut (11%)	263
Maredsous Bruin (8%)	243
McChouffe (8%)	363
Moinette Bio (7,5%)	335
Morpheus Undressed (6,9%)	391
Mort Subite Oude Gueuze (7%)	312

O

Oerbier (9%)	349
Oesterstout (8,5%)	370
Omer (8%)	287
Orval (6,2%)	248
Oud Beersel Oude Gueuze (6%)	317
Oude Gueuze Cuvée René (5,5%)	312

P

Palm Hop Select (6%)	255
Pannepot (10%)	303
Paix-Dieu Pleine Lune (10%)	287
Petrus Oud Bruin (5,5%)	346
Pauwel Kwak (8,4%)	260
Primus (5,2%)	332

R

Reninge Oud Bruin (6%)	348
Rochefort 8 (9,2%)	248
Rodenbach Grand Cru (6%)	348
Rulquin (7%)	395

S

Safranaise (La) (7%)	271
IV Saison (6,5%)	335
Saison d'Erpe Mere (6,9%)	338
Saison Dupont (6,5%)	338
Scotch de Silly (7,5%)	363
St Feuillien Grand Cru (9,5%)	244
St-Louis Gueuze Fond Tradition (5%)	311
St Bernardus Abt 12 (10%)	303
Stella Artois (5,2%)	332
Straffe Hendrik Quadrupel (11%)	304
Surfine (6,5%)	338

T

Tilquin Oude Quetsche (6,4%)	321
Timmermans Oude Gueuze (5,5%)	317
Tongerlo Prior (9%)	244
Trignac XII (12%)	374
Tripel Karmeliet (8,4%)	294
Tripel Kanunnik (8,2%)	294
Triple d'Anvers (8%)	294
Tuverbol (10,6%)	396

V

Val-Dieu Triple (9%)	244
Vapeur Cochonne (La) (9%)	287
Vedett IPA (5,5%)	388
Vicaris Generaal (7%)	396

W

Waterloo Récolte (6%)	339
Westmalle Dubbel (7%)	252
Westmalle Tripel (9,5%)	252
Westvleteren Abt (10,2%)	252
Wilderen Goud (6,2%)	272
Wild Jo (5,8%)	391
Wipers Times (6,2%)	272
Witkap Pater Stimulo (6%)	272

X

XO La Binchoise (12%)	374
XX Bitter (6,2%)	388

Z

Zinnebir (6%)	260
Zwarte Pol (6,5%)	370

BREWERIES

A

AB Inbev (Artois)	601
Abbaye des Rocs (Brasserie d')	559
Achel (Abdij)	647
Achouffe (Brasserie de)	521
Alken-Maes	647
Alvinne	577
Amai	647
Angerik	604
Anker (Het)	533
Art d'en brasser (L')	559
Augrenoise	559
Authentique Brasserie	559
Averbode	604

B

Barbiot	560
Bastogne (Brasserie de)	521
Bellevaux (Brasserie de)	657
Bertinchamps (Ferme de)	667
Bie (De)	577
Binchoise (La)	560
Blaugies (Brasserie de)	563
Boelens	633
Boon	604
Bosteels	633
Botteresse de Sur-les-bois (La)	657
Bouillon (Brasserie de)	524
Bourgogne des Flandres	577
Brasse & Vous	657
Brasserie à Vapeur	563
Brasserie Artisanale du Flo	657
Brasserie C (Curtius)	658
Brasserie de la Lienne	658
Brasserie des Géants (Brasserie des Légendes)	563
Brasserie du Bocq	667
Brasserie Ellezelloise Brasserie des Légendes)	563
Brasse-Temps (Le) Bergen	566
Brasse-Temps (Le) Louvain-la-Neuve	604
Brogne (Abbaye Saint-Gérard de)	667
Brouwershuis ('t)	533
Brussels Beer Project	606
Bryggja Brewery	580
Brunehaut	566

C

Cantillon	606
Caracole	670
Carrières (Brasserie des)	566
Caulier	567
Cazeau (Brasserie de)	567
Chimay (Abbaye de)	568
Cnudde	636
Contreras	636
Cornelissen (Dorpsbrouwerij)	648

D

Danny	636
De Block	607
De Cam	607
De Brabandere	580
De Landtsheer (Malheur)	636
De Ryck	637
De Troch	607
Den Toeteler	648
Den Triest	607
Den Tseut	636
Demanez (Brasserie)	524
DijkWaert	533
Dilewyns	637
Dochter van de Korenaar (De)	533
Dolle Brouwers (De)	580
Domus (Huisbrouwerij)	607
Donum Ignis	637
Dorpsbrouwerij Humulus	538
3 Fonteinen	608
Dubuisson (Brasserie)	570
Dupont (Brasserie),	570
Duvel Moortgat	538

E

Elfique	658
Engilsen	650
En Stoemelings	608
Erquelinnes (Brasserie d')	570

F

Fagnes (Brasserie des)	670
Fantôme (Brasserie de)	524
Floreffe (Abbaye de)	671
Fort Lapin	580
Frasnoise (La)	570

G

Gaverhopke ('t)	580
Gengoulf (Brasserie)	524
Glazen Toren (De)	637
Grain d'Orge	658
Grimbergen	630
Gruut	640
Gulden Spoor (Het)	581

H

Haacht	608
Halve Maan (De)	581
Hanssens Artisanaal	612
Herberg (Den)	612
Herkenrode (Abdij)	655
Hoegaarden	612
Hofbrouwerijke ('t)	539
Hof Ten Dormaal	612
Hopperd (Den)	538
Huyghe	640

I

Inter-Pol	524

J

Jandrain-Jandrenouille	613
Jessenhofke	650
Jupille (Jupiler)	662

K

Kazematten (De)	584
Kerkom	650
Koninck (De)	543
Kortrijk-Dutsel	613
Kroon (De)	614
Kroontje ('t)	640

L

Lamot (Grand Café)	556
Leite (De)	584
Leffe (Maison)	675

Lesse (Brasserie de la)	671
Liefmans	640
Lindemans	614
Loterbol	619

M

Maenhout	584
Maredsous (Abbaye de)	672
Marsinne	662
Millevertus (Brasserie de)	695
Mort Subite	124

N

Nest (Het)	548
Nieuwhuys	619

O

Oud Beersel	619
Oude Maalderij (Brouwerij d')	588
Omer Vander Ghinste	584
Orval (Abbaye d')	528

P

Pairi Daiza	570
Pakhuis ('t)	548
Palm Belgian Craft Brewers	620
Perron Bieren	650
Pirlot – Kempisch Vuur	548
Plukker (De)	588

R

Ranke (De)	570
Rodenbach	588
Roman	644
Rulles (Brasserie de)	528

S

Seizoensbrouwerij Vandewalle	592
Senne (Brasserie de la)	
St-Feuillien (Brasserie de)	244
Saint-Monon (Brasserie de)	528
Sainte Nitouche (Brasserie de la Croix)	662
Sainte Hélène (Brasserie)	528
Scassènes (Brasserie de)	571
Silenrieux (Brasserie de)	672
Silly (Brasserie de)	574
Sint-Bernardus	592

Sint-Canarus	644
Slaghmuylder	644
Smisje	644
Strubbe	592
Struise Brouwers (De)	592

T

Ter Dolen (Kasteelbrouwerij)	650
Tilquin (Gueuzerie)	620
Timmermans	624
Toye (Brouwerij)	592
Triest (Den)	607
Troch (De)	607
3 Fourquets (Les)	528
Tubize (Brasserie de)	624

V

Val de Sambre (Brasserie du)	574
Val-Dieu (Abbaye de)	662
Van Campenhout	625
Van den Bossche	645
Van Eecke	596
Van Honsebrouck (Kasteelbrouwerij)	596
Van Steenberge	645
Verhaeghe-Vichte	596
Verzet (Brouwers)	596
Villers-la-Ville (Abbaye de)	625
Vissenaken	626
Vlier (De)	626

W

Warsage	662
Waterloo (Brasserie de)	626
Weldebrouck	548
Westmalle (Abdij)	552
Westvleteren (Sint-Sixtus abdij)	596
Wiels (Kunstencentrum)	630
Wilderen	650

BEER AND BREW MUSEA

Abbey beers museum Grimbergen	630
Beer museum Anthisnes	664
Beer museum Lustin	675
Beer museum Olen	556
Beer museum St Vith	664
Beer museum Schaarbeek	629
Bocholter brewery museum	655
Brewery museum De Snoek	599
Bruges Beer Museum	599
European Beer museum Stenay (France)	685
Hopmuseum Dilbeek	629
Hopmuseum Poperinge	599
Paenhuys (Het) Bokrijk	655
Visitors center De Lambiek	629

BEER FESTIVALS

Ambiorix Beer festival	680
BAB Brugs Beer festival	680
Belgian Beer weekend	678
Beer passion weekend	680
Brassigaume	683
Christmas Beer Festival	683
Modeste Bier Festival	681
North Sea Beer Festival	681
Zythos Beer festival	678

EVENTS

Hoppestoet Poperinge Ridders van de Roerstok	48
Brew in Bokrijk	685
European beer museum in Stenay	685
Red-Brown Ale Trail	684
Exchange fair for beer items	685
Toer de geuze	684

CAFÉS

Aigle d'Or (L')	145
Antwaerps Bierhuyske ('t)	113
Apostelken ('t)	110
Bahnhove	112
Barbier (Den)	160
Been ('t)	113
BeerLovers' Café	145
Bier Central	113
Bier Circus	124
Bistro Léo	16
Boelekewis	154
Botteltje ('t)	151
Brasserie Lamborelle	116
Brugs Beertje ('t)	120
Café Le Coq	124
Café Rose Red	120
Café Vlissinghe	120
Cam (De)	154
Capital (The)	141
Chapître (Le)	151
Dairingman (Au)	124
Delirium Café	129
Dulle Griet (De)	131
Ekster (Den)	160
Gainsbar	138
Garre (De)	120
Gollem	113
Goudblommeke in Papier (Het)	128
Gouden Hoofd ('t)	134
Gouden Vis (De)	148
Hanekeef (D')	148
Hemelrijk (Het)	138
Huyze Vacas	157
In de Klein Hal	138
In De Verzekering Tegen De Grote Dorst	155
Kaffee Bazaar	138
Kastaar (De)	141
Klosken ('t)	155
Kulminator (De)	112
Labyrinth (Het)	157
Lorgnette (La)	116
Manuscript (Beertourism Café)	154
M-Café	141
Moeder Lambic	125
Monk	129
Mort Subite (A La)	124
Oud Arsenaal ('t)	110
Poechenellenkelder (De)	128
Sherlock Holmes (Le)	116
St Arnoldus	138
Taverne Le Saint-Géry	116
Temps des Cerises (Le)	160
Trollekelder (De)	134
Vaudrée (Le)	145
Vie est Belge (La)	131
Waterhuis aan de Bierkant (De)	134
Wiering (De)	141

RESTAURANTS

AB Café & Resto	486
Als ik mijn ogen toe doe... Honoloeloe	492
Brigittines (Les)	486
Château du Mylord (Le)	492
Dock's Café	482
3 Fonteinen	486
Eau Blanche (L')	490
Grand Café De Rooden Hoed	482
Heeren van Liedekercke (De)	490
Hommelhof ('t)	498
In De Zon	496
Nüetnigenough	486
Postel Ter Heyde	496
Zilte ('t)	482

USEFUL LINKS

www.babblebelt.com
www.bapas.be
www.beeradvocate.com
www.beercapital.be
www.beerfestival.be
www.beerhunter.com
www.beerinfo.com
www.beermad.org.uk
http://beerme.com
www.belgianbrewers.be
www.beertourism.com
www.beerpubmap.be
www.beertrips.com
www.belgianbeerboard.com
www.belgian-beer-routes.com
www.belgian-beers.eu
http://belgischbier.2link.be
www.belgischebieren.eu
http://belgischebieren.startpagina.be
www.belgiumking.com
www.biercuisine.nl
www.bierebel.com
www.gambrinusclub.be
www.hierstroomthetbier.be
www.ober.be
www.pint.nl
www.ratebeer.com

www.realbeer.com
www.tastingbeers.com
www.tastings.com
www.thedrinksbusiness.com/tag/beer/
www.wikibeeria.com
www.worldbeercollection.com
www.zythos.be

MAGAZINES

Bier Grand Cru (BE)
Bier Magazine (NL)
BierPassie Magazine (BE)
Belgian Beer and Food (BE)

Bière Magazine (FR)
De Zytholoog (BE)
Pint (NL)
Draft Magazine (US)
All About Beer (US)
BeerAdvocate (US)
Hops Magazine (CN)
The Beer Link (CN)

TELEVISION

Tournée générale, Season 1
Tournée générale, Season 2
Tournée générale, Season 3

In den hemel is geen bier... daarom drinken wij het hier!

BOOKS

Amato, M. *Beerology*. Apetite by Random House, Vancouver, 2014.
Bauweraerts, C. *My Chouffe Story*. Ballon Media, Antwerpen, 2012.
Beaumont, S. *Brewpub Cookbook*. BA, Boulder, 1998.
Beaumont, S. *The Beer Food Companion*. Jacqui Small, London, 2015.
Beckett, F. & Beckett, W. *An Appetite for Ale*. Camra, ST. Albans, 2007.
Becuwe, F. *Bier aan het Ijzer Front*. De Klaproos, Brugge, 2009.
Bergström, A. *Proef Bier*. Koken met Krullen, 's-Gravenhage, 2015.
Berstein, J. *The complete Beer Course*. Sterling Publishing, New York, 2013.
Berthelsen, C. *Olrejesen*. Turbine, Berlin, 2013.
Beysen, E. *Bier op Tafel*. Uitgeverij Helios, Kapellen, 1981.
Boon, JL. *Eten op zijn Vlaams*. De Arbeiderspers, Amsterdam, 1972.
Brillat-Savarin, J.M. *The Physiology of Taste*. Vintage Books, New York, 1949.
Brown, P. *Hops and Glory*. Pan Books, London, 2009.
Brown, P. *Three Sheets to the Wind*. Pan Books, London, 2006.
Bueltmann, F. *Beerevangelist's Guide to the galaxy*. Black Lake Press, Holland, 2013.
Burns, D. & Jarnit-Bjergso, J. *Food & Beer*. Phaidon Press Limited, London, 2016.
Buytaert, J. *Bier ZKT vis*. Njam, Antwerpen, 2013.
Calagione, S. & Old, M. *He said beer, she said wine*. DK, New York, 2009.
Calderon, A. *Verdwenen Brouwerijen van België*. Mens & Cultuur Uitgevers, Gent, 2013.
Canham-Nelson, M. *Teachings from the tap*. Beer Trekker Press, Carmel Valley, 2012.
Cantwell, D. & Bouckaert, P. *Wood & Beer. A Brewer's Guide*. Brewers Publications, Boulder, 2016.
Cattoor, M. *De Belgische Bierkeuken*. Borgerhoff & Lamberigts, Gent, 2008.
Cattoor, M. *Mario's Vlaamse Keuken*. Borgerhoff & Lamberigts, Gent, 2011.
Chartier, F. *Taste Buds and Molecules*. Houghton Mifflin Harcourt, London, 2012.
Cole M. *Let me tell you about Beer*. Pavilion Books, London, 2011
Coninx, A. *Bier & Gastronomie*. Linkeroever Uitgevers, Antwerpen, 2010.
Corneille, T. & EA. *Koken met Trappistenbier*. Davisdfonds, Leuven, 2014.
Coutteneye, S & Van Hemeldonck, J. *De bierkeuken van 't Hommelhof*. Roularta, Roeselare, 1999.
Coutteneye, S. & Van Den Steen, J. *De smaak van Bier*. Davidsfonds, Leuven, 2006.
Couttenye, S. *Biergastronomie uit de Westhoek 't Hommelhof in Watou*. Stichting kunstboek, Oostkamp, 2013.
Crauwels, D. & ea. *Caudelier. Kok voor Burger en Koning*. Oogachtend, 's Gravenwezel, 2005.
Crombecq's, P. *Bijzondere Bieren van België, Nederland & Luxemburg*. Kosmos-Z&K Uitgevers, Antwerpen, 1996.
Crouch, A. *Great American Craft Beer*. Running Press Book Publishers, Philadelphia, 2010.
D'eer M. *Epousailles Bières et Fromages*. Trécarré, Outremont, 2000
Daeninck, S. *Chimay: Verhaal/Producten/Recepten*, Lannoo, Tielt, 2014.
Daeninck, S. *Duvel à la Carte*. Lannoo, Tielt, 2005.
Darchambeau, N. *Chimay, une cuisine festive*. Editions Les Capucines, Limelette, 1994.
Darchambeau, N. *Het Genot van Orval*. Editions Les Capucines, Limelette, 1994.
Dawson, P. *The Beergeek Handbook*. Storey Publishing, North Adams, 2016.
Dawson, P. *Vintage Beer*. Storey Publshing, North Adams, 2014.
De Benedetti C. *The Great American Ale Trial*. Running Press, Philadelphia, 2011.
De Kimpe, S. *Vlaamse biergerechten proeven*. Uitgeverij Het Volk, Gent, 1983.
De Lange, F. & Vaessen, J. *Bier & Spijs. 70 inspirerende gerechten bij Nederlands Speciaalbier*. Caplan, Arnhem, 2014.
De Lange, F. *Ontdek de smaak van Bier*. Caplan, Arnhem, 2015.
De Meyer, V. & De Meyer M. *Lindemans. Koken met Bier*. Standaard Uitgeverij, Antwerpen, 2008.
De Plus, J. *Bier van 800°*. Weyrich, Neufchâteau, 2014.
De Prins, D. & Mertens, N. *De Belgische Keuken*. Standaard Uitgeverij, Antwerpen, 1995.
De Weert, T. *Bier als drank bij gastronomische gerechten*. Alken-Maes, Waarloos, 1994.
Deglas, C. *De Smaak van Belgisch Bier*. J.M. Collet, Braine-l'Alleud, 1995.
Delvaille, A. & Chavanne, P. *Recettes aux Bières de Wallonie*. Editions du Perron, Liège, 2005.
Deweer, H. *Alle Belgische Bieren*. Stichting Kunstboek., Oostkamp, 2015.
Dodd, J. *The Craft Beer Cookbook*. Adams Media, Avon, 2013.
Dornbush, H. *Beer Styles from Around the World*. Cervevisia Communications, West Newbury, 2015.
Dornenburg, A. & Page, K. *What to drink with what you eat*. Bulfinch Press, New York, 2006.
Draper, A. EA. *Craft Union*. Thornbridge Brewery Bakewell, 2012.
Dredge, M. *Beer and Food*. Ryland Peters & Small LTD, London, 2014.
Duponcheel, I. & Rivière, N. *Belgian Bites*. Dolce Publsihing, Brussel, 2012.

EA. *Antwerpen Bierstad*. Pandora Publishers., Brasschaat, 2013.

EA. *Beer Sommelier: A Journey Trough the Culture of Beer*. White Star Publishers, Novara, 2014.

EA. *Belgische Bieren in de Keuken en het Glas*. Colruyt, Halle, 2011.

EA. *Belgische Bieren*. Test Aankoop, Brussel, 2009.

EA. *Hop in the Saddle*. Into Action Publications, Portland, 2013.

EA. *La Fine Mousse. Le meilleur. De La Bière Artisanale*. Tana Editions, Paris, 2015.

EA. *Topchefs & Westmalle*. Davidsfonds, Leuven, 2005.

Fal, A. & Cantwell, D. *Barley Wine*. BA, Boulder, 1998.

Fayt, A. *La cuisine à la Bière*. En Stoemelings Editions, Brussel, 2011.

Flectcher, J. *Cheese & Beer*. Andrews McMeel Publishing, Kansas City, 2013.

Foster, T. *Porter*. Brewers Publications, Boulder, 1992.

Ganzenmüller, S. & Priller-Riegele, S. *Bier & Genuss*. BLV, München, 2013.

Garret, O. (ed) *The Oxford Companion to Beer*. New York, 2012

Garret, O. *The Brewmaster's Table*. Ecco, New York, 2003

Gatz, S. *De vier Seizoenen van het Belgisch Bier*. Uitgeverij, Van Halewyck, Leuven, 2012.

Glassman, B. *Brew Food*. Chefs Press Inc, San Diego, 2012.

Grossman, K. *Beyond the Pale*. John Wiley & Sons, Hoboken, 2013.

Hampson, T. *Beer Book*. DK, London, 2008.

Hampson, T. *World Beer*. DK, London, 2013.

HenDrickx, B. *340 Originele Cafés in Vlaanderen*. Uitgeverij EdiPA, Lier, 2013.

Herz, J. & Conley, G. *Beer Pairing*. Voyageur Press, Minneapolis, 2016.

Hieronymus, S. *For the Love of Hops*, BA, Boulder, 2012.

Hildago, H. *Biertapas*. Terra, , Arnhem, 2011.

Hildago, H. *The taste of Bier, Jazz & Blues*. Birdy Publishing BV, Zwijndrecht, 2013.

Holl, J. *The American Craft Beer Cookbook*. Storey Publishing, North Adams, 2013.

Jackson, M. *Grote Belgische Bieren*. Lannoo, Tielt, 2006.

Joye, M. *Bier op het bord*. Lannoo, Tielt, 2001.

Kempen, R. & Philipsen, M. *Minder Trameland in Bierland*. Mitra, Doesburg, 2007.

Kempen, R. *Beer best kept secrets*. Bier & Co, Amsterdam, 2009.

Kerkhoven, P. *Bier & Food*. Xander Uitgevers, Amsterdam, 2015.

Klosse, P. *Het Proefboek: De Essentie van Smaak*. Utrecht, 2011

Klosse, P. *The Essence of Gastronomy*. CRC Pres, New York, 2013.

Koch, G. & EA. *The Craft of Stone Berwing CO*. Ten Speed Press, Berkeley, 2011.

Kopp, S. *Barley & Hops*. Gestalten, Berlin, 2014.

Koster, B. *500 favorite kazen*. Stichting Kunstboek, Oostkamp, 2012.

Kunath, B. *Zelf Bier Brouwen*. Vetlman Uitgevers, Utrecht, 2012.

Lapanja, M. *Een godin in de keuken*. Arena, Amsterdam, 2003

Larson, M. *The Beer Select-O-Pedia*. Camra, ST. Albans, 2014.

Leventhal, J. *Gids voor de Bier Liefhebber*. Black Dog & Leventhal publishers, New York, 1999.

Lévesque Gendron, d. & Thibault, M. *Les Saveurs Gastronomiques de la Bière*. Druide, Montréal, 2013.

Lewis, M. J. T. *Stout*. Brewers Publications, Boulder, 1995.

Magerman, B. *36 Merkwaardige Belgische Bieren*. Media Marketing Communications, Ekeren, 2009.

Magerman, B. *Belgisch Bier Boek*. Lannoo, Tielt, 2002.

Marchand, B. & Delos, G. *Les Grands Chefs et la Bière*. Somogy, Paris, 2003.

Mc Quad, Tasty. *The Art and Science of What We Eat*. Scribner, New York, 2015.

McCalman, M. & Gibbons, D. *Mastering Cheese*. Clarkson Potters Publishers, New York, 2009.

McGee, H. *Over Eten en Koken: Wetenschap en Cultuur in de keuken*, Nieuw Amsterdam Uitgevers, Amsterdam, 2012.

Meilgaard, M.C, ea. *Sensory Evaluation Techniques*. CRC Press, New York, 2007.

Mercurio, P. *Koken met Bier*. Veltman Uitgevers, Utrecht, 2012.

Meus, J. EA. *Tussen Pot & Pint*. Lannoo, Tielt, 2009.

Mikkel Bjergso, B. & Pang, P. *Mikkellers Bogom OL*. Gyldendal, Copenhagen, 2014.

Mornin, B @Beaumont, S. *The Beer Bistro Cookbook*. Key Porter Books, Bolton, 2009.

Mosher, R. *Mastering Homebrew*. Chronicle Books LLC, San Francisco, 2015.

Mosher, R. *Tasting Beer: An insider's guide to the world's greatest Drink*. North Adams, 2009

Nachel, M & Ettlinger, S. *Bier voor Dummies*. Addison Wesley, Foster City, 2003.

O'Brien, C.M. *Fermenting Revolution*. New Society Publishers, Gabriola Island, 2006.

Otte, A. *H2O Verander Water in Bier*. Brouwland, Beverlo, 2011.

Page, K. & Dornenburg, *The flavor bible*. Little Brown, New York, 2014.

Papazian, C. *The Complete Joy of Homebrewing*. William Morrow, New York, 2014.

Patroons, W. *Bier*. Standaard Uitgeverij, Antwerpen, 1979.

Pauwels, L. *Bier Brouwen voor starters*. Standaard Uitgeverij, Amsterdam, 2012.

Perozzi, C. & Beaune, H. *The Naked Pint*. Penguin Group, New York, 2009.

Perreir-Robert, A. & Fontaine, C. *België door het Bier. Het Bier door België*. Uitgeverij Schortgen, Esch-sur. Alzette, 1996.

Pierre, E & Pham A & Denturck, M. *Bierographie*. Hachette, Paris, 2015.

Pierre, E. *Bières. Leçons de Dégustation*. Editions de la Martinière, Paris, 2015.

Pierre, E. *Le Guide Hachette Des Bières*. Hachette Livre, Vanves, 2014.

Pini, U. *Bières*. Feierabend, Berlin, 2003.

Protz, R. *De Hemelse Smaak van Abdijbier*. Deltas, London, 2002.

Raymaekers, J. *België Feest. Een geschiedenis van Bourgondisch tafelen*. Uitgeverij Van Halewyck, Leuven, 2005.

Reuchlin, H. *Van brood tot Brood. Bier in de beeldende kunst door de eeuwen heen*. Birdy Publishing, Zwijndrecht, 2013.

Routson, A. *The Beer Wench's Guide to Beer*. Quarto Publishing Group, Minneapolis, 2015.

Saunders, L. *The best of American Beer and Food*. BA publications, Boulder, 2007.

Schepers, A. *Een wereld vol bier*. ASCR, Zutphen, 2013.

Schiffner, K & Wejmar S. *Bier kombineert*. AV, Buch Wenen, 2010.

Schmeinck, A. *Smaakvrienden groenten*. Karakter Uitgevers B.V, Uihoorn, 2012.

Schultz, S. *Beer, Food and Flavor*. Skyhorse Publishing, New York, 2012.

Seminel, L. *Umami De vijfde smaak*. Terra Lannoo, Houten, 2012.

Shepherd, G. *Neurogastronomy*. Columbia University Press; New York, 2012.

Simpkins, J. *Allagash. The Cookbook*. Blue Tree, Portsmouth, 2012.

Smeets, R. *Schuim van mijn dagen, schenk me gedachten*. Uitegverij P, Leuven, 2014.

Stuckey, B. *Taste. What you 're Missing*. Free Press, New York, 2012.

Swinnen, J. *The economics of beer*. Oxford university Press, Oxford, 2011.

Tierney-Jones, A. *1001 Beers. You must taste before you die*. Universe Publishing, New York, 2010.

Van den Steen, J. *Belgian Family Brewers*. Davidsfonds, Leuven, 2009.

Van den Steen, J. *Adbijbieren: Geestrijk erfgoed*. Davidsfonds, Leuven, 2004.

Van den Steen, J. *Geuze & Kriek: Het geheim van de Lambik*. Lannoo, Tielt, 2011.

Van den Steen, J. *Geuze en Kriek: de Champagne onder de bieren*. Davidsfonds, Leuven, 2006.

Van den Steen, J. *Meer dan 150 verrassende cocktails*. Davidsfonds, Leuven, 2008.

Van den Steen, J. *Trappist: Het bier en de monniken*. Davidsfonds, Leuven, 2003.

Van den Steen, J. *Trappist: De tien heerlijke bieren*. Davidsfonds, Leuven, 2015.

Van den Steen, J. *Trappist: De zeven heerlijke bieren*. Davidsfonds, Leuven, 2010.

Van der Auwera, F. *Hop in het bord*. Standaard Uitgeverij, Antwerpen, 1995.

Van Hove, H. *Bier & Bord*. Roularta Books, Roeselare, 2007.

Van Hove, H. *Bier aan tafel*. Roularta Books, Roeselare, 2002.

Van Laere, S. *De smaak van kaas*. Davidsfonds, Leuven, 2007.

Van Lierde, G. *Bier in België*. Lannoo, Tielt, 1992.

Van Malderen, K., EA. *Bapas. Belgische Biertapas*. Standaard Uitgeverij, Antwerpen, 2011.

Van Malderen, K. *Bapas. Belgische Biertapas*. Manteau, Antwerpen, 2015.

Van Tricht M. & Declercq M. *Kaas & Wijn*. Lannoo, Tielt, 2003.

Van Uytven, R. *Geschiedenis van de dorst*. Davidsfonds, Leuven, 2007.

Vanraefelgem, S. *Bier. Vrouwen weten waarom*. Uitgeverij Van Halewyck, Leuven, 2013.

Vansteenbrugge, G. EA. *Bier & Chocolade*. Inni Publishers, Heule, 2016.

Verdonck, E. *Con Gusto*. Standaard Uitgeverij, Antwerpen, 2008.

Verdonck, E. *Bij de Brouwer*. Davidsfonds, Leuven, 2013.

Verdonck, E. *Bordje bier*. Davidsfonds, Leuven, 2014.

Verdonck, E. *Lekker Waals*. Davidsfonds, Leuven, 2012.

Verdonck, E. *Proef België*. Linkeroever Uitgevers, Antwerpen, 2011.

Verlinden, M. *Ambachtelijke bieren in België*. Lannoo, Tielt, 2015.

Vinken, B. *Belgische Bieren*. Lannoo, Tielt, 2007.

Vinken, B. *Bier op het Menu*. Lannoo, Tielt, 2009.

Vinken. B. & Van Tricht, M. *Bier & Kaas 50 speelse combinaties met Vinken en Van Tricht*. Lannoo, Tielt, 2015.

Vinken. B. & Van Tricht, M. *Vinken & Van Tricht: 50 Bier & Kaas Combinaties*. Lannoo, Tielt, 2011.

Walsh, D. *Bier Typen Gids*. Kosmos-Z&K Uitgevers, Utrecht, 2002.

Webb, T. & Pattyn, J. *100 Belgian Beers to try before you die*. Camra, ST. Albans, 2008.

Webb, T. Beaumont, S. *The World Atlas of Beer*. Octopus Publishing, London, 2012.

Webb, T. EA. *Lambicland*. Cognan & Mater Limited, Lavemham, 2010.

Wiesman A. & Westphal T. *Jong bier in oude vaten*. Fontaine uitgevers. 's Gravenland, 2010.

Woods, J. & Rigley, K. *The Beers of Wallonia*. The Artisan Press, Oxford, 1996.

Wouters, P. *Plaisirs Culinaires à la Bière*. Broquet, ST. Constant, 2013.

Wynants, P. & Rigolet, l. *Fijnproeven in België*. Standaard Uitgeverij, Antwerpen, 2001.

THANKS

Oh well, the glass is empty and the book is written/finished. Not before time, we'd like to thank all of these people for their kind collaboration:

Stephen Beaumont (beer author Canada)
Carsten Berthelsen (beer author Denmark)
Yannick Boes (ex-CEO Alken-Maes Belgium)
Hans Bombeke (beerexpert Belgium)
John M. Brauer (Executive Officer European Brewery Convention)
Peter Buelens (Public Relations Manager Palm Belgian Craft Brewers)
Matthew Carrigan (professor Santa Fe College USA)
Melissa Cole (beer author United Kingdom)
Estelle Comte (director European Beer museum Stenay France)
Thomas Costenoble (sommelier and organisator Brussels Beer Challenge Belgium)
Lorenzo Dabove (bierexpert Italy)
Thomas Debelder (manager restaurant 3 Fonteinen Belgium)
Denis Dekeukeleire (hop expert and professor University of Ghent Belgium)
Charles and Bruno Delroisse (brewers La Frasnoise Belgium)
Freddy en Filip Delvaux (yeast experts Belgium)
Sven Deman (master chocolatier and hobbybrewer Belgium)
Mieke Dockx (chef restaurant Marie Belgium)
Marjorie Elich (beer tasters association La Bière des Femmes Belgium)
Eric Fernez (chef restaurant Eugénie à Emilie Belgium)
Dominiek Geers (Dranken Geers)
Viki Geunes (chef 't Zilte Belgium)
Christophe Gillard (beer sommelier and trader Mi-Orge Mi-Houblon Belgium)
Cas Goossens (eigenaar café-restaurant De Rooden Hoed Belgium)
Sven Gatz (ex-directeur Belgische Brewers)
Tim Hampson (beer author United Kingdom)
Julie Herz (US Brewers Association)
John Holl (editor *All About Beer Magazine*, USA)
Hans Lachi (owner café-restaurant De Rooden Hoed Belgium)
Bart Lamon (sommelier Le Château du Mylord Belgium)
Catherine and Antoine Malingret (beer sommeliers and traders Ça Brasse Pour Moi Belgium)
Eric Martin (chef restaurant Lemonnier Belgium)
Laurent Martin (chef restaurant La Frairie Belgium)
Aaron Moeraert (sommelier 't Zilte Belgium)

Masayoshi Kaji (beer expert Japan)
Marc Lemay (commercial manager Brasserie Dubuisson Belgium)
Muriel Lombard (beer tasters association La Bière des Femmes Belgium)
Lisa Morrison (beer author USA)
Jurgen Nobels (cocktail expert Uncle Babe's Burger Bar Belgium)
Wilfried Patroons (beer author Belgium)
Luc Pauwels (brew teacher Belgium)
Elisabeth Pierre (beer author France)
Robert Putman (ex-director production Alken-Maes Belgium)
Henri Reuchlin (president European Beer Consumers Union and Beer author the Netherlands)
Marc Struyf (brewer Den Triest Belgium)
Jean-Baptiste and Christophe Thomaes (chefs Le Château du Mylord Belgium)
Jef Van den Steen (beer author Belgium)
Jean-Louis Van de Perre (president Belgian Brewers)
Bart Van der Perre (photographer Belgium)
Willem Van Herreweghen (brewer at Timmermans, Brasserie de Waterloo and Bourgogne de Flandres Belgium)
Stijn Van Laere (brewer Castle Brewery Van Honsebrouck Belgium)
Karl Van Malderen (beer author Belgium)
Piet Vannieuwenhuyse (sommelier and ex-owner Dock's Café Belgium)
Hildegard Van Ostade (brewer and chef at De Hoppeschuur Belgium)
Lio Verdonck (illustrator Belgium)
Ben Vinken (beer sommelier, beer author and publisher *BierPassie Magazine* Belgium)
Fedor Vogel (publisher and chef-editor *Bier! Magazine* The Netherlands)
Korneel Warlop (press department AB Inbev Belgium)
Frank Wiens (professor University of Bayreuth Germany)
Anne and Pierre Zuber (beer sommeliers and traders Délices & Caprices Belgium)

If there is anyone we have forgotten to acknowledge, please forgive us. Our omission was not intentional. Once again, we are grateful to everyone. Santé!

www.lannoo.com
Register on our web site and we will regularly send you a newsletter
with information about new books and interesting, exclusive offers.

Text: Erik Verdonck, Luc De Raedemaeker
Photography: Erik Verdonck, Bart Van der Perre, Roos Mestdagh (cover)
English translation: Cora Hackwith
Graphical design and illustrations: Patrizia Enna

If you have observations or questions, please contact our editorial office:
redactielifestyle@lannoo.com

© Lannoo Publishers, Tielt, 2016
D/2016/45/505 – NUR 440
ISBN: 978 94 014 3552 9

All rights reserved. Nothing from this publication may be copied, stored in an automated database and/or be made public in any form or in any way, either electronic, mechanical or in any other manner without the prior written consent of the publisher.